Joseph Ratzinger

Life in the Church and Living Theology

MAXIMILIAN HEINRICH HEIM

Joseph Ratzinger

*Life in the Church
and Living Theology*

Fundamentals of Ecclesiology
with Reference to *Lumen Gentium*

With a Foreword by
Joseph Cardinal Ratzinger

Translated by Michael J. Miller, M.A. Theol.

IGNATIUS PRESS   SAN FRANCISCO

Original German title:
Joseph Ratzinger—Kirchliche Existenz und existentielle Theologie
Second corrected and expanded German edition
© 2005 by Peter Lang GmbH, Frankfurt am Main, Germany

Unless otherwise indicated, citations from
Church documents are taken from
the Vatican website.

Cover photograph by Alessandra Benedetti/CORBIS

Cover design by Roxanne Mei Lum

© 2007 by Ignatius Press, San Francisco
ISBN 978-1-58617-149-0
Library of Congress Control Number 2006924095
Printed in the United States of America ∞

With gratitude
to my mother

CONTENTS

Foreword by Joseph Cardinal Ratzinger   1
Preface to the First Edition   5
Preface to the Second Edition   7
Introduction   9

PART ONE
THE CHURCH'S SELF-UNDERSTANDING
ACCORDING TO *LUMEN GENTIUM*

Section 1: *Lumen Gentium* amid the Tensions between
Tradition and Innovation   21

Chapter 1: The Theme of "Church" in the Dogmatic-Pastoral
Concern of the Council   21
§ 1. Church in a Time of Transition   21
§ 2. The Tension between the Pastoral Goal of *Aggiornamento*
and the Council's Doctrinal Purpose   24

Chapter 2: From the Schema *De Ecclesia* to the Dogmatic
Constitution *Lumen gentium*   29
§ 1. On the Dynamics at the Council   29
§ 2. What Was "New" about *Lumen Gentium*   31
  1. *Revitalization of the entire tradition of the Church*   31
  2. Lumen gentium *as "the work of the Council"*   32

Section 2: The Main Ideas of *Lumen Gentium*   39

Chapter 1: The Mystery of the Church   39
§ 1. The Term "Mystery"   39
§ 2. "Mystery"—The Disputed Overall Perspective   42
§ 3. Three Particular Perspectives: "Christ and the Church",
"Sacrament", and "Unity"   44
  1. *Christ and the Church*   44
    a. On distinguishing between Christ and the Church   44

    b. Church as the work of the trinitarian economy of
       salvation   45
    c. The Church—Seed and beginning of Christ's
       kingdom   46
    d. Biblical metaphors for the Church with a
       christological reference   49
  2. *The Church as sacrament*   52
    a. *Veluti sacramentum*   52
    b. One complex reality   55
    c. "Universal sacrament of salvation"   58
    d. The Church as the sacramental re-presentation of
       Jesus Christ   59
  3. *The Church's unity*   60
    a. Sacramental structure as sign and instrument of
       communio   63
    b. Trinitarian *communio* as the source and goal of
       ecclesial *communio*   65
    c. Church as mystery of the trinitarian *communio*   69
  4. *First excursus: "Una sancta catholica ecclesia"—The
  question of subsistence*   74
  5. *Second excursus:* Communio *as* participatio *in* suffering   76

Chapter 2: The People of God   78
  § 1. From a Marginal Phenomenon to the Central Concept   78
  § 2. The People of God in the Continuity of Salvation History   80
    1. *Election and formation of the assembly of the saved*   80
    2. *Church in continuity with the Old Testament People of
    God and as something qualitatively new*   81
    3. *Toward a sacramental-pneumatic foundation of the new
    People of God*   82
  § 3. The Participation of the People of God in Christ's
  Priestly, Prophetic, and Kingly Mission   84
    1. *The common priesthood of all the baptized*   85
    2. *The essential difference between the common priesthood and
    the ministerial priesthood*   87
    3. *The actuation of the common priesthood in the sacraments
    and in the life of virtue*   90
    4. *The prophetic ministry of the People of God*   92

a. The supernatural sense of faith belonging to the
whole People of God   92

b. The diaconal orientation of the charisms for the
upbuilding of the People of God   94

  5. *Kingly service in the People of God*   95

a. The dignity of the freedom of the children of God   95

b. Responsibility before God as responsibility for
creation and the world   96

§ 4. The Laity in the Church   97

§ 5. The Call to Holiness   101

§ 6. Religious   103

§ 7. Mary in the Mystery of Christ and of the Church   105

  1. *Mary's role in the economy of salvation*   106

  2. *Mary—Model for the Church*   107

  3. *The Cult of the Blessed Virgin in the Church*   107

§ 8. Excursus: The Catholicity of the People of God and
Ecumenism   108

  1. *The one People of God from many peoples*   108

  2. *Various degrees of membership in the Church*   109

  3. *The eschatological character of the Church and ecumenism*   111

  4. *Summary*   112

Chapter 3: The Hierarchical Structure of the Church and in
Particular the Episcopate   114

§ 1. Premises for Chapter 3 of *Lumen Gentium*   114

  1. *The Church as* Mysterium *and as the People of God is
the foundation for her socially visible constitution*   114

  2. *Continuing the themes of the First Vatican Council*   115

§ 2. The Main Themes in Chapter 3 of *Lumen Gentium*   117

  1. *The existence and function of the college of bishops*   117

a. The college of bishops in succession to the
apostolic college   117

b. The relationship between the college of bishops
and the Petrine office   118

c. Mutual relations among the bishops in the college   120

  2. *The sacramentality of episcopal consecration*   125

a. Sacramental understanding of the episcopal office
as the "fullness of the sacrament of orders"   125

b. On distinguishing "function" (*munus*) and
"power" (*potestas*)   126
3. *The three interwoven munera of the bishop are rooted in
sacramental ordination*   127
    a. The office of preaching   129
    b. The office of sanctifying   130
    c. The office of governing   130
§ 3. The "Preliminary Note of Explanation" to the Schema
on the Church   131
    1. *Historical perspective*   131
    2. *Central points of the* nota praevia   133
§ 4. Priests and Deacons   135
    1. *Priests and presbyterium*   135
       a. "Stepchildren of the Council"   135
       b. Participation in the consecration and in the
threefold mission of Christ   136
       c. One priesthood in union with the bishop   138
    2. *The permanent diaconate*   139
§ 5. Review—Church as a "Complex Reality"   140

PART TWO
JOSEPH RATZINGER:
LIFE IN THE CHURCH AND LIVING THEOLOGY

Section 1: Outline of the Ecclesiological Plan
from a Biographical Perspective   145

Chapter 1: From the Private Ego to the Ecclesial "I"   147
§ 1. Church as the Locus of the Faith   147
§ 2. The Church's Creed as the Form and Content of the
Existential Plan   150
Chapter 2: The Path of Joseph Ratzinger the Theologian   154
§ 1. Living in the Light of the Easter Mystery   154
§ 2. The Path to a Professorship   158
    1. *In the footsteps of the Fathers*   158
    2. *The* habilitation *thesis on Bonaventure's theology of history*   160
§ 3. Theological Advisor to Cardinal Frings   163
§ 4. Conciliar Theologian (*Peritus*): From Euphoria to Sober
Skepticism   166

§ 5. University Professor in Münster, Tübingen, and
Regensburg   169
     1. *Divided between Münster and Rome*   169
     2. *In Tübingen—The dramatic upheaval of 1968*   170
     3. *In Regensburg—Productive collaboration and separation
from* Concilium   174
        a. Appointed to the International Theological
Commission   175
        b. Founding of the *International Catholic Journal
Communio*   176
        c. Break with the journal *Concilium*—Opposing the
reduction of truth to sociology   178

Chapter 3: Consistency in Ratzinger's Theological Thought
Despite a Change of Perspective?   184
   § 1. The Council: "The Beginning of the Beginning"?   186
   § 2. Betrayal of His Former Positions?   190
   § 3. Corrections through a Change of Perspective   192
   § 4. Ratzinger's View of Church Renewal   194
   § 5. The Discussion about the Term "Restoration"   197

Chapter 4: Archbishop and Cardinal   206
   § 1. Archbishop of Munich and Freising: *Cooperatores Veritatis*   206
     1. *Consolidation through the Word of God*   207
     2. *Critique of flawed developments and the search for dialogue*   209
   § 2. Prefect of the Roman Congregation for the Doctrine of
the Faith   211
     1. *The teacher of theology is under obligation to the truth*   211
     2. *The office of prefect: Service to the unity of the faith*   214
        a. Catechesis and the *Catechism*   214
        b. On the debate with liberation theology   217
        c. The debate with traditionalism   222
        d. Ecumenism: Sober realism   222

   Section 2: Recurring Themes in Ratzinger's Ecclesiology   229

Chapter 1: The Church—Sign of Faith and Mystery of Faith   230
   § 1. The Reception of the New Ecclesiological Approaches
of the Renewal Movements   230

1. *The dynamic of the whole as the proper form*   230

2. *Not a functional, but a sacramental, perspective of the
Ecclesia*   234

3. *The Semitic understanding of* σῶμα Χϱιστου *as the bridge
between christological and pneumatological ecclesiology*   238

§ 2. "Body of Christ" as the Key to the Ecclesiology of
Lumen gentium   243

   1. *The patristic interpretation of* Corpus Christi *as the point
of departure*   244

     a. The Church as the true Body of Christ   244

     b. *Caritas* as the consequence of unity   246

   2. *The Pauline teaching about the Church as the Body of
Christ: Christological and pneumatological understanding of
the Church*   248

     a. Not an organization, but the organism of the
Holy Spirit   250

     b. The Pauline theme of nuptiality   254

     c. Unity in the Spirit as the goal of all the gifts   256

   3. *Consequences of the Body of Christ doctrine for
ecclesiology*   260

     a. The question of identification with the Church   260

     b. Roots of the current crisis in the Church   262

     c. The Church's identity crisis as an ecclesiologically
encrypted God crisis   265

     d. Jesus Christ's Church, not men's   268

§ 3. Eucharistic Ecclesiology   271

   1. *The Last Supper as the act of founding the Church*   272

   2. *Eucharistic communities as the realization of the Church*   276

     a. Legitimacy as union with the pastors   276

     b. The fulfillment of the whole Church in each
celebration of the Eucharist   283

   3. *The Church is constituted as the Body of Christ through
the Eucharist*   284

§ 4. The Church as a *Communio* Unity   286

   1. *Toward an understanding of the concept of* communio   288

     a. The secular roots—The semantics of κοινωνια   288

     b. Trinitarian *communio* as an essential feature of the
Church   288

2. *Consequences of the* communio *ecclesiology*   291
   a. Ecclesial *communio* as a response to the dichotomy
     caused by individualism   291
   b. *Communio* as liturgical community   292
   c. The content of the unity: "The teaching of the
     apostles"   294
   d. Church as *communio*: Open to the world   296
3. Communio *and membership in the Church*   300
   a. Three "historical rings" of the Body of Christ
     concept in relation to Church membership   300
   b. Membership in the Church   303
   c. The plural "churches" and the one Church of
     Jesus Christ   306
4. *The question of subsistence*   310
   a. The difference between *subsistit* and *est*   312
   b. The *subsistit* formula as an alternative to
     ecclesiological relativism   320
   c. Subsistence and the question of truth   326

Chapter 2: Church as People of God   331
§ 1. The Image of the "People of God" as a Revision of the
Body of Christ Idea   333
   1. *On the ecumenical significance of understanding the*
   Church as "the pilgrim people of God"   333
   2. *The inner continuity of salvation history through the one*
   People of God   335
   3. *The eschatological character of the pilgrim Church*   339
§ 2. The Biblical Root *Qāhāl* and the Church's Description
of Herself as Εκκλησια   344
   1. *Εκκλησια as the assembly of the people*   344
   2. *Jesus Christ as the sacramental center of the People of God* 346
§ 3. Jesus Christ as the Origin and Goal of the Church   348
   1. *Proclamation of the kingdom of God as eschatological*
   gathering and cleansing   348
   2. *Jesus Christ as the patriarch of the new People of God* 351
     a. "The family of God" as a favorite image of Jesus   352
     b. Jesus "appointed twelve" (Mk 3:14)   353
     c. Jesus as patriarch of the new Israel   354

§ 4. The Ontological Priority of the Universal Church   357
   1. *Universal Church, not sum of Churches*   359
     a. On the danger of an increasingly horizontal
       understanding   361
     b. The accusation of Roman centralism   364
   2. *The inner predestination of creation for the Church*   368
     a. The importance of the Torah's and Israel's
       preexistence for an understanding of the *Ecclesia*   368
     b. On the christological development of the image
       of the preexistent People of God   370
   3. *On the ontological precedence of the universal Church over*
   her concrete empirical realizations   373
     a. The first beginnings in the New Testament   374
     b. Arguments for an ontological priority of the
       universal Church over the local Churches in
       Lumen gentium   379
§ 5. On the Critique of the Sociological Misunderstanding
of the "People of God"   382
   1. *The transformation of the People of God concept into*
   something political   383
   2. *Relativism a prerequisite for democracy?*   389
   3. *On the problem of the majority principle*   392
§ 6. The Universal Call to Holiness   396
   1. *An increase in faith, hope, and charity as the aim of*
   conciliar ecclesiology   396
   2. *On the meaning of the Marian statements*   399
     a. Ratzinger's position during the Council   399
     b. Later complementary statements by Ratzinger   400
   3. *"I am black but beautiful"*   414
     a. *Ecclesia peccatrix?*   416
     b. The nature of true reform   425
     c. Morality, forgiveness, and atonement—The
       personal heart of reform   426

Chapter 3: The Hierarchical Constitution of the Church, in
Particular with Regard to Episcopal Collegiality   430
   § 1. The Idea of Collegiality as an Ecumenical Paradigm   432
     1. *Unity through multiplicity*   432

2. *Ratzinger's critique of the new paradigm, the priority of*
praxis   436
§ 2. Hierarchy as Holy Origin   440
 1. *The making present of a beginning*   440
 2. *On the sacramental basis of episcopal collegiality*   442
§ 3. Collegiality and Primacy   444
 1. *Dogmatic foundations of collegiality*   444
  a. The "collegiality" of the apostles   445
  b. The collegial character of spiritual ministry in the
   early Church   449
  c. The collegiality of the bishops and the primacy of
   the pope   450
 2. *Pastoral implications of the episcopal-collegial structure*   454
  a. Collegiality as the expression of the "we"
   structure of the faith   455
  b. The witness structure of ministry   457
  c. Unity in multiplicity as a structural question for
   the Church   460
§ 4. Aspects during the Council in Tension with the Later
Perspective   461
 1. *The "shadow" of the "Preliminary Note of Explanation"*   461
 2. *Concrete forms of episcopal collegiality, as variously*
interpreted   467
  a. Unbraiding the three papal offices—The totality
   of the Church in her universal dimension   467
  b. "Patriarchal districts"—On the theological status
   of the episcopal conferences   472
  c. The "episcopal synod" (synod of bishops) as
   congubernium—The commission on behalf of the
   universal Church cannot be delegated   482
 3. *Critical review*   493

PART THREE
SYNOPSIS AND SUMMARY

1. *Comparison between the main lines of* Lumen Gentium *and of*
Ratzinger's ecclesiology   497
 a. Preliminary remark: On the compromises in the conciliar
 documents   499

b. Comparison with regard to "mystery"   501

c. Comparison with regard to the "People of God"   504

d. Comparison with regard to "collegiality"   507

2. *Ratzinger's ecclesiology against the background of issues in intellectual history*   509

a. The paradigm of historical thinking   510

b. Harking back to patristic theology   514

c. Ecumenical perspective   516

3. *Liturgy as a topic for theological ecclesiology*   517

a. The demand that liturgy be "consistent with being"   518

b. Liturgy as an expression of the "universal"   520

c. Liturgy as *actio* of the Completely Other   521

Abbreviations

1. Abbreviations for the Working Documents of the Second Vatican Council   525

2. Abbreviations of Other Magisterial Documents   526

3. Abbreviated Titles of Frequently Cited Works by Ratzinger in Alphabetical Order   526

4. Other Abbreviated Titles   531

Bibliography

I. Church Documents and Sources   537

  1. Councils   537

  2. Papal Pronouncements in Chronological Order   537

  3. Magisterial Documents in Chronological Order   538

II. The Works of Joseph Ratzinger   539

  1. Separate Publications in Chronological Order   539

  2. Pieces in Collective Works and Periodicals in Chronological Order   544

    A. Essays, Interviews, and Letters   544

    B. Introductions, Forewords, and Epilogues   553

III. Secondary Literature on Vatican II   553

IV. Secondary Literature on Joseph Ratzinger   564

V. Additional Literature   567

Index   579

FOREWORD

The quarrel over Vatican II continues. What did it really mean to say? What is the right way of assimilating it into the life of the Church? This is not a dispute that remains in the rarefied atmosphere of academic theories—the destiny of the living Church is at stake. Father Maximilian Heim has made a remarkable contribution to this debate with his dissertation, which is appearing now in a second edition. He inquires into the correct interpretation of the Dogmatic Constitution on the Church, which, together with the Constitution on the Sacred Liturgy, the [Dogmatic] Constitution on Divine Revelation, and the Pastoral Constitution on the Church in the Modern World, makes up the essential patrimony of the Council. He does this by examining the theological works I have written in the four decades since the Council and contrasting them with the conciliar documents. I need not point out the fact that it was an absorbing reading experience for me to see the paths and detours of my own thinking, in its continuity and in its alterations, carefully illuminated here and held up against the standard of the Council. Yet the real purpose of this book extends far beyond the interpretation and synoptic presentation of my theological efforts; ultimately it is concerned with coming to a better understanding of Vatican II and, thus, of the Church herself and, thus, with comprehending more profoundly the things that matter to us all in the end—regardless of our individual theologies.

In my considered opinion, Father Heim has succeeded in formulating a convincing interpretation of the ecclesiology of the Second Vatican Council. In the Constitution *Lumen gentium* the Church does not speak about herself in the final analysis, does not reflect on herself, as one might conclude from a superficial reading. The first sentence of the document reads: "Christ is the light of humanity." This light is reflected upon the face of the Church. She is—as the Fathers of the Church say—the moon that receives all of its light from the sun, from Christ. Correctly understood, the Church's essence is found, not in the Church herself, but rather in her orientation [*Verwiesensein*]

I

and her referring [*Verweisen*] to One beyond herself. Father Heim shows this christological structure of the Council's teaching about the Church, which is necessarily a theo-logical structure: In Christ, man—human nature—is united with God. Through him, humanity has been taken up into the trinitarian dynamic: The Son leads to the Father in the Holy Spirit. It is about God, and only in this way do we treat the subject of man correctly.

But was not the emotional debate about episcopal collegiality and its relation to the primacy really about social structures in the Church and about the division of power? That may very well have been an essential element in what many were thinking and saying, and—human nature being what it is—this element will recur again and again. Father Heim makes it clear, however, that the conciliar text itself, which naturally goes into the subject of the concrete structures of the Church and necessarily made substantial decisions, nevertheless does not lose sight of the central theological point. A christologically centered ecclesiology means understanding the Church in terms of sacrament. More specifically, it means a eucharistic ecclesiology. It means the inclusion [*Einordnung*] and subordination of human sociological systems in the fundamental order [*Grundordnung*] of the *communio*, as this develops from the Eucharist. For those who believe, Christ is not a figure from the past, nor has he been taken far away from us into heaven. Through his Word and his corporeal presence in the Eucharist, he is always our contemporary. In the Eucharist the Church is constantly born again from the pierced heart of the Lord. And in the Eucharist we find also, in this place and at this hour, the nucleus of the Church's constitution, its meshing of unity and multiplicity, of universality and concrete moorings in the here and now. For the Eucharist, on the one hand, is always celebrated "on site". The Lord is here totally, not just a part of him; hence, in the celebration of the Eucharist we always find as well the Church in her totality, the whole Church. But just as the Lord is invariably present in his totality, so too is he invariably *one*, and hence the many celebrations of the Eucharist constitute only *one* Eucharist; only in the fellowship of all with all do we celebrate it properly. The subject of this liturgical act is only one community, insofar and inasmuch as it is intrinsically one with the universal Church, to the extent that the latter lives and works within it. Only along these lines can the questions about the relationship between primacy and episcopacy be understood correctly.

Well, now, I will not attempt to present the entire contents of an extraordinarily copious book in a short foreword. Rather, I merely wanted to try to arouse the reader's curiosity about a truly worthwhile and, for all its erudition, well-written book. I am glad that it is possible to publish a second edition of it within such a short time—something quite unusual for a dissertation. I wish the book the success that is also of interest to its author: that it might contribute to a better understanding of our faith and to more joy in believing.

Rome,
Feast of [the Presentation of the Lord and] the Purification of Mary
February 2, 2005

Joseph Cardinal Ratzinger

PREFACE TO THE FIRST EDITION

A church that causes people to speak much too much about herself
is not speaking about what she should be speaking about.

—"Demokratisierung 1"

The present work was completed in October 2002, forty years after the opening of the Second Vatican Council, and was accepted by the Catholic Theological Faculty of Karl Franz University in Graz, Austria, as a dissertation in the winter semester 2002–2003. It deals from a historical and a systematic theological perspective with the ecclesiology of Joseph Ratzinger with reference to *Lumen gentium*. In so doing, it examines critically the publications of Ratzinger the theologian up to the present day.

The beginnings of this study go back to the colloquia conducted by Dr. Hermann J. Pottmeyer for doctoral candidates in the field of fundamental theology. Shortly before my appointment as novice master of Heiligenkreuz [Holy Cross Abbey] in 1996, I had begun doctoral studies at the Ruhr University in Bochum, where as one of the founding monks of the new Cistercian abbey in Bochum-Stiepel I collaborated in setting up a center for spirituality. I am obliged and grateful to Prof. Pottmeyer for the lively interest in the subject of the reception of the Second Vatican Council that he awakened in me by his lectures and seminars and also for his initial suggestions for narrowing down the topic. My reassignment to Heiligenkreuz, together with a course for superiors of religious communities that I attended in 1997–1998 in the *Kardinal-König-Haus* (Vienna-Lainz), made it necessary to interrupt my doctoral studies.

I enrolled in the 1998 summer semester in the Karl Franz University in Graz so as to continue work on my doctorate at the Institute for Moral and Dogmatic Theology under the direction of Dr. Bernhard Körner. As my academic advisor, he deepened my interest in *Lumen gentium* and shaped this dissertation by his prudent supervision. I am especially indebted to him. I thank Dr. Gerhard Larcher, a professor at the Institute for Fundamental Theology and Dean of the Catholic Theological Faculty in Graz, for taking upon himself the trouble of being the second reader of my dissertation in spite of his many obligations. I am glad that he, like Prof. Körner, has declared his interest in publishing it.

My sincere thanks go to Dr. Hilda Steinhauer. As a former assistant professor at the Institute for Dogmatic Theology of the Catholic Theological Faculty of the University of Vienna, she accompanied the progress of this dissertation at the decisive stage by her critical proofreading, intensive discussions, and helpful suggestions. My confrere Fr. Dominicus Trojahn, O.Cist., guided my study by his profound philosophical knowledge. Furthermore, I would like to mention Fr. Alkuin Schachenmayr, Ph.D., who helped me with proofreading as I began to prepare the manuscript. I am much obliged to Mrs. Ursel Buchmüller for the final proofreading and corrections according to the new German spelling rules. I should also thank Dr. Karl Wallner, the Dean of the Philosophical-Theological Academy in Heiligenkreuz, for his kindness and for the initial formatting of the text. The reformatting of the text for publication by Peter Lang Verlag was undertaken by Br. Philipp N. Gschanes. I am much obliged to him also for this painstaking, detailed work. I would like to thank the editors of the *Bamberger Theologische Studien*, who unanimously voted to include my dissertation in the series. As someone born in Upper Franconia in the Diocese of Bamberg, I am happy that the treatise has thus gained recognition in my native region. For this my particular thanks go to Dr. Wolfgang Klausnitzer, Professor of Fundamental Theology and the Theology of Ecumenism at the Otto Friedrich University in Bamberg.

Above all, however, I am obliged to thank my superiors and all my confreres of the Cistercian Abbey of Heiligenkreuz: Abbot Emeritus Gerhard Hradil, who commanded me to write a dissertation, and Abbot Gregor Henckel-Donnersmarck, who despite my appointment as prior in 1999 encouraged me to complete the work. In the years 2001–2002 he arranged as necessary for me to be relieved of my conventual duties. The pastor of our monastery parish Mönchhof in Burgenland, Dr. Marian Gruber, generously gave me the opportunity to study without interruptions in his rectory. My heartfelt thanks to all the confreres who substituted for me during my absence from the Abbey.

Ut in omnibus glorificetur Deus

Heiligenkreuz, August 2003   Fr. Maximilian Heinrich Heim, O.Cist.

PREFACE TO THE SECOND EDITION

Therefore We, too, at the beginning of Our service as the Successor of Peter, wish to declare our firm and resolute intention to continue implementing the Second Vatican Council by following Our Predecessors and faithfully maintaining the two-thousand-year tradition of the Church.

— Pope Benedict XVI on the day after his election during his sermon in the Sistine Chapel

My thanks first of all to the successor of Peter, our Holy Father Pope Benedict XVI, for personally writing an extensive preface to this volume on the Feast of the Purification of Mary, February 2, 2005, while he was still prefect of the Congregation for the Doctrine of the Faith and dean of the college of cardinals. On March 1, 2003, I had the privilege of meeting him in person at the Vatican and giving him a copy of my unpublished dissertation, which had already been approved and which appeared later in the spring of 2004 as volume 22 in the series *Bamberger Theologischen Studien* published by Peter Lang Verlag. In the autumn of 2004, when the first edition was already sold out, the publisher informed me that a new edition was planned. Encouraged by Msgr. Helmut Moll (Cologne) to ask Joseph Cardinal Ratzinger to write a short preface for a revised second edition, it was a great joy for me that this request could actually be granted, despite the Cardinal's enormous workload.

Besides a repagination, the new edition incorporates improvements and small corrections to the format. Particular attention was paid to providing citations from critical editions of the Church Fathers. I have also proofread again and supplemented the index of proper names at the end of the book. For their help in proofreading I am particularly grateful to Mrs. Hildegard Schmitz and my confreres Fr. Bruno Hannöver and Fr. Rupert Fetsch.

The fact that in the year 2004 Christoph Cardinal Schönborn of Vienna conferred the Cardinal Innitzer Prize upon this book and Mayor Manfred Raum in my hometown of Kronach awarded it the Johann Kaspar Zeuss Prize honors not only me but also my dissertation adviser, Dr. Bernhard Körner, Dean of the Catholic Theological Faculty of the University of Graz, as well as our Philosophical-Theological Academy at Heiligenkreuz.

Bochum-Stiepel, on the Solemnity of the Ascension of the Lord, 2005
Fr. Maximilian Heinrich Heim, O.Cist.
Prior of the Cistercian Abbey in Stiepel

INTRODUCTION

We cannot return to the past, nor have we any desire to do so. But
we must be ready to reflect anew on that which, in the lapse of time,
has remained the one constant. To seek it without distraction and to
dare to accept, with joyful heart and without diminution, the fool-
ishness of truth—this, I think, is the task for today and for tomorrow.[1]

Joseph Ratzinger is considered by some to be the representative of a
"petrified theology",[2] whereas for others[3] he is a voice that claims to
speak the truth and makes it possible to perceive "the whole in its
depth dimension".[4] This dissertation places him—amid the tensions
of present-day disputes within the Church about the patrimony of the
Second Vatican Council—as an ecclesiologist at the center of this discourse, by setting forth his statements about the Church as a central
aspect of an existential theology. Because theology and ecclesial life
have been melded into one in an unusual way in Ratzinger's work, his
theological thought can be characterized as "existential", without thereby
relegating it to the realm of the merely subjective. Ratzinger is in fact
concerned about a theology that proceeds, not from a private being,
but rather from an existence that has surrendered itself to the Church,[5]
in other words, "a theology of *ex-sistere*, of that exodus by which the
human individual goes out from himself and through which alone he
can find himself",[6] a theology, therefore, that seeks God in the Church

---

[1] J. Ratzinger, "Der Weltdienst der Kirche: Auswirkungen von *Gaudium et spes* im letzten
Jahrzehnt", *IKaZ* 4 (1975): 439–54. Reprinted in *Principles*, 373–93, as the epilogue, "Church
and World: An Inquiry into the Reception of Vatican Council II". Citation at 393.

[2] Häring, *Ideologie*, 21.

[3] We should mention here, for example, Stephan Otto Horn and Vinzenz Pfnür as representatives of Ratzinger's "circle of students". The names of the members of this *Schülerkreis*
and of those who presented papers at their gatherings were published in *Mitte*, 316f.

[4] See Stephan Otto Horn and Vinzenz Pfnür, "Introduction", in *Pilgrim Fellowship*, 9–16,
citation at 12.

[5] See the foreword of W. Baier et al., eds., *Weisheit Gottes—Weisheit der Welt: Festschrift
für Joseph Kardinal Ratzinger zum 60. Geburtstag* (Sankt Ottilien: EOS-Verlag, 1987), 1:v.

[6] *Principles*, 171–90, citation at 189.

and through the Church as its preexisting center. Consequently, its task consists of "keeping what is earthly and human so that it is transparent toward the truly fundamental reality, the divine reality that opens itself to us through Christ in the Holy Spirit".[7]

If we understand theology this way, it becomes clear that Ratzinger's thought, in keeping with the patristic tradition, is defined, not by an opposition[8] between salvation history and its ontological unfolding,[9] but rather by a mutual ordering of the two that constantly adheres to the "*prae* [logical and temporal priority] of God's action".[10] This means that "faith in an *actio Dei* is antecedent to all other declarations of faith", because for God,

> it is precisely relationship and action that are the essential marks; creation and revelation are the two basic statements about him, and when revelation is fulfilled in the Resurrection, it is thus confirmed once again that he is not just one who is timeless but also one who is above time, whose existence is known to us only through his action.[11]

Defending this "primacy of God"[12] brings about a development in Ratzinger's theology—as Dorothee Kaes explains—from a theology that originally had a more pronounced orientation toward salvation

---

[7] Horn and Pfnür, "Introduction", 9–14, citation at 10.

[8] In this way, Ratzinger decisively distances himself from Bultmann's thesis that "the word, the kerygma, is the real salvation-event, the 'eschatological event', that leads man from the alienation of his existence to its essence. This word is present wherever it makes itself heard; it is the always-present possibility of salvation for mankind. It is clear that, in the last analysis, this primacy of the word that, as such, can always be spoken and thus can be posited as always present, cancels the notion of a continuous series of salvation-historical events" (*Principles*, 176), in that it separates a theologically insignificant history from a theologically relevant "story". The latter remains, in Bultmann's scheme, a "word-event" unconnected with the historical events. Compare Kaes, 89f. Ratzinger sees in this opposition between salvation history and metaphysics a problem that did not come so acutely to the fore until after the Second Vatican Council. The reason for this may be explained by the fact that "Vatican Council II did not link its debate on salvation to the already existing patristic term *dispositio* (or *dispensatio*) but rather coined for itself, as a borrowing from the German, the expression *historia salutis*. Therewith we have also an indication of the source of the problem that, in our century, has entered Catholic theology by way of Protestant thought" (*Principles*, 172).

[9] See ibid.

[10] Ibid., 185.

[11] Ibid.

[12] *Pilgrim Fellowship*, 284–98, citation at 287.

history[13] to thinking that is more characteristically metaphysical,[14] and this development occurs as a response to the intellectual debates of a given time period.[15]

Since my dissertation on Ratzinger's ecclesiology is situated within the context of the postconciliar developments in the Church, I was confronted with the question about an adequate reception of that image of the Church that the Second Vatican Council had outlined. In this regard, Ratzinger is not only a contemporary witness, but also a theologian who, as Thomas Weiler[16] has attempted to demonstrate, was himself able to exert influence on the Council's ecclesiology. Although it is not my purpose simply to reverse Weiler's approach and to maintain that the Council influenced Ratzinger the theologian, it is still undeniable that there was a reciprocal effect[17] and that consequently Ratzinger must be understood not only as an expert in the conciliar ecclesiology, as one of those who helped to shape it, but at the same time also as one of its most resolute defenders and as someone who continues to interpret and apply it concretely in his writings.

Thus two sets of questions result for the development of my theme: first, an inquiry into the Church's understanding of herself in *Lumen gentium* and, secondly, an investigation of Ratzinger's ecclesial life and the main lines of his ecclesiology, which has been shaped by his career. The first part of the dissertation, about *Lumen gentium*, will set out to provide the conceptual frame of reference for the discussion of Ratzinger's ecclesiological outline in the second part, whereby the fundamental themes of *mystery*, the *People of God*, and *collegiality*, which are structural elements of *Lumen gentium*, serve as the main coordinates for the systematic development of the subject. I have chosen them as guidelines for presenting Ratzinger's theology as well, because he himself associates them with the authority of the Second Vatican

---

[13] Along with G. Söhngen, Ratzinger stresses "emphatically that the truth of Christianity is not the truth of a universally accepted idea but the truth of a unique fact" (*Principles*, 174). Cf. G. Söhngen, *Die Einheit in der Theologie* (Munich: Zink, 1952), 347.

[14] For particulars, see Kaes, 86–88.

[15] See pt. 3, sec. 2, of this book, "Ratzinger's Ecclesiology against the Background of Issues in Intellectual History".

[16] Cf. Weiler, 151–283, esp. 281–83.

[17] See J. Ratzinger, "Geleitwort" [preface], in Weiler, xiii; similarly: G. Alberigo, "Die konziliare Erfahrung: Selbständig lernen", in Wittstadt, 2:679–98, esp. 688f.

Council's Constitution on the Church.[18] In any case the second part does not intend to make a detailed comparison with *Lumen gentium*; rather, it intends to show the importance of the main ecclesiological themes of the Constitution on the Church in Ratzinger's work, to note points of agreement or differences and modifications, and, where appropriate, to point out changes in Ratzinger's approach. In this regard, the question of how and when Ratzinger articulated the ambiguities[19] in *Lumen gentium* will serve as a litmus test for whether or not there was a change in his perspective. For this reason it is necessary to pay special attention to the historical factor in our discussions. This is accomplished, on the one hand, by tracing the principal stages of development both for *Lumen gentium* and for Ratzinger and, on the other hand, by explicitly examining the historical context at pivotal points of the systematic treatment of the subject. In this I am guided by the following suggestion of Weiler:

> A thorough study of Ratzinger's postconciliar ecclesiological writings would of course have to investigate which of Ratzinger's ideas remained unchanged and where, if at all, a change can be noted. Why did that happen? And with regard to the ideas that remained the same, one should ask whether they, in being brought into a new historical and theological context, do not acquire a different significance. Finally: Does the fact that Ratzinger's ideas remained the same really correspond thoroughly to the Second Vatican Council, which was, after all, in Ratzinger's view as well, "only the formulation of a task", which is to say, the beginning of a fundamental change, the accomplishment of which was (and is) still in the future?[20]

---

[18] See *Church* 3–20; "Ecclesiology", 123–52.

[19] Cf. pt. 2, sec. 2, chap. 3, § 4, "Aspects during the Council in Tension with the Later Perspective", and pt. 3, sec. 1, "Comparison between the Main Lines of *Lumen gentium* and of Ratzinger's Ecclesiology".

[20] Weiler, 315. In the same passage, Weiler cites J. Ratzinger, *Die letzte Sitzungsperiode des Konzils* (Cologne: Bachem, 1966), 73; cf. *Highlights*, 183. In 1996, Weiler declared (11f.) that, even though the theme of "Church" is an important focal point in Ratzinger's work as a whole, "it is astounding that so far relatively few publications have been dedicated to this important aspect.... A monograph on Ratzinger's ecclesiology has not yet appeared." Weiler did not consider the unpublished dissertation of K.-J. E. Jeon, *Die Kirche bei Joseph Ratzinger: Untersuchungen zum strukturierten Volk Gottes nach der Kirchenlehre Joseph Ratzingers* (unpublished dissertation, Innsbruck, 1995). An extensive list of further publications on Ratzinger's theology can be found in Weiler, 11f. Worth noting also is the bibliography of secondary literature

Before I outline the structure and division of my investigation, I should clarify why I take up *Lumen gentium* and not *Gaudium et spes* as the frame of reference for my discussion of Ratzinger's ecclesiology, even though the latter, in my opinion, would also be quite possible and reasonable.[21] The answer is twofold: First, in keeping with Ratzinger's approach, I attempt to shed light on the Church's intrinsic nature. For this purpose *Lumen gentium* is a suitable reference. Moreover, according to Wolfgang Beinert, the "other fifteen constitutions, decrees, and declarations lead to this Council document or are derived from it".[22] The second reason for my decision is related to the first. It can be expressed precisely by means of a programmatic statement by Ratzinger of his position in the year 1975:

> An interpretation of the Council that understands its dogmatic texts as mere preludes to a still unattained conciliar spirit, that regards the whole as just a preparation for *Gaudium et spes* and that looks upon the latter text as just the beginning of an unswerving course toward an ever greater union with what is called progress—such an interpretation is not only contrary to what the Council Fathers intended and meant, it has been reduced *ad absurdum* by the course of events. Where the spirit of the Council is turned against the word of the Council and is vaguely regarded as a distillation from the development that evolved from the "Pastoral Constitution", this spirit becomes a specter and leads to meaninglessness.[23]

Ratzinger traces the cause of this subsequent influence of *Gaudium et spes*, which he regards as problematic, back to the spirit of the preface.[24] In his opinion, the text of the Pastoral Constitution serves

---

compiled by Helmut Moll under the title "Rezeption und Auseinandersetzung mit dem theologischen Werk von Joseph Cardinal Ratzinger", in *Mitte*, 309–15.

[21] It seems to me that Ratzinger's stance with regard to *Gaudium et spes* deserves separate study, since Ratzinger has grappled with this document on several occasions. He declared in 1975, for example, that *Gaudium et spes* is "the most difficult and, [along] with the 'Constitution on the Sacred Liturgy' and the 'Decree on Ecumenism', also the most [consequential]" Council document, on account of the problem of finding a suitable concept of "the world" (*Principles*, 378).

[22] W. Beinert, "Kirchenbilder in der Kirchengeschichte", in *Kirchenbilder, Kirchenvisionen: Variationen über eine Wirklichkeit*, ed. Beinert, 58–127, citation at 111 (Regensburg: Pustet, 1995).

[23] *Principles*, 390.

[24] Cf. ibid., 379. For a more detailed discussion, see pt. 2, sec. 1, chap. 3, § 1, of this book, "The Council: 'The Beginning of the Beginning'?"

as "a kind of countersyllabus" for many theologians, who imagine that it "represents, on the part of the Church, an attempt at an official reconciliation with the new era inaugurated in 1789".[25] But since "the world, in its modern form" cannot be regarded as a homogeneous entity, the Church's progress cannot consist of "a belated embrace of the modern world".[26] From this insight Ratzinger derives the following basic rule, ten years after the end of the Council: "We must interpret Vatican Council II as a whole and ... our interpretation must be oriented toward the central theological texts."[27]

The two reasons just outlined, Ratzinger's preference for an essential ecclesiology and his partiality for the dogmatic documents of the Council, led me to select *Lumen gentium* as the background against which to present his ecclesiology. This means simultaneously, however, that the "outward-looking" perspectives are considered only in passing in this dissertation. This is true, specifically, with regard to Ratzinger's statements on the complicated question of the relation between the Church and the world[28] and his writings concerning ecumenism[29] as well as interreligious dialogue[30] and, last but not least, concerning the relation between the Church and Judaism.[31] My subject is further limited by the fact that I concentrate above all on the initiatives Ratzinger has taken as a scholar, and not on the contributions he has made to theological discussion in his official,

---

[25] *Principles*, 381, 382.

[26] Ibid., 390.

[27] Ibid.

[28] See, for example, "Weltoffene Kirche? Überlegungen zur Struktur des Zweiten Vatikanischen Konzils", in *Volk Gottes*, 107–28. Cf. also "Der Christ und die Welt von heute: Überlegungen zur Pastoralkonstitution des Zweiten Vatikanischen Konzils", in *Dogma*, 183–204, along with the commentary on articles 11–22 of *Gaudium et spes*, in *LThK.E*, vol. 3 (Freiburg im Breisgau: Herder, 1968), 313–54.

[29] One example is the striking essay entitled "Prognosen für die Zukunft des Ökumenismus", in *Mitte*, 181–94. It also contains the so-called Ratzinger formula, which states that "Rome must not demand more from the East by way of doctrine on the primacy than was formulated and practiced during the first millennium." We will treat this subject more thoroughly in this book in pt. 2, sec. 2, chap. 3, § 4.2, entitled "Concrete Forms of Episcopal Collegiality, as Variously Interpreted".

[30] See, for example, *Salt of the Earth*, 243–55.

[31] See the first volume of the Urfelder series, which especially promotes dialogue between Jews and Christians: J. Ratzinger, *Many Religions—One Covenant*, trans. Graham Harrison (San Francisco: Ignatius Press, 1999).

magisterial capacity, even though it was impossible to avoid some overlapping on certain questions.

After these preliminary remarks concerning methodology, I would like to define now more precisely the principal points of this dissertation and to explain its structure. *Part 1*, on the Church's self-understanding according to *Lumen gentium*, comprises two sections, one historical and one systematic. The latter is subdivided, following the sequence of the first three chapters of *Lumen gentium*, under the headings of "The Mystery of the Church", "The People of God", and "The Hierarchical Structure of the Church and in Particular the Episcopate". Because of their intrinsic relatedness, the themes of chapters 4 through 8 of *Lumen gentium* on the laity (4), on the universal call to holiness in the Church (5), on consecrated religious (6), on the eschatological character of the pilgrim Church and her union with the Church in heaven (7), and finally on the Blessed Virgin Mary, the Mother of God, in the mystery of Christ and of the Church (8) are considered in the chapter on the People of God. In *chapter 1*, on the mystery of the Church, an essential point is the aspect of *communio*; here the trinitarian *communio* is presented as the origin and purpose of Church unity. In *chapter 2*, in keeping with the Dogmatic Constitution, I will elaborate on the participation of the People of God in the priestly, prophetic, and kingly mission of Christ—an aspect that plays a relatively insignificant role in Ratzinger's ecclesiology. In *chapter 3*, the college of bishops takes center stage in my discussion. There I will examine above all the sacramental understanding of the episcopal ministry and inquire about how the "Preliminary Note of Explanation" added to *Lumen gentium* should be evaluated, both historically and with regard to its contents—a problem that was of decisive importance especially for Ratzinger as one of the theologians at the Council.

Part 2 of this book deals with Ratzinger's ecclesiology. It is structured along the lines of *Lumen gentium* and treats in succession the principal themes of the Dogmatic Constitution on the Church. In it I intend to show which fundamental ideas Ratzinger adopts in his ecclesiology, which themes he prefers, and which ones he modifies in his presentation or does not take into account at all. As in the first part of this dissertation, the systematic section is preceded by a historical *section 1*, which discusses the "Outline of the Ecclesiological

Plan from a Biographical Perspective". In this "prelude", the question
of the consistency in Ratzinger's theological thought is especially explosive. *Section 2* deals at first, in *chapter 1*, with the Church as sign of
faith and mystery of faith. Three central concepts of Ratzinger's ecclesiology are examined therein, namely, *Body of Christ, Eucharist*, and *communio*. The chapter concludes with critical reflections on the question
of the subsistence of the Catholic Church. *Chapter 2* is devoted to the
Church as the People of God. In it I will point out Ratzinger's references to rabbinical theology so as to demonstrate by means of concrete examples the ecclesiological consequences of the scriptural unity
of the Old and New Testaments that he insists upon. In particular,
this line of Ratzinger's reasoning is important also for the controversial question of the ontological priority of the universal Church. The
chapter goes on to deal with his oft-repeated claim that the term "People of God" has been misunderstood in a sociological sense, and the
problem of democratic structures in the Church is discussed along with
the themes of "relativism" and "majority rule". Comments on the
section "The Universal Call to Holiness" conclude the chapter. In
this context the importance of the mariological declaration for Ratzinger's ecclesiology is stressed, but also the problem of the Church's
sinfulness, with reference to the verse from the Song of Solomon "I
am black but beautiful",[32] which has been applied to the Church, and
with the assistance of the image of the *casta meretrix*. The conclusion
of the main part of my work is *chapter 3*, on Ratzinger's understanding
of the hierarchical constitution of the Church and, especially, of episcopal collegiality. By way of introduction, the latter is set forth as an
ecumenical paradigm, and then it is examined with regard to its origin, to the inherent tension between collegiality and primacy, and to
its pastoral implications. The last part of this chapter is devoted to
those emphases in Ratzinger's thought that have changed so much
over the course of time that one can speak of an early and a later
Ratzinger. Specifically, from his judgments on the value of bishops'
conferences and of the synod of bishops, it will become evident how
the later Ratzinger assigns a different theological weight to collegial
formations than the earlier Ratzinger did.

---

[32] Song 1:5.

Part 3 presents a "synoptic" overview. In summarizing, it compares the ecclesiology of *Lumen gentium* with that of Ratzinger. My concluding essay on the problematic position of modernity in intellectual history, which is behind Ratzinger's ecclesiology, attempts to sketch an outline of his thought against this backdrop and to pave the way toward a more nuanced answer to the question of its continuity or discontinuity. Finally, in a concluding remark, the liturgy is depicted as the hermeneutic locus of theological ecclesiology, in keeping with the axiom *lex orandi—lex credendi*, so as to emphasize and reflect critically on what is distinctive about Ratzinger's markedly eucharistic theology of *communio*.

PART ONE

THE CHURCH'S SELF-UNDERSTANDING
ACCORDING TO *LUMEN GENTIUM*

LUMEN GENTIUM AMID THE TENSIONS BETWEEN
TRADITION AND INNOVATION

———————

Chapter 1

The Theme of "Church" in the Dogmatic-Pastoral
Concern of the Council

§ 1. Church in a Time of Transition

Being part of human society, the Church participates in the revolutionary changes of the present. Since her founding, she has stood amid the tensions between tradition and innovation. On the one hand, she relies on what has already been handed down; on the other hand, she can pass on tradition only if she is ready to innovate. For tradition does not mean salvaging and studying the past like an archaeologist; it is instead "a process by which the past shapes the present and reaches out to the future".[1] As seldom before, this lively tension between the two poles of preserving the heritage and carrying it on became apparent during the Second Vatican Council (1962–1965), because there for the first time the Church took herself comprehensively as her theme in her own self-understanding.[2] Consequently, in the conciliar

———————

[1] Georg Schmuttermayr et al., eds., *Im Spannungsfeld von Tradition und Innovation: Festschrift für Joseph Kardinal Ratzinger* (Regensburg: Pustet, 1997), 5.

[2] O. González Hernández, "Das neue Selbstverständnis der Kirche und seine geschichtlichen und theologischen Voraussetzungen", in Baraúna, 1:155–85, citation at 155, n. 1. O. González Hernández points out in the same passage that the Church had already been challenged by the Reformation to ponder her nature anew, "and not merely with regard to one of her aspects or one of her structures, but rather in her totality as a domain of the Spirit, of the gospel, and of salvation. Might not the Council of Trent have been the providential *kairos* in which to give a timely answer to this fundamental question?" This

documents no one particular question of ecclesiology is central; instead, the saving mystery of Christ, which God causes to shine forth in the Church, is supposed to be proclaimed anew to all men. The term *mysterium*, which was still absent from the first draft of the Dogmatic Constitution on the Church,[3] marks a change in theological vocabulary, which left its impression on the final version of *Lumen gentium* and also influenced other conciliar documents.[4] Whereas formerly the juridical perspective determined the way in which Catholic theologians pictured the Church, now the ecclesiology of Vatican II was stamped by the metaphorical and symbolic theological discourse of Sacred Scripture and the Church Fathers.

This change was at the same time the product of an ecclesiastical renewal that had already begun during the First World War and had made inroads especially in the liturgical and ecumenical movements as well as in the (Catholic) youth movement, which led to an enlivening of the Church.[5] As early as 1922, Romano Guardini described this "enormous process" as an "awakening of the Church in the soul".[6] The experience of the Church as the living "Body of Christ" corresponded to a new theological interest in her form, and this in an interdenominational way: In 1924 Karl Adam, a theologian from Tübingen, published his book *Das Wesen des Katholizismus*[7] [*The Spirit of Catholicism*], a best seller that ran to thirteen editions (the most recent appearing in 1957), and in 1927 the Lutheran-Evangelical bishop Otto Dibelius came out with a work entitled *Das Jahrhundert der Kirche*[8]

---

thought is expressed in a similar manner in Gérard Huyghe's essay, "Autorität der Kirche durch Dienst an den Mitmenschen", in *Die Autorität der Freiheit: Gegenwart des Konzils und Zukunft der Kirche im ökumenischen Disput*, ed. J.C. Hampe, 1:251 (Munich: Kösel-Verlag, 1967), and by P. Neuner, "Die Kirche: Mysterium und Volk Gottes", in *Erinnerungen an einen Aufbruch: Das II. Vatikanische Konzil*, ed. N. Kutschki, 37 (Würzburg: Echter, 1995).

[3] Cf. G. Philips, "Die Geschichte der Dogmatischen Konstitution über die Kirche *Lumen gentium*", in *LThK.E*, vol. 1 (Freiburg am Breisgau: Herder, 1966), 139–55.

[4] Cf. *SC* 2, 35, 102; *OT* 9, 14, 16; *PO* 22; *CD* 12; *UR* 4; *NA* 4.

[5] For a more detailed treatment of this subject, see Pesch, 136.

[6] Romano Guardini, *Vom Sinn der Kirche*, new ed. (Mainz and Munich, 1990), 1. Reprinted as an excerpt in *tztD5/II*, 153–55.

[7] Karl Adam, *Das Wesen des Katholizismus*, 13th ed. (Düsseldorf: Patmos-Verlag, 1957). Cf. *tztD5/II*, 155f.

[8] Otto Dibelius, *Das Jahrhundert der Kirche*, 6th ed. (Berlin: Furche-Verlag, 1928). Cf. *tztD5/II*, 156–58. See also M. Plate, *Weltereignis Konzil: Darstellung-Sinn-Ereignis* (Freiburg im Breisgau: Herder, 1966), 166.

[The century of the Church], which was already in its sixth edition one year later. The Second Vatican Council is a continuation of these contemporary new beginnings,[9] yet it acknowledges, of course, its obligation to what the Church has handed down.

Although it produced the most voluminous writings of any council in Church history, Vatican II itself declared no dogmas; nevertheless, its documents are a binding[10] expression of the present Magisterium of the Church. This is especially true of the two dogmatic constitutions, one on the Church, *Lumen gentium*, and the other on revelation, *Dei Verbum*; yet the Constitution on the Sacred Liturgy *Sacrosanctum Concilium* and the Pastoral Constitution *Gaudium et spes*, as well as the other decrees and declarations of the Council, are, in varying degrees of importance,[11] components of its doctrinal wealth. At the same time they are all shaped by the pastoral concern about dialogue with contemporary people.[12] This concern gives rise to the problematic question: In what language can the Church best gain a hearing for her message in a pluralistic society? In addressing this concern, an expression of John XXIII became increasingly decisive: *aggiornamento*.[13]

---

[9] K. Wittstatt, "Perspektiven einer kirchlichen Erneuerung—der deutsche Episkopat und die Vorbereitungsphase des II. Vatikanums", in *Vatikanum II und Modernisierung: Historische, theologische und soziologische Perspektiven*, ed. F.-X. Kaufmann and A. Zingerle, 86 (Paderborn: Schöningh, 1996).

[10] Cf. "Bekanntmachungen", dated November 16, 1964, in *LThK.E* 1:349.

[11] Cf. the "hierarchy of truths" formulated by the Council in *UR* 11.

[12] H. Vorgrimler, "Zur Einführung", in *LThK.E* 1:7f., notes the ecclesiological systematization of the conciliar texts by Karl Rahner and also by A. Grillmeier. The former author went about his work by subdividing it under the headings of "Ecclesia ad intra" (the nature of the Church) and "Ecclesia ad extra" (the activity of the Church).

[13] See *AAS* 51 (1959): 68. Pope John XXIII had already used the term *aggiornamento* on January 25, 1959, in the Basilica of St. Paul Outside-the-Walls, when he unexpectedly announced the Council as well as a Roman diocesan synod and the reform of the *Codex Iuris Canonici* [*CIC* = Code of Canon Law]. "Suddenly ... an inspiration sprang up within Us like a flower that blooms in an unanticipated spring. Our soul was illumined by a great idea.... A solemn and binding word was formed upon Our lips. Our voice expressed it for the first time—a council!" (cf. Pesch, 22–24, esp. 23). In this speech, John XXIII used the term *aggiornamento* in reference to the adaptation of the *CIC*; the synod and the council were to "lead happily to the desired and expected *aggiornamento* of the *Codex Iuris Canonici*". See *AAS* 51 (1959): 68; cf. also Paul VI, *Ecclesiam suam*, in *AAS* 56 (1964): 626–36; English translation in *The Papal Encyclicals: 1958–1981*, ed. by Claudia Carlen, I.H.M. (Ann Arbor, Mich.: Pierian Press, 1990), 135–60.

This first encyclical of Pope Paul VI, like the encyclical *Pacem in terris* of John XXIII, is addressed not only to the Catholic bishops and all other Catholics, but also to "all

§ 2. The Tension between the Pastoral Goal of *Aggiornamento* and the Council's Doctrinal Purpose

Against the backdrop of radical societal changes, it was the main goal of the Second Vatican Council to promote "the growth of the Catholic faith, the restoration of sound morals among the Christian flock, and appropriate adaptation of Church discipline to the needs and conditions of our times".[14] This fundamental *pastoral* orientation, however, does not diminish the doctrinal purpose of the Council,[15] as specifically emphasized by the so-called Note that was placed at the beginning of the Pastoral Constitution *Gaudium et spes* and that "was confirmed by the Council with the same votes that approved the Constitution as a whole":[16]

> Although it consists of two parts, the Pastoral Constitution "The Church in the World Today" constitutes an organic unity. The

people of good will". The entire second part of *Ecclesiam suam* is shaped by the theme of the Church's renewal. "We cannot forget Pope John XXIII's word, *aggiornamento*, which We have adopted as expressing the aim and object of Our own pontificate. Besides ratifying it and confirming it as the guiding principle of the Ecumenical Council, We want to bring it to the notice of the whole Church. It should prove a stimulus to the Church to increase its ever-growing vitality and its ability to take stock of itself and give careful consideration to the signs of the times, always and everywhere 'proving all things and holding fast that which is good' (1 Thess 5:21) with the enthusiasm of youth." See *Ecclesiam suam* 50 in Carlen, *Papal Encyclicals*, 135–60, citation at 146. On this subject, see also G. Alberigo, "Die Ankündigung des Konzils: Von der Sicherheit des Sich-Verschanzens zur Faszination des Suchens", in Wittstadt, 1:1–7.

[14] John XXIII, encyclical *Ad Petri cathedram*, in *AAS* 51 (1959): 497–531. An English translation of the inaugural encyclical of John XXIII can be found in *The Encyclicals and Other Messages of John XXIII*, arr. and ed. the staff of *The Pope Speaks* magazine (Washington, D.C.: TPS Press, 1964), 24–56, citation at 37, and also at the Vatican website, http://www.vatican.va/holy_father/john_xxiii/encyclicals/documents/hf_j-xxiii_enc_29061959_ad-petri_en.html. This citation is from no. 61. Cf. *AD* 1, 1:5. See also H. Reuter, *Das II. Vatikanische Konzil: Vorgeschichte—Verlauf—Ergebnisse, dargestellt nach Dokumenten und Berichten* (Cologne: Wort und Werk, 1966), 11. The solemn public announcement of the Council by Pope John XXIII did not take place until December 7, 1959, in the Basilica of the Twelve Apostles (*AD* 1, 1:60f.).

[15] Cf. K. Rahner and H. Vorgrimler, "Allgemeine Einleitung" [General introduction], in *KlKK* 26. The fact that there were apprehensions on this account is noted by Alberigo, "Die Ankündigung des Konzils: Von der Sicherheit de Sich-Verschanzens zur Faszination des Suchens", in Wittstadt, 1:20–29; see also *AD* 1, 1:114–49.

[16] G. Alberigo, "Die Konstitution in Beziehung zur gesamten Lehre des Konzils", in *Die Kirche in der Welt von heute: Untersuchungen und Kommentare zur Pastoralkonstitution "Gaudium et spes" des II. Vatikanischen Konzils*, ed. G. Baraúna, 73 (Salzburg: Müller, 1967).

Constitution is called "pastoral" because, while resting on doctrinal principles, it seeks to set forth the relation of the Church to the world and to the men of today. In Part I, therefore, the pastoral emphasis is not overlooked, nor is the doctrinal emphasis overlooked in Part II.[17]

Whereas *Gaudium et spes* takes up the fundamental concerns of the Church's dialogue with the world and the men of today,[18] *Lumen gentium* characterizes the nature of the Church and her universal mission from a dogmatic perspective. Yet Giuseppe Alberigo is correct in emphasizing the relationship between the two Council documents; they do not intend to present a complete system, but they are, rather, "an organic, coherent complex that focuses on a few main ideas yet for that very reason is capable of giving rise to a developing interpretation that is aimed at growth".[19] Accordingly, even *Lumen gentium*, the "principal document of Vatican II", is not an "isolated monolith" among the conciliar texts; rather, as Alois Grillmeier puts it, it is "a synthesis of the understanding of the Church in the past and today and the product of various movements in the present".[20] This is evident, among other ways, from the fact that Pope Pius XI and his successor Pope Pius XII had already started preparations for the resumption of the interrupted First Vatican Council. When John XXIII, following "a kind of heavenly inspiration",[21] considered that the time had come "to give the Catholic Church and the whole human family the gift of

---

[17] Footnote on the title, "Pastoral Constitution ..." at the beginning of the document *Gaudium et spes*, in *Vatican Council II: The Basic Sixteen Documents: Constitutions, Decrees, Declarations*, Austin P. Flannery, O.P., gen. ed. (Northport, N.Y.: Costello; Dublin, Ireland: Dominican Publications, 1996), 903.

[18] The themes and central ideas of the Pastoral Constitution are as follows: The situation of man in the world today; the dignity of the human person; the community of mankind; man's activity in the universe; the role of the Church in the modern world; the dignity of marriage and the family; proper development of culture; economics and social life (the human person, social structures, and culture); the political community; avoidance of war; the establishment of an international community and the role of international organizations; ecumenical perspectives.

[19] Cf. Alberigo, "Konstitution in Beziehung", 50.

[20] A. Grillmeier, "Geist, Grundeinstellung und Eigenart der Konstitution 'Licht der Völker' [*Lumen gentium*]", in Baraúna, 1:140. On this theme, see also the preceding § 1.

[21] John XXIII, apostolic constitution *Humanae salutis*, in *AAS* 54 (1962): 7–10; English translation in *Encyclicals and Other Messages of John XXIII*, 386–97, citation at 389. See also the Opening Address of John XXIII on October 11, 1962, in *Council Daybook: Vatican II,*

a *new* Ecumenical Council",[22] this announcement stirred up great expectations and hopes. It was anticipated, above all, that the Council would take up the challenges posed by the changed circumstances and living conditions of mankind from a political, sociological, cultural, religious, and economic perspective and would reduce the truth of the gospel "to action in our lives"[23] according to these changing realities. This concern is expressed also in the Apostolic Constitution *Humanae salutis* dated December 25, 1961, with which John XXIII announced the convocation of the Council in October 1962.

> But We prefer to place Our unshakeable trust in the divine savior of the human race, who has not deserted the human beings whom he has redeemed. As a matter of fact, in keeping with the advice of Christ the Lord who urged us to recognize the *signs . . . of the times* (Mt 16:4), We can, in the midst of all the hideous clouds and darkness, perceive a number of things that seem to be omens portending a better day for the Church and for mankind.[24]

As further reasons for convoking the Council, the Constitution mentions first the ambivalence of the contemporary situation—which John XXIII describes as a "twofold picture: on the one hand, human society laboring under a great need for spiritual goods; on the other, the Church of Christ flourishing with a fullness of life"[25]—and secondly, in order to strengthen the faith and then to promote Church unity,[26] the sanctification of her members, the propagation of revealed truth,

---

Sessions 1 and 2, ed. Floyd Anderson (Washington, D.C.: National Catholic Welfare Conference, 1965), 25ff.

[22] John XXIII, *Humanae salutis*, in *Encyclicals and Other Messages of John XXIII*, 389.

[23] John XXIII, encyclical *Ad Petri cathedram*, no. 19, in *Encyclicals and Other Messages of John XXIII*, 28–29.

[24] *Humanae salutis*, 387. The motu proprio by John XXIII entitled *Concilium*, dated February 2, 1962, in *AAS* 54 (1962): 65f., set the date for the beginning of the Council as October 11, 1962 [English in *Council Daybook*, 1:10]. Cf. J.A. Komonchak, "Der Kampf für das Konzil während der Vorbereitung (1960–1962)", in Wittstadt, 1:190f.

[25] *Humanae salutis*, 389.

[26] Ibid., 390–91. Here it should be noted that Pope John XXIII understood "the way to unity with separated Christians" to mean their return to the Catholic Church. The latter, however, must "point up such aspects of doctrine and show such an example of fraternal charity as will enkindle among Christians separated from the Apostolic See a keener enthusiasm for that unity and, in a sense, prepare the way for its achievement" (ibid., 391).

as well as world peace.[27] These concerns underscore the necessity of a contemporary presentation of the Christian faith. The pope elaborated on this in his opening address at the first session of the Council:

> What is needed at the present time is a new enthusiasm, a new joy and serenity of mind in the unreserved acceptance by all of the entire Christian faith, without forfeiting that accuracy and precision in its presentation which characterized the proceedings of the Council of Trent and the First Vatican Council. What is needed ... is that this doctrine shall be more widely known, more deeply understood, and more penetrating in its effects on men's moral lives. What is needed is that this certain and immutable doctrine, to which the faithful owe obedience, be studied afresh and reformulated in contemporary terms. For this deposit of faith, or truths which are contained in our time-honored teaching, is one thing; the manner in which these truths are set forth (with their meaning preserved intact) is something else. This, then, is what will require our careful, and perhaps too our patient, consideration. We must work out ways and means of expounding these truths in a manner more consistent with a predominantly pastoral view of the Church's teaching office.[28]

In a similar manner, the Council makes this pastoral program its own at the beginning of the Constitution on the Sacred Liturgy *Sacrosanctum concilium*:

> This sacred Council has several aims in view: it desires to impart an ever-increasing vigor to the Christian life of the faithful; to adapt more suitably to the needs of our own times those institutions which are subject to change; to foster whatever can promote union among all who believe in Christ; to strengthen whatever can help to call the whole of mankind into the household of the Church.[29]

---

[27] The three fundamental themes of truth, unity, and peace, along with the renewal and promotion of them through love, were already contained in the inaugural encyclical of John XXIII, *Ad Petri cathedram*, passim.

[28] Opening address of John XXIII at the first session in *AAS* 54 (1962): 791; English version from Trinity Communications, http://www.catholicculture.org/library/view.cfm?id=3233&repos=1&subrepos=&searchid=18710; cf. *Council Daybook*, 1:25ff., citation at 27.

[29] *SC* 1; compare this also with the basic tone of John XXIII's first encyclical, *Ad Petri cathedram*, which is an expression of his pastoral concern. [English text cited above in n. 14.]

Therefore, a new awareness about the Church's vitality, both *ad intra* and *ad extra*, should be promoted, for the renewal of the Church, according to Jesus' promise in Matthew 28:19–20, still has "a redemptive significance in the modern world as well".[30] Therefore John XXIII emphasized in his Radio Message to the Catholics of the World:

> The Church should be sought for as she is in her intrinsic structure— vitality *ad intra* [inwardly]—as she presents, especially to her children, the treasures of illuminating faith and sanctifying grace.... Considered in relation to her vitality *ad extra*, that is, the Church in relation to the needs and afflictions of peoples ... , she senses the obligation to fulfill her responsibility through her teaching: "that ... we may so pass through temporal things, as not to lose those which are eternal" (Prayer for the Third Sunday after Pentecost).[31]

The years of debates over the successive drafts of the Constitution on the Church demonstrated how difficult this attempt to develop a contemporary formulation of the nature and mission of the Church proved to be.[32]

---

[30] J. A. Komonchak points out that the expressions "ad intra" and "ad extra" were incorrectly understood in a formalistic sense, "as though one could easily separate internal ecclesiastical questions from those involving the Church's relationship to the world". See Komonchak, "Kampf für das Konzil", 1:193.

[31] John XXIII, Radio Message to the Catholics of the World (September 11, 1962), in *AAS* 11 (1962): 678–85; English translation of excerpts in *The Pope Speaks*, vol. 8, no. 3 (1963): 233–34; citation translated from Italian.

[32] A chronological overview of the stages of the development of the Constitution on the Church, from the appointment of the Preparatory Theological Commission (see *AD I*, 1:95) by means of the motu proprio by John XXIII entitled *Superno Dei nutu* and dated June 5, 1960 (President: A. Ottaviani, Secretary: S. Tromp), to the solemn proclamation on November 21, 1964, by Pope Paul VI, is presented in *Constitutionis dogmaticae Lumen gentium Synopsis historica*, ed. G. Alberigo and F. Magistretti (Bologna: Istituto per le scienze religiose, 1975). See also the table, "Der Aufbau des Kirchenschemas vom I. Vatikanum bis zur Dogmatischen Konstitution 'Lumen Gentium'" in "Ekklesiologie: Die Lehre von der Kirche", by P. Neuner, in *Glaubenszugänge: Lehrbuch der katholischen Dogmatik*, ed. W. Beinert, 2:399–578, citation at 511 (Paderborn: Schöningh, 1995).

Chapter 2

From the Schema *De Ecclesia* to the Dogmatic Constitution *Lumen gentium*

§ 1. On the Dynamics at the Council

The first part of the schema on the Church, which had been composed during the two years prior to the Council by the Preparatory Commission *De doctrina fidei et morum* (for questions of faith and morals)[1] under the direction of Fr. Sebastian Tromp, S.J.,[2] was discussed at the end of the first session of the Council. After vehement debates,[3] a subcommission produced a second draft, which included substantial changes,[4] whereas the final text in the third draft incorporated modifications that were merely editorial in nature. A comparison of the structure of the first draft of the schema with the definitive outline of *Lumen gentium* shows the dynamic that had developed in the Council:

---

[1] This Preparatory Commission reported to the Holy Office and had also composed the document "On the Sources of Revelation", which was later rejected by the Council. See Hampe, *Konzil*, 137.

[2] Details concerning the first draft of a schema *De Ecclesia* by Fr. Sebastian Tromp can be found in J. A. Komonchak, "Der Kampf für das Konzil während der Vorbereitung (1960–1962)", in Wittstadt, 1:259–61.

[3] H. Reuter, *Das II. Vatikanische Konzil: Vorgeschichte—Verlauf—Ergebnisse, dargestellt nach Dokumenten und Berichten* (Cologne: Wort und Werk, 1966), 33, explains: "The protracted debate over the schema on the Church occupied to a great extent the General Congregations of the concluding phase of the first session, during which the work of the Holy Office was criticized, sometimes quite candidly. A verbal duel between two cardinals, Frings and Ottaviani, on this question during the second session garnered much public notice as well." See also G. Ruggieri, "Der schwierige Abschied von der kontroverstheologisch geprägten Ekklesiologie", in Wittstadt, 2:331–419.

[4] See Weiler, 213f.: "The subcommission *De Ecclesia* ... made the basis of its work a suggestion that had been circulating since the beginning of the Council, the outline by Gérard Philips, a dogmatic theologian from Lyons, who represented a sort of middle position between the Scholastic treatises of the Roman or Spanish cast and the unmistakably modern works of German or French theologians." Cf. also Teuffenbach, 352f., on the tense relationship between Tromp and Ottaviani.

Schema *De Ecclesia* (November 1962)	Constitution *Lumen gentium*
I. The nature of the Church Militant	I. The mystery of the Church
II. The members of the Church Militant and the necessity of the Church for salvation	II. The People of God
III. The episcopacy, as the highest degree of the sacrament of holy orders, and the priesthood	III. The hierarchical structure of the Church, in particular the episcopacy
IV. Residential bishops	IV. The laity
V. The states of evangelical perfection	V. The universal call to holiness in the Church
VI. The laity	VI. Consecrated religious
VII. The Church's Magisterium	VII. The eschatological character of the pilgrim Church and her unity with the Church in heaven
VIII. Authority and obedience in the Church	VIII. The Blessed Virgin Mary, Mother of God, in the mystery of Christ and the Church
IX. The relationship between Church and State	
X. The Church's duty to proclaim the gospel to all peoples throughout the earth	
XI. Ecumenism	
XII. (supplement, position in the document to be determined) The Virgin Mary, Mother of God and Mother of mankind	

A comparison of the two versions shows that the Constitution on the Church, as Karl Rahner remarked, "was not conceived from the start as a symmetrical and complete outline of a comprehensive ecclesiology". Rather, it "grew slowly and to some extent by chance through the supplementation of the preconciliar schema, which initially intended simply to treat certain particular themes"[5] that the Roman Curia considered to be of current interest. These topics were only loosely and unsystematically interconnected in the schema *De Ecclesia*. That is why, over the course of the Council, certain problematic subjects were taken out of the schema on the Church and discussed in separate decrees or declarations, for example, ecumenism in the decree *Unitatis redintegratio*; others received in-depth treatment in independent documents.[6]

---

[5] Karl Rahner, "Die Sünde in der Kirche", in Baraúna, 1:352.

[6] Cf., for example, the Decree concerning the Pastoral Office of Bishops *Christus Dominus*, the Decree on the Adaptation and Renewal of Religious Life *Perfectae caritatis*, the Decree on the Apostolate of the Laity *Apostolicam actuositatem*, or the Decree on the Mission Activity of the Church *Ad gentes*. The questions concerning the relation of the Church

Reference to *Lumen gentium* remains indispensable for the correct interpretation of these documents, inasmuch as they can be understood properly only in view of the image of the Church on which they are based. In the following section we will examine the points that the Council Fathers accentuated in *Lumen gentium* so as to provide new, contemporary insights into the nature of the Church and at the same time to maintain continuity with her tradition.

§ 2. What Was "New" about *Lumen Gentium*

1. *Revitalization of the entire tradition of the Church*

One objection to the original schema on the Church, *De Ecclesia*, was that "it was too rigid, too scholastic, too conventional and employed an excessively juridical, clerical, and triumphalist style."[7] That is why the Council Fathers attempted to formulate a synthesis of the Church's self-understanding with her biblical and patristic roots and thus to free ecclesiology from its narrow, juridical-hierarchical confines.[8] Specifically, as González Hernández explains, this happened through

> a rediscovery of forgotten aspects that had always been part of her heritage, a novel experience of new dimensions of this one Church by means of the conscious and renewed assimilation of her old contents. Thereby the Church is merely fulfilling her mission, which consists of maintaining the never-fading novelty of Christ as it constantly renews itself and making it accessible to all people of all times.[9]

---

to the world of today, which had already come up in chapter 9 of the *first* schema on the Church, among other places, were discussed primarily in the pastoral constitution *Gaudium et spes*.

[7] Concerning the discussion on the schema *De Ecclesia* (I), in *HerKorr* 18 (1963): 91; cf. *HerKorr* 17 (1963): 200.

[8] See the article by W. Kasper and J. Drumm, "Kirche, II. Theologie- und dogmengeschichtlich", in *LThK*, 3rd ed., vol. 5 (Freiburg im Breisgau: Herder, 1996), 1464. Cf. Kehl, *Kirche*, 49: The Second Vatican Council by no means intended "to break with tradition . . . , even though this had been marked very pointedly (since the Council of Trent in the fifteenth century) by Counter-Reformation tendencies and (since the First Vatican Council in the nineteenth century) by the anti-modernistic mind-set".

[9] O. González Hernández, "Das neue Selbstverständnis der Kirche und seine geschichtlichen und theologischen Voraussetzungen", in Baraúna, 1:165.

Accordingly, the distinctive feature in the renewal of ecclesiology by the Council consists precisely of the fact that this new formulation of the Church's self-understanding is carried out, not by delimiting or accentuating one particular historical epoch of ecclesiology, but rather through an attempt to integrate elements of her tradition that had been forgotten over the course of time.

This is especially true of the biblical and patristic beginnings of ecclesiology. In this way, the Church formulated in *Lumen gentium* a new self-understanding, which according to Guilherme Baraúna represents "an irrevocable step forward, an enrichment of her living patrimony".[10] Although the remarks set forth in *Lumen gentium* by the Council together with the Pope as the supreme teaching authority express no new dogma, they nevertheless bind the conscience of every member of the Church,[11] because they actualize for the present day her mission of proclaiming the gospel of Jesus Christ to all mankind.

2. Lumen gentium *as "the work of the Council"*

The definitive (third) version of the schema on the Church was finally passed on November 21, 1964, with 2,151 yes-votes against 5 nays, and it was solemnly promulgated on the same day. Gérard Philips, the chief editor of *Lumen gentium*, commented in retrospect on the work that had been accomplished:

> During the time between the 1963 and 1964 sessions, the Theological Commission made use of the interval to bring the text that had been presented into agreement with the wishes of the Council Fathers. More than is generally believed, the Constitution on the Church is the work of the Council itself and of its most active members.[12]

---

[10] Baraúna, "Vorwort", in Baraúna, 1:7.

[11] "Whatever else the Council sets forth must be accepted and adhered to by each and every Christian believer as the teaching of the highest Magisterium of the Church, in keeping with the intention of the Holy Synod itself, as this intention is determined from the subject being treated or from the manner of expression according to the principles of theological interpretation" (announcements made by the General Secretary of the Council in the 123rd General Congregation on November 16, 1964, in *KlKK* 197).

[12] G. Philips, "Die Geschichte der Dogmatischen Konstitution über die Kirche *Lumen gentium*", in *LThK.E*, vol. 1 (Freiburg im Breisgau: Herder, 1966), 150.

Now, by means of a brief survey of its individual chapters, we will show the extent to which the suggestions of the Council Fathers influenced the final form of the document. The purpose of this survey is, first, to mention several central modifications of the second version of the text of *Lumen gentium* and, secondly, to demonstrate the breadth of its image of the Church. Unlike the uncompleted Dogmatic Constitution *Pastor aeternus* of Vatican I (July 1870)[13] or even the schema *De Ecclesia* (November 1962), this image is no longer focused on the institutional dimension of the Church but rather makes evident—as Giuseppe Alberigo remarks—"the dynamic of a living body, which is constantly growing".[14]

1. The first chapter, "The Mystery of the Church", was not planned at all in the schema *De Ecclesia*. The original title and contents of the first chapter of that schema, "The Nature of the Church Militant", had been rejected by the majority of the Council Fathers already in the first session on account of the argument brought forward by Cardinals Frings, Liénart, and Döpfner: "The Church is a hidden mystery, and the study of it must be sustained by faith and love."[15] According to Charles Moeller, it is "as good as certain that this perspective owes its place in *De Ecclesia* to the influence of the German theologians". He mentions by name the Jesuit theologians Otto Semmelroth and Karl Rahner.[16] The expansion, in the second draft, of the passage about the "kingdom of God", which on earth has its beginning and core in the Church,[17] underscores the dynamic understanding of the Church in *Lumen gentium*.

---

[13] First Vatican Council, *Pastor aeternus*, in *DH* 3050–75. After Vatican I, as Klausnitzer observes, "it was forgotten, to a great extent, that *Pastor aeternus* developed from only the eleventh of a total of twelve chapters in the original schema.... Generally speaking, in the ordinary ecclesiology, catechesis, and preaching in Central Europe, the Church was presented almost exclusively from a juridical-hierarchical perspective" (Klausnitzer, 363). Cf. ibid., 363–81.

[14] G. Alberigo, "Das Zweite Vatikanische Konzil (1962–1965)", in *Geschichte der Konzilien: Vom Nicaenum bis zum Vaticanum II*, ed. Alberigo, 413–70, citation at 458 (Düsseldorf: Patmos, 1993).

[15] C. Moeller, "Die Entstehung der Konstitution, ideengeschichtlich betrachtet", in Baraúna, 1:76.

[16] Ibid., 1:82. See also: Wassilowsky, 329–35.

[17] Cf. *LG* 5.

A further central change in this first chapter concerns article 8, in which it is stated, by means of the concept of "subsistence",[18] that even though the one Church of Christ is "realized" (*subsistit*) in the Catholic Church, "many elements of sanctification and truth are found outside of its visible structure" also. "These elements, as gifts belonging to the Church of Christ, are forces impelling toward Catholic unity."[19] In contrast, the second draft of *De Ecclesia* (1963) had still read: "Haec igitur Ecclesia, vera omnium Mater et Magistra, in hoc mundo ut societas constituta et ordinata, *est* Ecclesia Catholica, *a Romano Pontifice* et Episcopis in eius communione directa."[20]

In his commentary on chapter 1 of *Lumen gentium*, Alois Grillmeier agrees with Heribert Mühlen that, in contrast to the exclusive character of the verb *est*, the new formula *subsistit in* "left open the question of the relationship of the one Church to the many churches".[21]

The concluding remarks of the first chapter of *Lumen gentium* about the "Church of the poor" as well as the emphasis on the path of penance and renewal the Church has to follow illustrate the way in which the Council perceived the authentic demands of the gospel.

---

[18] In Pesch's judgment, this "famous formulation in article 8 of the Constitution on the Church ... [contains] the most important statement by the Church of Rome relativizing herself, which strictly speaking is the only thing that lends authenticity to the Decree on Ecumenism in the first place" (219).

[19] LG 8. From the opposite perspective, the following is true: "The Church, precisely because it is Catholic, is open to dialogue with all other Christians, with the followers of non-Christian religions, and also with all people of good will, as John XXIII and Paul VI frequently said. *Lumen Gentium* explains convincingly and in depth the meaning of 'people of good will'. The Church wants to preach the Gospel *together with all who believe in Christ*. It wants to point out to all the path to eternal salvation, the fundamental principles of life in the Spirit and in truth" (John Paul II, *Crossing the Threshold of Hope*, ed. Vittorio Messori, trans. Jenny McPhee and Martha McPhee [New York: Alfred A. Knopf, 1994], 141).

[20] "Therefore this Church, the true Mother and Teacher of all, established and ordered as a society in this world, *is* the Catholic Church, governed *by the Roman Pontiff* and by the bishops in communion with him" (see Grillmeier, 1:174, n. 29).

[21] Ibid., 174. Cf. H. Mühlen, "Das Verhältnis zwischen Inkarnation und Kirche in den Aussagen des Vaticanum II", in *ThGl* 55 (1965): 171–90, ref. at 183. For a detailed discussion of the expression *subsistit in* as it is used in *Lumen gentium*, see pt. 1, sec. 2, chap. 1, §4, of this work; for Ratzinger's interpretation of it, see farther on, pt. 2, sec. 2, chap. 1, §4.

2. The second chapter, "On the People of God", was inserted into the second draft of the schema on the Church from the year 1963, immediately after the chapter on the episcopate. In the final version of the Constitution on the Church, it was placed before the chapter on the hierarchy so as to indicate that all Christians—ordained and lay— belong to the *one* People of God and share in the common priesthood of the baptized.[22] In this rearrangement, article 13 of *Lumen gentium* was completely rewritten. In it the foundation is laid for a universalism that is characteristic of the entire document and also builds an ecumenical bridge: "All men are called to belong to the new people of God. Where- fore this people, while remaining one and only one, is to be spread throughout the whole world and must exist in all ages."[23]

3. The composition of the third chapter of *Lumen gentium*, "On the Hierarchical Constitution of the Church and in Particular the Epis- copate", proved to be especially difficult because of its explosive theme. In retrospect, Gérard Philips recalled the tension in the great hall of the Council:

> On this question one group persisted in their fundamental opposi- tion. In view of the importance of the theme and the continuing controversy, the Secretariat of the Council had divided up the sub- mitted document into thirty-nine pieces, some of them containing only a single sentence, so as to put each to a vote. On the one hand, this involved the risk of losing the coherence of the reason- ing; on the other hand, this was supposed to ensure the greatest possible freedom.[24]

Another delicate subject was the reinstatement of the permanent diaconate. Enormous differences of opinion appeared here with regard to the celibacy obligation.[25] By a large majority, the Council Fathers rejected the motion to ordain as deacons *young* men who were not committed to celibacy.

---

[22] See O. Semmelroth, "Die Kirche, das neue Gottesvolk", in Baraúna, 1:365–79, esp. 371f. and 376.

[23] LG 13.

[24] Philips, "Geschichte der Dogmatischen Konstitution", 151.

[25] Cf. "Zur Diskussion über das Schema 'De Ecclesia' (II)—Der Diakonat", in *HerKorr* 18 (1963): 144. See also: D. A. Seeber, *Das Zweite Vaticanum: Konzil des Übergangs* (Freiburg im Breisgau: Herder, 1966), 124f.

4. The fourth chapter, "The Laity", was approved in the final vote by the largest majority.[26] It emphasized the particular importance of lay people by explaining that they share in their own way in the priestly, prophetic, and kingly office of Christ by living out their faith in the world. Through baptism, confirmation, and the Eucharist they are enabled to carry on their specific apostolate in the world:

> They must assist each other to live holier lives even in their daily occupations. In this way the world may be permeated by the spirit of Christ and it may more effectively fulfill its purpose in justice, charity, and peace. The laity have the principal role in the overall fulfillment of this duty. Therefore, by their competence in secular training and by their activity, elevated from within by the grace of Christ, let them vigorously contribute their effort, so that created goods may be perfected by human labor, technical skill, and civic culture for the benefit of all men according to the design of the Creator and the light of his Word. May the goods of this world be more equitably distributed among all men, and may they in their own way be conducive to universal progress in human and Christian freedom.[27]

5, 6, 7. The fifth chapter of *Lumen gentium*, "The Universal Call to Holiness in the Church", and the sixth, "Religious" (on consecrated religious), explain the essence of the Christian vocation: the sanctification of man. It follows logically that the eschatological goal is treated in the seventh chapter, "The Eschatological Nature of the Pilgrim Church and Its Union with the Church in Heaven".[28] This chapter was not planned originally and goes back to an intervention by John XXIII, who wanted to make sure that the veneration of the

---

[26] See Philips, "Geschichte der Dogmatischen Konstitution", 152. Out of a total of 2,236 votes cast, only eight were opposed.

[27] LG 36.

[28] The ambiguous word "eschatological" describes both the presence of the ultimate reality, in which the Church already shares now inchoatively, and also the expectation of the final fulfillment. Thus the term also addresses the Church's need for renewal. The traditional interpretation of "eschatological" was familiar to the Council Fathers under the heading of "The Last Things"—heaven, hell, purgatory—and of Christ's Second Coming at the end of time.

saints was anchored in ecclesiology,[29] since the Church "cannot speak only about the Church militant, but must also treat of her union with the Church 'triumphant' of the souls in heaven".[30]

8. Finally, the eighth and last chapter of *Lumen gentium*, "The Blessed Virgin Mary, the Mother of God, in the Mystery of Christ and the Church", became the subject of vehement debates between the representatives of two contrasting mariological movements:

> Some were in favor of a presentation that would be based on careful research of the sources and would take into account the development of salvation history as well as the development of dogma. . . . The others were accustomed to a "Mariology of privileges", which was largely based on abstract analyses and catered especially to the sentimental side of Marian devotion.[31]

As it is summarized precisely in the title of the Marian conclusion of *Lumen gentium*, "the Theotokos of the ancient tradition is the Virgin of Nazareth . . . , who in the Gospel says Yes to becoming the Mother of Christ and thus belongs to his mystery of salvation, which is continued and communicated by the Church." [32] The Council, by making room in its Mariology as well for the scriptural-patristic tradition and by refraining from any decision in controversial mariological questions,[33] not only follows a middle way[34] within the Catholic community, but also attempts at the same time to avoid provoking non-Catholics, especially Protestant Christians.[35]

---

[29] Cf. pt. 3, "Die dogmatische Konstitution über die Kirche *Lumen gentium*, Einleitung", in *KlKK* 120.

[30] Pesch, 192.

[31] Philips, "Geschichte der Dogmatischen Konstitution", 153f. To the latter type of Mariology belonged, among other things, the demand that the Council declare Mary as Mediatrix of all graces. Cf., for example, *AD* 1, 2.2: 22–80.

[32] Philips, "Geschichte der Dogmatischen Konstitution", 154.

[33] Cf. G. Söll, *Mariologie*, HDG 3/4 (Freiburg im Breisgau: Herder, 1978), 240.

[34] This applies in particular to the controversies about Mary's cooperation in redemption. Hence expressions that "could obscure the absolute transcendence of Christ in the work of redemption" are avoided. See G. Baraúna, "Die heiligste Jungfrau im Dienste des Heilsplanes", in Baraúna, 2:466. Cf. also *LG* 62.

[35] And so Cardinal Frings of Cologne suggested that, "in view of the various opinions evident today, everyone must sacrifice something of his personal preferences. We should limit ourselves to staking out the strictly dogmatic ground on which all can stand together.

In his commentary on the history of the development of *Lumen gentium*, Gérard Philips sums up the Constitution on the Church, saying that it gives us an overall view of the mystery of the Church, "the depth and richness of which have seldom been attained in all of her history".[36] Nevertheless, the consensus brought about by the Council Fathers was still largely determined by the tensions between different perspectives.[37] The controversies over the correct explanation of the conciliar documents and over an understanding of fidelity to the Council as a basis for further development in theology and Church are thus grounded in the Council documents themselves, and they lead logically to very different interpretations.[38] In an early reflection on the Constitution on the Church, Alois Grillmeier mentions two of its basic characteristics, namely, "moderation"[39] and "christocentrism",[40] whereby the first refers to the formal aspect, that is, the "tone" of the document, while the second pertains to its contents. Therefore in the next section we will turn our attention to the question: In what terms does *Lumen gentium* express the renewed self-understanding of Church in relation to the immediately preceding tradition?

Then not only will we be unassailable, but Mariology can also become fruitful in that way, both spiritually and even ecumenically" (Pesch, 194).

[36] Philips, "Geschichte der Dogmatischen Konstitution", 155.

[37] A more detailed discussion is found in H. J. Pottmeyer, "Die Zwiespältige Ekklesiologie des Zweiten Vatikanums: Ursache nachkonziliarer Konflikte", *TThZ* 92 (1993): 272–83.

[38] Cf. also, for example, J. B. Metz, "Das Konzil—'der Anfang eines Anfangs'?", in Richter, *Konzil*, 11–24. See also L. Bouyer, "Die Einheit des Glaubens und die Vielheit der Theologien: Eine historische Hinführung", in *Die Einheit des Glaubens und der theologische Pluralismus*, ed. Internationale Theologenkommission, 166–79, esp. 176 (Einsiedeln: Johannes Verlag, 1973).

[39] A. Grillmeier, "Geist, Grundeinstellung und Eigenart der Konstitution 'Licht der Völker'", in Baraúna, 1:153. By this Grillmeier means the new, noncondemnatory tone and the readiness to dialogue that were called for by John XXIII.

[40] Ibid., 154.

SECTION 2

THE MAIN IDEAS OF *LUMEN GENTIUM*

Chapter 1

The Mystery of the Church

§ 1. The Term "Mystery"

With the title "The Mystery of the Church", the first chapter of *Lumen gentium* announces an image of the Church that has been changed from that of the preconciliar schema *De Ecclesia*, inasmuch as it designates by the expression "mystery" the key theological concept that was decisive for the ecclesiology of the entire Constitution on the Church.[1] As Otto Hermann Pesch interprets it, the term "mystery" here attests to "an understanding whereby the Church is a part of the 'mystery' of God, and that means, according to the New Testament manner of speaking, the same thing as a part of God's *work of salvation*— the term μυστήριον is synonymous with οἰκονομία [in Latin: *dispensatio*] (cf. Eph 3:9)."[2]

In order to determine more precisely the understanding of "mystery" in *Lumen gentium*, we must briefly examine in this section the word's biblical and patristic provenance. The Greek word μυστήριον expresses one of the key concepts in the writings of Paul and post-Pauline

---

[1] On the gradual textual development of the first chapter *"De ecclesiae mysterio"*, see Alberigo/ Magistretti, 3–41. Cf. H.-J. Schulz, "Überlieferung—Wesensvollzug der Kirche", in *Mysterium Kirche: Sozialkonzern oder Stiftung Christi?* ed. W. Brandmüller, 63–83, ref. at 80 (Aachen: MM Verlag, 1996): "The rediscovery of the *Mysterium* Church is rightly judged to be the most important innovative feature of the ecclesiology of the Second Vatican Council." See also H. J. Pottmeyer, "Die Frage nach der wahren Kirche", in *HFTh* 3:159–84, at 171.

[2] Pesch, 161.

writings.[3] Paul proclaims Christ as the one and only eschatological sign of God's salvation for mankind. In Christ, God's eternal plan of redemption is realized once and for all. The recipient of this salvific mystery is the Church, the communion of those who have been called and sanctified by God. In Latin translations of the Bible, μυστήριον is most often rendered by the word *sacramentum*,[4] whereas the Latinized loanword *mysterium* occurs less frequently.[5] Μμυστήριον or *sacramentum* in this context designates the hidden mystery of God. Augustine[6] uses both terms (μυστήριον and *sacramentum*), often as synonyms. He associates with it "every state of affairs perceptible to the senses whose meaning is not limited to being what it immediately purports to be, but which refers beyond that to a spiritual reality".[7] In patristic theology, Christ himself, Scripture, the Church's liturgy, and the Church are termed a μυστήριον/*sacramentum*,[8] through which God himself intervenes in the historical reality of mankind.[9]

---

[3] Of the twenty-eight instances of μυστήριον in the New Testament, the post-Pauline letters to the Colossians and the Ephesians alone contain ten. Cf. R. Hoppe, "Das Mysterium und die Ekklesia: Aspekte zum Mysterium-Verständnis im Kolosser- und Epheserbrief", in *Gottes Weisheit im Mysterium: Vergessene Wege christlicher Spiritualität*, ed. A. Schilson, 81–101 (Mainz: Matthias-Grünewald-Verlag, 1989).

[4] Cf. F. Courth, *Die Sakramente: Ein Lehrbuch für Studium und Praxis der Theologie* (Freiburg im Breisgau: Herder, 1995), 26. Courth mentions three reasons why *sacramentum* eventually prevailed over the loanword *mysterium* in translations of the Bible: 1. It was not a foreign word. 2. It did not recall the pagan mystery religions. 3. It had ethical and religious connotations. Courth cites Tertullian (ca. 160–220) in this regard.

Originally the Latin word *sacramentum* meant "oath of allegiance". Because of its similarity to the baptismal promise, it was natural to translate *mysterium* as *sacramentum*; the Christian enlists in the *militia Christi*. On the meaning of the term *mysterium/sacramentum*, see J. Morawa, *Die Communio-Kirche als Sakrament des Heils in and für die Welt: Zum erneuerten Verständnis der Sendung der Kirche in der Gegenwart im Werk Walter Kaspers* (Frankfurt am Main: Lang, 1996), 229–244.

[5] Cf. E.-M. Faber, "Mysterium. III. Systematisch-theologisch", in *LThK*, 3rd ed., vol. 7 (Freiburg im Breisgau: Herder, 1998), 579–81, citation at 580.

[6] Cf. Courth, *Sakramente*, 26–28.

[7] F.-J. Nocke, "I. Allgemeine Sakramentenlehre", in *Handbuch der Dogmatik*, ed. T. Schneider, 2:188–225, citation at 197 (Düsseldorf: Patmos-Verlag, 1992).

[8] Grillmeier, 1:156. Cf. C. Vagaggini, *Theologie der Liturgie* (Einsiedeln: Benziger, 1959), 342–48.

[9] V. Hahn, "Strukturen der Kirche: Zur Identitätsproblematik der Kirche", in *Weisheit Gottes—Weisheit der Welt: Festschrift für Joseph Ratzinger zum 60. Geburtstag*, ed. W. Baier et al., 2:985 (St. Ottilien: EOS Verlag, 1987).

Precisely this harking back to the scriptural and patristic concept of mystery was significant for the Council, because the concept enabled it to broaden the narrow Neoscholastic view of the term "sacrament". This view was rooted in the Counter-Reformation, which tried to ward off the spiritualistic tendencies of the Protestant concept of Church through an understanding of the Church that was markedly institutional and comprehensible in juridical terms.[10] Three factors should be mentioned that helped to overcome this one-sidedness and thus to apply the concept of sacrament in its original breadth to the Church:

1. New approaches in exegesis: Already in the years immediately before the Second Vatican Council, influential Scripture scholars returned to the New Testament concept of μυστήριον, especially the exegetes[11] who had again brought to light the Pauline concept of mystery.

2. The theology of mystery[12] of Odo Casel (d. 1948): This theology led to the discovery of new perspectives on the "Christian cultic mystery" and to an understanding of the liturgy as *the celebration of the mystery*.

3. Ecumenical overtures to the Orthodox: Encounters with theologians[13] who had emigrated from Russia provided access to the Eastern view of the Church as mystery.

In our first paragraph, we defined the concept of "mystery" in terms of its biblical and patristic origin. It became evident thereby that the Council's decision to return to the meaning that the word had had in the early Church (a decision that had been prepared for by exegetical research, by Odo Casel's theology of mystery, and by the encounter with Orthodox theologians) was supposed to help expand the

---

[10] Cf. ibid.

[11] A wealth of examples from exegetical scholarship on the theme of *mysterium* from a biblical perspective can be found in B. Rigaux, "Das Mysterium der Kirche im Lichte der Schrift", in Baraúna, 1:199–219.

[12] Cf. O. Casel, *Das christliche Kultmysterium*, 4th ed. (Regensburg: Pustet, 1960); see also I. Herwegen, *Lumen Christi* (Munich: Theatiner-Verlag, 1924); W. Warnach, "Mysterientheologie", in *LThK*, 2nd ed., vol. 7 (Freiburg im Breisgau: Herder, 1962), 729–31.

[13] O. Rousseau, "Die Konstitution im Rahmen der Erneuerungsbewegungen in Theologie und Seelsorge während der letzten Jahrzehnte", in Baraúna, 1:28, refers to S. Bulgakov, "Le Ciel sur la terre", in *US* 3 (1927): 43. For an example of a fruitful exchange of opinions with Orthodox ecclesiology, I refer the reader to Yves Congar, a theologian at the Second Vatican Council; see C. T. M. Vliet, *Das Kirchenverständnis von Yves Congar* (Mainz: Matthias-Grünewald-Verlag, 1995), 62f.

institutional-juridical notion of sacrament and of the Church. This
leads us, however, to a new problem: From a Neoscholastic perspective, an ecclesiology centered on the aspect of mystery would necessarily be liable to the objection that it was spiritualizing the Church.
That is why this insight of the early Church at first met with resistance, as will be made clear in the next section on mystery as the
disputed overall perspective.

§ 2. "Mystery"—The Disputed Overall Perspective

The title "The Mystery of the Church" for the first chapter of *Lumen
gentium* evoked opposition at first from some Council Fathers, since
they feared that the idea of the visibility of the Church, which in
particular had been stressed since the time of the Reformation in contrast to the Protestant view of the "hidden Church" and the doctrine
of predestination, might be lost. On the contrary, the purpose of *Lumen
gentium*, as Alois Grillmeier emphasizes, was to make possible "a more
comprehensive view of the 'complex' reality of the Church than
before"[14] through the concept *mysterium*. That is why it says in *Lumen
gentium*:

> [T]he society structured with hierarchical organs and the Mystical
> Body of Christ, the visible society and the spiritual community ...,
> are not to be considered as two realities; rather, they form one com-
> plex reality which coalesces from a human and a divine element.[15]

Lumen gentium explicitly states that Christ instituted his Church on
earth as a visible structure and unceasingly sustains her. In doing so,
the Constitution on the Church cites Pope Leo XIII and Pope Pius XII
as its authorities when it says: "As the assumed nature, inseparably
united to him, serves the divine Word as a living organ of salvation,
so, in a somewhat similar way, does the social structure of the Church

---

[14] Grillmeier, 1:156.

[15] LG 8. The problem of the analogy suggested here and in the following quotation
concerning the incarnation of the divine Logos will be dealt with in greater detail in pt. 1,
sec. 2, chap. 1, § 3.2b, of this book.

serve the Spirit of Christ, who vivifies it, in the building up of the body (cf. Eph 4:15–16)."[16]

In the Council's understanding, the sociological reality of the Church and her mystery are mutually complementary; indeed, they permeate one another, since the Church is "the kingdom of Christ now present in mystery", which "grows visibly through the power of God in the world".[17] As early as the founding of the Church at Pentecost, she is manifested as a work of the triune God: "Jesus ... poured out on his disciples the Spirit promised by the Father (cf. Acts 2:33). From this source the Church ... receives the mission to proclaim and to spread among all peoples the kingdom of Christ and of God and to be, on earth, the initial budding forth of that kingdom."[18]

This "trinitarian signature"[19] is explicitly set forth in the first four articles of *Lumen gentium*. Through the revelation of Jesus in the Holy Spirit, the Church is called to become herself a sacrament of the divine *communio* as well as the sacrament of unity among men. *Mysterium*, therefore, has nothing in common with puzzling or even esoteric things that are conventionally described as being "mysterious". Instead, the term *mysterium*, according to Raphael Schulte, is concerned

> with *the* reality of the Church, which has her foundation in God himself as *the* mystery of faith, absolutely speaking, which after all is *revealed*. That is why we also start from God, as the one who reveals and communicates himself, in order to disclose the true nature of the Church as *mysterium*, so that this nature will be recognized as such and, most importantly, lived out.[20]

The "*mysterium*-nature" of the Church is fundamentally brought into focus by three particular perspectives: "Christ and the Church", "Sacrament", and "Unity". We will highlight these in the next paragraphs.

---

[16] *LG* 8 and the accompanying n. 11.

[17] *LG* 3.

[18] *LG* 5.

[19] Kehl, *Kirche*, 66.

[20] R. Schulte, "Erneuertes Kirchen- und Priesterverständnis als aktueller Auftrag: Zur Wegweisung der Dogmatischen Konstitution *Lumen gentium*—Über die Kirche", in *Aufbruch des Zweiten Vatikanischen Konzils heute*, ed. J. Kremer, 73–102, citation at 77 (Innsbruck and Vienna: Tyrolia-Verlag, 1993).

§ 3. Three Particular Perspectives:
"Christ and the Church", "Sacrament", and "Unity"

1. *Christ and the Church*

a. On distinguishing between Christ and the Church

"Lumen gentium cum sit Christus", the programmatic opening words
of the Constitution, summarize the main idea of the Council, formulated by John XXIII[21] shortly before the beginning of Vatican II, that
the Church is the light of the nations only in and through *Christ*. At
the same time they declare the christological core of the Constitution's ecclesiology, in which the nature and the mission of the Church
are expressed: "Christ is the Light of nations. Because this is so, this
Sacred Synod gathered together in the Holy Spirit eagerly desires, by
proclaiming the Gospel to every creature (cf. Mk 16:15), to bring the
light of Christ to all men, a light brightly visible on the countenance
of the Church."[22]

Through this emphatic reference to Christ, the Council Fathers, on
the one hand, avoid an ecclesiocentrism[23] that makes the theme
"Church" the be-all and end-all; on the other hand, the Church is
held responsible for turning to Christ in a continual process of conversion. That is why, in a lecture on scriptural theology entitled
"Church—Founded by Jesus Christ" given thirty years after the Council, Anton Ziegenaus admonishes his listeners that the commission to
proclaim the kingdom of God has a condition attached: conversion.[24]
The light of the gospel can shine upon all mankind only if the Church
through her ministry of proclamation[25] reflects the glory of Christ,
the *new* light of creation (cf. 2 Cor 4:6). Thus, at the very beginning
of *Lumen gentium*, as Grillmeier remarks in his commentary on *Lumen*

---

[21] Cf. the reference to the Radio Message of John XXIII dated September 11, 1962, in
Grillmeier, 1:156.

[22] *LG* 1.

[23] Cf. G. Alberigo, "Das Zweite Vatikanische Konzil (1962–1965)", in *Geschichte der
Konzilien: Vom Nicaenum bis zum Vaticanum II*, ed. Alberigo, 413–70, ref. at 458 (Düsseldorf: Patmos, 1993).

[24] A. Ziegenaus, "Kirche—Stiftung Jesu Christi", in Brandmüller, *Mysterium Kirche*, 45.

[25] Grillmeier, 1:157.

gentium, the "ecclesiological and missionary reform program of the Council"[26] is indicated.

b. Church as the work of the trinitarian economy of salvation

According to *Lumen gentium*, the Church derives her authority to act from her origin as a work of the divine economy of salvation. "The eternal Father ... [chose] to raise men to a participation of the divine life."[27] He carried out this salvific plan in the work of redemption, "for the sake of which he sent his Son into our sinful flesh, to accomplish the work of salvation in his death on the Cross, in order 'to send the Holy Spirit on Pentecost' on the basis of and by virtue of the crucifixion, so that those who believe in Christ 'would have access through Christ in one Spirit to the Father'".[28] This occurs when the "Ecclesia of God", which is trinitarian in her constitution from her very origin,[29] being the assembly called together according to the Father's eternal plan,[30] participates in and through the Holy Spirit in the mission of Jesus Christ,[31] "[so] that he should be the firstborn among many brethren" (Rom 8:29).[32]

This mission of Christ is, on the one hand, the dynamic origin of the Church and, on the other hand, her ongoing task, for Christ, as the One sent by the Father, founded the kingdom of God on earth, revealed the mystery, and brought redemption for all mankind by his obedience unto death.[33] His loving self-abandonment on the Cross is

---

[26] Ibid.

[27] *LG* 2.

[28] Schulte, "Erneuertes Kirchen- und Priesterverständnis", 78. Schulte refers here to *LG* 4.

[29] Cf. Kehl, *Kirche*, 279ff.

[30] Cf. *LG* 2.

[31] Cf. *LG* 3.

[32] *LG* 2. O. Rousseau points out that the trinitarian aspect in articles 1–4 is likewise to be found in the Greek Fathers of the Church, for example, in the anaphora of St. Basil. "This reference back to the Trinity—*Ecclesia de Trinitate*—which was frequently emphasized by the Greek Fathers ..., was taken up again by J. A. Möhler in the nineteenth century and was repeated by Y. Congar in *Irénikon* (1937): 131ff." (Rousseau, "Die Konstitution im Rahmen der Erneuerungsbewegungen in Theologie und Seelsorge während der letzten Jahrzehnte", in Baraúna, 1:28; see esp. n. 9). In the same passage, Rousseau cites Cardinal G. Lercaro, "La Signification du Décret De Œcumenismo", *Irénikon* (1964): 467–86, 469.

[33] Cf. *LG* 3.

the sacramental origin of the Church, which becomes present in the celebration of the Eucharist and perpetually constitutes the Church. For through the sacrifice of Jesus Christ on the Cross, which is made present upon the altar, "the basis for the Church's origin continually remains constitutive of the Church" [34] until the Second Coming of Christ at the end of the ages. In the meantime, the Church is called to prepare for the coming of his kingdom.

In summary, we can state that articles 2–4 of *Lumen gentium* examine the mystery of the Church from the perspective of her involvement in the trinitarian work of salvation and thus from a comprehensive view of salvation history. Prepared since the beginning of human history as the "ecclesia ab Abel",[35] the Church was "established in this last age of the world and made manifest in the outpouring of the Spirit". Thus she is "a people made one with the unity of the Father, the Son and the Holy Spirit".[36] At the end of time, she will finally "be gathered together with the Father in the universal Church".[37] This understanding in terms of salvation history raises the new question of the eschatological dimension of the Church, that is, the relation between Church and kingdom of God.

c. The Church—Seed and beginning of Christ's kingdom

If the Church is regarded, not as a *societas perfecta*, but as an entity that figures in salvation history, then her existence in time takes place as a growth process leading to perfection at the end of time. This enabled the Council Fathers to mention both the identity and also the difference between the Church of Jesus Christ and the kingdom of God:

> The Church, or, in other words, the kingdom of Christ now present in mystery, grows visibly through the power of God in the world.

---

[34] Grillmeier, 1:160.

[35] See *LG* 2: "At that moment . . . , all the just from the time of Adam, 'from Abel, the just one, to the last of the elect', will be gathered together with the Father in the universal Church." By the expression "ecclesia ab Abel" was meant the continuity between the Old and the New Covenant. See also Y. Congar, "Ecclesia ab Abel", in *Abhandlungen über Theologie und Kirche: Festschrift für Karl Adam*, ed. M. Reding, 79–108 (Düsseldorf: Patmos-Verlag, 1952). The expression "ecclesia ab Abel" goes back to the Church Fathers, especially Gregory the Great, Augustine, and John Damascene (cf. n. 2 in *LG* 2).

[36] *LG* 4.

[37] *LG* 2.

This inauguration and this growth are both symbolized by the blood and water which flowed from the open side of a crucified Jesus (cf. Jn 19:34) and are foretold in the words of the Lord referring to his death on the Cross: "And I, if I be lifted up from the earth, will draw all things to myself" (Jn 12:32).[38]

Therefore, the exaltation of Jesus on the Cross is simultaneously the sacramental origin of the Church and the sacramental basis for the unity of all men with one another and with God. This unity was established through the sacrifice of Jesus Christ on the Cross, which is made present upon the altar: The *one bread* as the sign of the *one Body* constitutes in time the pledge of this eschatological unity in the kingdom of God.[39] From the very beginning, this kingdom shone out before men in the word, in the work, and in the presence of Jesus Christ.[40] For this reason the Council declares that Jesus' preaching about the kingdom of God stood at the beginning of the Church's historical formation: "For the Lord Jesus set [his Church] on its course by preaching the good news, that is, the coming of the kingdom of God, which, for centuries, had been in the Scriptures: 'The time is fulfilled, and the kingdom of God is at hand' (Mk 1:15; cf. Mt 4:17)."[41]

When the Church faithfully accomplishes her mission, she shows herself to be, "on earth, the initial budding forth of that kingdom".[42] She is destined for perfection and longs for it, while she, "with all [her] strength, hopes and desires to be united in glory with [her] King".[43] For through the sending of the Spirit, access to the Father was secured for all who believe in Christ. The Spirit, however, "dwells in the Church and in the hearts of the faithful, as in a temple", prays in them, unifying the Church "in communion and in the works of

---

[38] *LG* 3. Cf. *GS* 39: "On this earth that Kingdom is already present in mystery. When the Lord returns it will be brought into full flower."

[39] Cf. *LG* 3. See also pt. 1, sec. 2, chap. 1, § 3.2, below of this book, "The Church as Sacrament".

[40] Cf. *LG* 5.

[41] Ibid.

[42] Ibid.

[43] Ibid. Compare P. Molinari, "Der endzeitliche Charakter der pilgernden Kirche und ihre Einheit mit der himmlischen Kirche", in Baraúna, 2:435–56, esp. 450–56. In a thought-provoking way, Molinari notes that the eschatological character of the Church not only is described in chapter 7 of *Lumen gentium* but also runs as a theme through the entire constitution.

ministry",[44] and thus brings about that spousal attitude of the Church, in which the Bride prepares herself for Christ. Constantly the Holy Spirit renews the Church and "leads [her] to perfect union with [her] Spouse. The Spirit and the Bride both say to Jesus, the Lord, 'Come!' (cf. Rev 22:17)."[45] Concretely, this eschatological tension means that the Church, ever since her founding, has had the experience of being fulfilled already and of having still to wait. Through the Holy Spirit, which was bestowed upon her at Pentecost in the power of the cru-cifixion, she is sent to "proclaim and to spread among all peoples the kingdom of Christ and of God".[46] In this process of her constant growth, she travels toward that perfected kingdom, filled with that eschatological hope of being "united in glory with [her] King".[47]

The *eschatological dimension* of the Church that has just been out-lined had made its way into the ecclesiology of *Lumen gentium* at the express wish of many Council Fathers, and, in the view of Olegario González Hernández, it represents "probably the most important nov-elty"[48] in the ecclesiology of the Council:

> Although contemporary ecclesiology owes the rediscovery of the pneumatological and sacramental dimensions to the dialogue with Orthodox theology, among other things, we would venture to assert that the rediscovery of the christocentric and eschatological dimen-sion is a fruit of the rapprochement with Protestant ecclesiology. Together with its greatest exponent, Karl Barth, this ecclesiology has emphatically given prominence to the transcendence of the Spirit and the expectation of what is yet to come, as opposed to hasty identifications of the Church with the kingdom of God.[49]

The ecumenical importance[50] of the idea of the kingdom of God is manifested in the fact that the kingdom of God, which was proclaimed

[44] *LG* 4.

[45] Ibid.

[46] *LG* 5.

[47] Ibid. Cf. E. Schillebeeckx, *Besinnung auf das Zweite Vatikanum: Vierte Session: Bilanz und Übersicht* (Vienna: Herder, 1966), 13.

[48] O. González Hernández, "Das neue Selbstverständnis der Kirche und seine geschicht-lichen und theologischen Voraussetzungen", in Baraúna, 1:177.

[49] Ibid.

[50] Cf. Per Erik Persson, "Der endzeitliche Charakter der pilgernden Kirche und ihre Einheit mit der himmlischen Kirche", in *Die Autorität der Freiheit: Gegenwart des Konzils*

by Jesus Christ and shone forth from his person, continues to work in the Church, which carries on Jesus' mission in the power of the Spirit, so as to be the herald that prepares the way for his kingdom.[51]

The eschatological perspective, based on Jesus' preaching of the kingdom of God, is only one central dimension of the ecclesiology of *Lumen gentium*, which the Council has brought to our attention again through its determined recourse to Scripture. We have the Council to thank also for the universal acceptance of a series of New Testament metaphors for the Church, which culminate in the Pauline image of the Body of Christ. With that the question arises as to the status accorded in *Lumen gentium* to this metaphorical and symbolic theological discourse about the Church.

d. Biblical metaphors for the Church with a christological reference

Article 6 of the Constitution on the Church describes the Church's structure with the help of symbols and analogies from Sacred Scripture as an order that cannot be explained by a single metaphor. Rather, it requires a synoptic presentation of complementary images in order to do justice to its complexity. They all exhibit a christological form and disclose, in the Council's words, "the inner nature of the Church".[52] The individual metaphors are taken from shepherding and farming, speak of a structure after the pattern of a building, and are finally related to family and nuptials. Specifically, the Church is described as "sheepfold", "vineyard",[53] "building", "temple", "family", "mother", "bride", and finally as the "Body of Christ". Since the last-mentioned image is the high point of the series and assumes a central position in the further course of the Constitution on the Church, we will now turn our attention to it at greater length.

---

und Zukunft der Kirche im ökumenischen Disput, ed. J. C. Hampe, 1:338–43, esp. 341 (Munich: Kösel-Verlag, 1967). The theological development that is manifested here becomes especially evident in comparison with the First Vatican Council. The latter had presented a draft of a "Constitution on the Church" that was not passed. In chapter 5 it stated, "The Church is so completely defined and determined in her constitution that no society that is separated from the unity of faith or from communion with this body could be called in any way a part or member of the Church" (*NR*, 8th ed., 390).

[51] Cf. *LG* 5.
[52] *LG* 6.
[53] Cf. L. Scheffczyk, "Kirche als Weinstock und Leib Christi: Die Wurzel des Mysteriums", in Brandmüller, *Mysterium Kirche*, 85–106.

Whereas the biblical-patristic image of the "Bride of Christ" [54] accentuates above all the personal difference between Christ and his Church, the Pauline image [55] of the Body of Christ emphasizes the unity of Head (Christ) and members (Church). As previously in the encyclical of Pius XII *Mystici Corporis*, [56] in *Lumen gentium* 7 a parallel is drawn between the Incarnation of the divine Logos and the founding of the Body of Christ:

> In the human nature united to himself, the Son of God, by overcoming death through his own death and resurrection, redeemed man and remolded him into a new creation (cf. Gal 6:15; 2 Cor 5:17). By communicating his Spirit, Christ made his brothers, called together from all nations, mystically the components of his own Body. [57]

The image of the "Body of Christ" in *Lumen gentium* 7 points to the christological or even pneumatological center of the ecclesiology of the Constitution on the Church. That is why this precise passage is of decisive importance for an "appropriate hermeneutic of the Council". [58] Such a hermeneutic has to make sure, above all, that the concept

---

[54] Cf. Jn 3:29.

[55] See Gal 6:15; 2 Cor 5:17; 1 Cor 12:13, 10:17, 12:12, and 12:26; Col 2:19; Eph 4:11–16, 5:23–28, 1:22f., and 3:19; cf. *LG* 7 and 8. The biblical idea of the Body of Christ is based on the Semitic notion of a corporate personality. The body as man's self, however, implies more than the physical in this context. Cf. *Called to Communion*, 35f. In the writings of St. Paul and of the Church Fathers, the term "Body of Christ" is used for the Church without the modifier "mystical". See also "Wesen", 47–68, specifically at 61.

[56] Cf. J. Werbick, *Kirche: Ein ekklesiologischer Entwurf für Studium und Praxis* (Freiburg im Breisgau: Herder, 1994), 277–315. Of course, it should be noted that, according to Werbick, "*Mystici corporis* had introduced the idea of diversity of members with a heavy emphasis on their differences in rank: 'That those who exercise sacred power in this Body are its first and chief members must be maintained uncompromisingly. It is through them, by commission of the Divine Redeemer himself, that Christ's apostolate as Teacher, King, and Priest is to endure'" (ibid., 278).

[57] *LG* 7.

[58] M. Seybold, foreword to *"Corpus Suum mystice constituit" (LG 7): La Chiesa Corpo Mistico di Cristo nel primo capitolo della "Lumen gentium"; Storia del Testo dalla "Mystici corporis" al Vaticano II con riferimenti alla attività conciliare del P. Sebastian Tromp S.J.*, by Stefano Alberto, 13 (Regensburg: Pustet, 1996). Stefano Alberto was able to demonstrate in his dissertation *"Corpus Suum mystice constituit" (LG 7)* how "the various concepts and images elucidate and heighten one another (Body of Christ, Mysterium / Sacrament, People of God, Communio, membership in / affiliation with the Church, etc.) and how they converge in the *conscientia Ecclesiae* that was so dear to the heart of Paul VI—the Church's

"Body of Christ" is interpreted *sacramentally*, as the Church Fathers and the liturgy understand it. The Council thereby complies with the concern expressed in the encyclical *Mystici Corporis* of Pope Pius XII, who opposed the merely mysterious and therefore intangible image of the *Corpus Christi mysticum* that to a great extent was conventional in his day and who emphasized anew the corporate constitution of the Church: She is "something definite and perceptible to the senses".[59] *Lumen gentium* confirms this statement, when it says in article 8: "Christ, the one Mediator, established and continually sustains here on earth his holy Church, the community of faith, hope and charity, as an entity with visible delineation through which he communicated truth and grace to all."[60]

Lumen gentium, however, avoids not only a one-sidedly mystical understanding of the Church, but also an equally one-sided fixation on the visibility of the institution. Indeed, the Constitution on the Church is concerned about the unity in tension of the visible and the invisible in *one complex reality*, "which coalesces from a divine and a human element".[61] The Church, which Christ called together from all nations

---

faith-filled consciousness of herself as the mystery of Christ (or of the Trinity), which is concretely and corporeally made visible and lived out in her" (ibid., 16f.).

[59] Pius XII, *Litterae encyclice no. 2: De mystico Iesu Christi corpore deque nostra in eo cum Christo coniunctione "Mystici Corporis Christi"* (June 29, 1943), 4th ed. Uberrimisque documentis illustravit Sebastianus Tromp S.I. (Rome: Pont. Universitatis Gregorianae, 1963). English edition: *Encyclical Letter of His Holiness Pius XII on the Mystical Body of Christ and Our Union in It with Christ, Mystici Corporis*, June 29, 1943 (Boston: St. Paul Editions, 1943), par. 14. Pius XII, encyclical *Humani generis*, in *AAS* 42 (1950): 561–78, citation at 571. See also Weiler, 35f.

[60] *LG* 8; cf. *SC* 2. See also Bernard of Clairvaux, Sermon 27 on the Song of Songs, in *On the Song of Songs*, 4 vols., trans. Kilian Walsh (Spencer, Mass.: Cistercian Publications, 1971–1980). Original Latin text in *Sancti Bernardi Opera*, ad fidem codicum recensuerunt J. Leclercq, C. H. Talbot, H. M. Rochais (Rome: Editiones Cistercienses, 1957–1997), vol. 1.

[61] *LG* 8. Here the constitution cites Pius XII, *Mystici Corporis*, in *AAS* 35 (1943): 193–248, citation at 221, and Pius XII, *Humani generis*, in *AAS* 42 (1950): 571. Cf. Alberto, "*Corpus Suum mystice constituit*" (*LG* 7), 566: "In questo senso si dovrebbe parlare rispetto alla 'Mystici Corporis', più che di una correzione significativa, di un ampliamento di prospettiva, suggerito dalla intenzione del Concilio di sottolineare, con apertura ecumenica, sia che fuori della Chiesa Cattolica esistono elementi di santità e di verità, sia che lo Spirito Santo non ricusa di servirsi delle chiese e comunità separate come strumenti di salvezza." (In this sense, with respect to *Mystici Corporis*, one would have to speak about a significant correction rather than a broadening of perspective suggested by the Council's intention of underscoring—along with the ecumenical overture—both that there are elements of sanctity and truth outside the Catholic Church and also that the Holy Spirit does not hesitate to make use of the separated churches and communities as instruments of salvation.)

and made, so to speak, "his own Body", therefore has a visible component as well as a spiritual component. It is part of her fundamental conviction that "the Spirit of Jesus Christ gives witness to itself bodily and visibly in the Church's central act of self-becoming [*in ihren zentralen 'Selbst'-Vollzügen*]".[62] This becomes especially clear in the realization of the sacramental life in the Church. While the salvific mission of Jesus is depicted and made really present in the sacraments, a real (albeit mysterious) transformation into Christ in the power of the Holy Spirit is thereby accomplished:

> In that Body the life of Christ is poured into the believers who, through the sacraments, are united in a hidden and real way to Christ.... Through baptism we are formed in the likeness of Christ.... Really partaking of the Body of the Lord in the breaking of the eucharistic bread, we are taken up into communion with him and with one another.... In this way all of us are made members of his Body (cf. 1 Cor 12:27), "but severally members one of another" (Rom 12:5).[63]

In much the same way as in *Mystici Corporis*, we can declare in summarizing that in *Lumen gentium* the Church is localized sacramentally and pneumatologically as *Corpus Christi*. Her sacraments, as visible signs, are instruments of salvation, through which the Holy Spirit imparts divine life. When she acts, it is always Christ himself, as Head of the Body, who is the one acting. Thus it becomes apparent why the Church herself is a sign and instrument of grace and why she can be described in an analogous sense as the "sacrament" of salvation.

2. The Church as sacrament

a. *Veluti sacramentum*

In the effort to develop an authentic interpretation of the Council, the term "sacrament", according to Leo Scheffczyk, is the "most significant and expressive concept for the 'mystery character' of the Church", which "makes accessible and includes many other characterizations of the Church".[64] Nevertheless, the formula *veluti*

---

[62] Werbick, *Kirche*, 302.

[63] LG 7.

[64] Leo Scheffczyk, *Aspekte der Kirche in der Krise: Um die Entscheidung für das authentische Konzil*, Quaestiones non disputatae 1 (Siegburg: F. Schmitt, 1993), 24.

sacramentum in the first article of *Lumen gentium* seemed strange and unfamiliar to many Council Fathers:[65] "[T]he Church is in Christ like a sacrament [*veluti sacramentum*] or as a sign and instrument both of a closely knit union with God and of the unity of the whole human race."

The reason that this mode of expression in the Constitution on the Church seemed so novel[66] lies in the fact that, from about the twelfth century on, only certain salvific signs were termed sacraments.[67] Furthermore, the precise *definition that there are seven sacraments*, which was proposed in 1439 at the Council of Florence and was confirmed again by the Council of Trent,[68] was cause for dogmatic misgivings about a modified application of the term *sacramentum*. Accordingly, the new perspective, *veluti sacramentum*—that is, "quasi-sacrament"—raises questions, which Leo Scheffczyk summarizes as follows:

> How can an association of men be a sacrament? Or: Is there besides the seven particular sacraments yet another new sacrament, which then would have to be counted as the eighth? If the Church, like Christ, is seen as a sacrament, the further question arises: Is not the Church thereby placed on a par with Christ, so that she erroneously appears to be "deified"? Such a designation for the Church is not prevalent, either, in the general understanding of the faith.[69]

---

[65] Cf. P. Smulders, "Die Kirche als Sakrament des Heils", in Baraúna, 1:289.

[66] On the textual history of *Lumen gentium* in relation to a sacramental ecclesiology, see G. Wassilowsky, "Die 'Textwerkstatt' einer Gruppe deutscher Theologen auf dem II. Vatikanum", in *Die deutschsprachigen Länder und das II. Vatikanum*, ed. H. Wolf and C. Arnold, 61–87 (Paderborn: Schöningh, 2000). "One main motive for favoring the theologoumenon 'Church as Sacrament' will have to be sought in the German determination to make ecumenical progress" (ibid., 82).

[67] Scheffczyk, *Aspekte der Kirche in der Krise*, 25.

[68] See also *DH* 1310: "There are seven sacraments of the New Covenant: baptism, confirmation, Eucharist, penance, extreme unction, order, matrimony...." Cf. Council of Trent, 7th sess. (1547), can. 1: "If anyone shall say that the sacraments of the New Law were not all instituted by Jesus Christ our Lord, or that there are more or less than seven, namely baptism, confirmation, Eucharist, penance, extreme unction, order, and matrimony, or even that any one of these seven is not truly and strictly speaking a sacrament: let him be anathema" (*DH* 1601).

[69] L. Scheffczyk, "Die Kirche—das Ganzsakrament Jesu Christi", in *Christusbegegnung in den Sakramenten*, ed. H. Luthe, 67 (Kevelaer: Butzon und Bercker, 1981).

It was possible to counter these objections, however, by pointing out that it is a question of the intrinsic connection between the Church and those sacraments and not of an addition:

> Judging by the catechism definition of sacrament, the Church is *not* a sacrament but, rather, is *prior* to the sacraments. *If* she is a sacrament, then she is the "primordial sacrament", the "root sacrament" (Otto Semmelroth), the "fundamental sacrament" (Karl Rahner), the "universal sacrament" (*Lumen gentium* 1). *In* it and *from* it the seven sacraments are produced. The Church shares with these particular sacraments, however, two important features that the Council of Trent also mentions expressly: being a visible form of invisible grace (*visibilis forma invisibilis gratiae*), which is one of Augustine's formulations.[70]

If, however, the Church is not only the administrator of the sacramental means of grace,[71] but is herself *like a sacrament*, then she is never an end in herself. Her "visible, tangible hierarchical constitution ... is at the service of the *invisible* reality of grace and faith that is communicated in her in a worldly, historical manner".[72] Hence the expression *veluti sacramentum*, according to Walter Kasper, offers one

> conceptual means, among others, of overcoming ecclesiological triumphalism, clericalism, and legalism and of setting forth the mystery of the Church, which is concealed in the visible form and comprehensible only in faith, so as to express and indicate, on the one hand, that the Church is derived entirely from Christ and permanently related to him and, on the other hand, that she is there as a sign and instrument but also to be entirely at the service of mankind and of the world. The concept lends itself especially to coordinating and distinguishing in a differentiated way the visible structure and the spiritual nature of the Church.[73]

---

[70] Pesch, 165. Cf. *DH* 1639; *NR*, 8th ed., 571. See also Scheffczyk, "Kirche—das Ganzsakrament Jesu Christi", 68: "The expression 'in the nature of' [*gleichsam*, referring to *LG* 1] indicates, at any rate, that the designation 'sacrament' does not apply to the Church without some degree of ambiguity."

[71] Cf. *LG* 7. See also K. Rahner, *Kirche und Sakramente*, QD 10 (Freiburg im Breisgau: Herder, 1960), 9.

[72] Werbick, *Kirche*, 411.

[73] W. Kasper, "Die Kirche als universales Sakrament des Heils", in *Glaube im Prozess: Christsein nach dem II. Vatikanum: Festschrift für Karl Rahner*, ed. E. Klinger and K. Wittstadt, 221–39, citation at 228–29 (Freiburg im Breisgau: Herder, 1984).

To express this nuanced way of looking at the Church, the Council in
Lumen gentium 8 chose the concept of *una realitas complexa*, of one
complex reality.

b. One complex reality

In order to "add depth to the visible, this-worldly side of the Church
through her spiritual dimension",[74] the intertwining of temporal-
social structure and transcendent reality must be reflected. In much
the same way as Pius XII had done,[75] *Lumen gentium* 8 emphasizes
that the visible together with the spiritual society of the Church make
up one complex reality. In order to explain the significance of this
mystery, theologians refer to the parallel, Incarnation—Church, with
the important proviso, of course, that this parallel is to be understood
analogously, as a comparison that is "no weak analogy", as it says literally in *Lumen gentium* 8.

> The society structured with hierarchical organs and the Mystical
> Body of Christ are not to be considered as two realities, nor are the
> visible assembly and the spiritual community, nor the earthly Church
> and the Church enriched with heavenly things; rather they form
> one complex reality which coalesces from a divine and a human
> element. For this reason, by no weak analogy, it is compared to the
> mystery of the incarnate Word. As the assumed nature inseparably
> united to Him serves the divine Word as a living organ of salvation,
> so, in a similar way, does the visible social structure of the Church
> serve the Spirit of Christ, who vivifies it, in the building up of the
> body (cf. Eph 4:16).

---

[74] Courth, *Sakramente*, 18.

[75] Cf. Pius XII, *Mystici Corporis*, in *AAS* 35 (1943): 193–248, citation at 221ff. Pius XII,
Humani generis, in *AAS* 42 (1950): 561–78, citation at 571. The schema *De Ecclesia Christi*,
which had been completed for the First Vatican Council but was never officially approved
because of the premature discontinuance of the Council, taught in its first chapter "that
men are purified from their sins through baptism and become members joined with one
another, that they are united with Christ, their Head, in faith, hope, and love and are
enlivened by the Holy Spirit. In the third chapter the Church is called a spiritual and
supernatural society by reason of this union. Subsequently the fourth chapter warns against
the teaching that the members of the Church are joined to one another only by invisible
bonds, as it were. For that would make the Church an entirely invisible society" (cf. F. van
der Horst, *Das Schema über die Kirche auf dem I. Vatikanischen Konzil* [Paderborn: Bonifacius-
Druckerei, 1963], 175f.).

From the passage just cited, it follows that someone who regards the Church only as a sociological entity cannot understand her, for her visibility is not simply that of a worldly institution; her social structure serves the Spirit of Christ, who enlivens it for the extension of his kingdom. The pioneers of this renewed sacramental view of the Church were, as early as the nineteenth century, Johann Adam Möhler (1796–1838) and—building upon his work—Matthias Joseph Scheeben (1835–1888). The former explained the reason for the unity of the spiritual and the visible in the Church with the idea of *incarnatio continua*.[76] Scheeben, in turn, spoke of the Church as "a great sacrament".[77]

Hence, in the opinion of Leo Scheffczyk, we can conclude that the sacramental aspect of the Church in *Lumen gentium* introduces no "formal innovation in the idea of Church", since the Council thereby "merely won recognition once again for an originally biblical idea that was anchored in tradition".[78] Nevertheless, the Second Vatican Council overcame a certain fixation that "too hastily and uncritically equated what is divine and what is human in (and about) the Church" and treated as sacred "claims to power and traditional structures [that were] all too human".[79] Hermann Josef Pottmeyer sees in the differentiation of this unity reason for hope that the structure of the Church

---

[76] Cf. J. A. Möhler, *Symbolik oder Darstellung der dogmatischen Gegensätze der Katholiken und Protestanten nach ihren öffentlichen Bekenntnißschriften* (Regensburg: Manz, 1882), 332f.: "Thus the Church is ... the Son of God, who continues to appear among men in human form, ever renewing and eternally rejuvenating himself, his ongoing incarnation, just as the faithful, too, are called the Body of Christ in Sacred Scripture. Now it is evident from this that the Church, even though she is made up of men, is not merely human. Rather, just as the divine and the human elements can be distinguished in Christ, although the two are united, so it is also in the Church as an undivided totality."

[77] M. J. Scheeben, *Die Mysterien des Christentums* (Freiburg: Herder, 1941), 461. See also Smulders, "Kirche als Sakrament", 290: "This association of the Church, on the one hand, with the Incarnation, and, on the other hand, with the sacraments in the narrow sense, especially with the Eucharist, is precisely one of the fundamental accomplishments of the theological understanding of the Church in the biblical and patristic periods."

[78] Scheffczyk, *Aspekte der Kirche in der Krise*, 33: "After all, the First Vatican Council had already described the Church as the 'ensign [raised up] for the nations' (alluding to the word of the prophet Isaiah 11:12, who awaits an especially visible exaltation of the community of believers in the end times)." Cf. Scheffczyk, "Zur Einführung" [By way of introduction], in the German edition of *Dominus Iesus* (Stein am Rhein: Christiana-Verlag, 2000), 6–10.

[79] Werbick, *Kirche*, 407.

can be reformed[80] in response to the signs of the time. At the same time, he refers in this context to the Pastoral Constitution *Gaudium et spes*, in which the spiritual and social realities of the Church are likewise distinguished but not separated:

> Since the Church has a visible and social structure as a sign of her unity in Christ, she can and ought to be enriched by the development of human social life, not that there is any lack in the constitution given her by Christ, but that she can understand it more penetratingly, express it better, and adjust it more successfully to our times.[81]

The recognition of the "plurality of forms of expression and schools of thought in the Church"[82] should be viewed as a further consequence of this development. Thus *Lumen gentium* 13 accentuates the *diversity* that should lead to the fullness of *unity*, in a "coexistence of different ecclesial and spiritual traditions, which originate in different cultural characters".[83] This universality becomes clearest in the vocation of all mankind to salvation,[84] which ultimately represents the "theological foundation for the relation between the Church and the world".[85] In the description of the Church as the *universal sacrament of salvation*, precisely this complex connection[86] between the Church's social constitution and her spiritual dimension finds its expression. But if the Church herself is constituted socially as well, the question arises how she can then be the sacramental sign and instrument of God's salutary gift to his creation. *Lumen gentium* answers it by underscoring the eschatological character of the Church as the universal sacrament of salvation.

---

[80] Cf. H.J. Pottmeyer, "Modernisierung in der katholischen Kirche am Beispiel der Kirchenkonzeption des I. und II. Vatikanischen Konzils", in *Vatikanum II und Modernisierung: Historische, theologische und soziologische Perspektiven*, ed. F.-X. Kaufmann and A. Zingerle, 142 (Paderborn: Schöningh, 1996): "The traditionalist opposition to the renewal of the Church, which began to make its voice heard after the Council, allows us to gauge what a formidable blockade the false sacralization of structures had been, now that it was being lifted."

[81] GS 44.

[82] Pottmeyer, "Modernisierung", 143.

[83] Ibid. Cf. GS 44.

[84] Cf. LG 3, 9, 16.

[85] Pottmeyer, "Modernisierung", 143.

[86] GS 1 paraphrases it as "linked ... with the deepest of bonds"; GS 40 describes the way in which "the earthly and the heavenly city penetrate each other."

c. "Universal sacrament of salvation"

The discussion about the eschatological character of the Church at
the beginning of the third session of the Council[87] revealed a certain
hesitancy to ascribe to the Church, as a sign and instrument, the quality of being provisional as well. Yet not only the individual human
being is destined for salvation, but the pilgrim Church, too, which
"in her sacraments and institutions ... has the appearance of this world,
... and she herself dwells among creatures who groan and travail in
pain until now and await the revelation of the sons of God".[88] As
sacrament, the Church is at the same time, however, an "eschatological reality in the sense that the *eschaton*, the heavenly reality of salvation that is yet to be attained, has already irrupted into this world in
the sacramental sign and is captured in a worldly character as though
in a seal".[89]

The theme of the Church as a sign of hope, which, on the one
hand, even now effectively testifies to God's presence and, on the other
hand, acknowledges her own provisional nature, so as to be for all
mankind the forerunner of the Lord who is to come again, is part and
parcel of the description of her as the *universal sacrament of salvation*. In
the power of the Holy Spirit,[90] "who is the guarantee of our inheritance",[91] the Church represents the eschatological reality, which continues the mission of the Son of God on earth and leads the faithful
onward toward her goal of "restoration":

Rising from the dead (cf. Rom 6:9), he sent his life-giving Spirit
upon his disciples and through him has established his Body which
is the Church as the universal sacrament of salvation. Sitting at the
right hand of the Father, he is continually active in the world that
he might lead men to the Church and through [her] join them to
himself and that he might make them partakers of his glorious life
by nourishing them with his own Body and Blood. Therefore the
promised restoration which we are awaiting has already begun in

---

[87] Cf. O. Semmelroth, "Kommentar zu *LG* Kap. 7", in *LThK.E*, vol. 1 (Freiburg im
Breisgau: Herder, 1966), 315f.
[88] *LG* 48. Cf. Rom 8:19–22.
[89] Semmelroth, "Kommentar", 317.
[90] Cf. *LG* 59.
[91] Quotation from Eph 1:14 in *LG* 48.

Christ, is carried forward in the mission of the Holy Spirit and
through him continues in the Church in which we learn the meaning of our terrestrial life through our faith, while we perform with
hope in the future the work committed to us in this world by the
Father, and thus work out our salvation (cf. Phil 2:12).[92]

The eschatological salvation begun in the Church strives toward perfection, toward that transfigured form "wherein that which was con-
cealed in its worldly form has no more need of a sign, but will be
experienced unveiled and in itself".[93]

In this section we have demonstrated, on the basis of *Lumen gentium*, that the eschatological reality that has already dawned in the
Church is dynamically ordered toward the salvation of the whole world.
Because this salvation is found only in Christ, however, the Church is
sacrament precisely by the fact that Christ is present in her throughout history. *Lumen gentium* defines this presence as a sacramental presence, as we will explain in the next section.

d. The Church as the sacramental re-presentation of Jesus Christ

Lumen gentium regards the Church as "the re-presentation [*das Gesche-
hen der Vergegenwärtigung*, literally: "the actual making-present"] of Jesus
Christ and of his definitive salvation for mankind".[94] This self-
understanding, in the opinion of Medard Kehl, avoids both a "mys-
tifying over-exaltation of the Church" and also a drifting into mere
functionalism.

> If this re-presentation is understood sacramentally, then the Church
> in her proclamation and her activity does not simply point like a
> signpost to a salvation that can be found somewhere else, apart from
> her (for instance, with God who remains absolutely transcendent or
> only in the kingdom of God perfected in the end times or in fol-
> lowing Jesus anonymously in the midst of the world, and so on).
> Conversely, though, the Church cannot simply direct mankind's search
> for salvation to herself, either, as if she were salvation per se, Christ
> present here and now, or the kingdom of God which has arrived.[95]

---

[92] *LG* 48.
[93] Semmelroth, "Kommentar", 317.
[94] Kehl, *Kirche*, 83. Cf. Courth, *Sakramente*, 19.
[95] Kehl, *Kirche*, 83.

The latter position would imply an undifferentiated identification of the Church with the kingdom of God or with Christ (the Church as "Christ living on") or else with the Holy Spirit. The latest council[96] opposed this notion precisely by "applying the term *sacrament* to the Church again, in order to define her specific relation to God's salvific action for the world".[97]

The remarks in this second section can be summarized as follows: The understanding of the Church as sacrament enabled the Council to express the unity and the difference between the social constitution of the Church and the transcendent reality present within her, between her concrete form and her universal mission, as well as between her temporal task and her provisional character as an eschatological sign. That is why the Church, according to *Lumen gentium*, cannot be identified either with Christ or with the kingdom of God (which would lead to her becoming absolutely an end in herself), yet neither can she be reduced to a mere reference to a transcendent reality. If the Church is supposed to be the universal sacrament of salvation for the world in the way just described, then this leads to the question of how we should understand her mark of unity, which is already anchored in the Apostles' Creed.[98]

3. *The Church's unity*

Against the background of the previous explanations, it becomes clear that unity, as an essential mark of the Church, is now identified with the rediscovered concept of *communio*. This concept defined Vatican II to such an extent that one can speak of it as the leitmotiv of the Council.[99] It conveys

> a concentration on the inmost nature of the Church, a reduction of her self-understanding, without however giving up the essential thing that is expressed precisely by the term "sacrament", as well as the

---

[96] See *LG* 1, 9, 48, 59; *SC* 5, 26; *GS* 42, 45; *AG* 1, 5.

[97] Kehl, *Kirche*, 82. See also: H. J. Pottmeyer, "Der eine Geist als Prinzip der Einheit der Kirche in Vielfalt: Auswege aus einer christomonistischen Ekklesiologie", *PthI* 5 (1985): 253–84, ref. at 263ff.

[98] Cf. *LG* 8.

[99] On this subject, compare K. Hemmerle, "Einheit als Leitmotiv in *Lumen gentium* und im Gesamt des II. Vatikanums", in Klinger and Wittstadt, *Glaube im Prozess*, 207–20.

affirmation of her task in the world, which ... is seen in fraternal service to the unity of all mankind.[100]

The Extraordinary Synod of Bishops that met in Rome from November 24 to December 8, 1985, took stock of the understanding of *communio* for which foundations had been laid by the Council, so that it [the Synod] might determine the position of and chart a course for "the Church today and tomorrow".[101] In the "triad" of *mysterium*, *communio*, and *missio*,[102] the Synod heard the leitmotivs of the Council's ecclesiology (which had been variously received) and, twenty years after its conclusion, gave fuller expression to the concept of *communio* than had the conciliar documents themselves:

> The *communio* ecclesiology is the central and fundamental idea of the conciliar documents. *Koinonia / communio*, which has its basis in Sacred Scripture, was highly regarded in the early Church and is so to this day in the Eastern Churches. Much has happened since the Second Vatican Council to make the Church as *communio* better understood and implemented more concretely in everyday life.[103]

This is necessary, because the concept *communio* is of decisive importance for the correct understanding of the relation between unity and multiplicity in the Church. Its importance in the Bible and in the early Church "obviously influenced a large number of the Council Fathers".[104] According to this concept, unity does not mean uniformity—that would be at variance with a legitimate multiplicity

[100] K. Rahner and H. Vorgrimler, "III. Die dogmatische Konstitution über die Kirche *Lumen gentium*", in *KlKK* 106.

[101] *Zukunft der Kirche aus der Kraft des Konzils: Die außerordentliche Bischofssynode '85: Die Dokumente mit einem Kommentar von W. Kasper* (Freiburg im Breisgau: Herder, 1986), 5.

[102] On this subject, see the keynote paper [*Grundsatzreferat*] "Ist das Konzil schon angekommen? Zum Schlussdokument der Außerordentlichen Bischofssynode 1985", read by K. Hemmerle at the plenary assembly of the Central Committee of German Catholics, which was published as a revised transcript from audio tape in K. Hemmerle, *Gemeinschaft als Bild Gottes: Beiträge zur Ekklesiologie*, ed. R. Feiter, Ausgewählte Schriften 5 (Freiburg im Breisgau: Herder, 1996), 60–84; see also ibid., 85–103: "Pilgerndes Gottesvolk—Geeintes Gottesvolk: Eine Weg-Skizze".

[103] Ibid., 32.

[104] K. Kienzler, "'Communio' zwischen Gott und den Menschen—zum Kirchenbild des 2. Vatikanischen Konzils", in *Zweites Vatikanisches Konzil: Das bleibende Anliegen*, ed. J. Piegsa, 122 (St. Ottilien: EOS Verlag, 1991).

of charisms—but rather a gift of God that, as *Lumen gentium* points out, is upheld by the visible bond of ecclesiastical order: Creed, sacraments, and hierarchy.[105] Like the Synod, Alois Grillmeier had already recognized *communio* as a pervasive theme of the Constitution on the Church in his commentary on the first chapter of *Lumen gentium*:

> The Church is the unity of communion in the Holy Eucharist, in the Holy Spirit, in the visible (hierarchical) administration, and in the various ministries. She is the animated [*beseelt* = "ensouled"] unity of the body in the diversity of the members and ministries. Not only the charismatic gifts, but the hierarchical order, too, is a self-communication of the Spirit. He thus becomes incarnate in the Church and forms a mystical person, so to speak, out of many persons.[106]

When the Council speaks about *communio*, it is not dealing primarily "with questions about the Church's structure", as Walter Kasper remarks. "The word *communio* refers rather to the actual 'thing' (*res*) from which the Church comes and for which she lives."[107] All men are called by God "to a participation of the divine life",[108] in which their most profound dignity consists.[109] That means, as Gisbert Greshake says, "the *communio* in which the triune God exists should be clearly marked on the fellowship of disciples redeemed by Christ and spread throughout the world by them."[110]

Consequently, the concept of *communio* leads again to the *mysterium* of the Church, upon which the Constitution on the Church elaborates in a Pauline manner as the mystery of *communio* under the three following headings: (a) The Church in her sacramental nature is the sign and instrument of *communio*. (b) The origin and the end of Church unity is the trinitarian *communio*. (c) The Church herself constitutes a mystery of trinitarian *communio*.

---

[105] Cf. *LG* 14.

[106] Grillmeier, 1:161.

[107] W. Kasper, "Kirche als communio: Überlegungen zur ekklesiologischen Leitidee des Zweiten Vatikanischen Konzils", in *Die bleibende Bedeutung des Zweiten Vatikanischen Konzils*, ed. F. König, 62–84, citation at 66 (Düsseldorf: Patmos, 1986).

[108] *LG* 2.

[109] Cf. *GS* 19.

[110] G. Greshake, *An den drei-einen Gott glauben* (Freiburg im Breisgau: Herder, 1998), 89.

a. Sacramental structure as sign and instrument of *communio*

The key to understanding the Church as *mysterium* is her sacramental structure. As the work of the triune God, the Church constitutes one and only one People of God, which "is to be spread throughout the whole world and must exist in all ages, so that the decree of God's will may be fulfilled: [namely] ... that all his children, scattered as they were, would finally be gathered together as one".[111] This conception of unity as union with God and as unity of men with one another,[112] which is mediated through the Church as the sign and sacrament of salvation, runs through the entire Constitution *Lumen gentium*.[113] On the basis of her sacramental constitution, the Church is never an end in herself; she serves, rather, as the "instrument" of redemption and the "seed of unity, hope and salvation".[114] That is why she is also the type, model, and example of the *communio* of all men and all peoples.[115] In accordance with her divine mission of renewing all things in Christ, the Church has the task of being a *sacrament for the world*, so as to prepare for the definitive kingdom of God.[116] Her commitment to justice and peace and to a new civilization of love is consequently "a fundamental perspective for the Church today. Precisely as a *communio* unity, as unity in reconciled diversity, the Church is the messianic people, the universal sign of salvation."[117]

---

[111] LG 13. Compare also GS 78: "For by the cross the incarnate Son, the prince of peace, reconciled all men with God ... , thus restoring all men to the unity of one people and one body." See also LG 26; SC 1, 2; GS 33, 45, 92; UR 2, 3, 4, 8, 22; AA 8, 18, 27; GE 1.

[112] Cf. LG 1.

[113] Cf. LG 3, 5, 9, 28.

[114] LG 9.

[115] AG 11, 23; GS 39; NA 1: "In her task of promoting unity and love among men, indeed among nations...."

[116] The sacramental character of the Church for the world manifests itself in the fact that the Church—as Klaus Hemmerle remarks in his commentary on *Lumen gentium*—"must be brought by us as the icon of redeemed humanity into the midst of humanity in such a way that this humanity comes thereby to the knowledge of its unity and to faith in the one who redeemed it" (K. Hemmerle, "Erste Überlegungen zu möglichen Themen für den Dresdener Katholikentag", in *Klaus Hemmerle: Weggeschichte mit dem Zentralkomitee der deutschen Katholiken*, edited by the Generalsekretariat des Zentralkomitees der deutschen Katholiken (Bonn: Generalsekretariat des Zentralkomitees der deutschen Katholiken, 1994), 39–52, citation at 48.

[117] Kasper, "Kirche als communio", 82. Cf. LG 9.

Based on the Church's mission in salvation history, it is understandable that important passages at the beginning of chapter 2 ("On the People of God") are in agreement with corresponding passages in the opening chapter ("The Mystery of the Church"), for only by virtue of her *mysterium* can the Church be the messianic people and as such serve the cause of unity.

> Christ ... [called] together a people made up of Jew and Gentile, making them one, not according to the flesh but in the Spirit. This was to be the new People of God.... So it is that that messianic people, although it does not actually include all men, and at times may look like a small flock, is nonetheless a lasting and sure seed of unity, hope and salvation for the whole human race. Established by Christ as a communion of life, charity and truth, it is also used by him as an instrument for the redemption of all, and is sent forth into the whole world as the light of the world and the salt of the earth (cf. Mt 5:13–16)....
>
> [Christ] has bought it for himself with his blood (cf. Acts 20:28), has filled it with his Spirit and provided it with those means which befit it as a visible and social union. God gathered together as one all those who in faith look upon Jesus as the author of salvation and the source of unity and peace, and established them as the Church that for each and all it may be the visible sacrament of this saving unity. While it transcends all limits of time and confines of race, the Church is destined to extend to all regions of the earth and so enters into the history of mankind.[118]

The characterization of the Church as the *sacramentum unitatis* became one of the most important leitmotivs throughout the composition of *Lumen gentium*.[119] The term *sacramentum* or *mysterium* designates here the inseparable unity and "the unconfused difference between the Church and God's self-communication in Jesus Christ and in the Holy Spirit".[120] Thus it expresses the unity of the visible and the invisible, of the knowable and the hidden.[121] For the Church, this means that

---

[118] *LG* 9.

[119] J. L. Witte, "Die Kirche 'Sacramentum unitatis' für die ganze Welt", in Baraúna, 1:420–52, citation at 424.

[120] Kehl, *Kirche*, 82.

[121] Cf. Pius XII, encyclical *Mystici Corporis*, in *AAS* 35 (1943): 193–248, ref. at 221ff. Pius XII, encyclical *Humani generis*, in *AAS* 42 (1950): 561–78, ref. at 571. See also *LG* 8.

on the basis of her sacramental structure she refers from the very start
to her origin and her goal, namely, unity in God, to which every true
communio is oriented and from which the trinitarian constitution of
the Church, her unifying structure, receives life and meaning.

b. Trinitarian *communio* as the source and goal of ecclesial *communio*

The Church of Jesus Christ is by her very nature unique.[122] How, though,
is her unity and uniqueness to be accounted for? Where does she have
her origin? Articles 2 through 4 of *Lumen gentium* give an answer to this
question from the perspective of the economy of salvation. The unity
of the Church, her existence, her nature, as well as her historicity have
their basis in the triune God. He himself is the prototype for this unity[123]
and desires to include men in his divine life.

1) *The Father calls men to share in the trinitarian* communio

The mystery of the Church's *communio* already has its foundations in
creation, for from the beginning the Father destined men to take part
in his divine life. Those whom he elected, before time began, he " 'predestined to become conformed to the image of his Son, that he should
be the firstborn among many brethren' [Rom 8:29]." [124] The Council
understands this *participatio* as personal fellowship[125] that proceeds from
the Father, who calls together in the Church those who believe in
Christ:

> Already from the beginning of the world the foreshadowing of the
> Church took place. It was prepared in a remarkable way throughout
> the history of the people of Israel and by means of the Old Cov-
> enant. In the present era of time the Church was constituted and,
> by the outpouring of the Spirit, was made manifest. At the end of
> time it will gloriously achieve completion.[126]

---

[122] Cf. *LG* 8.

[123] Cf. *UR* 2: "It is a mystery that finds its highest exemplar and source in the unity of
the Persons of the Trinity: the Father and the Son in the Holy Spirit, one God."

[124] *LG* 2. Cf. Col 1:15.

[125] Cf. *DV* 1 with the reference to 1 Jn 1:2–3; *DV* 2 with the reference to Eph 2:18;
2 Pet 1:4.

[126] *LG* 2.

That all-encompassing Church which the Father calls together begins as the "ecclesia ab Abel" [127] and attains its full specificity in the Incarnation, death, and Resurrection of Jesus Christ, in whom the *communio* is realized in a unique manner.

2) *In Christ the divine-human* communio *is realized*

Communio as origin and goal of the entire mystery of salvation has already "been realized in Jesus Christ in a historically unique and unsurpassable manner".[128] In becoming man, he wills to unite himself, so to speak, with every human being,[129] so as to lead every individual into the fellowship of the triune God through his redemptive work. Standing therefore at the center of the christological aspect of *communio* (which should not be detached from its trinitarian aspect) is soteriology:

> To carry out the will of the Father, Christ ... by his obedience ... brought about redemption. The Church ... grows visibly through the power of God in the world. This inauguration and this growth are both symbolized by the blood and water which flowed from the open side of a crucified Jesus (cf. Jn 19:34).[130]

Medard Kehl points out that the Fathers of the Church interpret the blood and water flowing from the Lord's open side as the source of the Eucharist and of baptism, that is to say: "Here the incarnate love of God comes to its completion (Jn 13:1); for the gift of the Spirit is embodied tangibly in these two ecclesial signs, through which the new life of the crucified and risen Christ is imparted in the Spirit to those who believe." [131] From what has just been said, it is clear that the unity of *communio* is realized in the eucharistic *communio*. That is

---

[127] Grillmeier, 1:159.

[128] Pesch, 187.

[129] Cf. *GS* 22: "He Who is 'the image of the invisible God' (Col. 1:15), is Himself the perfect man. To the sons of Adam He restores the divine likeness which had been disfigured from the first sin onward. Since human nature as He assumed it was not annulled, by that very fact it has been raised up to a divine dignity in our respect too. For by His incarnation the Son of God has united Himself in some fashion with every man." See also *AG* 3.

[130] *LG* 3.

[131] Kehl, *Kirche*, 74.

why *Lumen gentium* says: "Really partaking of the body of the Lord in the breaking of the eucharistic bread, we are taken up into communion with him and with one another [ad communionem cum Eo ac inter nos]." [132]

3) *The Church as the Bride of Christ in the Holy Spirit*

This unity of the Church in Christ that is brought about by the Spirit is expressed with particular clarity in the image of the Bride and the Bridegroom. With Irenaeus, *Lumen gentium* uses in this connection the metaphor of the rejuvenating power of the gospel, which leads the ever-young Church as Bride to perfect union with her Bridegroom (cf. Rev 22:17). [133]

> Christ loves the Church as his bride, having become the model of a man loving his wife as his body (cf. Eph 5:25–28); the Church, indeed, is subject to [her] Head (cf. Eph 5:23–24). "Because in him dwells all the fullness of the Godhead bodily" (Col 2:9), he fills the Church, which is his body and his fullness, with his divine gifts (cf. Eph 1:22–23) so that [she] may expand and reach all the fullness of God (cf. Eph 3:19). [134]

Because the Spirit unites the entire Body with Christ and gives it life, the Church becomes the Bride of Christ in this act of union. [135] A distinctive feature of the internal association of the members through the charity granted by the Holy Spirit is the fact that this solidarity does not dissolve the interpersonal encounter of Christ and the Church. [136] The conformity of all with Christ unites them with him and with one another, inasmuch as they are set free for their nuptial personal encounter.

---

[132] *LG* 7. Cf. *UR* 2; *AA* 8; see also *PO* 6.

[133] On this subject, see *LG* 4: "By the power of the Gospel He makes the Church keep the freshness of youth. Uninterruptedly He renews it and leads it to perfect union with its Spouse. The Spirit and the Bride both say to Jesus, the Lord, 'Come!' [cf. Rev 22:17]."

[134] *LG* 7.

[135] Ibid.

[136] Cf. Grillmeier, 1:169f. Grillmeier refers to the erroneous interpretations of the Body of Christ concept, which understand the relation between Christ as Head and the Church as Body "precisely as a new hypostatic union or simply as the extension thereof".

4) *The Holy Spirit effects the* communio

As the invisible and perpetual fundamental principle of the Church's unity, the Holy Spirit[137] continues to guide the work of Christ until "the promised restoration which we are awaiting",[138] which has already begun in Christ:

> When the work which the Father gave the Son to do on earth (cf. Jn 17:4) was accomplished, the Holy Spirit was sent on the day of Pentecost in order that he might continually sanctify the Church, and thus, all those who believe would have access through Christ in one Spirit to the Father (cf. Eph 2:18).[139]

That is why he lives in the Church and in the hearts of the faithful "as in a temple",[140] brings about their communion in God, bears witness to their adoptive sonship, and unifies the Church "in communion and in works of ministry [in communione et ministratione]".[141] Article 4 of *Lumen gentium*, which sets forth the pneumatic dimension of the Church and in this respect relies especially on John and Paul, acknowledges the working of the Holy Spirit both in the charisms and also in the hierarchical offices of service: "The Church, which the Spirit guides in way of all truth (cf. Jn 16:13) and which he unified in communion and in works of ministry, he both equips and directs with hierarchical and charismatic gifts and adorns with his fruits (cf. Eph 4:11–12; 1 Cor 12:4; Gal 5:22)."[142] According to *Lumen gentium*, the Holy Spirit joins the different hierarchical and charismatic gifts into a unity, and therefore his working "is manifested anew in every age, not only in the

---

[137] Cf. *UR* 2: "It is the Holy Spirit, dwelling in those who believe and pervading and ruling over the Church as a whole, who brings about that wonderful communion of the faithful. He brings them into intimate union with Christ, so that He is the principle of the Church's unity."

[138] *LG* 48.

[139] *LG* 4.

[140] Ibid.; cf. 1 Cor 3:16; 6:19.

[141] *LG* 4. Cf. *AG* 4: "Throughout all ages, the Holy Spirit makes the entire Church 'one in communion and in ministering; He equips her with various gifts of a hierarchical and charismatic nature,' a giving life, soul-like, to ecclesiastical institutions and instilling into the hearts of the faithful the same mission spirit which impelled Christ Himself."

[142] *LG* 4. Cf. Grillmeier, 1:161. A detailed presentation of this theme can be found in H. Mühlen, *Una mystica Persona: Die Kirche als das Mysterium der Identität des Hl. Geistes in Christus und den Christen* (Munich: Schöningh, 1964).

personal, variously applicable charisms of individual Christians",[143] but also and precisely in the sacramental structures of *Ordo*, that is, of holy orders, which are constitutive of the Church:

> As all the members of the human body, though they are many, form one body, so also are the faithful in Christ (cf. 1 Cor 12:12). Also, in the building up of Christ's Body various members and functions have their part to play. There is only one Spirit who, according to his own richness and the needs of the ministries, gives his different gifts for the welfare of the Church (cf. 1 Cor 12:1–11). What has a special place among these gifts is the grace of the apostles to whose authority the Spirit himself subjected even those who were endowed with charisms (cf. 1 Cor 14).[144]

According to our reflections thus far, it is characteristic of the unity that is bestowed on the Church in the Holy Spirit that it binds together all the members (who are independent persons capable of communication)[145] with the Head of the Body and with one another into a *communicatio*, without canceling the difference between them.[146] Thus, "the man who is perfected individually and socially ... is capable of participating in the *communio* of the love of the Father, the Son, and the Spirit and of sharing actively in the life of the Divine Persons",[147] inasmuch as the Church understands herself to be the image of the triune God.

c. Church as mystery of the trinitarian *communio*

In the previous section, we considered the derivation of the Church from the *communio* of the triune God. Now we will outline how this origin is reflected in the Church herself. This occurs in two steps, the first of which sets forth the patristic understanding of the Church in the writings of Cyprian (which influenced *Lumen gentium*) as a *communio* united by the Trinity, whereas the second focuses on the fact

---

[143] Kehl, *Kirche*, 393.

[144] LG 7.

[145] Cf. on this subject Kienzler, " 'Communio' ", 130.

[146] Cf. Eph 5:23ff.

[147] Gerhard Ludwig Müller, *Katholische Dogmatik für Studium und Praxis der Theologie* (Freiburg im Breisgau: Herder, 1996), 612.

that the *communio* unity of the Church is modeled on the trinitarian *communio*.

1) *Acceptance of the idea of* communio *in the early Church, according to Cyprian: The Church as "a people brought into unity from the unity of the Father, the Son, and the Holy Spirit"*

According to *Lumen gentium*, the Church is the place in which and the means by which "the decree of God's will may be fulfilled: In the beginning God made human nature one and decreed that all his children, scattered as they were, would finally be gathered together as one." [148] This happens when the Church unites people "from all tribes and peoples and tongues" [149] in herself into the one People of God, as a sign and instrument of God's salvific action in history: "Thus, the Church has been seen as 'a people made one with the unity of the Father, the Son and the Holy Spirit'." [150] As Alois Grillmeier notes in his commentary to chapter 1 of the Constitution on the Church, this last sentence of *Lumen gentium* 4 is "the summary of the trinitarian origin of the Church in salvation history and of her unity". [151] This sentence has formulated the Church's constitution with an expression of St. Cyprian and thus has "made a strong and momentous statement ... that is rooted deep in the tradition of the Church". [152] Yet *Lumen gentium* does not stop with Cyprian. He was referring only to the visible unity of the Church, especially under the authority of the legitimate bishop, [153] whereas the Council interprets the unifying function of the Church as a *universal* task that should unite *all* men with God

[148] LG 13.

[149] Rev 7:9.

[150] LG 4 with the reference to St. Cyprian, *De Orat. Dom.* 23, in CSEL 3, 1, 285; CCL 3 A, 105; PL 4, 553. See also UR 2: "The Church, then, is God's only flock; it is like a standard lifted high for the nations to see it: for it serves all mankind through the Gospel of peace as it makes its pilgrim way in hope toward the goal of the fatherland above. This is the sacred mystery of the unity of the Church, in Christ and through Christ, the Holy Spirit energizing its various functions. It is a mystery that finds its highest exemplar and source in the unity of the Persons of the Trinity: the Father and the Son in the Holy Spirit, one God."

[151] Grillmeier, 1:161.

[152] Scheffczyk, *Aspekte der Kirche in der Krise*, 16.

[153] St. Cyprian, *Ep.* 69, 6, in CSEL 3, 2, 754; CCL 3 C, 477f.; PL 3, 1142 B. Contrary to the heretics, Cyprian emphasizes that unity with the Church is necessary for the salvation of the soul. Compare on this subject Scheffczyk, *Aspekte der Kirche in der Krise*, 17.

and with one another. On the contrary, Cyprian maintains that those who are "outside the Church" do not belong to this unity:

> How inseparable is the sacrament of unity, and how hopeless are they, and what excessive ruin they earn for themselves from the indignation of God, who make a schism, and, forsaking their bishop, appoint another false bishop for themselves without [that is, outside of the Church], Holy Scripture declares.... And dares any one to say that the saving water of baptism and heavenly grace can be in common with schismatics, with whom neither earthly food nor worldly drink ought to be in common?[154]

Significant in this connection is Leo Scheffczyk's remark that "the Council does not quote Cyprian's rule, 'No salvation outside the Church', which goes farther." Nevertheless, the Council "still has basically the same image of the Church, combining the features of the uniqueness of the Church, her necessity for salvation, and the fullness of redemption that has been given to her in Christ and in the Holy Spirit".[155] Before we turn to the important question of the "una sancta catholica ecclesia", however, we should direct our attention to the Church as the icon of the Trinity.

2) The communio unity of the Church as an image of the Trinity

The Church is, in Gisbert Greshake's words, "within the realm of creation the clearest icon of the Trinity".[156] Lumen gentium 4 is seconded by the Decree on Ecumenism as well: "This is the sacred mystery of the unity of the Church, in Christ and through Christ,

---

[154] St. Cyprian, *Ep.* 69, 6, in BKV, 2nd ed., 60, 311f.; English version from *The Early Church Fathers on CD-ROM* (Gervais, Ore.: Harmony Media) [originally published in the United States by Charles Scribner's Sons, 1900]. Note the markedly paraenetic form of Cyprian's statement. The sixty-ninth letter of St. Cyprian is the first in the series of his writings in the dispute about baptism by heretics. Cyprian argues against Novatian and his followers, denying that they have any right whatsoever to baptize. The quotation cited in the text already suggests that the juridical structure of the Church as a *communio* in union with the bishop ultimately has a *sacramental* basis. We will discuss this subject farther on in the chapter "The People of God", pt. 1, sec. 2, chap. 2, § 2.3, "Toward a Sacramental-Pneumatic Foundation of the New People of God".

[155] Scheffczyk, *Aspekte der Kirche in der Krise*, 17.

[156] G. Greshake, *Der dreieine Gott: Eine trinitarische Theologie* (Freiburg im Breisgau: Herder, 1997), 377. Cf. Kasper, "Kirche als communio", 284. In that passage, Kasper refers to B. Forte, *La Chiesa—icona della Trinità: Breve ecclesiologia* (Brescia: Queriniana, 1984).

the Holy Spirit energizing its various functions. It is a mystery that finds its highest exemplar and source in the unity of the Persons of the Trinity: the Father and the Son in the Holy Spirit, one God."[157] These terse statements, however, not only have theological relevance but are also decisive in practical applications to the Church's life, in which her *communio* form is realized concretely as a unity in multiplicity. If, on the contrary, one reduces this trinitarian form, for instance,

> by forgetting the relation to the Father, [then] one overlooks the common dignity and mission, which are the foundation of the *communio*. If the Church is no longer understood as the Body of Christ, the *communio* ... of believers fragments when they assert opposing claims to possess the Spirit. Finally, if one forgets that the Church is the temple of the Holy Spirit, then it hardens into a hierocracy [that is, rule by sacred ministers].[158]

Participation and shared responsibility, transparency and the freedom to speak up, and peace in productive diversity have their deepest roots here, for the Church is "by her very nature communion and dialogue".[159] In this process of communication, particularity and generality do not cancel each other out; rather, they are mutually dependent, like two poles that "have to be reconciled as in a perichoresis".[160] That is why, according to Gisbert Greshake, the Church's *communio* unity, which has a trinitarian structure, consists "of the perichoresis of what has been distinguished, in the mutual recognition, communication, and sharing of what is proper to each",[161] and he goes on to explain:

> Ecclesial *communio*, which in this way is an image of the Trinity, consequently is realized as *communicatio*, which is thus based likewise on the divine *communio*. *Communicatio* or communication thus consists,

---

[157] UR 2.

[158] H.J. Pottmeyer, "Die Zwiespältige Ekklesiologie des Zweiten Vatikanums: Ursache nachkonziliarer Konflikte", *TThZ* 92 (1993): 283.

[159] P. Neuner, "Die Kirche: Mysterium und Volk Gottes", in *Erinnerungen an einen Aufbruch: Das II. Vatikanische Konzil*, ed. N. Kutschki, 46 (Würzburg: Echter, 1995).

[160] Greshake, *Dreieine Gott*, 391.

[161] Ibid., 393. Cf. Greshake, "Weltkirche und Ostkirche: Bemerkungen zu einem problematischen Verhältnis", *ThGl* 91 (2001): 528–42, esp. 530–36.

not in the mere conveyance of content ... , but rather in the communication of persons to one another. Just as the triune God lives out his interior life in the mutual self-communication of the Divine Persons, and just as by his very nature he proves himself to be self-communication with respect to the world also, so too the Church has to live out her life as self-communication: What she is and what each individual has received in her ... is to be handed on in a process of mutual communication and converted into practical action.[162]

From the previous discussion, it is evident that the ecclesiology of the Constitution on the Church is conceived in terms that are as pneumatological as they are christocentric,[163] since they are ultimately theological. Alois Grillmeier stresses in this connection that no perspective can be subsumed by another, since each one "has as its scope the Church in her entirety".[164] For this reason a *communio* ecclesiology "cannot be reduced to purely organizational questions and problems that concern merely the powers in the Church", even though, in the words of the 1985 Extraordinary Synod of Bishops, the Council's *communio* ecclesiology is "the foundation for the continuance within her of the right relation between unity and multiplicity".[165]

---

[162] Greshake, *Dreieine Gott*, 385. Cf. *DV* 6: "Through divine revelation, God chose to show forth and communicate Himself and the eternal decisions of His will regarding the salvation of men."

[163] In his encyclical *Ecclesiam suam*, dated August 6, 1964, Pope Paul VI emphasized that the first fruit of the deepening of the Church's sacramental awareness is a living relationship with Jesus. He refers to *Mystici Corporis*: "We must grow accustomed to seeing Christ himself in the Church. For it is Christ who lives in his Church, who teaches, governs and sanctifies through her; it is Christ, also, who reveals himself in various ways in his social members" (*AAS* 56 [1964]: 626–36; English trans. in *The Papal Encyclicals: 1958–1981*, ed. Claudia Carlen, I.H.M. [Ann Arbor, Mich.: Pierian Press, 1990], 135–60). See also *Mystici Corporis*, in *AAS* 35 (1943): 193–248, ref. at 238; English trans., *Encyclical Letter of His Holiness Pius XII*.

[164] Grillmeier, 1:161. Cf. H. J. Pottmeyer, "Der Heilige Geist und die Kirche: Von einer christomonistischen zu einer trinitarischen Ekklesiologie", *Tutzinger-Studien* 2 (1981): 44–55, ref. at 51. Pottmeyer criticizes the Council's failure to "advance to a trinitarian substantiation" for the Church, which would compensate for "the pneumatological deficiency of the preconciliar ecclesiology".

[165] *Zukunft aus der Kraft des Konzils: Die außerordentliche Bischofssynode '85*, the documents of the 1985 Extraordinary Synod of Bishops with a commentary by W. Kasper (Freiburg im Breisgau: Herder, 1986), 33f.

4. *First excursus: "Una sancta catholica ecclesia"—The question of subsistence*

If we ponder the statements on *communio* in *Lumen gentium*, it is obvious that a purely juridical notion of unity does not do justice to the trinitarian *communio*.[166] But how can we proceed along the path to unity in ecumenism?

The Second Vatican Council explicitly teaches: "This is the one Church of Christ which in the Creed is professed as one, holy, catholic and apostolic."[167] But in contrast to the preconciliar interpretation, *Lumen gentium* 8 no longer attempts to set up a direct equation with the words "est Ecclesia catholica"; rather, it deliberately speaks of *subsistence*: "Haec Ecclesia ... subsistit in Ecclesia catholica." Heribert Mühlen comments on the explosive ecumenical impact of this formulation:

> In the first days of December in the year 1962, as the debate about the prepared schema "On the Church" began, something like an initial thunderclap resounded through the great hall of St. Peter's in the words of the first speaker, Cardinal Achille Liénart of Lille: The Roman Church, he said, could not be identified with the Mystical Body of Christ, as the draft proposed. The Church was, instead, "a mystery of the Holy Spirit", and hence the relationship of non-Roman-Catholic Christians to the one Body of Christ had to be considered also.[168]

The Council Fathers finally agreed in 1964 on the previously mentioned formulation from *Lumen gentium* 8: "This Church ... subsists in the Catholic Church [subsistit in Ecclesia catholica], which is governed by the successor of Peter and by the bishops in communion with him [in eius communione]." As Alexandra von Teuffenbach[169] points out, it was Sebastian Tromp who resolved the dispute about the original verb *est* ["is"][170] and the later expression *adest in* ["is present in"] by introducing the definitive term *subsistit in* during

---

[166] On this subject, see farther on in this work, pt. 2, sec. 2, chap. 1, § 4.4, "The Question of Subsistence".

[167] LG 8.

[168] H. Mühlen, "Der Kirchenbegriff des Konzils", in Hampe, *Autorität der Freiheit*, 1:291–313, citation at 291.

[169] See Teuffenbach, 379–88.

[170] Cf. Grillmeier, 1:174f.

the decisive discussion of the Theological Commission about *Lumen gentium* 8 on November 26, 1963.[171] At that session, over which Cardinal Ottaviani presided, Gérard Philips was the discussion leader. As Teuffenbach demonstrates in her dissertation, there were no debates[172] about the expression *subsistit in*, since "the whole 'process' of including this word, which was so controversial later on, probably lasted less than a minute!"[173] Teuffenbach's conclusion, however, that *subsistit in* "can only be synonymous with *est*"[174] seems in my opinion to disregard the difference between the two concepts and also to neglect the ecumenical profile of *Lumen gentium* 8. It is precisely through this profile that the exclusive claim with respect to the idea of *communio* is transformed and broadened and thus "opened up to a greater variety",[175] so that "a gradation of Church membership becomes conceivable."[176]

This fundamental opening showed the way for the postconciliar reception process, which communicated the insight that the Catholic Church, while she is "of course *the* institutionally perfect realization" of the Church of Jesus Christ, does not completely exhaust the latter, so that "many elements of sanctification and of truth (the phrase 'and of truth' was added deliberately after lengthy discussion) can be found outside the Catholic Church as gifts belonging to the Church of Christ"[177] that impel believers toward Catholic unity.[178]

---

[171] Not only Tromp but many other members of the commission as well had already "crossed out the word *adest* and written *subsistit in* in the margin" (Teuffenbach, 380).

[172] Ibid., 382–87. Teuffenbach bases her claim on three sources: the minutes for the session of the Theological Commission held on November 26, 1963, the corresponding entry in Tromp's diary, and a marginal note that Tromp wrote by hand on his mimeographed copy of *LG* 8.

[173] Ibid., 392.

[174] Ibid., 393. This would call for translating *subsistere* with the German verb *bleiben* [remain], but that would not do justice either to the metaphysical concept of subsistence.

[175] H. Fries, "Das Konzil: Grund ökumenischer Hoffnung", in König, *Bleibende Bedeutung*, 107–21, citation at 113.

[176] B. Körner, "*Extra ecclesiam nulla salus*: Sinn und Problematik dieses Satzes in einer sich wandelnden fundamentaltheologischen Ekklesiologie", *ZKTh* 114 (1992): 274–92, citation at 280.

[177] K. Rahner and H. Vorgrimler, "III. Die dogmatische Konstitution über die Kirche *Lumen gentium*", in *KlKK* 107. See also H. Döring, "Der ökumenische Aufbruch", in Kutschki, *Erinnerungen*, 66–79, ref. at 72.

[178] Cf. Pesch, 219–23.

Hermann Josef Pottmeyer speaks in this connection of an ecclesiological turning point[179] and a change of direction made by Vatican II.
The marks of the true Church (*notae ecclesiae*) are to be read off, not simply from the "epoch-making form in which the post-Tridentine Church
was realized", but rather "from God's word and his will, against which
one should verify the true ecclesiality of the Catholic Church as well".[180]
Thus subsistence becomes a gift and a responsibility for the Catholic
Church. The crucial thing is no longer the emphasis on exclusivity, but
rather fidelity to Jesus' commission to spread the kingdom of God in the
world. This consideration, nonetheless, presupposes in our understanding of *Lumen gentium* 8 the clear knowledge that the Church herself is
not a historical work, not only a mission in time (as though she were
always somewhere off in the future), but rather is established ontologically in history, in the midst of which she can never be lost. The Council expresses this with the metaphysical concept[181] of subsistence.

5. *Second excursus:* Communio *as* participatio *in suffering*

The concern of one group of Council Fathers is addressed at the end
of chapter 1 of *Lumen gentium* and incorporated into the description
of the nature and mystery of the Church; today we call this the "preferential option for the poor". Gisbert Greshake sees therein a "very
important and quite essential characteristic of the Church.... If it is
true that there is no longer an 'immanent Trinity', but only one that
is involved in and remains in the history of mankind, which is marked
by sin, suffering, and death, then the Church, too, can be the image
of the Trinity only in this manner",[182] that is, by sharing powerlessness, poverty, and compassion with her God. "Just as Christ carried
out the work of redemption in poverty and persecution",[183] so the
Church, too, is called to walk the way of *kenosis*, of the self-emptying
of Jesus Christ, which in a similar manner becomes a criterion for her
own mission. Beset by human weakness, the Church is "always in

---

[179] Cf. H. J. Pottmeyer, "Die Frage nach der wahren Kirche", in *HFTh* 3:164.
[180] Ibid., 219.
[181] On this topic, see the subheading pt. 2, sec. 2, chap. 1, § 4.4.a., "The Difference
between *subsistit* and *est*".
[182] Greshake, *Dreieine Gott*, 381.
[183] *LG* 8.

need of purification", and she herself must follow the path of penance and renewal.[184] The Church testifies thereby that she is the pilgrim People of God, which "presses forward amid the persecutions of the world and the consolations of God", so that she may reveal in the world "faithfully though darkly, the mystery of [her] Lord, until, in the end, it will be manifested in full light".[185]

---

[184] K. Rahner, "Die Sünde in der Kirche", in Baraúna, 1:346–61.
[185] LG 8.

Chapter 2

The People of God

§ 1. From a Marginal Phenomenon
to the Central Concept

Already in *Lumen gentium* 4, that is, in the first chapter about the *mysterium* of the Church, we encountered *People of God* as a title for the Church—one that was of decisive importance for the postconciliar reception of Vatican II. It is rather surprising today, therefore, to learn that this biblical term did not find a place in the ecclesiology of the Second Vatican Council as an expression for the Church until the Council was under way,[1] and then only because numerous Council Fathers requested a special chapter on the *People of God* in the Constitution on the Church.[2] For the first draft of the schema on the Church, *De Ecclesia*, mentions the concept "People of God" only in passing, and in the encyclical *Mystici Corporis* of Pius XII the metaphor does not appear at all. In the two documents just mentioned, the image of the *Body of Christ* is the focus of the discussion. Through the new perspective of the Church as the People of God, it was possible for "the entire Church, laity and

---

[1] On this topic, see Stefano Alberto, "Begriff und Wesen der Kirche in der Entstehung der Kirchenkonstitution *Lumen gentium*: Einige Anmerkungen zu drei Voten der Fuldaer Bischofskonferenz (1960–1963)", in *Ex latere: Ausfaltungen communialer Theologie*, ed. E. Naab, 149–75, ref. at 161f. (Eichstätt: Franz-Sales-Verlag, 1993). Stefano Alberto points out the systematic subordination of the term "People of God" to the concept of the Body of Christ.

[2] Cf. B. Kloppenburg, "Abstimmungen und letzte Änderungen der Konstitution", in Baraúna, 1:108. Cf. G. Philips, "Die Geschichte der Dogmatischen Konstitution über die Kirche *Lumen gentium*", in *LThK.E*, vol. 1 (Freiburg im Breisgau: Herder, 1966), 150: A separate chapter, "The People of God", in *Lumen gentium* "corresponded to the effort to show the actualization of the mystery of the Church on her path through history and in the unfolding of the catholicity that is proper to her".

clergy, to become aware of their election, vocation, and mission and to understand their ministries, offices, and charisms as being those of the whole People".[3]

When we examine the frequency with which this concept then appeared in the documents of the last council, we can conclude with Werner Berg that the expression "People of God" was used around eighty times, especially in the Constitution on the Church,[4] but also in the Decree on Missionary Activity,[5] in the Decree on the Ministry and Life of Priests,[6] in the Pastoral Constitution [on the Church],[7] "and here and there in other documents as well",[8] in a different context in each instance.

The image of the pilgrim People of God (LG 9) directs our attention to the salvation-history dimension of the Church[9] as an analogy that—as Henri de Lubac remarks—"the Council wanted to emphasize, because it completes the analogy of the Body of Christ".[10] In order to determine the significance of the concept "People of God" for the image of the Church in Lumen gentium, we will investigate in the second section the question of the continuity and the distinction between the Old Testament and the New Testament People of God.

---

[3] L. Hödl, "'Die Kirche ist nämlich in Christus gleichsam das Sakrament . . .': Eine Konzilsaussage und ihre nachkonziliare Auslegung", in Kirche sein: Nachkonziliare Theologie im Dienst der Kirchenreform: Für Hermann Josef Pottmeyer, ed. W. Geerlings and M. Seckler, 163–79, citation at 170 (Freiburg im Breisgau: Herder, 1994).

[4] LG 4, 9, 11 (three times), 12 (three times), 13 (five times), 16, 17, 18, 22, 23, 28, 30, 31, 32 (twice), 33, 40, 41, 44, 45, 68, 69.

[5] AG 1 (twice), 10, 14 (three times), 15 (twice), 19 (twice), 21, 35, 37, 38.

[6] PO 1, 3, 4 (twice), 5, 7, 9, 11, 12 (twice), 18, 19, 20, 21.

[7] GS 3, 11 (twice), 44, 45, 92. The relatively infrequent use of the expression in Gaudium et spes is striking.

[8] W. Berg, "'Volk Gottes'—ein biblischer Begriff?", in Geerlings and Seckler, Kirche sein, 13–20, citation at 13.

[9] Cf. H. Mühlen, "Der Kirchenbegriff des Konzils", in Die Autorität der Freiheit: Gegenwart des Konzils and Zukunft der Kirche im ökumenischen Disput, ed. J. C. Hampe, 1:291–313, ref. at 309 (Munich: Kösel-Velag, 1967).

[10] Henri de Lubac, interview conducted by Angelo Scola: De Lubac: A Theologian Speaks (Los Angeles: Twin Circle Publishing, 1985), 8. He goes on to say (and we quote his exact words): "It does so by bringing out the fact that this Body is growing—in other words, that there is such a thing as 'salvation history'. But just as the Body of Christ is not a fleshly body, so this history is not a profane history."

§ 2. The People of God in the Continuity of Salvation History

1. *Election and formation of the assembly of the saved*

The central concern, that God's call always signifies a calling together
of a community of salvation, runs through chapter 2 of *Lumen gentium*: "God ... does not make men holy and save them merely as
individuals, without bond or link between one another. Rather has it
pleased him to bring men together as one people.... He therefore
chose the race of Israel as a people unto himself. With it he set up a
covenant".[11] The Old Testament describes *Israel* as the "People of God",
"because according to its faith experience (through its deliverance at
the Red Sea and the establishment of the Covenant) it owes its national
and religious existence to Yahweh through his historical act (and not
through a merely natural event) and *therefore* is his creation and his
property."[12] The call of Israel, however, that first-chosen People of
God, is the prefiguration of the New Covenant, which Christ established "in his blood" and which constitutes the New Testament People of God, which is no longer bound to one nation or to one land,
but rather embodies the universality of salvation for all mankind. The
Constitution on the Church attests to this continuity in salvation history at the beginning of its second chapter:

> All these things, however, were done by way of preparation and as a
> figure of that new and perfect covenant, which was to be ratified in
> Christ, and of that fuller revelation which was to be given through
> the Word of God himself made flesh.... Christ instituted this new cov-
> enant, the new covenant, that is to say, in his blood (cf. 1 Cor 11:25).[13]

According to *Lumen gentium*, the Church is connected within the
history of salvation with the Old Testament covenant people, from whom
the universality of the divine salvific will was, however, still hidden.
Nevertheless there are indications of this universality in the Old Testament as well. It already dawns upon the Patriarch Abraham[14] and

---

[11] *LG* 9.

[12] K. Rahner, "Volk Gottes", in *Herders Theologisches Taschenlexikon*, ed. Rahner, 8:65
(Freiburg im Breisgau: Herder, 1973).

[13] *LG* 9.

[14] Cf. Gen 12:3; 17:4–6.

bursts all national restrictions in the eschatological discourse of the prophets. Christ, the Head of the new covenant people, by sending his disciples out to all nations,[15] fulfilled this eschatological hope and "[called] together a people made up of Jew and Gentile, making them one, not according to the flesh but in the Spirit. This was to be the new People of God."[16] Of course, the pilgrim People of God of the New Covenant, too, is not yet at its goal: "Its end is the kingdom of God, which has been begun by God himself on earth, and which is to be further extended until it is brought to perfection by him at the end of time".[17]

2. Church in continuity with the Old Testament People of God and as something qualitatively new

Like the People of Israel chosen by God, the *Ecclesia Christi*, too, is, "not the democratic assembly of the people in the sense in which that was understood in antiquity, but rather the congregation gathered to worship and to be saved in the presence of the covenant God".[18] This awareness of *continuity* is found in quite a few New Testament passages, especially in the Pauline and Deutero-Pauline writings, which no longer relate the People of God concept (solely) to the first-chosen People of Israel, but already apply it to the Christian community.[19] Nevertheless, as Karl Kertelge remarks, we cannot conclude from this that the New Testament People of God represents merely a "prolongation" of the Old Testament People of God in salvation history; instead, it is the eschatological "reestablishment" of the latter "in the saving intercession of Christ 'for us' (Rom 8:34)".[20] The Church as the new

[15] Cf. Mt 28:16–20; 24:14.

[16] LG 9.

[17] Ibid. Cf. Hödl, " 'Die Kirche' ", 177: "The Church is not the first thing or the last thing. She does not exist for her own sake! She is a historical sign and instrument of salvation; she is provisional, not definitive. Therein the greatness and the limitations of the Church become clear in her history."

[18] Grillmeier, 2:179.

[19] Cf. Rev 15:14; 18:10; Rom 9:25f.; 2 Cor 6:16; Tit 2:14; 1 Pet 2:9f.; Heb 4:9; 8:10; 10:30; 13:12; Rev 18:4; 21:3. See A. Seigfried, "Volk Gottes als ekklesiale Gestalt der Gnade", in *Im Spannungsfeld von Tradition und Innovation: Festschrift für Joseph Kardinal Ratzinger*, ed. G. Schmuttermayr et al., 249–68, esp. 251–56: "Neues Volk in Jesus Christus" (Regensburg: Pustet, 1997).

[20] K. Kertelge, "Kirche: I. Neues Testament", in *LThK*, 3rd ed., vol. 5 (Freiburg im Breisgau: Herder, 1996), 1453–58, citation at 1454.

People of God is "not a continuation of the old Israel without intensification or interruption: its newness lies in the fact that Christ won it as his possession through his death on the Cross, blessed it with his Spirit, and unified it through the establishment of visible social bonds" [21] and promised that he would remain with it always. Hence, with Adam Seigfried we can summarize as follows:

> People of God expresses at the same time in biblical terms both continuity and difference of God's grace and favor between Old and New Covenant, between promise and fulfillment. The term λαοσ is equivalent to the Pauline term εκκλησια. . . . Unfortunately in the Middle Ages the title People of God is increasingly forgotten and is to a great extent replaced by the Body of Christ image. This does not change again until Vatican II.[22]

For this Council, as Hermann Joseph Pottmeyer has shown, the images "People of God" and "universal sacrament of salvation for the world" [23] became the fundamental concepts on the basis of which the mystery of the Church can be grasped. It is crucially important that these concepts are not in opposition to each other but rather are complementary and mutually dependent. Therefore, at this point in our argument, the question arises of why "People of God", according to *Lumen gentium*, is an especially appropriate image for the Church and, more particularly, what specific definition it acquires through the simultaneous understanding of the Church as the "universal sacrament of salvation for the world".

3. Toward a sacramental-pneumatic foundation of the new People of God

In the previous section it already became evident that the New Testament People of God is established essentially through Christ's saving work. Christ himself, in his earthly life as well as in his exaltation in

---

[21] Grillmeier, 1:179.

[22] Seigfried, "Volk Gottes", 256. J. Werbick, *Kirche: Ein ekklesiologischer Entwurf für Studium und Praxis* (Freiburg im Breisgau: Herder, 1994), 52, explains that the Church—as she declares in *NA* 4—no longer associates the expression "new People of God" with the idea that the first covenant was ineffective for salvation.

[23] H.J. Pottmeyer, "Modernisierung in der katholischen Kirche am Beispiel der Kirchenkonzeption des I. und II. Vatikanischen Konzils", in *Vatikanum II und Modernisierung: Historische, theologische und soziologische Perspektiven*, ed. F.-X. Kaufmann and A. Zingerle, 131–45, citation at 142 (Paderborn: Schöningh, 1996).

glory, is the sign of salvation, that is, the sacrament for all mankind. His sacramental being is continued in and through the Church.[24] For the *Ecclesia*, this means that she has been established as the assembly of those "who in faith look upon Jesus as the author of salvation and the source of unity and peace ... [so] that for each and all [she] may be the visible sacrament of this saving unity".[25] Even though the People of God "at times may look like a small flock", it is nevertheless "a lasting and sure seed of unity, hope and salvation for the whole human race".[26] Even those men who "do not belong to the Church in her historical and social dimension"[27] are supposed to be saved through her, the instrument of salvation.[28] Elected now to be the new People of God, the Church becomes on that account the sign of God's love and mercy toward all mankind. In her the new commandment of love is in force, through which the People of God is called to set out toward its own perfection in the kingdom of God, "which has been begun by God himself on earth".[29] This communion was established by Christ, who "has bought it for himself with his blood, has filled it with his Spirit and provided it with those means which befit it as a visible and social union", and this communion is called to be, in time, "the visible sacrament of this saving unity".[30]

From this sacramental foundation of the People of God, which we have already discussed in the chapter on the mystery of the Church[31] and therefore outline briefly here, arise the questions about the dignity of all Christians and the universal vocation to holiness, the mission of the laity, as well as the priestly and prophetic dimension of the

---

[24] Cf. L. Scheffczyk, *Aspekte der Kirche in der Krise: Um die Entscheidung für das authentische Konzil*, Quaestiones non disputatae 1 (Siegburg: F. Schmitt, 1993), 29: "In identifying Christ as a sacrament, which reveals a remarkable agreement among the Christian denominations, the sacramentality of the Church is still not touched on or attained. Here a gap between the theological outlooks opens up.... The same Karl Barth who acknowledges in Christ the (sole) sacramental being has misgivings about 'representing or repeating the reality of this sacrament in the Church or putting it into effect in her own action', because then the Church would have to be understood as a 'sort of prolongation of the Incarnation'."

[25] *LG* 9.

[26] Ibid.

[27] K. Rahner, "Das Volk Gottes", in Sandfuchs, 27–37, citation at 30.

[28] For a more nuanced expression of this thought, see below, §8.

[29] *LG* 9.

[30] Ibid.

[31] Cf. pt. 1, sec. 2, chap. 1, § 3.2.c., of this book, "Universal Sacrament of Salvation".

People of God. We will turn to the last-mentioned topic first, since this question is of decisive importance for our further discussion of *Lumen gentium*.

§ 3. The Participation of the People of God in Christ's Priestly, Prophetic, and Kingly Mission

One important insight in the ecclesiology of the Council is the doctrine concerning the participation of all Christians in the saving mission of the People of God. Not only those who are ordained and hold office, but also the laity, bear the responsibility for the building up of the Church as well as for her mission in the world, and accordingly they continue Christ's saving mission through their testimony of faith (*martyria*), in their celebration of the liturgy (*leiturgia*), and through their share in Christ's kingly office (*diakonia*). In its presentation of the fundamental defining acts of the New Testament People of God, *Lumen gentium* follows the plan of this *threefold office of Christ* and applies it in articles 10–12 to the Church as the People of God. In this passage it emphasizes the aspect of the common dignity of all the Church's members by referring to Revelation 1:6; 5:9–10, and 1 Peter 2:4–10,[32] thus accentuating active *participatio* in the one priesthood of Jesus Christ through prayer, witness, and service. This means that every baptized Christian, in keeping with his own vocation, has a share in the one priestly, prophetic, and kingly mission of Jesus Christ:

> It was for this purpose that God sent his Son, ... that he might be teacher, king and priest of all, the head of the new and universal people of the sons of God. For this too God sent the Spirit of his Son as Lord and Life-giver. He it is who brings together the whole Church and each and every one of those who believe, and who is the well-spring of their unity in the teaching of the apostles and in fellowship, in the breaking of bread and in prayers (cf. Acts 2:42).[33]

In our further remarks we will turn first to the *common priesthood* of all the baptized. In the Constitution on the Church a relatively large

---

[32] Cf. Ex 19:6: "You shall be to me a kingdom of priests...."
[33] *LG* 13.

amount of space is devoted to it, in comparison to the themes of
sharing in Christ's kingship and in his prophetic office; one reason is
for the sake of relating and clearly distinguishing between the common priesthood of all the baptized and the priesthood based on the
sacrament of holy orders.

1. The common priesthood of all the baptized

The idea of a common participation of all the baptized in the priesthood of Christ was not readily accepted by all the Council Fathers.
Behind their hesitation was the fear that this could result in a leveling
of the Church's ordained priesthood.[34] In order to express the fact
that the common priesthood is the lot of all the baptized and consequently is not obliterated in an ordained minister,[35] the expression
sacerdotium universale, which was still being used in the 1963 draft of
the schema on the Church, was changed to *sacerdotium commune*. As
Otto Hermann Pesch explains, *Lumen gentium* 10 presented "in a sen-
sational way the *priesthood of all the baptized* for the first time in an
official Church document".[36]

> Christ the Lord, High Priest taken from among men (cf. Heb 5:1–5),
> made the new people "a kingdom and priests to God the Father"
> (Rev 1:6; cf. 5:9–10). The baptized, by regeneration and the anoint-
> ing of the Holy Spirit, are consecrated as a spiritual house and a holy
> priesthood, in order that through all those works which are those of
> the Christian man they may offer spiritual sacrifices and proclaim
> the power of him who has called them out of darkness into his
> marvelous light (cf. 1 Pet 2:4–10). Therefore all the disciples of Christ,
> persevering in prayer and praising God (cf. Acts 2:42–47), should present
> themselves as a living sacrifice, holy and pleasing to God (cf. Rom 12:1).
> Everywhere on earth they must bear witness to Christ and give an
> answer to those who seek an account of that hope of eternal life
> which is in them (cf. 1 Pet 3:15).[37]

---

[34] Furthermore, the concept of *sacerdotium commune* is rather foreign to Eastern Christians. Cf. Grillmeier, 2:180.

[35] Cf. ibid., 181.

[36] Pesch, 174.

[37] LG 10.

It is instructive that Alois Grillmeier begins his commentary on
the second chapter of *Lumen gentium* with the clarification: "By 'People of God' is meant here, not the multitude of the faithful in contrast to the hierarchy, but rather the Church as a whole, with all the
groups of her members."[38] The Council was anxious to avoid all
opposition between hierarchy and laity in the Church and therefore
spoke in *Lumen gentium* about the commonality of all members of
the People of God before it discussed any differentiation:

> Therefore, the chosen People of God is one: "one Lord, one faith,
> one baptism" (Eph 4:5); sharing a common dignity as members
> from their regeneration in Christ, having the same filial grace and
> the same vocation to perfection; possessing in common one salvation, one hope and one undivided charity. There is, therefore, in
> Christ and in the Church no inequality on the basis of race or
> nationality, social condition or sex, because "there is neither Jew
> nor Greek: there is neither bond nor free: there is neither male
> nor female. For you are all 'one' in Christ Jesus" (Gal 3:28, Greek;
> cf. Col 3:11).[39]

The common vocation of all to holiness, based on their equal dignity as children of God, does not rule out, nonetheless, the fact that
there are different ministries among the members of the one people.
Lumen gentium emphasizes that "[t]he distinction which the Lord made
between sacred ministers and the rest of the People of God"[40] involves
a genuine *communio*. "Thus in their diversity all bear witness to the
wonderful unity in the Body of Christ."[41]

---

[38] Grillmeier, 2:176. Cf. E. Schillebeeckx, *Besinnung auf das Zweite Vatikanum: Vierte
Session: Bilanz und Übersicht* (Vienna: Herder, 1966), 14: "Within this People of God are
found various ministries, clerical and non-clerical. Certainly, there is in the Church the
special ecclesial office, that of the ministerial priesthood, such as the office held by the
pope with the bishops, the priests (presbyters), and deacons. This ecclesial office, indeed,
is essentially different from the priesthood of all believers, but its function is one of service
precisely with regard to the common priesthood and it is essentially ordered to it, so that
one cannot speak of a fundamental opposition; on the contrary, a unity arises from the
mutual association of the two."

[39] *LG* 32.

[40] Ibid.

[41] Ibid.

2. *The essential difference between the common priesthood and the ministerial priesthood*

Priests and lay people share in the common priesthood of all the baptized in cooperating with the saving mission of the Church.[42] That does not diminish the fact that the common priesthood is clearly distinguished from the ministerial or hierarchical priesthood.[43] "Though they differ from one another in essence and not only in degree, the common priesthood of the faithful and the ministerial or hierarchical priesthood are nonetheless interrelated: each of them in its own special way is a participation in the one priesthood of Christ." [44] The Council, therefore, speaks, not just about a difference in degree, but about an essential difference. As Raphael Schulte remarks, the correct understanding of the two types of participation in the one priesthood of Jesus Christ was "debated at length, with the advantageous result that we have a very clear orientation about the Council's intention".[45]

---

[42] *LG* 33; *CIC*, can. 225; cf. H. Hallermann, "Priesterliche Identität gewinnen in Abgrenzung oder in Kooperation?" *Diak* 29 (1998): 200: "The essential foundation for acquiring a new priestly identity, therefore, is the internal acceptance of the article of faith newly presented by the Council, that the laity share in the salvific mission of the Church herself and are appointed to that work by the Lord through baptism and confirmation."

[43] Adam Seigfried comments: "So far, unfortunately, full recognition of these statements of the Second Vatican Council on the common priesthood has not yet been achieved. Instead, there are evident and repeated efforts to qualify them.... Consequently, nothing is conceded to the common priesthood except what is left over after taking away the ordained priesthood. Today we are far from having successfully integrated the ordained priesthood into the common priesthood, because instead of finally investigating the questions about what form the sacramental priesthood should take within the People of God and what the admission requirements should be, many merely complain about the priest shortage.... Really taking seriously the common priesthood of the People of God would bring about a change in the principles of the ordained priesthood. It would be understood as an integral part of the common priesthood." See Seigfried, "Volk Gottes", 264. Here we should ask whether such an interpretation of *Lumen gentium* corresponds to the hermeneutic of the Council, since *Lumen gentium* is concerned, not about the "integration of the ordained priesthood into the common priesthood", but rather about the participation of both in the one priesthood of Jesus Christ. Cf. also W. Löser, " 'Jetzt aber seid ihr Gottes Volk' (1 Petr 2:10): Rechtfertigung und sakramentale Kirche", *ThPh* 73 (1998): 321–33, ref. at 328f.

[44] *LG* 10.

[45] R. Schulte, "Erneuertes Kirchen- und Priesterverständnis als aktueller Auftrag: Zur Wegweisung der Dogmatischen Konstitution *Lumen gentium*—über die Kirche", in *Aufbruch des Zweiten Vatikanischen Konzils heute*, ed. J. Kremer, 73–102, esp. 90ff. (Innsbruck and Vienna: Tyrolia-Verlag, 1993).

Nevertheless Schulte finds fault in the official German translation[46] of *Lumen gentium* 10, because in it

> the statement concerning the one priesthood of Christ (*de uno Christi sacerdotio*) is simply omitted, even though the Christian understanding of the priesthood in all of its participatory modes is founded on the fact that Jesus Christ is the one and only priest of the New Covenant, who allows the faithful to share in his one priesthood and to collaborate therein.[47]

This sharing in the priesthood of Jesus Christ occurs, according to Alois Grillmeier, in mutual dependence and does not cancel out what is distinctive to either sort of participation in Christ's priesthood.[48] Medard Kehl, nevertheless, is of the opinion that the conciliar distinction between the common priesthood and the ministerial priesthood as an essential difference and "not only"[49] one of degree constitutes a "very misleading formulation",[50] since it "does not exclude a 'gradation' in the sharing in the priesthood of Jesus and thus within Christian life itself".[51] It is questionable whether this conclusion can be drawn as an interpretation of *Lumen gentium*. In line with *Lumen gentium*, on the other hand, is Kehl's finding that the chief concern of the Council Fathers was, "not to put the significance of the ministerial priesthood on a par with that of the common priesthood, but rather to emphasize its proper character, which cannot simply be derived from the common priesthood".[52] Gisbert Greshake, too, observes that,

---

[46] This translation was commissioned by the German bishops and approved in the 1966 version.

[47] Schulte, "Erneuertes Kirchen- und Priesterverständnis", 100, n. 4.

[48] See Grillmeier, 2:182.

[49] *LG* 10.

[50] Kehl, *Kirche*, 114.

[51] It is debatable whether Kehl's interpretation corresponds to the intended meaning of *LG* 10. Even more problematic is his view about the essential difference: ". . . but that still implies that the ministerial priesthood is ontologically higher qualified, which, however, is by no means within the intended scope of this text" (see Kehl, *Kirche*, 114).

[52] Kehl, *Kirche*, 114. After this lucid insight, it is astonishing to read that Kehl sees in the ministry of the priest only a "sacramentally enhanced sign of that which is granted substantially (that is, on the level of the *res sacramenti* of the salvation that is communicated) and in common to all the faithful, namely, the making present of Christ's salvific ministry in our world". See also Werbick, *Kirche*, 375. In view of the "very vague language nowadays about the 'nature' or 'essence' of a thing", Werbick wonders whether we still should

in keeping with the Council's intention, it is not a question of more or less priesthood; instead,

> the difference between the two is *"essentia"*, "essential", which means that the two are in fact dependent on each other, but on another level altogether, which cannot be described adequately in terms of superiority and subordination, "more" and "less". The distinction between the ministerial and the lay priesthood is not primarily of a jurisdictional but rather of a sacramental nature.[53]

The fact that they are sacramental signs demands that ordained ministers not be rulers of the congregation but, rather, servants, like Christ, if they are to live up to their mission.[54] This means, in the words of Ferdinand Klosermann, that the figure of the servant (Phil 2:7) is "at the same time the figure of the brother":[55] "Now if Christ became the brother of all Christians, and therefore of the laymen as well, indeed, a brother who came to serve, then those who are appointed to the sacred ministry, too, are the brothers of those whom they serve."[56]

Of course this brotherhood demands a fraternal manner, a culture of love and respect in relations between the ordained ministers and the lay people.[57] Conversely, to cordon off the official ministers in any way from the People of God is an unacceptable politicization of a

---

speak about an "essential difference". In his opinion, there is a "specific responsibility of the ordained ministers for the uncurtailed presence of the divine truth".

[53] G. Greshake, *Priestersein* (Freiburg im Breisgau: Herder, 1982), 75. On this topic, see also the Congregation for the Doctrine of the Faith, *Instruction on Certain Questions regarding the Collaboration of the Non-Ordained Faithful in the Sacred Ministry of Priests* (*L'Osservatore Romano*, English ed., no. 47 [November 19, 1997], special insert). "Thus the essential difference between the common priesthood of the faithful and the ministerial priesthood is not found in the priesthood of Christ, which remains forever one and indivisible, nor in the sanctity to which all of the faithful are called.... This diversity exists at the *mode* of participation in the priesthood of Christ and is essential in the sense that 'while the common priesthood of the faithful is exercised by the unfolding of baptismal grace—a life of faith, hope and charity, a life according to the Spirit—the ministerial priesthood is at the service of the common priesthood ... and directed at the unfolding of the baptismal grace of all Christians.'" Here [p. III] the *Instruction* quotes *CCC* 1547.

[54] Cf. *LG* 32: "Pastors of the Church, following the example of the Lord, should minister to one another and to the other faithful."

[55] F. Klostermann, "Kommentar zu *LG* Kap. 4", in *LThK.E* 1:267.

[56] Ibid.

[57] See ibid., 267f.

theological concept.[58] The *common* priesthood belongs to *all* the members of the People of God[59]—laymen and priests—and therefore must not be called the "priesthood of the laity", since "the faithful who have received the sacrament of holy orders retain this original priesthood. It is the prerequisite for that further consecration."[60] That is why the common vocation to holiness remains essential for the operation of the common priesthood. This vocation is reflected in the life of virtue through which the Church herself becomes a credible sign and instrument of grace.

3. *The actuation of the common priesthood in the sacraments and in the life of virtue*

The realm of personal morality and Christian formation in life is inseparably connected with the actuation of the sacramental life. In an ecclesiological survey of the seven sacraments in *Lumen gentium* 11, it is demonstrated that the People of God is built up through the sacraments and also through the appropriately virtuous life of individual believers. This means that every "sacramental grace corresponds to a (particular) behavior".[61] Thus, for example, the "indelible character" of baptism demands that believers "must confess before men the faith which they have received from God".[62] Consequently, the main focus of *Lumen gentium* 11 is on the sacramental actuation of the common priesthood in the People of God. The Constitution on the Liturgy had already stated: "All the faithful should be led to that fully conscious and active participation in liturgical celebrations ... [to which] the Christian people as 'a chosen race, a royal priesthood, a holy nation, a redeemed people' ... [have a] right and [therefore also the] duty, by

---

[58] Therefore the current contrast between "ministerial Church" and "Church of the people" can claim no theological basis. It is counterproductive, in that it reinforces the so-called hierarchical schism that *Lumen gentium* clearly strove to overcome.

[59] Cf. P. Neuner, "Die Kirche: Mysterium und Volk Gottes", in *Erinnerungen an einen Aufbruch: Das II. Vatikanische Konzil*, ed. N. Kutschki, 44f. (Würzburg: Echter, 1995).

[60] E. J. De Smedt, "Das Priestertum der Gläubigen", in Baraúna, 1:381. Thus it is understandable that in *LG* 11, in the list of the sacraments that are related to the operation of the common priesthood, "holy orders" is also mentioned, since it cannot be validly administered or received without baptism.

[61] Ibid., 385.

[62] *LG* 11.

reason of their baptism".[63] Contrary to all leveling tendencies in carrying out the liturgy, *Lumen gentium* clearly speaks of participation in the eucharistic sacrifice in a manner *corresponding* to one's vocation:

> Taking part in the eucharistic sacrifice, which is the fount and apex of the whole Christian life, they offer the Divine Victim to God, and offer themselves along with It. Thus both by reason of the offering and through Holy Communion all take part in this liturgical service, not indeed, all in the same way but each in that way which is proper to himself.[64]

Thus the reception of the sacraments always has an ecclesiological significance as well, for—in the words of Karl Rahner—"in the reception of the sacraments we not only receive a gift of God's grace from the hand of the Church, but also actively build up the Body of Christ."[65] According to *Lumen gentium* 10, this happens through "spiritual sacrifices", through prayer and thanksgiving, through the witness of a holy life, through self-denial and acts of charity. *Lumen gentium* 11 says that the source and summit of Christian life in its entirety is participation in the eucharistic sacrifice, for in it the unity of the faithful attains its real purpose: "Strengthened in Holy Communion by the Body of Christ, they then manifest in a concrete way that unity of the people of God which is suitably signified and wondrously brought about by this most august sacrament."[66]

The other sacraments, too, even penance and the anointing of the sick, have an ecclesial dimension, in that by their efficacy they not only pertain to the individual as a member of the People of God but also contribute, each in its own way, to the building up of the entire Christian community. That is why ordination, too, that is, the sacrament of holy orders, is described primarily as a ministry to the People of God. A very special meaning for the Church is assigned, however, to the sacrament of matrimony, which signifies "the mystery of the unity and faithful love between Christ and the Church": First, the Christian marital covenant points as a sacrament to God's faithful

---

[63] *SC* 14, quoting 1 Pet 2:9, 4–5.
[64] *LG* 11.
[65] Rahner, "Volk Gottes", 28.
[66] *LG* 11. The following explanations are also based on this article.

covenant with his People, which God has established in Christ with his Church. Second, from the marital covenant proceeds the family as the "domestic church", which is the sacramental locus where the spouses sanctify one another and accept and raise children. It follows from this, third, that parents are the first to proclaim the gospel to their children, whereby they foster unity as well as the vocation proper to each one and thus reflect the Church in miniature.

With the last-mentioned aspect of the testimony of faith, we already touch on a further, prophetic dimension of the People of God.

4. *The prophetic ministry of the People of God*

The Constitution on the Church restores an awareness of the prophetic ministry of the People of God. To the People of God that he had founded, Christ gave a share in his prophetic office in a twofold way: in living *witness*, which attains its full development in the *sensus fidei*, the inerrant sense of faith possessed by the People of God as a whole, and in the *charisms*, which "are seen as being one with the sacraments, offices, and the entire life of virtue, which are likewise produced by the Spirit".[67]

a. The supernatural sense of faith belonging to the whole People of God

In the discussion of infallibility, especially since the First Vatican Council, the gift of infallibility was centered one-sidedly on the office of the successor of Peter, "and, furthermore, on a papal primacy that was viewed in isolation from the episcopate as a whole",[68] without taking into account the fact that the reality of revelation and salvation was established by Christ as a living gift and an imperishable possession for the faithful witnesses, the entire People. That is why chapter 4 of *Lumen gentium* says with regard to the laity:

> Christ, the great Prophet, who proclaimed the Kingdom of his Father both by the testimony of his life and the power of his words, continually fulfills his prophetic office until the complete manifestation

---

[67] Grillmeier, 2:189.
[68] Ibid. Cf. also Pesch, 183–85.

of glory. He does this not only through the hierarchy who teach in
his name and with his authority, but also through the laity whom
he made his witnesses and to whom he gave understanding of the
faith (*sensus fidei*) and an attractiveness in speech (cf. Acts 2:17–18;
Rev 19:10) so that the power of the Gospel might shine forth in
their daily social and family life.[69]

This supernatural sense of the faith (*sensus fidei*) belonging to the whole
People had been described previously in article 12 in similar terms:[70]

The holy people of God shares also in Christ's prophetic office; it
spreads abroad a living witness to him, especially by means of a life
of faith and charity and by offering to God a sacrifice of praise, the
tribute of lips which give praise to his name (cf. Heb 13:15). The
entire body of the faithful, anointed as they are by the Holy One
(cf. 1 Jn 2:20 and 27), cannot err in matters of belief.

In this passage the Council Fathers cite Augustine,[71] in whose view
the supernatural sense of faith of the whole People exists when the members of the Church, "from the bishops down to the last of the lay faithful ... show universal agreement in matters of faith and morals".[72] As
Hermann Josef Pottmeyer explains, the Magisterium "does not stand unilaterally in contrast to the faithful; rather, its infallibility in teaching about
matters of the faith (*infallibilitas in docendo*) has one of its roots in the infallibility of faith (*infallibilitas in credendo*) of the whole People of God."[73]
Endowed with the sense of faith, believers are "permitted and sometimes even obliged to express their opinion on those things which concern the good of the Church.... [R]everence and charity toward those
who by reason of their sacred office represent the person of Christ"[74]
is a fundamental prerequisite for this. That is why *Lumen gentium* emphasizes obedience to the Church's Magisterium:

---

[69] *LG* 35.
[70] Cf. M. Seckler, "Glaubenssinn", in *LThK*, 2nd ed., vol. 4 (Freiburg im Breisgau:
Herder, 1960), 945–48.
[71] Cf. Augustine, *De Praed. Sanct.* 14, 27, in PL 44, 980.
[72] *LG* 12.
[73] H.J. Pottmeyer, "Die Mitsprache der Gläubigen in Glaubenssachen: Eine alte Praxis
und ihre Wiederentdeckung", *IKaZ* 25 (1996): 134–47, esp. sec. "5. Die Lehre des 2.
Vatikanums vom Glaubenssinn und Glaubenskonsens", 142–45, citation at 143.
[74] *LG* 37.

That discernment in matters of faith is aroused and sustained by the Spirit of truth. It is exercised under the guidance of the sacred teaching authority, in faithful and respectful obedience to which the people of God accepts that which is not just the word of men but truly the word of God (cf. 1 Thess 2:13). Through it, the people of God adheres unwaveringly to the faith given once and for all to the saints (cf. Jude 3), penetrates it more deeply with right thinking, and applies it more fully in its life.[75]

Even though this passage clearly underscores the Magisterium's competence to govern, the statement about the *sensus fidei* of the whole People of God signifies an extension or a concretization of "what the First Vatican Council had already said and what the followers of the disappointed minority at that time now wanted to commit to writing: the fact that the pope is infallible, not outside of the Church and over against her, but rather as one bound up with her."[76]

Besides this supernatural sense of the faith belonging to the People of God, which cannot be understood as something antithetical to the Magisterium, the Holy Spirit has endowed the Church with charisms, which similarly are not granted in opposition to the official structures of the Church, but rather serve like them (and likewise in them) the unity of the Church.[77] Along these lines, Michael Figura speaks of an abiding *charismatic structure* of the Church, "which, however, cannot be played off against her hierarchical structure. The two are mutually dependent, for they originate from the same Spirit of God and serve the upbuilding of the Church."[78]

b. The diaconal orientation of the charisms for the upbuilding of the People of God

The fact that every individual in the People of God is charismatically gifted serves the renewal and upbuilding of the Church. Those who hold office and are equipped with authority to govern have the respon-

---

[75] *LG* 12. Cf. also *LG* 37.

[76] Pesch, 185.

[77] Cf. ibid., 184f. See H. Küng, "Die charismatische Struktur der Kirche", *Conc(D)* 1 (1965): 282–90.

[78] M. Figura, "Kirche und Eucharistie im Licht des Geheimnisses des dreifaltigen Gottes", *IKaZ* 29 (2000): 100–119, citation at 107.

sibility of testing, coordinating, and preserving the gifts given by the Holy Spirit. These gifts are not bound up with a particular state of life; instead, the Holy Spirit "distributes special graces among the faithful of every rank".[79] The criterion for the genuineness of a spiritual gift is its usefulness for the whole People of God: "These charisms, whether they be the more outstanding or the more simple and widely diffused, are to be received with thanksgiving and consolation for they are perfectly suited to and useful for the needs of the Church."[80] This charismatic structure of the Church implies "neither enthusiasm, which degenerates into arbitrariness and disorder, nor legalism, which hardens into routine and uniformity".[81] The crucial thing is that the whole People receives a share in the spiritual gifts that the Spirit of the Church desires to grant.

5. Kingly service in the People of God

The dignity and the freedom of the children of God have been awarded to *all* members of this People on the basis of their common vocation, and God's Spirit dwells in the hearts of individual believers as in a temple. That is why it is emphasized once again in *Lumen gentium* 32 that among them "all share a true equality with regard to the dignity and to the activity common to all the faithful for the building up of the Body of Christ"; this is the case even though "by the will of Christ some are made as teachers, pastors and dispensers of mysteries on behalf of others."[82] This share in Christ's kingship is characterized, according to *Lumen gentium* 36, by two essential marks, namely, by the dignity of the freedom of the children of God and by their responsibility before God.

a. The dignity of the freedom of the children of God

Through redemption in Jesus Christ, the crucified and glorified Lord, all those who have been baptized into the death of the Lord have a share in his "royal freedom", so that they might "by true penance and

---

[79] *LG* 12. Cf. De Smedt, "Priestertum der Gläubigen", 1:388f.
[80] *LG* 12; cf. *LG* 13.
[81] Küng, "Charismatische Struktur", 289.
[82] *LG* 32.

a holy life ... conquer the reign of sin in themselves (cf. Rom 6:12) ... so that serving Christ in their fellow men they might by humility and patience lead their brethren to that King for whom to serve is to reign." [83] This freedom in Christ demands apostolic zeal, so as to spread the "kingdom of holiness and grace, a kingdom of justice, love and peace". [84] From this develops the responsibility for the entire creation of God, which is a further hallmark of the kingly responsibility of every baptized person.

b. Responsibility before God as responsibility for creation and the world

Creation, too, should be brought under Christ's rule by the members of the People of God; that is to say, it should be liberated "into the freedom of the glory of the sons of God". [85] This involves "recognizing the inmost nature of the world and the fact that it is ordered to God" [86] and healing it of its disorder, so that it can receive the seed of God's Word. It is true that service to the world and the work of salvation obey their own respective laws, yet neither can be accomplished in isolation from the other. Responsibility for the world is entrusted in a special way to the laity, who in this endeavor are expected as members of the Church and of human society to allow themselves to be guided by their Christian conscience. In doing so, they should distinguish carefully between ecclesial and secular rights and duties yet harmonize them, "since even in secular business there is no human activity which can be withdrawn from God's dominion." [87] Hans Waldenfels refers to the Christian authenticity demanded here when he speaks of an "authority of life" that is manifested in the way in which believers comport themselves "as the faith-filled People of God in the everyday routine of human life". [88]

Thus we can conclude this §3 as follows: In its discussion of participation in the threefold mission of Christ, *Lumen gentium* emphasizes that it is granted not only to ordained ministers but to all baptized Christians and, therefore, to the laity as well. Common to all members

---

[83] LG 36.

[84] Ibid. Here *Lumen gentium* cites the preface for the feast of Christ the King.

[85] LG 36; cf. Rom 8:21.

[86] A. Auer, "Die Laien", in Sandfuchs, 55–71, citation at 63.

[87] LG 36.

[88] H. Waldenfels, "Autorität und Erkenntnis", *Conc(D)* 21 (1985): 255–61, citation at 259.

of the People of God are the vocation to exercise the common priesthood through the celebration of the sacraments and in living a life of
virtue, the prophetic ministry of acknowledging the faith and implementing the charisms, as well as the preservation of their royal dignity
through a holy life in imitation of Christ and with responsibility for
the world. Within this commonality, in which lay people and ordained
ministers are dependent on each other, the latter receive in a special
way a share in the one priesthood of Jesus Christ by virtue of their
ordination. Their sacramental priesthood is essentially different from
that of all the baptized, and as such it is at the service of the People of
God for their edification. This implies, at the same time, a recognition that the laity have a specific task in their responsibility for the
world. This is the subject of the next section.

§ 4. The Laity in the Church

Because of its textual history,[89] chapter 4 of *Lumen gentium*, entitled
"The Laity", is closely associated with chapter 2, "On the People of
God", but the two chapters are thematically connected as well: "Everything that has been said above concerning the People of God is intended
for the laity, religious and clergy alike. But there are certain things
which pertain in a special way to the laity, both men and women, by
reason of their condition and mission."[90] Those to whom chapter 4
of *Lumen gentium* is addressed are "defined negatively" at first; that is,
they are described by what they are *not*: "all the faithful except those
in holy orders and those in the state of religious life specially approved
by the Church".[91] Alfons Auer points out that this perspective "was
in the forefront for centuries and prevented for all too long the emergence of a positive self-awareness of the laity".[92] Medard Kehl evalu-
ates this circumstance as a significant expression of the "basic pastoral
schism" existing between the hierarchy and the "simple faithful". The
former "are to a great extent still considered in the Church's consciousness to be the ones who really act, have responsibility, and make

---

[89] On this subject, see Klostermann, "Kommentar zu *LG* Kap. 4", 1:260–62.
[90] *LG* 30.
[91] *LG* 31. Cf. Pesch, 204.
[92] Auer, "Laien", 57.

decisions in the Church, which is therefore in many instances simply identified with them (*Amtskirche*, 'the official Church')",[93] while the role of the latter was thought to be that of obeying and carrying out the plans of the authorities. The Council itself, however, both in *Lumen gentium* 30–38 and especially in the Decree on the Lay Apostolate *Apostolicam Actuositatem*, tried to do justice to the growing self-awareness of the laity and to their specific mission. Therefore it would be wrong to overlook the positive stance manifested in the observation that the laity, by virtue of their baptism and confirmation, are responsible representatives of the Church's mission and carry on their mission in the Church and in the world, each in his particular way.[94]

In *Lumen gentium* 31, the mission of the laity is immediately characterized by a threefold reference to the "world":

> What specifically characterizes the laity is their secular [that is, worldly] nature. . . . They live in the world, that is, in each and in all of the secular professions and occupations. . . . They are called there by God [so] that by exercising their proper function and led by the spirit of the Gospel they may work for the sanctification of the world from within as a leaven.[95]

But what does "world" mean here? For the lay person it is the "totality of his personal concerns and limits as well as his social and material ties";[96] within this context he is capable of actualizing his Christianity and his humanity. In the world, the laity are called to "enthusiastically lend their joint assistance to their pastors and teachers".[97] In emphasizing

---

[93] Kehl, *Kirche*, 117f. In n. 68, Kehl refers to works by P. M. Zulehner, *Sie werden mein Volk sein: Grundkurs gemeindlichen Glaubens* (Düsseldorf: Patmos-Verlag, 1986); Zulehner, "Das geistliche Amt des Volkes Gottes", in *Priesterkirche*, ed. P. Hoffmann (Düsseldorf: Patmos-Verlag, 1987); Zulehner, *Pastoraltheologie*, vol. 2, *Gemeindepastoral: Orte christlicher Praxis* (Düsseldorf: Patmos-Verlag, 1989); P. Weß, *Ihr alle seid Geschwister: Priester und Kirche* (Mainz: Matthias-Grünewald-Verlag, 1983); E. Klinger and R. Zerfaß, eds., *Die Kirche der Laien: Eine Weichenstellung des Konzils* (Würzburg: Echter, 1987); P. Neuner, *Der Laie und das Gottesvolk* (Frankfurt: Knecht, 1988); W. Beinert, "Autorität um der Liebe willen", in *Priester heute*, ed. K. Hillenbrand, 32–66 (Würzburg: Echter, 1990).

[94] Cf. *LG* 31; cf. Pesch, 205.

[95] *LG* 31.

[96] Auer, "Laien", 59.

[97] *LG* 32.

the secular character of the mission of the laity, the Council is "well aware that it intends no theological ranking thereby".[98] Through "this very diversity of graces, ministries and works", both laity and consecrated persons "bear witness to the wonderful unity in the Body of Christ",[99] so that the variety becomes a component of the unity.

After these basic reflections on the Council's view of the laity, we turn to the question of their task in the world. According to *Lumen gentium*, the laity are called, above all, "to make the Church present and operative in those places and circumstances where only through them can [she] become the salt of the earth".[100] Besides this, the Constitution mentions "a more direct form of cooperation in the apostolate of the Hierarchy".[101] Ferdinand Klostermann mentions also the "taking on of apostolic activities and tasks that in and of themselves pertain to the hierarchy as their responsibility but that as a matter of principle can also be delegated to lay persons, because [these activities require] no ordination or jurisdiction of divine right".[102] The Constitution on the Church characterizes the manner of this collaboration between the laity and their pastors as a "familiar dialogue".[103] For their dialogue with each other, "truth, ... courage and ... prudence" as well as "reverence and charity"[104] are necessary.

In articles 34–36 of *Lumen gentium*, the apostolate of the laity is viewed as a share in the priestly, prophetic, and kingly office of Christ.[105] In a special way, however, lay persons are called to collaborate in the work of creation and to sanctify the world for God. They accomplish this consecration when they allow "all their works, prayers and apostolic endeavors, their ordinary married and family life, their daily occupations, their physical and mental relaxation"[106] to be filled with life

---

[98] Kehl, *Kirche*, 122. Cf. *LG* 31.

[99] *LG* 32.

[100] *LG* 33; cf. Pius XI, *Quadragesimo anno*, in *AAS* 23 (1931): 177–228, ref. at 221f.

[101] *LG* 33.

[102] Klostermann, "Kommentar zu *LG* Kap. 4", 271.

[103] *LG* 37.

[104] Ibid. Cf. pt. 1, sec. 2, chap. 2, § 3.4.a., of this work, "The Supernatural Sense of Faith Belonging to the Whole People of God".

[105] See pt. 1, sec. 2, chap. 2, § 3, "The Participation of the People of God in Christ's Priestly, Prophetic, and Kingly Mission".

[106] *LG* 34.

in the Holy Spirit, while at the same time understanding their "hard-ships of life" as "spiritual sacrifices". The latter, as it says in *Lumen gentium* 34, are offered "in the celebration of the Eucharist" to God along with the Body of the Lord. "Thus, as those everywhere who adore in holy activity, the laity consecrate the world itself to God." Therefore the ministry of a lay person cannot "be limited to being acquainted with the laws and values of secular fields and applying them for the good of human society".[107]

The last article of chapter 4 summarizes once more the mission of the lay person in the Church and in the world by citing the letter to Diognetos, which understands Christians to be the "soul of the world":

> Each individual layman must stand before the world as a witness to the Resurrection and life of the Lord Jesus and a symbol of the living God. All the laity as a community and each one accord-ing to his ability must nourish the world with spiritual fruits (cf. Gal 5:22). They must diffuse in the world that spirit which animates the poor, the meek, the peace makers—whom the Lord in the Gospel proclaimed as blessed [cf. Mt 5:3–9]. In a word, "Christians must be to the world what the soul is to the body." [108]

But if all the baptized are called to allow themselves to be guided by the spirit of the gospel in human society and thus to "work for the sanctification of the world from within as a leaven",[109] in a life that is informed by faith, hope, and love, then this means nothing less than their vocation to holiness. This vocation is granted to all the members of the People of God as a gift and a duty.

---

[107] Auer, "Laien", 59.

[108] *LG* 38.

[109] *LG* 31. Cf. Klostermann, "Kommentar zu *LG* Kap. 4", 1:283: "The remark (in *LG* 38) also recalls the interpretation of the parable of the leaven in the dough (Mt 13:33) by John Chrysostom: 'As the leaven communicates its own power to the mass of dough, so you too will change the whole world.' For that to happen, of course, it is not enough for the leaven merely to touch the dough; it must be mixed in with it, indeed, be covered over by it. The ineffectiveness of many Christians is our own fault, 'since we should be instead enough to serve as leaven for a thousand worlds' [John Chrysostom, *Hom. in Mt* 46:2 in PG 58, 477–479]."

§ 5. The Call to Holiness

Within the framework of this dissertation, chapter 5 of *Lumen gentium*, "The Universal Call to Holiness in the Church", can be discussed only in outline form. It differs from chapters 3, 4, and 6 of the Constitution on the Church in that it focuses on no particular state of life in the Church but rather on the sanctification of all through God's saving work in the Church. This purpose has already appeared in other passages[110] of *Lumen gentium*. What was the reason for the decision to have a special chapter on the theme of the call to holiness? Friedrich Wulf gives the following answer:

> The Church is caught up in an immense transformation. She is changing her face. In the Constitution on the Church that was prepared for Vatican I, the idea of holiness was scarcely mentioned, or at best parenthetically. The fifteen chapters of that draft dealt with the Church chiefly as a juridical institution. . . . Now [in *Lumen gentium*] a correction is clearly being made. . . . The more the Church appears now as a little flock in the midst of a non-Christian humanity, and the more obvious the diaspora situation of Christians becomes, the more important the testimony of her holiness, of her devotion to the Lord, and of her fraternal charity will be, in order to win a hearing for her message and to ensure her credibility. Hence it is immediately clear why this theme has such central significance.[111]

The chapter itself begins with an article of faith: The Church is "indefectibly holy".[112] She receives this holiness from Christ, who "loved the Church as his Bride, delivering himself up for her. He did this that he might sanctify her (cf. Eph 5:25–26). He united her to himself as his own body and brought it to perfection by the gift of the Holy Spirit for God's glory."[113] It follows that the holiness of the individual Christian is always only a share in the one holiness of Jesus Christ,[114]

---

[110] Cf. *LG* 11: "Fortified by so many and such powerful means of salvation, all the faithful, whatever their condition or state, are called by the Lord, each in his own way, to that perfect holiness whereby the Father Himself is perfect."

[111] F. Wulf, "Kommentar zu LG Kap. 5 und 6", in *LThK.E* 1:288f.

[112] *LG* 39: "Ecclesia . . . indefectibiliter sancta creditur". Cf. K. Rahner, "Die Sünde in der Kirche", in Baraúna, 1:346–62, in particular, 358–61.

[113] *LG* 39.

[114] Ibid. Compare the Gloria of the Mass: "Tu solus sanctus".

through whose redemptive work the individual member in the People of God is "called ... and justified in the Lord Jesus",[115] not on the basis of his own works, but by grace. Here it is clearly evident "that the nature of the Church is by no means the sum of her individual members".[116] From this "indicative of being sanctified by God"— as Hermann Josef Pottmeyer puts it—"follows the imperative of a holy life".[117] Consequently, holiness is a gift of the Holy Spirit, who produces "fruits of grace ... in the faithful".[118] God's gift becomes the Christian's duty, whereas failure in this regard means sin; this is why in *Lumen gentium* 40 the Council quite explicitly connects failure and guilt: "Since truly we all offend in many things (cf. Jas 3:2) we all need God's mercies continually and we all must daily pray: "Forgive us our debts" (Mt 6:12)."[119] The call to holiness is *universal*: "The classes and duties of life are many, but holiness is one",[120] whether it is cultivated as a cleric or as a layman. Love, "as the bond of perfection and the fullness of the law (cf. Col 3:14; Rom 13:10), rules over all the means of attaining holiness and gives life to these same means".[121] The highest testimony of love, today as ever since the first days of Christianity, consists of martyrdom, which in a special way conforms the individual to Christ.[122] Furthermore, "the holiness of the Church is fostered in a special way by the observance of the counsels proposed in the Gospel by our Lord to his disciples."[123]

With its reference to the evangelical counsels of virginity (in this connection celibacy is explicitly mentioned), poverty, and obedience (through the renunciation of self-will), the Constitution makes a transition to the sixth chapter, "Religious".

---

[115] *LG* 40.

[116] K. Rahner, "Sünde in der Kirche", 1:346–62, citation at 359.

[117] H. J. Pottmeyer, "Die Frage nach der wahren Kirche", *HFTh* 3:182. Cf. *LG* 40.

[118] *LG* 39.

[119] *LG* 40; cf. *LG* 8.

[120] *LG* 41.

[121] *LG* 42.

[122] See ibid. Cf. F. Wulf, "Die allgemeine Berufung zur Heiligkeit in der Kirche: Die Ordensleute", in Sandfuchs, 72–85, citation at 82: "Of all these gifts of grace, the first to be mentioned is Christian martyrdom, and it is no accident that the suggestion for this came from a bishop of the Eastern Bloc countries."

[123] *LG* 42.

§ 6. Religious

Chapter 6 of *Lumen gentium*, "Religious", forms a unit with the previous chapter, "The Universal Call to Holiness in the Church". At the Council there were certain disagreements[124] about whether or not a separate chapter of the Constitution on the Church should be devoted to religious. Friedrich Wulf considers the compromise— the closely connected chapters 5 and 6—a successful one, since, "on the one hand, the call to religious life is aligned with the grace of baptism and with the unsurpassable vocation contained within it ... ; therefore consecrated religious are correctly mentioned in the context of the universal call to holiness. On the other hand, however, the conciliar document does not remain silent about the greatness and importance of their gift."[125] The Council calls this devotion to God in the religious state "consecration" (*consecratio*)[126] and thus underscores the significance of this special mission in the Church.

In the very first sentence of the chapter the focus is on the charism of choosing and practicing the evangelical counsels "of chastity dedicated to God, poverty and obedience".[127] Since this form of life is based on the word and example of Jesus and are "a divine gift which the Church received from [her] Lord and which [she] always safeguards with the help of His grace",[128] the religious state "is an integral part of the Church".[129] The Lord bestows this gift upon both *clerics* and *lay people*, which is why the religious state cannot be characterized as a "middle way" between the two. Rather, "the faithful of Christ are called by God from both these states of life" to this

---

[124] Several Council Fathers from Europe, North America, Australia, and Malaysia for theological reasons would have preferred to include consecrated religious in the chapter on the call to holiness. For details, see J. Schmiedl, *Das Konzil und die Orden: Krise und Erneuerung des gottgeweihten Lebens* (Vallendar-Schönstatt: Patris-Verlag, 1999), 369–76, esp. 370.

[125] Wulf, "Allgemeine Berufung", 85. Cf. Wulf, "Theologische Phänomenologie des Ordenslebens", *MySal* 4/2 (1973): 450–87.

[126] LG 44.

[127] LG 43.

[128] Ibid.

[129] Wulf, "Allgemeine Berufung", 84. Friedrich Wulf expressly points out that a particular order is not an integral component of the Church, but rather the imitation of Christ in poverty, chastity, and obedience.

exemplary form of life for the benefit of the Church's mission.[130] In this ecclesial connection, following the evangelical counsels becomes the expression of an undivided love for God and neighbor.

The most important purpose of this special form of life is to commend to God the person who is called to it: "In this way, that person is ordained to the honor and service of God under a new and special title."[131] At the same time, this form of life unites the religious "to the Church and [her] mystery".[132] Consequently, "[f]rom this arises their duty of working to implant and strengthen the Kingdom of Christ in souls and to extend that Kingdom to every clime. This duty is to be undertaken to the extent of their capacities and in keeping with the proper type of their own vocation. This can be realized through prayer or active works of the apostolate."[133] In this connection *Lumen gentium* speaks about the authority of the Church's hierarchy over religious orders, about the usefulness of [the privilege of] exemption, and also about the reception of vows by the Church, especially during the Eucharistic Sacrifice.[134] Religious orders, by continually making present "the form of life which ... the Son of God accepted in entering this world to do the will of the Father",[135] acquire an additional and specifically symbolic character, which *Lumen gentium* admonishes religious also to preserve:

> Religious should carefully keep before their minds the fact that the Church presents Christ to believers and nonbelievers alike in a striking manner daily through them. The Church thus portrays Christ in contemplation on the mountain, in his proclamation of the kingdom of God to the multitudes, in his healing of the sick and maimed, in his work of converting sinners to a better life, in his solicitude for youth and his goodness to all men, always obedient to the will of the Father who sent him.[136]

---

[130] *LG* 43: cf. R. Schulte, "Das Ordensleben als Zeichen", in Baraúna, 2:383–414, ref. at 396f.

[131] *LG* 44.

[132] Ibid.

[133] Ibid.

[134] *LG* 45. On exemption, see also *CD* 35; *AG* 30.

[135] *LG* 44.

[136] *LG* 46.

Consecrated life, as an expression of the free response to Christ's call, promotes the development of the human person, despite "the renunciation of certain values which are to be undoubtedly esteemed".[137] In this, Mary,[138] through her virginal, poor, and obedient way of life, is the example and guide for all religious.

§ 7. Mary in the Mystery of Christ and of the Church

It is necessary to discuss chapter 8 of *Lumen gentium*, at least in outline form, because Mary holds a central place within the pilgrim People of God. She is, "on the one hand, a member of the Church, and, being the first of the redeemed, she is the archetype and model of the Church. At the same time, however, she also surpasses the Church as the Mother of God's Son who is united with the saving work of Jesus Christ from the beginning."[139] I have already referred to the disputes that arose concerning the Marian schema.[140] Therefore I can devote this section to the actual theme of the concluding chapter of the Constitution on the Church: "The Blessed Virgin Mary, Mother of God, in the Mystery of Christ and the Church". In keeping with the structure of the chapter, I will examine three core concepts in greater detail. First, I will look at Mary's role in the economy of salvation; second, I will turn my attention to Mary as the type of the Church; and third, I will turn to Marian devotion in the Church.

---

[137] Ibid.

[138] Cf. ibid.

[139] Gerhard Ludwig Müller, *Katholische Dogmatik für Studium und Praxis der Theologie* (Freiburg im Breisgau: Herder, 1996), 478.

[140] See pt. 1, sec. 1, "*Lumen gentium* amid the Tensions between Tradition and Innovation", chap. 2, § 2.2.b, "*Lumen gentium* as 'The Work of the Council'". Cf. O. Semmelroth, "Kommentar zu *LG* Kap. 8", in *LThK.E* 1:326f. See also Pesch, 192–95; G. Baraúna, "Die heiligste Jungfrau im Dienste des Heilsplanes", in Baraúna, 2:459–76, ref. at 460. The results of the voting on October 29, 1963, were as follows: 1,114 were in favor of including the Marian schema in the Constitution on the Church, 1,074 were against it, and five votes were invalid. Baraúna explains: "Both Cardinal R. Santos, who spoke against the inclusion before the vote, and Cardinal F. König, who spoke in favor of it, had made it clear that neither possibility involved an attack against the integrity of Catholic doctrine. What they were trying to do ... was to avoid giving the impression that Mary is an isolated component in the divine order of creation and salvation—an impression that a certain type of Mariology ... was incapable of effacing, especially among the separated brethren."

1. *Mary's role in the economy of salvation*

The chapter begins by taking up the one and only statement about Mary in the letters of St. Paul: "Wishing in his supreme goodness and wisdom to effect the redemption of the world, 'when the fullness of time came, God sent his Son, born of a woman, ... that we might receive the adoption of sons' (Gal 4:4–5)."[141] In this passage—as Otto Semmelroth demonstrates—"Mary is associated with the person and with the work of Christ in such a way that the meaning of both figures is set forth precisely through their relation to one another."[142] The Constitution gives expression to Mary's association with her Son through his Incarnation, life, death, and exaltation,[143] as well as to her association with the mystery of the Church.[144] The latter is based on the fact that no one "can be associated with the person and the work of Christ through God's grace and a personal decision without that entailing at the same time a connection with the Church".[145] Christ, the sole mediator with the Father,[146] selected Mary in a unique manner to become his "associate" in the work of salvation:

> She conceived, brought forth and nourished Christ. She presented him to the Father in the temple and was united with him by compassion as he died on the Cross. In this singular way she cooperated by her obedience, faith, hope, and burning charity in the work of the Savior in giving back supernatural life to souls. Wherefore she is our mother in the order of grace.[147]

Her participation in Christ's work was not concluded when she was taken up into heaven, for in her maternal love she "cares for the brethren of her Son, who still journey on earth.... Therefore the Blessed Virgin is invoked by the Church under the titles of Advocate, Aux-

---

[141] LG 52.

[142] O. Semmelroth, "Maria im Geheimnis Christi und der Kirche", in Sandfuchs, 102–14, citation at 108.

[143] See *Lumen gentium*, chap. 8, sec. 2: "The Role of the Blessed Mother in the Economy of Salvation".

[144] See *Lumen gentium*, chap. 8, sec. 3: "On the Blessed Virgin and the Church".

[145] Semmelroth, "Maria", 111.

[146] LG 60; cf. 1 Tim 2:5–6.

[147] LG 61.

iliatrix, Adjutrix, and Mediatrix." [148] This assistance, however, is always part of Christ's redemptive work. Therefore it should be understood in such a way "that it neither takes away from nor adds anything to the dignity and efficaciousness of Christ the one Mediator". [149]

2. Mary—Model for the Church

The conviction that Mary personally is a shining example for the Church is already established in the introduction to chapter 8 of *Lumen gentium*:

> At the same time, however, because she belongs to the offspring of Adam she is one with all those who are to be saved. She is "the mother of the members of Christ . . . having cooperated by charity that faithful might be born in the Church, who are members of that Head." Wherefore she is hailed as a pre-eminent and singular member of the Church, and as its type and excellent exemplar in faith and charity. The Catholic Church, taught by the Holy Spirit, honors her with filial affection and piety as a most beloved mother. [150]

In her twofold fundamental mystery as Virgin and Mother, Mary is the unique type [151] of the Church. In her virginity, Mary is mother, like the Church, which in bridal submission faithfully preserves Christ's words and works and communicates them as Mother to the faithful. For through preaching and baptizing, the Church becomes a mother to her children, who are conceived of the Holy Spirit and born of God. [152]

3. The Cult of the Blessed Virgin in the Church

As the Council says, there has been "a remarkable growth" [153] in devotion to Mary in the Church, according to the prophetic words of the Magnificat, "Behold, henceforth all generations will call me blessed." [154]

---

[148] LG 62.

[149] Ibid.; cf. Ambrose, *Ep.* 63, in PL 16, 1218.

[150] LG 53; here *Lumen gentium* quotes Augustine, *De sancta virginitate* 6, 6, in CSEL 41, 239f.; PL 40, 399; cf. Scheffczyk, *Aspekte der Kirche in der Krise*, 107; see also H. Rahner, *Maria und die Kirche* (Innsbruck: Tyrolia-Verlag, 1962), 118.

[151] See LG 63.

[152] Cf. LG 64.

[153] LG 66. The following citations are also found in this article.

[154] Lk 1:48.

"This cult ... differs essentially from the cult of adoration", which belongs to God alone.

> The various forms of piety toward the Mother of God, which the Church within the limits of sound and orthodox doctrine, according to the conditions of time and place, and the nature and ingenuity of the faithful has approved, bring it about that while the Mother is honored, the Son, through whom all things have their being (cf. Col 1:15–16) and in whom it has pleased the Father that all fullness should dwell (cf. Col 1:19), is rightly known, loved and glorified and that all his commands are observed.

From an ecumenical perspective, the Council cautions against exaggerated forms of Marian devotion as well as against false disparagement of it.[155] The latter would occur—as Otto Semmelroth remarks—if someone "out of a well-intentioned yet excessively narrow-minded concern for God's sovereignty wanted to overlook the fact that the grace of redemption works also in the redeemed for the precise purpose of making them fruitful, through their share in Christ's work for the salvation of their fellowmen in a new, supernatural solidarity".[156]

With the view of Mary "as a sign of sure hope and solace to the People of God during its sojourn", *Lumen gentium* concludes in the eschatological confidence that through the intercession of Mary, the Mother of God and "Mother of men",[157] all men might one day be "gathered together in peace and harmony into one People of God", for the glory of the Holy Trinity.

§ 8. Excursus: The Catholicity of the People
of God and Ecumenism

1. *The one People of God from many peoples*

Through Christ, "the head of the new and universal People",[158] God calls all men from all the peoples of the earth to the unity of the

---

[155] See *LG* 67.
[156] Semmelroth, "Maria", 113f.
[157] Cf. *LG* 69.
[158] *LG* 13.

Church. This produces a tension between the unity and catholicity of the People of God and the multiformity and diversity of the peoples.[159] This diversity in unity and unity in multiformity corresponds also to the relation of the particular Churches to the one Church. On this subject, Alois Grillmeier remarks:

> The full catholicity of the Church is realized only when this unity resulting from a sharing of natural and supernatural goods is brought into the universal Church through the individual and particular Churches in mutual communion. The Council rediscovered the universal Church as the sum total and *communio* of the particular and local Churches, taken in their fullness, just as it also finds the universal Church anew in the local Church.[160]

Now, if the People of God has a universal mission and is meant to embrace all men, then the question arises of their membership in the Church and the conditions for it.

2. *Various degrees of membership in the Church*[161]

According to *Lumen gentium*, the Church comprises, in different degrees of association, all men whom God wills to call to salvation.[162] The Council, nevertheless, avoids the concept of "membership in the Church",[163] which was defined by Pope Pius XII in *Mystici Corporis*[164] in such a way that only those believers are members of the Church who are united in *one baptism* and in *one faith* and are not separated from the *ecclesiastical authority*. In *Lumen gentium*, in contrast, the criteria for life in communion with the Church are listed as "first, the possession of the Spirit of Christ, but then also unity with the visible Church, through the bonds of 'the profession of faith, the

---

[159] Cf. *LG* 13.

[160] Grillmeier, 2:192.

[161] See pt. 1, sec. 2, chap. 1, §3.4, Excursus 1 of this work, " '*Una sancta catholica ecclesia*': The Question of Subsistence".

[162] *LG* 13–17.

[163] Cf. K. Rahner and H. Vorgrimler, "III. Die dogmatische Konstitution über die Kirche *Lumen gentium*", in *KlKK* 108. See also Grillmeier, 2:196–98: "II. Die Zugehörigkeit oder das Verbundensein mit der Kirche".

[164] *DH* 3802. *Mystici Corporis* thus follows the post-Reformation line of argument found in Bellarmine, which was also continued by Vatican I.

sacraments, and ecclesiastical government and communion' (LG 14)".[165] As always, *Lumen gentium* teaches the doctrine that the Church is necessary for salvation, yet without excluding from salvation those who are not in the same *communio*.[166] It should be noted, nevertheless, that the Constitution on the Church speaks of the "possibility of not being saved" for those who know better yet ignore the necessity of the Church for salvation:

> This Sacred Council wishes to turn its attention firstly to the Catholic faithful. Basing itself upon Sacred Scripture and Tradition, it teaches that the Church, now sojourning on earth as an exile, is necessary for salvation. Christ, present to us in his Body, which is the Church, is the one Mediator and the unique way of salvation. In explicit terms he himself affirmed the necessity of faith and baptism (cf. Mk 16:16; Jn 3:5) and thereby affirmed also the necessity of the Church, for through baptism as through a door men enter the Church. Whosoever, therefore, knowing that the Catholic Church was made necessary by Christ, would refuse to enter or to remain in it, could not be saved.[167]

The Church is, "according to the Council's understanding, the concretization and historical manifestation of God's universal will for salvation in the world".[168] Through this emphasis on her historicity, nevertheless, the necessity of the Church for salvation was accentuated in a new way: as the universal sign of salvation, the Church is God's gift and offer, which becomes, for someone who has grasped it, an obligatory call from God. Bernhard Körner speaks of an admonishment "to follow the truth and the light, when they make themselves known as

---

[165] B. Körner, "*Extra ecclesiam nulla salus*: Sinn und Problematik dieses Satzes in einer sich wandelnden fundamentaltheologischen Ekklesiologie", *ZKTh* 114 (1992): 274–92, citation at 280.

[166] See *LG* 15 and 16.

[167] *LG* 14. Körner notes in this connection that the Council no longer takes up the doctrine of the *votum ecclesiae*, since "criticism of this dogmatic construct ... has made its weaknesses all too evident.... The abandonment of the theologoumenon *votum* makes it clear that the Council, by its very nature, is interested in formulating the faith but that it does not undertake to present a theological synthesis on salvation, the mediation thereof, and the possibility of salvation. That remains the task of the theologians." See Körner, "*Extra ecclesiam nulla salus*", 281.

[168] Grillmeier, 2:194.

such".[169] Inasmuch as the Church humbly acknowledges the difference between her sign-character (as Church) and what is signified (the perfection of God's kingdom), she articulates the fact that since she prepares the way for the kingdom of God, she will not experience her fulfillment until the end of time. This also includes the possibility that her sign-character may be obscured because of the sinfulness of her members.

3. The eschatological character of the Church and ecumenism

As the pilgrim People of God, the Church has a provisional character, which means that she is only making her way toward her fulfillment.[170] That is why one should—as Yves Congar recommends—"mention at the same time her attributes that are in tension with one another, for instance, her holiness and her need for reform, the fact that she is the seed of the kingdom of God but without the glory of the kingdom, that she is universal, yet busy extending her boundaries with great effort".[171] This emphasis on the eschatological character of the Church contributed in an important way toward giving the Constitution on the Church an ecumenical dynamic, which was then articulated especially in the Decree on Ecumenism,[172] produced under the auspices of the newly established Secretariat for Promoting Christian Unity. This emphasis found expression, furthermore, in the Declaration on the Relation of the Church to Non-Christian Religions and finally in the Declaration on Religious Liberty.

---

[169] Körner, "*Extra ecclesiam nulla salus*", 280. The same formula is found in M. Seckler, "Außerhalb der Kirche kein Heil?" in *Hoffnungsversuche*, by Seckler, 105–115, ref. at 115 (Freiburg im Breisgau: Herder, 1974).

[170] H. Döring, "Der ökumenische Aufbruch", in Kutschki, 66–79, citation at 71: "Against the comprehensive background of the eschatological Church, the non-Catholic Churches, too, have their place, even if it is not further specified."

[171] Y. Congar, "Schlusswort", in Baraúna, 2:589–97, citation at 594. Cf. H. Heinz, "Wer steht der Ökumene im Wege? Einsprüche gegen einen ökumenischen Stillstand", in *Zweites Vatikanisches Konzil: Das bleibende Anliegen*, by J. Piegsa, 77–115, ref. at 82: "Das Konzil als 'kopernikanische Wende' " (St. Ottilien: EOS Verlag, 1991).

[172] Originally the Decree on Ecumenism also dealt with questions concerning the relationship with non-Christian religions and freedom of religion. These controversial topics were later isolated and developed in separate declarations. Cf. F. König, "Das Vatikanum II—wegweisend für die Zukunft der Kirche", in *Die bleibende Bedeutung des Zweiten Vatikanischen Konzils*, ed. König, 131–42, ref. at 136 (Düsseldorf: Patmos, 1986).

4. *Summary*

In summarizing, we can say that, inasmuch as *Lumen gentium*, on the one hand, rediscovered the People of God[173] as an image for the Church and thus articulated also the fact that she is different from the kingdom of God and has an eschatological character and, on the other hand, took up again the concept of *communio*[174] from the early Church, it set the ecumenical movement on a new track. For in paving the way for the kingdom of God, the Church has a "this-worldly, sacramental form" that is not definitive, but rather "oriented ... toward her 'termination' in the *eschaton*".[175] Through this view of Christ who will come again and of his kingdom, it became possible to see the working of the Holy Spirit outside the limits of the Catholic Church as well.[176] Therefore, the Council focuses more on what unites the Catholic Church with the other Churches and ecclesial communities than on what separates them:

> The Church recognizes that in many ways she is linked with those who, being baptized, are honored with the name of Christian, though they do not profess the faith in its entirety or do not preserve unity of communion with the successor of Peter. For there are many who honor Sacred Scripture, taking it as a norm of belief and a pattern of life, and who show a sincere zeal. They lovingly believe in God the Father Almighty and in Christ, the Son of God and Savior. They are consecrated by baptism, in which they are united with Christ. They also recognize and accept other sacraments within their own Churches or ecclesiastical communities.[177]

---

[173] Cf. Y. Congar, "Die Kirche als Volk Gottes", *Conc(D)* 1 (1965): 5–16, citation at 11: "The advantage of the concept of the People of God for ecumenism is indisputable, especially for the dialogue with the Protestants." Cf. Klausnitzer, 377f.: "The advantage of the People of God concept for ecumenical dialogue".

[174] Grillmeier, 2:177: "Toward a more profound realization of the Church as *communio*, κοινωνια: Archbishop Ziadé saw in this second chapter (of *Lumen gentium*) the union of Eastern and Western ecclesiology."

[175] O. Semmelroth, "Kommentar zu *LG* Kap. 7", in *LThK.E* 1:315.

[176] Cf. Heinz, "Wer steht der Ökumene im Wege?" 85: "With the renunciation of the Catholic Church's claim to exclusivity in representing solely and entirely the Church of Jesus Christ, the goal of an 'ecumenism of return' to the bosom of the Catholic Church also became invalid."

[177] *LG* 15.

One expression of this union is *dialogue*. As Hanspeter Heinz observes, this word occurs twenty-four times in the conciliar documents (and what it means, much more often!), "and tellingly, it is found with particular frequency in the documents that deal with the encounter with other Christian churches, with the young Churches in mission lands, and with today's world".[178]

Out of respect for the history of religions, the Council speaks of various relations to the People of God even among non-Christians, especially Jews and Muslims.[179] The Council acknowledges the strongest relation with Jews, the people first chosen by God, "to whom the testament and promises were given and from whom Christ was born according to the flesh".[180] Conscious that, by God's decree, Christ is the source of salvation for all mankind, the Church is impelled by the Holy Spirit to carry out the missionary mandate of Jesus. Here the Council quotes Paul, the Apostle to the Gentiles: "Woe to me if I do not preach the gospel" (1 Cor 9:16). The Church as a whole and every individual member of the Church, according to his station, has this missionary duty to participate in the apostolate. The inculturation of the gospel, however, should ennoble the good that is already present as a seed sown "in the minds and hearts of men" or "in the religious practices and cultures of diverse peoples".[181]

---

[178] Heinz, "Wer steht der Ökumene im Wege?" 101f.
[179] See *LG* 16; cf. Thomas Aquinas, *Summa Theologiae* III, q. 8, a. 3 ad 1.
[180] *LG* 16.
[181] *LG* 17.

Chapter 3

The Hierarchical Structure of the Church
and in Particular the Episcopate

§ 1. Premises for Chapter 3 of *Lumen Gentium*

1. *The Church as* mysterium *and as the People of God is the foundation
for her socially visible constitution*

In the outline for *Lumen gentium*, chapter 3, "On the Hierarchical
Structure of the Church and in Particular on the Episcopate", was
deliberately placed after chapter 2, "On the People of God" for the
purpose of emphasizing the unity of this people[1] and of assigning to
the holders of office their place in the midst of this people. Through
this arrangement of the chapters, the Council "programmatically
places"—in Klausnitzer's words—"the social and visible constitution
that belongs to the Church from the very beginning *after* the biblically
based view of the communion of salvation".[2] In his commentary on
articles 18–27 of *Lumen gentium*, Karl Rahner had already pointed out
the subordinate position of chapter 3 after chapter 1, "De Ecclesiae
mysterio", and chapter 2, "De populo Dei":

> Chapter 3 ... is deliberately situated as the *third* chapter, after a
> discussion in the first two chapters of the proper nature of the Church,
> which is prior to her social constitution, not in a temporal manner
> (for the Church is always socially and "hierarchically" constituted),
> but rather objectively, with regard to the history of salvation. Only
> *because* there *is* communion in the Spirit as the fruit of redemption

---

[1] Cf. K. Rahner and H. Vorgrimler, "III. Die dogmatische Konstitution über die Kirche
Lumen gentium", in *KlKK* 107: "Chapter 2, with nine articles on the People of God, was
deliberately placed before the discussion of the hierarchical 'degrees' (chap. 3), so as to
speak first about the unity of the whole Church before discussing any hierarchical distinctions."

[2] Klausnitzer, 396.

among those who are redeemed by Christ can this communion also
be hierarchically constituted as a society and thus be established as
the means of salvation and primordial sacrament for the world, and
this entire institutional character is maintained by the Spirit.[3]

Although first place is not allotted to the institutional character of
the Church in defining her nature, special attention was given to chapter 3 in the discussions about *Lumen gentium* in order to highlight the
status of the local Churches,[4] in contrast to the so-called preconciliar,
centralist-universalistic understanding of the Church. Thus it is understandable that, given the importance of the subject and the controversial points of view, the text was divided up during the final phase
of the deliberations into thirty-nine parts to be voted on. A minority
of the Council Fathers opposed especially the statements on the collegiality of the apostolic as well as of the episcopal ministry, and they
had objections about classifying episcopal consecration as a sacrament.[5]

2. Continuing the themes of the First Vatican Council

A second essential presupposition for the drafting of the Constitution
on the Church was the continuation of the themes of the First Vatican
Council, which had defined the pope's primacy of jurisdiction and
papal infallibility in the Dogmatic Constitution *Pastor aeternus.*[6] That
is why the main emphasis was placed now on the *episcopal office* in the
conciliar reflections on the hierarchical constitution of the Church.
Lumen gentium contains no new theology on this subject but rather
harks back, on the one hand, to the tradition of the early Church
while intending, on the other hand, to preserve continuity with the
First Vatican Council.[7]

---

[3] K. Rahner, "Kommentar zu *LG* Artikel 18 bis 27", in *LThK.E*, vol. 1 (Freiburg im
Breisgau: Herder, 1966), 210.
[4] Cf. H.J. Pottmeyer, "Kirche als *Communio*: Eine Reformidee aus unterschiedlichen
Perspektiven", *StZ* 117 (1992): 579–89, ref. at 583. Cf. also J. Werbick, *Kirche: Ein ekklesiologischer Entwurf für Studium und Praxis* (Freiburg im Breisgau: Herder, 1994), 322.
[5] Cf. B. Kloppenburg, "Abstimmungen und letzte Änderungen der Konstitution", in
Baraúna, 1:106–39, specifically 110–23.
[6] See *DH* 3050–75.
[7] On this point, see *LG* 18. Cf. Pottmeyer, *Rolle*, 96: "In this chapter the continuity with
Vatican I is most conspicuous. The papacy is discussed almost exclusively in quotations from

And all this teaching about the institution, the perpetuity, the meaning and reason for the sacred primacy of the Roman Pontiff and of
his infallible magisterium, this Sacred Council again proposes to be
firmly believed by all the faithful. Continuing in that same undertaking, this Council is resolved to declare and proclaim before all
men the doctrine concerning bishops, the successors of the apostles, who together with the successor of Peter, the Vicar of Christ,[8]
the visible Head of the whole Church, govern the house of the
living God.[9]

Hermann Josef Pottmeyer sees in this look backward both the strength
and weakness of the statements in *Lumen gentium*:

> It is their strength, because it broke the spell of a one-sidedly cler-
> ical and juridical view of the Church, which in its exaggerated anti-
> Reformation and anti-Gallican form had made obedience to the
> pope the decisive feature of the Catholic Church. This look back-
> ward is also their weakness, however, for as a result ... little was
> said in this Constitution about relevance to today's world.[10]

Walter Kasper sees this twofold intention as the reason for the difficulty of interpreting *Lumen gentium* unambiguously, for, on the one
hand, "the Council, along the lines of the early Church, wanted to
counterbalance the First Vatican Council's doctrine on primacy with
teaching on the episcopal office and thus also to overcome the centralization of the Curia",[11] while, on the other hand, the teaching of
the First Vatican Council was reaffirmed, which represented, in Klausnitzer's words, "a one-sided ecclesiology that upsets the equilibrium
between the two highest authorities in the Church".[12]

In concentrating on the office of the bishop, chapter 3 of *Lumen
gentium* revolves around three main themes:[13] (1) the existence and

---

the First Vatican Council; the doctrine of the college of bishops was advocated by Vatican I
as well, even though it was unable to define it further."
  [8] Cf. Council of Florence, *Decretum pro Graecis*, in *DH* 1307, and First Vatican Council,
Pastor aeternus, in *DH* 3059.
  [9] *LG* 18.
  [10] Pottmeyer, *Rolle*, 96.
  [11] Kasper, "Theologie", 26f.
  [12] Klausnitzer, 397.
  [13] Cf. Rahner, "Kommentar zu *LG* Artikel 18 bis 27", 1:210.

function of the college of bishops;[14] (2) the sacramental character of episcopal consecration;[15] and (3) the intrinsic interrelatedness of the bishop's various *munera* [offices], which are rooted in the sacramental consecration.[16] The most important debates were conducted about these three questions, which is surprising, since "the first two main themes are contained in the schema of the Preparatory Commission, which had been composed principally by theologians of the Roman school ... and had been adopted almost unchanged, apart from minor modifications."[17] This resistance resulted especially from a changed ecclesiastical situation, which, according to Karl Rahner, "displayed an entirely new motivating force for the life and praxis of the Church".[18]

§ 2. The Main Themes in Chapter 3 of *Lumen Gentium*

1. *The existence and function of the college of bishops*

a. The college of bishops in succession to the apostolic college

The basis for the doctrine of the episcopacy is the calling and sending of the Twelve, to which Scripture attests.[19] In *Lumen gentium* 19, the Constitution on the Church uses the word *collegium* for the first time in reference to the apostles, whom the Lord appointed "in the form of a college" with Peter at the head. The concept of "college" is to be understood here, not in the juridical sense, "as though it were a question of a group in which all are equal",[20] but rather as a "stable group".[21] Hermann Josef Pottmeyer explains that the Second Vatican Council adopted *collegium*, "a term from legal language, without meaning it as such"; instead, the Council adheres "to the usage of this term in the

---

[14] Cf. *LG* 22f.
[15] See *LG* 21.
[16] Cf. ibid.
[17] Klausnitzer, 397.
[18] Rahner, "Kommentar zu *LG* Artikel 18 bis 27", 1:210.
[19] Cf. *LG* 19.
[20] Kloppenburg, "Abstimmungen", 112.
[21] *LG* 19.

Church's tradition since the third century".[22] This delimitation of the term *collegium* as used in the conciliar text, so as to prevent understanding it in a strictly juridical sense, was dealt with in the "Nota explicativa praevia" [the Preliminary Note of Explanation][23] to *Lumen gentium*.

Since the mission of the apostles will "last until the end of the world"[24] (that is, has an eschatological character), after the death of the apostles it was necessary that "other approved men would take up their ministry."[25] The Council teaches that "bishops by divine institution have succeeded to the place of the apostles, as shepherds of the Church".[26] For this reason, the office of bishop is an irrevocable and essential component of the Church's structure. It can "neither be dispensed with nor so limited in its functions—either by the Petrine office or by bishops' conferences or by the postconciliar diocesan councils—nor made so dependent upon them that de facto it can no longer fulfill the proper and lawful pastoral responsibility conferred upon it by Jesus Christ".[27] But it is not the individual bishop (with the exception of the pope) who "stands in an—ultimately imaginary—historical succession to one of the first apostles; rather, the college of bishops as a whole succeeds the apostolic college."[28] Describing this collegial union of the bishops with one another—and especially with the successor of Peter—is a central concern of the Council.[29]

b. The relationship between the college of bishops and the Petrine office

The problem of "whether there is one subject of the supreme authority in the Church or two"[30] was one of the most important questions dealt with by the Council. The minority of the Council Fathers turned against

---

[22] H. J. Pottmeyer, "Der theologische Status der Bischofskonferenz—Positionen, Klärungen und Prinzipien", in Müller/Pottmeyer, 44–87, citation at 73.

[23] See pt. 1, sec. 2, chap. 3, § 3, of this work, "The 'Preliminary Note of Explanation' to the Schema on the Church".

[24] *LG* 20; cf. Mt 28:20.

[25] *LG* 20.

[26] Ibid.

[27] Kasper, "Theologie", 27f.

[28] Ibid., 28.

[29] Cf. P. Stockmeier, "Kirche unter den Herausforderungen der Geschichte", in *HFTh* 3:106–8.

[30] Klausnitzer, 403.

the central point of the doctrine of collegiality, namely, that the bishops receive a share of the supreme and universal power of jurisdiction through their episcopal consecration, as members of the college of bishops. For then ... they would be receiving their power of jurisdiction directly from Christ, and the pope would be obliged to give them a share in the government of the universal Church.[31]

As Walter Kasper declares, these antitheses could not be reconciled, so that in fact in the definitive text "two different series of statements stand side by side."[32] Finally, by means of the "Nota explicativa praevia", Pope Paul VI brought about a wider consensus among the Council Fathers.

According to the doctrine of the Church presented by the Council, the Petrine office has been since apostolic times the principle of unity and of *communio* in the Church: "And in order that the episcopate itself might be one and undivided, he placed Blessed Peter over the other apostles, and instituted in him a permanent and visible source and foundation of unity of faith and communion."[33] As the successor of Peter, the bishop of Rome, "in virtue of his office, that is as Vicar of Christ and pastor of the whole Church, ... has full, supreme and universal power over the Church. And he is always free to exercise this power".[34] Together with the pope, nevertheless, the college of bishops is also responsible for unity of faith in the Church and for upholding the common discipline.[35] Unless there is unity with the successor of Peter, however, the college has no authority:

> The order of bishops ... is also the subject of supreme and full power over the universal Church, provided we understand this body together with its head the Roman Pontiff and never without this head. This power can be exercised only with the consent of the Roman Pontiff. For our Lord placed Simon alone as the rock and the bearer of the keys of the Church (cf. Mt 16:18–19) and made him shepherd of the whole flock (cf. Jn 21:15ff.); it is evident, however, that the power of binding and loosing, which was given to

---

[31] Pottmeyer, *Rolle*, 97.
[32] Kasper, "Theologie", 28.
[33] *LG* 18. Cf. First Vatican Council, *Pastor aeternus*, in *DH* 3050f. Cf. *LG* 19; *LG* 23.
[34] *LG* 22; cf. *CD* 2.
[35] Cf. *LG* 23.

Peter (Mt 16:19), was granted also to the college of apostles, joined
with their head (Mt 18:18; 28:16–20).[36]

As Klausnitzer notes, the question of whether one or two subjects
(the pope alone or the college with the pope) hold supreme authority
in the Church is answered by theology today in two ways:

> First, in the traditional way, namely that these two subjects of the
> supreme and full authority are only inadequately distinguished sub-
> jects, since the pope himself belongs to the college of bishops, and
> secondly in the thesis championed by Karl Rahner, that the college
> constituted under the pope as its primatial head is the *sole* subject of
> supreme ecclesial authority.[37]

The latter would mean that every action taken by the pope for the
universal Church would have to be assessed collegially.[38] Despite the
divergent positions on this question that continue to exist, it should
be emphasized that "the supreme authority to govern is structured
collegially, but not the primacy",[39] and that the successor of Peter is
always an independent authority.

c. Mutual relations among the bishops in the college

As the Council understands it,[40] the *communio* of the bishops among
themselves, in particular with the successor of Peter, is one of the
essential components of Church discipline. The following paragraphs
will outline three aspects of the way in which this *communio* is realized.

1) Collegial exercise of supreme authority in the Church

A special manifestation of *communio* is, first, the exercise of supreme
ecclesial authority by a collegial act, which is furthermore narrowly
circumscribed:

---

[36] LG 22.
[37] Klausnitzer, 407.
[38] Cf. Pottmeyer, *Rolle*, 108–11.
[39] Ibid., 99. Pottmeyer adds: "Nevertheless the minority achieved one thing: the pope's
independence and freedom of action was emphasized—in the text of the Constitution as
well as in the 'Preliminary Note'—in a way that is not found even in the definition by
Vatican I." Pottmeyer suspects that behind this maximalistic interpretation of Vatican I was
the reaction of the minority of the Council Fathers at Vatican II to the "specter" of participation in government by the college of bishops.
[40] Cf. LG 22.

The supreme power in the universal Church, which this college enjoys, is exercised in a solemn way in an ecumenical council. A council is never ecumenical unless it is confirmed or at least accepted as such by the successor of Peter; and it is the prerogative of the Roman Pontiff to convoke these councils, to preside over them and to confirm them. This same collegiate power can be exercised together with the pope by the bishops living in all parts of the world, provided that the head of the college calls them to collegiate action, or at least approves of or freely accepts the united action of the scattered bishops, so that it is thereby made a collegiate act.[41]

Accordingly, there are two possible varieties of a collegiate act: the general council and another form of collegiate act that is not further defined.[42] Both forms require approval or at any rate voluntary acceptance by the pope.

2) *Collegial unity of the particular Churches with one another and with the universal Church*

Collegiality is realized, secondly, above all in the mutual relations of the bishops and their particular Churches with one another;[43] that is, collegiality means that each individual bishop has "responsibility and a role for the whole Church".[44] Given this responsibility, the bishop of a particular Church, which is constituted after the model of the universal Church, is the visible principle and foundation of the unity of his diocese as well as the representative of this particular Church and her pastor.[45] Quite significant—in an ecumenical perspective[46] also—is the plural in the Council's formulation in reference to the particular Churches: "In and from which churches comes into being the one and only Catholic Church."[47] This way of seeing the Church in *Lumen*

---

[41] Ibid.
[42] Klausnitzer, 406, mentions in this connection the synod of bishops or a "council by correspondence" [*Briefkonzil*]. In the age of modern networking through the Internet, one could also make use of the new means of communicating. Klausnitzer (ibid.) points out that according to Karl Rahner there is yet a third way in which the college can act, namely, "through the pope 'alone', who exercises his authority as the primatial head of the college".
[43] Cf. *LG* 23.
[44] Klausnitzer, 406.
[45] See ibid.
[46] Cf. Rahner, "Kommentar zu *LG* Artikel 18 bis 27", 1:244.
[47] *LG* 23.

gentium, which takes as its point of departure the universal Church as such, widens the view to include the local congregation, in which Christ's Church is present:

> This Church of Christ is truly present in all legitimate local con-
> gregations of the faithful [in omnibus legitimis fidelium congrega-
> tionibus localibus], which, united with their pastors, are themselves
> called churches in the New Testament. For in their locality these
> are the new People called by God, in the Holy Spirit and in much
> fullness (cf. 1 Thess 1:5).[48]

It follows that the one Church of Jesus Christ "is neither the subsequent sum of confederation of the particular Churches (*ex quibus*)"
nor a super-Church, whose particular Churches "would merely be
provinces of a universal Church".[49] On this point, Walter Kasper
explains:

> Particular Church and universal Church realize one another in a
> perichoresis [or circumincession]; they are mutually internal (*in qui-
> bus*). In this phrase, "ex quibus et in quibus", is expressed the spe-
> cifically ecclesial constitutional structure, the like of which is found
> in no secular constitution. It can "function" only by a miracle based
> on the working of the Holy Spirit.[50]

Finally, another facet of collegial unity is the missionary responsibility "of proclaiming the Gospel everywhere on earth".[51] A bishop
should confront the problems beyond the limits of his diocese and
come to the aid of the Church's worldwide saving work by promoting
the spiritual, charitable, social, and cultural aspects of the missions.[52]

---

[48] *LG* 26. Cf. *LG* 28: "Becoming from the heart a pattern to the flock (cf. 1 Pet 5:3),
let them so lead and serve their local community that it may worthily be called by that
name, by which the one and entire people of God is signed, namely, the Church of God
(cf. 1 Cor 1:2; 2 Cor 1:1, and passim)." Cf. Rahner, "Kommentar zu *LG* Artikel 18 bis
27", 1:243: "Now it should be admitted objectively that the other perspective from traditional theology was a premise for the Council and almost unavoidably influenced the proceedings and that it was almost impossible to use both aspects equally as a structural principle
in one and the same decree."

[49] Kasper, "Theologie", 33.

[50] Ibid., 32f.

[51] *LG* 23.

[52] See ibid. Cf. L. Scheffczyk, "Die Kollegialität der Bischöfe unter theologischem und
pastoral-praktischem Aspekt", in *Episcopale Munus: Recueil d'études sur le ministère épiscopal*

3) *Inter-ecclesial structures at the regional level*

Thirdly, through mutual relations within the ecclesial *communio*, "larger ecclesial units"[53] developed on the regional level. They are seen in relation to the ancient patriarchal Churches, which the Council describes as "parent-stocks of the Faith":

> By divine Providence it has come about that various churches, established in various places by the apostles and their successors, have in the course of time coalesced into several groups, organically united, which, preserving the unity of faith and the unique divine constitution of the universal Church, enjoy their own discipline, their own liturgical usage, and their own theological and spiritual heritage. Some of these churches, notably the ancient patriarchal churches, as parent-stocks of the Faith, so to speak, have begotten others as daughter churches, with which they are connected down to our own time by a close bond of charity in their sacramental life and in their mutual respect for their rights and duties. This variety of local churches with one common aspiration is splendid evidence of the catholicity of the undivided Church. In like manner the episcopal bodies of today are in a position to render a manifold and fruitful assistance, so that this collegiate feeling may be put into practical application.[54]

The outcome of this web of relations is multiplicity in unity and unity in multiplicity; therein the Council indirectly recognizes a result of divine providence, since these patriarchal structures are not only to be understood as a historical reality but should also be brought into connection with a new form of episcopal collegiality in the form of bishops' conferences.[55] Nevertheless, the Council allocated no clearly defined theological place to the conferences of bishops.[56] As Karl Rahner notes, in *Lumen gentium* 22 or 23 it would have been possible to mention the synod of bishops also (*Synodus Episcoporum pro Universa*

---

offertes en hommage à Son Excellence Mgr J. Gijsen, ed. P. Delhaye and L. Elders, 83–99, ref. at 98 (Assen: Van Gorcum, 1982).

[53] Cf. Rahner, "Kommentar zu *LG* Artikel 18 bis 27", 1:233.

[54] *LG* 23.

[55] See *CD* 37f. Cf. J. Orlandis Rovira, *Stürmische Zeiten: Die katholische Kirche in der zweiten Hälfte des 20. Jahrhunderts*, trans. from Spanish by G. Stein (Aachen: MM-Verlag, 1999), 69f.

[56] Cf. Pottmeyer, "Theologische Status der Bischofskonferenz", 44.

Ecclesia), "since with respect to constitutional law it is the most important realization of the synodal principle".[57] The majority of the bishops had voted also for a form of ongoing participation in the government of the universal Church, so that the Council decided in *Christus Dominus* to establish a permanent synod of bishops:[58]

> Bishops chosen from various parts of the world, in ways and manners established or to be established by the Roman pontiff, render more effective assistance to the supreme pastor of the Church in a deliberative body which will be called by the proper name of Synod of Bishops. Since it shall be acting in the name of the entire Catholic episcopate, it will at the same time show that all the bishops in hierarchical communion partake of the solicitude for the universal Church.[59]

Many were disappointed when Pope Paul VI allowed the synod of bishops to have essentially only an advisory role when it was established in September 1965. Thereby the collaboration of the bishops fell "far short of the original ideas of the majority",[60] who had hoped to have a much greater say in running the Church. For "the very ancient practice" was that the "bishops duly established in all parts of the world were in communion with one another and with the Bishop of Rome in a bond of unity, charity and peace"[61] and came together for councils, in order to find joint settlements in questions of major importance to the Church, always in *communio* with the successor of Peter, so as to promote the unity of the People of God.[62] Noteworthy

---

[57] Rahner, "Kommentar zu *LG* Artikel 18 bis 27", 233.

[58] Cf. Orlandis Rovira, *Stürmische Zeiten*, 70f.: "The synod was established by Paul VI on September 13, 1956, immediately before the beginning of the last session of Vatican II. It is dependent on the Roman Pontiff, essentially has an advisory function, and convenes at intervals previously agreed upon. A General Secretariat consisting of fifteen members—twelve elected by the synod and three appointed by the pope—carries out its mandate between the synods."

[59] *CD* 5. Cf. Paul VI, motu proprio *Apostolica sollicitudo*, in *AAS* 57 (1965): 775–80; cf. *LG* 23.

[60] Pottmeyer, *Rolle*, 101; cf. P. Hebblethwaite, *Paul VI: The First Modern Pope* (New York: Paulist Press, 1993), 432f.

[61] *LG* 22.

[62] Cf. ibid., and also Pottmeyer, *Rolle*, 105: "In these texts, no doubt, the main lines of a *communio* ecclesiology are evident. This provides the framework for the teaching about the college of bishops and the primacy. Since both ideas of collegiality are found in the Council document and both types are concerned with overcoming centralism, they are both significant for the development of a *communio* primacy."

in this connection is the invitation by Pope John Paul II in his 1995 encyclical *Ut unum sint* (no. 95) to bishops and theologians, particularly in an ecumenical context, "to find a way of exercising the primacy which, while in no way renouncing what is essential to its mission, is nonetheless open to a new situation".[63] Hermann Josef Pottmeyer sees in this initiative by the Pope "an opportunity to commence a new epoch in the history of Christianity".[64]

The Petrine office, as Walter Kasper concludes, can "rightly exercise its ministry of unity only when it understands itself as strengthening the authority of the bishops and thus allows for a legitimate multiplicity in the unity".[65] This authority of the bishops is ultimately grounded in their sacramental consecration, through which they are admitted into hierarchical communion with the head and the members of the college.

2. The sacramentality of episcopal consecration

a. Sacramental understanding of the episcopal office as the "fullness of the sacrament of orders"

With great unanimity the sacramentality of the episcopal office was proclaimed, with reference to the special gift of the Spirit to the apostles on Pentecost.

They passed on this spiritual gift to their helpers by the imposition of hands (cf. 1 Tim 4:14; 2 Tim 1:6–7), and it has been transmitted down to us in episcopal consecration. And the Sacred Council teaches that by episcopal consecration the fullness of the sacrament of orders is conferred, that fullness of power, namely, which both in the Church's liturgical practice and in the language of the Fathers of the Church is called the high priesthood, the supreme power of the sacred ministry.[66]

Through this doctrinal statement, which comes close to being a solemnly proclaimed dogma, "the medieval Scholastic opinion going back

---

[63] John Paul II, *Ut unum sint*, Vatican trans. (Boston: Pauline Books & Media, 1995).
[64] Pottmeyer, *Rolle*, 9.
[65] Kasper, "Theologie", 39.
[66] LG 21.

to Peter Lombard (who cites Jerome), that episcopal consecration is
only a sacramental because it does not bestow an increase in power
over the Eucharistic Body of the Lord, but only an increase in authority over the Mystical Body",[67] is superseded. Contrary to that opinion, the Council emphasizes that "the fullness of the sacrament of
orders" is conferred, that is, "the supreme power of the sacred ministry".[68] On this point, Klausnitzer remarks:

> The Council does not see the episcopate ... as the "highest degree"
> of the priesthood, but rather views the simple ministerial priest-
> hood as a limited participation in the full priesthood of the bishop.
> Hence episcopal consecration is a sacrament, indeed, it is the sac-
> rament of holy orders absolutely speaking.[69]

From what has been said we can conclude with Karl Rahner: "The
full and entire office in what it contains, in its collegial form, and in
its unity with the pope is ... *divina institutione*",[70] since the bishops as
successors to the apostles have assumed their place as shepherds of the
Church "by divine institution".[71] The fact that the bishops collectively stand in succession to the apostles has far-reaching consequences for the rightful exercise of the episcopal office.

   b. On distinguishing "function" (*munus*) and "power" (*potestas*)

As successors of the apostles, the bishops are united with one another
in a *hierarchica communio*. This term opens the way to understanding
the distinction between function and power, for the *hierarchica communio*, together with the *sacramental consecration*, is the prerequisite for
the elected man to become a member of the "body of bishops".[72]
The power (*potestas*), which is bestowed on the bishop only in this
communio, can therefore be exercised as well only in communion with

---

[67] Kasper, "Theologie", 29.
[68] *LG* 21.
[69] Klausnitzer, 401. Klausnitzer points out that in order to demonstrate the sacramentality of episcopal consecration, *LG* 21, n. 54, cites the statement by the Council of Trent
that *Ordo* (!), that is, holy orders, is a real sacrament (*DH* 1766).
[70] Rahner, "Kommentar zu *LG* Artikel 18 bis 27", 1:217.
[71] *LG* 20.
[72] *LG* 22. Cf. "Preliminary Note of Explanation", no. 2. Cf. also K.M. Becker, "Das
Sacerdotium Episcopi nach der Lehre des Zweiten Vatikanischen Konzils", in Delhaye and
Elders, *Episcopale Munus*, 63–82, passage at 71ff.

the bishop of Rome. Whereas the bishop receives an indelible character through his consecration, hierarchical communion with the head and members of the college can be taken away from him.[73] The result of this, however, according to Karl Rahner, is that "the totality of the bishops and the power of this totality are not the subsequent sum of the individual bishops and of their powers, but rather this comprehensive unity, being morally legitimate, sacramentally grounded (article 21), and thus produced by the Spirit, (objectively) preexists the individual bishop as such."[74]

3. *The three interwoven* munera *of the bishop are rooted in sacramental ordination*

As distinct from the power (*potestas*), the three *munera* (functions or offices) of teaching, sanctifying, and governing are bestowed upon the bishop through ordination.[75]

> But episcopal consecration, together with the office [*munus*] of sanctifying, also confers the office of teaching and of governing, which, however, of its very nature, can be exercised only in hierarchical communion with the head and the members of the college. For from the tradition, which is expressed especially in liturgical rites and in the practice of both the Church of the East and of the West, it is clear that, by means of the imposition of hands and the words of consecration, the grace of the Holy Spirit is so conferred, and the sacred character so impressed, that bishops in an eminent and visible way sustain the roles of Christ Himself as Teacher, Shepherd and High Priest, and that they act in His person.[76]

In *Lumen gentium* 21 and also in *Lumen gentium* 24, the *hierarchical communio* is emphasized again, in the discussion of the canonical mission of the bishops. It "can come about by legitimate customs that have not been revoked by the supreme and universal authority of the Church, or by laws made or recognized by that authority, or directly

---

[73] Cf. K. Mörsdorf, "Der hierarchische Aufbau der Kirche", in Sandfuchs, 38–52, ref. at 45f.
[74] Rahner, "Kommentar zu *LG* Artikel 18 bis 27", 1:225.
[75] Cf. Kasper, "Theologie", 28.
[76] *LG* 21.

through the successor of Peter himself".[77] That means, for example, in the case of a diocesan bishop, that "appointment to the hierarchical communion occurs through a canonical mission (*missio canonica*), which only then allows him to exercise the *munera* that have been bestowed on him sacramentally".[78,79] As Klausnitzer observes, *Lumen gentium* nonetheless avoided "relating the doctrine of the three offices to the classical distinction between *potestas ordinis* and *potestas iurisdictionis*".[80]

The Council deliberately described ecclesial offices as *ministries*; with regard to the threefold office of the bishop, this central concern corresponds to the emphasis of its collegial, pastoral, and sacramental character. Consequently the bishop's task is to work so that "all who are of the People of God ... , working toward a common goal freely and in an orderly way, may arrive at salvation."[81] The holders of office, who "are endowed with sacred power",[82] are at the service of their brothers and sisters and share in the mission of the eternal shepherd Jesus Christ, who willed that his pastoral ministry be carried on until the consummation of the ages through the successors to the apostles, the bishops:[83] "Bishops ... have taken up the service of the community, presiding in place of God over the flock, whose shepherds they are, as teachers for doctrine, priests for sacred worship, and ministers for governing."[84]

---

[77] LG 24.

[78] Klausnitzer, 407.

[79] Cf. "Preliminary Note of Explanation", no. 2: "In his consecration a person is given an ontological participation in the sacred functions [*munera*]; this is absolutely clear from Tradition, liturgical tradition included. The word 'functions [*munera*]' is used deliberately instead of the word 'powers [*potestates*],' because the latter word could be understood as a power fully ready to act. But for this power to be fully ready to act, there must be a further canonical or juridical determination through the hierarchical authority."

[80] Klausnitzer, 402. In a rather long excursus, Klausnitzer poses questions regarding the bishop's *potestas* and *munera* that demand further elucidation. For example: "If all three *munera* are conferred by ordination, then what is the status of nonresident bishops, for instance, auxiliary bishops or titular bishops?"

[81] LG 18.

[82] Ibid. Cf. LG 24: "And that duty, which the Lord committed to the shepherds of His people, is a true service, which in sacred literature is significantly called 'diakonia' or ministry (cf. Acts 1:17 and 25; 21:19; Rom 11:13; 1 Tim 1:12)."

[83] Cf. LG 20; see also LG 21.

[84] LG 20.

In the following sections, we will describe in more detail the particular dimensions of the episcopal office.

a. The office of preaching

The preaching ministry, according to *Lumen gentium*, is one of the principal tasks of the bishop: The bishops are "preachers of the faith, ... authentic teachers", and above all, "witnesses to divine and Catholic truth".[85] The faithful are bound to submit with religious obedience to their instruction in matters of faith and morals. These statements pertain to the ordinary teaching authority of the bishop. In this connection, *Lumen gentium* 25 describes the ordinary teaching authority of the pope, whose utterances have varying weight:

> This religious submission of mind and will must be shown in a special way to the authentic magisterium of the Roman Pontiff, even when he is not speaking ex cathedra; that is, it must be shown in such a way that his supreme magisterium is acknowledged with reverence, the judgments made by him are sincerely adhered to, according to his manifest mind and will. His mind and will in the matter may be known either from the character of the documents, from his frequent repetition of the same doctrine, or from his manner of speaking.

According to the teaching of *Lumen gentium*, there are strictly defined limits that guarantee infallibility for the extraordinary (*ex cathedra*) Magisterium of the pope, as well as for the *ordinary* and general teaching authority of the college of all the bishops *in communio* with the pope, and also for the *extraordinary* and general Magisterium of the bishops assembled with the successor of Peter at an *ecumenical council*:[86] "Tantum patet quantum divinae Revelationis patet depositum".[87] That means that the scope of the doctrine must always correspond to the Church's deposit of

---

[85] *LG* 25.
[86] On this subject, compare Klausnitzer, 409: "The infallible doctrinal declaration by the pope now appears, however, more emphatically than in *Pastor aeternus*, to be one of several possible definitive acts of the Magisterium, since *Lumen gentium* sees infallibility as present in the college of bishops as well, 'when, together with Peter's successor, they exercise the supreme teaching office'." Klausnitzer goes on to summarize: "The infallibility of the pope, along with that of the college of bishops and of the Church, is ultimately one and the same, since there is only one infallibility" (ibid.).
[87] *LG* 25.

faith, which cannot be enlarged, but only unfolded or developed. Assent to the infallible Magisterium is granted through the working of the Holy Spirit. He preserves the Church in unity and leads her to her goal.[88] In this respect, *Lumen gentium* "transcends the legalistic view of juridical reception"[89] and arrives at a pneumatological perspective.

b. The office of sanctifying

Article 26 of *Lumen gentium* describes the bishop's sanctifying ministry. The bishop is "'the steward of the grace of the supreme priesthood,' especially in the Eucharist, which he offers or causes to be offered, and by which the Church continually lives and grows".[90] He is also responsible, however, for the sacramental life in the parishes. To what extent the latter can be put into practice concretely is a question that requires further elaboration.[91] It also touches directly upon the bishop's office of governing.

c. The office of governing

Bishops are in turn leaders, legislators, and judges for the dioceses entrusted to their care. They "govern the particular Churches entrusted to them by their counsel, exhortations, example, and even by their authority and sacred power".[92] Despite the preeminence of the pope, the bishops are "not subordinate functionaries";[93] rather, "[their] power, which they exercise personally in Christ's name, is proper, ordinary and immediate, although its exercise is ultimately regulated by the supreme authority of the Church."[94]

That means that the local bishop is "pastor proprius, ordinarius et immediatus"[95] of his flock. As Walter Kasper underscores in reference to *Lumen gentium* 27, his rights "must not be preempted, beyond what

---

[88] See ibid.

[89] Yves Congar, on the contrary, objects to the lack of a pneumatological ecclesiology at the First Vatican Council: Y. Congar, *Die Lehre von der Kirche: Vom Abendländischen Schisma bis zur Gegenwart*, HDG 3/3d (Freiburg: Herder, 1971), 107.

[90] *LG* 26. Here it is evident that the Council again calls special attention to the fundamental episcopal structure of the Church.

[91] Cf. Klausnitzer, 411.

[92] *LG* 27.

[93] Klausnitzer, 411.

[94] *LG* 27.

[95] Cf. *CD* 11.

is absolutely necessary, by superior authorities and their rights of res-
ervation." Quite to the contrary, the task of the Petrine office is, "not
to diminish the authority of the bishops, but rather to confirm,
strengthen and defend it".[96]

§ 3. The "Preliminary Note of Explanation"
to the Schema on the Church

1. Historical perspective

There is a binding interpretation for chapter 3 of *Lumen gentium* in
the form of a "Nota explicativa praevia". This Preliminary Note of
Explanation is the centerpiece of the "Announcements Communicated by the General Secretary of the Council in the 123rd General
Congregation on November 16, 1964".[97] It was produced by the Theological Commission and added to the Acts of the Council by an authoritative command of the pope:

> On the part of the higher authority, a preliminary note of expla-
> nation to the suggestions for changes to the third chapter of the
> *schema on the Church* is communicated to the Council Fathers; the
> teaching set forth in this third chapter must be interpreted and under-
> stood according to the intent and meaning of this note.[98]

Klausnitzer appraises the explanatory *nota* as "an aid to understanding the thirty-one *accepted* modifications to the third chapter of the
Constitution proposed by the Council Fathers and the pope".[99] Such
a note was deemed necessary because the proposed modifications (*modi*)
manifested a profound disagreement among the Fathers on the central
question of collegiality. David Andreas Seeber, at that time a full-time
correspondent of *Herderkorrespondenz* [a German Catholic news agency

---

[96] Kasper, "Theologie", 28. Cf. First Vatican Council, *Pastor aeternus*, in *DH* 3061.

[97] From the Acts of the holy ecumenical Second Vatican Council, announcements made
by the General Secretary of the Council in the 123rd General Congregation on November
16, 1964, in *LThK.E* 1:348–59.

[98] Ibid., 351 [translated from the German].

[99] Klausnitzer, 420.

and publisher], reports on the hidden difficulties in the production of this papal intervention,[100] which was no doubt extraordinary:

> On November 10, Secretary of State Cardinal Cicognani sent to Cardinal Ottaviani, the president of the Theological Commission, a letter instructing him to preface the final text of the schema on the Church with a "note of explanation" on the changes incorporated by the Commission. In contrast to earlier papal interventions, this time it was not a question of a papal *modus*, but rather a command— indeed, the pope made his consent to the schema on the Church dependent upon the execution of that command. Enclosed with the letter of the Cardinal Secretary of State were several requests for clarifications in the text of the schema and an opinion paper composed by the canonist W. Bertrams, S.J., concerning the difficulties that were brought to bear by the minority. The pope expressly demanded a clear statement in the requisite note of explanation to the effect that the consent of the pope is to be considered as "constitutive" for the accomplishment of a collegial act of the college of bishops. The Theological Commission was charged with formulating the note of explanation.[101]

Through his intervention, Pope Paul VI gave expression to the conviction that "one must grant the minority a hearing to the very end, so that finally they too can have a share in this unanimity."[102] In contrast to the First Vatican Council, at which practically no one listened to the minority, at the Second Vatican Council such

---

[100] Klausnitzer, ibid., however, suggests that the addition of an explanatory note is actually in keeping with conciliar practice: "At Vatican I the committee on the faith [*Glaubensdeputation*] had explained also through a representative on July 16, 1870, that is, two days before the promulgation of *Pastor aeternus*, how several points of the dogmatic constitution were to be construed." See also U. Betti, "Die Entstehungsgeschichte der Konstitution", in Baraúna, 1:45–70. The same essay cites interesting voting results that shed light on the development of the constitution. Betti (69) likewise defends the view that the addition of an explanatory note is in keeping with "conciliar practice" and cites Betti, *La costituzione dommatica "Pastor aeternus" del Concilio vaticano I* (Rome: Pontificio Ateneo "Antonianum", 1961), 466, 479, 495, 498, 597–601, 621–23, 641–44.

[101] D. A. Seeber, *Das Zweite Vaticanum: Konzil des Übergangs* (Freiburg im Breisgau: Herder, 1966), 227f.

[102] C. Moeller, "Die Entstehung der Konstitution, ideengeschichtlich betrachtet", in Baraúna, 1:71–105, citation at 100. On Pope Paul VI, see Quinn, *Reform*, 87f., 91. This "Preliminary Note of Explanation" was signed by the General Secretary of the Council, Archbishop P. Felici.

concessions were made to the minority view that it "was able to subscribe [to the resulting documents] without animosity".[103] After this
historical look back at the composition of the *nota*, the question now
arises of its essential contents.

2. *Central points of the* nota praevia

The *nota praevia* basically contains the following four main points:
Point 1: The term "college" is to be understood, not in the juridical sense as a group of equals, but rather as a "stable group whose structure and authority must be learned from revelation".[104] The parallel
between Peter and the other apostles, on the one hand, and the pope
and the bishops, on the other, "does not imply the transmission of the
apostles' extraordinary power to their successors".[105] Accordingly, neither can one speak of an equality, but only of "a proportionality between
the first relationship (Peter—apostles) and the second (pope—bishops)".[106]
Point 2 emphasizes once again that a man is admitted to the college
through episcopal consecration *and* by *hierarchical* communion,[107]
whereby jurisdiction[108] is allocated by the pope.

For this reason it is clearly stated that hierarchical communion with
the head and members of the church is required. Communion is a

---

[103] Moeller, "Entstehung der Konstitution", 101. Cf. R. Aubert, *Vaticanum I*, German
trans. K. Bergner (Mainz: Matthias-Grünewald-Verlag, 1965), 135–45 and 283–92.

[104] "Preliminary Note of Explanation", no. 1.

[105] Ibid.

[106] Ibid.

[107] Cf. *LG* 22. Giuseppe Alberigo notes further that the expression "hierarchical communion", "a term foreign to theological tradition", was coined specially for this second
point of the *nota*. See G. Alberigo, "Das Zweite Vatikanische Konzil (1962–1965)", in
Geschichte der Konzilien: Vom Nicaenum bis zum Vaticanum II, ed. Alberigo, 454 (Wiesbaden:
Fourier, 1998).

[108] Cf. Pottmeyer, *Rolle*, 102. Pottmeyer recognizes that there are theological difficulties
in distinguishing between office or function (*munus*) and power (*potestas*), for "in order to
be able to carry out the duties connected with the office at the universal and the local
Church levels, a legal act of the pope is required, which confers the authority to exercise
the functions, as it says in the 'Preliminary Note of Explanation'. There is a tension between
this distinction and the sacramental-theological foundation of the episcopal office, according to which 'the fullness of the sacrament of orders is conferred by episcopal consecration
... [and] bishops, in a resplendent and visible manner, take the place of Christ himself,
teacher, shepherd, and priest' (*LG* 21)."

notion which is held in high honor in the ancient Church (and also today, especially in the East). However, it is not understood as some kind of vague disposition, but as an organic reality which requires a juridical form and is animated by charity.[109]

Point 3 reiterates that only together with the successor of Peter is the college the subject of supreme and entire power, without prejudice to his own authority as head of the college, which entitles him to accomplish such acts alone. This means: "It is not a distinction between the Roman Pontiff and the bishops taken collectively, but a distinction between the Roman Pontiff taken separately and the Roman Pontiff together with the bishops."[110]

Point 4 confirms again the "pope's independence of conditions placed by the college of bishops and, conversely, the dependence of the college upon the pope".[111] Klausnitzer points out that numbers 3 and 4 of the "Note of Explanation" present an enhanced understanding of the primacy, in comparison with the First Vatican Council.

> In numbers 3 and 4 the "Note of Explanation" guarantees ... the primacy of the pope ... and yet ventures several statements that surpass even Vatican I (no. 3: *secundum propriam discretionem*; no. 4 *ad placitum*). These formulas, which are somewhat overdrawn, give the impression of arbitrariness and are not very felicitous; ... [yet the *nota*] also seems to take them back (no. 3: *intuitu boni Ecclesiae*; no. 4: *sicut ab ipso suo munere requiritur*). An emergency power of the episcopate with regard to the pope—which even those theologians in the Church's tradition who favored the papacy allowed for in certain cases (heresy, schism, mental illness)—is not taken into consideration and is rendered almost impossible (no. 4: *deficiente actione Capitis, Episcopi agere ut Collegeium nequeunt*).[112]

Finally, in a short postscript, the "Note of Explanation" attempts to allow for the situation of the separated Eastern Churches with respect to the liceity and validity of the actions of their episcopate and leaves the question to theological research.

---

[109] "Preliminary Note of Explanation", no. 2.
[110] Ibid., no. 3.
[111] Alberigo, "Zweite Vatikanische Konzil", 454.
[112] Klausnitzer, 421.

The focus of the "Preliminary Note of Explanation", as well as of the entire third chapter of the Constitution on the Church, was on determining the relation between primacy and episcopate. The fact that a total of 5,606 suggested modifications were submitted by the bishops for chapter 3 of *Lumen gentium* demonstrates that "the project and the internal difficulties were immense and nerve-wracking behind the scenes."[113] This was especially true for the juridical definition of the *hierarchical communio* of the Church, wherein the correct understanding of episcopal collegiality was debated so as to supplement the statements of Vatican I. In keeping with the basic pastoral approach of the Council, these refinements—as Alois Grillmeier demonstrates at length—"revoke nothing of the primacy of the ministry of sanctifying service in the episcopal office. Instead, this service is explicitly set forth as the prior reality. The juridical determination is then added to the office that is sacramentally conferred and turns the capability that is in principle already given into a readily applicable authority, which is intended to serve uniquely and solely the salvation and the welfare of the family of God."[114] The ministries of the priest and the deacon, to which the conclusion of chapter 3 of *Lumen gentium* is devoted, are to be understood in this spirit as well. They will be described in greater detail in the following section.

§ 4. Priests and Deacons

1. *Priests and presbyterium*

a. "Stepchildren of the Council"[115]

In October 1963 the schema *De Ecclesia* still contained only a few lines on the subject of priests. That is why Bishop Rénard of Versailles declared:

---

[113] Kloppenburg, "Abstimmungen und letzte Änderungen der Konstitution", in Baraúna, 1:106–39, esp. 130ff.

[114] A. Grillmeier, "Geist, Grundeinstellung und Eigenart der Konstitution 'Licht der Völker'", in Baraúna, 1:140–54, citation at 152. Cf. also Quinn, *Reform*, 92f.

[115] Pesch, 264.

Many priests experience a certain sadness at the thought that they
have been forgotten by the Council, that it speaks so much about
bishops and about deacons.... Our silence could cause them to
doubt their priesthood and make the cost of the sacrifices that are
demanded of them seem too high. Let this Council take note of the
fact that without priests we can do nothing.[116]

Certainly the importance of the priestly ministry is not to be measured by the number of articles in which the Constitution speaks about
priests. Nevertheless, there was a feeling that they were the "stepchildren of the Council", although they have to do the "everyday detail
work in the Church in preaching, pastoral care, and administering the
sacraments".[117]

Only *Lumen gentium* 28 is devoted to the ministry of the sacramental priesthood. The article is divided into three larger sections. First, it
deals with priests' relation to Christ on the basis of their share in the
Church's official ministry. Secondly, it speaks about the special connection of priests with their bishop and with one another in the presbyterium.[118] Finally, the third section looks at the priest in his ministry
to the People of God. Thus it is made clear that the priest has his
place in the structured relationships of the Church as *communio*.[119] For
that reason, too, this relatively short text about the priesthood "should
not be considered apart from the Constitution in its entirety".[120]

b. Participation in the consecration and in the threefold mission of Christ

The foundation of *communio* is participation in the consecration and
mission of Jesus Christ, which "becomes present and effective in the

---

[116] J. Giblet, "Die Priester 'zweiten Grades' ", in Baraúna, 2:189–213, citation at 189.

[117] Pesch, 264f. Originally the conciliar Decree on the Ministry and Life of Priests,
Presbyterorum ordinis, was not foreseen, either. In it, as in the Decree on Priestly Training,
Optatam totius, the relatively brief presentations on the priesthood are elaborated in a pastoral-
theological and practical way.

[118] In the Latin conciliar text, the priest is usually referred to as *presbyter* and only seldom as *sacerdos*. Cf. Pesch, 264.

[119] Giblet, "Priester 'zweiten Grades' ", 192. Giblet recalls that the image of the priest in
Lumen gentium cannot be understood "unless one keeps clearly in mind the doctrine about
the *ordo episcoporum* that was presented previously" (ibid.).

[120] A. Grillmeier, "Kommentar zu *LG* Artikel 28", in *LThK.E* 1:250.

Church, in each case in its respective way, in the common priesthood of all the faithful and in the special ordained priesthood".[121]

> Christ, whom the Father has sanctified and sent into the world (Jn 10:36), has through his apostles, made their successors, the bishops, partakers of his consecration and his mission. They have legitimately handed on to different individuals in the Church various degrees of participation in this ministry. Thus the divinely established ecclesiastical ministry is exercised on different levels by those who from antiquity have been called bishops, priests and deacons.[122]

The Church of Christ has the authority to impart ordination in this stepwise manner, since the *fullness and unity* of the ministerial priesthood that he founded was handed on by his apostles to the bishops. Even though priests do not have "the highest degree of the priesthood", by virtue of the sacrament of holy orders they are appointed "to preach the Gospel and shepherd the faithful and to celebrate divine worship".[123] In this triad of the preaching, governing, and sanctifying ministry on the basis of their ordination, there is a deliberate parallel to the description of the episcopal ministry: (1) through the anchoring of these three ministerial functions in the sacrament of holy orders and (2) through the same sequence in this triad, whereby the preaching of the gospel holds first place. The high point of priestly ministry, and also of ecclesial life, is of course the sacramental celebration of the death and Resurrection of Jesus Christ. Just as Jesus' abandonment of himself on the Cross sealed his testimony and "accomplished our redemption in his death and Resurrection, so, too, the center of priestly ministry remains the celebration of the Holy Eucharist."[124]

> They exercise their sacred function especially in the eucharistic worship or the celebration of the Mass by which acting in the person of Christ and proclaiming His Mystery they unite the prayers of the faithful with the sacrifice of their Head and renew and apply in the sacrifice of the Mass until the coming of the Lord

---

[121] Ibid.
[122] *LG* 28.
[123] Ibid.
[124] Grillmeier, "Kommentar zu *LG* Artikel 28", 250.

(cf. 1 Cor 11:26) the only sacrifice of the New Testament, namely that of Christ offering Himself once for all a spotless Victim to the Father (cf. Heb 9:11–28).[125]

As convincing witnesses,[126] they "should lead and serve their local community"[127] in an exemplary manner, so that it can rightly be called "Church". Before all men—believers and unbelievers alike—priests "bear witness to the truth and life"[128] and must be ready "under the leadership of the bishops and the Supreme Pontiff [to] wipe out every kind of separateness, so that the whole human race may be brought into the unity of the family of God."[129] This unity is manifested in a special way in the bond between the priests and their respective local bishop.

c. One priesthood in union with the bishop

Although their individual duties vary, priests "constitute one priesthood [*presbyterium*]".[130] The Council speaks about the priest's role of representing the bishop, indeed, of making the chief pastor present while acknowledging him as his father in reverence and obedience:

> They make him present in a certain sense in the individual local congregations, and take upon themselves, as far as they are able, his duties and the burden of his care, and discharge them with a daily interest. And as they sanctify and govern under the bishop's authority that part of the Lord's flock entrusted to them, they make the universal Church visible in their own locality and bring an efficacious assistance to the building up of the whole body of Christ (cf. Eph 4:12). Intent always upon the welfare of God's children, they must strive to lend their effort to the pastoral work of the whole diocese, and even of the entire Church.[131]

---

[125] *LG* 28.

[126] Ibid., with an allusion to 1 Pet 5:3: "... not as domineering over those in your charge but being examples to the flock".

[127] *LG* 28; cf. *LG* 26.

[128] *LG* 28; cf. H.J. Pottmeyer, "Die Frage nach der wahren Kirche", in *HFTh* 3:182: "the sign-character of their practice of the faith".

[129] *LG* 28.

[130] Ibid.

[131] Ibid.

It is significant, furthermore, that not only diocesan priests are included as members of the presbyterium, but religious priests as well. All priests should be united in true brotherhood and mutual charity.[132]

2. The permanent diaconate

The Council restored the permanent diaconate for the Latin Church "as a proper and permanent rank of the hierarchy".[133] The Council delegated to the episcopal conferences the authority to decide (with the approval of the pope) whether they will introduce the *permanent* diaconate into their respective territories. In *Lumen gentium*, deacons are explicitly included in the hierarchy, specifically "at a lower level" than priests. Accordingly, deacons "receive the imposition of hands, not unto the priesthood, but unto the ministry". The deacon's office is "*mutatis mutandis*, like that of the priest, only a limited participation in the one and complete ministry in the Church, the fullness of which belongs to the bishop alone".[134] "For strengthened by sacramental grace, in communion with the bishop and his group of priests, they serve in the diaconate of the liturgy, of the word, and of charity to the people of God."[135]

For this reason, the functions of the deacon[136] were expanded by *Lumen gentium*, along with the criteria for admission to ordination.[137] Thus allowances were to be made for the fact that the diaconate is an established ministerial office in the Church. We can

---

[132] Cf. ibid.

[133] LG 29. The next two citations are also from this article.

[134] H. Vorgrimler, "Kommentar zu LG Artikel 29", in *LThK.E* 1:257. Cf. Klausnitzer, 412: "The triad of episcopate-presbyterate-diaconate, which is presupposed by the Council, is not definitively traced back to its biblical, historical, or dogmatic origins (for example, the question about the *ius divinum* of a degree [that is, whether it is of 'divine right']), but is explained instead in terms of the underlying unity of the ecclesial ministry". See LG 28.

[135] LG 29.

[136] New duties include assisting at and blessing marriages, administering sacramentals, and officiating at funeral services. Cf. Mörsdorf, "Hierarchische Aufbau der Kirche", 53.

[137] See LG 29: "With the consent of the Roman Pontiff, this diaconate can, in the future, be conferred upon men of more mature age, even upon those living in the married state. It may also be conferred upon suitable young men, for whom the law of celibacy must remain intact."

forgo a more detailed presentation of this degree of holy orders[138]
within the context of our presentation, which is focused on the main
ideas of *Lumen gentium*.

§ 5. Review—Church as a "Complex Reality"

Looking back at the section on the hierarchical constitution of the
Church, and also at the discussion thus far on the Church's self-
understanding according to *Lumen gentium*, we should reiterate once
again a central statement in the Constitution on the Church by way
of summarizing:

> But, the society structured with hierarchical organs and the Mysti-
> cal Body of Christ are not to be considered as two realities, . . . nor
> [are] the earthly Church and the Church enriched with heavenly
> things; rather they form one complex reality which coalesces from
> a divine and a human element. For this reason, by no weak analogy,
> it is compared to the mystery of the incarnate Word.[139]

Through the ministry of the Church the Word of God admits us to
communion with the Father and the Spirit and unites us—not in an
egalitarian uniformity, but in various sorts of participation in the one
mission of Christ[140]—to that new People of God which, as the likeness of the *trinitarian communio*, becomes the sacrament of unity for all
mankind and the sign of salvation for the whole world.

Mirroring the trinitarian *communio* means also "that the indispensable (!) shared responsibility of all members in the Church must be
clearly distinguished from the official authority and that neither one
can be absorbed by the other".[141] Therefore, on the one hand, the

---

[138] I refer the reader to G. L. Müller, *Priesthood and Diaconate: The Recipient of the Sacrament of Holy Orders from the Perspective of Creation Theology and Christology*, trans. Michael
J. Miller (San Francisco: Ignatius Press, 2002).

[139] LG 8.

[140] Cf. B. Körner, "Mitgestaltung, nicht Demokratisierung? Eine erste Auswertung des Forschungsschwerpunktes 'Demokratische und synodale Strukturen in der Kirche' ", in *Bischofsbestellung: Mitwirkung der Ortskirche?* ed. Körner, 124–60, ref. at 146 (Graz: Styria, 2000).

[141] Ibid., 155, with a reference to H. U. von Balthasar, "Mitverantwortung", in *Klarstel-
lungen*, by Balthasar, 87–93 (Einsiedeln: Johannes Verlag, 1978); English trans.: "Our Shared
Responsibility", in *Elucidations*, trans. John Riches, 140–51 (San Francisco: Ignatius Press,
1998).

freedom of obedience in realizing one's own vocation and mission is essential for the individual member of the People of God—an obedience of which Christ gave his Church a living example even unto death. On the other hand, it requires of all members of the Church, as Hermann Josef Pottmeyer says, that they "set one another free, so that each can carry out his own mission—the *communio* structures are supposed to serve precisely this purpose."[142] In his book *The Office of Peter and the Structure of the Church*, Hans Urs von Balthasar shows how this reciprocal release can be accomplished concretely; in doing so, he goes against contemporary trends and advocates the freedom of the Petrine office as well:

> This [liberation through integration] now has a good chance to succeed, as the last two Councils have directed the whole *communio* of the Church, as well as the entire college of bishops, to allow the Petrine office space in which to exercise its function. If both things take place in the spirit of mutual eucharistic *communio*, the pilgrim Church will be able to be an anticipatory reflection of the perfect Church, without overplaying her role (i.e., in eschatological-pneumatic exaggeration) as pilgrim and penitent. Let us say it once again: the authoritative form of office that Christ established in the pilgrim Church is not an obstacle to her but the indispensable prerequisite if she is to be *communio* in the Spirit of Christ here on earth.[143]

At the conclusion of my reflections on *Lumen gentium*, I place a judgment by Hans Urs von Balthasar on the last two ecumenical councils. It could be read at the same time as the distillation of all that the Constitution on the Church singles out for emphasis: "What took place in the two Vatican Councils is nothing less than the liberation of the *Catholica*, enabling her to fulfill her unique potential of living under the headship of Christ in his Spirit."[144] The more the Church grasps this, the more luminous will be her witness to Christ and the more his glory, which is reflected upon the face of the Church,[145] will be able to enlighten all mankind.

---

[142] Pottmeyer, *Rolle*, 146.

[143] H. U. von Balthasar, *The Office of Peter and the Structure of the Church*, trans. Andrée Emery (San Francisco: Ignatius Press, 1986, 2007), 237–38.

[144] Ibid.

[145] *LG* 1.

PART TWO

JOSEPH RATZINGER:
LIFE IN THE CHURCH AND LIVING THEOLOGY

SECTION 1

OUTLINE OF THE ECCLESIOLOGICAL PLAN
FROM A BIOGRAPHICAL PERSPECTIVE

In order to understand what sort of roots nourish a theology and guide
its decisions, giving it stability and at the same time growth, so that it
makes progress but sometimes stops or perhaps even gives the impression of regressing, it is good to know how it came about. This is especially true in the case of Joseph Ratzinger, for two reasons: His
ecclesiological publications extend, chronologically first of all, from the
period of new beginnings in systematic theology based on a return to
the Church Fathers and the Franciscan tradition, which made a deep
impression on Vatican II, through the euphoria of the conciliar period
and the upheaval of 1968—a turning point in intellectual history—
down to the present day with its trends of renewal[1] in theology and its
debate over the correct "hermeneutic" or interpretation of the Council. Ratzinger's works take their particular emphasis from their respective historical context and, especially, from the author's evaluation thereof.
Furthermore, and this is the second point, Ratzinger undertakes his reflections from such different perspectives as that of a university professor, of
a theologian at the Council, of a bishop, and finally of the prefect for
the Congregation of the Doctrine of the Faith.[2] Therefore much light
is shed on his theological and, above all, his ecclesiological thought precisely by his autobiographical publications in recent years.

When, for the aforementioned reasons, I turn my attention in the
following pages to Ratzinger's life and work, it is not for the purpose

---

[1] On Ratzinger's understanding of "renewal", see pt. 2, sec. 1, chap. 3, of this work,
"Consistency in Ratzinger's Theological Thought Despite a Change of Perspective?"

[2] Instead of the official title, "Congregation for the Doctrine of the Faith", the more
familiar but not quite precise name, "Congregation for the Faith" is used most often in
this book. I am aware that all Roman Congregations are at the service of the Catholic
faith; nevertheless the original and proper task of the *Congregation pro Doctrina Fidei* is to
teach the faith of the Church authentically.

of producing a comprehensive biography or an exhaustive survey of his published work.[3] This sketch of his intellectual development is guided, rather, by the intention of demonstrating the ecclesial dimension of his life in its various expressions. The biographically oriented section 1 of part 2 of our dissertation, therefore, not only serves as a preamble to Ratzinger's ecclesiology, but already reveals one of its central aspects, namely, the "existential" ecclesiality, the habit of life in the Church that is prior to and indispensable for all ecclesiological reflection.

The discussion in this first section is divided into four chapters, the first of which demonstrates Ratzinger's rootedness, as a matter of principle, in the faith of the Church. In the second chapter, I will illuminate the path of the theologian up to his break with the journal *Concilium*. This raises the question of the consistency of Ratzinger's theological thought and, consequently, of his ecclesiology. The question will be investigated in the third chapter. The fourth chapter, finally, will deal with Ratzinger as archbishop and cardinal; within the framework of this dissertation, the focus is not on his official activity and, hence, not on the magisterial documents that he helped to compose, but rather on the scholarly theological contributions to ecclesiology that he produced during this period and on the emphases and nuances in them that were conditioned by his official post.

---

[3] A bibliography covering up to 2002 is found in *Pilgrim Fellowship*, 299–379.

Chapter 1

From the Private Ego to the Ecclesial "I"

§ 1. Church as the Locus of the Faith

In retrospect we recognize how thoroughly the Church formed Ratzinger's life and work, not in the sense of "a restricted ecclesiality that merely revolves around itself, but always in the sense of a 'catholic' ecclesiality, the dimensions of which are those of creation, redemption, and perfection themselves".[4] For this it is necessary, as Ratzinger said in 1985, "to find again the meaning of the Church as Church of the Lord, as the locus of the real presence of God in the world".[5] It is the mystery about which *Lumen gentium* says: "The Church ... [is] the kingdom of Christ now present in mystery"[6] and therefore not primarily a theory,[7] but rather the gospel lived out and witnessed to, since she "continues in [her] innermost being to be the faithful, the locus of faith, the guarantee of faith"[8] in the triune God:

> Belief in the Trinity is *communio*; to believe in the Trinity means to become *communio*. Historically, this means that the "I" of the credo-formulas is a collective "I", the "I" of the believing Church, to which the individual "I" belongs as long as it believes. In other words, the "I" of the credo embraces the transition from the individual "I" to the ecclesial "I". In the case of the subject, the "I" of the Church is a structural precondition of the creed: this "I" utters itself only in the *communio* of the Church; the oneness of the

---

[4] W. Baier et al., eds., *Weisheit Gottes—Weisheit der Welt: Festschrift für Joseph Ratzinger zum 60. Geburtstag* (St. Ottilien: EOS Verlag, 1987), 1:v (foreword by the editors).

[5] *Report*, 48.

[6] *LG* 3.

[7] Cf. *Salt of the Earth*, 20.

[8] J. Ratzinger, J. B. Metz, J. Moltmann, and E. Goodman-Thau, "The Provocation of Talking about God: A Discussion, Moderated by Robert Leicht", in Peters/Urban, 78–99, citation at 96. Cf. *Principles*, 23f.

believing subject is the necessary counterpart and consequence of
the known "object", of that "Other" who is known by faith and
who thereby ceases to be merely the "Other".[9]

Accordingly, the individual does not believe out of his own resources
but, rather, as Ratzinger stresses, always believes "along with the whole
Church".[10] Because the "I" of the believer exists only as a result of
the "we", the profession of the triune God in the ecclesial *communio*
constitutes the faith of the Church,[11] with which personal faith is
then bound up. For this reason, the Church, as a living memory,[12] is
the locus of faith, through which the unity of history is established.
The subject that holds everything together is the Church, and this is
true also in relation to the articles of faith, for without her these would
be only a more or less lengthy "catalogue of things to be believed;
within and by the Church, they are made one." [13] Hence Ratzinger
considers it to be "the decisive question . . . whether that memory can
continue to exist through which the Church becomes Church and
without which she sinks into nothingness".[14] With that he addresses
the central theme of the Eucharist. For Church is not built up as a
theory or as "a superfluity of unheeded words"; rather, "she came

---

[9] *Principles*, 23. Cf. *Einheit*, 17–51, esp. 36–42. See also Nachtwei, 187–93, "Kirche als
Erkenntnisort des dialogischen Personenverständnissen" [The Church as the epistemological locus of the dialogical understanding of persons], esp. 187: "The experience of the 'I'
as the 'I' in the 'We' of the Church" is for Ratzinger "not a detached locus alongside the
knowledge of the trinitarian God".

[10] *Einheit*, 36. Here Ratzinger bases his argument on Henri de Lubac, "Der Glaube in
der Kirche", in *Geheimnis aus dem wir leben* (Einsiedeln: Johannes Verlag, 1967), 49–82, esp.
68ff.; cf. de Lubac, *The Christian Faith: An Essay on the Structure of the Apostles' Creed* (San
Francisco: Ignatius Press, 1986), 203–26. See also *Salt of the Earth*, 34: "Believing with the
Church and knowing that I may entrust myself to this knowledge [of the faith] and knowing that the other things I know receive light from it and, conversely, can deepen it—that
does hold me together. Above all, the foundational act of faith in Christ, and the attempt
to bring one's life into unity in terms of that faith, unifies the tensions, so that they do not
become a fissure, a fracture."

[11] Cf. *Principles*, 26–27.

[12] Cf. Ratzinger et al., "Provocation", 96. In this passage Ratzinger takes up the expression "elephant's memory", which Metz first used in the discussion, ibid., 91: "All these
questions involve one having patience: not just patience, but certainly patience too, when
dealing with the Church's 'elephant's memory,' a memory that is salvific, since we can
only still talk about religion in a substantive sense at all because of its lasting guarantee."

[13] *Principles*, 23–24.

[14] Ibid., 24.

into existence because someone lived and suffered his word; by reason
of his death, his word is understood as word par excellence, as the
meaning of all being, as logos."[15] In the solemn remembrance of the
Church, the central mystery of salvation, namely, the death and Resurrection of the Lord, is present and mightily effective:

> This [central mystery] is not . . . merely a "timeless truth"—an eter-
> nal idea hovering independently over a realm of changing facts. This
> [central mystery], which is inseparably bound to the act of "faith
> in", introduces us into the dynamic circle of trinitarian love that
> not only unites subject and object but even brings individual sub-
> jects together without depriving them of their individuality.[16]

This saving event, which simultaneously universalizes and personalizes
and into which the individual enters through the Church, is for Ratzinger the most fascinating thing about being a Catholic:

> . . . that I, living within this great communion, can know that I am
> in communion with all the living and the dead; and that I also find
> in it a certainty about the essence of my life—namely, God who has
> turned to me—on which I can found my life, with which I can live
> and die.[17]

To sum up we can say: For Ratzinger, the Church is the transtemporal subject of faith, a subject that is rooted in the trinitarian mystery and testifies to its identity along with its origin in Christ. As such,
the Church is and professes the unity of believers from the various eras
over the course of history. For this reason, she is also "the condition for
real participation in Jesus' *traditio*, which without this subject exists, not
as a historical and history-making reality, but only as a private recollection".[18] Therefore the individual always believes by believing along
with the whole Church. The core of this faith is a very simple act: It is
a question of "sharing in the basic decision of Jesus Christ through a participation in the basic decision of the Church".[19] Within this sphere of

---

[15] Ibid., 26.
[16] Ibid.
[17] *Salt of the Earth*, 21.
[18] *Dogma*, 265.
[19] "Identification", 27. See also J. Meyer zu Schlochtern, *Sakrament Kirche: Wirken Gottes im Handeln der Menschen* (Freiburg im Breisgau: Herder, 1992), 153–90, ref. at 182.

the believing Church, which testifies to the Word of God and is centered on the celebration of the mystery of the death and Resurrection of Jesus Christ, Ratzinger's faith biography and hence his theology also have their foundations from the very beginning.[20] This means, more specifically, that he does not pursue his ecclesiological reflections from a perspective of critical distance from the Church; instead, they explicitly derive their orientation from the Creed of the universal Church and are placed at her service. For this reason, Ratzinger sees holding together theological research and the faith of the "simple folk" as one of his fundamental concerns.[21]

§ 2. The Church's Creed as the Form and Content of the Existential Plan

When asked what Jesus Christ means to him,[22] Ratzinger answered that even before he penetrated the faith in a scholarly way, the lived creed shaped his life, specifically the belief in Jesus Christ as the Son of God:

> I encountered him initially not in philosophy or theology but in the faith of the Church. This means that from the beginning I knew him not as a great figure of the past ... but as someone who is alive and at work today, someone whom people can encounter today. It means, above all, that I have come to know him within the history of the faith that has its origin in him, and according to the vision of faith as given its most enduring formulation by the Council of Chalcedon.

---

[20] Cf. *Spirit of the Liturgy*, 7: "One of the first books I read after starting my theological studies at the beginning of 1946 was Roman Guardini's first little book, *The Spirit of the Liturgy*.... This slim volume ... helped us to rediscover the liturgy in all its beauty, hidden wealth, and time-transcending grandeur, to see it as the animating center of the Church, the very center of Christian life. It led to a striving for a celebration of the liturgy that would be 'more substantial' (*wesentlicher*, one of Guardini's favorite words). We were now willing to see the liturgy—in its inner demands and form—as the prayer of the Church, a prayer moved and guided by the Holy Spirit himself, a prayer in which Christ unceasingly becomes contemporary with us, enters into our lives."

[21] *Principles*, 336. See also V. Pfnür, "Einführung", in *Mitte*, 17.

[22] See *Dogma and Preaching*, 6–10.

In my view Chalcedon represents the boldest and most sublime simplification of the complex and many-layered data of tradition to a single central fact that is the basis of everything else: Son of God, possessed of the same nature as God *and* of the same nature as us.[23]

Even these few sentences indicate that this faith, which is convincing in its simplicity, knows that it is obliged to Scripture and "tradition in its entirety".[24] In particular, it is characterized—as Peter Seewald,[25] a formerly fallen-away Catholic journalist, noted in a 1996 conversation with Ratzinger—by "a unity and integration of thought and faith that is no longer familiar to us skeptical and errant moderns".[26] It is rooted in a personal relationship with Christ, in which it becomes clear that the Church's Creed embraces "the totality of one's life plan",[27] that is, one's way of thinking, speaking, understanding, and acting, the way in which one relates to God and to others. Therefore, it cannot be compared, for example, with a political party platform, in which social concerns have top priority.[28] Essential to the comprehensive answer of faith are, on the one hand, "Being with and in the Church ... , [in which] the Holy Scriptures can be both lived and appropriated"[29] and, on the other hand, as Ratzinger emphasized at a 1972 conference of the International Theological Commission[30] entitled "The Unity of the Faith and Theological Pluralism", the duty to fit in with the diachronic as well as the synchronic Creed of the Church:

---

[23] Ibid., 7–8. Cf. *Introduction*, 11–29, esp. 20–29.

[24] *Dogma and Preaching*, 9.

[25] Peter Seewald, a native of Passau, was an editor for the German periodicals *Spiegel*, *Stern* and *Süddeutsche Zeitung*. At the time of his interviews with Cardinal Ratzinger, he was working as a free-lance journalist.

[26] *Salt of the Earth*, 33. The book entitled *Salt of the Earth: Christianity and the Catholic Church at the End of the Millennium* originally appeared in German and immediately proved to be an international best seller with editions in fourteen languages.

[27] Ibid., 19.

[28] Cf. *Dogma and Preaching*, 8. Cf. *Introduction*, 13ff.

[29] *Salt of the Earth*, 20.

[30] The Latin title Commissio Theologica Internationalis is frequently translated into German as Internationale Theologenkommission [International Commission of Theologians], whereas the correct translation is International Theological Commission. One reason for this is that some members are historians or philosophers. On this subject, see H. Moll, "Die Internationale Theologische Kommission im Spiegel ihrer Publikationen", *ThG* 33 (1990): 284–90, esp. 285.

The fact that the Christian makes his act of faith along with the transtemporal subject "Church" means the relativizing of every "today", which must be recognized as part of the whole history of the faith; it must be measured by what has already been received and remain open to the guidance tomorrow of the Spirit, who teaches us to understand what we cannot yet bear now (cf. Jn 16:12f.).[31]

Just as in the secular sphere an individual receives his manner of speaking and thinking, his intellectual and cultural cast from the milieu in which he grows up and finds his way in life,[32] so too in the realm of Christian faith the Church is for Ratzinger the place of basic religious experiences, through which he enters into the sacramental realization of the common Creed and is formed by it.[33] Concretely, this means for Ratzinger believing in the one who says about himself, "I am the truth",[34] and it also means believing in the revelation of this truth[35] as well as in the "communion that comes from the truth and thereby frees us from the unauthorized arrangements of human custom, in which man becomes his own creature, his own God, and thus a slave to himself".[36] Seen in this way, Ratzinger's faith testimony, which has been pondered theologically, can provide orientation amid the tensions between the pluralism of modern world views and the transtemporal unity that we call "Church"[37] and show us where the fundamental direction of Christian life should lead: to Jesus Christ, in whom God truly became man and who as "our contemporary in our today"[38] desires to dwell with men. At the same time, however, the question arises: To what extent can Ratzinger, with his integrated view,

---

[31] *Einheit*, 33.

[32] Cf. ibid., 36.

[33] Cf. ibid., 37.

[34] Jn 14:6.

[35] Cf. *Introduction*, 20: Through certain forms of dialogue among religions, faith in Christ, as the Truth in which God has revealed himself to man in a unique and unsurpassable manner, is relativized. Alluding to this in his preface, Ratzinger says that it becomes merely a question of "contact with the ineffable, with the hidden mystery. And to a great extent people agree that this mystery is not completely manifested in any one form of revelation, that it is always glimpsed in random and fragmentary ways and yet is always sought as one and the same thing." See also Häring, *Ideologie*, 43–45 and 145–54.

[36] *Einheit*, 50.

[37] Cf. ibid., 36. See also *Principles*, 23f.

[38] *Introduction*, 29.

give adequate attention to the skepticism and doubts of contemporary people and to the concrete problems they formulate?

In this first chapter, "From the Private Ego to the Ecclesial 'I' ", we have sketched the main lines of the understanding of ecclesiality to which Ratzinger owes allegiance with all his being. The purpose of the following biographical insights is to make this existential ecclesiality concrete by examining the more important stops along his path through life and to point out their significance for his ecclesiological thinking.

Chapter 2

The Path of Joseph Ratzinger the Theologian

§ 1. Living in the Light of the Easter Mystery

On a Holy Saturday, April 16, 1927, Joseph Ratzinger was born in Marktl am Inn in Upper Bavaria. On the same day he was baptized at the Easter Vigil, which at that time was still celebrated on Holy Saturday morning:

> I have always been filled with thanksgiving for having had my life immersed in this way in the Easter mystery, since this could only be a sign of blessing. To be sure, it was not Easter Sunday but Holy Saturday, but, the more I reflect on it, the more this seems to be fitting for the nature of our human life: we are still awaiting Easter; we are not yet standing in the full light but walking toward it full of trust.[1]

The child was baptized with the name Joseph, after his father. The latter, who was employed as a police commissioner, was originally from Rieckering in Lower Bavaria but for job-related reasons had to move repeatedly: including to Tittmoning, then to Aschau in the vicinity of Kraiburg, until he retired in 1937 and was able to obtain an old, very simple farmhouse in Hufschlag near Traunstein.[2]

---

[1] *Milestones*, 8. Cf. *Salt of the Earth*, 42f.

[2] Cf. *Salt of the Earth*, 45. Ratzinger speaks (ibid., 51) about his close relationship with his father and remarks that "the Third Reich went terribly against his grain." At that time he recognized that the resistance of the institutional Church to the regime was productive only when there were people to support this institution "from inner conviction" (on this subject, see *Milestones*, 13–20, ref. at 15). In contrast, John L. Allen, the author of *Cardinal Ratzinger: The Vatican's Enforcer of the Faith* (London: Continuum, 2000), writes in the first chapter of this biography, entitled "Growing Up in Hitler's Shadow": "More important is the question of what conclusions Ratzinger draws from the war. Having seen fascism in action, Ratzinger today believes that the best antidote to political totalitarianism is ecclesial totalitarianism. In other words, he believes the Catholic Church serves the cause of human

Joseph Ratzinger's mother, Maria, née Paintner, was born in Mühl-bach near Rosenheim. She was a skilled cook and still went to work after Joseph's father's retirement so as to earn money for the schooling of their three children, Maria, Georg, and Joseph. Joseph, who at first attended the *gymnasium* [a secondary school offering a classical edu-cation] in Traunstein while living at home, entered the archdiocesan minor seminary in Traunstein at Easter of 1939. This involved a great financial burden for the family, for his brother, Georg, too, was already at boarding school there.[3] Cardinal Ratzinger recalls:

> If in the next few years I familiarized myself with the idea of a priestly vocation, in a development that to a great extent paralleled that of my brother, although somewhat later in time, then the deci-sive factor—besides the more sentimental piety of our mother—was the strong and resolutely faith-oriented personality of our father. He thought differently from the way people were supposed to think, and did so with a calm composure and superiority that were persuasive.[4]

---

freedom by restricting freedom in its internal life, thereby remaining clear about what it teaches and believes" (3). Allen's subjective way of interpreting the facts is evident here along with his tendentiousness. This may be the reason why, in the German translation by Hubert Pfau [Düsseldorf, 2002], the entire first chapter from the original American edi-tion (pp. 1–44) was omitted, with no indication whatsoever from the translator or the publisher, even though this chapter can be viewed as the hermeneutic key to the whole book. If one reads, however, the section "Guilt and Reconciliation" in *God and the World*, 420–24, esp. 421f., one recognizes the absurdity of Allen's assumption. [In the interests of fairness, it should be noted that Allen completely revised his views in his second biography of Ratzinger, *The Rise of Benedict XVI: The Inside Story of How the Pope Was Elected and Where He Will Take the Catholic Church* (New York: Doubleday, 2005).—TRANS.] See also Ratzinger's article "Das Gewissen in der Zeit", *IKaZ* 1 (1972): 432–42, citation at 432: "For that man [Hitler], conscience was a chimera from which mankind had to be liber-ated: the freedom he promised would be freedom from conscience.... The destruction of conscience is the real prerequisite for totalitarian obedience and totalitarian rule. Where conscience holds sway, there is a limit to the dominion of human commands and human arbitrariness, something sacred that necessarily remains inviolable and, having an ultimate sovereignty, eludes all efforts—including my own—to control or manipulate it. Only the unconditional character of the conscience is the absolute antithesis to tyranny." See also *Prüfsteine*, 25–62, esp. 33f. Cf. also the lengthy review of the German edition of *Salt of the Earth*, by A. Batlogg, "Christentum als Neuheitserlebnis: Zur Veröffentlichung von Joseph Ratzinger", *ZKTh* 119 (1997): 323–32, esp. 331, where Batlogg establishes that Ratzinger's theology is pro-Semitic.

³ Cf. *Milestones*, 25.
⁴ Wagner/Ruf, *Kardinal Ratzinger*, 54f.

At the age of sixteen, in 1943 during the war, he became a *flakhelfer* (assistant in anti-aircraft defense) in the vicinity of Munich. During this time he was enrolled in the reduced curriculum at the Maximilians-Gymnasium in Munich.[5] In 1944 he was drafted into the *Reichsarbeitsdienst* [work service for the Reich], followed by infantry training in Traunstein. At the end of the war, he spent a few weeks in American custody as a prisoner of war. But soon after, in 1946, he entered the major seminary and attended the Philosophical-Theological College [*Hochschule*] in Freising. Ratzinger associates with this place two memories that made a lasting impression. First he mentions the postwar situation of that time:

> This was a very mixed group indeed, the 120 or so seminarians. . . .
> The span of ages ranged from some who were nearly forty down to
> a few of us who were nineteen. . . . It was understandable that many
> of the older combatants looked down on us youngsters as immature
> children who lacked the sufferings necessary for the priestly minis-
> try, since we had not gone through those dark nights that alone can
> give full shape to the radical assent a priest must give.[6]

Nevertheless, all were united by a great sense of gratitude and love for the Church, which was "the locus of all our hopes" and "the alternative to the destructive ideology of the brown[-shirted] rulers".[7]

A second event took place almost unnoticed and yet was decisive for the future of the young students: Alfred Läpple gave Ratzinger a copy of Henri de Lubac's book *Catholicisme*, which Hans Urs von Balthasar had translated into German:

> This book was for me a key reading event. It gave me not only a
> new and deeper connection with the thought of the Fathers but
> also a new way of looking at theology and faith as such. Faith had
> here become an interior contemplation and, precisely by thinking
> with the Fathers, a present reality. In this book one could detect a
> quiet debate going on with both liberalism and Marxism, the dra-
> matic struggle of French Catholicism for a new penetration of the
> faith into the intellectual life of our time. De Lubac was leading his

---

[5] Cf. *Milestones*, 30ff.
[6] Ibid., 41.
[7] Ibid., 42.

readers out of a narrowly individualistic and moralistic mode of faith and into the freedom of an essentially social faith, conceived and lived as a *we*—a faith that, precisely as such and according to its nature, was also hope, affecting history as a whole, and not only the promise of a private blissfulness to individuals.[8]

If von Balthasar indeed managed, in his 1943 introduction to this book, to summarize de Lubac's central ideas, then we can judge from it how these ideas later sank in and became part of Ratzinger's thought as well:

We are grateful that he [de Lubac] has taught us this: that he knows how to live and think out of the self-evident character of the entire Catholic sphere, that he can therefore (without the strain of historicist posturing) inquire into the whole living tradition that he owns, so as to overhear in it the complete answer to the most burning questions of the day, and, finally, that his movement dispenses with even so much as the appearance of pitting factions within the Church against each other—something that not infrequently bedevils the German [Catholic] movements. In this superiority to all protest and exclusivity, he is more deeply and more naïvely Catholic—if, indeed, the real name of Catholicism is communion.[9]

Impressed by this perspective, Ratzinger completed the two-year program of philosophy in Freising[10] and then continued his education at the Theological Faculty of the University of Munich, which on account of the damage from bombardments had been transferred to the small castle at Fürstenried, where the seminarians' living quarters were very crowded and there was a shortage of classrooms.[11]

---

[8] Ibid., 98.

[9] Hans Urs von Balthasar, "Geleitwort", in Henri de Lubac, *Katholizismus als Gemeinschaft* (Einsiedeln and Cologne: Benziger, 1943), 5. This is a German translation of *Catholicisme: Les Aspects sociaux du dogme*; English trans.: *Catholicism: Christ and the Common Destiny of Man* (San Francisco: Ignatius Press, 1988).

[10] See *Milestones*, 41–45. Among Ratzinger's teachers in Freising, besides Alfred Läpple, were Arnold Wilmsen and Jakob Fellermeier.

[11] Cf. *Milestones*, 47ff., esp. 48: "Since we had no lecture hall at our disposal, classes had to be held in the greenhouse of the castle garden. Here, we at first baked in the glowing heat that could be rivaled only by the freezing cold of the winter."

§ 2. The Path to a Professorship

1. *In the footsteps of the Fathers*

During the years of his theological studies, Ratzinger experienced the
revival of the intellectual impulses of the period between the two world
wars, which had been produced by the liturgical, biblical, and patristic movements. Teaching on the theological faculty in Fürstenried were,
among others, the exegete Friedrich Wilhelm Maier[12] and the dogmatic theologian Michael Schmaus, "who had become renowned
throughout Germany on account of his novel textbook of dogmatic
theology. He had parted ways with Neoscholastic schemas and composed a living presentation of the Catholic doctrine of the faith."[13]
Schmaus came from Munich and brought two noted scholars with
him: the young canonist Klaus Mörsdorf and the pastoral theologian
Josef Pascher, "who kicked open for us the doors of the liturgical
movement; and then the high-spirited and ingenious Gottlieb Söhngen, who familiarized me with the world of the Church Fathers".[14]
Ratzinger recalls the latter with special admiration:

> Characteristic of Söhngen . . . was the fact that he always developed
> his thought on the basis of the sources themselves, beginning with
> Aristotle and Plato, then on to Clement of Alexandria and Augus-
> tine, Anselm, Bonaventure, and Thomas, all the way to Luther and
> finally the Tübingen theologians of the last [that is, nineteenth] cen-
> tury. Pascal and Newman, too, were among his favorite authors.[15]

No sooner had Ratzinger taken his first test for a course with Gottlieb Söhngen in 1947 than the opportunity was offered to him to
pursue graduate studies. After the final examination in theology in the
summer of 1950, it so happened that Söhngen announced a competition for dissertations on the subject "The People of God and the

---

[12] He had been disciplined by Rome before the First World War on account of approaches
to exegesis that were still forbidden then. See Wagner/Ruf, 64.
[13] *Milestones*, 49.
[14] Wagner/Ruf, 62.
[15] *Milestones*, 56.

House of God in Augustine's Doctrine on the Church".[16] Within the allotted time of only nine months, Ratzinger completed his dissertation, which won first prize. That marked the beginning of his lifelong occupation with the subject of ecclesiology. In retrospect, he writes in 1992 about the present importance of this work in his foreword to the new edition of his dissertation:

> As for its relation to the theological debate today, the book ... acquired an unexpected relevance precisely in the postconciliar dispute about the Church. The Council ... assigned new significance to the concept "People of God" and devoted to it a whole chapter in the Constitution on the Church. If one reads this chapter in the context of the entire document, it becomes evident that the "People of God" statements are connected inseparably and organically with all the other great themes of the ecclesiological tradition and are combined with them into a synthesis, in which I find a complete confirmation of the essential conclusions of my book, a fully intrinsic unity in the foundational way of seeing the Church. Calling the Church a sacrament, a practice that Vatican II adopted from the preceding theology of the period between the wars, clearly indicates the christological-pneumatological transposition of the People of God concept; for Vatican II also, ecclesiology is inseparably bound up with Christology and Pneumatology, whereby the trinitarian character of God's action in history, as set forth in the Constitution on the Church, is addressed at the same time.[17]

After completing his dissertation, Joseph Ratzinger, together with his brother, Georg, was ordained a priest on June 29, 1951, by Cardinal Michael Faulhaber in the Freising Cathedral.[18] In 1952, after

---

[16] In the preface to the new edition of his dissertation, *Volk und Haus Gottes*, Ratzinger writes: "It was quite clear, though, that the main emphasis in the study that I was assigned to write would be on the People of God as a new hermeneutic key for the purpose of clarifying the patristic view of what the Church is.... It became evident that Augustine (like the Fathers of the Church generally) was completely in line with the New Testament, in which the expression 'People of God' appears mostly in quotations from the Old Testament and almost exclusively designates the people of Israel and, thus (if you will), the Church of the Old Covenant. The new community called together by Christ, in contrast, was named *Ecclesia*, which means assembly, a term having both an eschatological and a cultic aspect" (ibid., xiii).

[17] Ibid., xix.

[18] See *Milestones*, 99.

serving for a year as an assistant pastor, he was appointed an instructor at the major seminary in Freising, and from 1954 on he taught as a professor of dogmatic theology.

2. The habilitation *thesis on Bonaventure's theology of history*

Meanwhile, Ratzinger began his *habilitation* thesis, which at the suggestion of his academic supervisor, Gottlieb Söhngen, he devoted to St. Bonaventure's theology of history. This *habilitation* thesis had key importance for Ratzinger in the later debate about the eschatological aspects of the Constitution on the Church[19] and about the different ways in which it was received in ecumenical circles as well as by proponents of Latin American liberation theology.[20] For this reason it is necessary in the following pages to look more closely at two of its central statements.

The first point concerns how revelation is understood. Ratzinger's analyses—which did not go unchallenged[21]—said:

> in Bonaventure (as well as in theologians of the thirteenth century) there was nothing corresponding to our conception of "revelation", by which we are normally in the habit of referring to all the revealed contents of the faith: it has even become a part of linguistic usage to refer to Sacred Scripture simply as "revelation". Such an identification would have been unthinkable in the language of the High Middle Ages. Here, "revelation" is always a concept denoting an act. The word refers to the act in which God shows himself, not to the objectified result of this act. And because this is so, the receiving subject is always also a part of the concept of "revelation".... These insights, gained through my reading of Bonaventure, were later on very important for me at the time of the conciliar discussion on revelation, Scripture, and tradition. Because,

---

[19] Cf. "Einleitung", 15–17.

[20] Cf. the preface to the new German edition of *Geschichtstheologie*: "The question of whether someone as a Christian can imagine a sort of this-worldly perfection, whether something like a Christian utopia and eschatology is possible, can perhaps be described as the very theological core of the debate over liberation theology."

[21] They led first to the rejection of the thesis by the reader Michael Schmaus. Ratzinger himself relates the difficulties he had in gaining accreditation as a university lecturer in "The Drama of My *Habilitation*" in *Milestones*, 103–5.

if Bonaventure is right, then revelation precedes Scripture and becomes deposited in Scripture but is not simply identical with it. This in turn means that revelation is always something greater than what is merely written down.[22]

Therefore, according to Ratzinger, revelation always contains "the fact that it *arrives* and *is perceived*"[23] in the *Ecclesia*. Since "revelation is more than Scripture", it follows that "the living organism of the faith of all ages is then an intrinsic part of revelation."[24] According to Bonaventure—as Ratzinger demonstrates—the Word of revelation recorded in Scripture is indeed definitive; nevertheless, new depths are uncovered in every age through its reception by the Church.[25]

---

[22] Ibid., 108–9. Ratzinger uses similar expressions in another passage, ibid., 127.

[23] Ibid., 127. On this subject, see also the title essay by Ratzinger in *Revelation and Tradition*, by K. Rahner and Ratzinger, trans. W. J. O'Hara, 26–49 (New York: Herder and Herder, 1966); the passage cited is on pages 35–39, esp. 35: "Revelation means God's whole speech and action with man; it signifies a *reality* which scripture makes known but which is not itself identical with scripture."

From the perspective of Bonaventure's concept of revelation, the limitations of historical-critical exegesis appear clearly. Cf. Ratzinger's argument in *Milestones*, 127f., and also in his article "Das Christentum wollte immer mehr sein als nur Tradition. Die Kirche muss den Glauben vernünftig auslegen, damit er an den Enden der Erde verstanden werden kann. Ein Gespräch mit Joseph Kardinal Ratzinger" [Christianity always intended to be more than a mere tradition. The Church must expound the faith reasonably, so that it can be understood to the ends of the earth. A conversation with Cardinal Joseph Ratzinger], *FAZ* 57 (March 8, 2000): 52: "The revelation of Jesus Christ is ... not a meteor that has fallen to the earth, which now lies around somewhere as a mass of stone, from which one can take mineral samples to be analyzed in a laboratory. Revelation, that is, God's approach to man, is always greater than what can be grasped in human words, greater that the words of Scripture, also. Scripture is the essential testimony of revelation." See also Ratzinger, "Schrift-auslegung im Widerstreit: Zur Frage nach Grundlagen und Weg der Exegese heute", in *Schriftauslegung im Widerstreit*, ed. Ratzinger, 15–44, ref. at 41, QD 117 (Freiburg im Breisgau: Herder, 1989).

[24] *Milestones*, 127.

[25] See *Theology of History*, 62–63: "At no time does Bonaventure refer to the Scriptures themselves as 'revelation'. He speaks of *revelare* and *facies revelata* primarily when a particular understanding of Scripture is involved, namely that 'manifold divine wisdom' which consists in grasping the three-fold spiritual sense of Scripture—the allegorical, the anagogical and the tropological. These three are understood in analogy with the three divine virtues of faith, hope and love." See Bonaventure, *Hex[aemeron]* 13–17, 338. In his late work, *Collationes in Hexaemeron*, Bonaventure grapples with the problems of Joachimism and the Franciscan *Spirituales*, which had led to the resignation of his predecessor, John of Parma; see *Theology of History*, 3–9. Cf. *Milestones*, 109: "And this again means that there can be no such thing as pure *sola scriptura* ... , because an essential element of Scripture is

Therefore the Holy Spirit is at work in *every* age, and he shows the Church how she can proclaim this Word anew again and again.

By means of this understanding, Bonaventure distinguishes his position from the opinion of the Cistercian abbot Joachim of Fiore[26]—and with that we arrive at a second central statement about the theology of history in Ratzinger's *habilitation* thesis. Joachim had related the working of the Holy Spirit to a very specific age; in his reckoning, the age of the Father (Old Testament) and the age of the Son (New Testament) would be followed by a third phase of revelation, the age of the Holy Spirit.[27] From this third phase, the Calabrian abbot expected the eschatological fulfillment, indeed, a *this-worldly* fulfillment, a promise within history, "a synthesis of utopia and eschatology".[28] As Ratzinger demonstrates, "Joachim concretely formulated such a promise and so prepared the way for Hegel.... Hegel, in turn, furnished the intellectual model for Marx." [29]

In his *habilitation* thesis, Ratzinger shows that Bonaventure had quite a nuanced view of Joachim's thought and "by no means condemned it as a whole".[30] Bonaventure was, however, "implacable in his rejection

---

the Church as understanding subject, and with this the fundamental sense of tradition is already given."

[26] Cf. *God and the World*, 362. Cf. Ratzinger, *The God of Jesus Christ*, trans. Robert J. Cunningham (Chicago: Franciscan Herald Press, 1979), 97–106, esp. 97–99. See also Ratzinger, *Seek That Which Is Above* (San Francisco: Ignatius Press, 1986), 69f. Bonaventure—as Ratzinger explains in *Theology of History*, 105—rejects the restriction of the New Testament and the time of Jesus to the second age, since the New Testament for him is the eternal covenant (*testamentum*). Furthermore, Joachim's threefold division of history is admitted by Bonaventure only "to a very limited extent", and he emphasizes, in contrast to Joachim, that Christ is the axis around which the world turns and the center of everything (*Theology of History*, 118).

[27] See *Theology of History*, 109f. Cf. *Salt of the Earth*, 61f.: In this reckoning of the phases, the age of the Holy Spirit coincided with years during which St. Francis of Assisi lived (1181–1202).

[28] See the foreword to the new German ed. of *Geschichtstheologie* (no page numbers). Cf. *Report*, 173: With reference to the postconciliar theology of liberation, Ratzinger speaks of an element "that the secularist liberation programs ... have in common: they are attempting to achieve this liberation exclusively in the immanent plane, in history, in this world."

[29] *Salt of the Earth*, 63. Cf. *Milestones*, 110: "In a late two-volume work, Henri de Lubac has studied the subsequent history of Joachim's idea, which reaches out to Hegel and the totalitarian systems of our own [twentieth] century." It is manifested also, for example, in the expression "Third Reich". Cf. also Ratzinger, *God of Jesus Christ*, 97–106, ref. at 99–100.

[30] *Geschichtstheologie*, foreword to the new German ed.

of efforts to divide Christ and the Spirit, the christologically and sacramentally ordered Church from the pneumatological and prophetic
Church of the poor, all the while claiming that they themselves could
bring about a utopia by their way of life".[31] This distillation of the
contents of Bonaventure's theology of history displays ecclesiological
parallels to the debate about present-day liberation theology, but they
cannot be further developed in this biographical part of my dissertation.
    The second part of his originally voluminous *habilitation* thesis, which
dealt with Bonaventure's theology of history as outlined above, was
finally accepted in February 1957 after "weeks of restless waiting".[32]
As of January 1, 1958, Ratzinger was appointed *Privatdozent* [univer-
sity lecturer] at the University of Munich and professor for fundamental and dogmatic theology in the Philosophical-Theological College
in Freising. A half year later he was surprised by the call to fill a chair
for fundamental theology at the University of Bonn, where he began
lecturing in 1959.

§ 3. Theological Advisor to Cardinal Frings

During his years in Bonn (1959 to 1963) Ratzinger became acquainted
with the archbishop of Cologne at the time, Cardinal Joseph Frings,
with whom—according to his own statement—he had always had a
good understanding. The following incident illustrates this as well:

> Occasionally [Cardinal Frings] attended a lecture, and he also lis-
> tened to my presentation in Bensburg about the theology of the
> Council. We met in Cologne ... where he asked me to provide
> him with an outline on "The Council and the Modern Intellectual
> World" for a presentation that he was going to give in Genoa. Car-
> dinal Frings adopted the text ... almost verbatim. Then, however,
> the matter took a dramatic turn. In Italy, where misgivings had been
> voiced as well, the cardinal's speech had become known. And one
> day he received the summons to appear before the Holy Father. As

---

[31] Ibid. Cf. the positions Ratzinger has taken with regard to liberation theology, for
example, in *Principles*, 378–93, esp. 382–89; *Church*, 237–54; "Eschatology and Utopia";
Report, 169–90.
[32] *Milestones*, 111.

the secretary vested him with the cardinalatial insignia, the former archbishop of Cologne said, "Perhaps I am putting these on for the last time." But then everything turned out differently. Pope John XXIII quickly went over to the cardinal, embraced him, and said, "Dear Cardinal, you have said everything that I have thought and wanted to say but could not say myself." [33]

That was the start of years of close collaboration between Ratzinger and Frings, who at the beginning of the Second Vatican Council took Ratzinger along to Rome as his official theological advisor. Even before that, Cardinal Frings, as a member of the Central Preparatory Commission for the Council,[34] regularly sent Ratzinger *schemata* (drafts of documents) for his opinion. Looking back on that time, Ratzinger writes:

Naturally I took exception to certain things, but I found no grounds for a radical rejection of what was being proposed, such as many demanded later on in the Council and actually managed to put through. It is true that the documents bore only weak traces of the biblical and patristic renewal of the last decades, so that they gave an impression of rigidity and narrowness through their excessive dependency on scholastic theology. In other words, they reflected more the thought of scholars than that of shepherds. But I must say that they had a solid foundation and had been carefully elaborated.[35]

---

[33] Wagner/Ruf, 66. Cf. *Milestones*, 128f.; Weiler, 166–74. The speech can be found in J. Frings, *Das Konzil und die moderne Gedankenwelt* (Cologne: Bachem, 1962); also in "Kardinal Frings über das Konzil und die moderne Gedankenwelt", *HerKorr* 16 (1961/62): 168–74. See also J. Frings, *Für die Menschen bestellt: Erinnerungen des Alterzbischofs von Köln* (Cologne: Bachem, 1973), 247; cf. K. Wittstadt, "Perspektiven einer kirchlichen Erneuerung— der deutsche Episkopat und die Vorbereitungsphase des II. Vatikanums", in *Vatikanum II und Modernisierung: Historische, theologische und soziologische Perspektiven*, ed. F.-X. Kaufmann and A. Zingerle, 85–106, ref. at 96f. (Paderborn: Schöningh, 1996).

[34] Frings proved to be an independent thinker. For example, in the meeting of the Preparatory Commission for the schema *De Ecclesia* on June 19, 1962, he asked critically whether anyone perhaps feared the Council's authority (see *AD* 2, 2/4:638). Cf. also the discussion by Weiler, 162–74. A few pages later (178), Weiler speaks of Frings' spirited appearance at the very first General Congregation of the Council on October 13, 1962 (see *AS* 1/1:208). The talk given by Frings has been published in Latin and German in *Kardinal Frings: Leben und Werk*, ed. D. Froitzheim, 2nd ed., 214–17 (Cologne: Wienand, 1980).

[35] *Milestones*, 121. Cf. Ratzinger, "Geleitwort", in Weiler, xiii–xvi.

What form did Ratzinger's influence take, then, in this conciliar period? To say, in retrospect, that "crucial points that found their expression in the Second Vatican Council's Constitution on the Church"[36] can be attributed to him would probably overestimate somewhat his influence at that time.[37] The evolution of the conciliar documents was much too complex[38] for such a claim, because—as Ratzinger himself emphasizes—the "contributions of many individuals and meetings of those individuals at all possible levels"[39] went into it:

In this collaboration, a declaration matured, in which the whole is substantially more than the individual parts and the particular contribution of each individual has been absorbed and surpassed in the dynamic of this whole, which also transformed its own character and shaped it into a synthesis that did not originate in it.[40]

[36] Wagner/Ruf, 67 (caption). In reading this text, one should keep in mind that the book cited is a biography in photos.

[37] Cf. G. Alberigo, "Die konziliare Erfahrung: selbständig lernen", in Wittstadt, 2:679–98, ref. at 689: "It took only a few weeks for the assembled Council to be able to recognize the real principal players: from Bea and Ottaviani—who were already well known—to Ruffini, Frings, Léger, Suenens, and Lercaro; but also the Chilean Larraín and the African Malula; no less important were the periti like Tromp, Schillebeeckx, Congar, Ratzinger, Rahner, and Daniélou—to mention only a few—and organizers like the Jesuit Greco, who knit the African episcopate into one, or the rector of the Belgian College in Rome, Prignon, the indefatigable shadow of Suenens."

[38] For an example of the many-layered influences upon the Constitution on the Church, see Wassilowsky, 369, which contains a graphic illustrating the development of the second schema (1963). Cf. also Wassilowsky's statement (ibid., 404ff.): "Anyone who perceives the Council as an event made up of an infinite number of interpersonal communications, on the most varied levels, will quickly realize that structural prerequisites are needed, too, in order to get content and convictions adopted. . . . In investigating the role played by the Council theologians in the process of shaping opinions at Vatican II, therefore, scholars had to make use of reflections and insights that had already demonstrated their empirical validity in modern historical research. For example, in order to explain the development and the significance of the groups among the periti, the analytical concept of 'networking' could be useful to conciliar scholarship."

[39] Ratzinger, preface, in Weiler, xiii. Cf. Salt of the Earth, 71: "You should never, as Karl Rahner often said, overestimate the role of an individual. Now, the Council was a very large body, and while individuals certainly generated decisive impulses, the reason they could do so was that others desired the same thing. Perhaps others couldn't formulate it, but the willingness was there; people were on the lookout for something."

[40] Ratzinger, preface, in Weiler, xiii.

§ 4. Conciliar Theologian (*Peritus*): From Euphoria
to Sober Skepticism

Besides recognizing the personal advisors to the individual bishops at
the Council, the procedural rules of the Council[41] also recognized
the so-called *periti*,[42] who were appointed as official theologians at
the Council by virtue of papal authority through a letter from the
cardinal secretary of state. Ratzinger, who accompanied Cardinal Frings
to the Council together with Herbert Luthe,[43] the archiepiscopal
secretary at the time, was appointed an official conciliar theologian
toward the end of the first session at the request of the archbishop of
Cologne.[44]

---

[41] H. Jedin, "Die Geschäftsordnung des Konzils", in *LThK.E*, vol. 3 (Freiburg im
Breisgau: Herder, 1968), 610–23. During the second session of the Council, further
rules were enacted for the *periti*, which they were strictly obliged to follow. See *AS*
3/1:24; German translation, 25: "In keeping with the task entrusted to them, the *periti*
should answer knowledgeably, wisely, and objectively the questions submitted to them
by the commissions for study. They are forbidden to organize particular movements
or trends or to grant interviews and publicly state their personal views about the Council. Furthermore, they should refrain from criticizing the Council and communicating
with outsiders about the activity of the commissions, thus heeding the regulations
set down by the Holy Father with respect to conciliar confidentiality." See also Weiler,
207.

[42] Weiler, 206–34, describes Ratzinger's activity as *peritus* in several conciliar commissions, esp. 208ff. Ratzinger, among other things, collaborated in the subcommission of the
Theological Commission that was assigned to compose articles 22–27 of chapter 3 of the
1964 schema on the Church, "De constitutione hierarchica ecclesiae et in specie de epis-
copatu" (ibid., 208ff.). Cf. *AS* 3/1:260. See also Wassilowsky, 243f. According to his account,
Ratzinger, along with K. Rahner, Salaverri, and Maccarone, was substantially involved in
developing chapter 3 of the schema on the Church in 1963.

[43] Today Hubert Luthe is bishop emeritus of the diocese of Essen, Germany.

[44] See *AS*, indices, 946. Cf. J. Ratzinger, *Die erste Sitzungsperiode des Zweiten Vatikanischen Konzils: Ein Rückblick* (Cologne: Bachem, 1963), 5: "I owe a very special debt of
gratitude to the archbishop of Cologne, His Eminence Cardinal Frings, who made it possible for me to participate in the Council and who through his profound humanity and
kindness lent to those days in Rome the splendor that surrounds my memory of them."
See also *Milestones*, 121. Cf. G. Ruggieri, "Der schwierige Abschied von der kontroverstheologisch geprägten Ekklesiologie", in Wittstadt, 2:331–419, esp. 333, 392f. Concerning
Ratzinger's influence on Frings, see also H.J. Pottmeyer, "Die Voten und ersten Beiträge
der deutschen Bischöfe zur Ekklesiologie des II. Vatikanischen Konzils", in *Der Beitrag der
deutschsprachigen und osteuropäischen Länder zum Zweiten Vatikanischen Konzil*, ed. K. Wittstadt and W. Verschooten, 143–55, ref. at 152 (Louvain: Bibliotheek van de Faculteit der
Godgeleerdheid, 1996).

During the Council and afterward, a series of Ratzinger's ecclesiological publications appeared;[45] particularly noteworthy are the four collections of memoirs from the individual sessions of the Council,[46] which describe concrete questions, debates, trends, and results from his perspective.

The report constitutes merely the external framework for a presentation that was concerned with putting in a somewhat clearer light several theological questions that came up, so as to go behind the Council's external purposes, which are indicated only in a few short strokes, and to reveal its inner workings, which at the same time may be considered the lasting and essential thing about the whole event. Of course it was necessary . . . to make a selection that, . . . though guided at first simply by the author's preference, nevertheless has hit upon several problems, I believe, that deserve attention with regard to the future of Christianity.[47]

Although on the eve of the Council Ratzinger shared the euphoria of that great beginning,[48] which was fed above all by the optimism of John XXIII, his commentaries soon became more restrained; indeed, as early as 1966 traces of skepticism began to appear in his assessment of the postconciliar period:

[45] See the bibliography of Ratzinger's work (up to 1996) in Weiler, 358–66, esp. 359–61. Cf. also the comprehensive bibliographical presentation (up to 1986) by Helmut Höfl in *Weisheit Gottes—Weisheit der Welt: Festschrift für Joseph Kardinal Ratzinger zum 60. Geburtstag*, ed. W. Baier et al., 2:1*–77* (St. Ottilien: EOS Verlag, 1987). Furthermore, see the selected bibliography, arranged by subject, in *Mitte*, 291–308, as well as the bibliography up to February 1, 2002, in *Pilgrim Fellowship*, 299–379.

[46] These four booklets were translated into English by Henry Traub, S.J. (pt. 1), Gerard C. Thormann (pts. 2 and 3), and Werner Barzel (pt. 4) and published with only one new foreword as J. Ratzinger, *Theological Highlights of Vatican II* (New York: Paulist Press, 1966). The four volumes originally appeared as J. Ratzinger, *Die erste Sitzungsperiode des Zweiten Vatikanischen Konzils: Ein Rückblick* (Cologne: Bachem, 1963); Ratzinger, *Das Konzil auf dem Weg: Rückblick auf die zweite Sitzungsperiode des Zweiten Vatikanischen Konzils* (Cologne: Bachem, 1964); Ratzinger, *Ergebnisse und Probleme der dritten Konzilsperiode* (Cologne: Bachem, 1965); and Ratzinger, *Die letzte Sitzungsperiode des Konzils* (Cologne: Bachem, 1966).

[47] *Rückblick*, 7f.

[48] Cf. *Highlights*, 30: "On the other hand, the Council had so often done the impossible that it was natural enough to become affected by Pope John's really contagious optimism and to take new hope."

What is the spiritual situation of the Church among us today after
the Council and as a result of it? ... Let us put it bluntly—a
certain unease prevails, a mood of disillusionment and disappointment as well. ... Catholics, however, are less united than before:
For some the Council accomplished too little, ... a conglomera-
tion of cautious compromises, a victory of diplomatic circumspec-
tion over the driving wind of the Holy Spirit, who does not want
complicated syntheses but rather the simplicity of the gospel message; for others, though, the results are a scandal, the capitulation
of the Church to the pernicious spirit of a dark age that is far
from God because it is so fiercely and obstinately set on worldly
things.[49]

In 1966, at the Catholic Congress in Bamberg, Ratzinger admon-
ished the gathering "to recognize that what made us so joyful and
grateful at the Council actually has another side to it and, thus, to
understand the responsibility that it entails".[50] He then warned against
a new triumphalism of the new over the old, which, as he puts it,
could "become more dangerous than peacock fans and tiaras [former
accoutrements of the papacy], which are more a cause for amusement,
anyway, than for pride".[51] With regard to the true meaning of *aggiornamento*, he challenged his listeners to have the courage to face "the
scandal of the Cross". The goal of this new beginning cannot be the
world, because as long as "the world is the world, the Church is on
pilgrimage, on the way to the Lord".[52]

Ratzinger's work as advisor during the Council had already brought
him both joy and anxiety. This conflict was intensified by a new challenge: He was called to Münster to fill the professorial chair vacated
by the dogmatic theologian Hermann Volk, who had been appointed
bishop of Mainz.

---

[49] *Volk Gottes*, 129–51: "Catholicism after the Council", lecture given at the Bamberg
Catholic Congress in 1966, citation at 130f. Cardinal Julius Döpfner marveled at the "conservative streaks" in Ratzinger's talk; see *Milestones*, 134. On June 18, 1965, Ratzinger gave
a lecture to the Catholic Student Union in Münster on true and false renewal of the
Church, but it received little attention as an "initial warning signal", as he puts it; see *Volk
Gottes*, 91–106: "What Does Renewal of the Church Mean?"
[50] *Volk Gottes*, 150.
[51] Ibid., 151.
[52] Ibid.

§ 5. University Professor in Münster, Tübingen, and Regensburg

1. Divided between Münster and Rome

During the summer semester of 1963, Ratzinger began lecturing at the University of Münster. Meanwhile, his work as conciliar advisor continued unabated. He himself describes the situation at that time:

> I lived and worked dividing my time between Münster and Rome. . . . Now and then, on returning from Rome, I found the mood in the Church and among theologians to be quite agitated. . . . More and more the Council appeared to be like a great Church parliament that could change everything and reshape everything. . . . Very clearly resentment was growing against Rome and against the Curia, which appeared to be the real enemy of everything that was new and progressive.[53]

At that time one could already detect signs of the "fermentation of the early postconciliar period"[54] that indicated a complete reorganization fraught with tensions. The year 1968 became a "particularly important milestone"[55] in this revolutionary change. It should be noted—as Ratzinger points out in a review of the Council written in 1982—that "the postconciliar crisis in the Catholic Church coincided with a global spiritual crisis of humanity itself or, at least, of the Western world."[56] Similarly, in 1972 he explained the crisis in the world

---

[53] *Milestones*, 132. See also Ratzinger, "Buchstabe und Geist des Zweiten Vatikanums in den Konzilsreden von Kardinal Frings", *IKaZ* 16 (1987): 251–65, ref. at 262. Ratzinger warns about hasty "categorizations" when he says in reference to Cardinal Joseph Frings: "Just as in the first session of the Council the cardinal was critical of the proposed schemata, which had been drawn up largely in terms of the Neoscholastic tradition, so now he proved to be critical of texts in which it was possible to detect the ardor of a rash modernity."

[54] *Introduction*, 13.

[55] Cf. ibid., 11ff.

[56] *Principles*, 367–93, citation at 370. Cf. *Dogma*, 439–47: "The most important thing of all, it seems to me, is that fact that the conclusion of the Council was connected, in the general intellectual situation of mankind, especially of the Western world, with the passing of a generation that was of crucial importance: with the change from the first postwar generation to the second. To the extent that this is accomplished, what determines the consciousness [of the day] is no longer the energy of a world that must be reconstructed out of nothing, but rather the oppressive force of an already fully constructed world where

and in the Church as the result of "the interaction between the spiritual and intellectual tremors caused by the transition to the second postwar generation and the ideological and theological movements that were playing into each other's hands".[57] Ratzinger himself experienced the unrest of the year 1968 at the University of Tübingen.

2. In Tübingen—The dramatic upheaval of 1968

In the summer semester of 1966 Ratzinger accepted the newly established second professorship for dogmatic theology in Tübingen. From today's perspective, it is astonishing[58] that "Hans Küng had vigorously supported such an appointment"[59] and was able to win over his colleagues to the idea. During Ratzinger's years in Tübingen (1966 to 1969), there was a sudden and dramatic "change in the ideological 'paradigm' by which the students and a part of the teachers"[60] in the humanities faculties directed their thinking. Ratzinger characterizes it as follows:

> While until now Bultmann's theology and Heidegger's philosophy had determined the frame of reference for thinking, almost overnight the existentialist model collapsed and was replaced by the

---

everything has already been done but that offers no meaning. And postwar theology, too, was at least partly responsible for this absence of meaning. Under the guidance of existential thought, it had taken refuge in the idea that there can be no objective basis for faith and meaning, thus abandoning the world to sheer relevance" (ibid., 440).

[57] *Dogma*, 443.

[58] Cf. H. Küng (a theologian very critical of the Vatican): "This pope talks with Haider [a contemporary Austrian politician thought by some to be a dangerous reactionary], but not with Küng!" Quoted from D. Hemberger's interview with Hans Küng in *Die Furche* 57 (2001/1): 11: "Along with Cardinal Ratzinger, I am among the few surviving theologians of the Council and hence know how the decrees were intended—namely, to be an initial advance.... Since his about-face, the former conciliar theologian, henceforth a curial theologian, has made this door to the future into a door to the past by attempting to reduce everything to Roman absolutism." Cf. H. Küng, "Kardinal Ratzinger, Papst Wojtyla und die Angst vor der Freiheit (1985): Nach langem Schweigen ein offenes Wort", in *Katholische Kirche—wohin? Wider den Verrat am Konzil*, ed. N. Greinacher and H. Küng, 389–407 (Munich: Piper, 1986).

[59] *Milestones*, 135. Cf. pp. 392f. of Küng's "public statement after a long silence", referenced in n. 58 above.

[60] *Milestones*, 136. Cf. "Demokratisierung 1", 13f. See also *Principles*, 382–89, and Häring, *Ideologie*, 22–30.

Marxist. Ernst Bloch was now teaching in Tübingen and made Heidegger contemptible for being petty bourgeois. At about the same time as I arrived, Jürgen Moltmann came to the Faculty for Lutheran Theology....

Existentialism fell apart, and the Marxist revolution kindled the whole university with its fervor, shaking it to its very foundations. A few years before, one could still have expected the theological faculties to represent a bulwark against the Marxist temptation. Now the opposite was the case: they became its real ideological center.[61]

Social and political factors were among the more important causes of the student demonstrations of 1968. They resulted from "a latent uneasiness and made clear the institutionalized constraints of a system that followed only the laws of production and consumption".[62] Not long after the Council, it became quite clear that more and more relations between Church and society, which through the message of *Gaudium et spes* were supposed to establish a new relationship, were breaking off. On the presupposition that new situations demand a new linguistic expression of the faith,[63] political theology was developed.

---

[61] *Milestones*, 136–37. Cf. *Salt of the Earth*, 77f.: To give an impression of the atmosphere at the time, Ratzinger quotes his Lutheran colleague Peter Beyerhaus, a theologian of the missions who suffered as he did as a result of this upheaval and [recalled] the following "sign of the times": " 'So what is Jesus' Cross but the expression of a sado-masochistic glorification of pain?' And the 'New Testament is a document of inhumanity, a large-scale deception of the masses.' These two citations came, not from the polemics of Bolshevist atheist propaganda, but from a flyer disseminated among fellow students in the summer of 1969 by the union of Protestant theology students at the University of Tübingen." See P. Beyerhaus, "Der kirchlich-theologische Dienst des Albrecht-Bengel-Hauses", *Diakrisis* 17 (1969): 9f. Ratzinger joined with Peter Beyerhaus and Ulrich Wickert (a Lutheran professor of patristics) in a "common course of action" (*Milestones*, 138). Cf. also *Introduction*, 11.

[62] L. de Vaucelles, "Der Katholizismus in der Zeit nach dem Konzil: Veränderungen des gesellschaftlichen Umfelds", in *Die Rezeption des Zweiten Vatikanischen Konzils*, ed. H.J. Pottmeyer, G. Alberigo, and J.-P. Jossua, 66–84, citation at 78 (Düsseldorf: Patmos-Verlag, 1986).

[63] P. Hünermann defended this thesis in his essay "Zu den Kategorien 'Konzil' und 'Konzilsentscheidung': Vorüberlegungen zur Interpretation des II. Vatikanums", in *Das II. Vatikanum—christlicher Glaube im Horizont globaler Modernisierung: Einleitungsfragen*, ed. Hünermann, 67–82, ref. at 78 (Paderborn: Schöningh, 1998).

In Tübingen, Jürgen Moltmann devised "a wholly new and different conception of theology from Bloch's perspective".[64] Granted, in the volume *Eschatologie*, which was published in 1977 in the series Kleine Katholische Dogmatik, Ratzinger acknowledges that individual gleams of real gold[65] can be found among the different outlines of political theology,[66] whereby he refers explicitly to Jürgen Moltmann's "rich and complex" theological model,[67] which he cannot reject outright. But in his critique of political theology, he opposes first of all the transformation of eschatology into political utopia, which "involves the emasculation of Christian hope", leaving behind a "deceptive surrogate".[68] His second objection concerns the pseudo-mystification of politics, which is likewise falsified thereby, because "the mystery of God is invoked in order to justify political irrationalism." [69]

In this time of upheaval, which was heralded by the student revolt of 1968, Ratzinger was Dean of the Faculty for Catholic Theology in Tübingen, a member of the Greater and Lesser Academic Senate, and also a member of the commission in charge of drawing up a new constitution for the university;[70] thus he experienced how the university turned "into a seething cauldron" in which even "assaults against

---

[64] *Milestones*, 136. In Bloch's writings, biblical thought was combined with an expressionistic and poetical language that was rich in imagery. Cf. the article by M. Eckert on "Bloch, Ernst", in *LThK*, 3rd ed., 2:527.

[65] Cf. J. Ratzinger, *Eschatology: Death and Eternal Life*, trans. Michael Waldstein (Washington, D.C.: Catholic Univ. of America Press, 1988), 57–60.

[66] Here Ratzinger is referring in particular to the outlines by J.B. Metz, *Zur Theologie der Welt* (Mainz: Matthias-Grünewald-Verlag, 1968); J. Moltmann, *Theologie der Hoffnung* (Munich: Kaiser, 1964); Moltmann, *Der gekreuzigte Gott* (Munich, 1972); and S. Wiedenhofer, *Politische Theologie* (Stuttgart: Kohlhammer, 1976). Cf. also N. Lobkowicz, *Was brachte uns das Konzil?* (Würzburg: Naumann, 1986), 97; Lobkowicz is of the opinion that Ratzinger's *Eschatology: Death and Eternal Life* is an outstanding presentation of the dubiousness of political theologies. With reference to Jürgen Moltmann and Johann Baptist Metz, Nikolaus Lobkowicz writes (and I cite him verbatim): "Both are obsessed with the idea, which in turn goes back to the Marxist Ernst Bloch, that the revolutionary will of the Marxists is a concrete fulfillment of eschatological hope."

[67] See Ratzinger, *Eschatology*, 58. Cf. Ratzinger, J.B. Metz, J. Moltmann, and E. Goodman-Thau, "The Provocation of Speaking about God: A Discussion, Moderated by Robert Leicht", in Peters/Urban, 78–99, esp. 92.

[68] See Ratzinger, *Eschatology*, 59.

[69] Ibid.

[70] Cf. *Milestones*, 138.

professors"[71] were not unheard of. Ratzinger goes on to explain that "it was actually a small circle of functionaries who drove developments in the direction I have described."[72]

Despite the unrest, Ratzinger was able to complete in 1967 a project he had been planning almost since the beginning of his teaching career: the *Introduction to Christianity: Lectures on the Apostles' Creed.* When it appeared in book form, it was extraordinarily well received, so that only a year later the tenth edition was published and eventually the book was translated into seventeen languages. In the preface to the 1968 edition, Ratzinger compares the development of this restless time with the fairy tale "Lucky Hans":

> Has our theology in the last few years not taken in many ways a similar path? Has it not gradually watered down the demands of faith, which had been found all too demanding, always only so little that nothing important seemed to be lost, yet always so much that it was soon possible to venture on the next step? And will poor [Hans], the Christian who trustingly let himself be led from exchange to exchange, from interpretation to interpretation, not really soon hold in his hand, instead of the gold with which he began, only a whetstone that he can safely be advised to throw away?[73]

Ratzinger himself declares, however, that with these provocative questions he does not intend to pass an unjust judgment on "modern theology"[74] as a whole; instead, he means to portray a widespread mood in the late sixties and the related trend of adapting the Christian message to the spirit of the age, as was manifested (among other ways), in his opinion, in the protest within the Church against the publication of *Humanae vitae.*[75]

---

[71] Wagner/Ruf, 66. Cf. *Salt of the Earth*, 76f.

[72] *Milestones*, 138.

[73] *Introduction*, 31. *Salt of the Earth*, 78. See also H. Häring, "Eine katholische Theologie? J. Ratzinger, das Trauma von Hans im Glück", in Greinacher and Küng, *Katholische Kirche—wohin?* 241–58; Häring, *Ideologie*, 192–95.

[74] *Introduction*, 32.

[75] Cf. W. Beinert, "Eine Kirche, die so bleibt, bleibt nicht: Tradition und Wandel in der Glaubensgemeinschaft", in *Im Spannungsfeld von Tradition und Innovation: Festschrift für Joseph Kardinal Ratzinger*, ed. G. Schmuttermayr et al., 219–48, citation at 229 (Regensburg: Pustet, 1997): "The student revolution of 1968 that broke out immediately after the Council, along with its consequences, which continue to this day, as well as the storm unleashed

The atmosphere at the Theological Faculty in Tübingen, which was troubled on account of the 1968 student revolt, and a desire to be closer to his family[76] prompted Ratzinger to make yet another change of university.

3. In Regensburg—Productive collaboration and separation from Concilium

After the exhausting years in Tübingen, in 1969 Ratzinger answered the call to go to Regensburg to take the second professorial chair for dogmatic theology. In that way he was able to collaborate in the construction of the fourth Bavarian state university, which had just been founded in 1967. During this period he published important works that focus on ecclesiology and other subjects. Particularly noteworthy are *Das neue Volk Gottes: Entwürfe zur Ekklesiologie* [The new People of God: Sketches of an ecclesiology] (1969); *Demokratie in der Kirche: Möglichkeiten, Grenzen, Gefahren* [Democracy in the Church: Possibilities, limits, dangers] (1970, co-written with Hans Maier); *Zwei Plädoyers: Warum ich noch ein Christ bin. Warum ich noch in der Kirche bin"* (1971, together with Hans Urs von Balthasar; English translation: *Two Say Why: Why I Am Still a Christian; Why I Am Still in the Church* [Chicago: Franciscan Herald Press, 1973]; *Dogma und Verkündigung* (1973; English translation: *Dogma and Preaching* [Chicago: Franciscan Herald Press, 1985]); and *Eschatologie—Tod und ewiges Leben* (1977; English translation: *Eschatology: Death and Eternal Life* [Washington, D.C.: Catholic University of America Press, 1988]).

The remarkable thing is that Ratzinger's writings, beyond their didactic character, repeatedly exhibit a markedly spiritual purpose—or, as Michael Fahey described it, an "essentially eschatological feature".[77] In a widely acclaimed presentation to the Catholic Academy in Bavaria on the question of Church renewal, Ratzinger himself declared in 1971:

---

within the Church by the encyclical *Humanae vitae* (published that same year), which has not yet been calmed, can be regarded as signals that prompted the highest authorities in the Church and those lower down to apply the brakes."

[76] Cf. *Milestones*, 140f.

[77] Cf. Fahey, 82. Cf. J. Ratzinger, *Faith and the Future* (Chicago: Franciscan Herald Press, 1970), 89–106. On this subject, see the systematic presentation of Ratzinger's eschatology by G. Nachtwei, *Dialogische Unsterblichkeit: Eine Untersuchung zu Joseph Ratzingers Eschatologie und Theologie*, EThSt 54 (Leipzig: St. Benno Verlag, 1986).

A man becomes a Christian only by repenting.... When reform is dissociated from the hard work of repentance, and seeks salvation merely by changing others, by creating ever fresh forms, and by accommodation to the times, then despite many useful innovations it will be a caricature of itself. Such reform can touch only things of secondary importance in the Church. No wonder, then, that in the end it sees the Church itself as of secondary importance.[78]

a. Appointed to the International Theological Commission

As early as 1969, Ratzinger had been appointed to the newly established International Pontifical Theological Commission. He remarks that it was extremely interesting to see how the individual members of this Commission—almost all of whom "had taken part in the Council, and, within the theological configuration that then obtained, ... could all be said to have a progressive orientation"—had taken "the experiences of the postconciliar period and had defined their own position within them".[79] Ratzinger describes this circumstance in his memoirs as follows:

Henri de Lubac, who had suffered so much under the narrowness of the neoscholastic regime, showed himself to be a decided fighter against the fundamental threat to the faith that now was changing all previous theological positions. Something similar may be said of Philippe Delhaye. Jorge Medina, a theologian from Chile the same age as myself, saw the situation as I did. New friends were arriving: M.-J. Le Guillou, a great expert in Orthodox theology, was fighting for the theology of the Fathers against the dissolution of the faith into political moralism. A mind with a very special character was that of Louis Bouyer, a convert with an extraordinary knowledge of the Fathers, the history of the liturgy, and biblical and Jewish traditions.[80]

In particular, the theological debate about the foundation and contents of Christian ethics struck "the very nerve of the Christian life"[81] at that time. In 1974, Ratzinger sharply criticized the general trend of

---

[78] J. Ratzinger, "Why I Am Still in the Church", in *Two Say Why: Why I Am Still a Christian; Why I Am Still in the Church*, by Hans Urs von Balthasar and Joseph Ratzinger, trans. John Griffiths, 70 (Chicago: Franciscan Herald Press, 1973).

[79] *Milestones*, 142.

[80] Ibid., 142–43.

[81] Ratzinger, *Principles of Christian Morality*, trans. Graham Harrison (San Francisco: Ignatius Press, 1986), 7.

the time, "to view Christianity primarily not as 'orthodoxy' but as 'orthopraxy'",[82] for then "the truth ... [is considered] unattainable, and the insistence on truth is regarded as the ploy of interest groups seeking to confirm their position. According to this view, only praxis can decide the value or worthlessness of theories."[83] To this, Ratzinger opposes the argument that

> Christian praxis is nourished by the core of Christian faith, that is, the grace that appeared in Christ and that is appropriated in the sacrament of the Church. Faith's praxis depends on faith's truth, in which man's truth is made visible and lifted up to a new level by God's truth. Hence, it is fundamentally opposed to a praxis that first wants to produce facts and so establish truth.[84]

By placing the question about truth in the center, Ratzinger provides a response to the overemphasis on orthopraxis, which in his opinion has clearly manifested itself as a trend in theological debate[85] since the plenary assembly of the World Council of Churches in Uppsala in the year 1968.

b. Founding of the *International Catholic Journal Communio*

This concern about giving voice to the primacy of the truth was addressed also by the founding of the *International Catholic Journal*

---

[82] Ibid., 47–73, citation at 47.

[83] Ibid., 48. There is little room—in the mind-set that Ratzinger is depicting—for a Magisterium, since it would appear "as a symptom of particular interests hiding behind the slogan of 'orthodoxy' and opposing the onward march of the history of freedom" (ibid., 49).

[84] Ibid., 70.

[85] Cf. ibid., 47f. See also Fahey, 82. Despite this critique by Ratzinger, the fact that the Catholic Church has been more open to ecumenical dialogue and for the first time sent official representatives (and not just observers) to Uppsala can be taken as a positive sign of the times. Cf. R. Girault, "Die Rezeption des Ökumenismus", in Pottmeyer, Alberigo, and Jossua, *Rezeption des Zweiten Vatikanischen Konzils*, 180–217. A further step in ecumenical *rapprochement* was the 1969 visit of Pope Paul VI to the World Council of Churches in Geneva, where the Pope spoke of that organization as a "wonderful Christian movement" (ibid., 185). See also Ratzinger's report on the conference of the WCC Commission for Faith and Church Constitution in Louvain from August 2 to 12, 1971. This conference left Ratzinger with an overall positive impression, even though he noted the trend "of regarding the faith as indefinable anyway and seeking the unity of Christians in common programs of action instead". See J. Ratzinger, "Einheit der Kirche—Einheit der Menschheit: Ein Tagungsbericht", *IKaZ* 1 (1972): 78–83, citation at 81.

Communio,[86] which appeared for the first time in 1972. The initiative for this process came from Hans Urs von Balthasar,[87] who like Ratzinger belonged to the International Theological Commission, although he had not participated in the Council. According to Ratzinger, two events were decisive for Balthasar in founding the new publication: first, Balthasar's encounter with the blossoming movement *Communione e liberazione*, which had been founded in Italy by Don Giussani. In it Balthasar found "the energy, the willingness to take risks, and the courage of faith that were needed".[88] The second important circumstance was that the last editor of the magazine *Hochland*, Franz Greiner, was willing to bring all of his journalistic experience to bear on behalf of the new *International Catholic Journal Communio*. As editor in chief, he described the stance taken by the new publication as follows in the first issue [of the German edition]:

The abundant ... and often bewildering supply [of ideas] in post-conciliar Catholicism ... has not remedied the need but exacerbated it. Therefore a critical examination of the supply must be ventured. In our ecclesial communion we are increasingly experiencing the formation of fronts, a polarization not only of opinions, but also of faith perspectives and attitudes, which endangers the very

---

[86] On this subject, see the foreword to the first issue of the German edition of *Communio*: F. Greiner, "Vorwort", *IKaZ* 1 (1972): 1–3. One purpose is to address mankind's crisis of faith and of meaning through a new approach that "rises above" the polarization between "right" and "left". Greiner mentions three prerequisites for this: "Catholicity, an international scope, and a new sense of responsibility [*Trägerschaft*]". "*Catholicity* means what is 'universal' in the sense in which Church tradition uses the term; furthermore it means "all-embracing", both globally and regionally, rising above particular denominations and living in and with them; 'embracing the whole truth', and thus those truths also that are not within the parameters of theological thought" (ibid., 2f.).

[87] Cf. J. Ratzinger, "Communio—ein Programm", *IKaZ* 21 (1992): 454–63, ref. at 456. Their first meeting took place as early as the autumn of 1969. Besides Balthasar and Ratzinger, the founding members included Henri de Lubac, Louis Bouyer, Jorge Medina, and M.J. Le Guillou, who later dropped out because of a serious illness. Karl Lehmann likewise supported the project.

[88] Ibid., 456. See also *Milestones*, 145: "In Germany we won the support of Karl Lehmann, a dogmatic theologian then in Freiburg who is now [1998] bishop of Mainz. For a publisher we found Franz Greiner.... To our number were added: Hans Maier, then Bavarian minister of culture, ... the psychologist A. Görres, and O.B. Roegele, professor of journalism in Munich and founder of the *Rheinischer Merkur*."

foundation of the faith that carries us all. We are not willing to accept this development as an inevitable process.[89]

Looking back on those years, one recognizes, despite everything, Ratzinger's joy over this "collaboration in a team of friends", which he numbers among the "most stimulating experiences"[90] of that time. The founding of *Communio* marks at the same time a turning point[91] in Ratzinger's relationship to the theological journal *Concilium*. It gives evidence of a different evaluation of the spirit of the modern age and thus also a different view of the task of theology. This will be explained in more detail in the following paragraphs.

c. Break with the journal *Concilium*—Opposing the reduction of truth to sociology

As publishers of the new international journal *Concilium*, Karl Rahner and Edward Schillebeeckx formulated their purpose in founding the publication in the foreword to the first issue in 1965 as follows:

> In this journal, real scholars in theology want to address the men who do the practical work in the Church, for much in the Church

---

[89] Greiner, "Vorwort", 1; see also Fahey, 82.

[90] Wagner/Ruf, 67.

[91] Cf. H. Vorgrimler, "Vom 'Geist des Konzils'", in Richter, *Konzil*, 40. See Vorgrimler, "Theologische Positionen Karl Rahners im Blick auf Hans Urs von Balthasar", a lecture given on January 12, 2000, in the Karl Rahner Akademie in Cologne, which was accessed at: www.kath.de/akademie/rahner/vortrag/Vorgrim_rahner.htm (March 17, 2002). In the first section of his lecture, Vorgrimler mentions some interesting details concerning the development of the journal *Communio* in opposition to *Concilium*, referring to von Balthasar's relationship to Rahner: "Then I had to witness his estrangement from—indeed, his hostility toward—Karl Rahner, after the publication of his little book *Cordula oder der Ernstfall* in 1966, which was about Rahner's theory of 'being an anonymous Christian', and their clashes in the International Theological Commission in 1969–1970 over the question of the ordained priesthood and its reform. I tried in vain, with the help of Joseph Ratzinger, to change von Balthasar's mind. In 1972 they parted ways, after a twelve-year friendship. Von Balthasar realized, practically overnight, his cherished plan of founding an international theological journal that was supposed to become a deliberate alternative to the Second Vatican Council and the journal that resulted from it, *Concilium*, produced by Rahner and Metz, which I helped to edit also. Together with Joseph Ratzinger, Karl Lehmann, and the politician Hans Maier (among others), he lifted the journal *Communio* out of the baptismal font, massively supported by Church funding. It seemed impossible for me to stand on both sides of the fence, especially since von Balthasar's star was in the ascendant after decades of non-observance in the Vatican, while Rahner's star was beginning to sink there."

depends on the decisions and actions of the latter, and they know, having learned from the experiences of the Council, that practical decisions and the preaching of the gospel today must also learn something from real theological scholarship (and, of course, vice versa).[92]

Concilium deliberately intended to distance itself from the so-called textbook theology of past decades, by declaring Scripture, salvation history, and especially the *condition humaine* as the decisive criteria for its theological work, and it did so with the purpose of seeking "on the basis of our own situation the way ... to a better understanding of God's Word concerning the people and the world of our time".[93] This new understanding of theology already finds expression in the title *Concilium*. It is supposed to have a threefold meaning. First, it is a reference to Vatican II with the intention of continuing to build upon it. Second, the title stands for "the theologians who consult with one another and collaborate (*concilium, con-kalium, concalare*)", and finally it was selected "in gratitude for the initiative of Pope John XXIII, which was so successfully continued by Pope Paul VI".[94] In summary, it means that the publication was supposed to be understood as an instrument of a "never-ending dialogue".[95]

As "the new *Internationale* [Communist anthem] of progress",[96] as Ratzinger dubbed *Concilium* in 1975, the journal intended to be a "permanent organ"[97] for the perpetuation of what Pesch calls "the spirit of the Council".[98] From 1965 to 1972, Ratzinger himself belonged to the editorial board of *Concilium*, as a member of the section for dogmatic theology.[99] At that time Edward

---

[92] K. Rahner and E. Schillebeeckx, "Wozu und für wen eine neue internationale theologische Zeitschrift?", *Conc(D)* 1 (1965): 1–3, citation at 1.

[93] Ibid.

[94] Ibid., 2.

[95] Ibid.

[96] *Principles*, 383.

[97] Ibid.

[98] Cf. Pesch, 160: "Geist und Buchstabe" [spirit and letter]. See also Häring, *Ideologie*, 36f., n. 17.

[99] In April 1971, the general assembly of the editorial board of *Concilium* decided on a reorganization of the journal, which went into effect on January 1, 1973. One substantial innovation was the plan to structure each issue around a theme; that is, in each issue one topic would be treated in an interdisciplinary manner. See "Das neue Gesicht des 'Concilium'", trans. A. Berz, in *Conc(D)* 8 (1972): 705–7, ref. at 705f.

Schillebeeckx[100] from Nijmegen was editor in chief for that section. As Ratzinger explains in retrospect, the international editorial staff, scattered throughout the world, originally pursued the following goal:

> They wanted to be, as it were, a permanent council of theologians that would increasingly realize the promise of this beginning in a constant exchange with all the vital forces of the present. If conciliarity as the new form of Catholicity meant to internationalize national tendencies, this automatically implied that from now on the tendencies of the varied particular churches would also have a determinative impact and that it could no longer be expected that the direction would be set by a single central source.[101]

Ratzinger observes that tensions among the staff who collaborated on *Concilium* became increasingly evident,[102] particularly between the Latin American theologians, whose experience of the spirit of Western capitalism had been anything but "liberating",[103] and the theologians from western Europe and North America, who viewed reconciliation with the spirit of modernity as "a return home from the ghetto".[104] Consequently, the genuine international collaboration that had been expected proved, in Ratzinger's opinion, to be flawed, because "its very foundation, namely, union in the spirit of the modern era",[105] could no longer support the weight of the structure. Interestingly enough, this difficulty is pointed out also in an essay by Michael Fahey that appeared in 1981 in the journal *Concilium*; Fahey, like Ratzinger, recognizes

---

[100] At that time Edward Schillebeeckx, O.P., was a professor of dogmatic theology in Nijmegen (1953–1983).

[101] *Principles*, 383.

[102] On this subject, see ibid., 385.

[103] Cf. A. García, "Die lateinamerikanische Theologie der Befreiung", *IKaZ* 2 (73): 400–423, esp. 406f. The rise of liberation theology signifies a crisis of modernity, because Latin America recognized no vision of liberation in Western-style "progress" but rather saw in this spirit of the Enlightenment precisely the reason for its reduction to poverty.

[104] Cf. *Principles*, 385.

[105] See ibid.: "In view of these circumstances, it seemed only logical that progressive Latin Americans should level sharp criticism precisely against the representatives of progressive European and North American thought. Hans Küng was accused of a shockingly reactionary political attitude and of being blind to the practical dimensions of the problem. The theology of secularization was criticized for its lack of clarity and its political naiveté."

that the cause of the crisis in the late sixties was the reduction of truth to a sociological issue.

During those years, Ratzinger began to take a stance against political theology and the various views of liberation theologians. He warned about those who borrowed much too much from the philosophers—from Marx to Marcuse—and gave the impression that we could have a world without suffering, but only through societal reforms.... In 1972, however, he cites as the cause for confusion and conflict the "new consciousness" that is based essentially on the increasing "socialization of the question of truth". "Thus ... in this new situation a most important task could devolve upon the Church's liturgy: to counter the retreat into positivism and sociology, to keep open the question of truth, and to insist on addressing it." [106]

The secularization, relativization, and subjectivization of the question of truth [107] in the modern era, which acknowledges only what is empirically demonstrable, showed—as Ratzinger puts it—that "the concept of truth had practically been abandoned and replaced by that of progress." [108] But when man's ability to apprehend truth is called into question or abolished, all truth propositions become optional as well.

In many places today, people no longer ask *what* a person thinks. They have their judgment upon his thinking ready at hand if they can assign him to the appropriate formal category: conservative,

---

[106] Fahey, 82. Fahey quotes here J. Ratzinger: "Was eint und was trennt die Konfessionen?" *IKaZ* 1 (1972): 171–77, citation at 173.

[107] Ratzinger, "Ohne Glaube an Christus zerfällt alles in reine Tradition: Die anderen Religionen, die Ökumene, der Dialog mit den Juden; ein Gespräch mit Kardinal Joseph Ratzinger über den Wahrheitsanspruch des Christentums", *Die Tagespost* 52, no. 127 (October 23, 1999): 5.

[108] *Prüfsteine*, 45. Cf. Ratzinger, "Die Situation der Kirche heute—Hoffnungen und Gefahren", in *Festvortrag beim Priestertreffen (J. Ratzinger) und Ansprache beim Pontifikalamt (Kardinal J. Höffner) anlässlich des 60-jährigen Priesterjubiläums von Kardinal Josef Frings*, ed. Presseamt des Erzbistums Köln, 18 (Cologne, 1971). Ratzinger points out in his lecture that with the loss of transcendence (in the "God is dead" mentality), "truth, justice, and love necessarily disappear.... When there is no longer a nature of things and of men that is established by God, but only successive developments and functions; when the mind is only a product of material developments, ... then no lasting point of reference remains by which to distinguish between true and untrue, good and evil. All that is left is the function of development and the pragmatic decision of man, for which he himself sets the standards according to his particular perspective."

reactionary, fundamentalist, progressive, revolutionary. The sche-
matic classification suffices, making it unnecessary to deal with the
substance.[109]

In this connection Ratzinger complains with uncharacteristic bit-
terness about the role of public opinion, which also locks theologians
into the factional framework: It "needs to have clear-cut rules, and
admits of no nuances: a person has to be either a progressive or a
conservative."[110]

As early as 1962, Ratzinger contrasted the various forms of relativizing the question of truth with the demand for a "sober obedience
... that comes from the truth and leads into the truth".[111]

What the Church of today (and of all times) needs is not eulogists
for the status quo, but rather men whose humility and obedience is
as great as their passion for the truth; men who give witness despite
all sorts of misunderstandings and opposition; in a word, men who
love the Church more than comfort and an uncontested path through
life.[112]

Passion for the truth and love for the Church are expressed in that
sentire cum ecclesia [thinking with the Church] which seemed in danger
of shattering precisely in the time immediately after the Council. In
an allusion to Romano Guardini, Ratzinger therefore laments that the
Church was being extinguished in the souls of believers.[113] Against
the background of what we have just presented, the much-disputed
question[114] arises of whether the collapse of ecclesial and social

---

[109] *Prüfsteine*, 48. Cf. *Turning Point*, 174. The following remark by Ratzinger can serve
to illustrate the situation in theology: "Horkheimer and Adorno, with the clear sight of the
outsider, have denounced the attempt by theologians to sneak past the core of the faith,
removing the provocatory character of the Trinity and life beyond death as well as of the
biblical narratives by reducing these to the level of symbols. They tell us that when theologians bracket off dogma, what they say has no validity; they bow to that 'fear of the
truth' in which the spiritual and intellectual decline of the present day has its roots."
[110] Ratzinger, "Why I Am Still in the Church", 68.
[111] *Volk Gottes*, 71–90: "Freimut und Gehorsam", citation at 87.
[112] Ibid.
[113] See Ratzinger, "Why I Am Still in the Church", 67.
[114] On this subject, see the introductory article by D. Mieth and C. Theobald, "Unbeantwortete Fragen", *Conc(D)* 35 (1999): 1–3, citation at 1, concerning the first issue in the
volume that is dedicated to the theme of "Unfinished Business after the Council". "The

paradigms,[115] which in Ratzinger's opinion also drew *Concilium* in its wake, brought about a change in his own theological thought, from a progressive stance to one in favor of restoration. A preview of the chapter on his understanding of the hierarchical constitution of the Church[116] shows that modifications can be noted in Ratzinger's ecclesiology. Whether they are the expression of an altered perspective or whether they indicate a change in his thinking will be examined in more detail in the following chapter.

Second Vatican Council was a transitional Council. It was well aware that not only would new questions surface very quickly, but also new paradigms and new procedures would have to be found; this was so precisely on account of its open perspective (the pastoral orientation of its teaching, *aggiornamento*, and so on). The Council was then actually received in two different ways. The 'official reception' continues to rely on the classical distinction between doctrine and discipline, so as to fit the new (Second Vatican Council) gradually into the old (Council of Trent and First Vatican Council). Simultaneously the 'practical reception' brings to light new problems from the base and, along with them, new experiences and attempts, which in turn open up paths to new solutions. The turbulent history of our journal *Concilium*, founded thirty-five years ago, is a reflection of this process in which there are so many tensions, in which it has become more and more difficult to connect the historical and cultural differences of the various contexts with the normative structure of the Christian tradition."

[115] Cf. H.J. Pottmeyer, "Kirche—Selbstverständnis und Strukturen: Theologische und gesellschaftliche Herausforderung zur Glaubwürdigkeit", in *Kirche im Kontext der modernen Gesellschaft*, ed. Pottmeyer, 99–123 (Munich and Zurich: Schnell und Steiner, 1989).

[116] See pt. 2, sec. 2, chap. 3, in this work "The Hierarchical Constitution of the work: Church, in Particular with Regard to Episcopal Collegiality".

Chapter 3

Consistency in Ratzinger's Theological Thought Despite a Change of Perspective?

As a matter of principle for Ratzinger, there is no contradiction between tradition and progress. "Tradition properly understood is, in effect, the transcendence of today in both directions. The past can be discovered as something to be preserved only if the future is regarded as a duty; discovery of the future and discovery of the past are inseparably connected, and it is this discovery of the indivisibility of time that actually makes tradition." [1] With reference to the reception of the Council, he says that this implies that one should not subscribe to an "anti-historical, utopian interpretation" [2] of Vatican II that strays ever farther from its point of departure, that is, the actual conciliar documents. By that he means "an increasingly narrow postconciliar progressivism" that derives its initial approach from "the theology of the world . . . that J. B. Metz developed by combining Karl Rahner's transcendental-philosophical reinterpretation of Thomism with Friedrich Gogarten's explanation of the world, which was inspired by Luther". [3] According to Ratzinger's analysis, such a "theology of the world" developed under the influence of Ernst Bloch into the "theology of hope", which then led to "political theology". From this, in turn, proceeded the pragmatic approach to theology, that is, the primacy

---

[1] *Principles*, 87. On p. 101 of the same book, Ratzinger reflects that "the most rabid forms of progressivism are forms of archaeologism", because in form they resemble statements by traditionalists, who likewise close off tradition at some point or other. Cf. also Ratzinger, *Faith and the Future* (Chicago: Franciscan Herald Press, 1971), 93–106.

[2] *Dogma*, 439–47: "Epilog—Zehn Jahre nach Konzilsbeginn—wo stehen wir?" citation at 443.

[3] Ibid.

of orthopraxis over orthodoxy. When, however (in Ratzinger's words), "Christianity is interpreted as 'orthopraxy' not only pragmatically but in principle, the basic issue is the question of truth, of what is reality."[4]

In contrast to this, ten years after the beginning of the Council, Ratzinger himself was already calling for a "creatively spiritual understanding [of Vatican II] in vital unity with authentic tradition".[5] At the same time, he characterized selectivity of any sort—for example, affirming the Second Vatican Council while departing from the Council of Trent or Vatican I, or else acknowledging the Council of Trent and the First Vatican Council while rejecting the most recent Council—as being destructive for the Church, because anyone who rejects one council denies the authority of the others also.[6] In Ratzinger's view, "to defend the true tradition of the Church today means to defend the Council."[7] Therefore the habit of speaking about the preconciliar and postconciliar Church is to him absurd. All the more so, since the Second Vatican Council itself did not intend this dichotomy, because it was always concerned with progress on the basis of tradition.[8]

Now critics repeatedly raise the objection that there was a discontinuity[9] in Ratzinger's theological development; if this could be proved, it would contradict the notion of tradition that was just outlined, that is, the transcendence of today in both directions, toward the past and toward the future. Therefore the two-part question arises of whether Ratzinger remained faithful to his understanding of tradition or whether a break can be noted in the development of his theology.

---

[4] Ratzinger, *Principles of Christian Morality*, trans. Graham Harrison (San Francisco: Ignatius Press, 1986), 51.

[5] *Dogma*, 443.

[6] Cf. *Report*, 28.

[7] Ibid., 31.

[8] Cf. ibid., 35.

[9] Cf. H. Vorgrimler, "Vom 'Geist des Konzils' ", in Richter, *Konzil*, 25–52. Regarding a concrete change in Ratzinger's position vis-à-vis the status of the bishops' conference, see H.J. Pottmeyer, "Der theologische Status der Bischofskonferenz—Positionen, Klärungen und Prinzipien", in *Die Bischofskonferenz: Theologischer und juristischer Status*, with contributions by I. Führer et al., ed. H. Müller and H.J. Pottmeyer, 44–87, esp. 56f. (Düsseldorf: Patmos, 1989).

§ 1. The Council: "The Beginning of the Beginning"?

Not infrequently Ratzinger is accused of subscribing more and more to the conservative movement[10] in the Church, which is characterized by a "serious loss of any sense of reality",[11] in Herbert Vorgrimler's judgment. Ratzinger himself, on the contrary, emphasizes the consistency[12] of his theological thinking. During his interview with Vittorio Messori, published as a book entitled *The Ratzinger Report*, which started a lively debate in 1985, the interviewer asked Ratzinger whether his collaboration in the past with *Concilium*, in comparison to his position today, was "a false step [or] a youthful transgression".[13] Ratzinger made a lapidary reply:

> It is not I who have changed, but others. At our very first meetings I pointed out two prerequisites to my colleagues. The first one: our group must not lapse into any kind of sectarianism or arrogance, as if we were the new, the true Church, an alternative magisterium with a monopoly on the truth of Christianity. The second one: discussion has to be conducted without any individualistic flights forward, in confrontation with the reality of Vatican II, with the

---

[10] Cf. Häring, *Ideologie*, 29. In Häring's judgment, the content of Ratzinger's theology has not changed, but "his determination has hardened, along with his decision to follow uncompromisingly the line of alleged service to the Church. As for the contents, he has buried himself in his conventional convictions. Yet he has heightened the urgency with which he has been drawing the battle lines."

[11] Vorgrimler, "Vom 'Geist des Konzils'", 25–52, esp. 40–47. Vorgrimler summarizes "the theses of Cardinal Ratzinger" set forth in the book *The Ratzinger Report* as follows: "All in all, what emerges from this 'analysis of the crisis [in the Church]' is the picture of a serious loss of any sense of reality. The remedies for the crisis that Ratzinger mentions here are no less problematic than the portrayal of the crisis" (ibid., 42).

[12] The question of consistency was raised again in Häring, *Ideologie*, 57. Häring passes the following judgment: "Now Ratzinger certainly is right about one thing: Personally he has not changed at all, not even in the least. The spirit of Vatican II has hardly inspired him. Unfortunately he does not see the rigidity and immobility of the system and of his own theological biography as a problem." Weiler makes a contrary statement (315): "As I have shown, with regard to ecclesiology, [Ratzinger] was one of the ones responsible . . . for the 'spirit', that is, the theological perspectives and emphases of the Council. . . . Already during the Council and especially afterward, Ratzinger never tired of criticizing this 'spirit of the Council', by stating basically the same ecclesiological ideas that a few years before had earned him the reputation of being a 'progressive' conciliar theologian."

[13] *Report*, 18.

true letter and the true spirit of the Council, not with an imaginary Vatican III.[14]

Ratzinger determines that around the year 1973 there was a change in the theological treatment of the documents of the Second Vatican Council. In his judgment, for quite a few theologians they were now no longer an obligatory point of reference, but only a "point of departure", "the beginning of a beginning",[15] so as to "surpass" the Council and to "move forward".[16] For this reason, in 1975 Ratzinger posed the question:

> Are we, then, to interpret the whole Council as a progressive movement that led step by step from a beginning that, in the "Dogmatic Constitution on the Church", was only just emerging from traditionalism to the "Pastoral Constitution" and its complementary texts on religious liberty and openness to other world religions—an interpretation that makes these texts, too, become signposts pointing to an extended evolution that will permit no dallying but requires a tenacious pursuit of the direction the Council has finally discovered?[17]

The basis for this account of the influence of *Gaudium et spes*—to Ratzinger's way of thinking, a problematic account—was principally, as he says, the "spirit of the preface" of the Pastoral Constitution and its "ambiguity", which lies especially in its use of the terms "world", "dialogue", and "optimism".[18] The "world" is interpreted in that document largely "in a pretheological stage"[19] as something distinct from the Church, so that there is a striving for cooperation between the

---

[14] Ibid., 18–19. Ratzinger makes this claim in his own behalf: "I have always tried to remain true to Vatican II, to this *today* of the Church, without any longing for a *yesterday* irretrievably gone with the wind and without any impatient thrust toward a *tomorrow* that is not ours" (ibid., 19).

[15] Cf., for example, J. B. Metz, "Das Konzil—'der Anfang eines Anfangs'?" in Richter, *Konzil*, 11–24, citation at 11. "Which will prevail: an offensive or a defensive form of fidelity to this Council and to the preservation of Church traditions? Karl Rahner, himself an influential conciliar theologian, spoke of this Council as the 'beginning of a beginning', as the seed of a spiritual awakening to a new epoch in Church history, which must be taken into account in a daring fidelity."

[16] *Report*, 19.

[17] *Principles*, 378.

[18] Ibid., 379–81.

[19] Ibid., 379.

Church and the world, whereby the Church can emerge from her
ghetto of closing herself off from the world. This interpretation of
Gaudium et spes, then, in connection with *Nostra aetate* and *Dignitatis
humanae*, presents—in Ratzinger's words—"a revision of the *Syllabus*
of Pius IX, a kind of countersyllabus".[20] Thereby, in Ratzinger's judgment, a fundamentally new definition of the relationship of the Church
to the world would be undertaken. Ratzinger understands the second concept from the preface of *Gaudium et spes*, "dialogue",[21] as a
sort of colloquium, "as a speaking with one another and as a mutual
search for solutions in which the Church brings to bear her own
particular contributions and hopes that with the contributions of others progress will be made".[22] Since the goal of dialogue is the building of a humane society, in his view a "concentration on current
pragmatic, economic, political and social tasks"[23] comes to the fore.
Finally, the third characteristic theme of the preface to *Gaudium et
spes* to be noted is "optimism". Ratzinger says in retrospect, ten
years after the end of the Council, that people believed that if the
world and the Church worked together, nothing would be impossible any more:

> The affirmation of the present that was sounded in Pope John
> XXIII's address at the opening of the Council is carried to its
> logical conclusion; solidarity with today seems to be the pledge of
> a new tomorrow. The basic determining factor of the whole seems
> to me to lie in the relationship between goal and means. The
> Church cooperates with the world for the building up of society.
> She hopes in this way "to carry on the work of Christ": namely,
> "to bear witness to the truth", "to serve and not to be served".....
> The social commitment evidenced in this dialogue with the world
> is presented here as a task directly imposed by the gospel so that
> its truth can exert its full influence.... Its relationship with social
> action is thus a unique one of tension between goal and means in

---

[20] Ibid., 381.

[21] Cf. *GS* 3, where it says: "Hence, giving witness and voice to the faith of the whole
people of God gathered together by Christ, this council can provide no more eloquent
proof of its solidarity with, as well as its respect and love for, the entire human family with
which it is bound up than by engaging with it in conversation about these various problems."

[22] *Principles*, 380.

[23] Ibid.

which social activity is to be understood predominantly as concrete action.[24]

Thus, as early as 1975, Ratzinger distrusts this amalgamation of truth
with pragmatism. Precisely this emphasis on what is "praxeological"
leads to a "farewell to the metaphysics" of history.[25] As he sees it, the
two contrary phenomena just mentioned (the study of praxis/the truth)
are typical of the debate about genuine fidelity to the Council[26] during the postconciliar phase.[27] They explain why "the actual statements and purposes of Vatican II could be consigned to oblivion, so
as to be replaced first by the utopia of a forthcoming Vatican III and
then by synods, which would at any rate honor the 'spirit' but not the
documents of Vatican II."[28] But if these documents are only the point
of departure or only a dynamic forward movement and no longer the
crystallization of the Church's faith convictions,[29] then in Ratzinger's
opinion one can sneak past the conciliar text itself and cite instead as
one's authority this indefinite "spirit of the Council". That is why he
asks in 1975:

Does this mean that the Council itself must be revoked? Certainly
not. It means only that the real reception of the Council has not yet
even begun. What devastated the Church in the decade after the
Council was not the Council but the refusal to accept it.... The
task is not, therefore, to suppress the Council but to discover the

---

[24] Ibid., 380–81.

[25] On this subject, see *Dogma*, 441.

[26] Metz, on the contrary, interprets fidelity to the Council, for example, as the duty to
make "the history of the Council's influence within the Church, in short, the conciliar
tradition that has already been established within the Church" as the standard for interpreting it. By this he understands first and foremost the development of the Church into
a "polycentric World Church", as well as the discovery of the new "dignity and authority
attributed by the Council to the lay faithful themselves". See Metz, "Das Konzil—'der
Anfang eines Anfangs'?" 12.

[27] This phase extends to the beginning of the year 1989.

[28] *Dogma*, 441. By "synods" here are meant, not the postconciliar synods of bishops, but
rather imaginary synods that would deliberately distance themselves from the actual statements and purposes of Vatican II. Cf. "Demokratisierung 2", 84: "At synods and diocesan
forums there is a great temptation to give in to pastoral slogans and to parrot their standardized demands."

[29] On this subject, see Pesch, 160. Pesch, in contrast, views it as a positive development
if the conciliar dynamic no longer prescribes a specific "praxis".

real Council and to deepen its true intention in the light of present experience.[30]

As Pesch rightly remarks, Ratzinger had "counted on 'the future elaboration and development' of the conciliar compromises",[31] in the sense in which the majority understood them, of course. In 1965, Ratzinger was in agreement with Karl Rahner in saying that everything that the Council decided "can serve [only] as a beginning; its real importance is achieved only in its translation into the realities of everyday Church life."[32] At this point in my dissertation, then, the problem arises of whether the claim that Ratzinger abandoned his own earlier positions corresponds to reality or not.

§ 2. Betrayal of His Former Positions?

Ratzinger replies to the accusation that he has betrayed his own positions by pointing out that it never was his purpose to develop "a system of my own, an individual theology".[33] The peculiar feature of his theology is its ecclesial dimension, that is, the intention "to think in communion with the faith of the Church" and especially "with the great thinkers of the faith".[34] In doing so, he is concerned with concentrating, simplifying, and deepening the faith; he wants to update [aggiornieren] the faith,[35] as Pope John XXIII intended. This fundamental attitude of Ratzinger, however, does not exclude differently nuanced expressions of his theological findings. These are conditioned also by biographical vicissitudes:

---

[30] Principles, 390–91.
[31] Pesch, 160. See "Kommentar", 349. Cf. also M. Seckler, "Über den Kompromiss in Sachen der Lehre", in Seckler, Im Spannungsfeld von Wissenschaft und Kirche: Theologie als schöpferische Auslegung der Wirklichkeit (Freiburg im Breisgau: Herder, 1980), 99–103.
[32] Highlights, 131. See also ibid., 183: "What happened in Rome was only the formulation of a mandate whose execution must now be undertaken."
[33] Salt of the Earth, 66. Concerning criticism leveled against Ratzinger, see, for example, H. Häring, "Eine katholische Theologie? J. Ratzinger, das Trauma von Hans im Glück", in Katholische Kirche—wohin? Wider den Verrat am Konzil, ed. N. Greinacher and H. Küng, 241–58 (Munich: Piper, 1986).
[34] Salt of the Earth, 66.
[35] Cf. ibid., 73.

Although the constellations in which I have found myself—and naturally also the periods of life and their different influences—have led to changes and development in the accents of my thought, my basic impulse, precisely during the Council, was always to free up the authentic kernel of the faith from encrustations and to give this kernel strength and dynamism. This impulse is the constant of my life. It would also have ruled out my withdrawing into an anti-Church opposition. Naturally the office gives an accentuation that isn't present as such when you are a professor. But nonetheless what's important to me is that I have never deviated from this constant, which from my childhood has molded my life, and that I have remained true to it as the basic direction of my life.[36]

In this resolute loyalty to the Church, Ratzinger was opposed, even before the end of the Council, to an *aggiornamento* that consists exclusively of modernization[37] and does not bring the uniquely Christian message to bear.[38] For him, *aggiornamento* is "a process that presupposes the faith and takes place within the faith".[39] This faith "is more laborious because it has become more exposed and defenseless",[40] Ratzinger remarked in 1966 at the Catholic Congress in Bamberg. Within the faith, the mystery of the Cross shines forth, because in every age the faith is bound up with the scandal of the Cross, for this scandal is "irrevocable . . . if we are not to abolish Christianity".[41]

Thus Ratzinger was concerned with the essentials of the faith that should not be called into question by *aggiornamento*. As early as 1970, he remarked in a jubilee lecture in honor of Cardinal Frings that "the consequences of the Council were quite different" from what had been expected "in the struggles of those days in Rome".[42] That was also the reason why corrections on the part of the Magisterium were delayed for so long. When the Congregation for the Doctrine of the Faith

---

[36] Ibid., 79.
[37] See the essay "Was heißt Erneuerung der Kirche", in *Volk Gottes*, 91–106, ref. at 93.
[38] Ibid., 94f.
[39] Ibid., 95.
[40] Ibid., 129–51: "Der Katholizismus nach dem Konzil", citation at 130.
[41] Ibid., 146f.
[42] Ratzinger, "Die Situation der Kirche heute—Hoffnungen und Gefahren", in *Festvortrag beim Priestertreffen (J. Ratzinger) und Ansprache beim Pontifikalamt (Kardinal J. Höffner) anlässlich des 60-jährigen Priesterjubiläums von Kardinal Josef Frings*, ed. Presseamt des Erzbistums Köln, 21 (Cologne, 1971).

condemned erroneous ecclesiological teachings on June 24, 1973, with
the instruction *Mysterium Ecclesiae*, Ratzinger as a theology professor
reacted approvingly:

> Everyone knows that the Catholic Church today has entered a stage
> of momentous internal tensions. It really ought to be clear also that
> the organs of Church government cannot simply remain silent in
> this situation, but must do their part in order to overcome the cri-
> sis. The people in the Church are calling more and more urgently
> for clear lines to be drawn, but so far the Pope and the bishops have
> been unable to make the decision to do so.[43]

Against the background of this statement arises the new question of
whether Ratzinger perhaps corrected the stances he had taken earlier
precisely in order to react to the paradigm shift in the Church and in
the world in the late sixties.

§ 3. Corrections through a Change of Perspective

In a loyalty to the Magisterium that has been matured by critical
reflection—especially loyalty to the declarations of the Council—it is
possible, as Ratzinger admits, for new perspectives to result through a
change in the spatial and temporal coordinates of one's points of reference, and the fresh perspectives can relativize earlier ways of looking
at a subject.

> Let's put it this way: time can certainly bring correction. I can sim-
> ply learn through dialogue that I haven't seen this or that matter
> properly. On the other hand, I couldn't deny a present conviction
> that I had reached to the best of my abilities. That isn't possible,
> you see. On the other hand, a development through further learn-
> ing that also brings a correction of past views is entirely within the
> realm of possibility.[44]

Adjustment, change, and maturation are even necessary, as signs of
life, in order to preserve one's own continuity, which is a sign of

---

[43] Ratzinger, "Ökumenisches Dilemma? Zur Diskussion um die Erklärung *Mysterium Ecclesiae*", *IKaZ* 3 (1974): 56–63, citation at 56.

[44] *Salt of the Earth*, 15.

consistency: "I don't deny that there has been development and change in my life, but I hold firmly that it is a development and change within a fundamental identity and that I, precisely in changing, have tried to remain faithful to what I have always had at heart."[45] This continuity in Ratzinger's thought, acknowledged by M. Fahey[46] and also by G. Lohaus,[47] D. Seeber,[48] R. Frieling,[49] and G. Nacht-wei,[50] is denied, however, by some theologians, who accuse Ratzinger of deviating from his earlier theological views.[51] In contrast, Hermann Häring takes up a middle position. In his opinion, Ratzinger's "writings from 1965 to 1970" can be judged "unambiguously only in connection with his later development".[52] For this reason Häring

---

[45] Ibid., 116.

[46] Cf. Fahey, 79.

[47] Lohaus, 243f.: "Even in his *preconciliar* publications, Ratzinger's concern is clear: to show that the Church is a sacramental, eucharistic communion. . . . Insofar as the 'theme' of Church is concerned, the Prefect of the Congregation for the Faith argues no differently from the theologian." Given the "(over-)emphasis on the local Church at that time", the fact that Ratzinger stresses the universal Church could offer "a necessary corrective, so to speak" (ibid., 244).

[48] Cf. D. Seeber, "Kardinal Ratzinger: Wechsel nach Rom", *HerKorr* 36 (1982): 4–7, ref. at 6: "Both as a theologian and as a bishop—contrary to many suppositions, changes in this regard can be noted that correspond to the atmospheric highs and lows in the Church, but these are by no means ruptures—Ratzinger always proved to be a man of the Church."

[49] R. Frieling, "Der Ökumenismus Ratzingers", *MdKI* 33 (1982): 64–70, ref. at 64.

[50] Nachtwei, 284, cites the judgment by M. Fahey.

[51] S. Toiviainen speaks of a clear transformation in Ratzinger's thought. On this subject, compare the German-language summary of his dissertation, *Subjektista objektiin: Painopisteen muutos Joseph Ratzingerin transsendentaalisessa ajattelumuodossa 1954–1981* (Helsinki: Helsinki Suomalainen teologinen kirjallisuusseura, 1993), 290–305: "Vom Subjekt zum Object: Verschiebung des Schwerpunktes in der transzendentalen Denkform von Joseph Ratzinger in den Jahren 1954–1981" [From the subject to the object: The shift of emphasis in the transcendental form of Joseph Ratzinger's thought in the years 1954–1981], esp. ibid., 303. Hans Küng claims that the early Ratzinger, a theological reformer, changed into an anxious prophet of doom: H. Küng, *Kardinal Ratzinger, Papst Wojtyla und die Angst vor der Freiheit* (1985). "Nach langem Schweigen ein offenes Wort", in Greinacher and Küng, *Katholische Kirche—wohin?* 389–407, ref. at 392. See also U. F. Schmälzle, "Bekehrung oder Neurose? Der Weg der Kirche nach dem II. Vatikanum unter dem Anspruch der Selbstevangelisierung", in Richter, *Konzil*, 119–39, esp. 121. Here Schmälzle contrasts Ratzinger's commentary on article 20 of *Gaudium et spes* (Ratzinger, "Kommentar zu Artikel 11–22 der Pastoralkonstitution *Gaudium et spes*", in *LThK.E*, vol. 3 [Freiburg im Breisgau: Herder, 1968], 313–54, ref. at 340–43), with his discussion of "The Status of Church and Theology Today" (*Principles*, 367–393, esp. 372f.).

[52] Häring, "Eine katholische Theologie?" 243. Häring develops the same line of argument in *Ideologie*, 29f.

sees Ratzinger "as the strategist for the turn back"[53] that was already defined in Ratzinger's *Introduction to Christianity*.

In her dissertation, Dorothee Kaes demonstrates that Ratzinger's theology developed from a primacy of salvation history "to a stronger emphasis on the metaphysical level".[54] This development, however, does not disrupt his fidelity to his overall concept that the Church is the place where the faith is authenticated as times change.[55] Christoph Schönborn, too, showed in an unpublished talk that, in interpreting the Council, Ratzinger has always remained faithful to his principle; that is, he has conscientiously distinguished between "mere adaptation to the spirit of the age" and "genuine renewal, the renewal of what is essentially Christian".[56]

Ratzinger himself tried to answer the question of what genuine reform means to him in a lecture he gave in June 1965 to the Catholic Student Union in Münster. We will turn to his discussion of this question in the following paragraphs.

§ 4. Ratzinger's View of Church Renewal[57]

John XXIII had already made it clear that the goal of the reform movement of Vatican II could not be a different, new Church, but only her renewal in the power of the Holy Spirit.[58] The Council itself speaks of the Church in *Gaudium et spes* as the "faithful spouse of her Lord", but also about her members' lack of fidelity.[59] Therefore, Ratzinger says, the reform of the Church begins with the personal renewal of the individual, so that "what belongs to Christ" will not be obscured

---

[53] Häring, "Eine katholische Theologie?" 244.

[54] Kaes, 95–120, citation at 97.

[55] Ibid., 119.

[56] Ibid., 20. Kaes refers to Schönborn's talk "Theology—Magisterium—Faith: A Chronic Conflict? Introduction to the Theological Thought of Cardinal Ratzinger", given on September 14, 1985, in St. Georgen/Längsee.

[57] See *Volk Gottes*, 91–105.

[58] Pope John XXIII hoped that the Council would bring about a new Pentecost in the Church; on this subject, see *AD* 1, 1:19 and 24.

[59] *GS* 43.

by sinful human structures.[60] Hence in June 1965, even before the end of the Council, Ratzinger opposed a twofold misunderstanding of reform. First he distanced himself from a form of "Pharisaism" that tries to reduce the essence of ecclesial renewal to external, demonstrable change and action; reform "does not consist in an abundance of external exercises and arrangements, but rather in one thing: being fully in the brotherhood of Christ".[61] Secondly, he warns about the "Sadducean misunderstanding" of reform. Her renewal is understood as a kind of simplification that makes things *trite* instead of simple.[62] Viewed positively, renewal in the Spirit has two dimensions, according to Ratzinger. First, it is unthinkable without man's cooperation—herein is manifested the historical dimension of the Church—and secondly, it must be open to the mystery of Christ. In the first instance, it becomes apparent that reform, as God's work through the cooperation of men, always bears the historical traits of incompleteness and striving for what is yet to come. Therefore the Church must not close herself off from the signs of the times but, rather, must constantly seek an appropriate answer in the particular time and in the particular situation in which she proclaims God's Word. And this specific mission of the Church conceals within it a dynamic that is based on the Word of God itself. For the Word of God, which has come into the world, brings about transformation and not conformity with the world.

Only in this poverty of a desecularized Church, which has opened herself to the world so as to free herself from its entanglement, will her missionary aspiration also become completely credible again. . . . She advertises and recruits, not for herself, but for him whose lot she has drawn: "The Lord is my lot and my portion . . .". Only the desecularized Church can devote herself to the whole world in a truly Christian manner, not so as to win it over to an institution with its own claims to power, but rather so as to bring it back to

---

[60] *Report*, 49–53, esp. 53: "Hence, true 'reform' does not mean to take great pains to erect new façades (contrary to what certain ecclesiologies think). Real 'reform' is to strive to let what is ours disappear as much as possible so what belongs to Christ may become more visible." Cf. also *Called to Communion*, 140–47.

[61] *Volk Gottes*, 104. Cf. ibid., 101: "The important thing is not that a lot happens, but rather that the truth should come to pass in truthfulness, for without truthfulness, truth has lost its soul and has become ineffective even as truth."

[62] Ibid., 105f.

itself by bringing it to the one about whom every man can say: *Interior est intimo meo, superior superiori meo*—the one who is so infinitely above me is nevertheless so fully within me that he is my true inmost being.[63]

Thus Ratzinger characterizes the "openness to the world", of the individual as well as of the whole Church, as a "desecularizing opening-up of the world" and asks critically whether the opening-up of the Church by Vatican II did justice to this demand, which is valid for all times. This implies another thought: whether the last Council with its interpretation of "openness to the world" was itself in continuity or discontinuity with the previous Council and with the Magisterium. Ratzinger answers this question as follows:

> Compared with certain trends of development in the nineteenth and the first half of the twentieth century, it [the Council] no doubt constitutes a rupture, yet it is a rupture within a common basic intention. One could say that the Council marks the transition from a conservationist to a missionary attitude, and the conciliar alternative to "conservative" is not "progressive", but rather "missionary". In this antithesis is found basically the precise meaning of what conciliar "opening-up to the world" means and what it does not mean. It does not provide the Christian with greater comfort by setting him free to conform to the world in a fashionable mass culture—the Council could never do that, because as a Christian event it was bound to the nonconformism of the Bible: "Do not be conformed to this world" (Rom 12:2).[64]

According to Ratzinger, this "desecularized openness to the world" results in a second dimension for renewal in the Spirit, namely, opening oneself for the mystery of Christ, so as to participate in his freedom, for "where the Spirit of the Lord is, there is freedom".[65] In this second dimension, a Christian dialectic takes effect: The more united to the Lord the Church is, the freer she is. The more she participates

---

[63] Ibid., 107–28, citation at 126f.

[64] Ibid., 128. In this tension between missionary duty and confronting a world that is closed in on itself, the Crucified, "the Lamb [that] . . . had been slain" (Rev 5:6), becomes the place where the world is broken open, where guilt is transformed into grace.

[65] 2 Cor 3:17; see *Volk Gottes*, 71–90, ref. at 90.

in his divine freedom, the more authentic her human features become.[66] For this reason, renewal, as Ratzinger understands it, does not mean "the reconstruction and restoration of particular historical forms", but rather orientation to the Lord, "who is our origin [*Herkunft*] as well as our future [*Zukunft*]".[67]

§ 5. The Discussion about the Term "Restoration"[68]

From the exposition thus far, it is clear that Christ is the origin, the way, and the goal of every ecclesial renewal. Given this premise, the "leap forward" and the "return to the origins and the beginnings"[69] are not contradictory, since the Church is founded upon and lives on the unique fact of the Incarnation and redemption in Jesus Christ. Therefore, even though she advances toward her perfection in the kingdom of God, she is always bound to events that occurred two thousand years ago: "to what happened then and only once".[70]

Hence renewal can only mean for her [the Church] a new orientation to this origin which alone is authoritative. She cannot be manipulated arbitrarily. It is not within the Church's control to be "with the times" whenever she wishes. She cannot measure Christ and Christianity according to the standard of the time and its trends; instead, she must subject the times to the measure of Christ.[71]

This does not mean, however, that the Church must rely on a particular historical form that she has assumed; rather, she must rely on the living Word of God, whose incarnational mystery endures. Therefore, renewal is never a glorification or a new edition of the past in the sense of a *restoration*, "which in fact would be just as unchristian as

---

[66] *Called to Communion*, 146.

[67] *Volk Gottes*, 43–70: "The pastoral implications of the doctrine of the collegiality of bishops", citation at 70.

[68] See Henri de Lubac, interview conducted by Angelo Scola: *De Lubac: A Theologian Speaks* (Los Angeles, Calif.: Twin Circle Publishing, 1985), 40.

[69] *Volk Gottes*, 68.

[70] Ibid.

[71] Ibid.

mere modernization".[72] But do these statements not contradict opinions expressed by Ratzinger in the mid-1980s, in which he considered a restoration desirable? A *complete* citation of the passage in question from the interview with Vittorio Messori should be informative in this regard:

> If by "restoration" is meant a turning back, no restoration of such kind is possible. The Church moves forward toward the consummation of history, she looks ahead to the Lord who is coming. No, there is no going back, nor is it possible to go back. Hence there is no "restoration" whatsoever in this sense. But if by *restoration* we understand the search for a new balance after all the exaggerations of an indiscriminate opening to the world, after the overly positive interpretations of an agnostic and atheistic world, well, then a *restoration* understood in this sense (a newly found balance of orientations and values within the Catholic totality) is altogether desirable and, for that matter, is already in operation in the Church. In this sense it can be said that the first phase after Vatican II has come to a close.[73]

To this quotation Ratzinger adds a footnote[74] clarifying the word "restoration", which in its German form [*Restauration*] had caused misunderstandings. In everyday German usage, this term is associated with a retrograde reproduction of past conditions; Ratzinger, on the contrary, wants it to be understood according to its semantic content as "a recovery of lost values, within a new totality", and he believes "that this is precisely the task that imposes itself today in the second phase of the post-conciliar period".[75]

Looking back at the Council and its reception in 1984, shortly before his death, Karl Rahner used the expression "restoration" in quite a different way, when he noted "certain restorational [*restaurative*]

---

[72] Ibid., 69. A little farther on in the same essay, Ratzinger writes: "The Church that strives for renewal does not brush aside the creeping vines of a historical period so as to restore some ideal condition, but rather so as to go to meet the Lord, so as to be free to answer his call."

[73] *Report*, 37–38.

[74] Ibid., 38.

[75] Ibid., n. 5.

tendencies" that "puzzled him",[76] or when he spoke about a "rather weary and wintry time of the Church".[77] Herbert Vorgrimler alludes to this image again in his essay "On 'the Spirit of the Council'" when he states that "the 'wintry' spirit and the spirit of springtime that has been wafting since the Council to this day are in stark contrast to each other."[78] Critical comments about the catchword "restoration" used by Ratzinger were made also in 1986 by Cardinal Franz König in an interview with the journalist Gianni Licheri:

> If you put the emphasis on the concept of "restoring", then that conveys a sense of nostalgia for the past. We must keep in mind, however, the fact that the Second Vatican Council was held almost one hundred years after the previous Council. The Church of the past regarded every new development in history with great fear; she felt that she was separated from the world, in which she saw evil. The Council turned this view completely around: the Church opened herself up to history, to non-Christians, to the ecumenical movement.[79]

Cardinal König's objection provides food for thought. Yet Cardinal Henri de Lubac[80] arrives at a completely different evaluation of Ratzinger's statements. He finds the "stir which was made recently ... about the word 'restoration' ... ridiculous",[81] because in his interview with Prof. Angelo Scola he understands this expression as one possible translation for the Latin word *instauratio*:

> Let me note in passing that this word, which has suddenly become so controversial, is a conciliar word. It is the French translation ... of the word *instauratio*, which occurs in the very title of one of the council constitutions and several times afterward. All the translations I have been able to consult agree on this point. Moreover, the

[76] P. Imhof and H. Biallowons, eds., *Glaube in winterlicher Zeit: Gespräche mit Karl Rahner aus den letzten Lebensjahren* (Düsseldorf: Patmos, 1986), 224–26, citation at 226.

[77] Ibid., 11–26, citation at 18.

[78] Vorgrimler, "Vom 'Geist des Konzils'", 25–52, citation at 48.

[79] F. König, *Der Weg der Kirche* (Düsseldorf: Patmos-Verlag, 1986), 116f.

[80] It is unfair to claim that de Lubac's opinion was the result of "his gratitude for the change in his personal status": see Vorgrimler, "Vom 'Geist des Konzils'", 25–52, citation at 46f., n. 41. Cf. also de Lubac, *De Lubac: A Theologian Speaks*, last two paragraphs on p. 40.

[81] Ibid., 40.

word is so far from being backward-looking that it fits in well with
another word in the conciliar text, translated by "progress": *"ad instau-
randam atque fovendam ...".*[82]

If we look at Ratzinger's statements in context, therefore, we see
that reform, as he understands it, means the "recovery of lost values",
"renewal from the source, directed toward hope".[83] Even though certain formulations are more nuanced now than in the early statements
by the conciliar theologian, he remains true to his fundamental statement that "a return to the past ... a restoration understood thus is not
only impossible but also not even desirable".[84] In 1981, Michael Fahey
posed the question of whether the term "neo-conservatism" could be
applied to Ratzinger and summarized his findings:

> In many respects this expression would surely be a strange misno-
> mer. Ratzinger is a theologian well acquainted with the classical
> theology of the West, who has advocated collegiality and liturgical
> reform and is known for his openness to Eastern Orthodoxy. He
> was always apprehensive about the negative influence of Archbishop
> Lefèbvre's followers. The expression "neo-conservative" would apply
> to him only if one understood it to mean this theologian's specific
> understanding of pastoral theology and his conviction that much of
> the Gospel is overlooked by those theologians who are fascinated
> by structural reform in the Church, or else if one were willing to
> include within this expression his emphasis on prayer, the liturgy,
> and self-denial.[85]

Most importantly, the voices critical of Ratzinger have become louder
again[86] in reaction to the declaration *Dominus Iesus* issued by the Congregation for the Faith. For example, Leonardo Boff, in his book

---

[82] Ibid.

[83] *Volk Gottes*, 68.

[84] *Report*, 38n.

[85] Fahey, 84.

[86] Cf. P. Hünermann, "Theologische Reflexionen zu einem umstrittenen römischen
Lehrdokument", in *Was ist heute noch katholisch? Zum Streit um die innere Einheit und Vielfalt
der Kirche*, ed. A. Franz, 65–86, ref. at 65, QD 192 (Freiburg im Breisgau: Herder, 2001).
See also M.J. Rainer, ed., *"Dominus Iesus": Anstößige Wahrheit oder anstößige Kirche? Dokumente, Hintergründe, Standpunkte und Folgerungen*, 2nd ed. (Münster: Lit, 2001). In this volume (336–45) there is a bibliographical overview of more than one hundred opinions on
Dominus Iesus, compiled by M. Mühl and J.-H. Tück.

Manifesto for Ecumenism, describes the cardinal and member of the Roman Curia as "an angel of death for the future of ecumenism",[87] who "is turning the Council on its head".[88] In a very similar vein, Hermann Häring accuses Ratzinger of imposing a "dictatorship of opinion".[89] In contrast to the voices that call Ratzinger an opponent of ecumenism, Stephan Horn demonstrates that an ecumenical commitment has characterized his theological work from the beginning.[90] In the mid-1970s he even took decisive ecumenical initiatives that today [in 2003] have the complete support of the present papal Magisterium.[91] At that time, in a lecture in Graz, Austria, on "Prognoses for the Future of Ecumenism", which attracted much attention, Ratzinger proposed the thesis: "Rome must not demand more from the East by way of doctrine on the primacy than was formulated and practiced during the first millennium."[92] This "Ratzinger formula" has become, in the words of Walter Kasper,[93] foundational for ecumenical dialogue.

Ratzinger has a different approach[94] to the denominations that resulted from the Reformation. With regard to them, he refers more often to

---

[87] L. Boff, *Manifest für die Ökumene: Ein Streit mit Kardinal Ratzinger* (Düsseldorf: Patmos-Verlag, 2001), 73, 76, 105.

[88] Ibid., 89ff.

[89] See Häring, *Ideologie*, 195–98.

[90] Stephan O. Horn, "II. Ökumenische Dimensionen—Einführung", in *Mitte*, 175–80, ref. at 175.

[91] Cf. John Paul II, *Ut unum sint*, Vatican trans. (Boston: Pauline Books & Media, 1995).

[92] J. Ratzinger, "Prognosen für die Zukunft des Ökumenismus", in *Mitte*, 181–94, citation at 188. First published in *Ökumenisches Forum: Grazer Hefte für konkrete Ökumene* 1 (1977): 31–41. See also Quinn, *Reform*, 31: "Commenting on the final report of the Anglican-Roman Catholic International Commission I, Cardinal Joseph Ratzinger wrote: 'The early Church did indeed know nothing of Roman primacy, in practice, in the sense of Roman Catholic theology of the second millennium.'" Cf. also *Church*, 65–87, "Anglican-Catholic Dialogue: Its Problems and Hopes". Particularly noteworthy here is the expression "hermeneutics of unity" (82), which relativizes the above-cited speech from the year 1976. That ecumenical advance in 1976 was interpreted, contrary to Ratzinger's intention, to mean that the councils and dogmatic definitions of the second millennium should be regarded, not as ecumenical, but rather as particular developments of the Latin Church.

[93] Cf. Kasper, "Auseinandersetzung", 798.

[94] Cf. *Volk Gottes*, 148–51: "Wende zur Ökumene", ref. at 149. During a speech given at the 1966 Catholic Congress in Bamberg, Ratzinger said: "Who would have ventured to suppose even ten years ago that the official language of the Church would consciously and deliberately begin to designate as churches not only the Churches of the East, but also

the divergences in controverted questions than to the convergences and sees in them "unsolved differences".[95] In 1983, when volume 100 of the series Quaestiones disputatae, entitled *Reunion of the Churches: A Real Possibility*, was published as a counterpart to the "Ratzinger formula",[96] this "Fries-Rahner plan" elicited vigorous opposition from Ratzinger. Karl Rahner and Heinrich Fries had intended their ecumenical reflections as a bridge to all denominations, but especially to those ecclesial communities that resulted from the Reformation. The reason for Ratzinger's critique of this approach lay in Rahner's thesis of "epistemological tolerance":[97] "In no particular Church may any proposition be rejected and excised from the profession of faith which is a binding dogma in some other particular Church."[98] In Ratzinger's judgment, through this formula Rahner had managed "to skip the question of truth ... by means of a few manoeuvres of ecclesial politics".[99] For this reason he describes this plan as "a forced march towards unity".[100] According to his understanding, Church unity by its nature can be understood, not as "unity in action", but rather as "the unity of fundamental decisions and fundamental convictions".[101] Therefore, Ratzinger cautions against "a hectic chase after reunion", even though he reminds us at the same time that "division and separation [can] no longer [be] a reason for opposition but rather a challenge to an inward understanding and acceptance of the other that

those communities that resulted from the Reformation?" For this, Ratzinger said, we must give thanks. Even then, however, he was not unaware of the analogous use of the term "Church".

[95] *Church*, 99–121, citation at 108.

[96] Cf. H. Fries and K. Rahner, *Einigung der Kirchen—reale Möglichkeit*, QD 100 (Freiburg im Breisgau: Herder, 1983), 51. In this passage, Karl Rahner explains that they (Fries and Rahner) took their inspiration for the new project from Ratzinger's formulation: "If the Prefect of the Roman Congregation for the Faith today declares that the Eastern Churches could reunite with Rome while remaining at that stage of doctrinal development where they were when the separation occurred, then this declaration does indeed imply the thesis propounded here."

[97] *Church*, 122–34, citation at 124. On this subject, see Fries and Rahner, *Einigung der Kirchen*, 17.

[98] Fries and Rahner, *Einigung der Kirchen*, 17. K. Rahner describes this fundamental statement as a "realistic principle of faith". Cf. ibid., 35–53.

[99] *Church*, 114.

[100] Ibid., 108.

[101] Ibid.

means more than mere tolerance—a belonging to each other in loyalty to Jesus Christ." [102]

When we examine Ratzinger's contrasting positions to the Eastern Churches and to the denominations of the Reformation, we can find consistency in his writings on the question of ecumenism as well. [103] Basically he is attempting to counteract denominationalism and separation by setting up a "hermeneutics of unity", which consists of "reading the statements of both parties in the context of the whole tradition and with a deeper understanding of scripture". [104] According to Stephan Horn, this means "constantly purifying oneself and deepening one's understanding with a view to it [unity], and thereby helping others as well, along this same path of purification and meditation, to recognize the common middle and to find themselves in it." [105]

In this struggle for a hermeneutics of unity, according to Wiedenhofer, Ratzinger is convinced that faith is a path "that must be followed staunchly, trusting in the promise—a path that demands great responsibility and resolve in avoiding the detours that lead astray, a path along which one must repeatedly start out again in a constant willingness to do penance and in the hope of forgiveness." Finally, it is due to the spiritual character of [Ratzinger's] ecclesiology that "every attempt to reify the Church and render her absolute" [106] is prevented. This does not mean, however, giving up with respect to the question of truth, as Ratzinger himself reaffirmed in 1972 in an ecumenical reflection. [107] Rather, he subscribes to the principle that "progress that

[102] Ibid., 121.

[103] Cf. Highlights, 61–76.

[104] Church, 65–98, citation at 82. Here it becomes clear that Ratzinger is concerned with a principled, well-considered affirmation of ecumenism-in-truth, which is Christ himself.

[105] Horn, "II. Ökumenische Dimensionen", 175–80, citation at 178f. Cf. Highlights, 66–67: "Furthermore the pneumatological aspect was reinforced. Speaking of union in the Holy Spirit, the text said that his sanctifying power also works in those [Protestant] Christians, and that Catholics, in turn, are in constant need of purification and renewal."

[106] S. Wiedenhofer, "I. Theologische Grundlegung—Einführung", in Mitte, 123–26, citation at 125.

[107] J. Ratzinger, "Was eint und was trennt die Konfessionen: Eine ökumenische Besinnung", IKaZ 1 (1972): 172.

is based on forgetting is deceptive; unity that finds embarrassment in truth is transitory."[108]

As the result of this chapter, we can state: In the first place, Ratzinger does not understand the Council as the "beginning of a beginning" in the sense of a movement that distances itself from its point of departure; he regards it, rather, as a constant point of reference.[109] In contrast, as far as the reception of its decisions is concerned, he declared as early as 1965 that everything that "a Council decides . . . can serve [only] as a beginning; its real importance is achieved only in its translation into the realities of everyday Church life".[110]

Secondly, Ratzinger answers the question of the continuity between his work as a professor and as a cardinal and prefect of the Congregation for the Faith in an exchange of letters between Metropolitan Damaskinos and himself from the year 2000 through 2001,[111] by pointing out, to start with, that his own theological statements should be distinguished from the documents of the Congregation for the Faith. As a professor, he says, he still takes part today in theological discussion while being responsible to the truth of the faith[112] and with an awareness of his own limitations.[113] In the role of prefect of the

---

[108] Ratzinger, "Ökumenisches Dilemma? Zur Diskussion um die Erklärung *Mysterium Ecclesiae*", *IKaZ* 3 (1974): 56–63, citation at 63; also published in *Principles* as "Ecumenism at a Standstill? Explanatory Comments on *Mysterium Ecclesiae*", 228–37, citation at 237.

[109] Cf. *Principles*, 378–93, esp. 390.

[110] *Highlights*, 131.

[111] Metropolitan Damaskinos and Cardinal Joseph Ratzinger, "Exchange of Letters between Metropolitan Damaskinos and Cardinal Joseph Ratzinger", originally published in *IKaZ* 30 (2001): 282–96; English translation in *Pilgrim Fellowship*, 217–41, citation at 230f.: "The Professor and the Prefect are the same person, but the two terms refer to two offices that correspond to different tasks. In that sense, then, there is a difference but no contradiction. The Professor (and I am still the Professor) is concerned with knowledge, and in his books and lectures he presents what he thinks he has found and opens himself not only to other theologians disputing it but also to the judgment of the Church. . . . What he writes or says springs from his personal journey of faith and understanding and locates him in the shared journey of the Church. The Prefect, on the other hand, is not supposed to expound his personal views. On the contrary, he has to leave them in the background so as to make room for the common message of the Church. . . . The Congregation's documents are not infallible, yet they are still more than contributions to the discussion—they are signposts intended to speak to the believing consciences of pastors and teachers." See also de Lubac, *De Lubac: A Theologian Speaks*, 39f.

[112] Cf. Damaskinos and Ratzinger, "Exchange of Letters", 230.

[113] Cf. ibid.

Congregation for the Faith, he must "see to it that the organs of the teaching Church carry on their work with a high degree of responsibility, so
that in the end a document is purged of everything that is merely personal and truly becomes the common message of the Church".[114] Thirdly,
the "common yardstick of the faith",[115] which determines Ratzinger's
theology existentially, is the clamp or bracket that holds together the different areas of his ecclesial existence. For him this standard is a synonym
for fidelity to the truth. He acknowledges his obligation to it as professor, as archbishop of Munich-Freising, and finally as prefect of the Congregation for the Faith. In all stages of his life, the connection between
theology and the Church's Magisterium is essential, since without theology the Church becomes poor and blind. But a theology without
Church "melts away into caprice".[116] Finally, Ratzinger's theology is
characterized by a constant ecclesiality, which embraces the whole
tradition of the Church. For himself personally, he does not exclude gradually developing corrections of his theological knowledge and thus different accentuations as well. They are at the service of a renewal as a
transformation through God's Word, which for him is simultaneously
the orientation to Christ, the incarnate Word of God. Hence labels like
"conservative" or *restaurativ*—in my opinion—misrepresent the christological foundation and the goal that motivate Ratzinger. He is concerned with the missionary spirit that Christ bestowed on his Church.
That is why reform for Ratzinger always means renewal coming from
the origin, that is, through Christ and in the hope directed toward
him. On the basis of their christological orientation, both mission and
reform are characterized by a hermeneutics of unification.

---

[114] Ibid. Gitta Marnach does not adequately distinguish between the person (theologian) and the office (prefect). In her short biography of Ratzinger, she repeats negative
stereotypes, objecting, for example, to his alleged inability at dialogue, when she comes to
speak about the Congregation for the Faith: "The Congregation for the Doctrine of the
Faith is no dialogue partner.... By the way in which he has conducted himself in office,
Cardinal Ratzinger has earned for himself the reputation of an implacable judge of the
faith and is regarded as a sort of Cerberus [mythical three-headed watchdog] of the pope,
which is not exactly flattering for him." See G. Marnach, "Wächter des Glaubens: Joseph
Kardinal Ratzinger", in *Wie sie wurden, was sie sind: Zeitgenössische Theologinnen und Theologen im Portrait*, ed. L. Baucherochse and K. Hofmeister, 210–29, citation at 227 (Gütersloh: Gütersloher Verlag-Haus, 2001).
[115] Damaskinos and Ratzinger, "Exchange of Letters", 231.
[116] *Nature*, 48.

Chapter 4

Archbishop and Cardinal

By its very nature, this section of the biography can be only a fragment, since we stand with it at the threshold of the present. Furthermore, it would exceed the parameters of this dissertation to give a
comprehensive account of Cardinal Ratzinger's work.[1] Consequently,
I write this chapter as a biographical note, divided into two parts corresponding to the chronological sequence of Ratzinger's appointment
as archbishop of Munich and Freising and next as prefect of the Roman
Congregation for the Doctrine of the Faith.

§ 1. Archbishop of Munich and Freising:
Cooperatores Veritatis

In looking back on the past decades, Cardinal Ratzinger describes the
time of his professorship, especially his years in Regensburg, as "a time
of fruitful theological work",[2] despite all the controversies in the period
immediately after the Council. He was trying then, "after the decisive
turning point of the Council", to formulate his own theological view-
point in a new way. He was striving "to be able to say something of
my own, something new and yet completely within the faith of the

---

[1]Scholarly discretion demands a certain reserve in commenting on a period of time that
continues into the present. In this, my dissertation corresponds to what Ratzinger writes
at the end of his book *Milestones—Memoirs: 1927–1977*, which appeared in German [and
English] in 1998: "The episcopal consecration brings me into the present period of my
life.... This is why I cannot write any memoirs about it but can only attempt to fill in this
Now" (see *Milestones*, 153). The original edition of his autobiography appeared first in
Italian with the title *La mia vita: Ricordi (1927–1977)* (Milan, 1997).

[2]*Milestones*, 149.

Church",[3] by means of a theological project but was unable to accomplish this according to his own plans. "When on July 24, 1976, the news of the sudden death of the archbishop of Munich, Julius Cardinal Döpfner, was broadcast, all of us were shocked. Rumors at once began circulating that I was among the candidates to succeed him." [4]

1. Consolidation through the Word of God

After the premature death of Cardinal Julius Döpfner,[5] Ratzinger was appointed archbishop of Munich and Freising[6] by Pope Paul VI on March 24, 1977, and promptly received episcopal consecration on May 28, 1977, the eve of Pentecost, from Bishop Josef Stangl[7] of Würzburg along with the co-consecrators Rudolf Graber, bishop of Regensburg, and Auxiliary Bishop Ernst Tewes of Munich;[8] on this occasion [Bishop Stangl] invited all his diocesan priests, in keeping with his own motto, to be "Co-workers of the Truth",[9] to place themselves under God's

---

[3] Ibid., 150.

[4] Ibid., 150–51.

[5] See the biographical information about Cardinal Döpfner in E. Tewes, ed., *Kardinal Julius Döpfner: Weggefährte in bedrängter Zeit: Briefe an Priester* (Munich: St.-Michaels-Bund, 1986), 153f., and also information about the events of that time, ibid., 147–51. See also J. Ratzinger, *Christlicher Glaube und Europa*, twelve homilies (Munich: Pressereferat der Erzdiözese München-Freising, 1981), 137–44: "Offener Blick auf Christus: Julius Kardinal Döpfner".

[6] Cf. *Milestones*, 152. See also the text of the papal letter announcing the appointment in Wagner/Ruf, 7f.: "In the Spirit We look upon you, beloved son: you are endowed with superior intellectual gifts, above all you are a distinguished master of theology, which you have wisely, zealously, and fruitfully handed on to your students as a teacher of theology."

[7] After the death of Cardinal Julius Döpfner, Bishop Josef Stangl became the president of the Freisinger (or Bavarian) Bishops' Conference for the interim. There was no obligation for Bishop Stangl to be the principal consecrator, since a candidate for episcopal ordination is completely free in his choice of consecrators.

[8] Cf. *Milestones*, 152f. See also the text of the papal letter announcing the appointment in Wagner/Ruf, 24. In the homily at his consecration, the new archbishop said, among other things, "My thoughts go back once again to the hour in which we accompanied Cardinal Döpfner to his grave.... On this day I cannot avoid the question of whether the faith will still be a feature on the face of our land when someday they accompany me on my final journey."

[9] See J. Ratzinger, "Der Bischof ist ein Christus-Träger: Predigt bei der Bischofsweihe im Münchener Liebfrauendom am 23. Juli 1977", in Wagner/Ruf, 36–40, ref. at 38. Cf. *God and the World*, 262f.: "I must say that I felt very strongly within myself the crisis of the claim of truth during the decades of my teaching work as a professor. What I feared was that the way we use the idea of the truth of Christianity was sheer arrogance, yes, and even

Word and, together with their bishop, to become "beasts of burden"
for the living Word of God. Alluding to the ritual of episcopal consecration, he said:

> When we look more closely, we can recognize even more clearly
> in the [liturgical] gesture of the opened book the nature and the
> demands of the episcopal ministry. Three things become evident:
> The man who is consecrated in this way is covered, as it were, by
> the book. . . . This means that the bishop does not act in his own
> name but, rather, is the trustee of someone else, of Jesus Christ
> and his Church. . . . The Word . . . protects him; it is his help and
> his salvation. Hence the Word is also called the helmet of salva-
> tion. . . . There is yet a third meaning hidden in the sign of the
> book that is imposed. This book . . . stands for the Word of God,
> which in turn comes from the radiant power of the Holy Spirit
> and wishes to draw the person that it touches into the force field,
> so to speak, of the Holy Spirit.[10]

A few weeks after his episcopal consecration, the young archbishop
was elevated, along with four other appointees,[11] to the college of
cardinals by Pope Paul VI in Rome in the consistory of June 27, 1977.
During his years as archbishop of Munich and Freising, he published,
in addition to a series of smaller works, the volume entitled *Feast of
Faith*. With this book, Ratzinger meant, not to distract his readers

---

a lack of respect for others. The question was, how far may we still use it? . . . Christianity
makes its appearance with the claim to tell us something about God and the world and
ourselves—something that is true and that enlightens us. On this basis I came to recognize
that, in the crisis of an age in which we have a great mass of communications about truth
in natural science, but with respect to the questions essential for man we are sidelined into
subjectivism, what we need above all is to seek anew for truth, with a new courage to
recognize truth. In that way, this saying handed down from our origins, which I have
chosen as my motto, defines something of the function of a priest and a theologian, to wit,
that he should, in all humility, and knowing his own fallibility, seek to be a co-worker of
the truth." And indeed, he should do so in the knowledge that he is together with others
"in a greater whole . . . that helps to support [them all] but is itself supported as well"
(Wagner/Ruf, 53).

[10] Wagner/Ruf, 37f.

[11] This group consisted of the administrator of the Archdiocese of Prague, František
Tomášek, as a representative of the then-persecuted Church, who had already been named
a cardinal *in pectore* on May 24, 1976, and also the black African curial Archbishop Bernardin Gantin, curial theologian Luigi Ciappi, and Giovanni Benelli, who until then had
served as substitute in the Papal Secretariat of State (see Wagner/Ruf, 27).

from the crises that had shaken the contemporary world, but rather to press on to the worship of God as the center of human life, precisely out of a concern for humanity. In it he expresses the certainty that "[o]nly if man, every man, stands before the face of God and is answerable to him, can man be secure in his dignity." [12]

2. Critique of flawed developments and the search for dialogue

The courage to criticize for the sake of the truth is plainly evident in Ratzinger's New Year's Eve homily of 1979, in which he pointed out the powerlessness of the ecclesial officeholder with respect to public opinion:

> Anyone who exercises authority in the Church today has no power. On the contrary, he stands against the prevailing power, against the force of an opinion that regards faith in the truth as an offensive disturbance of that certainty with which people in large measure have subscribed to arbitrariness. This public power will not hesitate to strike anyone who contradicts it in the face—but this is precisely what Paul described as the lot of the apostle, the witness to Jesus in the world (1 Cor 4:12f.).[13]

At that time the *Süddeutsche Zeitung* [a Bavarian newspaper] judged that Ratzinger was, "of all conservatives in the Church, ... the one with the greatest capacity for dialogue".[14] It may be that we should take such characterizations with a grain of salt, since they are often as short-lived as the topical interest of a daily newspaper. Nevertheless, the point here is that he confronted the problems:

> Even today I am glad that in Munich I didn't dodge conflicts, because letting things drift is ... the worst kind of administration I can imagine. From the very beginning it was clear to me that during my time in Rome I would have to carry out a lot of unpleasant tasks.

---

[12] *Feast of Faith*, 7.

[13] Ratzinger, "Was ihr von Anfang an gehört habt, soll in euch bleiben: Silvesterpredigt 1979" [homily on New Year's Eve 1979], published by the Press Office of the Archdiocese of Munich and Freising (Munich, 1980), 19f.

[14] See *Salt of the Earth*, 83.

But I think I may say that I have always sought dialogue and that it
has also been very fruitful.[15]

For Ratzinger, entering into dialogue meant acknowledging a legitimate pluralism in modern society, without falling into a value-free
neutrality. For this reason, he insisted on the greatness that God had
given man—the opportunity to enter into the dialogue of love—and
warned against alienating man from his proper calling by permissiveness and selfishness.[16] As archbishop of Munich and Freising, Ratzinger saw that he had been "thrown right into the midst of this situation
of crisis and turmoil".[17] In this situation he was especially concerned
about the formation of future priests.

> The number of seminarians in the archdiocese had decreased; they
> lived as guests in the ducal Georgianum. . . . I knew from the very
> beginning that it was my most pressing duty to give the diocese its
> own seminary again, even though many doubted that such an under-
> taking made any sense in the changed Church.[18]

In summarizing, we can state that Ratzinger sees it as a bishop's
duty, not only to be "open" to the people's concerns, but also to be
"capable of opposing the world and its negative tendencies in order to
improve them, check them and to warn the faithful against them".[19]
The "world", which he often speaks of negatively in the Johannine
sense (as opposed to "universe"), could be defined as the complex

---

[15] Ibid. Cf. ibid., 82: "The words of the Bible and of the Church Fathers rang in my
ears, those sharp condemnations of shepherds who are like mute dogs; in order to avoid
conflicts, they let the poison spread."

[16] Cf. Ratzinger, "Lasst das Netz nicht zerreißen: Silvesterpredigt 1980" [homily on
New Year's Eve 1980], published by the Press Office of the Archdiocese of Munich and
Freising (Munich, 1981) [no page numbers].

[17] Song, 162. For personal reasons, also, Ratzinger had doubts about his appointment to
an episcopal see: "I had little pastoral experience. I felt that, in principle, I was called from
the beginning to teach and believed that at this period of my life—I was fifty years old—I
had found my own theological vision and could now create an oeuvre with which I would
contribute something to the whole of theology. I also knew that my health was fragile and
that this office would involve a great physical demand on me" (Salt of the Earth, 81).

[18] Song, 162.

[19] Report, 65. Statistical trends should not upset us, since in the Church there is always
a new beginning through sanctification, "which statistics cannot take into account, because
they cannot calculate freedom". See Ratzinger, Zeitfragen und christlicher Glaube, 2nd ed.
(Würzburg: Naumann, 1983), 90.

totality of man's behaviors that are contrary to the faith. Defending man against bad influences was Ratzinger's concern as bishop. He understood that this involved rescuing man from his lack of orientation and directing him toward God, so that he would not "sink down into an empty freedom: the freedom to choose death, loneliness, and the darkness of the absence of truth".[20] Two points seem to me to be particularly relevant to the theme of this dissertation: Ratzinger's conviction that he was always under an obligation to *the* truth and that he was serving the cause of Church unity through dialogue in a critical exchange of opinion with opposing points of view.

§ 2. Prefect of the Roman Congregation for the Doctrine of the Faith

1. *The teacher of theology is under obligation to the truth*

Pope John Paul II appointed Cardinal Ratzinger the prefect of the Congregation for the Faith in 1981. Once again Ratzinger viewed his motto, *Co-workers of the Truth*, as the unifying element between his duties thus far as archbishop of Munich and Freising and his new calling. He depicts this transition in his career as follows:

> Despite all the differences in modality, what is involved was and remains the same: to follow the truth, to be at its service. And, because in today's world the theme of truth has all but disappeared, because truth appears to be too great for man and yet everything falls apart if there is no truth, for these reasons this motto also seemed timely in the good sense of the word.[21]

Despite the great demands upon him in the Curia, Ratzinger published a considerable number of writings, by which he directly intervened in and enlivened the ongoing scholarly discussion between the Magisterium and theology. Thus in 1982, shortly after he was called to the Vatican, he published his *Theologische Prinzipienlehre* [*Principles*

[20] Ratzinger, "Lasst das Netz nicht zerreißen".
[21] *Milestones*, 153. See also Nachtwei, 238–42.

of Catholic Theology], a compilation of "building blocks" in fundamental theology that had grown over the previous decade. The questions
raised in it about the center of the faith, the source of the characteristic features of the Christian message, lead to the principles that are
true for every Christian, insofar as he stands by the Creed of the Church.
In the small volume entitled *Wesen und Auftrag der Theologie*, which
appeared in 1993 [*The Nature and Mission of Theology*, 1995], Ratzinger set forth the prerequisites and foundations for theological work,
with a view to the question of academic freedom:

> The Magisterium of the Catholic Church ... presupposes that Chris-
> tianity, especially in its Catholic variety, has a determinate content
> and thus confronts our thinking with a prior given.... Theology is
> born when the arbitrary judgment of reason encounters a limit, in
> that we discover something which we have not excogitated our-
> selves but which has been revealed to us. For this reason, not every
> religious theory has the right to label itself as Christian or Catholic
> theology simply because it wishes to do so; whoever would lay claim
> to this title is obliged to accept as meaningful the prior given which
> goes along with it.[22]

The theologian has to realize that he is bound to the faith of the
Church, for "the subject who pursues theology is not the individual
scholar but the Catholic community as a whole, the entire Church."[23]
In the book *Auf Christus schauen: Einübung in Glaube, Hoffnung und
Liebe* [*To Look on Christ: Exercises in Faith, Hope and Love*], Ratzinger
repeats that faith in the Christian sense is "necessarily ... ecclesial

---

[22] *Nature*, 7–8. In his foreword, Ratzinger first describes contemporary expectations:
"Two things are expected of the theologian in the modern world. On the one hand, he is
supposed to subject the traditions of Christianity to critical examination by the light of
reason, to distill from them the essential core which can be appropriated for use today, and
thereby also place the institutional Church within her proper limits. But at the same time
he is also expected to respond to the need for religion and transcendence, a need which
simply refuses to be ignored, by giving guiding orientations and meaningful content which
can be responsibly accepted today. In the emerging [global community] an additional task
devolves upon him: he must promote interreligious dialogue and contribute to the development of a planetary ethos.... Finally, however, the theologian should also be a com-
forter of souls.... The institutional Church often appears to be an annoying impediment.
This is especially true of the Magisterium of the Catholic Church" (7).

[23] *Report*, 71.

faith".[24] Only in the " 'We' of the Church" can the individual become one with the "I" of Jesus Christ: "In this new subject, the wall between myself and others falls down.... In this new subject I am contemporaneous with Jesus, and all the experiences of the Church are mine, too, and have become my own".[25]

For this reason, as Gerd Lohaus summarizes Ratzinger's understanding, the "I", interpreted ecclesially, is "a Not-'I', and *in this way* it is an 'I' that is inserted into the Church and thus into Christ".[26] When the individual abides in the "we" of the Church, then dogmas are "not walls that prevent us from seeing. On the contrary, they are windows that open upon"[27] expansive vistas and speak to us about eternity and time, about the origin and future of mankind.[28] The prerequisite for this, in Ratzinger's opinion, is a conversion to the truth, because "from the very beginning it was a constitutive element of the Christian faith that its teaching appealed to man in terms of his ultimate bond, his bond to the truth."[29] If this commitment in the sphere of the Church is replaced with merely pragmatic social or political standards and values, then—Ratzinger says—new constraints[30] arise with ruinous consequences for ecclesial communion.[31] For this reason, unity of faith in the truth and Church unity are not mutually exclusive but, rather, mutually dependent. With Ratzinger we can conclude that faith and truth are therefore always a prior gift that we do not invent but to which we convert.[32]

---

[24] Ratzinger, *To Look on Christ: Exercises in Faith, Hope and Love* (New York: Crossroad, 1991), 37 [where the German *kirchlich* is translated as "churchly" instead of "ecclesial"].

[25] Ibid., 37–38.

[26] G. Lohaus, "Kirche und Pastoral bei Joseph Ratzinger: Die pastoraltheologische Relevanz seines konziliaren Kirchenbegriffs (Teil 1)", in *Pastoralblatt für die Diözesen Aachen, Berlin, Essen, Hamburg, Hildesheim, Köln, Osnabrück* 53 (2001/5): 134. Cf. also Kaes, 141, 145f. Cf. also *Nature*, 50f.

[27] *Report*, 72.

[28] Cf. Ratzinger, "Geleitwort", in Christoph Schönborn, *Leben für die Kirche* (Freiburg in Breisgau: Herder, 1997), 9.

[29] *Nature*, 80.

[30] Cf. ibid., 82.

[31] Cf. interview with Joseph Cardinal Ratzinger, in *Handing on the Faith in an Age of Disbelief*, with conferences by Archbishop Dermot J. Ryan (Dublin), Godfried Cardinal Danneels (Malines/Brussels), and Franciszek Cardinal Macharski (Krakow) (San Francisco: Ignatius Press, 2006), 65–82, ref. at 72–73.

[32] On the theme of "Conversion, Faith and Thought", see *Nature*, 55f.

Together with Hans Urs von Balthasar, Ratzinger formulated an imperative that sums up his understanding of his task as a teacher of theology in the postconciliar situation of the faith and the Church. It reads: "Do not presuppose the faith but propose it",[33] present the faith, as Ratzinger says, "in its unity and simplicity".[34] The prefect of the Congregation for the Faith is concerned about this catholicity of faith not only in questions of catechesis and the catechism but also in the debate with liberation theology or with the traditionalist movement, and in ecumenical relations. Within the framework of this biographical retrospect, we will now highlight each of these questions briefly, so as to shed more light simultaneously on the complexity of the duties of the prefect of the Congregation for the Faith. A central concern, in Ratzinger's own view, is to recognize the office of prefect as a service to the unity of the faith and of the Church.

2. The office of prefect: Service to the unity of the faith

a. Catechesis and the Catechism

At the invitation of the archbishops of Paris and Lyons, Jean-Marie Lustiger and Albert Decourtray, respectively, Cardinal Ratzinger gave talks at Notre Dame in Paris and at Fourvière in Lyons in 1983 on overcoming the crisis in catechesis, offering an analysis that met with considerable displeasure.[35] Now as always he considers the four classic principal divisions of catechesis as the foundation for Christian life: (1) the Creed (what we must believe); (2) the Our Father (what we must hope); (3) the Ten Commandments (what we must do); and (4) the sacraments and the Church (the environment in which all of

---

[33] See Ratzinger, Gospel, Catechesis, Catechism: Sidelights on the Catechism of the Catholic Church (San Francisco: Ignatius Press, 1997), 23.

[34] Ibid., 24.

[35] H. U. von Balthasar, "Introduction" (by the translator of the 1983 German edition), in Ratzinger, Handing on the Faith, 7: "Of the four distinguished testimonials in Paris and Lyons (January 1983) concerning what is essential for a truly ecclesial catechesis in the countries of the West and of the Eastern bloc, only Cardinal Ratzinger's lecture met with displeasure, partly because he came from Rome, and partly because he candidly pointed out things that were still lacking in catechetical textbooks in France, despite many years of efforts to develop proper materials for religious instruction."

this is anchored).[36] With these four pillars of catechetical instruction, "it was a question, not of an artificial system, but of a simple arrangement of the requisite memorized material of the faith, which at the same time mirrors the elements of the Church's life."[37] They are "the *loci* or centers of activity for interpreting the Bible", or, as contemporary scientific language puts it, "successive points in a thematic organization and hermeneutic of Scripture".[38] "This fundamental structure", however, as Ratzinger observes, "is neglected in extensive areas of present-day catechesis."[39] But this leads ultimately to the loss of the *sensus fidei*.

In 1992, thirty years after the beginning of the Council, Pope John Paul II entrusted to the Church the *Catechism of the Catholic Church*[40] as a major, binding compendium of the faith;[41] two years later, Ratzinger had to lament the lack of acceptance that it met with in a "significant portion of German-language theology". This poor reception tended to "'shut out' the book and to declare it a fundamental mistake".[42] Ratzinger counters the objection that it is actually a "Roman partisan catechism"[43] by reiterating the right "to affirm jointly

---

[36] Cf. Ratzinger, "Handing on the Faith and the Sources of Faith", in Ratzinger, *Handing on the Faith*, 13–40, ref. at 33.

[37] Ibid., 33.

[38] Ibid., 34.

[39] *Report*, 73.

[40] *Catechism of the Catholic Church*, 2nd ed. (Vatican City: Libreria Editrice Vaticana; Washington, D.C.: United States Catholic Conference, 2000).

[41] Cf. Joseph Ratzinger and Christoph Schönborn, *Introduction to the Catechism of the Catholic Church* (San Francisco: Ignatius Press, 1994), 7: "Preaching and proclamation have yet to discover in it an aid to comprehending and communicating the faith as a living, organic whole. Furthermore, the Catechism is meant to assist theology, which is becoming sterile and cold on account of overspecialization and rationalistic dessication, to realize anew 'the admirable unity of the mystery of God' (John Paul II in the Apostolic Constitution on the Catechism).... Catechesis must be encouraged to recognize that its paramount task is the transmission of knowledge of the faith." Cf. C. Schönborn, "Major Themes and Underlying Principles of the Catechism of the Catholic Church", in *Introduction to the Catechism*, 37–57, esp. 39. As Schönborn mentions, at the beginning of the Extraordinary Synod of Bishops in 1985, Cardinal Bernard Law introduced talk about the world as a "global village" into the discussion, which was supposed to recall also the worldwide unity of the faith. The participants in this 1985 Extraordinary Synod of Bishops were soon unanimous in their conviction that such a compendium of the faith was necessary for the entire Church.

[42] Ratzinger, *Gospel, Catechesis, Catechism*, 7. See also H. Verweyen, *Der Weltkatechismus: Therapie oder Symptom einer kranken Kirche?* (Düsseldorf: Patmos-Verlag, 1993).

[43] Cf. H. Küng, "Ein Welt-Katechismus?" *Conc(D)* 29 (1993): 273f.

something held in common".[44] In saying this, he is concerned with handing on the faith, that is, with the proclamation of the gospel, and not primarily with themes that are dictated by current opinion. In such stereotypes of a "pastoral approach by slogans",[45] we can recognize a symptom of the dwindling ecclesial consciousness, especially in the German-speaking world.

> Wherever you go, wherever a diocesan forum meets or some other event takes place, you know already what questions will be raised: celibacy, the ordination of women, and divorce and remarriage. These are certainly serious questions. But there is, so to speak, a constant preoccupation with a few fixed points. Meanwhile, there is too little attention to the fact that out there 80 percent of the world's population are non-Christians; they are waiting for the gospel, or in any case the gospel is intended for them.[46]

In Ratzinger's view, the reasons for the contemporary crisis of faith lie particularly in the lack of ecclesial consciousness, in the fact that "the authentically Catholic meaning of the reality 'Church' is tacitly disappearing, without being expressly rejected. Many no longer believe that what is at issue is a reality willed by the Lord himself."[47] Confronted with this complex problem, catechesis as an ecclesial commitment plays an important role, and now in the *Catechism of the Catholic Church* it has a guideline for maintaining ecclesial unity in a multicultural, globalized world.[48]

---

[44] Ratzinger, "Introduction to the Catechism of the Catholic Church", in Ratzinger and Schönborn, *Introduction to the Catechism*, 9–36, citation at 20.

[45] "Demokratisierung 2", 84.

[46] Ibid., 88. Cf. Ratzinger's discussion of the "canon of criticism" from the 1995 "Petition of the People of the Church" in *Salt of the Earth*, 181–213. Ratzinger begins his response (ibid., 181–82) to these standardized questions with a contrary consideration: "These issues are resolved in Lutheran Christianity. On these points it has taken the other path, and it is quite plain that it hasn't thereby solved the problem of being a Christian in today's world and that the problem of Christianity, the effort of being a Christian, remains just as dramatic as before. Metz, if I recall correctly, asks why we ought to make ourselves a clone of Protestant Christianity. It is actually a good thing, he says, that the experiment was made. For it shows that being Christian today does not stand or fall on these questions."

[47] *Report*, 45.

[48] Ratzinger himself admits that the *Catechism* cannot be considered a *catechismus minor* that is ready to use for instruction in the schools and parishes, "inasmuch as cultural

b. On the debate with liberation theology

Ratzinger sees as another service to the unity of the Church his critique of liberation theology,[49] a deliberately praxis-oriented approach that grappled with social and political grievances in Latin America.[50] In 1984, when the *Instruction of the Congregation for the Doctrine of the Faith concerning Certain Aspects of Liberation Theology*[51] was not yet published but had already caused quite a stir because of a journalistic indiscretion,[52] Ratzinger said in his interview with Vittorio Messori that "the defense of orthodoxy [is] really the defense of the poor, saving them pain and illusions which contain no realistic prospect even of material liberation."[53]

---

differences spawn a corresponding diversity of teaching methods"; see Ratzinger, "Introduction to the Catechism", 9–36, citation at 17.

[49] Liberation theology is the specifically Latin American path taken by a "theology" that understands itself as a preferential option for the poor and hence as a "praxeology". "Theology as the praxis of the people means an active faith that takes as its point of departure the concrete situation as it is experienced historically, and its principal theme is: How can this situation be overcome?" (Leonardo Boff). See H. Kirchner, *Die römisch-katholische Kirche vom II. Vatikanischen Konzil bis zur Gegenwart* (Leipzig: Evangelische Verlagsanstalt, 1996), 87. See also the work by Gustavo Gutiérrez, *A Theology of Liberation: History, Politics, and Salvation*, trans. and ed. Sr. Caridad Inda and John Eagleson (Maryknoll, N.Y.: Orbis Books, 1973), which he presented in 1971 as a systematic outline of liberation theology. In 1968 he first formulated the expression "theology of liberation".

[50] Cf. Kirchner, *Römisch-katholische Kirche*, 87: "With that approach ... the 'theology of liberation'—more accurately we should speak of a plurality of 'liberation theologies'—was vulnerable on several counts to criticism and contradiction from the start. Many saw in the very use of the term *liberación* nothing but an adaptation of the key word of the political left, based on a one-sidedly Marxist analysis of society. Particularly in its ecclesiology 'from below', however, critics saw an abandonment of the current hierarchical model, and with its political option for the poor, 'liberation theology' by definition stood in opposition to the ruling class."

[51] Congregation for the Doctrine of the Faith, *Instruction concerning Certain Aspects of Liberation Theology*, August 6, 1984. Two years later, another document was published: *Instruction of the Congregation for the Doctrine of the Faith on Christian Freedom and Liberation*, March 22, 1986. As Hubert Kirchner points out, the theme of liberation in this second document is set in a larger context, "so that the expression 'liberation theology' scarcely appears any more as a theme, although to a large extent there is room for its concerns" (Kirchner, *Römisch-katholische Kirche*, 120f.). Cf. John Paul II, encyclical *Sollicitudo rei socialis* (1988).

[52] Cf. *Report*, 169.

[53] Ibid., 170. Cf. Ratzinger, "Probleme von Glaubens- und Sittenlehre im europäischen Kontext", in *Zu Grundfragen der Theologie heute*, ed. Erzbischöfliches Generalvikariat Paderborn, Presse- und Informationsstelle, 7–17, citation at 10 (Paderborn, 1992): "The widespread

The main point in Ratzinger's critique of liberation theology was its adoption of Marxist theorems, whereby it thought that it could "build a bridge between Marx and the Bible".[54] Thus—according to Ratzinger's interpretation—the biblical concepts of "righteousness", "law", and "judgment", for example, which are variants on the Hebrew word *mishpat* and are among the most frequently recurring terms of the Old Testament, are interpreted in a this-worldly sense, in accordance with Old Testament usage.[55] This, he says, is an essential hallmark of the liberation-theology approach:

> The New Testament is taken back into the Old; redemption becomes the Exodus, interpreted in a political way, as the secular act of liberation, and thus the Kingdom of God becomes the product of the human act of liberation. In this process, it is not only Christology that totally loses its own features; the Old Testament itself is deprived of its dynamic that points ahead and upward, and it is turned around even in its own direction of movement.[56]

Accordingly, eschatology, too, then undergoes a political reinterpretation. The "kingdom", a central code word in all the variations of liberation theology, is built up as a future vision of this world:

> It is characteristic that one now speaks simply of the "kingdom"—without mentioning God—and that this is understood now as the ideal human society. It is the aim of faith and the task of all theology to work to bring about the "kingdom". The central word of faith becomes a political concept.... Faith itself thereby becomes political ideology. Politics has absorbed faith into itself.[57]

Ratzinger, on the contrary, is convinced that the Christian faith "goes beyond the social and political realm", and therefore, "precisely

---

approval that the political explanation of Christianity has met with, as we find it in liberation theology, which meanwhile has failed in practice, is based on the same causes. Redemption is replaced by liberation in the modern sense, which can be understood more in an individual psychological sense or in a collective political sense and which is also readily combined with the myth of progress."

[54] *Turning Point*, 72. Cf. G. Collet, "Befreiungstheologie. I. Historische, geographische und politische Wurzeln", in *LThK*, 3rd ed., 2:130–32, ref. at 132.

[55] *Turning Point*, 72.

[56] Ibid., 71.

[57] Ibid., 69.

in this, it is a faith in social responsibility." [58] Social responsibility is an essential part of Christian social doctrine, which is concerned with "making the faith operative, that is, relating the ethos of the faith to economic and political reason". [59] According to Ratzinger, such a responsibility must be guided by reason and will, so as to make God's law concrete and realize it

> in changing historical situations, always in the essential imperfect-ability of man's action within history. It is not permitted to man to set up the "Kingdom", but he is charged to go toward the Kingdom through justice and love. . . . Faith's hope always goes infinitely farther than all our realizations, reaching into the realm of the eternal; but precisely the fact that this hope is given to us gives us the courage to take up again and again, despite all inadequacy, the struggle for a just order that is the form of freedom and builds up a dam against the tyranny of injustice. [60]

Ratzinger's own response to the distress of poverty is guided by a comprehensive vision of man, which formulates what is distinctive in the Christian idea of freedom in a perspective that is historical and yet also goes beyond history. He is convinced that man's freedom "can exist only in the correct mutual allocation of these freedoms, and this is possible only if they all take the freedom of God and his truth as their criterion." [61] Therefore, in his opinion the only free person is the one who

> takes the criteria for his . . . action from within and needs to obey no external compulsion. For this reason the person who has become at one with his . . . essential nature, at one with the truth itself, is free. The person who is at one with the truth no longer acts according to external necessities and compulsions; in him . . . , nature,

---

[58] Ibid., 76. Cf. *Report*, 172–73: "Taking note of the signs of the times also means rediscovering the courage to look reality in the face, to see what is positive and what is negative. And if we take this objective line, we shall see that the secularist liberation programs have one element in common: they are attempting to achieve this liberation exclusively in the immanent plane, in history, in this world. But it is precisely this limited view, restricted to history and lacking an opening to transcendence, that has brought man to his present state."

[59] *Mitte*, 249–65, "Politik und Erlösung", citation at 262f.

[60] *Turning Point*, 77.

[61] Ibid., 73.

desire and action have come to coincide. In this way man within the finite can come into contact with the infinite, [can] bind himself ... to it and thus, precisely by recognizing his ... limits, [can] himself ... become infinite. Thus at the end it becomes [evident] once again that the Christian doctrine of freedom is not some petty moralism.[62]

In contrast, when progress is regarded merely as "a necessary process of the legitimate development of history, it is located below the level of what is genuinely human and in its depths it is conceived against man."[63] This deficiency is, according to Ratzinger, one reason for the dramatic upheavals of the year 1989, which not only changed the political landscape of Europe but also convulsed Marxist ideology worldwide.[64] At any rate, the idea of liberation has a wealth of other facets. It is manifested, for example, in feminism as well:

You might say that, here, political liberation theology has been superseded by an anthropological one. What is meant by liberation in this instance is not simply liberation from imposed social roles but, ultimately, a liberation that aims to free man from his human biological determination. . . . The idea that "nature" has something to say is no longer admissible; man is to have the liberty to remodel himself at will. He is to be free from all the prior givens of his essence. He makes of himself what he wants. . . . Man is to be his own creator—a modern, new edition of the immemorial attempt to be God, to be like God.[65]

Within the parameters of this section, it would take us too far afield to attempt to examine in more detail these individual problems and

---

[62] *Church*, 274–75.

[63] *Turning Point*, 89. Cf. "New Questions", 116: "Wherever politics tries to be redemptive, it is promising too much. Where it wishes to do the work of God, it becomes, not divine, but demonic."

[64] Cf. *Introduction*, 11ff., 18. Ratzinger refers here to the increasing perplexity and skepticism with regard to great ideals. See also "New Questions", 117–19.

[65] *Salt of the Earth*, 132–33. See also Elizabeth Schüssler Fiorenza, *Bread, Not Stones: The Challenge of Feminist Biblical Interpretation* (Boston: Beacon Press, 1984). See also the essay by the same author: "Ecclesia semper reformanda: Theologie als Ideologiekritik", *Conc(D)* 35 (1999): 70–77.

their cross-connections to the questions of the concept of God, interfaith dialogue,[66] the problem of inculturation, or the New Age movement.[67] Common to all these themes is that ultimately they are concretely related to the question about truth, which (according to Ratzinger) cannot be the result of votes or polls; instead, the Church must preserve her diachronic and synchronic unity in the service of the truth.[68]

In summarizing, Ratzinger admits that the various approaches of liberation theology also contain "really ... worthwhile insights",[69] in that they attempt "to rethink and elaborate the connections between faith and work, given today's assumptions".[70] Their basic problem, however, is their "faith in politics as a salvific force"[71] and the related notion that the idea of God has no practical purpose.[72]

---

[66] Cf. *Many Religions*, 17: "Liberation theology, understood in political terms, had given a new, political shape to questions about redemption and about the world's hope, questions that had long been pushed to one side." After the historical turning point of 1989, the basic themes of liberation theology, such as the search for freedom, justice, and protecting the environment, "are still current, [of course,] but now they are conceived in more modest terms and within a different framework. This different framework is, above all, the dialogue with the world religions, a dialogue that has become increasingly necessary in a world where cultures are more and more encountering and interpenetrating one another." Cf. Ratzinger, "Christentum: Der Sieg der Einsicht über die Welt der Religionen", *30 Tage* 18, no. 1 (2000): 33–44: lecture given on November 27, 1999, at the Sorbonne in Paris on the theme "Deux milles ans après quoi?"

[67] *Salt of the Earth*, 132–34.

[68] For him, this is one essential reason why the Church's Magisterium cannot simply follow the spirit of the age but must first recognize the limits of its own authority and, therefore, cannot approve, for example, of the ordination of women. On this subject, see *Report*, 93–96, citation at 94: "Evidently, Christian intuition understood that the question was not secondary, that to defend Scripture (which in neither the Old nor the New Testament knows women priests) signified once more to defend the human person, especially those of the female sex." Cf. Ratzinger, "Grenzen kirchlicher Vollmacht: Das neue Dokument von Papst Johannes Paul II. zur Frage der Frauenordination", *IKaZ* 23 (1994): 337–45.

[69] *Introduction*, 16.

[70] *Mitte*, 265. Cf. ibid., 263: "In the attempt made by liberation theology to bring utopia into play as a middle ground between empirical reason and faith, there was an intuition of something right that was wrongly applied, because the predominance of the utopia swallows up reason and leaves faith without an object."

[71] *Introduction*, 16.

[72] Ibid., 16f.

c. The debate with traditionalism

The prefect of the Congregation for the Faith understands his dealings with the followers of the late Archbishop Lefèbvre (d. 1991) to be another service for the unity of the Church. As Hubert Kirchner observes in his presentation of recent Church history, as late as April 1988 a meeting of theologians and canonists from both sides made "satisfactory progress".[73] Shortly thereafter Cardinal Ratzinger met again with Archbishop Lefèbvre. On May 5, 1988, "they signed a preliminary agreement that already formulated substantial aspects of the anticipated reunion".[74] Probably due to pressure from his extremist collaborators, Lefèbvre recanted and consecrated four bishops without permission on June 30, 1988. Consequently, "Archbishop Lefèbvre and the four bishops whom he consecrated incurred excommunication *latae sententiae* in keeping with the Code of Canon Law (can. 1382): the schism was accomplished."[75] According to Michael Karger, it is to Ratzinger's credit that supporters of the old [Tridentine] rite were preserved from the schism of the traditionalists through the founding of the Priestly Fraternity of St. Peter.[76] Here, too, it is clear that concern for Church unity determined Ratzinger's course of action.

d. Ecumenism: Sober realism

In a letter to the *Theologische Quartalschrift* [Theological quarterly], which in 1986 published a volume on the progress of ecumenism edited by Max Seckler, Ratzinger wrote:

> The moment when the Second Vatican Council created new foundations for ecumenical activity in the Catholic Church was preceded by a lengthy process of joint struggle in which much matured that could now quickly be implemented. The speed with which so much ... suddenly became possible seemed to give ground for hope of a rapid and complete end to the division. But when everything

---

[73] Kirchner, *Römisch-katholische Kirche*, 131.

[74] Ibid.

[75] J. Orlandis Rovira, *Stürmische Zeiten: Die katholische Kirche in der zweiten Hälfte des 20. Jahrhunderts* (Aachen: MM-Verlag, 1999), 112–16 and 243–45, citation at 244.

[76] Cf. M. Karger, "Kirche als Leib Christi und als Volk Gottes verbunden: Zum siebzigsten Geburtstag von Kardinal Joseph Ratzinger, dem Präfekten der römischen Kongregation für die Glaubenslehre", *Deutsche Tagespost* 50, no. 46 (April 15, 1997): 5.

that had become possible in this way was translated into official forms
a kind of standstill had necessarily to occur.... The blame had
unavoidably to be allocated, and it was easy to lay it at the door of
the Church authorities.[77]

In the same letter, Ratzinger speaks, together with Heinrich Schlier,
of an eschatological inevitability of factions, according to the verse
from St. Paul, "there must be factions."[78] He recognizes in this "must"
not only an impoverishment, but also "a new wealth of listening and
understanding",[79] so that it is possible, by way of the *felix culpa*, "to
find unity through diversity. That means to accept what is fruitful in
these divisions, to take the poison out of it and to receive precisely
the positive element from this diversity."[80] According to this sober
realism, prayer and penance, besides the learned disputes, are important steps along the way to the goal—penance, too, because "an admission of unfaithfulness to Christ on the part of all Christians, not only
on the Catholic side",[81] is salutary. Ultimately the goal is not something man-made but something God-given.

In this connection, we should recall the great *mea culpa* that Pope John
Paul II vicariously made for all Christians during the Holy Year 2000.
In a press conference concerning the document "Remembrance and Reconciliation: The Church and the Faults of the Past", Ratzinger spoke about
the theme of the factions among Christians, noting that it is necessary
to promote mutual encounters "from which can grow—along with the
memory of the past—the spirit of reconciliation that all sides need, the
purification of memory as well as the necessity of a new beginning".[82]
In the person of the present pope [John Paul II], he sees a pastor of the
Church who is pressing forward dynamically, especially in ecumenism.
"For this reason, it has always been an absurd claim that he [John Paul
II] wants to go back [to the days] before the Council."[83]

---

[77] *Church*, 135–142, citation at 135f.
[78] 1 Cor 11:19.
[79] *Church*, 138.
[80] Ibid., 139.
[81] *Report*, 160.
[82] Ratzinger, "Nur die Wirklichkeit der Vergebung macht das Bekenntnis der Sünden
möglich", *30 Tage* 18, no. 3 (2000): 24–27.
[83] *Salt of the Earth*, 260. Ratzinger describes Pope John Paul II as follows: "He has always
been decidedly a Pope of the Second Vatican Council.... He had a very constructive role

Eloquent testimony to this assessment is the signing of the Joint
Declaration by the Catholic Church and the Lutheran World Federation on the Doctrine of Justification on October 31, 1999. Ratzinger
commented: "Even if you did not exactly understand the substance of
the proceedings, there was simply a sigh of relief that unity is growing, that the burden of separation is diminishing."[84] Nevertheless, Ratzinger's realistic view is striking here as well. He finds fault with the
fact that "to this day no one has really succeeded in expressing in
contemporary language the doctrine of justification."[85] For the religious experience of Martin Luther in his day, dread of God's wrath,
by which sinful man knew that he was threatened, is essentially different, after all, from today's picture of man's relation to God. It is not
"God's wrath [that] terrifies, but his absence. And so, of course, an
entirely new reassurance concerning salvation and healing becomes
necessary."[86] According to Ratzinger, this is significant for ecumenical dialogue.

The theological dialogue is not concerned with finding out what
can still be demanded of each party and what is still useful ... but
rather with discovering deeper points of convergence beneath the

---

in drawing up the Constitution *Gaudium et spes*.... So this document, which is probably
the most dynamic and forward-looking document of the Council as a whole, became
almost a sort of maxim for his life.... And he naturally also notices more and more that
there are diverse, countervailing interpretations of the Council. For this reason he speaks
of 'fidelity' to it, which is naturally a dynamic fidelity. It is not what we would like the
Council to have said that must determine our course, but what the Council really said"
(ibid., 260–61).

[84] Ratzinger, "Wie weit trägt der Konsens über die Rechtfertigungslehre?" *IKaZ* 29
(2000): 424–37, citation at 424.

[85] Ibid., 427. In this passage, Ratzinger points out that "a paradigm shift has taken place;
our position in the coordinate system of reality has put us into a completely different
perspective, from which we must reorganize our insights and experiences. This very fact is
our ecumenical opportunity today. The fact that today we can overcome our differences,
which formerly were abysmal, is not based on the fact that we have become wiser or
holier, ... but simply on the fact that our vantage point in reality has given us a different
view of the whole situation." (See also *God and the World*, 450f.)

[86] Ratzinger, "Wie weit trägt der Konsens", 430. See also "Absurd", 52: Points of convergence beneath different linguistic forms can be discovered when it is recognized that
the "context for the experience of God and the self" has changed, "and so the language
can be regarded from a distance and at the same time from a perspective that remains in
substantial identity, so that the foundational intuitions emerge from behind the passions
that divide, in each case purified, and can be related to one another."

different linguistic formulae and learning to distinguish what is historically incidental to a period from what is genuinely fundamental.[87]

Furthermore, the question of the authority of a "Magisterium" of the Churches or ecclesial communities—one that could testify authoritatively to the *sensus fidelium*—has become rancorous in the interdenominational dialogue. Here, in Ratzinger's opinion, arises the immediate question about the importance of tradition, whereby the Protestant principle of *sola Scriptura* is placed in a new light: "By itself, so to speak, from the intrinsic commission of the Church and from its vital requirements, something like a teaching authority (I do not say "Magisterium") has taken shape in the Protestant sphere as well. This is encouraging." [88]

Basically the unity of the Church, according to Ratzinger, is a *datum*, something given that is not brought about by ecumenical models for reunion or "restored by some kind of political coup",[89] since neither a pope nor a world council of churches can act unilaterally in this matter. The ecumenical task consists, rather, in this: "We can only humbly seek to essentialize our faith, that is, to recognize what are the really essential elements in it—the things we have not made but have received from the Lord—and in this attitude of turning to the Lord and to the center, to open ourselves in this essentializing so that he may lead us onward, he alone." [90]

The declaration *Dominus Iesus*, too, which caused a worldwide controversy in the fall of 2000, was quite obviously meant to promote this essentialization of the faith. According to Ratzinger's own words, it was the purpose of this declaration in particular to make "a great and solemn profession of the lordship of Jesus Christ at the climax of the Holy Year".[91] Unintentionally, however, the controversy centered on

---

[87] Ratzinger, "Absurd", 52.

[88] Ratzinger, "Wie weit trägt der Konsens", 436. Cf. "Absurd", 52: "... a practical example: In the dispute with Gerd Lüdemann, it became quite clear that the Lutheran Church cannot get by without a magisterium, either. In the dissolving of the contours of the faith through a chorus of contradictory exegetical efforts ... , we see that it is precisely continuity with the creeds, and thus with the living tradition of the Church, that guarantees the literalness of Scripture."

[89] *God and the World*, 453.

[90] Ibid.

[91] "Absurd", 51. Cf. 1 Cor 12:3 and Jn 6:68f.

the Catholic concept of Church, as the Second Vatican Council had
expounded it in the *subsistit* formula.[92] Many theologians were indig-
nant,[93] especially over the formulation in *Dominus Iesus* number 17
about the "Unicity and Unity of the Church":[94]

> On the other hand, the ecclesial communities which have not pre-
> served the valid Episcopate and the genuine and integral substance
> of the Eucharistic mystery, are not Churches in the proper sense. . . .
> "The Christian faithful are therefore not permitted to imagine that
> the Church of Christ is nothing more than a collection—divided,
> yet in some way one—of Churches and ecclesial communities; nor
> are they free to hold that today the Church of Christ nowhere really
> exists, and must be considered only as a goal."[95]

In an interview with the *Frankfurter Allgemeine Zeitung*, Ratzinger
confirmed that the *subsistit* formula means to say that the "being of
the Church as such" extends much farther "than the Roman Catholic
Church, but in her it has in a unique way the character of a proper
subject".[96] In that interview, he speaks also about the so-called reconciled diversity.[97] This cannot mean that the contents of the faith
become inconsequential, thereby dismissing the question of truth,

> so that we would all regard ourselves as one, even though we believe
> and teach contrary things. The term is correctly applied, as I under-
> stand it, when it means that despite all the differences—which do
> not allow us simply to make everything out to be fragments, as it
> were, of a Church of Jesus Christ that does not really exist—we
> encounter one another as people who have been reconciled with
> one another in the peace of Christ.[98]

---

[92] *LG* 8.
[93] On this subject, see M. Mühl and J.-H. Tück, "Stellungnahmen zu *Dominus Iesus*:
Ein erster bibliographischer Überblick", in *"Dominus Iesus": Anstößige Wahrheit oder anstößige
Kirche? Dokumente, Hintergründe, Standpunkte und Folgerungen*, ed. M.J. Rainer, 2nd ed.,
336–45 (Münster: Lit, 2001).
[94] *DI*, nos. 16f.
[95] Ibid., no. 17. Cf. *LG* 22; *UR* 3, 22; Congregation for the Doctrine of the Faith,
declaration *Mysterium Ecclesiae*, in *AAS* 65 (1973): 398.
[96] "Absurd", 51.
[97] Ibid., 52.
[98] Ibid.

In saying this, Ratzinger does not bow down to the "subjectivist and relativistic thesis that everyone can be saved in his own way".[99] The claim of truth demands, particularly in ecumenical dialogue, fidelity to the Lord, who is himself the truth.[100] This faith is "something living, ... and it can never, through any possible political manipulations, be brought to some kind of formula of compromise."[101] How is the question of the unity of the Church posed today, at the beginning of the third Christian millennium? Ratzinger, in an interview with Peter Seewald, summarizes the situation as follows:

> The formula that the great ecumenists have invented is that we go forward together. It's not a matter of our wanting to achieve certain processes of integration, but we hope that the Lord will awaken people's faith everywhere in such a way that it overflows from one to the other, and the one Church is there. As Catholics, we are persuaded that the basic shape of this one Church is given us in the Catholic Church, but that she is moving toward the future and will allow herself to be educated and led by the Lord. In that sense we do not picture for ourselves any particular model of integration, but simply look to march on in faith under the leadership of the Lord—who knows the way.[102]

This marching on with Christ in the service of Church unity, as "co-workers of the truth", as the motto says, visibly characterizes Ratzinger's episcopal ministry. His ascent to ministerial office prompted him to reflect on the metaphor of the beast of burden in Psalm 72 (73): "Ut iumentum factus sum apud te et ego semper tecum", which he is fond of translating as St. Augustine did: "I have become your donkey, and in just this way am I with you."[103]

[99] Ibid. Cf. K. Berger, "Keine Ohrfeige für Protestanten: Warum *Dominus Iesus* auch für protestantische Christen nützlich sein kann", *Die Tagespost* 53, no. 141 (November 25, 2000): 6.

[100] See *DI*, no. 2. Cf. Jn 14:6.

[101] *God and the World*, 453.

[102] Ibid., 452–53.

[103] *Milestones*, 154–56, esp. 156.

SECTION 2

RECURRING THEMES IN
RATZINGER'S ECCLESIOLOGY

Corresponding to the plan of part 1 of this book, "The Church's Self-Understanding according to *Lumen gentium*", this section will trace through several decades of Ratzinger's theological writings some of the principal themes in *Lumen gentium*: "mystery", "People of God", and "hierarchy". In this way it should become clear (1) to what extent his thought is in agreement with the statements of the Constitution on the Church; (2) where he takes up and elaborates on aspects of *Lumen gentium*;[1] and also (3) on what issues his position is different from that of *Lumen gentium*. Furthermore, we will be interested in pursuing the question already raised in the biographical part about the continuity or discontinuity in Ratzinger's theological approach. We intend to discuss this question with the help of concrete examples, so as to arrive at a nuanced conclusion. Finally, in the last chapter of this section, we will examine significant emphases in Ratzinger's ecclesiology so as to focus on their distinctive features.

---

[1] On this subject, see "Kollegialität", 70. Ratzinger concludes this 1966 essay with the statement that "it would be wrong if theologians were now to devote all their work and energies to interpreting the Council. The point of this document in particular is not to absorb the efforts of the theologians but rather to lead them beyond themselves and to guide them to the very sources of the perpetual rejuvenation of all theology: to Sacred Scripture and to the rich treasures that can be found anew in every generation in the writings of the Church Fathers" (ibid.).

Chapter 1

The Church—Sign of Faith and Mystery of Faith

§ 1. The Reception of the New Ecclesiological Approaches
of the Renewal Movements

As a young theologian, Ratzinger was impressed by the ecclesiological ideas of the renewal movements of his time. The first subdivision of this section shows how Ratzinger's thought was formed by
the dynamic of the whole that was fueled by the efforts for renewal
at that time. Especially important for his ecclesiology is the new
approach to the Church as a mystery. In November 1962, it was
included in the schema of the Constitution on the Church.[2] The
vision of the Church as a *mysterium* was accompanied by the rediscovery of her sacramental structure. We take this as our theme in a
second subdivision. Finally, the third subdivision of this section is
devoted exclusively to one of Ratzinger's concerns that also has ecumenical significance, namely, how to combine the Western Body of
Christ ecclesiology with the Eastern Churches' trinitarian understanding of the Church.

1. *The dynamic of the whole as the proper form*

The Second Vatican Council "articulated . . . what had matured in the
way of insight based on faith during those four decades full of hope
and new departures between 1920 and 1960".[3] So said Ratzinger in a
lecture in Foggia, Italy, on October 21, 1985. Twenty years before
that, the former conciliar advisor had already reached this conclusion

---

[2] Cf. Alberigo/Magistretti, 3.

[3] J. Ratzinger, "The Ecclesiology of the Second Vatican Council", reprinted in *IKaZ* 15
(1986): 41–52, and in *Church*, 3–28, citation at 3.

at the beginning of his commentary about the Constitution on the Church:

> The Constitution . . . is the result of a rather long project—or better: a process of intellectual renewal that went back many years. . . . The biblical movement, the liturgical movement, the ecclesiological movement, the ecumenical movement—all these taken together were the expression of a single new impulse, which . . . in the midst of the crisis expressed the new vitality that had simply been bestowed on the Church, which knows that in her origin are also hidden the enduring forces of her renewal.[4]

This dynamic is the inspiration for Ratzinger's ecclesiological *oeuvre* as well.[5] In 1956—that was the year when he was writing his *habilitation* thesis and first became personally acquainted with the theologian Karl Rahner[6]—he wrote an article quite in the spirit of that time with the title "The Church as the Mystery of Faith", which he later put at the beginning of his postconciliar book *Das neue Volk Gottes* [The new People of God].[7] In this essay, Ratzinger intended to give a "nonpolemical presentation of the main lines of the New Testament concept of Church",[8] taking into account the perspective of the Church Fathers[9] and in contrast to the view of the Church as a "societas perfecta".[10] This was supposed to overcome the narrowly juridical view of the Church and the reduction of her to her visible structure. This concern had developed earlier in the period

---

[4] "Einleitung", 7.

[5] Therefore, in looking back at the Council, he admits, with Karl Rahner, that "each individual could only make his own modest contribution to a totality that flowed together from many sources and would not tolerate a dedication to one author or another." See Ratzinger, "Geleitwort", in Weiler, xiii. Cf. K. Rahner, "Theologische Grundinterpretationen des II. Vatikanischen Konzils", in *Schriften zur Theologie*, by Rahner, 14:287–302 (Einsiedeln, Zürich, and Cologne: Benziger, 1980).

[6] *Milestones*, 107.

[7] Ratzinger, "Die Kirche als Geheimnis des Glaubens", *LebZeug* 4 (1956/57): 19–34; later reprinted under the title "Vom Ursprung und vom Wesen der Kirche", in *Volk Gottes*, 9–24.

[8] Ibid., 9, n. 1.

[9] Ibid., 20ff.

[10] Ibid., 9f. As a way of characterizing that antireform approach—which is at the same time apologetic—Ratzinger in his 1985 review of the Council quoted J. A. Möhler, who caricatured the one-sidedly juridical view of the Church in these terms: "Christ in the beginning established the hierarchy and by doing so did enough to look after the Church until the end of time" (cf. *Church*, 4).

between the two world wars, which was so full of enthusiasm for ecclesiology, with the rediscovery of the Church as the Body of Christ:

> People saw this as getting over a one-sidedly legal and institutional understanding of Church, which they liked to sum up with the term "hierarchology". Discourse about the Body of Christ moved the Church out of all those mere legalities and externals and into the realm of mystery with Christ as the center.[11]

That led, however, as Ratzinger recognized, to the problem of the unmediated juxtaposition of the new dogmatic teaching about the Church's mystery of faith and the previous apologetic ecclesiology:[12]

> Thus arose ... the danger of a disastrous two-track approach, a division of the Church into "the Church of law and the Church of love", as a widely used slogan put the distinction (citing Rudolf Sohm). Meanwhile the expression "Body of Christ" ran the risk of expressing the incorporeal quality of the Church (Koster). In reality, however, there is only one, single, indivisible Church, which is at the same time the mystery of faith and the sign of faith, mysterious life and the visible phenomenal form of this life.[13]

When the Second Vatican Council formulated its teaching about the Church as a consequence of the newly developed ecclesiological consciousness, the point, according to Ratzinger, was not "to outline a new theory about the Church", nor was it a question of the Church "reflecting on herself". Rather, it was supposed to help the Church "to be truly free for the Lord, or as the Church Fathers put it in a wonderful metaphor: The Church is like the moon, which does not have its light from itself or for itself; upon her face is reflected the light of Christ, and it shines for the people who need guidance in the night of this earthly age."[14] He uses the

---

[11] *Volk und Haus Gottes*, xi.

[12] Cf. *Volk Gottes*, 11.

[13] Ibid.

[14] "Einleitung", 8. Cf. *LG* 1. On the symbolism of the moon, see also Ratzinger, "Why I Am Still in the Church", in *Two Say Why: Why I Am Still a Christian; Why I Am Still in the Church*, by H. U. von Balthasar and J. Ratzinger, trans. John Griffiths, 65–90, ref. at

same metaphor in his apologia, "Why I Am Still in the Church", which was published in 1971 together with a similar essay by Hans Urs von Balthasar as a book entitled *Plädoyer für die Kirche* [*Two Say Why*, 1973]:

> The essence of the Church is that it counts for nothing in itself, in that the thing about it that counts is what it is not, in that it exists only to be dispossessed, in that it possesses a light that it is not and because of which alone it nonetheless is. The Church is the moon— the *mysterium lunae*—and thus exists for the faithful, for thus it is the place of an enduring spiritual decision.[15]

Summarizing, Ratzinger says that that is why the first message of the Church is "Christ" and not herself; "it is healthy to the extent that all its attention is directed towards him."[16] This fundamental insight was expressed by the Council in the first sentence of the Constitution on the Church *Lumen gentium*, to wit: Since Christ is the light of the world, the Church, being the mirror of his glory, can transmit his light. From this, Ratzinger draws the conclusion: "To understand Vatican II correctly one must always and repeatedly begin with this first sentence."[17]

As the conclusion of this first subsection, we can state that Ratzinger's ecclesiology is shaped by the rediscovery of the unique mystery of the Church, a theme that was incorporated in the Constitution on the Church as chapter 1 with the title "De Ecclesiae mysterio". For Ratzinger, who "during the Octave of Christmas in 1962 joined the circle of authors of the schema",[18] this sacramental dimension of the Church had a decisive status. The process by which the Council rediscovered it will be presented in the following paragraphs from Ratzinger's perspective.

76–79 (Chicago: Franciscan Herald Press, 1973). See also the section "Mysterium Lunae", in *Symbole der Kirche: Die Ekklesiologie der Väter*, by H. Rahner, 91–173 (Salzburg: Müller, 1964).

[15] Ratzinger, "Why I Am Still in the Church", 79. Ratzinger refers to Ambrose, *Hexaemeron* 4, 8, 32, in CSEL 32, 1, 137f.

[16] *Church*, 5.

[17] Ibid.

[18] Wassilowsky, 278. Cf. Weiler, 212.

2. Not a functional, but a sacramental, perspective of the Ecclesia

As Ratzinger observes, "the word *sacramentum* as a designation for the Church"[19] first occurred in March 1963 in an official text drafted by the competent conciliar commission. The draft contained "the words that survived all further alterations: *Cum vero Ecclesia sit in Christo signum et instrumentum seu veluti sacramentum intimae totius generis humani unitatis eiusque in Deum unionis . . . : '. . .* the Church is, in Christ, a sacrament, as it were, a sign and instrument of the most intimate union with God as well as of the unity of all mankind.'"[20] These words were introduced into the Constitution on the Church by the chief editor of *Lumen gentium*, the Belgian theologian Gérard Philips, who "may have adopted this formula from a draft that was composed by German theologians".[21] Through this new ecclesiological approach, he was able to uncover again the *sacramental* structure[22] of the Church.

As Ratzinger explains, the term "sacramental" is used here "in opposition to that superficial view which often enough tried to see the Church as established on the level of worldly legitimacy and to seek for the Church a place among worldly institutions".[23] Above all, the papacy, which for a long time had been regarded in isolation as a

---

[19] *Principles*, 44. Ratzinger elaborates, ibid.: "The word had not appeared in the first draft of the Theological Commission, which had been prepared by Sebastian Tromp, S.J., the principal author of Pius XII's encyclical on the Mystical Body. Nor had it occurred in the first alternative draft offered by the Belgian theologian Gérard Philips on November 22, 1962. Toward the end of 1962, Philips revised his text.... On March 6, 1963, the Commission accepted as the basis of further discussion this revision." It contains the important term *mysterium*. J. Grootaers remarks that it is difficult to trace the development of the schema by G. Philips. See Grootaers, "Zwischen den Sitzungsperioden: Die 'zweite Vorbereitung' des Konzils und ihre Gegner", in Wittstadt, 2:421–617, ref. at 475, n. 82; cf. ibid., 479.

[20] *Principles*, 44.

[21] Ibid. Ratzinger is one of the theologians who used this expression even before the Council: cf. *Volk Gottes*, 9–24; *Principles*, 50. As early as the 1930s, the concept of the Church as sacrament had "made a breakthrough" in the writings of Henri de Lubac; see de Lubac, *Catholicism: Christ and the Common Destiny of Man*, trans. Lancelot C. Sheppard and Sister Elizabeth Englund, O.C.D. (San Francisco: Ignatius Press, 1988). See also S. Alberto, "Begriff und Wesen der Kirche in der Entstehung der Kirchenkonstitution *Lumen gentium*", in *Ex latere: Ausfaltungen communialer Theologie*, ed. E. Naab, 156, 169f., n. 32 (Eichstätt: Franz-Sales-Verlag, 1993).

[22] Cf. *LG* 1.

[23] *Highlights*, 48.

purely juridical position, was to be rediscovered in its sacramental dimension.[24] In contrast to this externalized image of the Church, "as it had prevailed to a great extent at the beginning of the modern era, the Constitution of the Council attempts to set forth again the unique character of the 'communion of saints' that is mentioned in the Creed." [25] If the Church herself is a sacred sign "among men, then it does not exist for its own sake." [26]

Ratzinger proved to be disappointed, however, by the fact that a quarter-century after the Council, the Church was regarded not so much from the perspective of her being as under the aspect of her changing. The ecclesiological theme "has to a large extent become the question of how the Church can be changed and ameliorated. Yet even someone who wishes to improve upon a mechanical device, and all the more someone who wants to heal an organism, must first investigate how the apparatus is designed or how the organism is inwardly structured." [27] For Ratzinger, the fundamental question of the origin and the nature of the Church arises, *not in functional terms*, but always in terms of her *being*:

> What is the Church in the first place? What is the purpose of her existence? What is her origin? Did Christ actually will her, and, if so, how did he intend her to be? Only if we are able to reply properly to these basic questions do we have any chance of finding an adequate answer to the particular practical problems mentioned above.[28]

Hence the first thing needed is "to view the inside and the outside of the Church together as a unity again".[29] Concretely, that means that her inner mystery must not become detached from her external

---

[24] *Principles*, 195. Cf. "Einleitung", 8f.: "Every age is more or less dependent on its own presuppositions in its view of the Church. So it is not surprising that in Catholic theology of the modern period Church was understood to a great extent as an authoritarian state, with the pope at the top as the absolute monarch; then came the ecclesial aristocracy of the bishops and their assistants, the priests, and finally, in a purely passive role, the subjects, the faithful people."

[25] "Einleitung", 9.

[26] *Highlights*, 48.

[27] *Called to Communion*, 9.

[28] Ibid., 13. Cf. *LG* 5.

[29] *Volk Gottes*, 10.

(hierarchical) organization.[30] The nature of the Church is to be the Church of Jesus Christ, and not of men.[31] That is why, shortly after the Council, Ratzinger criticized the fact "that the concept of the Church as a sacrament is not yet deeply entrenched either in the consciousness of the Church or in theology".[32] Citing Origen, he states that this is related to the fact that "we discover the spiritual meaning of a *mysterium*, of a *holy* sign, only when we live the mystery."[33] Church as sacrament or mystery expresses a relationship, based on her own sign-character:

> I understand it as a sign only if I enter into its referential context, if I enter upon the way that it is. But if a sign, a visible reality, points to what is invisible, what is divine, it is eminently clear that I can discover its referential context only by identifying myself with it, by allowing myself to be incorporated into the relationship that makes the sign a sign.[34]

So that the Church can function as a sign of salvation, and thus be an instrument in bringing about the union of God and men with each other, she must have, according to Ratzinger, a "fullness of power" that is not derived from ourselves but is imparted by divine "institution".[35] This corresponds to the statement in *Lumen gentium* that Christ himself is her origin and her essential center.[36] From him is derived the unity of the Church's visible and invisible reality in her corporate constitution[37] as well as in her sacramental manner of existing.[38] Thus the one, unique, and indivisible Church is "at the same time a mystery

---

[30] Cf. ibid., 11.

[31] Cf. *Report*, 48f.

[32] *Principles*, 45.

[33] Ibid., 48.

[34] Ibid., 47–48. In Ratzinger's view, therefore, intellectual insight coincides with one's own conversion. Accordingly, the power of this spiritual process can transform a person radically (ibid., 51).

[35] Cf. ibid., 48.

[36] Cf. *LG* 3.

[37] Cf. *LG* 7.

[38] Cf. *LG* 1, 9, 48, 59. Especially *LG* 9: "God gathered together as one all those who in faith look upon Jesus as the author of salvation and the source of unity and peace, and established them as the Church that for each and all it may be the visible sacrament of this saving unity." On this question, see *Volk Gottes*, 11–24: "The Unity of the Two Aspects of the Church".

of faith and a sign of faith, mysterious life and the visible phenomenal form of this life".[39] For this reason, ecclesiology and Christology are directly related to each other. Christ produces the Church in the profession of faith, baptism, and the Eucharist and makes her into his body by filling her with his Spirit. In her trinitarian reality, the Church, as *Lumen gentium* says, is the People of the Father,[40] the Body of Christ,[41] and the Temple of the Holy Spirit.[42]

According to Ratzinger, both ecclesiology and Christology can be understood only in light of the trinitarian mystery.[43] In a lecture[44] given in 1967, he reported that during the Council, through the rediscovery of the Pneumatology of the Eastern Church, some of the inflexibility of Western theology, which had come about by neglecting it in the past, was progressively relaxed: "In the sight of the conciliar discussion, both the idea of the Church as the Body of Christ and the christological understanding of the Church appeared largely as the antithesis of a pneumatological understanding of the Church."[45]

In his opinion, that was due to the fact that the expression "Body of Christ" was interpreted "more in terms of the Incarnation, while actually skipping the Resurrection",[46] so as to emphasize what is corporeal, that is, institutional in the Church. The Church appears then—following Ratzinger's reasoning—"as the continuation of the fact that God once became flesh in history. . . . From this prior understanding, that *corpus* means first of all corporeality, results also the strict

---

[39] *Volk Gottes*, 11.

[40] On this subject, see *LG* 2.

[41] See *LG* 3.

[42] Cf. *LG* 4.

[43] On this subject, see "Geist und Kirche", 91–97.

[44] Ratzinger, "Kirche als Tempel des Heiligen Geistes" [The Church as temple of the Holy Spirit], in *Mitte*, 148–57. The original title of the lecture, which Ratzinger gave in Salzburg on September 29, 1967, was "Aspects of the Church".

[45] Ibid., 148.

[46] Ibid. See also ibid., 149f.: "From such a perspective we might say that the absence in Western ecclesiology of the basic ecclesiological themes of the freedom, charisms, and multiplicity of Churches in the one Church is the result of its narrow emphasis on Christology, of the absence of Pneumatology in its ecclesiology, and its reduction of Pneumatology to Christology, which the Eastern theologian then sees exemplified in the *Filioque* of the Creed, which after all was *the* or [at least] one source of the dispute, inasmuch as here, symptomatically and in principle, Pneumatology seems to be reduced to Christology."

limitation of the Church."[47] This "narrowing down" was broken up in "the renewed encounter with Scripture and the Church Fathers, as well as in the ecumenical discussions occasioned by Vatican II ... in favor of an idea of the Incarnation that was shaped more by Easter and in favor of a more emphatically trinitarian approach in Christology".[48]

In the course of this dissertation, therefore, the new question arises of the bridge between the Western *Corpus Christi ecclesiology* and the *trinitarian understanding of the Church* typical of the Eastern Churches. In order to demonstrate a connection between christological and pneumatological ecclesiology, Ratzinger takes his bearings, on the one hand, from Augustine, who in opposition to the Donatists had emphasized the indivisible unity of the Spirit and the Body of Christ: "Do you want to have the Spirit of Christ? Then be in the Body of Christ! You cannot have the Spirit as something separated and free-floating, so to speak; rather, it is the Spirit of Christ's Body",[49] and, on the other hand, from the holistic biblical and Semitic understanding of "body".

3. The Semitic understanding of σῶμα Χριστοῦ *as the bridge between christological and pneumatological ecclesiology*

Ratzinger presupposes that the two images of the Church, "Body of Christ" and "Temple of the Holy Spirit", are not contradictory but rather complementary and interdependent. That is to say, they explain each other and reciprocally articulate the trinitarian and the sacramental understanding of the Church.[50] He sees the demonstration of their intrinsic connection as a project for theology today.

---

[47] Ibid., 149. See also ibid., 154. Cf. *Introduction*, 333f.

[48] Ratzinger, "Geleitwort", in *Komm, Schöpfer Geist: Betrachtungen zum Hymnus Veni Creator Spiritus*, by R. Cantalamessa, 11–14, citation at 11 (Freiburg im Breisgau: Herder, 1999).

[49] Ratzinger, "Kirche als Tempel", 154.

[50] Cf. S. Wiedenhofer, "I. Theologische Grundlegung—Einführung", in *Mitte*, 123–26, ref. at 124. See J. Ratzinger, "Kirche", in *LThK*, 2nd ed., 6:172–83, citation at 176f.: "When categorizing and ordering the individual phenomena of ecclesial existence, we must keep in mind the Church's specific position within salvation history, which results from the correct understanding of the interrelationship and unity of her christological and pneumatological aspects." Cf. also Weiler, 84ff.: "Der christologische und pneumatologische Aspekt der Ekklesiologie Ratzingers", esp. 85: "According to Ratzinger, 'any direct and exclusive derivation of the institution from the Incarnation', as traditional ecclesiology used to attempt, would be 'unbiblical'."

Teaching about the Church must take its departure from teaching about the Holy Spirit and his gifts. But its goal lies in a doctrine of the history of God with men or, alternatively, of the function of the story of Christ for mankind as a whole. This indicates at the same time in what direction Christology must evolve. It is not to be developed as a doctrine of God's taking root in the world, a doctrine that, starting from Jesus' humanity, interprets the Church in an all too worldly fashion. Christ remains present through the Holy Spirit with all his openness and breadth and freedom, which by no means exclude the institutional form but limit its claims and do not allow it simply to make itself the same as worldly institutions.[51]

Where, though, does Ratzinger find the bridge, so that christological and pneumatological ecclesiology do not stand side by side as antitheses? His answer is: in the biblical perspective of the σῶμα Χριστοῦ. A precise analysis, in fact, shows that in Scripture there is

no such opposition between body and spirit, because the talk about σῶμα Χριστοῦ, about the Body of Christ, is in no sense taken to mean a direct continuation of the earthly corporeality of Jesus as a permanent corporeality; rather, the expression σῶμα Χριστοῦ, the Body of Christ, as applied to the Church in the New Testament, should be understood (a) with reference to the passages about the Last Supper and (b) in light of the Resurrection. And both of these, in turn, must be interpreted against the background of the Semitic biblical terminology and not according to the presuppositions of our concept of body.[52]

It is characteristic of the Semitic interpretation of the expression σῶμα Χριστοῦ used in the accounts of the Last Supper—"This is my body (σῶμα μου)"—that it makes no distinction between body and soul in our Western sense, and "consequently there is no word for body, as we understand it, that is, for the concept of body as considered separately from the soul."[53] When the New Testament speaks in terms of σῶμα, body, "the totality of corporeal man is meant, man as

---

[51] *Introduction*, 333–34.
[52] Ratzinger, "Kirche als Tempel", 150. See also Ratzinger, "Kommentar zu Artikel 11–22 der Pastoralkonstitution *Gaudium et spes*", in *LThK.E*, vol. 3 (Freiburg im Breisgau: Herder, 1968), 323.
[53] Ibid.

person, so that σῶμα often becomes the equivalent of person."[54] With reference to the Last Supper accounts, this means that the statement "This is my body [σῶμα μου]" expresses (as Ratzinger put it) the *whole reality* of the Lord.

It means Jesus himself, who is present with what is his own and with the uniqueness of his "I" and thus is fully, completely, and really present and devotes himself to man's "I" as the one who is complete, one, and indivisible. His statement at the Last Supper, "This is my body, which is given for you", therefore, does not mean something like, "Here you are receiving my body", but means to say, rather, "In this bread I give myself—that is the meaning of σῶμα—I give myself up for you, through it I am in your midst and there for you", whereby this expression "for you" specifies and defines what is proper to Jesus' "I", so to speak, the genuine substance, the core of the reality . . . his whole existence. The "I" of Jesus is precisely in its most authentic reality the act of self-giving, of service, of being open for all.[55]

In this mode of being present, "act and substance mutually interpenetrate."[56] At the same time, this is the place where the Last Supper is appreciated in the light of the Resurrection.[57]

By way of supplementing the term σῶμα, Ratzinger sheds light also on the Johannine term σάρξ, "flesh",[58] which "again does not designate the merely corporeal flesh as a physical element, separated from the spirit", but rather expresses human life in its earthly existence and, thus, a "form of corporeality that is a bridge and a boundary but is

---

[54] Ibid., 150f.
[55] Ibid., 151.
[56] Ibid.
[57] Ratzinger, "Geleitwort", in Cantalamessa, *Komm, Schöpfer Geist*, 11f.: "There was a new awareness of how closely [united to the Spirit] Paul and John see Christ as being. Think of the magnificent—albeit oft misunderstood—statement from the Second Letter to the Corinthians: 'The Lord is the Spirit' (2 Cor 3:17). Think of Jesus' discourse at the Last Supper, in which the Lord inseparably unites his coming again with the coming of the Holy Spirit and connects his word with that of the Holy Spirit. The Spirit of Truth will lead the disciples into the fullness of the truth that they cannot yet bear, not speaking on his own authority, but glorifying Christ, just as Christ does not speak on his own authority but glorifies the Father (cf. Jn 16:13f.)."
[58] See Jn 6:51ff.; cf. also Jn 1:14.

also and especially limit, isolation, and enclosure."[59] The biblical accounts of the institution [of the Eucharist], however, presuppose that "Jesus, because he was crucified and is risen, no longer exists in the form of σαρξ, but has left this historical form of existence behind"[60] and encounters us now in a completely new openness. The Gospel of John testifies to this openness in chapter 19, with its reference to the pierced side of Jesus.[61] In Ratzinger's view, the Johannine account of the Passion, indeed, all of Johannine theology, culminates here:

> Jesus' side is opened, and from it come forth blood and water, that is, the two fundamental sacraments of baptism and Eucharist and therein the Church. From this open side comes the fact that Jesus now exists as otherwise only spirit can exist, namely, as the one who is opened, the one who at all times can be there and is there for everyone. And that means, in biblical terminology, that the σωμα of Jesus, that is, his form of corporeality, is πνευμα.[62]

The peculiar formula σωμα is πνευμα is supposed to express the fact that Christ's body no longer continues to exist in the "form of intra-historical corporeality, which is enclosure, but rather continues to exist in a new manner, namely, as pure communication, as pure openness, as pure transcendence [Hyper], as pure being-for-others".[63] In such an understanding, the ecclesiological Body of Christ concept, which since Mystici Corporis had been referred corporately to the Catholic Church, is reconciled with the concerns of the ecumenical movement, for which a corporate interpretation of Corpus Christi was problematic. At that time—as Ratzinger observed—the consequences of this narrow interpretation (Body of Christ = Catholic Church) were weighty, manifesting themselves particularly in the question of membership in the Church.[64] In contrast, the pneumatic understanding of the Body of Christ concept results also in a new view of membership in the Church:

---

[59] Ratzinger, "Kirche als Tempel", 151.
[60] Ibid.
[61] See Jn 19:34.
[62] Ratzinger, "Kirche als Tempel", 152.
[63] Ibid.
[64] Ibid.

It is no longer faced with the exclusive alternative, "member or non-member", belonging to the Body or not belonging to it; instead, a completely different pair of concepts emerges, namely, belonging in a supportive and productive way [*tragend*] or belonging in a supported and derivative way [*getragen*].[65]

When the Church lives in this meshing of bearing and being borne, she merges, "on the one hand, with Christ, by bearing with him and thus becoming the Body of Christ in the narrower sense", and, on the other hand, she merges "with mankind, inasmuch as she, like it, is borne up by him".[66] The actual "subject is . . . 'Christ' himself",[67] and the Church is—as Ratzinger puts it—"nothing but the space of this new unitary subject, which is, therefore, much more than mere social interaction".[68]

In summary, we can observe that, by building a bridge from Christology to Pneumatology, Ratzinger opens up a new horizon, because in this way he demonstrates that there are many layers to the Church as the Body of Christ. With the help of the pneumatic understanding of *Corpus Christi*, he overcomes the corporate rigidity of that image of the Church and proposes in contrast to it a concept of the *Body of Christ* with multiple shadings of meaning. This multivalence characterizes both the eucharistic Body given by the Lord and also the

---

[65] Ibid., 152f.

[66] Ibid., 153. See also "Geist und Kirche", 91–97, esp. 95: "To become a Christian means to receive [*aufnehmen*] the whole Church into oneself, or rather, to allow oneself from within to be taken up [*aufnehmen*] into her. When I speak, think, or act, as a Christian, I always do it in and from that totality. So the Spirit gets a hearing, and so people come together. They come together exteriorly only if they have previously come together interiorly: if I have become inwardly broad, open, and mature; if I have received others into myself by believing with them and living with them, so that I am never alone any more, and my whole being bears the stamp of this With."

[67] *Nature*, 54.

[68] Ibid. When one reads this text, which was written about twenty years after the Council, one is struck by a certain nuancing of the earlier statement from the year 1967 (cited above), when Ratzinger in the original 1993 German edition underscores especially "the bodily and historical dimensions" of the subject that is Christ himself. See ibid., 54: "It is an application of the same christological singular found in the Letter to the Galatians. Here, too [in First Corinthians], it has a sacramental reference, though this time it points to the Eucharist, whose essence Paul defines two chapters before in the bold assertion: 'Because there is one bread, we who are many are one body' (1 Cor 10:17). 'One body': in accordance with the biblical significance of *soma*, this may be translated as 'one subject', provided we are sensitive to the connotations of bodiliness and historicity belonging to this word."

ecclesial communion founded by him, with the result that new light is thereby shed on the relationship between the Church and the world and a completely new horizon emerges for the question of membership in the Church. This pneumatic Christology, according to Ratzinger, has another consequence for ecclesiology: the latter must become more trinitarian, more "spiritual", so as to comprehend Christ and the Church as the Body of Christ associated with Easter and the Holy Spirit.[69] The understanding of *Corpus Christi* that we have just sketched is also the basis for the following section on the "Body of Christ" as the key to the ecclesiology of *Lumen gentium*.

§ 2. "Body of Christ" as the Key to the Ecclesiology[70]
of *Lumen gentium*

In Ratzinger's commentary to the first chapter of *Lumen gentium*,[71] it says: "Among the many images for the Church ... two have an unmistakably preeminent place",[72] namely, the Body of the Christ and the People of God. They are the metaphors through which "the hidden nature of the Church shines forth the most". The two complement each other to produce "a holistic view of the Church", for she is "the People of God only in and through the Body of Christ",[73] that is to say, "the People of God through communion with Christ in the Holy Spirit".[74] Thereby the Body of Christ image signifies a "spiritual union in the body",[75] which does not oppose institution and Spirit but rather acknowledges their interpenetration.[76] Seeing the Church as "the People

---

[69] Cf. Ratzinger, "Geleitwort", in Cantalamessa, *Komm, Schöpfer Geist*, 12.

[70] Cf. LG 7.

[71] Ibid.

[72] "Einleitung", 9. The two following quotations are also found there.

[73] *Volk und Haus Gottes*, xiv. See *Volk Gottes*, 15. Ratzinger stated this central idea of his ecclesiology as early as 1956 in the essay "Vom Ursprung und Wesen der Kirche". He published that earlier sketch again here, essentially unchanged.

[74] *Volk und Haus Gottes*, xiv.

[75] "Ecclesiology", 146.

[76] Cf. *Church*, 14: Ratzinger notes "the work of Henri de Lubac, who put the idea of the body of Christ in concrete terms as eucharistic ecclesiology and thus opened it up to the actual questions of the Church's legal order and the relationship between the local and the universal Church".

of God" only in and through the Body of Christ is for Ratzinger a central and fundamental decision. In interpreting *Lumen gentium*, this option results in a completely different understanding of the Church from the one that takes the perspective "People of God" alone as its point of departure.

To understand how Ratzinger arrives at his ecclesiological view, we should first sketch its patristic background. That can be done briefly, because Thomas Weiler[77] has already presented the main lines of it. In a second step, I will turn to the Pauline theology of the Body of Christ, which forms the basis for Ratzinger's ecclesiology, and finally I will also discuss the consequences of his teaching on the Body of Christ.

1. *The patristic interpretation of* Corpus Christi *as the point of departure*

a. The Church as the true Body of Christ

As Weiler demonstrates, Ratzinger's ecclesiology has its foundations in the biblical and patristic understanding of the Church.[78] Starting with his dissertation, *Volk und Haus Gottes in Augustins Lehre von der Kirche* [The People of God and the house of God in Augustine's doctrine of the Church], he devoted many, many pages to Augustine's *Corpus Christi* interpretation. His study of this theme led Ratzinger to the conclusion that Augustine sees the "authentic nature" of the Church in the fact that "she is a sacramental Body of Christ communion, that is, *corpus Christi*."[79] As understood by this Doctor of the Church, *Corpus Christi* is "neither 'mystical' nor confused"; instead, this Body is "quite concrete and by no means considered only metaphorically. Hence the axiom 'unus panis—unum corpus sumus multi' is actually the objective core of Augustine's concept of the Church."[80] In this sense,[81]

[77] Weiler, 41–68.
[78] Ibid., 273f.
[79] *Volk und Haus Gottes*, 324.
[80] Ibid., 324f.
[81] Cf. ibid., 211. Here Ratzinger quotes Augustine, *De civitate Dei* 10, 5: "Sacrificium ergo visibile invisibilis sacrificii sacramentum, id est sacrum signum, est" (CSEL 40, 1, 452; CCL 47, 277) and ibid., 10, 6: "Hoc est sacrificium christianorum: Multi unum corpus in Christo. Quod etiam sacramento altaris fidelibus noto frequentat ecclesia, ubi et demonstratur, quod in ea re quam offert, ipsa offeratur" (CSEL 40, 1, 456; CCL 47, 279), and also

Ratzinger can say: "The Church, which is this Body of Christ, ... has her sign, which, like the thing itself that is signified, is a holy sign: *sacrum signum*, that is, *sacramentum*. This means that the *sacramentum corpus Christi* corresponds to the *corpus Christi* by portraying it."[82]

According to Augustine, therefore, the Church is the true Body of Christ, *verum corpus*, whereas he describes the Eucharist as the sacrament of the Body of Christ, *sacramentum corporis Christi*.[83] Ratzinger maintains that this is a central idea of patristic ecclesiology in general.[84] The Fathers of the Church understand the Church herself as the *true Body of Christ*,[85] "that is, as really united with the Lord",[86] whereas they originally describe the Eucharist as *corpus mysticum*,[87] whereby

---

ibid., 10, 20: "Cuius rei sacramentum quotidianum esse voluit ecclesiae sacrificium: quae cum ipsius capitis corpus sit, se ipsam per ipsum discit offere" (CSEL 40, 1, 481; CCL 47, 294).

[82] *Volk und Haus Gottes*, 211.

[83] See Augustine, *De civ. Dei* 21, 25, 3, in CSEL 40, 2, 566; CCL 48, 795; PL 41, 742.

[84] In *Volk Gottes*, 21, Ratzinger cites as an example John Chrysostom's 24th Homily on First Corinthians, in PG 61, 200: "What is the bread? The Body of Christ. What do those who receive it become? The Body of Christ. Not many bodies, but one Body. Consequently, if we all live on the same thing and all become the same thing, why do we not then show the same love? Why do we, too, not become one in this sense?"

[85] Cf. Augustine, *De civ. Dei* 21, 25, 3, in CSEL 40, 2, 566; CCL 48, 795; PL 41, 742. Here—as Ratzinger explains—"Church and Eucharist are defined in their mutual relationship as *verum corpus Christi* [true Body of Christ] (Church) and *sacramentum corporis Christi* [sacrament of the Body of Christ] (Eucharist). The Catholic receives the 'sacramentum corporis Christi in vero Christi corpore'" (*Volk und Haus Gottes*, 211).

[86] *Volk Gottes*, 20.

[87] Cf. *Church*, 7. See also "Wesen", 49f. In the Middle Ages, the term *corpus mysticum* was transformed and applied to the Church; that is, during the thirteenth century the expression "mystical body" was no longer referred, as in the writings of the Church Fathers, to the Eucharist, which from then on was described as *corpus verum*. In contrast, the Church, understood as a corporate body, was now described as a *corpus ecclesiae mysticum*, meaning a corporation in the juridical sense. In the modern era, the expression underwent a further "modification": "mystical" was romantically derived from "mysticism". See "Wesen", 54: "[Theologians and preachers] had heaped upon this image of the Mystical Body all the glories of the supernatural, thus creating a highly unrealistic concept, which alongside the all-too-human reality of the Church appeared, necessarily, as a castle in the air." The Body of Christ theology in the period between the two world wars of the twentieth century, as Ratzinger demonstrates, had interpreted the word "mystical" in the current sense, as "an interior vision of the divine, as a mysterious interior communion with God". As the Church Fathers understood it, however, "the expression Body of Christ by no means has the character of interiority.... It refers, rather, to the Church as a reality concretely constituted in the Eucharist and built up by it, a reality that through the Eucharist is at the same time quite interior and quite public." See *Volk und Haus Gottes*, xv.

"the eucharistic celebration [is considered] as the concrete form in which our Christ-corporeality is effected." [88]

b. *Caritas* as the consequence of unity

An essential consequence of this real corporeal unity of baptized persons with Christ and with one another is brotherly love,[89] which cannot be separated from the Eucharist. This means, in turn—as Ratzinger says, echoing the Church Fathers—that "the Christ liturgy . . . in a certain sense is more realistically celebrated in everyday life than in the ritual execution of it." [90] To corroborate this, Ratzinger can refer also to the Angelic Doctor:

> Thomas Aquinas preserved this insight of the Church Fathers when he said that the *res sacramenti* of the Eucharist is the "communion of saints". Or in another passage when he noted: "In the Sacrament of the Altar, two things are signified, to wit, Christ's true body and Christ's mystical body." For the Fathers, indeed, . . . the everyday practice of charity is an essential part of the eucharistic event, and furthermore only in this way is the status of Christians as the Body of Christ fully achieved—a status that has in the eucharistic celebration its definitive and therefore also its demanding center.[91]

As Ratzinger says with Augustine, without love, "faith can indeed 'exist, but not save'—'esse, non prodesse'." [92] In this perspective, love, that is, the Holy Spirit, becomes the "distinguishing mark of what is Christian" [93] and thus the eschatological judgment. The

---

[88] *Volk Gottes,* 20.

[89] Cf. *Volk und Haus Gottes,* 200–205, where Ratzinger explicitly treats the theme of the connection between Eucharist and ethics. As proponents of this view, Ratzinger mentions Hilary, Chrysostom, and Cyril of Alexandria.

[90] *Volk Gottes,* 22.

[91] Ibid., with a reference to Thomas Aquinas, *Societas sanctorum,* in *Summa Theologiae* III, q. 80, a. 4, c.; ibid., q. 60, a. 3 *sed contra.* Cf. the reference in Nachtwei, 58: "The connection between Church and Body of Christ, as found especially in Augustine's writings, was—in Ratzinger's view—suppressed from St. Thomas on, inasmuch as the latter replaced the *Corpus Christi* idea with the notion of *Corpus Ecclesiae* that originated in legal language.... Admittedly Thomas, still relying on the patristic heritage, viewed the *res sacramenti* of the Eucharist as the unity of the Mystical Body of Christ."

[92] "Holy Spirit", 51.

[93] Ibid.

Church—the *Corpus Christi* created by the Holy Spirit—establishes this *communio* and thus becomes God's gift in this world. Anyone who leaves the communion of the Church terminates love. That is why for Ratzinger, following Augustine, "schism is . . . a pneumatological heresy",[94] which has come about as a departure "from the abiding that is of the Spirit, from the patience of *caritas*—a revocation of love in the revocation of abiding and, thereby, a renunciation of the Holy Spirit, who is the patience of abiding and being reconciled".[95]

The actual heart of this division, however, according to Ratzinger, is found in the fact that the fellowship of communion is shattered. With Augustine he interprets its destruction liturgically, when he sees the fundamental nature of the division in the fact that one altar is set up against the other: "erigere altare contra altare".[96] Here it becomes clear that every division is most profoundly and intrinsically "an offense against the Church understood in terms of the Eucharist".[97] This sacramental perspective of *Corpus Christi*, as understood in patristic theology, is in Ratzinger's view also the hermeneutic key to *Lumen gentium*, where it says: "Really partaking of the body of the Lord in the breaking of the eucharistic bread, we are taken up into communion with him and with one another."[98]

Before we turn, however, to this central point in Ratzinger's understanding of the Church, which culminates in his eucharistic ecclesiology,[99] it is necessary to point out the real basis for his *communio* ecclesiology, which goes even beyond its patristic roots: the Pauline doctrine of the Church as the Body of Christ.[100]

---

[94] Ibid., 52. On the following page, Ratzinger describes Augustine's experiences with the Donatists: "People said that they [the Donatists] washed clean the ground on which a Catholic had been standing. And what was worse, they controlled gangs, bands of embittered proletarians, who were perhaps dreaming of an earthly kingdom of God and who repeatedly attacked the *cellae*, or isolated farmhouses, the country houses, churches, and castles of the Catholics."

[95] Ibid., 52.

[96] *Volk und Haus Gottes*, 115.

[97] Ibid., 116.

[98] Ibid., 116.

[99] Cf. also *Volk Gottes*, 20.

[100] Cf. "Einleitung", 9f.

2. *The Pauline teaching about the Church as the Body of Christ: Christological and pneumatological understanding of the Church*

In 1956, when Ratzinger explained Paul's image of the Church in the lecture "On the Origin and Nature of the Church", he emphasized that "the question of the Pauline concept of the Church ... is extraordinarily spacious and many-layered".[101] He based his argumentation especially on the Letters to the Romans,[102] the Corinthians,[103] and the Galatians.[104] Ratzinger expresses the core of the apostle's statements in the formula: "Church is that communion which confirms and fulfills its invisible nature as the Body of Christ in the visible and ordered worship assembly."[105] This sacramental[106] understanding of the Church as *Corpus Christi* includes at the same time the presence of the Holy Spirit[107] in it and thus opens it up to the trinitarian *mysterium*: "For it is the risen Christ alone who can be this infinite breadth and openness; but of him Saint Paul says 'the Lord is the Spirit' (2 Cor 3:17). In the Spirit we say together with Christ 'Abba', because we have become sons (cf. Rom 8:15; Gal 4:6)."[108]

Inasmuch as the trinitarian mystery determines the development of the Church from the very beginning, it is expressed, according to

---

[101] *Volk Gottes*, 15.

[102] Ratzinger refers to Rom 12:4–8; cf. also Rom 5:12–21; 6:1–11; see *Volk Gottes*, 15.

[103] Ratzinger refers to 1 Cor 6:12–20; 10:14–22; 12:12–31; cf. also 1 Cor 15:21f., 44–49.

[104] Ratzinger refers to Gal 3:16, 26–28.

[105] *Volk Gottes*, 20.

[106] Sacramental because, according to Ratzinger, in First Corinthians Paul connects the celebration of the Eucharist with the *communio* of the Spirit: "Paul, [of all the New Testament writers,] who is certainly not suspected of having hierarchical ambitions (readers have attempted and still try today to find an office-free spiritual Church in his writings), this same Paul had to insist quite vehemently on order while discussing the celebration of the Eucharist in his Letter to the Corinthians. Consequently, though, a Church that understands herself in terms of the Eucharist as the Body of Christ is not just a Church of those who practice charity, but necessarily also a Church of holy order, a hierarchically organized Church (hierarchy = holy order)" (ibid., 23).

[107] Cf. *Volk und Haus Gottes*, xix; *Called to Communion*, 33f. Cf. LG 7: "Also, in the building up of Christ's Body various members and functions have their part to play. There is only one Spirit who, according to His own richness and the needs of the ministries, gives His different gifts for the welfare of the Church [cf. 1 Cor 12:1–11]." See also *Principles*, 132.

[108] *Called to Communion*, 33f.

Ratzinger, with the brief Pauline formula "Body of Christ".[109] Consequently, the Church is greater than her visible externals; that is, she cannot simply be equated with the sum of her members as though she were a merely sociological entity.[110] She does not become corporate through the association[111] of her members, as though in a club. Rather, her unity is a gift,[112] which is granted to her in the Holy Spirit. He unites all the members—despite their different qualities—with the Head of the Body, with Christ. For the Church is "the Body of Christ in the way in which the woman is one body, or rather one flesh, with the man. Put in other terms, the Church is the Body, not by virtue of an identity without distinction, but rather by means of the pneumatic-real act of spousal love." [113] This should be kept in mind when Ratzinger speaks of the Church as the "organism of the Holy Spirit" [114] yet, at the same time, refers to the Pauline theme of the love of Bride and Bridegroom as a definition of the relationship between Christ and his Church.[115] Both metaphors point to the sacramental unity of the Church, which is bestowed on her only in the Holy Spirit.

In the following discussion, the Spirit-effected unity of the Church will be defined in more detail in three ways. First, we will describe the Church as the organism of the Holy Spirit by taking up with Ratzinger the theme of her "corporate personality" and by examining

---

[109] Ibid.

[110] Cf. *Report*, 47.

[111] Cf. ibid., 49.

[112] Cf. *Called to Communion*, 41–42: "This convocation abides with one mind in prayer and thus receives its unity from the Lord."

[113] Ibid., 39. See Eph 5:23ff.

[114] "Einleitung", 9.

[115] See also "Marian Doctrine", 26: "Church is, not an organization, but an organism of Christ. If Church becomes a 'people' at all, it is only through the mediation of Christology. This mediation, in turn, happens in the sacraments, in the Eucharist, which for its part presupposes the Cross and Resurrection as the condition of its possibility. Consequently, one is not talking about the Church if one says 'people of God' without at the same time saying, or at least thinking, 'Body of Christ'. But even the concept of the Body of Christ needs clarification in order not to be misunderstood in today's context: it could easily be interpreted in the sense of a Christomonism, of an absorption of the Church, and thus of the believing creature, into the uniqueness of Christology. In Pauline terms, however, the claim that we are the 'Body of Christ' makes sense only against the backdrop of the formula of Genesis 2:24: 'The two shall become one flesh' (cf. 1 Cor 6:17)." On this topic see Ratzinger, "Kirche als Heilssakrament", in *Zeit des Geistes*, ed. J. Reikerstorfer, 59–70 (Vienna: Dom-Verlag, 1977).

the characteristic way in which she grows. Then we will turn to the Pauline theme of nuptials, so as to point out what is unique to the Church's union with Christ. Finally, we will look also at how the Spirit builds up this union from members and gifts that are quite different.

a. Not an organization, but the organism of the Holy Spirit

1) *"Corporate personality"*

The Pauline image of the Body of Christ says first of all "that the Church is more than an external *organization* for the attainment of interior salvation", that she is an *"organism* of the Holy Spirit".[116] For this reason, the Church is "something alive that embraces us all from within",[117] in which we are profoundly united by a "communal constitution of salvation".[118] Hence Ratzinger explains:

> Just as man can be human only as a fellowman, so too he can come to our common Father only as a fellowman, in the "we" of the children of God. The fact that we bear with one another, that we are for each other and from each other, ... acquires here its real depth, in that it enters into the being-for-us of Jesus Christ, into the "Body of Christ", which is the organism of the Spirit.[119]

As Ratzinger demonstrates by referring to the biblical sources, the idea behind this is "the Semitic conception of the 'corporate personality' ... [which] is expressed, for example, in the idea that we are all Adam, a single man writ large."[120] Christ as the new

---

[116] "Einleitung", 9. Cf. 1 Cor 12:12.

[117] *Church*, 3.

[118] "Einleitung", 10.

[119] Ibid.

[120] *Called to Communion*, 35. In this passage [35–36] Ratzinger notes that in the modern era, with its apotheosis (idolatry) of the personal subject, the thought of a "corporate personality" has become incomprehensible. "The 'I' was now a fortified stronghold with impassable walls. Descartes' attempt to derive the whole of philosophy from the *'cogito'* ... is typical in this regard. Today the concept of subject is gradually unraveling.... At the same time there is a renewed understanding that the 'I' is constituted in relation to the 'thou' and that the two mutually interpenetrate. Thus, the Semitic view of the corporate personality—without which it is difficult to enter into the notion of the Body of Christ— could once again become more easily accessible." See also *Volk und Haus Gottes*, 198f.: "the anti-Gnostic σῶμα theology of the apologists", esp. n. 32, where Ratzinger points out

Adam[121] makes us one, also, in the Holy Spirit. With him humanity begins anew. To be one in him means "to accept the love of God, which is our truth—that dependence on God which is no more an imposition from without than is the Son's sonship".[122] This new corporate entity becomes the Body of Christ "through the Pneuma making men into 'communion' ".[123] In this connection, Ratzinger asks us to consider that "accepting the whole community of believers is, indeed, part of being a Christian, ... for otherwise the Holy Spirit himself is missing, the One who unites." [124] The decisive thing in this regard is love for the Church, as Ratzinger puts it in Augustinian language:

> However much anyone loves the Church, that is how much he has of the Holy Spirit. The theology of the Trinity becomes a direct standard for ecclesiology; the designation of the Spirit as love becomes the key to Christian living, and at the same time love is interpreted in practical terms, as patience in the Church.[125]

The need for patience is a consequence of the experience that the Church is not yet perfected but is eagerly awaiting her one final union in the triune God. On her way toward this destination, she grows by "overcoming the boundary between I and Thou" through "self-transcendence leading into her foundation, into eternal love".[126] That is why the Church can never "be a national church or be identified with any race or class. If this is so, she must be catholic and gather God's scattered children into unity." [127] For this reason, the trinitarian

---

that Methodius assumes a complete identity between Adam and Christ and a "real, complete union of all men with the Logos".

[121] Cf. *LG* 2: "Fallen in Adam, God the Father did not leave men to themselves, but ceaselessly offered helps to salvation, in view of Christ, the Redeemer 'who is the image of the invisible God, the firstborn of every creature' [Col 1:15]. All the elect, before time began, the Father 'foreknew and predestined to become conformed to the image of His Son, that He should be the firstborn among many brethren' [Rom 8:29]." See also *AG* 3; *GS* 22.

[122] *In the Beginning*, 76.

[123] "Holy Spirit", 51.

[124] Ibid., 52.

[125] Ibid. Cf. *Volk und Haus Gottes*, 136–58.

[126] "Geist und Kirche", 91–97, citation at 94.

[127] Ibid.

mystery of unity, that is, the triune God himself, is the archetypal image of the Church:

> And from the perspective of the Trinity, the Spirit tells us what God's plan for us is: unity in the image of God. He also tells us, however, that we human beings can become one with each other only if we find ourselves in a higher unity, in a third person, so to speak. Only when we are one with God can we become one with each other. The way to the other leads through God.[128]

As the icon of the Holy Spirit,[129] the Church ought to illustrate this unity. He is actually the "element in which she lives", in which "opposition is reconciled and becomes fellowship and the shattered pieces of Adam are put back together to restore unity."[130]

2) The growth process

The process of growth brought about by the Spirit demands development and historical dynamism of the Church,[131] as Ratzinger explains in his retrospect on the Council from the year 1986:

> A body remains identical precisely by being continually renewed in the process of living. For Cardinal Newman the idea of development was in fact the bridge that made his conversion to Catholicism possible. My own belief is that it belongs in fact to the decisive fundamental concepts of Catholicism. . . . Anyone who wants to cling merely to the words of scripture or the patterns of the early Church banishes Christ to the past. The result is either a faith that is completely sterile and has nothing to say to today or an arbitrariness that jumps over two thousand years of history and throws it into the dustbin of failure while dreaming up for itself how Christianity was really meant to appear according to scripture or according to Jesus. . . . Genuine identity with the origin is only

---

[128] Ibid., 92.
[129] Ibid., 95.
[130] Ibid., 92.
[131] Cf. LG 7: "In order that we might be unceasingly renewed in Him [cf. Eph 4:23], He has shared with us His Spirit who, existing as one and the same being in the Head and in the members, gives life to, unifies and moves through the whole body."

to be found where there is also the living continuity that develops it and thus preserves it.[132]

In Ratzinger's view, Church grows in the tension between continuity and renewal.[133] These two attitudes—fixation on a particular form of the Church or ignoring tradition—are both mistaken; Ratzinger's judgment varies as to which one is the specific danger of the day. Whereas in the above-cited passage he mentions both errors, in 1970, confronting the feasibility craze of that time, he emphasizes that the Church cannot be understood as a project that we ourselves plan:

> The man of today looks towards the future. His slogan is "Progress," not "Tradition"; "Hope," not "Faith." He is moved, it is true, by a certain romanticism about the past. . . . For that to which he looks forward is not, as in the early Church, the kingdom of God, but the kingdom of man.[134]

On the contrary, in the Church, the *communio* established by God in the Holy Spirit, the principle holds true: "Let no one act merely on the basis of his own will. . . . Each one must act, speak, and think out of the communal character of the new 'we' of the Church, which is in a relationship of exchange with the 'We' of the triune God."[135] For this reason, Christ and the Church can never be exhaustively described in terms of what is our own; rather, they are rooted in the mystery of the Holy Spirit. This Spirit does not hinder progress; rather, he "leads into all truth, into what Jesus has not yet uttered, and precisely in this way he also announces what is to come".[136]

Inasmuch as the Church, through the working of the Spirit, is again and again reoriented toward receiving Christ, she assumes the form of the Bride, who awaits the Bridegroom and goes out to meet him.

---

[132] *Church*, 6–7. At that same time (1986) the discussions about Ratzinger's tendency to revise his opinions took place. See H. Vorgrimler, "Vom 'Geist des Konzils'", in Richter, *Konzil*, 25–52, esp. 40–44.

[133] Cf. *Song*, 146.

[134] Ratzinger, *Faith and the Future* (Chicago: Franciscan Herald Press, 1970), 81–82.

[135] "Geist und Kirche", 91–97, citation at 94f.

[136] Ibid., 95.

b. The Pauline theme of nuptiality

Ratzinger describes "the idea of nuptiality, or—to express it in profane terms—the biblical philosophy of love",[137] as one root of the
Pauline concept of the Body of Christ.[138] Just as man and woman
become "one flesh"[139] according to Genesis 2:24, so too Christ and
the Church are "one spirit" according to 1 Corinthians 6:17. Ratzinger spells this out as follows:

> Now if the community of the faithful (not the individual Christian)
> appears as the "Bride" (2 Cor 11:2; Eph 5:22–33), then accordingly
> this means, first, that this community claims to be the new People
> of God. Yet the Old Testament idea is modified considerably, in
> that the following is now true: The community is the People *of God*
> by virtue of the fact that it is the Bride *of Christ* and thus fused with
> him, the Son, into the unity of the one spirit-body (*pneuma*).[140]

Thus "we must not interpret the term 'spirit' with modern linguistic sensibilities"[141] but rather in terms of the biblical *pneuma*. According to Ratzinger, this denotes "a single spiritual existence together
with him who, in rising again, was made 'spirit' by the Holy Spirit

---

[137] *Called to Communion*, 37–38. Cf. *LG* 6; Hos 2:19–20: "And I will espouse you for
ever; I will espouse you in righteousness and in justice, in steadfast love, and in mercy. I
will espouse you in faithfulness; and you shall know the LORD." See also *God and the
World*, 352–53: "The tradition identifying the Church with a woman reaches far back into
the Old Testament, where Israel sees itself as the bride whom God wishes to take into his
confidence, to make his own, and to unite to himself in eternal love. That was adopted in
the Church, which in fact continues the life of the Old Testament. Paul talks about our
mother, the Jerusalem on high. He is thus discovering, from within the Jewish tradition,
the image of the Church as mother, this motherly city that has given birth to us all and
that gives us life and freedom. And so the Fathers took up this idea, which also appears in
the Apocalypse—the woman arrayed in the sun—and used it to portray the whole holy
being of the Church." See also *Church*, 20.

[138] Cf. *Weiler*, 74.

[139] See *Behold*, 49: "It is also the Holy Spirit who imparts new meaning to Adam's
becoming 'one flesh' with Eve, applying it to the Second Adam: 'He who is united to the
Lord becomes one spirit with him' (1 Cor 6:17)." For Ratzinger, this represents also an
important argument for the "ontological priority of the universal Church, of the one
Church and the one Body, of the one Bride, before the concrete empirical realizations in
the individual particular Churches" ("Gottesidee", 46). On this subject, see pt. 2, sec. 2,
chap. 2, §4, of this work: "The Ontological Priority of the Universal Church".

[140] *Volk Gottes*, 16.

[141] *Called to Communion*, 38.

while remaining bodily in the openness of this Spirit."[142] Since the Church becomes one body and one spirit "by means of the pneumatic-real act of spousal love",

> Christ and the Church are one body in the sense in which man and woman are one flesh, that is, in such a way that in their indissoluble spiritual-bodily union, they nonetheless remain unconfused and unmingled. The Church does not simply become Christ, she is ever the handmaid whom he lovingly raises to be his Bride and who seeks his face throughout these latter days.[143]

The "unconfused and unmingled" quality of the Church's union with Christ in the Spirit results in the "dynamic character" of the sacramental reality, "which is not an already accomplished physical fact but takes place as a personal event".[144] Through her response as the Bride of Christ, the Church abides in this "mystery of love"[145] and lives on her "devotion to Christ"[146] in the Holy Spirit. Insofar as the Bride must continually renew her response, however, she is also marked by the ability to fail, by infidelity. Furthermore, the Church, according to Ratzinger, must even be a "Church of sinners", because she is also still "the expression and unfolding of that love which in Christ sat down at table with sinners".[147] For this reason, the new Bride, which the Church Fathers had expected to be "without wrinkle or blemish, as the truly obedient and holy People of God", is in his opinion "in reality just as wrinkled and blemished and full of sinners".[148] Nonetheless it is true: "The Church must constantly become what she is through unitive love and resist the temptation to fall from her vocation into the infidelity of self-willed autonomy.... She is always on the way to union with Christ, which also includes the Church's own internal unity."[149] Hence, in summarizing, we can state that for Ratzinger the mystery of the Church, the sign of the most intimate union

---

[142] Ibid. The Church is the Body "not by virtue of an identity without distinction" (ibid., 39).

[143] Ibid., 39.

[144] Ibid.

[145] Ibid.

[146] Cf. *Principles*, 131f.

[147] Ratzinger, "Kirche als Tempel", 148–57, citation at 157.

[148] Ibid. See also *Introduction*, 338f.

[149] *Called to Communion*, 39–40.

with God and with one another, shines forth in the comparison of
the relationship of Christ with the Church to that of the Bridegroom
with the Bride.

c. Unity in the Spirit as the goal of all the gifts

If the internal unity of the Church is granted by God as the fruit of
her fidelity to Christ, then she herself becomes the leaven of unity in
the world. For this reason, it seems to Ratzinger absurd to separate
the Church, which is simultaneously the instrument of this unity,[150]
from Christ, who communicates his Spirit to her.[151] She is communion with Christ "in the life of prayer, in the life of the sacraments; in
the fundamental attitudes of faith, hope and love",[152] and she can be
the instrument of this unity only because she was born from the Paschal Mystery of Jesus Christ, from the "*one* Body of Christ that was
opened for us on the Cross".[153]

> From his side, that side which has been opened up in loving sac-
> rifice, comes a spring of water that brings to fruition the whole of
> history. From the ultimate self-sacrifice of Jesus spring forth blood
> and water, Eucharist and baptism, as the source of a new community.
> *The Lord's opened side is the source from which spring forth both the
> Church and the sacraments that build up the Church.*[154]

Therefore, Ratzinger understands baptism as an act of "being opened
up"[155] toward this *one Corpus Christi*, as a trinitarian process, and thus
as "much more than a process of socialization in the local Church".[156]

---

[150] Cf. *LG* 1; *GS* 42.

[151] Cf. Kaes, 145f.: "Ort der Gegenwart Christi im Heiligen Geist".

[152] *Church*, 5.

[153] "Ecclesiology", 141, citing Vinzenz Pfnür.

[154] *Eucharist*, 43.

[155] "Ecclesiology", 141; see also ibid.: "Baptism does not spring from the individual
congregation; rather, in baptism the door is opened for us into the one Church: baptism is
the presence of the one Church and can come only from her—from the Jerusalem that is
above, from our new mother."

[156] Ibid. See also "Gottesidee", 46: Like baptism, the Eucharist, too, cannot be reduced
to a limited *communio* of the local Church. For in the Eucharist Christ always gives his
Body for the whole Church and thus makes the individual congregation a place of universal *communio*, "which unites heaven and earth, the living and the dead, the past, present,
and future, and opens them up toward eternity". Thus the Paschal Mystery is rooted in the
Trinity, and Ratzinger sees in this also the reason for the ontological and temporal priority

He corroborates this idea with the reference made by Hugo Rah-ner[157] to John 7:37–39 and John 19:34:

> Both passages are an expression of the Paschal Mystery: from the Lord's pierced Heart proceeds the life-giving stream of the sacraments; the grain of wheat, dying, becomes the new ear, carrying the fruit of the Church forward through the ages. Both texts also express the connection between Christology and pneumatology: the water of life which springs from the Lord's side is the Holy Spirit, the spring of life which makes the desert blossom. This also brings out the connection between Christology, pneumatology and ecclesiology: Christ communicates himself to us in the Holy Spirit; and it is the Holy Spirit who makes the clay into a living Body, i.e., fuses isolated men into the one organism of the love of Jesus Christ.[158]

As Ratzinger discusses elsewhere,[159] Augustine connects the passage in John 7:37–39 ("'If any one thirst, let him come to me and drink. He who believes in me, as the Scripture has said, "Out of his heart shall flow rivers of living water."' Now this he said about the Spirit, which those who believed in him were to receive ...") with John 4:7–14, Jesus' conversation with the Samaritan woman at Jacob's well. The latter passage in Scripture is a central text for Augustine, since—as Ratzinger explains—here "the word 'gift' is a name for the Holy Spirit".[160]

Consequently, Ratzinger views as inadequate the argument that the image of the *Body of Christ* should be classified merely as a Stoic allegory,[161] even though Paul no doubt resorted to such ideas, "for

---

of the universal Church with respect to the local Churches (cf. ibid., 5). I will go into this in greater detail in pt. 2, sec. 2, chap. 2, §4, "The Ontological Priority of the Universal Church".

[157] On this subject, see H. Rahner, *Symbole der Kirche*, 177–235: "Flumina de ventre Christi".

[158] *Behold*, 48–49.

[159] "Holy Spirit", 47, with a reference to Augustine, *De Trinitate* 15, 19, 33, in CCL 50 A, 508f.; cf. ibid., 5, 14,15–15, 16, in CCL 50, 222–24.

[160] "Holy Spirit", 48.

[161] Cf. *Called to Communion*, 34: "The Stoic allegory compares the state to an organism whose members must all work together. This metaphor is an image for the reciprocal dependence of all on all and, therefore, also for the importance of the diverse functions that build up a commonwealth. This imaginative picture was used in order to calm agitated masses."

example, when he tells the quarreling Corinthians that it would indeed be ridiculous for the foot to want suddenly to be a hand, or for the ear to conceive a sudden desire to be an eye." [162] If the Body of Christ metaphor could be thoroughly explained by "considerations of sociology or moral philosophy such as these", then it would be "nothing but a marginal gloss on the actual substantive content of the notion of the Church".[163] But if these gifts "are in the end just one Gift in many forms, that is, the Spirit of God, and if the Spirit is the gift of Jesus Christ, which he gives and which he, in men, receives, then the inmost orientation of all the gifts is: unity." [164]

This unity is based on the *communio* of the triune God himself.[165] For he is, as Ratzinger declares, "the prototype of the new, unified humanity, the archetype of the Church, which we can regard as having been founded by the words of Jesus' prayer: 'That they may be one, even as we are one' (Jn 17:11, 21, 22)." [166] Consequently, Ratzinger finds in the Trinity the measure and the basis for the Church herself:

> She is supposed to bring to its fulfillment the word of the sixth day of creation: "Let us create man in our image and likeness." In her, humanity, which had become the antitype of God because of its rifts and divisions, shall again become the one Adam, whose image—as the Fathers of the Church say—was torn to shreds by sin and now lies scattered about. In the Church the divine measure of man shall again become evident: unity, "as we are one". Thus the Trinity, God himself, is the archetype of the Church; Church is not another notion over and above "man"; rather, she is man's journey to himself.[167]

As it says in the Decree on the Missions, this new Adam has been constituted "head of a renewed humanity".[168] Therefore, becoming a Christian, according to Ratzinger, is "becoming united: the shards of

---

[162] Ibid., 34; see 1 Cor 12:17ff.
[163] *Called to Communion*, 35.
[164] "Holy Spirit", 56.
[165] Cf. LG 4.
[166] "Geist und Kirche", 91–97, citation at 91.
[167] Ibid., 91f.
[168] AG 3.

the broken image of Adam must be put back together. To be a Christian is not self-affirmation; rather, it is a new beginning that leads into that great unity embracing humanity in all places and in all times." [169] The way to this unity is conversion, which consists, not in the superficial change of a few ideas, but rather in a "process of dying": [170]

> The boundaries of the "I" are broken up; the "I" loses itself so as to rediscover itself in a greater subject, which encompasses heaven and earth, the past, present, and future, and establishes truth itself therein. This "I and yet no longer I" is the Christian alternative to nirvana. We can also say: The Holy Spirit is this alternative. He is the power of openness and of the amalgamation in this new subject, which we call Body of Christ or Church. [171]

If, however, this Spirit-effected unity is the purpose of all the gifts, then this "coming to each other is not an inexpensive process.... Without the courage of conversion, of allowing oneself to be broken open like the grain of wheat, it does not work. The Holy One is fire; anyone who does not want to be burned should not get close to him." [172] The consequence of such a refusal of conversion is the deadly loneliness of egotism. The sort of communion, though, that "is sought apart from the fire ultimately remains trifling and empty appearance.... A saying of Jesus handed down by Origen reads: Whoever is close to me is close to the fire." [173] This saying shows the inner connection of Christ, the Holy Spirit, and the Church. For the Body of

---

[169] "Geist und Kirche", 94.

[170] Ibid., 95; cf. Gal 2:20: "I have been crucified with Christ; it is no longer I who live, but Christ who lives in me."

[171] "Geist und Kirche", 95f. Cf. also Ratzinger, *Images of Hope: Meditations on Major Feasts*, trans. John Rock and Graham Harrison (San Francisco: Ignatius Press, 2006), 63–73: "Pentecost: The Holy Spirit and the Church", citation at 68: "What does all this have to do with the Holy Spirit and the Church? The answer is that the Christian alternative to nirvana is the Trinity, that ultimate unity in which the distinction between I and Thou is not withdrawn but joined to each other in the Holy Spirit. In God there are Persons, and so he is precisely the realization of ultimate unity. God did not create the person so that he might be dissolved but so that he might open himself in his entire height and in his innermost depth—there where the Holy Spirit embraces him and is the unity of the divided persons."

[172] "Geist und Kirche", 96.

[173] Ibid. See also Ratzinger, *Ministers of Your Joy: Scriptural Meditations on Priestly Spirituality* (Ann Arbor, Mich.: Servant Publications, 1989), 35.

Christ doctrine, it means that it cannot be disengaged from the concrete reality of the Church.

3. Consequences of the Body of Christ doctrine for ecclesiology

Before turning with Ratzinger to the deeper dimension of eucharistic ecclesiology, that is to say, of the Church's *communio* structure, we should set forth the initial consequences of his Body of Christ doctrine. These (a) are related to the question of identification with the Church, (b and c) have to do with the roots of the present crisis in the Church, and (d) give a response to the sociological misunderstanding of Church.

a. The question of identification with the Church

For Ratzinger, the question of identification with the Church is concerned with one essential and yet simple act, namely, with "sharing in the basic decision of Jesus Christ through a participation in the basic decision of the Church".[174] How does that work? Ratzinger gives an answer that is simple, not in the sense of "naïve", but rather in the sense of something rudimentary: it means deciding for "identification with Him who identified Himself with us"[175] and who, as Son, is one with the Father.[176] Against this background, the slogan "Yes to Jesus, No to the Church" proves to be a fatal error, since it clings fast to an image of Jesus that relies on one's private interpretation and does not want to hear anything about "what the faith of the Church and, even more basically, the faith of the evangelists says about Jesus".[177] For this reason, the slogan ought to be "Yes to Jesus, No to Christ" or "Yes to Jesus, No to the Son of God".[178] Furthermore, it ignores the faith community, which through the ages and down to the present day gives living testimony to the gospel, thus making it accessible in the first place:

---

[174] "Identification", 27; cf. 28.

[175] Ibid., 28.

[176] Cf. ibid.

[177] Ratzinger, "Probleme von Glaubens- und Sittenlehre im europäischen Kontext", in *Zu Grundfragen der Theologie heute*, ed. Erzbischöfliches Generalvikariat Paderborn, Presse- und Informationsstelle, 7–17, citation at 8 (Paderborn, 1992).

[178] Ibid.

Christ exists not purely ideally but only in his body. This means with the others, with the community that has persisted through the ages and that is this body of his. The Church is not an idea but a body, and the scandal of the incarnation, over which so many of Jesus's contemporaries came to grief, is continued in the infuriating aspects of the Church. But here too the saying applies: "Blessed is he who takes no offence at me" (Mt 11:6).[179]

Although the Church cannot be separated from the concrete form in which she appears in every age, she must never—as Ratzinger emphasizes—be simply equated with it, either,[180] for she encompasses "the entire communion of saints, both the living and the dead ... or more exactly: all the living—those of yesterday, of today, and of tomorrow; and therefore the future of the Church which remains yet to be realized".[181] Moreover, he recalls the statement of St. Augustine "that there are some who are empirically within the Church though spiritually outside it, and *vice versa*".[182] In the Church, however, the ever-present Spirit and the solidarity with Christ testify to her supra-temporal dimension, which is a constitutive element in her real identity, because ultimately it delineates one aspect of her divine dimension, which brings forth the new quality of unity. Therefore, Ratzinger says, "In the strict sense, Church is present only where the Pauline identification formula is fully effective: 'All of you are one in Christ Jesus.' This is also the content of the Pauline designation of the Church as 'Body of Christ', which in Ephesians blends with the 'One-flesh' formula of Genesis 2."[183] An ecclesiology that ignores this act of identification is, in Ratzinger's view, "of no interest for anthropology or world history".[184]

---

[179] *Church*, 6.
[180] "Identification", 17. See *LG* 8.
[181] "Identification", 18.
[182] Ibid.
[183] Ibid., 24f.
[184] Ibid., 23. Ratzinger finds that the reason why Küng's Christology was problematic and ultimately failed was that he disregarded this act of identification. Küng, along with E. Topisch, had ironically asked the question, "Will aber heute noch ein vernünftiger Mensch Gott werden?" [Does any reasonable person today still want to become God?]; see H. Küng, *Christ sein* (Munich: Piper, 1974), 433.

b. Roots of the current crisis in the Church

The real problem of the present day, according to Ratzinger, is not an ecclesiological but a christological crisis. He sees an initial root cause for it in the construction of a so-called *historical Jesus*, "behind the Jesus of the Gospels, which is distilled from the sources and contrary to the sources according to the standards of the so-called modern world view and of the mode of historiography that was inspired by the Enlightenment".[185] It builds on the premise that the only thing that can be historic is "that which is always possible as a matter of principle; [on] the presupposition that the normal causal connection is never interrupted and that anything that violates this familiar system of laws is therefore unhistorical."[186] Ratzinger concludes from this in his 1992 essay on contemporary problems of theology:

> Thus the Jesus of the Gospels cannot be the real Jesus; a new one must be found, from which everything has to be removed that could only be comprehensible as coming from God. Thus the interpretive principle by which this Jesus is reconstructed openly excludes whatever in him is divine: This historical Jesus can only be a non-Christ, a non-Son.[187]

Obviously what comes to light here is the conflict with the theological opinion that dogmas themselves are to be understood historically as subsequent faith testimonies and that they require "in new epochs, on the basis of the given coherence and consensus"—as Peter Hünermann puts it—"a newly worked-out understanding",[188] which provides access to the original faith testimony of Scripture. For this reason, Hünermann suspects Ratzinger of tragically depreciating historical theology to the status of a mere ancillary science while maintaining that "real theology [results] from the magisterial interpretation of the data of revelation". He criticizes Ratzinger for continuing in this way "an understanding of theology that was cultivated in the Roman

---

[185] Ratzinger, "Probleme von Glaubens- und Sittenlehre", 9.
[186] Ibid.
[187] Ibid.
[188] P. Hünermann, "Rationale Begründungsverfahren in der Dogmatik und kirchliches Lehramt", in *Glaubenswissenschaft? Theologie im Spannungsfeld von Glaube, Rationalität und Öffentlichkeit*, ed. P. Neuner, 77–98, citation at 97, QD 195 (Freiburg im Breisgau: Herder, 2002).

Curia under Pius XII and Paul VI"[189] and ends up accusing him indirectly of fundamentalism. Here, however, the criticism seems, in my opinion, to be overstrained. When it is a question of the historical content of theological statements, then Ratzinger speaks on a different level from Hünermann about the "historical identity" of theology: Ratzinger means the working of God, revealed in history. Historicity becomes in his writings a "trademark" of divine revelation itself:

> Here there is a sort of "trademark", a historical identity which the Magisterium knows it is called to defend. As the facts stand, however, what is really an effort to protect a historical (and, as we believe, God-given) identity is constantly construed as an attack upon intellectual freedom, all the more so as this identity is often a stumbling block for the contemporary mind, inasmuch as certain of its contents irritate our mentality and lifestyle.[190]

For this reason, theology, according to Ratzinger's insight, comes about only by virtue of the fact that "the arbitrary judgment of reason encounters a limit, in that we discover something which we have not excogitated ourselves but which has been revealed to us".[191] It is a question of the historically comprehensible truth of revelation.

Ratzinger finds a second root cause of the christological crisis in the reinterpretation of redemption as liberation in the modern sense, "which can be understood in a more psychological-individual or a more political-collective way".[192] Jesus appears in this perspective only as a historical leading figure without mediating any grace. Accordingly, authority in the Church is reinterpreted as arrogated power. Instead, the Church should become

> a place of "freedom", understood in a psychological and political sense. She should be the space of our dreams and wishes . . . ; she

---

[189] Ibid. See also Hünermann's argument, in his "Hinweise zum theologischen Gebrauch des 'Denzinger' ", *DH* 9–13, esp. 9f. The evaluation of various Gospel testimonies "cannot be a simple process of quality control using the standard of preconceived formulas. The Gospel is 'the Word of life' (1 Jn 1:1) that sets us free for a 'new way of thinking and living'. Handing on the faith, which in a fundamental way is always the expansion of a language community, is therefore different from 'serving the letter'."

[190] *Nature*, 8.

[191] Ibid.

[192] Ratzinger, "Probleme von Glaubens- und Sittenlehre", 10.

cannot refer to anything otherworldly. . . . All that is unredeemed in my own life, all my dissatisfaction with myself and others redounds upon her.[193]

Lastly he locates a third root cause in the deism of the Enlightenment, which practically speaking has prevailed "in the general consciousness".[194] A God who cares about us, who for us becomes man and finally gives up his life for us, is inconceivable for many people. "But if God no longer has anything to do with us," says Ratzinger, "then the idea of sin also goes by the wayside", along with the awareness that "the cause for the misery in the world and in our own lives is to be sought in sin." Many people today cannot imagine at all that "a human deed could offend God." Such an attitude has its effects on one's understanding of Church, liturgy, and moral theology. The Church, in this view, can "only be a man-made organization" that—as Ratzinger ironically continues—is designed "more or less skillfully"[195] to be people-friendly. As for liturgy, the sacraments can now be little more than "signs of building up community, rituals that hold the community together and stimulate it to take action in the world", because how could there ever be, for example, the "Real Presence of this 'historical Jesus' in the Eucharist"?[196] Worship and liturgy undergo a fundamental transformation from a deist perspective:

> Their first subject is not God or Christ, but rather the "we" of those celebrating. And naturally [worship and liturgy] cannot have adoration as their primary meaning, since there is no reason for it in a deist understanding of God. Nor, of course, can they be about atonement, sacrifice, or the forgiveness of sins. Rather, it is all about those who celebrate, affirming their fellowship with one another and thus stepping out of the isolation into which modern life forces the individual.[197]

---

[193] Ibid., 10f. Ratzinger sees this as part of modern man's "shortage of experience": "The man of today no longer understands the Christian doctrine of redemption. . . . He simply cannot imagine what vicarious atonement and satisfaction are. What was meant by the word Christ, Messiah, does not occur in his life and thus remains an empty formula. In this way the profession of Jesus as the Christ vanishes quite automatically" (ibid., 10).

[194] Ibid., 11. The following citations are also found there.

[195] Ibid., 9.

[196] Ibid.

[197] Ibid., 11f.

As for moral theology, Ratzinger says, the fundamental option of the deist world view means that morality flattens out into an ethics without any reference to God.[198] Thus modern man is left to his own devices, caught up in the evolutionary system of power, struggle, and survival. Once the view of a God who cares about man is lost, however, the latter ends up in distress. For, as a logical consequence, one would have to deny man himself—says Ratzinger—and "reduce him to a series of states ... in which what is typically human and really moral also would disappear".[199]

This leads to the conclusion: Behind man's identity crisis in Western societies that are shaped by a deist world view is the cryptically disguised question about God. This societal crisis, in turn, has had repercussions on the Church, too, in the wealthy nations of Europe and North America, leading to insecurities that are ultimately rooted in the question about God.

c. The Church's identity crisis as an ecclesiologically encrypted God crisis

Based on the discussion thus far, we are now confronted with the crucial question: How is the Christian faith in God different from a deist view of God and the world? With the core Christian articles concerning the triune God as the Creator and Christ as the Redeemer of mankind and the Holy Spirit as the Giver of divine life, the revealed truth of faith is at stake, faith in Jesus as the Christ of the Gospels. This truth can be grasped only through a theological act of faith, whereby in Ratzinger's view everything ultimately depends on the question about God: "Faith is faith in God or else there is no faith. Ultimately it can be traced back to the simple belief in God, the living God, from which all the rest follows."[200] For this reason, the

---

[198] See ibid., 13. "What faith calls the commandments of God appears now to be the cultural shaping of historical forms of human behavior. We can note dependencies, connections with other cultures, developments, and contradictions. All this seems to show sufficiently that it is only a matter of rules for the game of life, which were formulated in those particular societies" (ibid.).

[199] Ibid., 15.

[200] Ibid. Ratzinger speaks about this crisis of God in his final pastoral letter as archbishop of Munich and Freising also. See Ratzinger, "Wagt den Lebensstil, der Zukunft hat", in *Wir leben vom ja: Dokumentation der Verabschiedung von Joseph Kardinal Ratzinger*, ed. Pressereferat der Erzdiözese München-Freising (Munich: Pfeiffer, 1982), 117–19, ref. at 118.

refusal to make this act of faith also precipitates a serious identity crisis of the Church. As Ratzinger declares along with Johann Baptist Metz,[201] today's crisis in the Church is an ecclesiologically encrypted "crisis of God",[202] in which the slogan "Yes to Jesus, No to the Church" has been transformed into "Religion: Yes; God: No".[203] In order to overcome this "crisis of God", it is necessary to understand that

> the Church is not there for her own sake but should be the instrument of God for gathering men to him, so as to prepare for the moment when God shall be "everything to every one" (1 Cor 15:28). The idea of God is the very thing that had been left aside . . . , and it had thereby been deprived of its entire meaning. For a Church that is there only for her own sake is superfluous. And people notice that straightaway.[204]

As Ratzinger observed in 1985, "the authentically Catholic meaning of the reality 'Church' is tacitly disappearing, without being expressly rejected."[205] More and more today, a notion of Church is gaining acceptance that resembles "the model of certain North American 'free churches', in which in the past believers took refuge from the oppressive model of the 'State Church' produced by the Reformation".[206] Those Christians established *their* churches, in each case according to their own ideas. But as they did so, the mystery, the supernatural view of the Church, necessarily went by the wayside:

> If the Church . . . is viewed as a human construction, the product of our own efforts, even the contents of the faith end up assuming an arbitrary character: the faith, in fact, no longer has an authentic, guaranteed instrument through which to express itself. Thus, without a view of the mystery of the Church that is also *supernatural* and

---

[201] Cf. "Ecclesiology", 124f.

[202] Cf. J. Ratzinger and J. B. Metz, "God, Sin, and Suffering: A Conversation", in Peters/ Urban, 47–53, citation at 48: "Ratzinger: . . . That the God theme, in all its dimensions, . . . in its urgency, is the core; that all the other crises can be explained only in terms of it. . . . —Metz: . . . I have used the phrase 'God crisis' not to distance myself from the problems facing the Church but in order to draw attention to the fact that behind the Church crisis there is a crisis that is probably more profound and more radical."

[203] Cf. "Ecclesiology", 124. See also *God and the World*, 68f.

[204] "Ecclesiology", 128–29.

[205] *Report*, 45.

[206] Ibid., 45–46.

not only *sociological*, christology itself loses its reference to the divine. . . . The Gospel becomes the *Jesus-project*, the social-liberation project or other merely historical, immanent projects that can still seem religious in appearance, but which are atheistic in substance.[207]

This sociological view of the Church can lead—as Ratzinger explained disapprovingly as early as 1971, in the midst of the post-1968 academic upheaval[208]—to the tendency to speak about "our church" rather than the Church of Jesus Christ:

His Church has been replaced by our Church, and hence by the many Churches—for everyone has his own. The Churches have become *our* enterprises, of which we are proud or else ashamed. Many small private properties are ranged alongside one another— nothing but *our* Churches, made by ourselves, our own work and property, and which we want to keep as they are or refashion as we think fit.[209]

As Ratzinger explains its main thesis, however, the Second Vatican Council deliberately tried to coordinate "talk about the Church with talk about God";[210] it intended to present an ecclesiology that is theological in the strict sense. For this reason, the Council is primarily concerned with Christ, the Light of the nations, whose glory is reflected on the face of the Church.[211]

---

[207] Ibid., 46.

[208] Cf. Ratzinger, "Die Situation der Kirche heute—Hoffnungen und Gefahren", in *Festvortrag beim Priestertreffen (J. Ratzinger) und Ansprache beim Pontifikalamt (Kardinal J. Höffner) anlässlich des 60-jährigen Priesterjubiläums von Kardinal Josef Frings*, ed. Presseamt des Erzbistums Köln, 9 (Cologne, 1971): "A Chinese proverb says: 'He who looks at himself does not shine', and indeed, a Church that looks predominantly to herself loses her splendor." Ratzinger describes the state of the Church here with a rather long quotation from Saint Basil, *On the Holy Spirit* (FC 12, 312–23).

[209] J. Ratzinger, "Why I Am Still in the Church", in *Two Say Why*, 79 . Cf. *Report*, 46: "Behind the *human* exterior stands the mystery of a *more than human* reality, in which reformers, sociologists, organizers have no authority whatsoever."

[210] "Ecclesiology", 132. Cf. ibid., 124: "The elderly Bishop [Buchberger] of Regensburg . . . said: 'My dear Brothers, at the Council you must above all talk about God. That is what is most important.' " See also "Gottesidee", 46: "The Church is not supposed to speak primarily about herself, but rather about God, and to make sure that this actually happens, there are corrections within the Church as well, whereby the course must be set by the right priorities in talking about God and about the common ministry."

[211] Cf. LG 1.

d. Jesus Christ's Church, not men's

It became clear in the previous section that with the disappearance of the concept of God, many Catholics also lost sight of the Church's christological-pneumatological origin, with the predictable result that Church became an association that is to be shaped by its members and degenerates into "a party of Christ".[212] To this Ratzinger responds, from his strictly theological perspective: The Church is "not a club, not a party, not even a sort of religious state within the secular state, but a body—Christ's Body. And this is why the Church is not of our making but is constructed by the Lord himself when he cleanses us by Word and sacrament and thus makes us his members."[213]

This very idea of union through reconciliation leads to the real heart of the Church, into "the ever renewed marriage of the Church with her Lord, actualized in the eucharistic mystery where the Church, participating in the sacrifice of Jesus Christ, fulfills its innermost mission, the adoration of the triune God".[214] Therefore, the schema on the liturgy had priority [at Vatican II] not only due to technical considerations, but also because of the primacy of worship, which according to Ratzinger determines the whole architecture of the Second Vatican Council.

> Worship, adoration, comes first. And thus God does. This beginning is in accordance with the rule of St. Benedict (XLIII): "Operi Dei nihil praeponatur" [Let nothing take precedence over the work of God, that is, liturgy]. The Constitution on the Church, which then followed as the Council's second text, should be seen as inwardly bracketed together with it. The Church derives from adoration, from the task of glorifying God. Ecclesiology, of its nature, has to do with liturgy. And so it is logical, too, that the third Constitution talks about the Word of God, which calls the Church together and is at all times renewing her. The fourth Constitution shows how the glory of God presents itself in an ethos, how the light we have received from God is carried out into the world, how only thus can God be fully glorified.[215]

---

[212] Cf. *Called to Communion*, 158.
[213] Ibid., 161–62.
[214] *Highlights*, 14.
[215] "Ecclesiology", 126.

If all the conciliar documents are subordinated to the primacy of wor-ship, the glorification of God, then this is true of ecclesiology, too, which has the mystery of Christ as its inmost core. But since the essen-tial characteristic of λατρεια is disappearing more and more nowadays, other self-made structures are taking the fore. This becomes especially clear in the liturgy: Ratzinger warns that "the more we do it for our-selves, however, the less it attracts people, because everyone can clearly sense that what is essential is increasingly eluding us."[216] Liturgy with-out an ecclesial form is a contradiction in terms, because "the Church . . . is the true subject of the liturgy."[217] Liturgy is for the Church, as Ratzinger says with Romano Guardini, "participation in the trinitar-ian dialogue of Father, Son, and Holy Spirit; only in this way is it not our 'doing', but opus Dei—God's action in us and with us."[218]

But if the Church's liturgy must be seen primarily as God's action upon us and with us, this leads at the conclusion of this second sec-tion to the finding that the term "Body of Christ", as Ratzinger under-stands it, proves to be the key concept for laying the foundation of ecclesiology. This designation leads "the Church out of merely legal and external considerations into the realm of mystery, with Christ at the center".[219] This phrase is from Ratzinger's foreword to the new [German] edition of his dissertation, which, as he himself puts it, "gained an unexpected relevance precisely in the postconciliar debate about the Church".[220] Indeed, unlike the twentieth-century Body of Christ theology during the period between the two world wars, which

---

[216] Ibid.

[217] Song, 118.

[218] Ibid. Cf. Church, 6.

[219] Volk und Haus Gottes, xi. Even before Mystici Corporis, misgivings about the image of the Mystical Body of Christ had been expressed. E. Przywara, S.J., and M. D. Koster, O.P., warned about a possible euphoria over this Pauline image, which in their opinion could not be applied to ecclesiology but rather belongs to the doctrine on grace (in the sense of life in Christ). In Koster's view, "Body of Christ" is a pure metaphor, which only makes a rhetorical comparison. The concept that does have ecclesiological relevance, based on Scripture and also the liturgy, is "People of God". Cf. M. D. Koster, Ekklesiologie im Werden (Paderborn: Bonifacius-Druckerei, 1940). Reprinted in the anthology of Koster's essays, compiled by H. D. Langer and O. H. Pesch under the title Volk Gottes im Werden (Mainz: Matthias-Grünewald-Verlag, 1971), 195–272.

[220] Volk und Haus Gottes, xix. Ratzinger expresses the hope, ibid., that with his disser-tation he might be able to promote a deeper understanding of the ecclesiology of Vatican II through the findings of biblical theology and the insights of the Church Fathers.

explained the attribute "mystical" largely in the sense of a mysterious interior communion with God, Ratzinger—with Augustine and in the patristic tradition—calls attention to the fact that "mystical" and "sacramental" are synonymous. From this he draws several conclusions for an accurate interpretation of the expression *Corpus Christi* in the ecclesiology of *Lumen gentium*: As the Church Fathers understood it, the "message about the Body of Christ was by no means characterized by interiority"[221] as opposed to an ecclesiology with a hierarchical stamp.[222] This expression, rather, depicts the Church as "the reality that is concretely constituted in the Eucharist and built up from it, a reality that is thereby simultaneously completely interior and completely public".[223] For this reason, the reality expressed by the term "Body of Christ" is for the Church the christological foundation of ecclesiology, which at the same time points to her sacramental structure, for the Church is—as Ratzinger formulated it in 1963 during the Council—"Body of Christ, because she receives the Lord in the Lord's Supper and lives on this core".[224]

Together with Gerd Lohaus,[225] we can thus summarize as follows: Ratzinger's understanding of the Church as Body of Christ has a distinctly eucharistic cast thanks to Augustine, since he understands the latter's concept of the Church in terms of "its characteristically liturgical core".[226] It is our task in the next section, therefore, to develop the theme of the Eucharist as the foundation of Ratzinger's ecclesiology. We will do this in three steps: (1) the Last Supper as the act of founding the Church; (2) eucharistic communities as the realization of the Church; and, finally, (3) the Church constituted as the Body of Christ in the Eucharist.

---

[221] Ibid., xv.

[222] Cf. *LG* 7: "As all the members of the human body, though they are many, form one body, so also are the faithful in Christ [cf. 1 Cor 12:12]. Also, in the building up of Christ's Body various members and functions have their part to play. . . . What has a special place among these gifts is the grace of the apostles to whose authority the Spirit Himself subjected even those who were endowed with charisms [cf. 1 Cor 14]. Giving the body unity through Himself and through His power and inner joining of the members, this same Spirit produces and urges love among the believers."

[223] *Volk und Haus Gottes*, xv.

[224] "Wesen", 46–78, citation at 59.

[225] Cf. Lohaus, 234–45, ref. at 236.

[226] Ibid.

§ 3. Eucharistic Ecclesiology[227]

Gerd Lohaus sums up Ratzinger's eucharistic ecclesiology in the formula: "Church, as the Body of Christ in the Eucharist, is the sacrament of God's *communio*."[228] Ratzinger himself, in his commentary on *Lumen gentium*, shows that the Church, from the perspective of the Body of Christ, points to the very heart of ecclesial life, to the mystery of the Eucharist, and that through this mystery she herself becomes a sacrament, the salvific sign of God in the world:

> The two meanings of Body of Christ, the eucharistic and the ecclesial, are not identical, yet they are thoroughly interrelated: The Church is built up from the eucharistic meal, and conversely the whole purpose of the Eucharist is to gather people into the Body of the Lord and thus into the Spirit of the Lord, so as to transform them into the living Body of Christ, the place of the concrete and mighty presence of Christ in the world.[229]

In Ratzinger's opinion, this eucharistic ecclesiology, which could also be called a *communio* ecclesiology, forms the real centerpiece of the ecclesiology of the Second Vatican Council, "the novel and at the same time the original element in what this Council wanted to give us".[230] Henri de Lubac, a forerunner of the conciliar ecclesiology,[231] made it clear, says Ratzinger, "in a splendid work of comprehensive scholarship that the term 'mystical body' originally meant the holy eucharist and that for Paul as for the Fathers of the Church the idea of

---

[227] Cf. *LG* 26.

[228] Lohaus, 236. See also ibid., 237: "'Sacrament' means that Church is Eucharist, and this essentially eucharistic way of actualizing herself is a sacred sign of the communion of men with God and with one another that is brought about in this actualization."

[229] "Einleitung", 10.

[230] *Church*, 7.

[231] Cf. K. Wittstadt, "Am Vorabend des II. Vatikanischen Konzils (1. Juli—10. Oktober 1962)", in Wittstadt, 1:457–560, ref. at 513. Here Wittstadt mentions the following French theologians who were particularly influential during the work of the Council: Fr. Yves Congar, O.P., Fr. Jean Daniélou, S.J., and Fr. Henri de Lubac, S.J. "All of the aforementioned theologians belonged to the *Nouvelle théologie*. As is well known, the 'New Theology' became a label for authors who were striving for a renewal in the method and content of theology and for that reason were accused of helping to bring about a revival of Modernism. In particular, the Jesuits of Lyons-Fourvière and the Dominicans of Le Saulchoir were suspected."

the Church as the body of Christ was indissolubly linked with the idea of the eucharist."[232] In her, Christ is really present and gives the *Ecclesia* his Body to be her food; in this act is accomplished simultaneously the re-presentation of her foundational event: "The Church came into being when the Lord had given his body and his blood under the forms of bread and wine, whereupon he said, 'Do this in memory of me.'"[233]

1. The Last Supper as the act of founding the Church

Just as "the first Passover night was the very hour in which the People Israel was born"[234] and the two foundational acts of Israel were accomplished with the Passover and with the making of the covenant at Sinai,[235,236] so too Christ understands himself to be "the new, true Paschal Lamb that dies vicariously for the whole world".[237] He

> thus elevates the meal in which his flesh is eaten and his blood is drunk to the status of the true, definitive Passover meal. That means that this meal has no other meaning than the one that was once characteristic of the Jewish Passover celebration. So it follows automatically that this meal appears as the source and basis of a new Israel and as its abiding core.[238]

In addition, Ratzinger says, "There is no longer any need for a center localized in an outward temple" since the "Body of the Lord,

---

[232] *Church*, 7. Cf. Henri de Lubac, *Corpus mysticum: L'Eucharistie et l'Église au Moyen Age, Étude historique* (Paris: Aubier, 1944).

[233] *Called to Communion*, 75.

[234] *Volk Gottes*, 13.

[235] Ratzinger refers to the exegetical assumption of Gerhard von Rad, "that the internal beginning of the Old Testament is to be found, not in a belief in creation, but rather in the reality of the covenant" (Ratzinger, "Difficulties in Teaching the Faith Today: Interview with Joseph Cardinal Ratzinger", in *Handing on the Faith in an Age of Disbelief*, by Ratzinger et al., trans. Michael J. Miller, 65–82, citation at 75 [San Francisco: Ignatius Press, 2006]).

[236] Cf. *Called to Communion*, 26f.

[237] *Volk Gottes*, 13. For this reason the heart of the Eucharist is the *"presentation of Jesus Christ's sacrifice on the Cross"* (*Eucharist*, 44; cf. LG 10, 11, 28; SC 2, 47).

[238] Ibid. In his presentation, Ratzinger relies on J. Jeremias, *Die Abendmahlsworte Jesu* (Göttingen: Vandenhoeck & Ruprecht, 1960).

which is the center of the Lord's Supper, is the one new temple that joins Christians together into a much more real unity than a temple made of stone could ever do."[239] For this reason, he advocates the view that "Jesus' last supper now [should be regarded] as the actual foundation of the Church."[240] Even though "exegetical works"[241] try to separate the Last Supper from the ecclesial sacrament, he insists on the institution of the Eucharist by Jesus Christ—granted, in a form that still functions within the Jewish Passover liturgy:[242]

Jesus gives those who are his own this liturgy of his death and resurrection and thus gives them the feast of life. In the last supper he recapitulates the covenant of Sinai, or rather what had there been an approximation in symbol now becomes reality: the community of blood and life between God and man. When we say this, [it] is clear that the last supper anticipates and at the same time necessarily presupposes the cross and the resurrection, since otherwise everything would remain empty gestures. Hence the Fathers of the Church were able to use a striking image to say that the Church sprang out of the wound in the Lord's side from which blood and water flowed. In reality this is the same, though seen only from another point of view, as when I say that the last supper is the origin of the Church.[243]

---

[239] *Called to Communion*, 27. Cf. *LG* 6: "As living stones we here on earth are built into it [that is, the New Jerusalem]."

[240] *Church*, 8. Cf. J. Meyer zu Schlochtern, *Sakrament Kirche: Wirken Gottes im Handeln des Menschen* (Freiburg im Breisgau: Herder, 1992), 152–90, ref. at 155.

[241] *Feast of Faith*, 33–60, ref. at 39, n. 8. See parallel passages, in J. Werbick, *Kirche: Ein ekklesiologischer Entwurf für Studium und Praxis* (Freiburg im Breisgau: Herder, 1994), 77: The historical-critical perspective "makes it quite unlikely that one could ever ascribe to the 'historical Jesus' in the first place the purpose of founding a Church or that it could have been within the 'horizon of his intentions'". See also H. Verweyen, *Gottes letztes Wort: Grundriss der Fundamentaltheologie* (Düsseldorf: Patmos-Verlag, 1991), 485.

[242] *Feast of Faith*, 33–60, ref. at 40f.

[243] *Church*, 8. Cf. *Called to Communion*, 75. The same argument appears in *Eucharist*, 29: "The institution of the Eucharist is an anticipation of his death. . . . For Jesus shares himself out, he shares himself as the one who has been split up and torn apart into body and blood. Thus the *eucharistic words* of Jesus are the answer to Bultmann's question about how Jesus underwent his death; in these words he undergoes a spiritual death, or, to put it more accurately, *in these words Jesus transforms death into the spiritual act of affirmation, into the act of self-sharing love*; into the act of adoration, which is offered to God, then from God is made available to men."

Accordingly, Ratzinger understands the origin of the Church in such a way that Jesus' words at the Last Supper, his death on the Cross, and his Resurrection form an indivisible trinity, which "gives us an inkling of the mystery of the triune God".[244] There is more: Because the Church in celebrating the Eucharist enters into Christ's prayer and thereby also into his self-abandonment to the Father in the Holy Spirit,[245] to celebrate the Eucharist also means to participate in the unity of the triune God and, thus, "to enter into union with the universal Church—that is, with the one Lord and his one Body. That is why there belongs to the Eucharist not only the anamnesis of the whole of sacred history but also the anamnesis of the whole community of the saints, of those who have died and of all living believers throughout the world".[246] This universal character of the Eucharist is particularly demonstrated by the First Eucharistic Prayer, the so-called Roman Canon, which developed from the Jewish Passover Haggadah. According to Ratzinger, it is

the direct descendant and continuation of this prayer of Jesus at the Last Supper and it is thereby the heart of the Eucharist. [The Roman Canon] is the genuine vehicle of the sacrifice, since thereby Jesus Christ transformed his death into verbal form—into a prayer—and, in so doing, changed the world. As a result, this death is able to be present for us, because it continues to live in the prayer, and the prayer runs right down through the centuries. A further consequence is that we can share in this death, because we can participate in this transforming prayer.[247]

---

[244] *Eucharist*, 44.
[245] Cf. *Feast of Faith*, 37f.
[246] *Principles*, 293.
[247] *Eucharist*, 49. In *Feast of Faith*, 37f., Ratzinger refers to and explains the concept of verbal sacrifice in late antiquity, which is echoed in the expression *oblatio rationabilis* in the Roman Canon of the Mass: "Sacrifice to the Divinity does not take place by the transfer of property but in the self-offering of mind and heart, expressed in word. This concept was adopted into Christianity without any difficulty. The eucharistic prayer is an entering-in to the prayer of Jesus Christ himself; hence it is the Church's entering-in to the Logos, the Father's Word, into the Logos' self-surrender to the Father, which, in the Cross, has also become the surrender of mankind to him. So, on the one hand, *eucharistia* made a bridge to Jesus' words of blessing at the Last Supper, in which he actually underwent, in an inward and anticipatory manner, his death on the Cross; and, on the other hand, it built

Wherever the Eucharist is celebrated, Christ is totally present in this way, in this re-presentation of his entire mystery, which is at the same time the mystery of the Church as well. Her "worship is [her] constitution, since of [her] nature [she] is [herself] the service of God and thus of men and women, the service of transforming the world."[248] Thereby the faithful enter into the structure of the *Communicantes* [prayer of the Roman Canon], which means concretely that they are united in "communion not only with the Lord but also with creation and with men of all places and all times".[249] For this reason, every celebration of the Eucharist inherently presupposes "a visible, concrete [*nennbare*, identifiable] ... unity"[250] as an essential structural element. Accordingly, the commemoration of the pope[251] and the bishop in the Eucharistic Prayer during the Mass is not something incidental; rather, it is an expression of this unity, for it means, in Ratzinger's opinion, "that we are truly celebrating the *one* Eucharist of Jesus Christ, which we can receive only in the *one* Church".[252]

This last-mentioned thought leads us immediately to the core of the conciliar declaration that the Church lives in all *legitimately organized* eucharistic communities.[253] Consequently, in the next section, I will examine with Ratzinger (a) the question of the legitimate organization of local communities; (b) the principle of totality that has already been noted, which states that the entire Church takes place in every Eucharist; and finally I will discuss (c) Ratzinger's ecclesiological conclusion that the Church, as the Body of Christ, is constituted on the basis of the Eucharist.

---

a bridge to the theology of the Logos and hence to a trinitarian deepening of the theology of Eucharist and of the Cross. Ultimately it facilitated the transition to a spiritual concept of sacrifice."

[248] *Church*, 8. Cf. *Called to Communion*, 20.

[249] *Eucharist*, 52.

[250] Cf. *Behold*, 93.

[251] Klemens Richter replies that the concept of eucharistic ecclesiology does not require an explicit commemoration of the pope "except as presider over a local Church"; see K. Richter, "Liturgiereform als Mitte einer Erneuerung der Kirche", in Richter, *Konzil*, 53–74, ref. at 63–65.

[252] *Eucharist*, 53.

[253] See *LG* 26.

2. Eucharistic communities as the realization of the Church

a. Legitimacy as union with the pastors

1) Successio apostolica

In his interpretation of *Lumen gentium*, Ratzinger ponders the fact that the conciliar document does not simply say, "The Church exists completely in every community celebrating the eucharist", but rather, "The Church of Christ is really present in all *legitimately organized* local groups of the faithful, which, *in so far as they are united to their pastors*, are . . . called Churches."[254] Two elements are crucial for this: "The community must be 'legitimately organized' for it to be the Church, and it is legitimately organized 'in union with its pastors'".[255] To be legitimately organized, as *Lumen gentium* understands it, means first, according to Ratzinger, that

> nobody can turn himself . . . into the Church. A group cannot simply come together, read the New Testament, and say: "We are now the Church, because the Lord is present wherever two or three are gathered in his name." An essential element of the Church is that of receiving. . . . For faith is the encounter with what I cannot think up myself or bring about by my own efforts but what must come to encounter me. The term we use for this structure of receiving and encounter is "sacrament". And part of the basic structure of a sacrament is that it is received and that no one administers it to himself. . . .
>
> The Church is not something one can make but only something one can receive, and indeed receive from where it already is and where it really is: from the sacramental community of his body that progresses through history.[256]

Without this sacramental communion, a community cannot be Church. As Ratzinger explains, Henri de Lubac had already "put the idea of the body of Christ in concrete terms as eucharistic ecclesiology and thus [applied it] to the actual questions of the Church's legal order and the relationship between the local and the universal Church".[257] The

---

[254] Ibid.; the emphasis in italics is from *Church*, 9–10.
[255] *Church*, 10. Cf. *Called to Communion*, 21.
[256] *Church*, 10.
[257] Ibid., 14. Cf. M. Figura, "Die Beziehung zwischen Universalkirche und Teilkirche nach Henri de Lubac", *IKaZ* 30 (2001): 468–83.

formula he devised twenty years before the Second Vatican Council's Constitution on the Church, "The Eucharist makes the Church",[258] should also be understood in this sense. Hence the Church's eucharistic constitution is very closely connected with the question of the ordained priesthood, which derives its legitimacy from the *successio apostolica*, "from within the 'Catholic' context, the Church as a whole and her sacramental power".[259] While asserting the *catholic* (universal) principle, he also accentuates the ontological primacy[260] of the universal Church over the particular Churches, which as communities are "always related to the whole"[261] and therefore also bear universality within themselves from the outset. Specifically, Ratzinger argues from the status of the apostle. He is "not the bishop of a community but rather a missionary for the whole Church"; he personally stands for the universal Church and "no local Church can claim him for herself alone."[262] As early as the apostolic age it is true that

the ministry concerned with the universal Church enjoys such a clear precedence over local offices that the concrete physiognomy of the latter is still overshadowed in the chief Pauline letters. It must be mentioned that the prophetic rank, invested with an equally supra-local mission, was active alongside the apostles. Still, these prophets are always designated in the Didachē as "your high priests" (13, 3). Only when we have grasped the meaning of this statement can we fully comprehend the import of the formula that the bishops are the successors of the apostles.... The fact that in the difficult formative process of the postapostolic Church the place of the apostles was also finally adjudged to them implies that they now assumed a responsibility whose scope transcended the local principle. It means that the catholic and missionary flame must not be extinguished even in this new situation. The Church cannot become a static juxtaposition of essentially self-sufficient local Churches.[263]

[258] Lubac, *Corpus mysticum*, 103.
[259] *Principles*, 287. On this theme, see also C. Böttigheimer, "Mysterium Christi und sakramentales Amt: Zur Problematik von Gemeinden ohne sonntägliche Eucharistiefeier", *StZ* 122 (1997): 117–28.
[260] See also Kasper, "Auseinandersetzung", 795–804.
[261] "Ecclesiology", 138.
[262] *Called to Communion*, 83.
[263] Ibid., 85.

At the beginning of the apostolic age—as Ratzinger demonstrates—the Church's episcopal ministry emerged and crystallized in a form that goes beyond the local community. In a way analogous to the college of apostles, the individual bishop was now not only the head of a local Church but also belonged to a collegial *communio*. By this, Ratzinger means that "the individual bishop stands in the apostolic succession and, hence, in every case only through his membership in this *collegium*."[264] This, however, has repercussions for the eucharistic understanding of the Church, for an essential part of the eucharistic structure of the local community is the horizontal relation of its bishop to the college of bishops.[265] For that reason, the Eucharist, too, always contains the "dimension of the sacrament *extra nos*",[266] which is to say that it "does not take its origin from the local Church, nor does it end there".[267] Consistently with this observation, Ratzinger remarks elsewhere:

> Here, too, the place, the geographical element, is less constitutive of the local church, of the "community", than is communion with the bishop—that is, the theological element; this theological element, in turn, is seen in conjunction with the reality of the "apostolic succession", which the bishop guarantees.[268]

With the reality of apostolic succession, we have returned again with Ratzinger to the point of departure of our reflections on the question of the legitimacy of eucharistic communities, and now we inquire into the importance he attributes to the *extra nos* of the sacrament for solving contemporary ecclesiological problems.

2) *The concrete application of the* extra nos *of the sacrament*

An initial consequence of the *extra-nos*, in Ratzinger's view, concerns the celebration of the Eucharist. Each time it is celebrated, the Eucharist declares "that Christ is coming to us from without, passing through our locked doors; ever and again it comes to us from without, from

---

[264] *Volk Gottes*, 38.

[265] See also pt. 2, sec. 2, chap. 3, § 3.1.b, of this work: "The Collegial Character of Spiritual Ministry in the Early Church".

[266] "Ecclesiology", 143. Cf. "Gottesidee", 46.

[267] "Ecclesiology", 143.

[268] *Principles*, 290.

the whole, one body of Christ, and draws us into that body".[269] That is why the community cannot give the Eucharist to itself.[270] This should be kept in mind so as to avoid that misunderstanding of eucharistic ecclesiology—resulting from "a one-sided contemporary interpretation of local Church tradition"[271]—which says "that there is nothing relevant to the constitution of the Church beyond the individual local bishops",[272] in other words, that the unity of the universal Church is only a "pleromatic enhancement but not a complement, not an augmentation of ecclesiality".[273]

We will return once more to this question in the course of our discussion of the hierarchical constitution of the Church. Nevertheless, it seems necessary to address it here in order to understand Ratzinger's argument that the Eucharist indeed happens at any given place, yet it "is at the same time universal, because there is only one Christ and only one body of Christ".[274]

This is connected to a second problem. In the contemporary discussion of the "community's right to the Eucharist",[275] Ratzinger discerns the legitimate desire to understand Church again in terms of her original center, for this option "recognizes the fact that the ecclesial community is centered around the Eucharist and, consequently, understands the Church herself in terms of her original liturgical context."[276]

"Community" is the new discovery of the post-conciliar period. We have called to mind once more that Eucharist, in the language of the ancient Church, was called, among other things, *synaxis*, the "meeting together", the assembly. It draws and binds men together, unites them, builds up community. Conversely, the community experiences Eucharist as fulfillment, as the center of its life, something in which

---

[269] "Ecclesiology", 143. Cf. *Principles*, 293.

[270] Cf. *Principles*, 287: "Where the Eucharist is claimed as the right of the community, there quickly follows the notion that the community can, in fact, confer it on itself, in which case it no longer needs a priesthood that can be bestowed only by ordination in the *successio apostolica*."

[271] *Called to Communion*, 89. Cf. Richter, "Liturgiereform als Mitte", 53–74.

[272] *Called to Communion*, 89. See also *Principles*, 292f.

[273] *Principles*, 292.

[274] "Ecclesiology", 131–32.

[275] Cf. J. Blank, P. Hünermann, and P. M. Zulehner, *Das Recht der Gemeinde auf Eucharistie* (Trier: Paulinus-Verlag, 1978); see *Principles*, 285–311.

[276] *Principles*, 285.

it shares as a totality. All this is true, but we must remember that the scope of *synaxis* is much wider than the individual community. Behind it stand those words from the Gospel of John: Jesus wanted to die for the nation, and not only for the nation but "to gather into one the children of God who are scattered abroad" (Jn 11:52).[277]

In order to clarify this scope of the Eucharist, Ratzinger contrasts the celebration of it to the sort of prayer services found in Islam. Even though the Liturgy of the Word makes up a considerable part of the Holy Mass, it considers itself, taken alone, "as incomplete",[278] since it is always directed toward the sacrifice of the New Covenant. The latter consideration is also, for Ratzinger, the intrinsic reason why the Eucharist is clearly distinct from the sort of assembly of the faithful found in the Jewish synagogue liturgy in the time when *there was no Temple*.

The synagogue service is the divine worship that takes place in the absence of the Temple and in expectation of its restoration. Christian worship, for its part, regards the destruction of the Temple in Jerusalem as final and as theologically necessary. Its place has been taken by the universal Temple of the risen Christ. . . . The new Temple already exists, and so too does the new, the definitive sacrifice: the humanity of Christ opened up in his Cross and Resurrection. The prayer of the man Jesus is now united with the dialogue of eternal love within the Trinity. Jesus draws men into this prayer through the Eucharist, which is thus the ever-open door of adoration and the true Sacrifice, the Sacrifice of the New Covenant.[279]

In pointing out this relation between the Eucharist and the Temple sacrifices in salvation history, Ratzinger is concerned with the intrinsic unity of the Old and New Testaments. For this reason, he objects to the modern approaches to the subject in which "the exclusive model for the liturgy of the New Covenant has been thought to be the synagogue—in strict opposition to the Temple".[280] He sees in them one cause for the fact that nowadays "priesthood and sacrifice are no

---

[277] *Feast of Faith*, 147–48. Cf. *Song*, 59–77, reference to 74ff.
[278] *Spirit of the Liturgy*, 48.
[279] Ibid., 48–49.
[280] Ibid., 49.

longer intelligible"[281] and that the indispensability of the ordained priesthood is debated again and again, especially in times of increasing priest shortages. Ratzinger has repeatedly spoken out on this set of problems, for example, on the topics of celibacy,[282] *viri probati*,[283] and the ordination of women,[284] which were also taken up in the so-called "Petition of the People of the Church" in Germany and Austria.[285] In this connection, he points out that another reason why the priestly state seems so strange in our democratic, secularized societies is that this ministry "is not based on the consent of the majority but on the representation of *another*".[286] Surely still other factors contributing to this crisis could be mentioned that Ratzinger does not take into account, since he thinks in terms of the nature of the priesthood and therefore accentuates the theological as opposed to other, for example, sociological causes. He is convinced that it is "a great temptation to pass from that supernatural 'authority of representation', the hallmark of the Catholic priesthood, to a much more natural 'service of

---

[281] Ibid. In contrast, Ratzinger himself emphasizes the "comprehensive 'fulfillment' of pre-Christian salvation history and the inner unity" of the Old and New Testaments.

[282] Cf. *Salt of the Earth*, 194–200. Ratzinger views the debate about celibacy in particular as one symptom of a crisis in faith. The priest should give witness to the kingdom of heaven with his whole life. Just as the priestly tribe of Levi in the Old Testament owned no land, so too the celibate life-style of the priest should indicate that God alone is his inheritance; cf. Psalm 16. Although Ratzinger's view may seem one-sided, it accurately formulates, in my opinion, a decisive reason for the contemporary lack of acceptance for the celibate life-style.

[283] As early as 1970 Ratzinger referred to the possibility of *viri probati* in the Church of the future; see Ratzinger, *Faith and the Future*, 101–2. Cf. *Salt of the Earth*, 256: "Let's leave open what forms will develop in this area. But the irreplaceability of the priesthood and of the deep inner connection between celibacy and priesthood are constants."

[284] Cf. *Salt of the Earth*, 208–13. For Ratzinger, participation in ministry means at the same time entering into a "relationship of subordination". This explanation contradicts the interpretation that claims to see ordination as an instrument for the exercise of ecclesial power. Ratzinger cites (ibid., 210) the exegete Elisabeth Schüssler Fiorenza: "At first she took a vehement part in the struggle for women's ordination, but now she says that that was a wrong goal. The experience with female priests in the Anglican Church has, she says, led to the realization that 'ordination is not a solution.... Ordination is subordination....' And on this point her diagnosis is completely correct."

[285] Cf. Herder Verlag, ed., *"Wir sind Kirche": Das Kirchenvolks-Begehren in der Diskussion* (Freiburg im Breisgau: Herder, 1995). Individual essays on the topic of the "Petition of the People of the Church" can be found in P. M. Zulehner, ed., *Kirchenvolks-Begehren (und Weizer Pfingstvision): Kirch auf Reformkurs* (Düsseldorf, Innsbruck, and Vienna: Tyrolia, 1995).

[286] *Report*, 56.

the coordination of consensus', that is to say, a comprehensible category, because it is only human and, besides, more in consonance with modern culture." [287]

The fact that this effort ultimately leads to a different image of the Church is plainly manifest in the practice of equating Sunday worship services without a priest, even when not absolutely necessary, with Sunday Mass, so as to emphasize the value of the local parish community. In Ratzinger's view, the right understanding of Church is at risk in such thinking. Only if Church is understood *from below*, that is to say, "congregationally" [288] and not episcopally, does it follow that the community itself holds all authority and thus constitutes itself. "But this approach inevitably destroys the public nature and the all-embracing reconciliatory character of the Church, both of which are represented in the episcopal principle and result from the essence of the Eucharist." [289] The saying of Jesus, "Where two or three are gathered in my name, there am I in the midst of them" (Mt 18:20), cannot be interpreted as an isolated authorization to found churches, since "it is not a definitive and exhaustive statement of the whole of the Church's reality. The assembly, even the informal togetherness of prayer groups, has an important role in the Church." [290] An essential part of the Church and the Eucharist, nevertheless, is the *successio apostolica*:

> It means that no group can constitute itself a church but *becomes* a church only by being received as such by the universal Church. It means, too, that the Church cannot organize herself according to her own design but can *become* herself again and again only by the gift of the Holy Spirit requested in the name of Jesus Christ, that is, through the sacrament.[291]

As a result of this point, we can state that Ratzinger sees apostolic succession as the guarantee for the *legitimacy* of the Eucharist, which is necessary for the fulfillment of its life-giving purpose. By virtue of apostolic succession, the bishop or the priest is not only the presider over the community that celebrates the Eucharist, but he is at the

---

[287] Ibid.
[288] *Called to Communion*, 81.
[289] Ibid.
[290] Ibid., 82. Cf. *Church*, 8f.
[291] *Principles*, 293.

same time bound up in the *extra-nos* [that which is "beyond us"] of the sacrament. Even though the ecclesiology of the local Church (led by the bishop), as set forth by the Second Vatican Council, follows from the intrinsic connection between Eucharist and community, this unity always has, according to Ratzinger, a *universal* structure. For this reason, he emphasizes that the episcopal ministry, because of its apostolic provenance and its collegial constitution, is at the same time service to the universal Church. Episcopal ministry and Eucharist belong together by their very nature, because the episcopal ministry is understood "as a service to unity that follows necessarily from the character of the Eucharist as sacrifice and reconciliation".[292] At the same time this forms the sacramental basis for episcopal collegiality, for a "Church understood eucharistically is a Church constituted episcopally."[293] The complicated questions concerning the episcopal ministry that are broached here will be examined in depth further on in the section on the hierarchical structure of the Church.[294]

b. The fulfillment of the whole Church in each celebration of the Eucharist

In contrast to the more juridical concept of Church in the West, in the Eastern Church[295] a eucharistic ecclesiology was developed that consists above all in an ecclesiology of the local Church. Its axiom is: The Church is built up from the Eucharist.[296] This fundamental principle is of decisive importance for the ecclesiology of Vatican II as well. In the real presence of Christ in the word and sacrament of the Eucharist, the Church experiences her most profound mission. Hence the whole Church is fulfilled in every gathering, "for the Body of the Lord is always whole . . . , and this is true also of the word of God."[297]

---

[292] *Called to Communion*, 79.
[293] Ibid.
[294] See pt. 2, sec. 2, chap. 3, of this work: "The Hierarchical Constitution of the Church, in Particular with Regard to Episcopal Collegiality".
[295] Cf. M. M. Garijo-Guembe, "Konsequenzen des Dialogs mit der Orthodoxie für die römische Ekklesiologie", in Richter, *Konzil*, 140–58, esp. 153. Here Garijo-Guembe judges the section on episcopal collegiality in Ratzinger's *Das neue Volk Gottes* as "one of the best works on collegiality".
[296] Cf. *Principles*, 292.
[297] Ibid., 252–53.

On the other hand, according to Ratzinger's argument, every community can receive the one Christ only within the communion of the Church, for "this Lord is always one, always undivided not only in one place but in the whole world."[298] In this respect, however, there is an intrinsic condition for unity: "I can only have the one Lord in the unity that he is himself, in the unity with the others who are also his body and are continually to become his body anew in the eucharist."[299]

For this reason, the fullness of the Church, according to Ratzinger, is always universal. This teaching of the Council excludes—as he says— all "self-sufficiency" and testifies that "the community of the faithful of all places and all times is not some external matter of organization but is grace springing from within and at the same time a visible sign of the power of the Lord who alone can give unity across so many barriers."[300] Together with Gerd Lohaus, we can distill from this the following quintessential conclusion: "Communities" are correctly understood "as being centered on the Eucharist" only when we recognize that this centering simultaneously points to their "*ecclesial* existence".[301] This insight leads us immediately to Ratzinger's next thesis: Church as *Corpus Christi* is always founded upon the Eucharist.

3. *The Church is constituted as the Body of Christ through the Eucharist*

The point of departure for this reflection is Ratzinger's conviction that being a Christian is nothing other than sharing in the mystery of the Incarnation, or to formulate it with an expression used by the Apostle Paul, "the Church, insofar as she is the Church, is the 'Body of Christ' (i.e., a participation on the part of men in that communion between man and God which is the Incarnation of the Word)."[302] This communion is accomplished foundationally in the Eucharist:

> The Lord becomes our bread, our food. He gives us his body, which, by the way, must be understood in the light of the Resurrection and of the Semitic linguistic background.... The body is a man's self,

---

[298] Ibid., 293.
[299] *Church*, 11.
[300] Ibid.
[301] Lohaus, 234–45, citation at 236.
[302] *Behold*, 88.

which does not coincide with the corporeal dimension but comprises it as one element among others. Christ gives us himself—Christ, who in his Resurrection has continued to exist in a new kind of bodiliness.[303]

The reception of the eucharistic gifts effects an inner penetration by the Risen One, who transforms us into his Body. The presence of Jesus in the sacrament is consequently "not something at rest but is a power that catches us up and works to draw us within itself".[304] Ratzinger illustrates this central idea, which has its roots in the *Confessions*[305] of St. Augustine, as follows:

> Communion means that the seemingly uncrossable frontier of my "I" is left wide open and can be so because Jesus has first allowed himself to be opened completely, has taken us all into himself and has put himself totally into our hands. Hence, Communion means the fusion of existences; just as in the taking of nourishment the body assimilates foreign matter to itself, and is thereby enabled to live, in the same way my "I" is "assimilated" to that of Jesus, it is made similar to him in an exchange that increasingly breaks through the lines of division. This same event takes place in the case of all who communicate; they are all assimilated to this "bread" and thus are made one among themselves—*one* body.[306]

In this intimate and eucharistic attachment of the Church, in which the Lord gives us his Body and makes us his Body, Ratzinger discerns the ever-abiding "place where the Church is generated", whereby the risen Lord "never ceases to found her anew; in the Eucharist the Church is most compactly herself—in all places, yet one only, just as he is one only." [307]

With this thought, we have broached the new theme of *communio* ecclesiology. "Its source lies in Christology: the incarnate Son is the 'communion' between God and men." [308] Through the ecclesial *communio*, he gives us a share in the mystery of the Incarnation, so that

---

[303] *Called to Communion*, 36–37.
[304] *Eucharist*, 77.
[305] Augustine, *Confessiones* 7, 10, 16, in CSEL 33, 1, 157f.; CCL 27, 103f.
[306] *Called to Communion*, 37. Cf. *Behold*, 88.
[307] *Called to Communion*, 37.
[308] *Behold*, 88.

we must proceed from the premise "that there can be no separation of Church and Eucharist, sacramental communion and community fellowship".[309] Hence eucharistic ecclesiology is called *communio* ecclesiology. According to Ratzinger, it is "the real core of Vatican II's teaching on the Church, the novel and at the same time the original element in what this Council wanted to give us".[310]

§ 4. The Church as a *Communio* Unity

Already at the beginning of my examination of Ratzinger's ecclesiology, I pointed out that for him the sacramental perspective is decisive in assimilating the teaching of the Council. We will now explore the depths of this perspective in relation to the Church as a *communio* unity.

Communio has become a fundamental concept of Ratzinger's own ecclesiology. Already in his dissertation on Augustine, we read the descriptive formula: *Church is communio*,[311] whereby this *communio* represents "the eucharistic relationship of love for the whole world".[312] This gives us to understand that his ecclesiology from the very outset (in keeping with Augustine)[313] understands *communio* in a eucharistic way, as Gerd Lohaus makes clear, writing in 1993:

---

[309] Ibid.

[310] *Church*, 7.

[311] See *Volk und Haus Gottes*, 138.

[312] Ibid. "But if the Catholic's *communio* is *caritas* and, on the other hand, Church is essentially *communio*, then *catholica* and *caritas* come so close together that it finally seems to allow us to address the *Catholica* as objective *caritas*, in which one acquires a share through participation in this *communio* that represents *caritas*. *Caritas* and *ecclesia* come together here so intimately that in a certain sense one can reckon them to be identical. For the individual, accordingly, it does not mean a subjective attitude, but rather membership in the Church, indeed, necessarily in that Church which herself abides in charity, that is, in the eucharistic relationship of love for the whole world" (ibid.).

[313] It is worth noting that in Augustine's writings, Christ is represented sacramentally by the entire *ecclesia sancta*, through the holy People of God, and not only unilaterally through the ordained ministers. See *Volk und Haus Gottes*, 149, esp. n. 55. In contrast, Hermann J. Pottmeyer maintains that the conciliar recognition of "the participation of all the faithful in the threefold ministry of Christ" is "plainly suppressed" by Ratzinger's eucharistic *communio* ecclesiology; Pottmeyer refers to Ratzinger's 1986 essay "The Ecclesiology of the Second Vatican Council" (in *Church*, 3–20); see also H. J. Pottmeyer, "Kirche als Communion: Eine Reformidee aus unterschiedlichen Perspektiven", *StZ* 117 (1992): 579–89, ref. at 589, n. 6. In my opinion, it only seems, of course, that Ratzinger conceals the priestly, kingly, and prophetic

In the celebration of the Eucharist, Church fulfills what she is and what she becomes again and again: *communio*. *Communio* is that "effect" of the eucharistic fulfillment of Church which she "manifests" in carrying out the Eucharist.... If the Church is *sacramentum*, then the grace communicated in the Eucharist as *the* fulfillment of Church has a communicative structure: unification with God is the content of the grace, and the unification has as its consequence the unity of men with one another.[314]

Communio as an essential feature of the Church had a decisive significance[315] in the early Church and finally made its way again into the ecclesiology of Vatican II,[316] even though—as Ratzinger remarks— "the term 'communion' does not occupy a central place in the Council."[317] Only in the course of the gradual process of understanding and implementing the Council's teachings did the expression become one of the most important theological concepts.[318] Twenty years after the Council, the Extraordinary Synod of Bishops in 1985 even describes the concept "*communio* ecclesiology" as "the central and fundamental idea of the conciliar documents".[319] Ratzinger himself expressly advocated this centering of ecclesiology on the word *communio*[320] and understands it to be the "synthesis for the essential elements of the conciliar ecclesiology".[321]

In the following paragraphs, we will look at the concept of *communio* as Ratzinger interprets it, first by defining more precisely this key word in his ecclesiology, secondly by demonstrating concrete

---

dignity of the People of God in his 1986 essay, since he recommends further reflection on this dignity in relation to the universal call to holiness (*LG* 10) (*Church*, 20).

[314] Lohaus, 234–45, citation at 237. Cf. "Ecclesiology", 130f.

[315] On this subject, see the exposition in Kehl, *Kirche*, 320–46.

[316] In the conciliar documents themselves, *communio* is used as a synonym for terms such as *communitas*, *societas*, and *participatio*, whereby the purpose of this *communio* is described as "a participation of the divine life" (*LG* 2).

[317] "Ecclesiology", 129.

[318] Cf. "Kirche—unter dem Wort Gottes—feiert die Geheimnisse Christi—zum Heil der Welt: Schlussdokument der zweiten außerordentlichen Synode, 9 Dezember 1985" [concluding document issued by the Second Extraordinary Synod of Bishops], in *Zukunft aus der Kraft des Konzils: Die außerordentliche Bischofssynode '85*, the synod documents with a commentary by Walter Kasper (Freiburg im Breisgau: Herder, 1986), 17–45, esp. 33–40.

[319] Ibid., 33.

[320] Cf. "Gottesidee", 46.

[321] "Ecclesiology", 130.

conclusions that follow from the *communio* ecclesiology in answer to contemporary problems, and thirdly by investigating the question about membership in the Church.

1. *Toward an understanding of the concept of* communio

a. The secular roots—The semantics of κοινωνια

As Ratzinger explains, *communio*, in Greek κοινωνια, is a word that originally had secular roots meaning community, fellowship (common property, common work, common values). In Hebrew, the corresponding term is *ḥabhûrâ*, which is likewise translated by fellowship, cooperative. In the Jewish context, three applications of this term should be considered:

> As early as the first century B.C. the group of the Pharisees call themselves *ḥabhûrâ*; since the second century A.D. the term is also used for the rabbis; and ultimately the word is applied to those (at least ten in number) assembled for the Passover meal. This latter usage shows quite clearly how easily it could be applied to the mystery of the Church: the Church is the *ḥabhûrâ* of Jesus in a very deep sense— the fellowship of his Passover, the family in which his eternal desire of eating the Passover with us (cf. Lk 24:15) is fulfilled.[322]

In Greek, we find in Plato's philosophy an antecedent for the Christian interpretation of κοινωνια. He speaks in the *Symposium* about a mutual κοινωνια between gods and men and even says that this "communion with the gods also brings about community among men."[323] Ratzinger explains that Plato thereby "coins a wonderful phrase, which could actually be taken as an intimation of the eucharistic mystery, when he says that the cult is concerned with nothing other than the preservation and the healing of love".[324]

b. Trinitarian *communio* as an essential feature of the Church

As an essential feature of the Church, *communio* is nevertheless not simply the synthesis of these semantic meanings; rather, it is the product

---

[322] *Behold*, 84. See also Ratzinger, *Ministers of Your Joy*, 108f.
[323] *Behold*, 86.
[324] Ibid. See n. 12 there with the reference to Plato's *Symposium* 188 b–c. Cf. *LG* 59.

of a new and heretofore nonexistent reality, which is revealed in the Incarnation of the Divine Word:[325]

> The one, transcendent God of the Old Testament unveils his innermost life and shows that, in himself, he is a dialogue of eternal love. Since he himself is relationship—Word and Love—he can speak, feel, answer, love. Since he is relationship, he can open himself and provide his creature with a relationship to him. In the Incarnation of the eternal Word there comes about that communion between God and the being of man, his creature, which up to now had seemed irreconcilable with the transcendence of the only God.[326]

Being at the service of this κοινωνια between God and men is the sacramental meaning of the Church. Consequently, Ratzinger can state the equation: Church *is* communion—"not only between human beings but, as a result of the death and Resurrection of Jesus, communion with Christ, the incarnate Son, and hence communion with the eternal, triune Love of God".[327] The encounter with Jesus Christ, the incarnate Word, is the point of departure and the center of the *communio*: "Fellowship with God is mediated by the fellowship of God with man, which is Christ in person; the encounter with Christ brings about fellowship with him and, thus, with the Father in the Holy Spirit; on this basis it unites men with one another."[328]

The goal of this *communio* is eschatological joy; here Ratzinger makes an immediate connection between perfect joy (cf. 1 Jn 1:3) and the Holy Spirit, for "in that saying about perfect joy there is a connection with the farewell discourses of Jesus and, thus, with the Paschal Mystery and with the coming again of the Lord in paschal contemplation, which is directed toward his perfect coming again in the new world."[329] Due to this interrelation of the *eschaton*,[330] the Paschal Mystery, and

---

[325] Cf. *LG* 1–4.

[326] *Behold*, 86–87.

[327] Ibid., 86.

[328] "Ecclesiology", 130. Cf. 1 Jn 1:3: "That which we have seen and heard we proclaim also to you, so that you may have fellowship with us, and our fellowship is with the Father and with his Son Jesus Christ. And we are writing this that our joy may be complete."

[329] "Ecclesiology", 130. Cf. Jn 15:20, 22, 24, with Lk 11:13.

[330] See "Ecclesiology", 131: In eucharistic ecclesiology the doctrine on the Church becomes "quite concrete in type and yet at the same time remains entirely spiritual, transcendent, and eschatological".

communio ecclesiology, the last-mentioned is understood "in its inmost nature"—already in Ratzinger's *Principles of Catholic Theology*—as "eucharistic ecclesiology":[331]

> The Church is *communio*; she is God's communing with men in Christ and hence the communing of men with one another—and, in consequence, sacrament, sign, instrument of salvation. The Church is the celebration of the Eucharist; the Eucharist is the Church; they do not simply stand side by side; they are one and the same. The Eucharist is the *sacramentum Christi* and, because the Church is *Eucharistia*, she is therefore also *sacramentum*—the sacrament to which all the other sacraments are ordered.[332]

Thus it becomes evident how the term *communio*, due to its ecclesial etymology by way of κοινωνια and *communicatio* (in the Vulgate), means both "Eucharist" and also "fellowship", "community", or "parish".[333] From the two meanings taken together results, according to Ratzinger, "the eucharistic dynamism of community within the Church",[334] which flows from the authority and the love of the Lord.[335] More precisely, this means, as Gerd Lohaus explains:

> The Eucharist as the fulfillment of the Church is ... the inclusion of the Church and thus of Christians in Christ's self-surrender to the Father. Church is thus ... simultaneously a trinitarian and a communicative happening. Hence Ratzinger's concept of *communio has a trinitarian character and is also informed by the wisdom of the Cross*.[336]

This distinctive character of the *communio* concept has a fourfold significance for his ecclesiology: (1) *Communio* becomes the answer that gives meaning to humanity, which at present is torn by modern individualism. (2) It is the intrinsic nature of the Church's liturgical celebration. (3) *Communio* bestows binding force by remaining in the teaching of the apostles. (4) It understands itself to be missionary, in the sense of carrying on a dialogue with the world.

---

[331] Ibid., 131.
[332] *Principles*, 53.
[333] See *Behold*, 75.
[334] Ibid., 76.
[335] Cf. ibid., 99.
[336] Lohaus, 234–45, citation at 238; italics in the original.

2. *Consequences of the* communio *ecclesiology*

a. Ecclesial *communio* as a response to the dichotomy caused by individualism

According to Ratzinger, the Church as *communio* is a "mystery of union" and, consequently, at the same time a response to "the split into individuality"[337] that is rooted in the nature of original sin. Furthermore, this *communio* perspective was meant to counteract the individualistic view of *Christian* salvation that was largely taken for granted in the first half of the twentieth century. De Lubac criticized this view by citing the following passage by Jean Giono:

Have I found joy? ... No, but I have found *my* joy and that is something wildly different....
The joy of Jesus can be personal. It can belong to a single man and he is saved. He is at peace, he is joyful now and for always, but he is alone....
When I am beset by affliction, I cannot find peace in the blandishments of genius. My joy will not be lasting unless it is the joy of all. I will not pass through the battlefields with a rose in my hand.[338]

This individualistic notion of Christian salvation—as Ratzinger summarizes de Lubac's own argument—is a "caricature of Christianity that, in the nineteenth and twentieth centuries, made possible the rise of atheism".[339] On the contrary, de Lubac's perspective makes it evident that the Church per se is the *sacrament of unity*[340] and is opposed to the narrow, self-centered perspective. This new view teaches us

to understand the sacraments as the fulfillment of the life of the Church; in doing so, it enriches the teaching about grace: grace is

---

[337] *Principles*, 49.
[338] See Henri de Lubac, *Catholicism: A Study of Dogma in Relation to the Corporate Destiny of Mankind*, trans. Lancelot C. Sheppard and Sister Elizabeth Englund, O.C.D. (San Francisco: Ignatius Press, 1988), 13.
[339] *Principles*, 49.
[340] Cf. also *SC* 26: "Liturgical services are not private functions, but are celebrations of the Church, which is the 'sacrament of unity,' namely, the holy people united and ordered under their bishops. Therefore liturgical services pertain to the whole body of the Church; they manifest it and have effects upon it; but they concern the individual members of the Church in different ways, according to their differing rank, office, and actual participation."

always the beginning of union. As a liturgical event, a sacrament is always the work of a community; it is, as it were, the Christian way of celebrating, the warranty of a joy that issues from the community and from the fullness of power that is vested in it.[341]

It follows from this that the Church as *communio* is the "sacrament of salvation"[342] through her relationship with the Lord, which "in turn founds a new relationship between men".[343]

b. *Communio* as liturgical community

The second consequence of ecclesial *communio*, according to Ratzinger, is directly connected with the first:

The Church is not merely an external society of believers; by her nature, she is a liturgical community; she is most truly Church when she celebrates the Eucharist and makes present the redemptive love of Jesus Christ, which, as love, frees men from their loneliness and leads them to one another by leading them to God.[344]

In this κοινωνια something new happens that simultaneously distinguishes it from all other communities.[345] It brings about the comprehensive unity, *unio* or *unitas*,[346] a communion between God and men, which is realized in the Person Jesus and in turn "becomes communicable in the Easter mystery",[347] that is, in the death and Resurrection of Jesus Christ. In this way, the Eucharist becomes "our participation in the Easter mystery, and hence it is constitutive of the Church, the Body of Christ."[348] For this reason, "*communio* ecclesiology is intrinsically eucharistic ecclesiology."[349] The *communio sacramentalis* so thoroughly determines the nature of the Church, according to Ratzinger, that it is permissible to express this in the formula: "Church is

---

[341] *Principles*, 50.
[342] Cf. *LG* 59.
[343] *Behold*, 90.
[344] *Principles*, 50.
[345] Cf. Ratzinger, *Ministers of Your Joy*, 57f.
[346] *Principles*, 51.
[347] *Behold*, 93.
[348] Ibid.
[349] "Gottesidee", 46.

communio":[350] "The Church is communion; she is the communion of the Word and Body of Christ and is thus communion among men, who by means of this communion that brings them together from above and from within are made *one* people, indeed, one Body."[351]

This bodiliness of the one Church is indivisible and presupposes the unity of the congregation celebrating the Eucharist with the universal Church. This is because "the Eucharist does not take its origin from the local Church, nor does it end there",[352] as it says in a key statement in the rather controversial essay[353] "On the Ecclesiology of the Constitution *Lumen gentium*", written by Ratzinger in the year 2000. He had already pointed out in an earlier work this connection between the unity of the sacrament and the indivisibility of the Church:

> While the Church is indeed constituted primarily by sacramentality and by her communion with Christ, precisely because she is the "Body of Christ", she is corporeal and is the corporation of Christians. The two things are not mutually exclusive but, rather, mutually conditioning. Because the Church is sacramental communion in the Body of the Lord and on the basis of his Word, it is the communion of sacred law.[354]

The adjective "sacred" makes clear that "the order of unity is not one of purely human law but that unity is a key characteristic of the Church's essence, so that the juridical expression of unity in the office of Peter's successor" and in the *communio* of the bishops with one another and with the pope "belongs to the core of her sacred order. Hence, the loss of this element wounds her at the point where she is most truly Church."[355] In dealing with this question, therefore, Ratzinger is concerned ultimately with the order of the Church, which was firmly

---

[350] *Principles*, 254: "The center of the oldest ecclesiology is the eucharistic assembly—the Church is *communio*." Cf. Meyer zu Schlochtern, *Sakrament Kirche*, 153–90, ref. at 158.

[351] *Called to Communion*, 76.

[352] "Ecclesiology", 143; cf. *LG* 7.

[353] See W. Kasper's reply to Ratzinger's comments, "Über die Ekklesiologie der Konstitution *Lumen gentium*", in Kasper, "Auseinandersetzung", 795–804, esp. 796, where Kasper conjectures that in Ratzinger's interpretation the relation between the universal Church and the local Church "has become unbalanced".

[354] *Called to Communion*, 93. Cf. *Church*, 7f.: In the writings of Paul and the Church Fathers, the Body of Christ concept is inseparable from the *communio sacramentalis*.

[355] *Called to Communion*, 94.

established by Christ in revelation and which is firmly adhered to in the teaching of the apostles.

c. The content of the unity: "The teaching of the apostles"

For this reason, the third consequence of *communio* ecclesiology is that the *communio* has a definite content, namely, the obligation to persevere in the teaching of the apostles. In keeping with the description of the infant Church in Acts 2:42: "They held steadfastly to the apostles' teaching and fellowship, to the breaking of the bread and to the prayers", Ratzinger explains that the *eucharistic communio* is inseparable from fellowship in the teaching of the apostles:

> That is, the unity has a content which is expressed in doctrine. The teaching of the Apostles is the concrete way in which they continue to be present in the Church. In virtue of this teaching, even future generations, after the death of the Apostles, will remain in unity with them and thus form the same, one, apostolic Church.[356]

Ecclesial office is required in order to maintain *communio* in the teaching of the apostles:

> So the indivisible presence of one and the same Lord, who is also the Father's Word, presupposes that every individual community is part of the entire, single Body of Christ. This is the only way the community can celebrate Eucharist at all.... It also presupposes that it is "continuing in the teaching of the Apostles", something manifested and guaranteed by the institution of the "apostolic succession".[357]

For Ratzinger, persevering in the teaching of the apostles has both an institutional and a personal character,[358] as he makes clear by quoting Origen's remark, "A mystery can be seen only by one who lives it."[359] He thereby makes the important point that doctrine transforms only when it is put into practice. Hence continuing in union with the teaching of the apostles is not a technique for making some-

---

[356] *Behold*, 74–75. In connection with this idea of persevering in the apostolic teaching, Ratzinger refers to Acts 20:18–35 (the farewell discourse of Paul in Miletus).

[357] Cf. *Behold*, 74–100, ref. at 99. See also *Principles*, 285–98.

[358] Cf. ibid., 75: "The 'presbyters' are entrusted with the responsibility of upholding the Apostles' teaching and ensuring that it remains a present reality. They are the personal guarantee for that 'continuing in' the original doctrine."

[359] *Principles*, 51.

thing;[360] it is—as Ratzinger repeatedly says—a process of conversion to what is inside, "a radical inner change in our thinking and being",[361] whereby the individual is cleansed of the sin that otherwise isolates him. But if he undergoes this conversion of heart,[362] something surprising happens: "The path that leads men within and the path that draws them together are not in conflict; on the contrary, they need and support one another. For it is only when men are united inwardly that they can really be united outwardly."[363]

What union, though, reaches into the depths of man, so that it supports him even in death, that is, embraces human life in its entirety? It is union with God, which proceeds from him, from his incarnate Word, which has identified itself with man. In accord with *Lumen gentium* 1, Ratzinger directs our attention to the whole human race when he emphasizes, together with Gérard Philips, the importance of the ecclesial *communio* for the whole world:

> The Church is, then, the sacrament of union with God and, for that reason, of the mutual union of the faithful in a single movement of love for him. She serves, therefore, as a sign for the whole human race.... If, then, a unified temporal order on the worldly level and the building of the universal kingdom of God by Jesus Christ must continue to be quite separate realities, man would, nevertheless, have to be blind indeed if he denied the interaction that links the two together.[364]

---

[360] Ratzinger recalls that "the Bible portrays this graphically in the story of the tower of Babel: the most advanced union in terms of technical skill turns suddenly into a total incapacity for human communication. Even from the inner structure of the episode, that is the logical outcome: where each person wants to be a god, that is, to be so adult and independent that he owes himself to no one but determines his own destiny simply and solely for himself, then every other person becomes for him an antigod, and communication between them becomes a contradiction in itself" (ibid., 52).

[361] Ibid., 51.

[362] Cf. *Behold*, 69, where Ratzinger speaks about the pierced Heart of the Crucified and Risen One, which "invites us to step forth out of the futile attempt of self-preservation and, by joining in the task of love, by handing ourselves over to him and with him, to discover the fullness of love".

[363] *Principles*, 52.

[364] Ibid., 53–54, referring to G. Philips, *L'Église et son mystère au II Concile du Vatican*, vol. 1 (Paris: Desclée, 1967), 74, 76.

In summary, we can state that Ratzinger recognizes ecclesial *communio* in word and sacrament as the sign through which the unity of all mankind throughout the world is to be brought about as well. For him this means that the Church can be the sacrament of unity for the world only through faithfulness to the teaching of the apostles and to the Eucharist, but also that she must not close herself off from the world.[365]

d. Church as *communio*: Open to the world

When Ratzinger addresses the Church's openness to the world, the question for him is this: "Does such a movement correspond to the nature of the Church and to her essential mission?"[366] In his opinion, a central element of the Christian faith is the fact that it has a "definite content" and therefore is not simply "an immersion in what is mystical and ineffable ... which ultimately does not depend on the contents".[367] This content is the Church's Creed, the fact that the triune God "has shown us his face and his heart in Jesus Christ".[368] Because the Church lives on the basis of this trinitarian mystery, "which has disclosed and confided itself to her quite concretely in Jesus Christ",[369] she is bound to fulfill this movement together with Christ, that is, to be "open to the world", and this by her very nature.

But here the question immediately arises about the *manner* of this openness to the world. By reason of the differences in their answers, great minds went their separate ways in the postconciliar debate.[370] God's self-disclosure *in Jesus Christ* cannot have the purpose of "affirming the world in its worldly existence and its worldliness";[371] by analogy, neither can the Church, according to Ratzinger, conform herself

---

[365] Cf. *Principles*, 50. Ratzinger sees in the concept of the "Church as sacrament of unity" a response to "contemporary man's search for the unity of mankind".

[366] *Volk Gottes*, 108. Cf. *Dogma*, 183–204. See also K.-J. E. Jeon, *Die Kirche bei Joseph Ratzinger: Untersuchungen zum strukturierten Volk Gottes nach der Kirchenlehre Joseph Ratzingers* (unpublished dissertation, Innsbruck, 1995), 197ff.

[367] "Absurd", 51.

[368] Ibid.

[369] *Volk Gottes*, 108.

[370] Ratzinger describes this topic (ibid.) as "the really decisive point of the dispute among the Council Fathers" that continues in the postconciliar period and will be resolved only through the process of assimilating and implementing the Council.

[371] Ibid., 109. The next two quotations are found there also.

to the world without betraying Christ's mission. Hence he considers the decisive feature of the Christ-event, as far as our subject is concerned, to be the concept of *commercium*, which, translated from Latin, is *exchange*. Part of the mystery of Christ is the unheard-of fact that "an exchange between God and the world" takes place, resulting in "something that can be described as 'dialogue'". This exchange has the form of God's self-giving love: God takes on what is ours, "so as to give us what is his in this way and not otherwise". The Church stands in the midst of this movement of Christ. For this reason, it is her authentic mission, not to isolate herself from the world, but to devote herself to it:

> The Church has no nature and no significance of her own besides Christ; instead, she must find her meaning in being the instrument of Christ's movement. If this is so, then on this basis her course and her mission are charted clearly enough. The Church has no option of becoming self-enclosed in her contentment about what she has already achieved. She is herself the gesture of self-opening and hence must continually place herself at the service of this gesture and must carry it out historically. But this gesture is by no means an end in itself; its real goal is to introduce [souls] into that *sacrum commercium*, into that holy exchange which began when God became man.[372]

God enters into dialogue with men by revealing himself in assuming flesh, and in this way he wills to lead the world to salvation. The sending of the incarnate Word is thoroughly in keeping with the dialogical structure of God's freedom and love, and, according to Ratzinger, it has the surprising effect that what is higher takes on what is low—something that was inconceivable in the intellectual world of antiquity.[373] For the Church, this results in a sort of twofold opening to the world: mission, in the sense of continuing Christ's mission in the world, and the "indifferent love that serves and participates in the love of God, which is poured out even in places where it finds no response".[374] If this is understood correctly, then mission can never serve a selfish quest for power. Its task remains always the same: "to

---

[372] Ibid., 110.
[373] Cf. ibid., 109.
[374] Ibid., 110.

hand on the message about divine love".[375] As opposed to the relativistic thesis that everyone can be saved in his own fashion, Ratzinger calls it "selfishness or criminal laziness or cowardice"[376] if the Church were to suppress the message of this incarnate Word, so as to operate "in a more humanitarian way".

Vatican II heralds the change from a situation "in which a maximum degree of christianization seemed to have been attained"[377] and had to be preserved to a new missionary life of love in a society in which Christians represent a minority. In Ratzinger's own words:

> The Council marks the transition from a conservationist to a missionary attitude, and the conciliar alternative to "conservative" is not "progressive", but rather "missionary". In this antithesis is found basically the precise meaning of what conciliar "opening up to the world" means and what it does not mean.[378]

Opening up to a non-Christian world means, last but not least, that the Christian "is exposed" "as sheep in the midst of wolves" (Mt 10:16) and thus shares Christ's fate of suffering and persecution. For Ratzinger, this has nothing to do with pessimism. The believer's confidence is founded on Christ, the Crucified, the Lamb once slain, "because he knows that nevertheless this Lamb torn apart by wolves holds in his hand the seals of world history and opens it".[379] The meaning of this opening up of the Church to the world is to be found in the Cross of Jesus Christ. For Ratzinger this becomes clear from the very fact that the Crucified prays Psalm 22. This is the prayer of the one who suffers, abandoned by God, who is nevertheless filled with the hope of the righteous. As it continues, however, this psalm is at the same time a prayer of promise for the poor and finally announces the conversion of all the ends of the earth to the Lord. Together with the early Christians, Ratzinger therefore interprets it in a eucharistic sense: From Christ's Passion proceeds "the feeding of the poor and the turning of the nations to worship the God of Israel".[380]

---

[375] Ibid., 111.
[376] Ibid.
[377] Ibid., 127.
[378] Ibid., 128.
[379] Ibid.
[380] Behold, 23.

In the eucharistic view of Christ's self-renunciation, the intrinsic connection between the Last Supper and Jesus' death on the Cross becomes evident once again: They are inseparable sacred signs of God's self-giving love, which definitively stands open for mankind:

> His dying words fuse with his words at the Supper, the reality of his death fuses with the reality of the Supper. For the event of the Supper consists in Jesus sharing his body and his blood, i.e., his earthly existence; he gives and communicates himself. In other words, the event of the Supper is an anticipation of death, the transformation of death into an act of love.... Death, which, by its very nature, is the end, the destruction of every communication, is changed by him into an act of self-communication; and this is man's redemption, for it signifies the triumph of love over death.[381]

When death, which otherwise "puts an end to words and to meaning, itself becomes a word, [and thus] becomes the place where meaning communicates itself",[382] man's redemption occurs. In participating in this mystery of redemption, which alone gives meaning to life, we recognize that the missionary task of the Church and her dialogical structure are not in opposition to one another but, on the contrary, are mutually dependent while acknowledging at the same time man's freedom, because both of them, mission and dialogue, are expressions of the one communicating love of God. Through redemption in Christ, the Crucified, God has called everyone to freedom, so as to enter into *communio* with all through him. In Ratzinger's opinion, this freedom safeguards the Church against the danger of "spiritual imperialism",[383] which would degrade mission and dialogue to a caricature of themselves. Freedom, however, does not mean arbitrariness, but rather becoming *one* spirit with Christ.[384] The more fully the Church lives in Christ in this *communio*, the more her own "internal unity"[385] grows.

---

[381] Ibid., 24f.

[382] Ibid., 25.

[383] *Volk Gottes*, 112; cf. 110–12.

[384] Cf. 1 Cor 6:17: "He who is united to the Lord becomes one spirit with him." Ratzinger understands "spirit" as used in 1 Corinthians 6:17, not in opposition to "body", but rather in a way related to the Pauline understanding of the Body of Christ. Cf. *Called to Communion*, 38f. See pt. 2, sec. 2, chap. 1 § 2.2.b, of this work, "The Pauline Theme of Nuptiality".

[385] *Called to Communion*, 40.

Conversely, the Church of Jesus Christ is painfully aware of the fragility of her unity the moment she moves away from the spirit of Jesus.[386]

3. Communio *and membership in the Church*

I will treat the theme "*communio* and membership in the Church", as Ratzinger understands it, from a threefold perspective. First the problem will be examined in light of history, whereby we will consider how each historical period understood the Church as *Corpus Christi*. After this brief synopsis of an important topic in the history of theology, as a second step I will look at the criteria determined by today's Magisterium for membership in the one Church. This leads finally to the third question, whether and in what way Ratzinger considers it possible to speak about the unity of the Church while at the same time using the plural form, "Churches".[387]

a. Three "historical rings" of the Body of Christ concept in relation to Church membership

The relationship between *communio* and Church unity and the question of membership in the Church have been subject to varying emphases over the course of history. According to Ratzinger, we can distinguish three historical responses to the question of who belongs to the Body of Christ or to the People of God. He describes them as three "historical rings":[388]

1. The sacramental perspective: During the time of the Church Fathers, the sacramental understanding was the decisive view of the Church. She is "the People of God, which is gathered up into the

---

[386] Cf. ibid.

[387] In this discussion, I will limit myself mainly to the fundamentals and the points of departure for the framing of the ecumenical question that Ratzinger regards as taken for granted in *Lumen gentium*. Ratzinger indicated during the Council that even the Constitution on the Church requires supplementing with passages from the other conciliar documents (*UR, AG, NA, DH*) that deal with the subject; he speaks of a "lacuna" left here by the schema on the Church. See *Highlights*, 67. See also ibid., 68: "We might even say that the closer a text came to theological perfection, the more restricted and closed it would be thought in the future."

[388] "Wesen", 61.

Body of Christ in the celebration of the Eucharist".[389] Ratzinger says that this *biblical-patristic* concept of Church can be expressed in the equation *ecclesia = communio = Corpus Christi*.[390] It is therefore a sacramental *communio* "of those who communicate with one another in the Body of Christ", whereby Ratzinger equates it as a matter of principle[391] with the *communio eucharistica*.

2. The institutional-hierarchical perspective: Unlike the biblical-patristic understanding, the corporate concept of the Church in the Middle Ages has an institutional-hierarchical character. The Church was regarded above all as a corporation comprehensible in legal terms, as a *corpus* ecclesiae *mysticum*, that is, "as a corporation of Christ (and not as the 'Body' of Christ!)".[392] This clearly circumscribed societal institution was so structured as to form a *societas perfecta* and as such was identified with the Roman Catholic Church.

3. The "mystical" perspective: In the modern era the concept *Corpus Christi mysticum* was interpreted as a "mysterious, mystical organism of Christ" in an ecclesiology tinged with romanticism from the nineteenth until the mid-twentieth century. Here the word "mystical" was derived from "mysticism". Ratzinger describes this as an "organological-mystical understanding".[393]

In the schema on the Church that was prepared for the Council[394] and also in the encyclical *Mystici Corporis*, the Body of Christ concept was still "imprecise and undefined"[395] and contained elements from all three historical phases. Furthermore, as Ratzinger observes critically, the expression "corpus Christi mysticum" used in *Mystici Corporis* is neither Pauline nor patristic, nor was it usual during the Middle Ages; it refers "primarily to the intellectual property of the nineteenth

---

[389] Ibid.

[390] Ibid.

[391] This *communio eucharistica*, according to Ratzinger, cannot be expressed "without provisos, because a certain association with the *communio* is characteristic of all baptized persons—an association that unequivocally distinguishes them from the situation of the unbaptized" ("Wesen", 63).

[392] Ibid., 61.

[393] Ibid., 61f.

[394] Cf. also J. A. Komonchak, "Der Kampf für das Konzil während der Vorbereitung (1960–1962)", in Wittstadt, 1:326f.

[395] "Wesen", 63. Ratzinger goes on to say that even "the enduring formula *corpus Christi mysticum*" caused interpretive problems in biblical as well as in juridical respects (ibid.).

and twentieth centuries".[396] This had its effects in 1963 on the deliberations of the Council concerning the schema *De Ecclesia*:

> Twenty years previously, in 1943, the encyclical *Mystici Corporis* had appeared, which was well received by everyone, not least of all because it taught us to understand the Church as the Body of the Lord. The new schema on the Church likewise built on this fundamental idea, but this is precisely what became the main starting point for criticism. Such a development is comprehensible only if one recognizes that the Church is a living thing that advances and grows in history.... From this viewpoint, one can understand that what was progress in 1943 was not necessarily progress any more in 1962. At the same time it becomes clear how difficult it is to arrive at a statement of the nature of the Church. Such a statement can be attempted only against the background of the historicity of this Church.[397]

This change, according to Ratzinger, marked a central point in the transformation of the way in which the Body of Christ concept was interpreted. Due to the challenge of the conciliar period, with its call for unity among Christians, the problem of presenting this concept of the Church adequately grew more complicated.[398] In terms of the Council's ecumenical mission, the following concerns motivated Ratzinger at that time: Given the new sensitivity for Church and unity, how could the Roman Church alone be identified with the Body of Christ?[399] The second question followed: Can the "hidden mystery of Christ's spiritual operation"[400] be confined to the limits of the visible Church?

Therefore, even during the Second Vatican Council, Ratzinger advocated reinstating the first, that is, the biblical-patristic concept of the Church as the Body of Christ in a *communio* union so as to eliminate, through this sacramental-ecclesiological interpretation, the opposition between the People and God and the Body of Christ:

---

[396] Ibid. Cf. Y. Congar, "Ecclesia ab Abel", in *Abhandlungen über Theologie und Kirche: Festschrift für Karl Adam* (Düsseldorf: Patmos-Verlag, 1952), 79–108.

[397] "Wesen", 47–68, citation at 49.

[398] Cf. G. Ruggieri, "Der schwierige Abschied von der kontroverstheologisch geprägten Ekklesiologie", in Wittstadt, 2:331–419, esp. 353, 387–95.

[399] Cf. "Wesen", 63.

[400] Ibid. Cf. Congar, "Ecclesia ab Abel", 79–108.

When the first concept is taken as the starting point, there is no contrast at all to the People of God concept. "People of God" has been taken up into "Body of Christ" like the Old Testament into the New. In this case, there is no dilemma, either, about whether the Church is "an institution or a form of mysticism". In the second and the third and in any other case, however, the result is a hopeless blockage of the various aspects of ecclesial reality. Reinstating the first concept means carrying out a real *reformatio* with regard to the second: overcoming the weight of history and purifying the present in terms of the origin.[401]

In summary, this means that this Body of Christ/People of God concept expands the possibilities of membership in the Church. We cannot elaborate these trains of thought in greater detail; we will concentrate instead in the following paragraphs on the problem of membership in the Church and thus also on the question of the visibility of the Church of Jesus Christ.

b. Membership in the Church

The question of membership in the Church had already occupied the Preparatory Commissions in the months leading up to the Second Vatican Council. In particular, Cardinal Augustine Bea, who was in charge of the Secretariat for Non-Catholics, spoke in favor of the view that Christians of non-Catholic denominations, too, were members of the Body of Christ by virtue of their baptism.[402] Cardinal Ottaviani, on the other hand, criticized this interpretation, since he assumed the identity "of the Catholic Church and the Mystical Body".[403] In a lecture given in February 1963, looking back at the first session of the Council, Ratzinger, too, dealt with this theme. He spoke in support of "recognizing the Christianity of the separated brethren and not ignoring the wound caused by separation".[404] As he saw it, the problem was whether the prerequisite for individual

---

[401] "Wesen", 62.
[402] See Komonchak, "Kampf für das Konzil", 1:329. Cardinal Bea's belief is said to have been close to the view of Pope John XXIII. Schmaus and Lécuyer, too, advocated a similar position.
[403] *AD* 2, 2/3:1024.
[404] "Wesen", 47–68, citation at 66.

membership in the Church is baptism alone,[405] or, as Robert Bellarmine, S.J.,[406] had declared in the debates of the Counter-Reformation,
the triad[407] of Creed, sacraments, and hierarchy (including the Petrine
ministry). Two years after the Council, in an essay entitled "Aspects of
the Church",[408] Ratzinger mentions another element that is crucial for
the conciliar hermeneutic, namely, the question of the Holy Spirit:

> According to the Constitution on the Church of the Second Vati-
> can Council, someone is a full member of the Church only when
> he has the spirit of Christ. This means that a non-institutional, non-
> juridical but rather pneumatic element belonging to the order of
> grace has been included in the definition of full membership in the
> Church; that Church membership is no longer defined in a way
> that is purely institutional, with no regard for the state of salvation,
> but rather in terms that are institutional as well as spiritual and pneu-
> matic, in keeping with the theology of grace.[409]

This development is exciting, because until then the Church had
always opposed spiritualistic tendencies in describing the Church and
had insisted "that there were also weeds in the field of the Church
... and consequently that the state of grace is not part of the definition

---

[405] Cf. CIC (1917), can. 87.

[406] Cf. Robert Bellarmine, Controversarium de conciliis 4/2, in Opera, ed. J. Fèvre (Paris, 1870) [photostatic reprint (Frankfurt, 1965)], 317: Bellarmine's definition of the Church reads as follows: "Nostra autem sententia est, Ecclesiam ... esse coetum hominum ejusdem Christianae fidei professione, et eorundem Sacramentorum communione colligatum, sub regimine legitimorum pastorum, ac praecipue unius Christi in terris Vicarii Romani Pontificis." (Our opinion is that the Church ... is the assembly of men bound together by the profession of the same Christian faith and by communion in the same sacraments, under the direction of lawful pastors, especially of the one Vicar of Christ on earth, the Roman Pontiff.) Besides the hallmarks of right faith and true sacraments (compare this with the Protestant understanding of the Church according to the Confessio Augustana), Bellarmine's definition emphasizes obedience to the bishops, particularly to the pope as the representative of Christ on earth. In the Counter-Reformation mentality, this leads to a progressive narrowing down of the classical marks of the Church—unity, holiness, catholicity, and apostolicity—to the via primatus, and consequently romanitas became the most important mark of the true Church. On this subject, see H.J. Pottmeyer, "Die Frage nach der wahren Kirche", in HFTh 3:159–84, ref. at 166–69.

[407] This dogmatic-apologetic line of argument was followed both in Mystici Corporis and in the schema De Ecclesia.

[408] Reprinted in considerably abridged and slightly rewritten form in J. Ratzinger, "Kirche als Tempel des Heiligen Geistes", Mitte, 148–57.

[409] Ibid., 153. See also Jeon, Kirche bei Joseph Ratzinger, 118.

of Church membership".[410] The Council, too, is far from promoting spiritualistic tendencies. For this reason, Ratzinger says, it supports the opinion that a person has the Holy Spirit only if he endures "the humiliation of the σωμα", according to St. Augustine's retort to the Donatists: "Do you want to have the spirit of Christ? Then be the Body of Christ!"[411]

Hence in *Lumen gentium*—as Ratzinger demonstrates—on the one hand, "the constant Catholic belief is formulated ... [that] the one Church of Jesus Christ really exists in the visible Catholic Church and not [as] an entity that remains hidden behind the concrete Christian ecclesial communities."[412] This statement relates to the communion of the Church as institution. On the other hand, *Lumen gentium* speaks about "many elements of sanctification and of truth" outside the Catholic Church as well, which as "gifts belonging to the Church of Christ ... are forces impelling toward catholic unity".[413] This, however, is tantamount to saying that

> not only the unity of the Church, but also the division of Christendom, is a reality, in other words, that whatever of Christianity exists outside the Catholic Church is nevertheless really "Christian" and—since there is no such thing as merely private, church-free Christianity—it is also a presence of Church.[414]

Finally, with the *subsistit* formula in 1964, the Council started out on a new path that speaks concretely about the Catholic Church as

---

[410] *Mitte*, 154.

[411] Ibid.

[412] "Einleitung", 12. See also *Church*, 99–134, esp. 120: In 1983 Ratzinger reflects that "the Catholic tradition, as it has been restated by the Second Vatican Council, is not characterized by the idea that all existing 'Churchdoms' [*Kirchentümer* = Christian denominations] are merely fragments of a true Church which does not exist anywhere but which one must now try to form by putting all these fragments together; this kind of idea would turn the Church into purely the work of man."

[413] *LG* 8. See "Absurd", 51. There Ratzinger admits that the expression "elements" was poorly chosen but that the intention was to allude to the fact that the Reformation conceived of the Church more as something that happened.

[414] "Einleitung", 13. Cf. *LG* 8; see also *LG* 15: "The Church recognizes that in many ways she is linked with those who, being baptized, are honored with the name of Christian, though they do not profess the faith in its entirety or do not preserve unity of communion with the successor of Peter." See *LG* 16: "Finally, those who have not yet received the Gospel are related in various ways to the people of God." See also *Highlights*, 66.

the subsistence of the Church of Jesus Christ,[415] without denying the ecclesial existence of other Christian denominations. Ratzinger, too, follows this development when in the same year he declares that now non-Catholic Christians, as the Council puts it, "exist not merely as *individuals* but in Christian *communities* which are given positive Christian status and ecclesial character".[416]

Before I turn to this *subsistit* formula, I should at least begin to sketch how Ratzinger himself deals with the reality of Church unity and the fact of a plurality of churches.[417] This is connected with a second question: Has Ratzinger's stance in this matter changed since the Council and moved toward an "ecumenism of return"?[418]

c. The plural "churches" and the one Church of Jesus Christ

Looking back on the second session of the Council, Ratzinger recognizes a certain ambivalence in the fact that the schema on the Church treated the ecumenical question only in passing.[419] He deems this, on the one hand, regrettable but, on the other hand, notes that it had one advantage: "The doctrinal text on the Church is clearly open to supplementation, and this is provided by the schema on ecumenism."[420]

> By merely juxtaposing the two texts, the second developing a view only hinted at in the first, the Council in effect characterizes the first—the doctrinal text on the Church—as an open and far from comprehensive text.... The doctrinal text on the Church is not a

---

[415] On the composition of *LG* 8, see Alberigo/Magistretti, 38. Ratzinger was present as *peritus*, along with other members of the Commission, at the decisive meeting of the Theological Commission on November 26, 1963, during which the word *subsistit* was inserted into the text of *LG* 8 (Teuffenbach, 379).

[416] *Highlights*, 67. See also Ratzinger's negative judgment on the theologoumenon *votum ecclesiae*, which had made its way into the first schema of the Constitution on the Church in 1962 (ibid., 54f.).

[417] Cf. Jeon, *Kirche bei Joseph Ratzinger*, 64, 119–22. Jeon presents Ratzinger's outlook during the Council without referring to later modifications of his position.

[418] On the problems raised by this charge of an "ecumenism of return", see Weiler, 317–20, 329f.

[419] In this regard, note Teuffenbach's axiom that *Lumen gentium* is "a document of the Catholic Church ... that is also addressed to the Catholic Church. It is not an ecumenical document" (Teuffenbach, 21). Nevertheless, in my opinion, we still should ask whether the fundamental option of the Council was not broader.

[420] *Highlights*, 67.

theological treatise or an all-encompassing theological description of the Church. It rather indicates a path to be followed. . . . In general, the texts of a Council are not meant to save work for theologians. Rather, they should stimulate such work and open new horizons. If necessary they should also mark off the boundaries between solid ground and quicksand.[421]

Therefore, Ratzinger considers the conciliar pronouncements on ecumenism as a mandate concerning ongoing developments that must still be put into practice. In the retrospect he wrote at that time, he recalls the fear on the Lutheran side that ecumenism would be seen exclusively as a movement resulting in absorption.[422] Yet for him there is no doubt that a Catholic cannot share the view "that none of the 'existing Churches' is *the* Church of Jesus Christ but rather that they are various concretizations of the one Church which does not exist as such".[423] Nevertheless, he spoke at that time about a legitimate plurality,[424] about "the churches", and did so for three reasons. First, he mentions a biblical reason: Just as the New Testament speaks about the "Church of God in Athens, in Corinth, in Rome", so too, analogously, she exists "in Trier, Mainz and Cologne".[425] These are Churches in the sense of liturgical communities, which are united with one another in their shared *communio*. This means that the New Testament is acquainted with a plurality of Churches, but of course not in denominational form, but rather "only within the unity of the one Church".[426] Secondly, this plurality has never been denied in Catholic theology, inasmuch as the Church always was made up of particular Churches. Nevertheless—and this is Ratzinger's third reason—this plurality of Churches was in practice increasingly repressed "in favor of a centralized system; in this process, the local Church of Rome has, so to speak, absorbed all the other local Churches".[427] At the same time, this situation—as the

---

[421] Ibid., 67–68.
[422] Ibid., 70.
[423] Ibid.
[424] See Ratzinger, *Der gegenwärtige Stand der Arbeiten des Zweiten Vatikanischen Konzils* (Bonn: Katholische Rundfunk- und Fernseharbeit in Deutschland, 1964), 10.
[425] *Highlights*, 71.
[426] Ibid., 74.
[427] Ibid., 72.

former conciliar theologian put it—was one cause of the development of the ecumenical movement:

> The plurality of Churches, which should have had a legitimate existence within the Church, had receded increasingly into the background. This explains why this plurality, for which there was no room *within* the Church, was developed *outside* of it in the form of autonomous separate Churches. The Council's recognition of this is tantamount to its seeing that uniformity and unity are not identical. Above all, it means that a real multiplicity of Churches must be made alive again within the framework of Catholic unity.[428]

Although Ratzinger, in this review of the second session of the Council, draws the conclusion that the Council attributed the honorific title "church" (in the sense of liturgical communities) to other denominations as well, he does not disregard the objective difference between the Catholic understanding of Church and that of other Christian communities, which *themselves* prefer to be listed among a plurality of churches. In particular, the communities that resulted from the Reformation have a highly diversified understanding of Church. So as not to ignore this objective difference and place them all on the same level, Ratzinger, out of consideration for the Protestant communities as well, prefers the expression *communiones ecclesiales* (ecclesial communities), which Cardinal Franz König originally suggested[429] and which at the time of the Council met with a much more positive reception than at the present.[430]

---

[428] Ibid.

[429] See ibid., 75.

[430] See "Absurd", 51: "To claim the title of Church in the same way for all existing ecclesial communities would contradict their own self-understanding. Luther did not see the Church, in the theological and spiritual sense, as being realized in the great institutional body of the Catholic Church, which he viewed, rather, as an instrument of the Antichrist.... Luther himself could not possibly have seen the Church in the national churches that were forming subject to the control of the princes: these were auxiliary structures that were needed but were not the Church in the spiritual sense.... Thus, upon sober reflection, it is clear that for Protestants the reality 'Church' is found, not in the institutions called national churches, but somewhere else.... It seems completely absurd to me, what our Lutheran friends to all appearances want at this time: that we should regard these accidental historical formations as Churches in the same sense in which we believe that the Catholic Church based on the successors to the apostles in the episcopal ministry is Church. The real debate would be if our Protestant friends were to say: We see the

In this way, on the one hand, their ecclesial dignity is recognized, and, on the other hand, enough room is allowed for the distinctive structures and different self-understanding in each case. The most important new step is that the Eastern Churches and the ecclesial communities that resulted from the Reformation have been described as positive ecclesial entities.[431]

Ratzinger spoke in very similar terms in 1966 at the Catholic Conference [*Katholikentag*] in Bamberg about a plural, "the Churches",[432] while warning against a euphoria "that forgets to make difficult demands on itself and overlooks the fact that the Catholic Church dares and must dare to take the paradoxical position of attributing to herself in a unique way the singular form, 'the Church', despite and in the midst of the plurality she has accepted".[433]

This insight of Ratzinger builds the bridge to the present-day debate about the statement in the declaration of the Congregation for the Doctrine of the Faith *Dominus Iesus*, which reaffirmed the exclusive Catholic claim to the "uniqueness and oneness of the Church" and thereby elicited protest, especially in the Reformation countries.[434] The reason for it was the formulation of article 17, which does not grant full ecclesial status to the ecclesial communities that resulted from the Reformation: "On the other hand, the ecclesial communities which have not preserved the valid Episcopate and the genuine and integral substance of the Eucharistic mystery are not Churches in the proper sense."[435] With the distinction between "Churches in the proper sense"

Church differently, more pneumatologically and not so much in institutions, not even in apostolic succession. After all, the question is not whether all existing churches are Church in the same way, since that is obviously not the case, but rather where and how the Church exists and does not exist."

[431] Translated directly from *Rückblick*, 70. Cf. *Highlights*, 75, where the summary translation misses many of the nuances in Ratzinger's appraisal.

[432] See *Volk Gottes*, 149: "Who would have ventured to suppose even ten years ago that the official language of the Church would consciously and deliberately begin to designate as Churches not only the Churches of the East, but also those [ecclesial] communities that resulted from the Reformation?"

[433] Ibid.

[434] On this subject, see M. Mühl and J.-H. Tück, "Stellungnahmen zu *Dominus Iesus*: Ein erster bibliographischer Überblick", in *"Dominus Iesus": Anstößige Wahrheit oder anstößige Kirche? Dokumente, Hintergründe, Standpunkte und Folgerungen*, ed. M.J. Rainer, 2nd ed., 336–45 (Münster: Lit, 2001).

[435] *DI* 23.

and ecclesial communities we arrive at a vast subject that encompasses the Council's framing of the ecumenical question and its many-layered postconciliar reception.[436] Within the parameters of my dissertation, I will discuss one aspect of this complicated question, namely, the theme broached in the final version of the 1964 Constitution on the Church: the subsistence of the *one* Church of Jesus Christ in the Catholic Church, which is viewed by Ratzinger from the Catholic perspective as the foundation for the ecumenical dialogue.

4. The question of subsistence

Subsistence is a central idea of the conciliar ecclesiology that cannot be overlooked,[437] if for no other reason than because of its explosive power. We do well to reflect on it now, on the one hand, in order to recognize, with Ratzinger, the progress that *Lumen gentium* made in this question and, on the other hand, to understand how a completely different value judgment could be made about the same statement a few years after the Council because of a change in consciousness throughout Christendom.[438] Ratzinger does not conceal his disappointment with a superficial ecumenism nowadays that forgets its own fundamental principles.[439] Nevertheless, his writings show a remarkable consistency in his positive assessment of the term *subsistit*, for today, four decades after the Council, in a time when "subjectivism is canonized"[440] and many people stitch their Christianity together like a patchwork to suit their taste, this formula has gained new relevance. In this regard, Ratzinger is dealing, not with a debate about Church policy, but rather with a question that goes to the substance of the faith.

---

[436] *Church*, 99–134, esp. 114f.

[437] In the study by Kwang-Jin Elmanus Jeon, the reader searches in vain for the conciliar theme of subsistence, which is so crucial for Ratzinger, in particular even when it belongs to the context of what is being discussed; see Jeon, *Kirche bei Joseph Ratzinger*, 64, 114–27. Compare my essay "Nur Tinte oder substantielle Erkenntnis? Zur ekklesiologischen Diskussion um den Begriff der Subsistenz", in *Auditorium Spiritus Sancti: Festschrift zum 200-Jahr-Jubiläum der Philosophisch-Theologischen Hochschule Heiligenkreuz*, ed. K.J. Wallner, 241–78 (Grevenbroich: Bernardus-Verlag Langwaden, 2004), the essential arguments of which have been incorporated also into my dissertation.

[438] Cf. *Principles*, 228–37, ref. at 232.

[439] Cf. ibid.

[440] "Absurd", 51.

The subsistence formula is, according to *Lumen gentium*, an essential foundation for ecumenical dialogue. At the conclusion of Vatican II, it was described by Ratzinger as "the genuinely ecclesiological breakthrough".[441] Its point of departure is the recognition that the Church, as the one Body of Christ and as a hierarchically organized society, is at the same time spiritual and visible, "one complex reality", which, in a way analogous to the mystery of the Incarnation, "coalesces from a human and a divine element".[442] This Church of Jesus Christ *subsists* in the Catholic Church, that is to say, has in her "her concrete form of existing".[443] What was considered at the time of the Council to be an ecumenical accomplishment[444] was soon called into question again[445] and is presently once more the subject of vexing debates.[446]

In the following paragraphs, I cannot present the full spectrum of the postconciliar discussion about the *subsistit*.[447] Therefore, I will concentrate on typical statements by Ratzinger and thereby allow those with contrary positions to have their say as well. Since I have already

---

[441] *Principles*, 228–37, citation at 232.

[442] See *LG* 8.

[443] This German translation of *subsistere* is found in "Einleitung", 35. See also Kasper, "Auseinandersetzung", 800.

[444] See G. Philips, "Die Geschichte der dogmatischen Konstitution über die Kirche *Lumen gentium*", in *LThK.E*, vol. 1 (Freiburg im Breisgau: Herder, 1966), 139–55, citation at 150: "The identity of this Body with the Roman Church, finally, had been expressed in such nuanced form in article 8 that sufficient consideration was given to the ecumenical efforts." Cf. also a Lutheran assessment of the schema on the Church from the time of the Council by H. Ott, "Das Mysterium der Kirche", in Hampe, *Konzil*, 164–70, citation at 169: "I think that we still can rejoice for the moment over the fact that the positive significance of the non-Roman Christian communities is set forth in the schema as never before in a magisterial document of the Roman Church. ... We must rejoice that the schema is unclear, contradictory, and hazy at precisely this point: it means that we are not running up against a fortified battle line here. When all is said and done, there is still ambiguity as to where the true Church is to be found." Cf. Pesch, 219–23. See also Weiler, 331f.

[445] Cf. J. Ratzinger, "Ökumenisches Dilemma: Zur Diskussion um die Erklärung *Mysterium Ecclesiae*", *IKaZ* 3 (1974): 56–63. See also L. Boff, *Church, Charism and Power: Liberation Theology and the Institutional Church*, trans. John W. Diercksmeier (New York: Crossroad, 1985).

[446] We should mention here two polemical works written attacking Ratzinger: L. Boff, *Manifest für die Ökumene: Ein Streit mit Kardinal Ratzinger* (Düsseldorf: Patmos-Verlag, 2001); Häring, *Ideologie*.

[447] On this subject, see Teuffenbach, 24–34. In the chapter of her dissertation entitled "Status Quaestionis", Teuffenbach consulted the following theologians on the *subsistit* formula: F. Ricken, W. Dietzfelbinger, H. Mühlen, J. Ratzinger, U. Betti, F. Sullivan, G. Mucci, M. M. Garijo-Guembe, and L. Boff.

examined the historical background of the subsistence formula in part 1 of my dissertation, with reference to *Lumen gentium*,[448] I would like now to select three questions in particular that are of importance for Ratzinger's ecclesiological thought: (a) the difference between *subsistit* and *est*; (b) the *subsistit* formula as an alternative to present-day ecclesiological relativism; and, finally, (c) subsistence and the question of truth.

a. The difference between *subsistit* and *est*

When it says in paragraph 8 of *Lumen gentium* that the Church of Jesus Christ "subsists in the Catholic Church, which is governed by the successor of Peter and by the bishops in communion with him", then the question arises of what *subsistit* is supposed to mean. In a 1974 essay entitled "Ecumenism at a Standstill?" Ratzinger alludes to the difficulty of translating the Latin verb *subsistere*:

No translation can fully capture the sublime nuance of the Latin text in which the unconditional equation of the first conciliar drafts—the full identity between the Church of Jesus Christ and the Roman Catholic Church—is clearly set forth: nothing of the concreteness of the conciliar concept of the Church is lost—the Church is there present where the successors of the Apostle Peter and of the other apostles visibly incorporate her continuity with her source; but this full concreteness of the Church does not mean that every other Church can be only a non-Church. The equation is not mathematical because the Holy Spirit cannot be reduced to a mathematical symbol, not even where he concretely binds and bestows himself.[449]

---

[448] See pt. 1, sec. 2, chap. 1, § 3.4, excursus 1 of my dissertation: "*Una Sancta Catholica Ecclesia*—The Question of Subsistence".

[449] *Principles*, 228–37, citation at 230–31. In my opinion, this interpretation by Ratzinger is completely in keeping with the *relatio* on *LG* 8 written by the subcommission in the fall of 1963, in which it says literally: "Hence the intention is to show that the Church, whose inmost mysterious nature is being described, can be found on earth concretely in the Catholic Church." Cited according to the [German] translation of Teuffenbach, 376. In contrast, Teuffenbach's conclusion, that according to this *relatio* "the main statement of the entire paragraph 8 [of the Constitution on the Church] reaffirms precisely this identification of the Catholic Church with the Church of Christ", does not quite express the intention of the *relatio* described above.

At the same time, Ratzinger emphasizes that it is not easy to maintain this tension that is inherent in the *subsistit* without immediately jumping to the conclusion that the concrete Churches are only "external institutionalizations in whose unavoidable plurality the unity of the Church was mirrored in a more or less fragmented fashion".[450] What, then, does "subsistence" mean?

Whereas Leonardo Boff, relying on the classical dictionary of the Latin language by A. Forcellini,[451] explains the expression *subsistit in* as something "concrete" and "historical",[452] Ratzinger's discussion aims at a hermeneutic examination from the perspective of ancient philosophy:

> The term *subsistit* derives from classical philosophy, as it was further developed in Scholasticism. The Greek word corresponding to it is *hypostasis*, which plays a central role in Christology, for describing the unity between divine nature and human in the Person of Christ. *Subsistere* is a special variant of *esse*. It is "being" in the form of an independent agent.[453]

Applied to the Church of Jesus Christ, this means that she "may be encountered in this world as a concrete agent in the Catholic

---

[450] *Principles*, 231.

[451] Forcellini, 5:707f. As a criticism of Boff, it must be noted that Forcellini refers his linguistic field analysis exclusively to pre-Christian and non-Christian classical Latin authors. The later Christian and theological reception history of the term *subsistere* is not taken into account by Forcellini. It is a different situation with the term *subsistentia*; in this case, besides Cassiodorus, Boethius in particular is cited (his fifth theological *opusculum*, "De duabus naturibus", in PL 64, 1337–54)—along the same lines as Ratzinger—as testifying to the relation between the Greek word υποστασις and the Latin *subsistentia*: "Longe vero illi (graeci) signatius naturae rationalis individuam substantiam υποστασεως nomine vocavere, nos vero per inopiam significantium vocum translatitiam retinuimus nuncupationem eam, quam illi υποστασιν dicunt personam vocantes" (Forcellini, 5:707). (Much more accurately, however, they [the Greeks] called an individual substance having a rational nature by the name of υποστασις [*hypostasis*]. We, however, for lack of terminology, have retained the customary way of naming it by calling 'person' what they express as υποστασις.) [English translation from the Latin, with reference to the German.] On the philosophical and theological reception history of this term "subsistence", see C. Horn, "Subsistenz", in *HWPh*, vol. 10, cols. 486–93.

[452] Cf. Boff, *Manifest für die Ökumene*, 95. But compare Forcellini, 5:707f.

[453] "Ecclesiology", 147. I find that Teuffenbach's attempt to make a linguistic analysis of the expression *subsistit in* lacks precisely this hermeneutic approach that proceeds from the metaphysical connotation of *subsistit* (Teuffenbach, 85–114), the only exception being a short citation from Thomas Aquinas (ibid., 103), which has no influence, however, on his findings.

Church".[454] According to Ratzinger, this concreteness means, above all, uniqueness, since "the view that *subsistit* should be multiplied fails to do justice to the particular point intended."[455]

If one accepts the fact that the Council Fathers were influenced by Neoscholastic philosophy in the terminology they used, then a hermeneutic appeal to this way of thinking could shed light on what was intended by the term *subsistit*. To me, this philosophical reflection seems necessary, especially since Ratzinger himself cites what the Council Fathers intended to say in using this terminology.[456] This does not mean applying Neoscholastic thought as the interpretive key to *Lumen gentium* in general. Our purpose here is simply to give an etymological, semantic outline of the Neoscholastic term *subsistere*. To do this, we should consult two classic manuals, one by Joseph Gredt and the other by Leovigildo Salcedo and Clemente Fernandez. In the *Philosophiae Scholasticae Summa*,[457] which was the official textbook of philosophy

---

[454] "Ecclesiology", 147.

[455] Ibid. S. Albert makes a similar argument, *"Corpus Suum mystice constituit"* (LG 7): La Chiesa Corpo Mistico di Cristo nel primo capitolo della Lumen gentium; Storia del Testo dalla Mystici corporis al Vaticano II con riferimenti alla attività conciliare del P. Sebastian Tromp S.J. (Regensburg: Pustet, 1996), 566: "Il Concilio ribadisce però con altrettanta chiarezza che solo per mezzo della Chiesa cattolica si può ottenere tutta la pienezza dei mezzi di salvezza e che solo in essa sussiste senza possibilità di essere perduta quell'unità dell'una e unica Chiesa che Cristo fin dall'inizio le ha donato (cf. UR 4)." (The Council emphasizes with equal clarity, however, that one can obtain the fullness of the means of salvation only through the instrumentality of the Catholic Church and that in her alone subsists, without the possibility of being lost, that unity of the one and only Church with which Christ endowed her from the beginning [see UR 4].)

[456] "Absurd", 51: "I myself was present when they developed the *subsistit* formula at the Second Vatican Council, and I can say that I am well acquainted with the topic."

[457] C. Fernandez, "Metaphysica Generalis", in *Philosophiae Scholasticae Summa*, ed. L. Salcedo and C. Fernandez, 3rd ed., vol. 1 (Madrid: Ed. Católica, 1964), 770. Fernandez makes a twofold distinction in defining the term "substance": "Substantia definitione etymologica dupliciter declarari potest: a.) a substare: tunc substantia est: res quae substat aliis, res quae stat sub aliis (nempe accidentibus) ut sustentaculum.... b.) a subsistere: tunc substantia est: res quae in se subsistit, quae est in se, non egens alio in quo sit. Sub hac significatione innotescit substantia absolute, in se ipsa, quoad suum modum essendi, scilicet, sufficientiam ontologicam, vi cuius est in se et non in alio." (Substance can be defined etymologically in two ways: a) From *substare*: then substance is a thing that stands firm for other things, something that underlies other things (namely, accidents) as their support.... b) From *subsistere*: then substance is a thing that subsists in itself, that *is* in itself, having no need of something else in which to exist. This second definition considers

at the Gregoriana[458] from the 1930s on, and also in the *Elementa Philosophiae Aristotelico-Thomisticae*[459] by Joseph Gredt, the term *subsistit* is classified under the concept of substance. Upon close inspection, it becomes clear that Neoscholasticism regards a substance's function of supporting attributes as being rooted in its independence. This corresponds to the classical mode of thinking in Scholastic philosophy not to designate functions without an ontological basis. Only because substance in itself means independence, and precisely therein is distinguished from accidents, can it assume the function of supporting accidents. In summary, this means that only because substance subsists can it also be a subject.

The result of all this, in my opinion, is the following situation with regard to the language used in *Lumen gentium*. Presupposing the terminological formation of the Council Fathers by the philosophical manuals of their time, that is, in the 1920s and 1930s, we can propose the thesis that the formula: "Haec Ecclesia, in hoc mundo ut societas constituta et ordinata, subsistit in Ecclesia catholica"[460] means: The Church of Jesus Christ is present, in an ultimate density of her reality,

---

substance absolutely, in itself, as to its mode of being, that is, its ontological sufficiency, by virtue of which it exists in itself and not in something else.)

[458] It is remarkable that Teuffenbach, in her second chapter, entitled "Linguistic Analysis of the Expression *Subsistit in*" (Teuffenbach, 85–114), does not take the philosophical connotations into account. Considering the fact that S. Tromp himself, who inserted the *subsistit* into the final version, lectured from 1929 to 1962 (with interruptions) as a professor for fundamental theology at the Pontifical Gregorian University (ibid., 63), Neoscholastic philosophy was for him the instrument with which he expressed himself theologically.

[459] J. Gredt, *Elementa Philosophiae Aristotelico-Thomisticae*, vol. 2 (Barcelona, Freiburg, and Rome: Herder 1961), 137: "Substantia est res, cuius quidditati debetur esse in se et non in alio. Contra substantiam distinguimus accidens, quod est res, cuius quidditati debetur non esse in se sed in alio seu inhaerere. Substantiam concipimus a) tamquam subjectum accidentium, cui haec inhaerent, seu tamquam substantem accidentibus; b) tamquam in se stantem seu subsistentem, id quod intelligimus per oppositionem ad inhaesionem accidentis, cui non convenit in se stare seu subsistere, sed inhaerere." (A substance is a thing that, due to its essence [*quidditas*], exists in itself and not in something else. We distinguish a substance from an accident, which is a thing that, due to its essence, does not exist in itself but exists or inheres in something else. We understand a substance (a) as the subject of the accidents that inhere in it or as the thing underlying and supporting the accidents; or (b) as existing in itself or subsisting, which we understand by way of contrast to the inherence of an accident, which is not apt to exist in itself or to subsist, but rather to inhere.)

[460] *LG* 8: "This Church, constituted and organized in the world as a society, subsists in the Catholic Church."

in the Catholic Church. Moreover, the term "subsistence" implies that ecclesiality in all its possible forms *has its basis* in the Catholic Church as the authentic realization of Christ's foundation. And this very subsistence, which is her own, makes it possible for her to support the "elementa plura sanctificationis et veritatis"[461] that can be found outside her boundaries. But this means simultaneously that the elements (outside the Catholic Church) do not exist in the manner of subsisting but, rather—expressed philosophically—exist *in alio*, which means, therefore, that they are dependent on the Catholic Church for their continued existence, since they can *be* only through her. There is no doubt whatsoever that these theological reflections on the term *subsistit* will have reached their limits when they lead to the conclusion that every Christian community outside the Catholic Church realizes its ecclesiality only in an accidental manner. In my opinion, it would be more appropriate—with regard to ecumenism as well—to speak in this connection about participation; this concept, however, is not taken up by *Lumen gentium* in this context.

Furthermore, the development in the schema on the Church leading from *est* to *subsistit*, which is traced in the *Synopsis historica* for *Lumen gentium* by G. Alberigo and F. Magistretti,[462] shows that the term *subsistit* was first introduced into the text during the process of composing the final version (March–July 1964/November 21, 1964). We can tell from this, in my opinion, that the ecumenical orientation [of the Council] caused the question of the Church both to be framed ontologically and also to be rendered more precise through the use of the philosophical term *subsistit*.[463] We must differentiate, however, this

---

[461] Ibid.: "the many elements of sanctification and of truth".

[462] On this subject, see Alberigo/Magistretti, 38.

[463] Cf. ibid. An initial, explicitly ontological definition of the *Ecclesia catholica* as the Church founded by Christ emerged in February–April 1963 ("est"), connected with the overview of the boundaries of the Church that was retained in later versions with slight modifications. In November 1962, in contrast, the identity of the Church with the Catholic Church was not emphasized in an explicitly ontological way: See ibid.: "his in terris ut societas organice constituta, Ecclesia nempe Catholica quae Romana est" (the Church that is organically constituted as a society here on earth, namely, the Catholic Church that is Roman). The verb *est* refers only to the *Romanitas*. And in the first draft of the schema on the Church (likewise from November 1962), "ideoque sola iure Catholica Romana nuncupatur Ecclesia" (and so only the Roman Catholic Church is rightly called the Church), it is a question only of the juridical exclusivity of the title "Church".

ontological definition of the unique subsistence of the Church of Jesus Christ in the Catholic Church from the concrete phenomenon of the latter, that is, the manner in which she appears. Precisely herein Ratzinger sees the possibility of identifying also her sinful defects in realizing her ecclesiality.[464] For this reason, he formulated in 1977 the thesis (not as a definition, but as a statement about the Church): "On the one hand, the Church should never be separated from her concrete, historical form; but on the other hand, she can never be fully equated with that form. This statement stands within a broad consensus of tradition which transcends the boundaries of ecclesiastical divisions."[465]

If we consult yet another explanation of the *subsistit* written by Ratzinger in the year 2000, we find that here, too, in keeping with *Lumen gentium*, he does not presuppose a complete identity between the Church of Jesus Christ and the Roman Catholic Church[466] but, rather, remains precisely in the tension that he described above:

> When the Council Fathers replaced the word *est* that was used by Pope Pius XII with the word *subsistit*, this had a very precise significance: The term "is" (from the verb "to be") is broader than the term "subsist". "Subsisting" is a particular way of being, namely, being an independent, self-contained subject. So the Fathers were saying: The being of the Church as such extends much farther than the Roman Catholic Church, yet in the latter she has in a unique way the character of an independent subject.[467]

---

[464] Cf. *Das neue Volk Gottes: Entwürfe zur Ekklesiologie* (Düsseldorf: Patmos-Verlag, 1969), 236f.

[465] "Identification", 17. Ratzinger concedes here that the connection between the empirical Church and the theological entity called Church did not completely disappear even in the lands that witnessed the Reformation. "The visible community nonetheless is still considered the place in which the real Church gathers. . . . On the other hand, post-Tridentine Catholicism had a very narrow understanding of the connection between the visible Church and the salvific reality 'Church'; as an extreme example of this, people like to cite Bellarmine's statement that the Church (namely, the real Church of God) is as visible as the Republic of Venice, that is, as visible as the national community" (ibid., 24). See also *Mitte*, 148–57, ref. at 154.

[466] Weiler, 329–32: "Does an 'ecumenism of return' necessarily follow from Joseph Ratzinger's eucharistic ecclesiology?"

[467] "Absurd", 51. See also Ratzinger, "Begegnung lutherischer und katholischer Theologie nach dem Konzil", *Oecumenica* 4 (1969): 251–70. Cf. also Häring, *Ideologie*, 122. It is revealing to note the way in which Häring cites his sources. He quotes Alois Grillmeier

What, then, is the cause of this paradox that allows us to distinguish between the uniqueness and concreteness of the Church, on the one hand, and the presence of ecclesial elements outside the one subject, on the other hand? Ratzinger explains the self-contradictory nature of divisions among Christians in terms of human sin:

> Because sin is a contradiction, this distinction between *subsistit* and *est* is, in the end, something that cannot be entirely explained logically. Reflected in the paradox of the distinction between the uniqueness and the concrete existence of the Church, on the one hand, and, on the other, the continuing existence of a concrete ecclesiastical entity outside of the one active agent is the contradictory element of human sin, the contradictory element of schism.[468]

Ratzinger's critique is directed against a benign view of divided churches. For one harmful result is that the division of Christendom loses its sting, because division is seen merely as "a representation of the multitudinous variations upon a theme, in which all the variations are in some sense right, and all in some sense wrong".[469] This leads to a second consequence, that even in this "relativistic dialectical process"[470] the necessary search for unity may be conducted in vain.

But how do matters stand, then, with the legitimate plurality of Churches advocated by Ratzinger during the Council? Ratzinger pleaded for what was then an almost revolutionary vision of the unity of Churches, in which the Churches "remain Churches, yet become *one* Church".[471] In doing so, he was hoping for a sort of Church unity that does not absorb,[472] that avoids confusing unity with uniformity,

---

without explaining the premises presupposed by the latter, with which Grillmeier prefaces his interpretation of the individual points as a brief summary. Because of their importance, we cite Grillmeier's premises here: "1. The true and unique Church of Christ exists in concrete historical form. As such she is therefore—despite her mysterious character—identifiable and recognizable. 2. The concrete existential form of this Church founded by Christ is the Catholic Church." See Grillmeier, 1:174.

[468] "Ecclesiology", 148.
[469] Ibid.
[470] Ibid.
[471] *Highlights*, 73.
[472] See *Volk Gottes*, 148f.: "Who would have dared to hope that such a passionate search for possibilities of *rapprochement* and understanding would begin, such a lively willingness to revise what was hitherto taken for granted and seemed to be the only possible phenomenon, so as to look beyond the mere demand for return and to arrive at the possibility

so that they "remain in existence as *Churches*, with only those modifications which such a unity necessarily requires".[473]

It would give a false impression if one were to try to speak about a fundamental contrast between these statements and Ratzinger's present understanding of unity. Back then, too, he left no doubt that "for Catholics, however, there is *the* Church, which they identify with the historic continuity of the Catholic Church."[474] Of course there is no question here of a self-wrought or deserved uniqueness of the Catholic Church. By sheer grace, she is called to be "the work of God, which he maintains despite the persistent demerits of the human officeholders".[475] We encounter this unswerving fidelity of God already in the Old Testament, when God calls his people into being despite their infidelity to his covenant. But the fact that his new People of God journeys on to meet the Lord in the form of the Church of Jesus Christ and the fact that this subsists in the Catholic Church can be perceived—as Ratzinger explains—only in faith.[476]

---

of a unification that is not absorption but rather a real encounter in the truth and love of the Lord." See also M. Volf, *Trinität und Gemeinschaft: Eine ökumenische Ekklesiologie* (Mainz: Matthias-Grünewald-Verlag, 1996), 42.

[473] *Highlights*, 73. Cf. Weiler, 329f. Weiler cites Ratzinger as saying that it is the duty of Catholic theology "to shed light on [the Church's] all-too-simple identification of herself with the Church of the Fathers and to take into account theologically as realities the intervening historical developments and shifts as well. . . . Between the patristic equation *ecclesia catholica* = *corpus Christi* and the equation in the 1943 encyclical there is a historical development, which gave to both entities a somewhat altered content, so that, first, the entity '*ecclesia catholica*' looks different now, something that is manifested quite externally in the fact that she is now called *ecclesia Romana-catholica*. In the addition of the adjective *Romana*, which no doubt signifies a certain restriction of the adjective *catholica*, we must perceive also [*mithören*] the whole message of Vatican I, the pointed meaning that this Council's teaching gave to the term Catholic. In being more precisely defined as 'Roman', in the sense of the papal primacy of jurisdiction, the adjective 'Catholic' was intrinsically narrowed down, a process that then does not allow a simple identification with the term 'Catholic' in patristic theology, even if one believes that the idea of primacy was implicitly present in the Church of the Fathers. On the other hand, though, the *corpus Christi* concept, too, underwent a far-reaching metamorphosis, so that both sides of the equation have been affected by the vicissitudes of history." On the metamorphosis of the Body of Christ understanding of the Church, see pt. 2, sec. 2, chap. 1, § 4.3.a, of this work: "Three 'Historical Rings' of the Body of Christ Concept in Relation to Church Membership".

[474] *Highlights*, 73. See also *Volk Gottes*, 149.

[475] "Ecclesiology", 149.

[476] Cf. ibid.

Christ's Church really exists, and not just scraps of her. And she is not a never-to-be-attained utopia; on the contrary, she is concrete. This is precisely what the *subsistit* means: The Lord guarantees her existence in spite of all our sins and failings, which no doubt are quite evident in the Catholic Church. The *subsistit* was also supposed to say, however, that although the Lord keeps his promise, there is ecclesial reality outside the Catholic communion as well, and this very contradiction is the strongest imperative to seek unity.[477]

Accordingly, the way indicated by the Council was not to act as though all Christian Churches and ecclesial communities added up to the Church of Jesus Christ. With such an ecclesiological relativism that claims "that the Church of Jesus Christ is *also* present in the Catholic Church, it would have been expressing a trite slogan, and there would have been no need to struggle in order to formulate it."[478] That is why, for Ratzinger, the *subsistit* formula is also a sign of the continuity of "the whole faith history of the Church".[479]

b. The *subsistit* formula as an alternative to ecclesiological relativism

In the present age, which is imbued with relativism, the uniqueness of the Church that Ratzinger highlights in his interpretation of the *subsistit* formula becomes a stumbling block, even within the Church. Thus Hermann Häring speaks in his analysis of *Dominus Iesus* about an "ideology of uniqueness and universality"[480] and also about an effort to turn the idea of unity into something sacred or even a sacrament,[481] and he suspects that a modern-day imperialistic model of unity[482] is behind it all. He interprets the *subsistit* formula as the expression of indecision and of the vague compromise "of a synod that is wavering between ecumenical openness and the old exclusivity".[483] He remarks critically, with reference to the way the formula is understood in Ratzinger's writings, that the latter has "violated at least the

---

[477] "Absurd", 51.
[478] Ibid.
[479] Ibid.
[480] Häring, *Ideologie*, 110.
[481] See ibid., 130.
[482] Cf. ibid., 131.
[483] Ibid., 121.

spirit of the declaration".[484] According to Häring, the *subsistit* refers solely to the spiritual side of the Church: "It is not concerned with the Catholic faith organization, but rather with the ecclesial reality willed by God, . . . which we profess in the Creed to be one, holy, catholic, and apostolic. This very Church is professed in the Creed and lived by the churches of the Reformation as well."[485] With this interpretation, however, Häring assumes a different sort of visibility of the Church from the one the Council spoke about when it related this visible character specifically to the subsistence of the Church in the Catholic Church. An interpretation of the *subsistit* formula must take into account the entire conciliar message. Furthermore, according to Ratzinger, it is necessary to note "the only official pronouncement of the Magisterium concerning this expression since the Council"[486] (that is, until the subsequent declaration *Dominus Iesus*), namely, the "Notification on the Book *Church: Charism and Power: Essay on Militant Ecclesiology*, by Father Leonardo Boff, O.F.M.",[487] dated March 11, 1985. In it the Congregation for the Faith deals specifically with the question of subsistence. Contrary to Boff's thesis[488] that the Church of Christ subsists in other Christian churches also, the declaration states:

> But the Council had chosen the word *subsistit*—subsists—exactly in order to make clear that one sole "subsistence" of the true Church exists, whereas outside her visible structure only *elementa ecclesiae*— elements of church—exist; these—being elements of the same Church—tend and conduct toward the Catholic Church (*Lumen gentium*, no. 8). The decree on ecumenism expresses the same doctrine (cf. *Unitatis redintegratio*, nos. 3–4), and it was restated precisely

---

[484] Ibid.

[485] Ibid.

[486] "Ecclesiology", 145.

[487] Congregation for the Doctrine of the Faith, "Notification on the Book *Church: Charism and Power: Essay on Militant Ecclesiology* by Father Leonardo Boff, O.F.M." Cf. Boff, *Church: Charism and Power*.

[488] See also Leonardo Boff's statement on this theme in Boff, *Manifest für die Ökumene*, 92–97. Unlike Häring, who neglects the visible character of the Church, Boff is very much concerned here with the concrete visible form of the Church, as it can be met with empirically and historically. From the realization that the Church of Jesus Christ and the Catholic Church are not completely identical, however, he draws a conclusion that does not do justice to the intended message of *Lumen gentium*: that there is a plurality of "subsistences" of the Church.

in the declaration *Mysterium Ecclesiae* (no. 1, AAS LXV (1973), pp. 396–98).[489]

In Boff's ecclesiology, which is influenced by liberation theology and sociology, an ontological or even a sacramental perspective has considerably less significance than in Ratzinger's writings. Boff's etymological interpretation of the word *subsistit* was already typical of this approach.[490] Ratzinger, in contrast, cautions in general against an ecclesiological relativism that would justify itself with the historical-critical argument that Jesus himself never thought of founding a Church. Accepting that premise would lead to the following conclusions:

> The concrete structure of the Church is said not to have developed until after the Resurrection, in the process of ridding Christianity of eschatology, through the more immediate sociological requirements of institutionalization; and it is said that at the beginning there was certainly no "catholic" Church, but merely various distinct local Churches with varying theologies, with offices that differed, and so on.[491]

---

[489] Congregation for the Doctrine of the Faith, "Notification on the Book *Church: Charism and Power* by Father Leonardo Boff", section entitled "The Structure of the Church". In the German edition of the CDF Notification (in *Verlautbarungen des Apostolischen Stuhls*, no. 67, ed. Sekretariat der Deutschen Bischofskonferenz, 6 [Bonn, 1985]), there is a footnote that reads: "In German there is no equivalent for the Latin word *subsistit*. It is an intensified form of the verb 'to exist' and denotes full and independent existence. In using this term, the Council meant to say that the true Church is not an invisible idea or a mere eschatological expectation but rather is present in the institutional form of the Catholic Church as such. In contrast, the non-Catholic Churches and ecclesial communities enjoy a different kind of participation in the being of the Church, which the Council described with the expression 'elements' of ecclesiality. On the one hand, it intended thereby to explain the presence of what pertains to the Church [*des Ekklesialen*] outside the Catholic Church as well, without, on the other hand, surrendering her unity and visibility. At the same time 'subsistence' and 'elements' were brought into a dynamic relationship of mutual affinity. The Notification points out that L. Boff's misunderstanding of the *subsistit* dissolves this dynamic synthesis and replaces it with an ecclesiological dialectic that necessarily brings in its wake a relativity in matters concerning the truth of the faith." Cf. also *DI*, nos. 16f.

[490] See pt. 2, sec. 2, chap. 1, § 4.4.a, in this work, "The Difference between *Subsistit* and *Est*".

[491] "Ecclesiology", 145. See also "Gottesidee", 46: Boff's ecclesiological relativism "justifies itself with the opinion that the 'historical Jesus' himself did not have a Church in mind, much less founded one. The real Church structure came into existence only

From this it follows logically that the subsistence refers, not exclusively to the Catholic Church, but also to other Churches and ecclesial communities,[492] a thesis that Leonardo Boff defended once again in his "Manifesto against Ratzinger".[493]

The Church of Christ and the Catholic Church are not completely identical. The Church of Christ is larger than the Catholic Church. On account of this fact, over the course of history and to this day the Church of Christ has been able to subsist in the other Christian churches and ecclesial communities as well, that is, to assume other historical and cultural forms. Together and in fellowship with one another, they constitute the Church of Christ in history, the Church of God through the ages.[494]

---

after the Resurrection, as part of the process of de-eschatologization and as a result of the inevitable sociological needs of institutionalization; furthermore, at the beginning there was no 'catholic' universal Church at all, but only various local Churches with different theologies, different ministries.... Hence all institutional constructs are ... as such human constructs that can or even must be radically changed again in new situations."

[492] Critiquing a completely different and trinitarian justification for ecclesiological relativism, for example, in the writings of Eberhard Jüngel, Ratzinger remarks "that the Church in the West, in translating the trinitarian formula into Latin, did not adopt the Eastern formula outright, which describes one God as one being in three hypostases ('subsistences'), but instead rendered the word *hypostasis* with the expression 'person', because the concept of subsistence as such did not exist in Latin and was not suited to formulating the unity and diversity of Father, Son, and Holy Spirit. Above all, though, I am decidedly against the increasingly fashionable trend of applying the trinitarian mystery directly to the Church. It does not work. We would end up believing in three Gods." See "Absurd", 51. Compare also E. Jüngel, "Nur Wahrheit befreit", *Deutsches Allgemeines Sonntagsblatt*, no. 37 (October 15, 2000): 20–22.

[493] That was the original title for the book *Manifesto for Ecumenism*: Boff, *Manifest für die Ökumene*.

[494] Boff, *Manifest für die Ökumene*, 96; see also ibid., 99: "'... by virtue of their ecclesial elements, the Church of Christ operates in a certain way within them.' Consequently the Church of Christ subsists in the non-Catholic churches." The latter inference appears to be illogical. In the course of his argument, L. Boff uses the term *sacramentum* (sign and instrument) as, in his words, "an extremely helpful category for designating the various degrees of density and concreteness of the complex reality of the one Church of Christ" (ibid., 101). Boff refers here (100) to a passage in J. J. Degenhardt, H. Tenhumberg, and H. Thimme, eds., *Kirchen auf gemeinsamem Wege* (Bielefeld and Kevelaer: Luther-Verlag, 1977), 26: "The realization of Church as the foundation of Jesus Christ occurs in varying degrees of density." On this subject, see also D. Sattler, "Ökumenische Annäherungen an die *Ecclesia ab Abel* vor dem Hintergrund *Dominus Iesus*", in *Was ist heute noch katholisch? Zum Streit um die innere Einheit und Vielfalt der Kirche*, ed. A. Franz, 87–113, esp. 95–99, QD 192 (Freiburg im Breisgau: Herder, 2001).

In opposition to such a view, Ratzinger cites Jesus' actions, as communicated in the tradition of the Church. In his opinion, it is obvious that Jesus proclaimed the kingdom of God, surrounded himself with disciples, and "not only imparted to them his message as a new interpretation of the Old Testament, but also gave them in the Sacrament of the Lord's Supper a new and unifying heart, through which everyone who confessed his name could become one with him in an entirely new way".[495] According to Paul, this *communio* in the Lord means being one body with Christ and becoming one spirit with him and with one another. Hence for anyone who places his faith in this apostolic tradition, Pentecost is no vague announcement, but instead proof of the fact "that the Church was not devised and built up by men"[496] but rather was created by the Holy Spirit. In this apostolic view, as Ratzinger summarizes, the pneumatic reality of the Church and her sacramental-hierarchical structure are not in opposition to each other but rather belong together inseparably.

> The institution is not then a structure we can rebuild or demolish just as we like, which has (allegedly) nothing at all to do with the business of believing.... The institution is not an unavoidable—although theologically irrelevant or even damaging—external phenomenon; it is, in its essential core, a part of the concrete character of the Incarnation.[497]

According to Ratzinger, it is a question of defending the belief that the Church of Jesus Christ can be encountered as a concrete reality in a unique way in the Catholic Church. To the question of whether this does not run counter to the ecumenical formula about the "reconciled diversity" of the Christian denominations, he replies:

> I can very well accept the idea of "reconciled diversity", if that does not mean indifference toward the contents [of faith] and thus dismissal of the question about truth, so that we would all regard ourselves as one, even though we believe and teach contrary things. The expression is correctly applied, as I understand it, when it

---

[495] "Ecclesiology", 146.
[496] Ibid.
[497] Ibid., 146–47.

indicates that, despite the differences that do not allow us simply to regard everything as fragments of a Church of Jesus Christ that does not really exist, we nevertheless meet in the peace of Christ as Christians reconciled with one another. When it means, furthermore, that we recognize that our divisions contradict the will of the Lord and allow the pain we experience over this to compel us to search for unity and to beg the Lord for it, knowing that we all need his forgiveness and love.[498]

Ratzinger understands Church unity to be a gift and a task that the Church has received from the Lord, because it is an essential mark of the one, holy, catholic, and apostolic Church. Yet the visible Church is wounded because, even though she is one, "the reality of salvation and of being saved, ecclesial reality",[499] exists outside her visible boundaries as well. Thus unity becomes a task, not in the sense of a utopian dream, but rather as a search for truth, for anyone who seeks the truth is, as Ratzinger puts it, "objectively on the way to Christ and thus also on the way to the communion in which he remains present to history—the Church".[500]

With that, we have arrived at that delicate point which is basically behind the problem of ecclesiological relativism. We are talking about the loss of the quest for truth[501] in an age when, as Ratzinger polemically remarks, "subjectivism is canonized"[502] and everyone ends up looking for a church that suits his taste. In a pluralistic, global society, the subsistence and truth claim of the Catholic Church is therefore a challenge to an overwhelming "universal paradigm"[503] of relativism at the beginning of the twenty-first century.[504]

---

[498] "Absurd", 52.

[499] Ibid.

[500] Ibid.

[501] See also A. F. Utz, "Der christliche Glaube als Voraussetzung des demokratischen Pluralismus: Eine sozialethische Würdigung der wissenschaftlichen Arbeiten von Joseph Kardinal Ratzinger", in *Glaube und demokratischer Pluralismus im wissenschaftlichen Werk von Joseph Kardinal Ratzinger: Zur Verleihung des Augustin-Bea-Preises 1989*", im Auftrag der Internationalen Stiftung *Humanum*, ed. Utz, 11–44, ref. at 30f. (Bonn: WBV, 1991).

[502] "Absurd", 51.

[503] G. L. Müller, *Mit der Kirche denken: Bausteine und Skizzen zu einer Ekklesiologie der Gegenwart* (Würzburg: Naumann, 2001), 8.

[504] Cf. "New Questions", 117–21.

c. Subsistence and the question of truth

Many people today—in Ratzinger's estimation—regard faith in a truth that is binding and valid for everyone, a truth that was revealed in human history uniquely and in an unsurpassable way in Jesus Christ and is guaranteed in history down to this day by the testimony of the Church, "as a kind of fundamentalism, as an attack upon the modern spirit, and as a threat to tolerance and freedom".[505] Against this background, it is not surprising that the relatively short chapter 4 of *Dominus Iesus*[506] "Unicity and Unity of the Church" has elicited the most protest,[507] even though the document is not primarily about ecumenical questions and how they are framed. It is concerned, rather, with bringing up the absolute claims of the truth that has shone forth in Jesus Christ,[508] and with them ultimately the question of the true religion. *Dominus Iesus* answers the latter question in its conclusion with a quotation from *Dignitatis humanae*, the conciliar Declaration on Religious Freedom:

We believe that this one true religion continues to exist in the Catholic and Apostolic Church, to which the Lord Jesus entrusted the

---

[505] Ratzinger, "Presentation of the Declaration *Dominus Iesus* in the Press Conference Room of the Holy See, on September 5, 2000", in *Pilgrim Fellowship*, 209–16, citation at 211. See also Kaes, 71. According to Dorothee Kaes, Ratzinger sees the problem "in the loss of the idea of being and in the relativizing of reality that is connected with it. Herein lies one of the chief reasons for the crisis in which the Christian faith finds itself. For an intellectual approach that regards historicity and stability as mutually exclusive, it seems impossible to adhere to a unity of faith in its historically transmitted form."

[506] Of the twenty-three articles in the declaration, only two (nos. 16 and 17) are applied to the question "Unicity and Unity of the Church". See the special insert, *L'Osservatore romano*, English ed., no. 36 (September 6, 2000): IIf.

[507] In reference to this chapter, Häring speaks of "the real nadir of the document"; see Häring, *Ideologie*, 127. Cf. ibid., 110f. See also Boff, *Manifest für die Ökumene*, 89–113: "III. Wer stellt das Konzil auf den Kopf?" (Who is standing the Council on its head?). See also "Absurd", 52. There Ratzinger points out that *Dominus Iesus* uses "the classical magisterial language . . . in keeping with the documents of the Second Vatican Council". At the same time he concedes that Walter Kasper "is quite correct in noting that the turmoil surrounding the document is really about a communications problem", since the magisterial language "is of course quite different from the language of the newspapers and the media. But then one should translate the document and not disparage it."

[508] *Dominus Iesus* is structured as follows: Introduction / I. The Fullness and Definitiveness of the Revelation of Jesus Christ / II. The Incarnate Logos and the Holy Spirit in the Work of Salvation / III. Unicity and Universality of the Salvific Mystery of Jesus Christ / IV. Unicity and Unity of the Church / V. The Church: Kingdom of God and Kingdom of Christ / VI. The Church and the Other Religions in Relation to Salvation / Conclusion.

task of spreading it among all people.... Especially in those things that concern God and his Church, all persons are required to seek the truth, and when they come to know it, to embrace it and hold fast to it.[509]

On the occasion of the presentation of *Dominus Iesus*, Ratzinger made it understood that, in a pluralistic society that portrays relativism, "under the banner of the encounter with other cultures, as the true and humane philosophy",[510] it is necessary to defend the core and center of the Christian faith; this means "that there is a universal, binding, and valid truth in history, which became flesh in Jesus Christ and is handed on through the faith of the Church".[511] It is a question of the fundamental insight that not all religions are equally valuable ways to salvation. Even though "seeds of truth and goodness"[512] can be found in other religions and cultures, the claim to originality and uniqueness of the revelation of Jesus Christ must not be diminished, and we should not weaken its missionary impetus to proclaim Christ to all men as *the* way, *the* truth, and *the* life (Jn 14:6).[513]

This same demand is described by Hermann Häring as Ratzinger's "ideology of uniqueness and universality".[514] But does not Häring thereby characterize the very concept of religious truth, which is considered absolute in other revealed religions as well, for example, in Islam or in Judaism, as ideology? The legitimate demand for tolerance

---

[509] *DH* 1, cited in *DI*, no. 23.

[510] Ratzinger, "Presentation of the Declaration *Dominus Iesus*", 209–16, citation at 212.

[511] Ibid., 211. See also Müller, *Mit der Kirche denken*, 7.

[512] Ratzinger, "Presentation of the Declaration *Dominus Iesus*", 214: "Goodness and truth, whever they may be, come from the Father and are the work of the Holy Spirit. The seeds of the Logos are cast abroad everywhere. Yet we cannot shut our eyes to the errors and illusions that are present in these religions." Ratzinger refers to *LG* 16: "Often men, deceived by the Evil One, have become vain in their reasonings and have exchanged the truth of God for a lie, serving the creature rather than the Creator." See also *NA* 2.

[513] Cf. *Einheit*, 17–51, ref. at 32–36, esp. 32f.: "The truth of what man is, what the world is, what God is, that is, the truth in general is real in the Person of Jesus Christ. Part of it, though, is the history from which it comes, in terms of which it interprets itself— that history, then, which goes back to the faith of Abraham, indeed, back to God's call to Adam. This, of course, does not justify speaking of a "historicity of the truth" as such, but it does mean that the truth comes to man in a movement that progresses through history and unfolds within it. The truth demands of man, in order for him to become aware of it, that he enter into this movement."

[514] Cf. Häring, *Ideologie*, 110.

toward individual persons, according to Ratzinger, must not be confused with the postulate of giving up the question of truth in the first
place. In his opinion, the result would be that no one would take
anyone else seriously. For him, it is axiomatic that "mission and dialogue should no longer be opposites but should mutually interpenetrate."[515] In order to keep dialogue from becoming "aimless
conversation",[516] the question of the truth must not be declared taboo:

> If the question of truth is no longer being considered, then what
> religion essentially is, is no longer distinguishable from what it is
> not; faith is no longer differentiated from superstition, experience
> from illusion. Unless claims to truth are considered, respect for other
> religions ultimately becomes contradictory and meaningless, because
> there is no criterion by which to distinguish what is of positive
> value in any religion and what is negative or is the product of super-
> stition and deception.[517]

For Christians, the fullness of truth has been revealed by God in
Jesus Christ. Ratzinger responds to the question of the transmission of
this truth in history by saying that the "transtemporal subject,
Church",[518] conveys it and testifies to it. As times change, the Church
retains her own identity, albeit "in a process of spiritual growth (or
else, under certain circumstances, spiritual decline)".[519] This does not
mean, however, "that truth itself would be cancelled out in historicity
(or temporality)",[520] because through Christ truth itself always precedes time. From this, Ratzinger draws the conclusion:

---

[515] *Many Religions*, 112.

[516] Ibid. But Ratzinger adds: "Conversely, mission activity in the future cannot proceed
as if it were simply a case of communicating to someone who has no knowledge at all of
God what he has to believe."

[517] Ratzinger, "Presentation of the Declaration *Dominus Iesus*", 213. With reference to
the interreligious question, the absolute claim of the truth meets with "the agreement of
many Protestant Christians", as even Hermann Häring admits (Häring, *Ideologie*, 110).

[518] *Einheit*, 17–51, citation at 33.

[519] Ibid., 34.

[520] Ibid., 35. Ratzinger refers here to the contrast between the Bible's understanding of
truth and that of Hegel: "The biblical faith in the Incarnation of the Logos and in his
participation in history is radicalized by Hegel in the notion of the temporality of the
Logos itself, which is Being only as Time and comes completely into its own only in a
temporal way. The ultimate logical consequence of this is that truth is surrendered to time.
Depending on one's way of looking at it, then, either the opportune as such becomes the

Christian faith measures itself instead in terms of the truth that already exists and thus becomes the crisis in every age. To that extent, there is no real temporality of truth, and, thus, neither is there any pluralism of truths, either in an evolutionary or in a revolutionary scheme of things. There is, of course, the historical transmission of truth in the historical subject Church; both her past and also her waiting for the future fulfillment of the promise belong to that subject. Within the reality of this subject lies the real mediation between Being and Time, between the eternity and the historicity of truth.[521]

Who, though, can lay claim to being the transtemporal subject of this transmission of the truth? In *Lumen gentium* 8 and *Nostra aetate* 1, the Council Fathers themselves gave the answer: the Church of Jesus Christ, which subsists in the Catholic Church and participates in the mystery of the Incarnation of the Divine Word. Yet according to Ratzinger, this does not mean identifying the Church with truth; rather, the Church remains "the space established by truth in which it can be known",[522] as Nachtwei summarizes it in his study of Ratzinger.

Chapter 1 in part 2, section 2, of this dissertation, entitled "The Church—Sign of Faith and Mystery of Faith", demonstrates that the Pauline Body of Christ concept provides the key to Ratzinger's ecclesiology and thus to explicating the mystery of the Church. This is possible because Ratzinger, influenced and assisted by the Orthodox tradition of the Eastern Churches, interprets the Body of Christ image more profoundly as a eucharistic ecclesiology and from this perspective demonstrates the intrinsic connection to the understanding of *communio* in the early Church. In this way, the "Body of Christ" image of the Church, which has been largely neglected since the Council, appears to be the connecting link to the key word of postconciliar ecclesiology, *communio*. By reason of its eucharistic-pneumatic specificity, Ratzinger's understanding of the "Body of Christ" (and here he agrees with the vision of *Lumen gentium*) opens up, in comparison to the

---

true, or else future potential becomes the standard for the truth: then anything that keeps the future open and makes it possible is true. Such a pragmatic concept of truth, which measures a statement solely in terms of what it accomplishes for today and tomorrow, basically means resignation with respect to the question of truth." See also Kaes, 67.

[521] *Einheit*, 17–51, citation at 36.

[522] Nachtwei, 239. Cf. J. Ratzinger, "Theologie und Kirchenpolitik", *IKaZ* 9 (1980): 425–34.

preconciliar interpretations of the concept, a new and comprehensive understanding of membership in the Church as well.[523] Inasmuch as her *communio* has a eucharistic foundation, her essential unity is once again at the center of attention, so that from an ecumenical perspective, the question about the true Church acquires a specific urgency. Together with *Lumen gentium*, Ratzinger defends the *subsistit* [subsistence] of this true Church in the Catholic Church so as to counter an ecclesiological relativism and to maintain Christianity's claim to truth. This does not prevent him—again, in keeping with *Lumen gentium*—from recognizing elements of the true Church in other Christian communities also, which as "gifts belonging to the Church of Christ"[524] impel Christians to unity.

In the next chapter of this dissertation on Ratzinger's ecclesiology, we will turn to the image of the Church that was predominant in the first phase of the implementation of the Council and even today holds a decisive status in understanding *Lumen gentium*: the Church as the new People of God.

---

[523] On this subject, see Alberto, *"Corpus Suum mystice constituit" (LG 7)*, 566.
[524] LG 8.

Chapter 2

Church as People of God

In order to understand the whole reality of the Church, it is necessary
to shed light on it, as *Lumen gentium* does, from different sides and by
means of various concepts. Each one allows us to recognize only partial aspects of her mystery, and therefore they can be adequately interpreted only in a comprehensive view.[1] Because of his study of Augustine's
ecclesiology,[2] the notion of the "People of God" had become for Ratzinger, even before the Council, a central concept[3] of his own ecclesiological research, with the resulting finding

that Augustine (and the Church Fathers in general) continued along
the same lines as the New Testament, in that the expression

---

[1] Cf. Internationale Theologenkommission, ed., *Mysterium des Gottesvolkes* (Einsiedeln:
Johannes Verlag, 1987), 24. "As many as eighty comparisons have been found in the New
Testament to describe the Church. This variety of images that the Council uses, therefore,
is intentional: It is supposed to emphasize the inexhaustible character of the *mysterium*
Church. To the one who contemplates her, she shows herself as 'a reality that is saturated
with the presence of God and for that reason is constituted in such a way that she allows
ever new and deeper interpretations of herself.'" See also Paul VI, "Address at Opening of
the Second Session of the Second Vatican Council on September 29, 1963", in *AAS* 55
(1963): 848 [English translation in *Council Daybook: Vatican II*, ed. Floyd Anderson, vol. 1
(Washington, D.C.: National Catholic Welfare Conference), 143–50, at 144b]. The desire
of Pope Paul VI for a deeper self-understanding of the Church through the adoption of a
series of biblical images—for ecumenical reasons as well—is found again in *LG* 6.

[2] Ratzinger's doctoral dissertation advisor, the fundamental theologian G. Söhngen, had
raised the question of whether "People of God" might be an ecclesiological theme running through the works of Augustine. The basis for his hypothesis was a passage from
Augustine cited in the *Roman Catechism: "Catechismus Romanus*, Pars I, capitulum IX 2:
'Ecclesia', ut ait S. Augustinus, 'est populus fidelis per universum orbem diffusus'" (cited
in Latin in *Volk und Haus Gottes*, xxii). In the English translation by John A. McHugh,
O.P., and Charles J. Callan, O.P.: "The Church, says St. Augustine, consists of the faithful
dispersed throughout the world" (*Catechism of the Council of Trent for Parish Priests*, 7th ed.
[New York: Joseph F. Wagner, August 1943), 97.

[3] *Volk und Haus Gottes*, vii.

331

People of God occurs predominantly in quotations from the Old Testament and almost exclusively designates the People of Israel and, thus (if you will), the Church of the Old Covenant.... Only in a christological transposition, or, as we could also say, in a pneumatological interpretation, does it become a reference to the Church.[4]

This background is a key to understanding Ratzinger's positions with regard to the People of God concept during the Council as well as in the postconciliar period. To his way of thinking, which is influenced by Augustine, the formula reads: "The People [of God] has its authentic character in the fact that it is a sacramental Body of Christ communion, that is, *corpus Christi*."[5] This corresponds, as I have shown in part 1 of my study, to the intended message of the Constitution on the Church, *Lumen gentium*.[6] The emphases and nuances that are specific to its understanding of the "People of God" are characterized by Ratzinger as follows:

If one wants to sum up in brief phrases the outstanding elements of the concept of the people of God that were important for the Council, one could say that here was made clear the historical character of the Church, the unity of God's history with mankind, the inner unity of the people of God even across sacramental class-distinctions, the eschatological dynamism, the provisional and fragmentary nature of this Church that is always in need of renewal, and finally also the ecumenical dimension, that is, the different ways in which being linked and related to the Church are possible and effective outside the boundaries of the Catholic Church.[7]

In the following six subsections I would like to give a systematic presentation of the "People of God" concept in Ratzinger's writings.

---

[4] Ibid., xiiif.

[5] Ibid., 324; cf. Weiler, 63–66.

[6] This thesis can be supported also by a reference made during the time of the composition of the schema on the Church. The plan then was to relate systematically the themes of the Body of Christ and the People of God; see S. Alberto, "Begriff und Wesen der Kirche in der Entstehung der Kirchenkonstitution *Lumen gentium*", in *Ex latere: Ausfaltungen communialer Theologie*, ed. E. Naab, 161, 173, n. 63 (Eichstätt: Franz-Sales-Verlag, 1993).

[7] *Church*, 17.

In order to make the transition from the previous chapter, I will look at it first as a revision of the Body of Christ idea. Second, I will investigate together with Ratzinger its roots in the New Testament, which are expressed by the Church's designation of herself as εϰϰλησια. Third, we will speak about Jesus Christ as the origin and goal of the Church. Fourth, in Ratzinger's perspective of salvation history, this theme is connected with the question of the ontological priority of the universal Church. Fifth, this results in a critique of the sociological misunderstanding of the Church as People of God. Sixth and finally, we will show the nature and the goal of every ecclesial existence, namely, the universal call of all its members to holiness, and thus demonstrate its eschatological character.

§ 1. The Image of the "People of God" as a Revision of the Body of Christ Idea

1. On the ecumenical significance of understanding the Church as "the pilgrim people of God"

No basic theological concept had so much resonance as the description of the Church as the "People of God". According to Ratzinger, this expression became a slogan even before the Council, after the Lutheran Scripture scholar Ernst Käsemann entitled his 1939 monograph on the Letter to the Hebrews *Das wandernde Gottesvolk* [The pilgrim people of God].[8] There were many reasons for the widespread acceptance of this expression, not the least of which was the fact that in it the eschatological element of the Church comes to the fore. The experience of the apocalyptic horrors of the First World War had produced a general longing for a real fellowship of peace and hope. The burgeoning spiritual movements of the period between the two world wars had made interdenominational dialogue possible among Catholics as well as among Protestants. During this *rapprochement*, the Catholic Church's understanding of herself as "Christ's continuing life on earth" or as "the incarnation of the Son continuing until the end of

---

[8] See ibid., 16.

time"[9] proved to be a stumbling block. From the perspective of that self-understanding, "any criticism could appear as an attack on Christ himself."[10]

That was also the reason why Protestant Christians, especially, could not accept the Body of Christ idea of the Church, as it had been presented in 1943 by Pope Pius XII in his encyclical *Mystici Corporis*. According to this encyclical, membership in the Church is based not only on baptism—as was said in the canon law that was in force at the time[11]—but also on right faith and juridical affiliation with the true Church. In retrospect, Ratzinger commented on these requirements:

> This made it clear that in certain circumstances a legal approach can offer more flexibility and openness than a "mystical" one. It was asked whether the image of the mystical body was not too narrow a starting-point to be able to define the multitude of different forms of Church membership that now existed thanks to the confusion of human history.[12]

In the image of the People of God, a concept had been rediscovered that was roomier and more flexible in the question of Church membership and that could serve as an "ecumenical bridge",[13] especially among the separated Christian brethren. It became possible thereby, as Ratzinger puts it, "to express the inner unity of the people of God", in which the fact that all are journeying toward God "[cuts] across all ... distinctions"[14] and makes them all pilgrims. Inasmuch as the Church, "the pilgrim people of God", is journeying through time toward its goal and hence is not yet perfected, "its own hope is still ahead of it."[15]

---

[9] Ibid.

[10] Ibid. Ratzinger speaks here of a "christological difference": "The Church is not identical with Christ but stands over against him. It is the Church of sinners that continually needs purification and renewal."

[11] Cf. can. 87 *CIC* (1917); see also "Wesen", 64–66.

[12] *Church*, 15.

[13] Ibid., 16. Cf. J. Ratzinger and K. Lehmann, *Living with the Church*, trans. Zachary Hayes, O.F.M. (Chicago: Francisco Herald Press, 1978), 9ff.

[14] *Church*, 17.

[15] Ibid.

2. The inner continuity of salvation history through the one People of God

The "People of God" therefore has significance in the history of theology, and this aspect of it, which points up the incompleteness of
what is temporal and interprets God's workings in human history as
the history of salvation that can be experienced in the world, reveals
the unity of the Old and the New Testaments[16] in the one People of
God, which God himself calls.[17] For Ratzinger this continuity means
more than a historical sequence. According to the Scripture verse "Salvation is from the Jews" (Jn 4:22),[18] the Church as the new People of
God has an Old Testament lineage, and "this heritage remains abid-
ingly vital."[19] As a consequence of this, "there is no access to Jesus,
and thereby there can be no entrance of the nations into the People of
God, without the acceptance in faith of the revelation of God who
speaks in the Sacred Scripture that Christians term the Old
Testament."[20]

---

[16] See *Nature*, 83–85. With the term *symphonia*, the Church Fathers and other writers
describe the totality of Scripture as a "polyphony" "composed of the many apparently
quite discordant strains in the contrapuntal interplay of law, prophets, Gospels and apostles". Ratzinger emphasizes that, according to the Fathers, heresy is the "reductive selection" of thematic elements, "because truth lies only in the whole and in its tensions"
(ibid., 84).

[17] Cf. *God and the World*, 146–51.

[18] See *Many Religions*, 28.

[19] Ibid. Ratzinger says that *CCC* 528 takes the same position: "The magi's coming to
Jerusalem in order to pay homage to the king of the Jews shows that they seek in Israel, in
the messianic light of the star of David, the one who will be king of the nations. Their
coming means that pagans can discover Jesus and worship him as Son of God and Savior
of the world only by turning toward the Jews and receiving from them the messianic
promise as contained in the Old Testament. The Epiphany shows that 'the full number of
the nations' now takes its 'place in the family of the patriarchs' and acquires *Israelitica
dignitas* (are made 'worthy of the heritage of Israel')." In *Many Religions*, 36f., Ratzinger
emphasizes that the *CCC*, with its understanding of the "inner continuity and coherence"
of the OT and the NT, "stands squarely within the Catholic tradition, especially as it was
formulated by Augustine and Thomas Aquinas. In this tradition the relationship between
the Torah and the proclamation of Jesus is never seen dialectically; God in the Law does
not appear *sub contrario*, as it were, in opposition to himself. In tradition, it was never a case
of dialectics, but rather of analogy, development in inner correspondence following the
felicitous phrase of Saint Augustine: 'The New Testament lies hidden in the Old; the Old
is made explicit in the New.'"

[20] Ibid., 28. See also "Gottesidee", 46.

This inner continuity already becomes evident in God's covenant with Abraham and the prophets when he gives them a universal promise[21] that he finally fulfills in Jesus Christ through the new and everlasting covenant. According to Ratzinger, in this promise-structure there is "only *one* will of God for men, only *one* historical activity of God with and for men",[22] in which "God's unfailing love"[23] was revealed. For this reason the following holds true for the Church: "It is not some new creation of Jesus. The People of God has been on its way since Abraham and can always only be one: through Jesus its boundary-posts have merely been extended to the ends of the earth and driven in more deeply—as far as the trinitarian love of God."[24]

On the basis of this unity in salvation history, in the diachronic sense, we can discern that the "People of God" exists "not simply in their empirical setting"[25] in the sense of belonging to a nation.[26] The decisive thing, in Ratzinger's view, is not the nation, but rather membership on the basis of the promise: God creates his people through divine election, by looking universally "toward the many sons who will be given to Abraham".[27] For this reason, "right from the beginning, the promise to Abraham guarantees salvation history's inner continuity from the Patriarchs of Israel down to Christ and to the

---

[21] Cf. *Many Religions*, 68f. Ratzinger distinguishes between the promise to Abraham and the Sinai Covenant, since the latter applies strictly to the People of Israel and provides this People with a legal and liturgical order. The Mosaic Law is surpassed only by Christ. Ratzinger says here (70): "It is characteristic of the Messiah—he who is 'greater than Moses'— that he brings the definitive interpretation of the Torah, in which the Torah is itself renewed, because now its true essence appears in all its purity and its character as grace becomes undistorted reality.... In this Torah, which is Jesus himself, the abiding essence of what was inscribed on the stone tablets at Sinai is now written in living flesh, namely, the twofold command of love. This is set forth in Philippians 2:5 as 'the mind of Christ'. To imitate him, to follow him in discipleship, is therefore to keep the Torah, which has been fulfilled in him once and for all."

[22] Ibid., 57.

[23] Ibid., 65.

[24] Ratzinger, *Ministers of Your Joy: Scriptural Meditations on Priestly Spirituality* (Ann Arbor, Mich.: Servant Publications, 1989), 64f.; cf. *Church*, 18.

[25] *Principles*, 55. Ratzinger substantiates this by citing Norbert Lohfink, "Beobachtungen zur Geschichte des Ausdrucks 'Am Jahwe'", in *Probleme historischer Theologie: Gerhard von Rad zum 70. Geburtstag*, ed. Hans Walter Wolff, 275–305 (Munich: Kaiser, 1971).

[26] Cf. "Demokratisierung 1", 28.

[27] *Many Religions*, 68.

Church of Jews and Gentiles." [28] The making of the covenant with
Abraham mysteriously hints at how God makes good his promise in
Jesus Christ: through his love even to the Cross. Ratzinger emphasizes this steadfast loyalty of God with a quotation from Augustine:
"God is faithful, for he has put himself under a debt to us, not as
if he had received anything from us, but by promising us so much.
The word of promise was too little for him: he wanted to bind
himself in writing, by giving us, as it were, a handwritten version of
his promises." [29] In Jesus' death out of love for mankind, the covenant agreement with Abraham is fulfilled.[30] Furthermore, Ratzinger interprets the ritual of walking between the halves of the animals
that Abraham had sacrificed (Gen 15:17) as a divine pledge that
prefigures the Cross: "Let it be to me as to these animals if I break
the covenant. Abraham has a vision of a smoking oven and a blazing
torch—images of theophany—passing between the animal parts. God
seals the covenant by guaranteeing his faithfulness in an unmistakable
symbol of death." [31]

When God's pledge is made good in Jesus Christ, the testament is
transformed into the fulfillment of the promise, in that a holy exchange
is accomplished: The Divine Word becomes flesh, and we mortal men
receive his divine life.[32] In the self-immolation of Jesus on the Cross,
he vicariously "takes us up and leads us into that likeness with God,
that transformation into love, which is the only true adoration".[33] In
this manner, Ratzinger, along with John 2:19, sees Jesus Christ simultaneously as the new Temple and

the definitive sacrifice: the humanity of Christ opened up in his
Cross and Resurrection. The prayer of the man Jesus is now united
with the dialogue of eternal love within the Trinity. Jesus draws
men into this prayer through the Eucharist, which is thus the

[28] Ibid.
[29] Ibid., 72, with a reference to Augustine, *En in ps* 109, 1 CChr [CCL] 40:1601.
[30] Cf. *Spirit of the Liturgy*, 37f.
[31] *Many Religions*, 73. In keeping with Near Eastern customs, the covenant partners
walked between the two halves of the sacrificed animals as a sign of the curse that they
would call down upon themselves if they were ever to break the covenant.
[32] Cf. ibid., 74. Ratzinger's idea of a holy exchange is influenced by the liturgy: See the
preface for Christmas III.
[33] *Spirit of the Liturgy*, 47.

ever-open door of adoration and the true Sacrifice, the Sacrifice of
the New Covenant, the "reasonable service of God".[34]

Thus the accomplishment of this sacrifice in and through Jesus Christ
is a real and universal eschatological sign for the reality toward which
the pilgrim People of God has been journeying since the days of Abraham: toward the heavenly Jerusalem, to the universal Temple of the
risen Christ, "whose outstretched arms on the Cross span the world,
in order to draw all men into the embrace of eternal love".[35] One
consequence of this, in Ratzinger's view, is that Christian worship,
that is, the celebration of the Eucharist, must always be universal in its
sacrificial character.

Within the parameters of this dissertation, we cannot thoroughly
examine the causes that, according to Ratzinger, have led in modern
times to an abrupt division between the Old Testament theology of
sacrifice and the New Testament liturgy of prayer. Nevertheless, it
seems to me appropriate to consider this subject briefly, because ultimately in the aforementioned gap the inner unity of the Old and the
New Testament is at stake.

> In modern theological discussion, the exclusive model for the lit-
> urgy of the New Covenant has been thought to be the synagogue—in
> strict opposition to the Temple, which is regarded as an expression
> of the law and therefore as an utterly obsolete "stage" in religion.
> The effects of this theory have been disastrous. Priesthood and sac-
> rifice are no longer intelligible. The comprehensive "fulfillment" of
> pre-Christian salvation history and the inner unity of the two Tes-
> taments disappear from view. Deeper understanding of the matter is
> bound to recognize that the Temple, as well as the synagogue, entered
> into Christian liturgy.[36]

Universality, therefore, is a distinctive feature of Christian worship:
It unites the Old and the New Testament, the Church in heaven with
the earthly assembly of the People of God, the horizontal and the
vertical dimensions, "mankind's movement toward Christ" and "Christ's

---

[34] Ibid., 48–49.
[35] Ibid., 48.
[36] Ibid., 49; cf. *Many Religions*, 30f.

movement toward men".[37] In this way, Christ "wants to unite mankind and bring about the one Church, the one divine assembly, of all men".[38] Thereby worship itself becomes the eschatological sign of this universal alliance, which makes visible the "already" and the "not yet" of the pilgrim Church. For this reason, liturgy is, as Ratzinger explains,

> a liturgy of promise fulfilled, of a quest, the religious quest of human history, reaching its goal. But it remains a liturgy of hope. It, too, bears within it the mark of impermanence. The new Temple, not made by human hands, does exist, but it is also still under construction. The great gesture of embrace emanating from the Crucified has not yet reached its goal; it has only just begun. Christian liturgy is liturgy on the way, a liturgy of pilgrimage toward the transfiguration of the world, which will only take place when God is "all in all".[39]

In summary, we can state that Ratzinger is concerned above all with the inner continuity of salvation history through the one People of God. As a result of the sacrifice of Jesus Christ, which as an eschatological sign wishes to draw all mankind into Jesus' vicarious submission to love, Christian worship and the liturgy must be universal, too. For this reason, the sacrifice of the New Covenant and the prefigurations of the Old Covenant must not be set in opposition. Another consequence of this universality that God grants in the accomplishment of the one sacrifice of Jesus Christ is the eschatological character of the liturgy, which already presents today a sign of the eternal fulfillment.

In the next subsection, we will turn to this eschatological character of the pilgrim People of God, which awaits its fulfillment at the end of time.

3. The eschatological character of the pilgrim Church

This study cannot aim to give a comprehensive picture of the complexity of the term "eschatological" in Ratzinger's works.[40] Therefore, as

[37] *Spirit of the Liturgy*, 49.
[38] Ibid.
[39] Ibid., 50.
[40] On this subject, see Nachtwei's dissertation. See also J. Ratzinger, *Eschatology: Death and Eternal Life*, trans. Michael Waldstein (Washington, D.C.: Catholic Univ. of America Press, 1988; *Principles*, 171–90: "Salvation History, Metaphysics and Eschatology"; *Church*,

our examination thus far of the connection between Israel and the Church in salvation history has already suggested,[41] I would like to discuss the importance of this eschatological character from an ecclesiological perspective: Just as Israel's faith is oriented both backward, toward its faith history, and also forward, toward the hope of the coming Messiah, so too the existence of the Church, according to Ratzinger, is always "bipolar", that is, related to yesterday as well as to the future: "*referring back* to her foundational event in the Lord's death and Resurrection, and *forward looking* to his coming again, when he will make good his promise and transform the world into the new heaven and the new earth."[42]

Thus the eschatological view of the Church becomes a deeper theocentric or christocentric perspective, since Christ, as the origin, is at the same time the Lord who is to come. From this, Ratzinger concludes: "A Christ-centered Church is thus oriented not merely toward past salvific events; it will always also be a Church moving forward under the sign of hope. Its decisive future and its transformation are still ahead."[43] For the Church, eschatological hope and the expectation of the Second Coming of the Messiah are identical. In Ratzinger's view, this is especially evident in the Eucharist. As the fulfillment of the Church's nature and life, it is the sign of the dawning Parousia, "the fulfillment of the risen life that has already begun but is not yet perfected",[44] as Gerhard Nachtwei puts it in his study of Ratzinger's eschatology. In her worship, the Church celebrates the crucified and risen Lord, who as the Pierced One continually comes to

---

237–54: "Eschatology and Utopia". See Ratzinger, "Damit Gott alles in allem sei und alles Leid ein Ende habe", in *Kleines Credo für Verunsicherte*, ed. J. Hoeren and N. Kutschki, 121–40 (Freiburg im Breisgau: Herder, 1993). See also *Eucharist*, 130–48. Cf. also K.-J. E. Jeon, *Die Kirche bei Joseph Ratzinger: Untersuchungen zum strukturierten Volk Gottes nach der Kirchenlehre Joseph Ratzingers* (unpublished dissertation, Innsbruck, 1995), 79–83: "Die eschatologische Dynamik der Kirche", and 95–97: "Die eschatologische Phase der Heilsgeschichte".

[41] On this subject, see also *Many Religions*, 106. In terms of eschatological hope, it is true "that the figure of Christ both links and separates Israel and the Church. It is not within our power to overcome this separation, but it keeps both of us to the path that leads to the One who comes. To that extent, the relationship between us must not be one of enmity."

[42] *Volk Gottes*, 69.

[43] *Highlights*, 47.

[44] Nachtwei, 58.

meet her.[45] According to Ratzinger, every Eucharist is "Parousia, the coming of the Lord, and every Eucharist is even more so the suspense of yearning for the revelation of his hidden splendor".[46] In this way, Christ does not "allow history to fall into the non-being of what is past"[47] but rather holds it and leads it to its goal.

Many people, however, deny such an eschatological hope, because they give priority to an imaginable utopia.[48] Unlike Christian hope, this sort of expectation, in Ratzinger's judgment, is built, on the one hand, on a mythological notion of history, "which will necessarily result in the emergence of the just society in the end",[49] and, on the other hand, on the idea that man effects this change by his own power, "which has no need of a transcendent God".[50] In contrast, since her foundation the Church has testified to eschatological hope, which is "the inner criterion by which we live, the hope that supports us in the present".[51] Along with the Letter to the Hebrews (Heb 11:13–16), Ratzinger therefore describes the Christian faithful of all times as "strangers" who are journeying arduously toward their future homeland.[52] The apocalyptic images of Scripture, such as the holy city, the heavenly Jerusalem, the wedding, and the feast,[53] widen our sight to look for a "real entity", as Ratzinger calls it, "the new homeland to which we are traveling".[54] By way of

---

[45] Cf. ibid. and also *Song*, 128–46, citation at 129: "For this reason the real focal point is the *Majestas Domini*, the risen Lord lifted up on high, who is seen at the same time and above all as the one returning, the one already coming in the Eucharist. In the celebration of the liturgy the Church moves toward the Lord; liturgy is virtually this act of approaching his coming. In the liturgy the Lord is already anticipating his promised coming. Liturgy is anticipated Parousia."

[46] KKD 9:167.

[47] *Many Religions*, 106.

[48] On this subject see *Prüfsteine*, 91: In the modern period, eschatological considerations are avoided, because, as Ratzinger explains here, "they seem to alienate man and keep him away from his task in this world, which is also political. 'Brothers, remain true to the earth' was Nietzsche's cry at the beginning of this [twentieth] century, and the vast Marxist movement drove home the point that we have no time to lose on heaven. Bertolt Brecht thought that 'we should leave heaven to the sparrows.'"

[49] *Eucharist*, 142.

[50] Ibid.

[51] *Prüfsteine*, 90.

[52] Cf. *Prüfsteine*, 90f.

[53] On this subject, see *Dogma*, 301–21, esp. 304–10.

[54] *Prüfsteine*, 90. Cf. LG 13, 48. See also Phil 3:20.

analogy,[55] these metaphors speak of the reality[56] "Church" within the context of salvation history as the embodiment of what is already definitive and the prefiguration and promise of the future.[57]

This important eschatological aspect became part of the Church's consciousness again thanks mainly to *Lumen gentium*.[58] Even though many commentators paid little attention to it,[59] it is in Ratzinger's opinion a key to a correct understanding of the Church as the People of God, because the Church is regarded, not in her earthly state of imperfection, but rather in her perfected form.[60] What does Ratzinger see now as the distinguishing feature of the eschatological perspective of *Lumen gentium*? He offers a sort of quintessential description in his commentary on the Constitution on the Church:

> The ambiguous word "eschatological" means here that the Church is "already" the presence of the ultimate but is "not yet" the fullness thereof, which instead is still concealed within her under the veil of this temporal existence. It means to say that the Church lives on the finality of God's effective and irrevocable grace, which has appeared in Christ, but also that she is still marked by human sins and failings and thus again and again stands in the reflected light of judgment and mercy.[61]

Hence this aspect of "already and not yet" [62] is simultaneously an indication of the Church's need for renewal: Again and again she must set aside her excessive attachments to earthly things "and whatever leads to feelings of self-satisfaction".[63] Moreover, *Lumen gentium* testifies that

---

[55] Cf. *Dogma*, 304.

[56] See also *LG* 2, 4, 5, 6, 8, 9, 13, 48, 49.

[57] Cf. "Ecumenical Situation", 268: Understood correctly in the biblical sense, eschatology, according to Ratzinger, is "not *later* in a chronological sense, something that with the succession of days will sometime arrive in an indefinitely distant future and is just not here yet today. No, what is eschatological is what is genuinely real, which will at some time be revealed as such but already sets its mark upon all our days."

[58] Cf. chapter 7 of *LG*: "The Eschatological Character of the Pilgrim Church and Her Unity with the Church in Heaven".

[59] This is the assessment of the International Theological Commission. See their publication *Mysterium des Gottesvolkes*, 79.

[60] Cf. *LG* 48; *GS* 40.

[61] "Einleitung", 15f.

[62] *Principles*, 156. Cf. *LG* 9.

[63] *Highlights*, 47.

the Church does not represent "a rounded-off and finished reality". Instead, within the coordinates of space and time—as Ratzinger puts it—she is "continually journeying with and toward the God" who calls her in the midst of human history.[64] Besides this perspective of what is already definitive but not yet fully visible, the traditional preconciliar understanding of eschatology as the doctrine about the "Last Things" is, in Ratzinger's judgment, relevant to *Lumen gentium* as well and should not be overlooked.[65] The interpretation of the *eschaton* along the lines of heaven, hell, purgatory, and the Last Judgment was "uppermost in the minds"[66] of the majority of the Council Fathers rather than the aspect of the Parousia as something already begun but not yet perfected.[67] Nevertheless, we can discern both old and new linguistic usage interwoven in the treatment of the theme of eschatology.[68] Even when "eschatological" is used in the traditional sense of the term,[69]

we soon notice a unique meshing of the future and the present. For the future of the Church has already begun (to use a modern slogan) in this respect as well: In her saints she has already arrived at the destination of her pilgrimage, even though their beatitude lacks its ultimate fullness, as long as they still await the fulfillment of the Body of Christ in the resurrection of the dead. This reaching over into the world of those who are already at home, or, to put it another way, this unbroken and unbreakable communion of all the members of Christ's Body, is essential to the Church.[70]

Inasmuch as the Church's liturgy is oriented toward the eschatological unification of the People of God, the union of those who are still on pilgrimage with those who are already perfected attains in the liturgy "its supreme actualization".[71] For this reason, according to Ratzinger,

---

[64] Ibid., 46.
[65] See *LG* 49, 50, 51.
[66] "Einleitung", 16.
[67] Cf. Nachtwei, 58f.
[68] Examples can be found also in Ratzinger's *Eschatology*; cf. the German ed., KKD 9:193, among other passages.
[69] For Ratzinger, this connotation of eschatology is "no less primary and essential" than the "modern" connotation ("Einleitung", 16).
[70] Ibid., 16.
[71] Ibid., 17.

it is tantamount to "entering into the liturgy of the heavens that has always been taking place", that is, entering into the communion of saints.[72]

In the next subsection, we will take up a broader perspective on the People of God concept by pointing out its continuity with reference to Israel and the Church[73] in terms of the semantic meaning of the biblical root *qāhāl*.

§ 2. The Biblical Root *Qāhāl* and the Church's Description of Herself as Ἐκκλησια

1. Ἐκκλησια *as the assembly of the people*

As a rule, the New Testament does not apply to the nascent Church the expression "People of God", which in its pages refers most often to Israel,[74] but uses instead the Greek word εκκλησια, which means "called out".[75] Besides this, the primitive Christian community described itself with expressions like "the saints" or "the assembly of God".[76] The latter is derived from the Old Testament root *qāhāl*. This means "to gather" and thus refers to how the People came into being. Therefore, according to Ratzinger, the Greek word εκκλησια, too, "in its

---

[72] *Song*, 128–46, citation at 129.

[73] Cf. *LG* 2: "He planned to assemble in the holy Church all those who would believe in Christ. Already from the beginning of the world the foreshadowing of the Church took place. It was prepared in a remarkable way throughout the history of the people of Israel and by means of the Old Covenant. In the present era of time the Church was constituted and, by the outpouring of the Spirit, was made manifest. At the end of time . . . , all the just, from Adam . . . will be gathered together with the Father in the universal Church."

[74] In his dissertation on the People of God in Augustine's works, Ratzinger demonstrated that although this concept occurs frequently in the NT, as a rule it designates Israel. Probably in only two NT passages is this term applied to the Church directly as a synonym. The christological or else pneumatological transfer of the OT concept "People of God" to the Church is brought about by the *Concordia testamentorum*, which is the heart of patristic scriptural interpretation. See the foreword to the new edition of *Volk und Haus Gottes*, xiv. See also *Church*, 17f.

[75] *God and the World*, 63.

[76] See R. Schnackenburg, "Kirche. I. Die Kirche im NT", in *LThK*, 2nd ed., ed. J Höfer and K. Rahner, 6:169f.

technical sense",[77] should be interpreted analogously as a gathering of the people.

The Greek term that lives on in the Latin loanword *ecclesia* derives from the Old Testament root *qahal*, which is ordinarily translated by "assembly of the people". Such "popular assemblies", in which the people was constituted as a cultic and, on that basis, as a juridical and political entity, existed both in the Greek and the Semitic world.[78]

As applied to the Church, *ecclesia* is, in Ratzinger's view, first a concept from "the allegorical (spiritual) interpretation of the Old Testament".[79] Hence it can be used suitably only in a "spiritualizing acceptation that never renounces the reference to what went before".[80] "The word has a justifiable meaning at all only within the referential framework of a spiritual transposition of an Old Testament reality, therefore only in the relation between letter and spirit, [that is,] in the spiritualization of the letter."[81]

With reference to the Church, this means that the term "People", according to Ratzinger, can be understood properly only from its Old Testament context. In his definition of the conceptual content of *qāhāl*, he points out two remarkable differences from the *Greek* assembly of enfranchised citizens. First, in Israel, women and children belong to the assembly of the people, whereas among the Greeks they were not allowed to participate actively in the political process. A second, more substantial difference (because it is religious) consists, then, in the fact that "Israel gathers 'to listen to what God proclaims and to assent to it' ",[82] because for Israel the assembly at Sinai is the "normative image" for the assembly of the People of God,[83] whereas in Greece the citizens

---

[77] *God and the World*, 63.

[78] *Called to Communion*, 30.

[79] "Demokratisierung 1", 28.

[80] Ibid.

[81] Ibid., 28.

[82] *Called to Communion*, 31. In *Principles*, 55, Ratzinger points out that "even in the Old Testament, the designation 'people of God' referred to the people of Israel not simply in their empirical setting but only at the moment in which they were addressed by God and answered his call." In this regard, he cites Lohfink, "Beobachtungen", 275–305.

[83] Cf. *Called to Communion*, 31. The assembly at Sinai "was solemnly reenacted after the Exile by Ezra as the refoundation of the people. But because the dispersion of Israel continued on and slavery was reimposed, a *qahal* coming from God himself, a new gathering

rule themselves. As Ratzinger explains it, the first Christians, who understand themselves in terms of this Jewish heritage, regard their *ecclesia*, their assembly, as the answer to Israel's prayers for the gathering of the People of God at the end of time, so that they can simultaneously say: "This petition is granted in us. Christ, who died and rose again, is the living Sinai; those who approach him are the chosen final gathering of God's people (cf., for example, Heb 12:18–24)." [84]

Thus Jesus Christ is the perpetual and unifying center for the Church from the very beginning. When we consider this intended message, Ratzinger says, it becomes clear why the general expression "People of God" did not come to be used in the New Testament as a title for the assembly of Christians, but *ecclesia* instead, a term for the action that God takes in Jesus Christ, the new Sinai—Christ, who stands for "the spiritual and eschatological center of the concept of 'people' ".[85]

2. *Jesus Christ as the sacramental center of the People of God*

Just as Israel was first elected to be God's people through listening to God's word, so too the new People of God is called together as εκκλησια through hearing Christ, the Son of God and the Son of Abraham, and is formed by his proclamation of the kingdom of God,[86] that is, by being gathered and cleansed in a "Christological process of transformation".[87] Viewed externally, the men whom God calls to communion with himself are a heterogeneous mass of humanity, or, as Ratzinger puts it, a "nonpeople".[88] In light of the crucified and risen Lord, however, they form an intrinsic unity in Christ that transcends all boundaries and differences:[89]

---

and foundation of the people, increasingly became the center of Jewish hope. The supplication for this gathering ... is a fixed component of late Jewish prayer" (ibid.).

[84] Ibid. See also *Many Religions*, 70: "The Torah of the Messiah is the Messiah, Jesus, himself." Ratzinger adopts this idea from H. Schlier, *Der Brief an die Galater* (Göttingen: Vandenhoeck & Ruprecht, 1962), 273.

[85] *Called to Communion*, 32.

[86] Cf. "Demokratisierung I", 28.

[87] *Church*, 18.

[88] *Principles*, 55.

[89] Cf. *Many Religions*, 33: "The unity between the good news of Jesus and the message of Sinai".

This nonpeople can become a people only through him who unites them from above and from within: through communion with Christ. Without this christological meditation it would be presumptuous, if not actually blasphemous, for the Church to designate herself the "people of God". One of the most crucial tasks in the study of the conciliar legacy today, then, will be to reveal anew the sacramental character of the Church and, in so doing, to call attention once again to what this really means: that union with God which is the condition of man's unity and freedom.[90]

A People of God concept devoid of this sacramental center would be, in Ratzinger's view, only a caricature of the ecclesiology presented in *Lumen gentium*.[91] Only five years after the Council, therefore, he was calling on theologians to let such a flattened, unbiblical concept of the People of God "vanish again from the debate as soon as possible".[92] Christology must remain the center of ecclesiology, so that the latter will not be misinterpreted sociologically. Specifically this means that the Church must be understood in terms of "the sacraments of baptism, the eucharist and holy orders"[93] and be seen in a living sacramental union with Christ. As Ratzinger discerns the authentic intention of the Council Fathers, they wanted to define the People of God always in terms of the Body of Christ and the Word of God, thus articulating the *differentia specifica*[94] of the new People of God.

> The Council very brilliantly made this connection clear when along with the term "people of God" it brought into prominence another fundamental term for the Church: the Church as sacrament. One only remains faithful to the Council if one always takes and reflects on these two core terms of its ecclesiology together, sacrament and people of God.[95]

Rediscovering Jesus Christ—who gathers his people around himself as εκκλησια through their listening to his Word and their celebration of the Eucharist—as the spiritual center of the concept "Church" was,

---

[90] *Principles*, 55. See also *Church*, 19.
[91] Cf. *Principles*, 54f.
[92] "Demokratisierung 1", 29.
[93] *Church*, 19.
[94] "Wesen", 59.
[95] *Church*, 19.

in Ratzinger's view, the chief concern of *Lumen gentium*. Accordingly, the term εϰϰλησια has a fourfold meaning that expands concentrically: the worshipping assembly, the local community, the Church "in a larger geographical area",[96] and the one Church of Jesus Christ himself. Moreover "there is a continuous transition from one meaning to another, because all of them hang on the christological center that is made concrete in the gathering of believers for the Lord's Supper."[97]

Together with Ratzinger, we wish to turn now to Jesus Christ as the origin of the Church. We will do so by making two points, the first of which discusses the proclamation of the kingdom of God. Ratzinger understands this as the eschatological sign of gathering and purifying the People of God in the end times, the sign through which the Church began. Afterward, in the second point, I will examine the patriarch theme as an Old Testament type of Jesus Christ, the founder of the new People of God.

§ 3. Jesus Christ as the Origin and Goal of the Church

1. *Proclamation of the kingdom of God as eschatological gathering and cleansing*

The point of departure for Ratzinger's comments on the origin of the Church is the realization that "what Jesus' message immediately announced was not the Church but the kingdom of God (or 'the Kingdom of the Heavens')."[98] Of course, he does not understand the latter in the same sense as in Alfred Loisy's *bon mot*: "Jesus proclaimed the kingdom; what came was the Church."[99]

---

[96] *Called to Communion*, 32.

[97] Ibid.

[98] Ibid., 21.

[99] A. Loisy, *L'Évangile et l'Église* (Paris: Fishbacher, 1902). See also *tztD5/II*, 134–36, citation at 135. This well-known saying of Loisy's was first applied in a Catholic sense in 1929 by E. Peterson. Ratzinger comments in a footnote: "I myself probably contributed to its spread by treating it in my [lectures] and by adopting it from Peterson and Schlier, though in a substantially modified form, in my article 'Kirche' in *LThK*. Unfortunately, these alterations have been wiped away in the process of popularization; the maxim was lined with an interpretation that found no support even in Loisy's original meaning" (*Called to Communion*, 21).

A historical reading of the texts reveals that the opposition of Kingdom and Church has no factual basis. For, according to the Jewish
interpretation, the gathering and cleansing of men for the Kingdom
of God is part of this Kingdom. "Jesus' very belief that the end was
near would have made him desire to gather the eschatological people of God" [citing Jeremias, *Neutestamentliche Theologie* (Gütersloh,
1971), 1:167].[100]

The proclamation of the kingdom of God, therefore, is "never merely
a verbal event";[101] rather, "the *sole* meaning of the entire activity of
Jesus is the gathering of the eschatological people of God."[102] This is
the theme also of the New Testament parables about growth, in which
"the 'soon' of the imminent eschatology characteristic of John the
Baptist and Qumran passes over with Jesus into the 'now' of Christology."[103] Therefore, "in Jesus' mouth, 'Kingdom of God' does not
mean some thing or place but the present action of God." Jesus himself "is God's nearness. Wherever he is, is the Kingdom." Accordingly,
Ratzinger recasts Loisy's statement to read: "The Kingdom was promised, what came was Jesus", and, indeed, he came "in order to gather
together what was dispersed (cf. Jn 11:52; Mt 12:30)."

From the foregoing discussion, Ratzinger derives two elements that
are essential for an understanding of Church:

First, the dynamism of unification, in which men draw together
by moving toward God, is a component of the new people of God
as Jesus intends it. Second, the point of convergence of this new

---

[100] Ibid., 21–22. See also *God and the World*, 344, where Ratzinger reflects that anyone who thinks that Jesus "was only intent on the kingdom of God, or he intended something else, in any case, not the Church", fails to recognize not only that "Jesus stands within the salvation history of the Jewish people, but also his intention to renew this people ... as a whole, to make it broader and more profound—and thereby to create what we call the Church."

[101] "Demokratisierung 1", 28. On this subject, see *LG* 3: "The Church, or, in other words, the kingdom of Christ now present in mystery"; *LG* 5: "The mystery of the holy Church is manifest in its very foundation. The Lord Jesus set it on its course by preaching the Good News, that is, the coming of the Kingdom of God, which, for centuries, had been promised in the Scriptures: 'The time is fulfilled, and the kingdom of God is at hand' (Mk 1:15; Mt 4:17). In the word, in the works, and in the presence of Christ, this king-dom was clearly open to the view of men."

[102] *Called to Communion*, 22, citing J. Jeremias, *Neutestamentliche Theologie*, vol. 1 (Güter-sloh: Gütersloher Verlagshaus G. Mohn, 1971), 167.

[103] This and the following quotations are found in *Called to Communion*, 22–23.

people is Christ; it becomes a people solely through his call and its response to his call and to his person.[104]

As a process of unifying sinners, this gathering is inseparably connected with purification. Ratzinger understands purification to mean true reform in the sense of *ablatio*, "the removal of what is not really part of the [image]",[105] a process that, as such, results in *congregatio*, that is, gathering:

> Reform is ever-renewed *ablatio*—removal, whose purpose is to allow the *nobilis forma*, ... the living Lord, to appear. Such *ablatio*, such "negative theology", is a path to something wholly positive. This path alone allows the divine to penetrate and brings about "*congregatio*", which as both gathering and purification is that pure communion we all long for.[106]

In this way, the proclamation of the kingdom of God creates "a communion of converted sinners who live by the grace of forgiveness and transmit it themselves".[107] For this reason, in Ratzinger's view, the forgiveness of sins in every case is "an active-passive event":[108] God's living Word "produces the pain of conversion and thus becomes an active self-transformation".[109] Given the importance that forgiveness has for the gathering of the People of God, Ratzinger considers it no accident that "in the three decisive stages of the birth of the Church that the Gospels recount to us",[110] *ablatio*, the forgiveness of sins, is central:

> The first episode is the consignment of the keys to Peter. The bestowal of the power to bind and to loose, to open and to shut, which the Gospel speaks of here is in its core an authority to let in, to bring home, to forgive (Mt 16:19). We find the same reality again at the

---

[104] Ibid., 23.

[105] Ibid., 141.

[106] Ibid., 142. Ratzinger mentions that Chiara Lubich, the foundress of the Focolare movement, presented very similar ideas in a talk entitled "L'arte del levare". See ibid., 141, n. 4.

[107] *Called to Communion*, 149.

[108] Ibid.

[109] Ibid. Cf. Ratzinger and J.B. Metz, "God, Sin, and Suffering: A Conversation", in Peters/Urban, 47–53, ref. at 51. Ratzinger remarks: "Shrinking from recognizing God [himself] as active has led to this overburdening of [man]. ... This is why it seems so important to me to hear once again that God [himself] addresses us and says, 'Your sins are forgiven.' "

[110] *Called to Communion*, 148.

Last Supper, which inaugurates the new communion from and in the Body of Christ. This communion is made possible by the Lord's shedding his blood "for many for the forgiveness of sins" (Mt 26:28). Finally, the risen Lord establishes the communion of his peace when he first appears to the Eleven. He does so by giving them full authority to forgive (Jn 20:19–23)."[111]

The proclamation of the kingdom of God as the gathering and purification of the People of God refers us to the holiness granted by God, to which all are called. For this reason, the expressions "kingdom of God" and "People of God", according to Ratzinger, are closely connected with the "divine activity of election".[112] If the *ecclesia*, the New Testament People of God, is understood as "the continuation of Israel", then the reason for it is that Christ, as the "Torah", the living Word of God, has become the patriarch of this people, and all of them, "by their descent from Christ … also become children of Abraham."[113]

2. Jesus Christ as the patriarch of the new People of God

Once again in the discussion thus far we have been able, with Ratzinger, to establish the continuity between Israel and the Church. For him, this unity between the Old and the New Covenant, which is founded in Scripture, is an important key and criterion for an understanding of divine activity in human history.[114] Accordingly, Ratzinger comprehends the reestablishment of the eschatological people of twelve tribes[115] as God's definitive salvific act.

---

[111] Ibid., 148–49.

[112] "Demokratisierung 1", 28.

[113] *Salt of the Earth*, 187.

[114] See *In the Beginning*, 9–10: "For the Christian the Old Testament represents, in its totality, an advance toward Christ; only when it attains to him does its real meaning, which was gradually hinted at, become clear. Thus every individual part derives its meaning from the whole, and the whole derives its meaning from its end—from Christ. Hence we only interpret an individual text theologically correctly (as the [F]athers of the [C]hurch recognized and as the faith of the [C]hurch in every age has recognized) when we see it as a way that is leading us ever forward, when we see in the text where this way is tending and what its inner direction is."

[115] Cf. J. Meyer zu Schlochtern, *Sakrament Kirche: Wirken Gottes im Handeln der Menschen* (Freiburg im Breisgau: Herder, 1992), 153–90, ref. at 156.

I will now examine this insight from three perspectives. First, I will discuss the communal character of the People of God, based on the image of the family of God. Second, we will turn our attention to the symbolism of the number twelve: In the calling of the Twelve, the New Testament People of God acquires a dimension in salvation history that encompasses all times. Furthermore, Ratzinger discerns in the number twelve the criterion of "the cosmic", which is a distinctive feature of his ecclesiology.[116] Finally, I will look at the Old Covenant theme of the patriarch, which finds its fulfillment in Jesus Christ as the patriarch of the new People of God.

a. "The family of God" as a favorite image of Jesus

Among the images that are used in the New Testament to describe the new People of God, such as the flock, wedding guests, a cultivated field, the building of God, and the city of God,[117] we find what Ratzinger calls Jesus' "favorite" image,[118] the family of God.

> God is the father of the family, Jesus the master of the house, and it therefore stands to reason that he addresses the members of this people as children, even though they are adults, and that to gain true understanding of themselves, those who belong to this people must first lay down their grown-up autonomy and acknowledge themselves as children before God (cf. Mk 10:24; Mt 11:25).[119]

For Ratzinger, family, Church, and kingdom of God are intimately interrelated. He sees the Church as the locus of a sort of extended

---

[116] Cf. *Church*, 13: "In this context people were aware that twelve was also a cosmic number, the number of the signs of the zodiac which together made up the year, mankind's time scale. This emphasized the unity of history and the cosmos, the cosmic character of the history of salvation: the twelve were to be the new signs of the zodiac of the final and definitive history of the universe." See also KKD 9:166f. Ratzinger suggests here that the cosmic imagery of the New Testament should be understood, not as "a cosmic depiction of the course of future events", but rather as a "representation of the Parousia mystery in the language of liturgical tradition. . . . The New Testament conceals and reveals what is humanly ineffable about Christ's [Second] Coming by speaking about it with words from that domain [that is, the liturgy] which in this world is privileged to express the place of contact with God."

[117] Cf. *LG* 5 and 6.

[118] *Called to Communion*, 23. See *LG* 6.

[119] *Called to Communion*, 23–24.

family, "which over the centuries does not lose its identity and sinks its roots into the ground of eternal truth itself".[120] Jesus likes to speak in terms of this familial image when he talks about his Father and describes his disciples as brothers. In Ratzinger's view, the group of Jesus' disciples is not an "amorphous mob"[121] but rather has a definite structure, which Jesus himself established in the circle of the Twelve. A sign of this is the new order of prayer that Jesus gives to his disciples, as manifested, for instance, in the Our Father. It becomes a distinctive characteristic of this community, in which the disciples demonstrate, as primordial cells, so to speak, "that the Church is a communion united principally on the basis of prayer".[122] Their order of prayer, which grew out of Israel's temple worship, is transformed by Jesus himself, especially in the understanding of his Passover as a covenant event,[123] into "an entirely new worship, which logically meant a break with the temple community".[124]

In the following point we focus first on the new community of the Twelve, which is a typological reference to the old twelve tribes of Israel.[125]

b. Jesus "appointed twelve" (Mk 3:14)

Out of the complex set of questions concerning Jesus' founding of the Church, Ratzinger selects—as he himself puts it—one small segment, "which marks the core of Jesus' idea of the Church".[126] Here the Marcan verse "He appointed twelve" (Mk 3:13), which is also taken

---

[120] Ratzinger, "Lasst das Netz nicht zerreißen: Ein Wort an die Familien", New Year's Eve homily 1980 (Munich: Pressereferat der Erzdiözese München-Freising, 1981), no pagination.

[121] Called to Communion, 24.

[122] Ibid. Cf. Song, 162ff.: "Let Yourself Be Built into a Spiritual House: Formation into the Family of God". On this subject, see also Song, 78ff.

[123] Cf. Called to Communion, 26f.

[124] Ibid., 26.

[125] See LG 2: "He planned to assemble in the holy Church all those who would believe in Christ. Already from the beginning of the world the foreshadowing of the Church took place. It was prepared in a remarkable way throughout the history of the people of Israel and by means of the Old Covenant." See also LG 6: "The Church, further, 'that Jerusalem which is above' is also called 'our mother'". See also Many Religions, 47–77: "The New Covenant: On the Theology of the Covenant in the New Testament".

[126] Volk Gottes, 11.

up in *Lumen gentium* 19 with the words "duodecim constituit",[127] plays an important role:

> Jesus intended to be more than the propagandist for a new morality;
> ... he wanted, instead, to found a new religious *community*, a new "peo-
> ple", and he declared this by means of a simple gesture, which Mark
> formulated as follows: "And he ... called to him those whom he desired
> ... and he appointed twelve ..." (Mk 3:13f.). Long before the title
> "apostle" existed ... there was the community of the "Twelve", whose
> name and nature it was, precisely, to be "the Twelve". How seriously
> this number twelve was taken became evident after Judas' betrayal. The
> apostles (under the direction of Peter) saw it as their first duty to restore
> their group to the number twelve (Acts 1:15–26). Indeed, this num-
> ber was anything but arbitrary or random.[128]

Furthermore, "none of the [Twelve] had significance by himself, but only when united with the eleven others, because only with them was he part of the intended symbolic gesture."[129] For this reason, Ratzinger derives from the number twelve that collegial principle which was a constitutive element of the new People of God from the very beginning. At the same time, the restoration of the perfect number "twelve" symbolized for Israel the dawning of the eschatological time of salvation. When Jesus chose this sign, this signal was comprehensible to everyone, as Ratzinger observes. Jesus himself is thereby understood to be the new Jacob/Israel, the patriarch of the new people consisting of twelve tribes, that is, the founder of the new Israel.

c. Jesus as patriarch of the new Israel

In order to shed more light on the question about the patriarchy,[130] we must look with Ratzinger once more to the Old Testament. If

---

[127] See *LG* 19: "The Lord Jesus, after praying to the Father, calling to Himself those whom He desired, appointed twelve (*duodecim constituit*)."

[128] *Volk Gottes*, 11.

[129] *Highlights*, 50. See further on in this work, pt. 2, sec. 2, chap. 3, § 3.1.a, "The 'Collegiality' of the Apostles".

[130] Cf. *LG* 9: "For those who believe in Christ, who are reborn not from a perishable but from an imperishable seed through the word of the living God [cf. 1 Pet 1:23], not from the flesh but from water and the Holy Spirit [cf. Jn 3:5–6], are finally established as 'a chosen race, a royal priesthood, a holy nation ... who in times past were not a people, but are now the people of God' [1 Pet 2:9–10]."

Jesus makes himself the patriarch of a new Israel by calling the Twelve, then there is a problem: how to resolve the question of fleshly descent, which in Judaism is decisive. Ratzinger answers: The Twelve become Jesus' progeny by "being with" him.[131] More particularly, this means that Jesus replaces the criterion of physical descent with election to membership in the group of Twelve. The latter involves a twofold duty for those who are called: Jesus wants them to be with him, so that he might send them.[132] Presupposing this symbolic character, "everything that Jesus does in the group of Twelve is always part of founding the Church as well, inasmuch as everything was arranged so as to enable them to become spiritual fathers of the new People of God."[133] Moreover, in Jesus' description of himself as the "Son of Man"—Ratzinger says—there are likewise overtones of the "theme of founding a Church", since this title is "a symbolic word for the People of God in the end times, due to its origin in Daniel 7".[134]

Besides these, there are other central points in the New Testament in which Jesus' "intention to establish a Church is clearly concentrated".[135] Among them, Ratzinger numbers the conferral of the power to bind and loose upon Peter (Mt 16:18f. and Jn 21:15–17) and to the apostles (Mt 18:18), the mission of the Seventy or the Seventy-two (Lk 10:1ff.),[136] and especially the Paschal meal of the New Covenant

---

[131] *Called to Communion*, 25.
[132] Cf. ibid. and Mk 3:14.
[133] *Volk Gottes*, 12.
[134] Ibid. Compare Daniel's vision of the four living creatures and the Son of Man in Daniel 7, esp. Daniel 7:13–14: "I saw in the night visions, and behold, with the clouds of heaven there came one like a son of man, and he came to the Ancient of Days and was presented before him. And to him was given dominion and glory and kingdom, that all peoples, nations, and languages should serve him; his dominion is an everlasting dominion, which shall not pass away, and his kingdom one that shall not be destroyed." Cf. also Rev 1:13; 2:26; 14:14.
[135] *Volk Gottes*, 12.
[136] See *Called to Communion*, 25–26: "The group of seventy, or seventy-two, of which Luke speaks supplements this symbolism; seventy (seventy-two) was, according to Jewish tradition (Gen 10; Ex 1:5; Dt 32:8), the number of the non-Jewish peoples of the world. The ascription of the Greek Old Testament produced in Alexandria to seventy (or seventy-two) translators was meant to express that, with the appearance of this Greek text, the sacred book of Israel had become the Bible of all the nations.... The seventy disciples signify the claim of Jesus on the whole of humanity, which is destined to become the great band of his followers; these seventy are an allusion to the fact that the new Israel will embrace all the peoples of the earth."

"as the real act of founding the Church".[137] The previous call of the Twelve and the singling out of Peter, though, "are not abolished in the Last Supper, but rather presupposed", and both acts acquire their full meaning only as a result of the Last Supper.[138] Within this celebration, Jesus reveals himself to the Twelve (Mk 14:17, 19) as the Mediator of a new and everlasting covenant:

> And as they were eating, he took bread, and blessed, and broke it, and gave it to them, and said, "Take; this is my body." And he took a chalice, and when he had given thanks he gave it to them, and they all drank of it. And he said to them, "This is my blood of the covenant, which is poured out for many. Truly, I say to you, I shall not drink again of the fruit of the vine until that day when I drink it new in the kingdom of God."[139]

This action of Jesus at the Last Supper is—as Ratzinger puts it— "something new" that is woven into the context of the Jewish Passover celebration, "but it is clearly recognizable as an independent entity."[140] At the same time, this distinctive act is meant to be repeated,[141] "which implies that it was separable from the immediate context in which it took place".[142]

Along with Ratzinger, we recognize at the same time this emerging action of Jesus as the eschatological fulfillment of the prototype based in the Old Testament. As the patriarch of the new People of God, Jesus calls the Church, which he establishes on the foundation of the group of Twelve, to proclaim the gospel of the kingdom of God to all men symbolically. The Church, as *Ecclesia ab Abel*,[143] was destined for this from all eternity. In this salvation-history perspective, Ratzinger even speaks about a preexistence of the Church,[144] which reaches even farther back, in that her foundations were laid even before creation. Based on this

---

[137] *Volk Gottes*, 12.
[138] Ibid. Cf. *LG* 26.
[139] Mk 14:22–25. Compare the parallel passage Mt 26:26–29.
[140] *Feast of Faith*, 40.
[141] Cf. Lk 22:19; 1 Cor 11:24f.
[142] *Feast of Faith*, 40.
[143] Cf. *LG* 2: "When ... all the just, from Adam and 'from Abel, the just one, to the last of the elect,' will be gathered together with the Father in the universal Church." See also *Volk und Haus Gottes*, 296.
[144] See "Gottesidee", 46.

approach, he infers, in keeping with patristic theology,[145] "the ontological priority of the universal Church, of the one Church and the one
Body, the one Bride, with respect to her concrete empirical realizations
in the particular Churches, considered individually".[146]

This theme has an important place in Ratzinger's contributions to
the present-day ecclesiological debate about a hermeneutic that is faithful to the Council, and therefore we will discuss it in the next subsection from three points of view. First, we will explicitly discuss the
totality of the Church that existed from the very beginning. Overlooking this, Ratzinger says, leads to a progressively more horizontal
understanding of ecclesiology. Conversely, Ratzinger's critics see in
this totality or fullness a means of establishing a Roman centralism. In
a second step, we will have to demonstrate that creation was intrinsically predestined for the Church. Ratzinger supports this thesis with
the idea of the preexistence of the Torah and of Israel and reflects
even more profoundly on it in christological terms. Thirdly and finally,
we will look at the ontological priority of the universal Church with
respect to her concrete realizations and, with Ratzinger, find the beginnings of this concept in the New Testament and the rationale for it in
Lumen gentium, whereby once again the question of an appropriate
interpretation of the Council is raised.

As a way of broaching the issue, we choose the letter written by the
Congregation for the Doctrine of the Faith *On Some Aspects of the
Church Understood as Communion*,[147] which plays an important role in
the contemporary debate about the ontological priority of the universal Church.

§ 4. The Ontological Priority of the Universal Church

Ever since the Extraordinary Synod of Bishops in 1985, which was
convoked by Pope John Paul II on the twentieth anniversary of the

---

[145] On this subject, see "Ecclesiology", 134. Cf. *Volk und Haus Gottes*, 296–301: "The
Two Testaments—The Supratemporal Character of the Church".

[146] "Gottesidee", 46.

[147] Congregation for the Doctrine of the Faith, *Letter to the Bishops of the Catholic Church
on Some Aspects of the Church Understood as Communion*, dated May 28, 1992. [At Vatican
website.]

conclusion of the Council,[148] the concept of *communio* has been the focus of interest in interpreting and implementing the Council and even threatens, as Hermann Josef Pottmeyer declares, to displace the key concept of "the People of God".[149] The years since 1985, however, have shown that the *communio* concept, too, can be associated with notions that, in the judgment of the Congregation for the Faith, tend to give too much importance to the particular Churches. Therefore, in 1992 they wrote a *Letter to the Bishops of the Catholic Church on Some Aspects of the Church Understood as Communion* criticizing that tendency.[150]

A treatment of the letter of the Congregation for the Faith in its entirety would go far beyond the parameters of this dissertation. Particularly informative for our purposes is article 9 of *Some Aspects of the Church Understood as Communion*, which should be regarded as a reference work on account of its significance in Ratzinger's current explanation of the controversial theme "the ontological priority of the universal Church". There it says:

> In order to grasp the true meaning of the analogical application of the term *communion* to the particular Churches taken as a whole, one must bear in mind above all that the particular Churches, insofar as they are "part of the one Church of Christ", have a special relationship of "mutual interiority" with the whole, that is, with the universal Church, because in every particular Church "the one, holy, catholic and apostolic Church of Christ is truly present and

---

[148] Cf. the German edition of the documents of the 1985 Extraordinary Synod of Bishops, *Zukunft aus der Kraft des Konzils: Die außerordentliche Bischofssynode '85*, with a commentary by Walter Kasper (Freiburg im Breisgau: Herder, 1986).

[149] Cf. H.J. Pottmeyer, "Kirche als Communio: Eine Reformidee aus unterschiedlichen Perspektiven", *StZ* 117 (1992): 579–89, ref. at 579. See also Congregation for the Doctrine of the Faith, *Some Aspects of the Church Understood as Communion*, art. 1. The document calls, on the one hand, for an appropriate integration of "the concept of *communion* with the concepts of *People of God* and of the *Body of Christ*" and, on the other hand, for due consideration of the intrinsic "relationship between Church as *communion* and Church as *sacrament*".

[150] Cf. Congregation for the Doctrine of the Faith, *Some Aspects of the Church Understood as Communion*, art. 8: "Sometimes, however, the idea of a 'communion of particular Churches' is presented in such a way as to weaken the concept of the unity of the Church at the visible and institutional level. Thus it is asserted that every particular Church is a subject complete in itself, and that the universal Church is the result of a *reciprocal recognition* on the part of the particular Churches."

active". For this reason, "the universal Church cannot be conceived as the sum of the particular Churches, or as a federation of particular Churches". It is not the result of the communion of the Churches, but, in its essential mystery, it is a reality *ontologically* and *temporally* prior to every individual particular Church.[151]

If you were to ask why the Congregation for the Faith and its prefect insist on this ontological priority, the answer given by Ratzinger would be: in order to acknowledge the mystery of the Church which comes from God and so as to center the concept of Church on God again, given the danger of an increasingly more horizontal view.[152]

1. *Universal Church, not sum of Churches*

In 1970, only five years after the Council, Ratzinger notes a change in the concept of Church due to a one-sided concept of the community or parish,[153] which in his judgment results from the fact that "community" was becoming detached from its essential moorings in the universal Church. In such a view, the universal Church was seen only as "a subsequent addition or an umbrella organization".[154] He expressed very similar concerns in the year 2000 in his essay "On the Ecclesiology of *Lumen gentium*", in which he refers in particular to the above-cited letter of the Congregation for the Faith, *Some Aspects of the Church Understood as Communion*:

> In the same measure as "communion" became the current buzzword, its meaning was distorted and rendered superficial. . . . "Communion" ecclesiology began to be reduced to the theme of the relationship between the local Church and the Church as a whole, and that in turn, more and more, declined into the question of the assignment of competent authority as between the one and the other. The theme of egalitarianism of course also once more took a large

---

[151] Ibid., art. 9.

[152] Cf. "Gottesidee", 46.

[153] It should be noted that in the postconciliar discussions, the terms "community" or "parish", "local Church", and "particular Church" are not always clearly defined but often are used synonymously.

[154] "Demokratisierung 1", 40.

place, and according to that there could only be perfect equality in "communion".[155]

In such a view of *communio*, which Ratzinger generally assumes to have been the ecclesiological trend since 1985, one can in fact no longer find anything of the *sacramentally* based, mutual interpenetration of particular Churches (*ecclesiae particulares*) and universal Church that *Lumen gentium* itself affirms when it speaks about the *collegial* association and unity of the particular Churches:

> This collegial union is apparent also in the mutual relations of the individual bishops with particular Churches and with the universal Church. The Roman Pontiff, as the successor of Peter, is the perpetual and visible principle and foundation of unity of both the bishops and of the faithful. The individual bishops, however, are the visible principle and foundation of unity in their particular Churches, fashioned after the model of the universal Church, in and from which Churches comes into being the one and only Catholic Church. For this reason the individual bishops represent each his own Church, but all of them together and with the pope represent the entire Church in the bond of peace, love and unity.[156]

A second passage in *Lumen gentium* likewise shows the interpenetration of local Churches and universal Church, in this case especially from the perspective of the Eucharist, which is bound up with the sacrament of orders: "This Church of Christ is really present in all legitimate local congregations of the faithful (*in congregationibus localibus*), which, united with their pastors, are themselves called Churches in the New Testament."[157]

From these two passages of *Lumen gentium*, we can determine that the interpenetration of local Church and universal Church is always seen by the Council in the context of Eucharist, the sacramental unity of the Church, and the collegiality of the bishops with one another, including the Petrine office. If this sacramental foundation is no longer acknowledged, the result is the "progressively more horizontal

---

[155] "Ecclesiology", 132.

[156] *LG* 23.

[157] *LG* 26; cf. K. Rahner, "Kommentar zu *LG* Kap. 3, Artikel 18 bis 27", in *LThK.E*, vol. 1 (Freiburg im Breisgau: Herder, 1966), 243f. Karl Rahner points out that this approach is especially important for ecumenism as well.

understanding"[158] of the People of God concept. This trend will be described in more detail as a first step in the next few pages. This will be followed by a second discussion devoted to the critiques of the Magisterium's reply. Here we will examine in particular the "centralistic-universalistic tendencies"[159] that are said to be found in the letter *Some Aspects of the Church Understood as Communion*, the objection being that the relation between universal Church and local Churches is no longer interpreted as a relationship of "reciprocal interiority or of mutual interpenetration"[160] but rather falls back into a "relationship of superiority and subordination"[161] when the universal Church is construed as having an ontological priority over the local Churches. Furthermore, of particular interest to us is the question of how Ratzinger as a theologian grapples with the accusation of Roman centralism, especially since as prefect of the Congregation for the Doctrine of the Faith he is [in 2003] one of those responsible for the situation.

a. On the danger of an increasingly horizontal understanding

What the Church is by her nature cannot be recognized from a purely sociological perspective, for ecclesiology has to transcend itself so as to address the decisive question about God. Therefore the real reason for the increasingly horizontal understanding of the "People of God" lies in the "omission of the concept of God",[162] which Ratzinger deliberately placed at the center of ecclesiology[163] as early as 1972 in the foreword to the monograph entitled *Die Frage nach Gott* in the series entitled Quaestiones desputatae: "Who is the God from whom the 'People of God' gets its name? What does it mean when men are 'People of God'? By whom are they then defined? Does this word and hence this people have any meaning at all?"[164]

---

[158] "Gottesidee", 46.
[159] Cf. Kasper, "Theologie", 34. See also M. Kehl, *Wohin geht die Kirche? Eine Zeitdiagnose* (Freiburg im Breisgau: Herder, 1996), 80–98.
[160] Pottmeyer, "Kirche als Communion", 579–89, citation at 583.
[161] Ibid.
[162] "Gottesidee", 46.
[163] See the parallels in "Ecclesiology", 124–26.
[164] Ratzinger, "Einleitung", in *Die Frage nach Gott*, ed. Ratzinger, 5–8, citation at 6, QD 56 (Freiburg im Breisgau: Herder, 1972).

According to Ratzinger, the People of God preserves its essential character only when it expresses the *communio* with God and thereby the *communio* among its members also. The point of departure for this unity is the encounter with Jesus Christ. Theories that render ecclesiology horizontal, that replace the question about God with the "primacy of politics",[165] as happened to some extent in the liberation theologies, leave God with "nothing to do"[166] and consequently reduce the relation between local Churches and the universal Church to the sociological level. It then becomes a question of organization in the sense of merely allotting competencies.[167] Similar consequences for ecclesiology result nowadays from the various forms in which the divinity of Jesus Christ is relativized.[168]

In his critique of the trends that horizontalize the faith and the Church, Ratzinger suggests that they are rooted above all in the religious subjectivism of the postmodern period. To counteract them, he advocates "the 'I' of the Creed",[169] that is, the diachronic faith of the Church. In this respect, the axiom holds: The content of the Church's faith is not herself, but rather "the Word that becomes flesh and calls men to itself".[170] According to Ratzinger, "the whole message of the gospel and the Lord in his totality are present" in the legitimate local Christian communities that have been called together by the Lord, and therefore "the fullness of Church is

---

[165] *Introduction*, 15.

[166] Ibid., 16.

[167] "Gottesidee", 46.

[168] We cannot examine here in greater detail the crisis of Christology, although it has ecclesiological importance. It would require an extensive analysis of its own. The introductory essay by Ratzinger for the new [2000] edition of his *Introduction to Christianity* provides a few leads (*Introduction*, 18–29). "The figure of Christ is interpreted in a completely new way, not only in reference to dogma, but also and precisely with regard to the Gospels. The belief that Christ *is* the only Son of God, that God really dwells among us as man in him, and that the man Jesus is eternally in God, is God himself, and therefore is, not a figure in which God appears, but rather the sole and irreplaceable God—this belief is thereby excluded. Instead of being the man who *is* God, Christ becomes the one who has *experienced* God in a special way.... If the figure of Jesus is taken out of this inevitably scandalous dimension, if it is separated from his Godhead, then it becomes self-contradictory. All that is left are shreds that leave us perplexed or else become excuses for self-affirmation" (ibid., 21–22).

[169] *Einheit*, 36–42, citation at 37.

[170] "Demokratisierung 1", 40.

present"[171] as well. The Church's faith in the presence of God in Jesus Christ contradicts the understanding implied in the deistic image of God, which puts God at a great distance away and relegates religion to the private domain.[172] This is how we should understand it when Ratzinger to a great extent blames the exclusion of the "theme of God" for the ecclesiological crisis of our time.[173]

The Church's profession of faith in God has contents that are valid for all times;[174] Ratzinger summarizes this profession in the formula: "The 'I' of the Credo is the Church."[175] Consequently, the individual Christian can be in the unity of the Creed only if he "is in union with the one Church".[176] The question then arises of whether this unity excludes every sort of plurality. According to Ratzinger, we should first distinguish "between illegitimate pluralism and positive plurality".[177] The decisive criterion[178] here is the relationship to the truth itself. By the latter we mean, not a thing, but rather the Person Jesus Christ, who says about himself: "I am ... the truth" (Jn 14:6).

> To believe in God means to believe in the truth; to believe in Christ means to believe in its accessibility and in the community that results from the truth and in that very way frees us from the arbitrary stipulations of human praxis, in which man becomes his own creature, his own God, and thus his own slave. Accordingly, we should defend the Christianity of Jesus Christ himself against such developments by means of the accessibility and expressibility of the truth.[179]

For Ratzinger the "accessibility of the truth", then, means, not "canonizing theological systems", but rather openness to that center "which gives those systems food for thought".[180] For this reason, unity must not be confused with uniformity. A legitimate "discussion about right

---

[171] Ibid. This means also for Ratzinger that the universal Church is present at the same time through the fact that the local community is sacramentally rooted in her.

[172] Cf. *Introduction*, 13.

[173] Cf. Ratzinger and Metz, "God, Sin, and Suffering", 47–53, ref. at 47.

[174] Cf. *Einheit*, 48–51, ref. at 50.

[175] Ibid., 36.

[176] "Demokratisierung I", 40.

[177] *Einheit*, 48.

[178] Cf. ibid.

[179] Ibid., 50.

[180] Ibid.

order and the allotment of responsibilities"[181] is necessary, for no doubt "there can be, again and again, factors that upset the equilibrium and require adjustments".[182] This leads us to the accusation of Roman centralism that was leveled in connection with the document *Some Aspects of the Church Understood as Communion.*

b. The accusation of Roman centralism

In 1999, when Walter Kasper wrote the essay "On the Theology and Praxis of the Episcopal Ministry",[183] in which he suggested that the 1992 letter of the Congregation for the Doctrine of the Faith *Some Aspects of the Church Understood as Communion,* practically speaking, reversed the conciliar definition of the relation between the universal Church and the local Church and thus leveled the accusation that this was "an attempt at a theological reinstatement of Roman centralism",[184] this led to a public debate between him and Ratzinger. It culminated on February 27, 2000, at a conference held in the Vatican on the Second Vatican Council, when Ratzinger, referring to Walter Kasper, declared:

> The resistance to the expression of the priority of the universal Church before the individual parts of the Church is difficult to understand in theological terms, perhaps indeed incomprehensible. It becomes comprehensible only out of a suspicion that is thus briefly formulated: "This formula becomes truly problematical if the one universal Church is covertly identified with the Roman Church and, de facto, with the pope and the curia. . . ." In this passage, the identification of the universal Church with the pope and curia is at first introduced just as a hypothesis, as a danger, yet afterward it nonetheless seems to be attributed to the letter of the Congregation for Doctrine. . . . This interpretative leap is astonishing, but there is no doubt it stands for a suspicion that is widespread; it gives expression to a complaint to be heard all around, and it probably also expresses a growing inability to imagine anything concrete at all under the

---

[181] "Gottesidee", 46.

[182] Ibid.

[183] Kasper, "Theologie", 18–39. The same article first appeared in *Auf neue Art Kirche sein: Festschrift für Bischof Homeyer,* ed. W. Schreer and G. Steins, 32–48 (Munich: Bernward bei Don Bosco, 1999).

[184] Kasper, "Theologie", 34.

heading of universal Church or that of the one, holy, catholic Church.[185]

The cause of the conflict was the way in which the "ontological precedence" of the universal Church was formulated in the [CDF] document *Some Aspects of the Church Understood as Communion*, where it says:

> From the Church, which in its origins and its first manifestation is universal, have arisen the different local Churches, as particular expressions of the one unique Church of Jesus Christ. Arising *within* and *out of* the universal Church, they have their ecclesiality *in* it and *from* it. Hence the formula of the Second Vatican Council: *The Church in and formed out of the Churches* (*Ecclesia in et ex Ecclesiis*), is inseparable from this other formula: *The Churches in and formed out of the Church* (*Ecclesiae in et ex Ecclesia*).[186]

The second formula cited there, "Ecclesiae in et ex Ecclesia", which originated with Pope John Paul II[187] as a supplement to the formula in *Lumen gentium* 23, "Ecclesia in et ex Ecclesiis", gave rise to the above-mentioned fear that "the one universal Church [might be] covertly identified with the Roman Church and, de facto, with the pope and the curia".[188] On this subject, Kasper wrote in 1999, and I quote him:

> If that is happening, then the document issued by the Congregation for the Doctrine of the Faith cannot be understood as an aid to clarifying *communio* ecclesiology; rather, it has to be understood as dismissing it and attempting to restore Roman centralism. This process seems in fact to be under way. The relation between the local Church and the universal Church has become unbalanced.[189]

---

[185] "Ecclesiology", 138–39.

[186] Congregation for the Doctrine of the Faith, *On Some Aspects of the Church Understood as Communion*, emphasis added by the author.

[187] John Paul II, Address to the Roman Curia, December 20, 1990, in *AAS* 83 (1991): 745–47.

[188] Kasper, "Theologie", 34. Ratzinger criticizes this statement of Walter Kasper in "Ecclesiology", 138; cf. "Gottesidee", 46.

[189] Kasper, "Theologie", 34.

In Ratzinger's estimation, this reproach of Kasper's was the expression of "a suspicion that is widespread' and "a complaint to be heard all around".[190] This is presumably the underlying reason for the tone struck by Ratzinger here, which, as Hermann Josef Pottmeyer writes in an essay from the year 2001, "betrays a sense of personal injury".[191] In his reply in the journal *Stimmen der Zeit* (December 2000) to Ratzinger's public message delivered in the Vatican in February 2000, Walter Kasper admits that it would be unfair "to suspect only the will to power of the Curia" as being behind the "centralistic trends" that had accelerated after the Council.[192] In Kasper's view, two circumstances are responsible for the Roman centralism that he criticizes: first, a sort of ecclesial nationalism and, second, the changes going on in a globalized world. The latter, of course, simplify the exchange of messages, yet as a "secondary effect" it can also make it easier to shirk one's own responsibility and saddle Rome with it.[193] Along these lines Kasper declares:

Behind this there is also the justified concern about the situation of many particular Churches, where there is often a glorification of pluralism and of the special characteristics of the local Churches that has the ideological features of an ecclesial nationalism; the emphasis on unity in the New Testament is then overlooked. Behind the trend toward standardization, furthermore, is the fact that in a world that is undergoing globalization, one that in many respects has become a "global village", isolated solutions in particular Churches have become more difficult. The modern means of communication, also,

---

[190] "Ecclesiology", 139.
[191] Pottmeyer, "Weg", 291.
[192] Kasper, "Auseinandersetzung", 796. Cf. Pottmeyer, "Weg", 296: "All that being said, the phenomenon of centralism, which is rightly lamented, is presented in a way that is more nuanced, with respect to its causes, than the usual view of it. Its causes are neither solely of an institutional sort nor to be sought in the Roman Curia alone. It can even be maintained that the undeniable contribution of Rome to this centralism is generally overestimated because it is the most conspicuous. The Curia is a very differentiated structure, and it is naïve to demonize it as a whole."
[193] Cf. Pottmeyer, "Weg", 297: "The greater responsibility for what is deplored as centralism belongs to the bishops themselves, or, more precisely, to a majority of them. They are insufficiently aware of their constitutional position and role, which have a sacramental basis, as Vatican II emphasized.... A reference to Rome's jurisdiction is not infrequently a pretext to distract attention from one's own perplexity and inaction."

have made it much easier to keep in touch with "headquarters". Finally, behind the tendency toward centralization there is also occasionally the temptation to shift one's own responsibility conveniently onto "Rome" and to hide behind it.[194]

A chronological review shows that it would be wrong to conclude that there are insuperable differences behind the exchange of opinions between Kasper and Ratzinger that is summarized here. Nonetheless, Ratzinger was still defending himself in September 2000 against the stereotyped criticism and regretted the lack of a "nuanced debate on the subject matter"[195] itself. He speculated that the reason for the lack of objectivity was the prejudice that immediately sees "everything that comes from Rome from political points of view, from the perspective of the division of power".[196]

In a conciliatory way, Walter Kasper described this dispute in December 2000 as "friendly".[197] At the same time, Ratzinger, in an essay for the *Frankfurter Allgemeine Zeitung* dated December 22, 2000, showed that he was open to criticism when he himself spoke of the possibility of an "extravagant Roman centralism" that "then must be identified as such and corrected".[198] In November 2001, he responded directly to Kasper's "friendly difference of opinion" from the previous December with a short reply in the American Jesuit magazine *America*, entitled "The Local Church and the Universal Church: A Response to Walter Kasper".[199] Finally, Ratzinger summed up the whole debate at the beginning of 2002 by remarking: "This exchange of views has, thank God, led to an extensive rapprochement of our respective stances."[200]

---

[194] Kasper, "Auseinandersetzung", 796. See also Pottmeyer, "Kirche als Communio", 579–89, ref. at 584. In his critique here, Pottmeyer emphasizes especially the common responsibility of all the faithful as "responsible co-supporters of Church".

[195] "Absurd", 51.

[196] Ibid.

[197] See the subtitle of W. Kasper, "Das Verhältnis von Universal- und Ortskirche: Freundschaftliche Auseinandersetzung mit der Kritik von Joseph Kardinal Ratzinger" (The relation between universal Church and local Church: A friendly difference of opinion with Cardinal Ratzinger's critique), *StZ* 125 (2000): 795–804.

[198] "Gottesidee", 46.

[199] J. Ratzinger, "The Local Church and the Universal Church: A Response to Walter Kasper", *America* 185, no. 16 (2001): 7–11.

[200] See n. 12 in Ratzinger's essay "The Ecclesiology of the Constitution *Lumen gentium*", in *Pilgrim Fellowship*, 123–52, ref. at 139, with additional nn. 7 through 12.

After this chronological listing of the various positions, the question still arises of why Ratzinger in his essay on *Lumen gentium* from the year 2000 harked back to the 1992 CDF document *Some Aspects of the Church Understood as Communion*, even though it had met with a "hailstorm of criticism"[201] after its publication. Pottmeyer sees the reason for this in the fact that he is concerned above all about "the unity of the Church in the mystery of her coming forth from God".[202] This is for Ratzinger, as the latter himself says, clearly "a reality that ontologically and temporally preceded the individual particular Churches".[203] In his emphasis on the ontological priority of the Church as a whole, he cites patristic theology, which discerned already in creation an inner teleology directed toward the Church, inasmuch as it transferred to the Church the rabbinical notion of the preexistence of the Torah and of Israel.

2. The inner predestination of creation for the Church

a. The importance of the Torah's and Israel's preexistence for an understanding of the *Ecclesia*

Together with the Church Fathers, Ratzinger assumes that there is an intrinsic interrelationship and continuity between the Old and New Testament.[204] Moreover, the Augustinian axiom "The New Testament lies hidden in the Old; the Old is made explicit in the New"[205] is for him an important key to understanding Scripture. Accordingly, the Old and the New Testaments cannot be regarded as opposed to one another, although their unity is fraught with tensions. For according to the patristic interpretation, "there is only *one* will of God for men, only *one* historical activity of God with and for men, though this activity employs interventions that are diverse and even in part contradictory—yet in truth they belong together."[206]

---

[201] "Gottesidee", 46.

[202] Pottmeyer, "Weg", 303.

[203] "Ecclesiology", 134.

[204] Cf. *In the Beginning*, 9: "For the Christian the Old Testament represents, in its totality, an advance toward Christ; only when it attains to him does its real meaning, which was gradually hinted at, become clear. Thus every individual part derives its meaning from the whole, and the whole derives its meaning from the end—from Christ."

[205] *Many Religions*, 36.

[206] Ibid., 57.

According to Ratzinger—and this idea is found in the letter *Some Aspects of the Church Understood as Communion* as well—the one and only Church *ontologically* "precedes creation, and gives birth to the particular Churches".[207] This thought is supposed to express the unity of God's action in creation and election. As it was for the Church Fathers, who refer to the rabbinical tradition, according to which "the Torah and Israel are conceived of as preexisting",[208] so also it is true for Ratzinger: God's creation is "planned for the purpose of providing a space for God's will". In creation, the one People of God has its place, for God's will "needs a people that lives for the will of God and makes it the light for the world". For the Church, which stands in a relation of "ultimate identity" to Israel, this means that the Church Fathers could not see, in the Church of Jesus Christ, "something that developed by chance at a later date but rather recognized in this assembly of peoples subject to God's will the inner teleology of creation."

At the beginning of the modern era this patristic knowledge about the intrinsic purposefulness of creation was lost, along with the Church Fathers' notion of the living unity of Scripture. As a result of "the new historical thinking", the individual biblical texts were isolated and read, as Ratzinger puts it, in their "bare literalness . . . with a view not to Christ but to the probable origins of those texts".[209]

But precisely the christological, holistic view is for Ratzinger the key to understanding the ontological[210] precedence of the People of

---

[207] Congregation for the Doctrine of the Faith, *On Some Aspects of the Church Understood as Communion*, see art. 9, n. 42, with references to St. Clement of Rome, *Epist. II ad Cor.*, 14, 2: Funck, 1, 200; *Shepherd of Hermas*, Vis. 2, 4: PG 2, 897–900.

[208] This and the following quotations are found in "Gottesidee", 46.

[209] *In the Beginning*, 17.

[210] On this subject, see Kaes, 124: "Since ontology is said to be the philosophical foundation for the continuity thesis, it is denounced as a Scholastic and later as a Greek evil. Such critics see their view confirmed in the finding that, with few exceptions, biblical thought is not in terms of being [*seinshaft*] but rather dualistic and thus opposed to the Greeks' metaphysical way of thinking. One can object that the Bible, in understanding Christ as the eschatological Adam, who in turn was created in God's image, establishes a lasting standard for the nature of man. Ratzinger knows, however, that this argument is dismissed by the opponents of ontological thinking, who note that Scripture speaks of the first and the second Adam and regards the first as the man who has been alienated by history. In Luther's writings, at least in many passages, the chasm is understood along these lines so radically that there is no bridge between historical man and the new life made possible in faith. Here the principle of discontinuity is consistently applied and thus

God. In contrast, describing the faith in a purely historical way while rejecting ontological categories[211] represents for him the real philosophical problem of the present day, which no longer thinks in terms of "the whole in the fragment" or "the fragments of the whole".[212] At the conclusion of this dissertation[213] I will sketch the intellectual-historical background that determines this way of thinking. Therefore, let it simply be noted here, in the quintessential formulation of Dorothee Kaes, that Ratzinger chooses an approach

> that assumes a continuity in history and thus makes room also for an ontological way of thinking. He sees himself justified in making such an assumption, inasmuch as Christian antiquity, for all the differences between the first and the second Adam, was nevertheless well aware of their unity. It has its foundations in God's plan of creation, which is not abolished by Christ, but fulfilled.[214]

To summarize, we can state that Ratzinger, together with the Church Fathers, sees the teleological aspect of an intrinsic predestination of creation for the *Ecclesia* as being rooted in the rabbinical notion of the preexistence of the Torah and Israel. In the next subsection, we will look more closely at the theme of its christological transformation.

b. On the christological development of the image of the preexistent People of God

In the Old Testament, creation and worship are most profoundly interwoven. That prompts Ratzinger to formulate the axiom that creation was called into being by God "for the sake of worship".[215] For creation itself, this means:

> Creation is oriented to the sabbath, which is the sign of the covenant between God and humankind. . . . Creation is designed in such

---

an ontology, in the sense of a continuity of nature that spans history is denied." See also *Principles*, 153–71, esp. 158–63.

[211] Cf. *Principles*, 162.

[212] J. Ratzinger, "Das Ganze im Fragment: Gottfried Söhngen zum Gedächtnis", *Christ in der Gegenwart* 23 (1971): 399.

[213] Cf. pt. 3, sec. 2, in this work: "Ratzinger's Ecclesiology against the Background of Issues in Intellectual History".

[214] Kaes, 125.

[215] *In the Beginning*, 28.

a way that it is oriented to worship. . . . As St. Benedict said in his Rule: *Operi Dei nihil praeponatur*—"Nothing must be put before the service of God." This is not the expression of an otherworldly piety but a clear and sober translation of the creation account and of the message that it bears for our lives. The true center, the power that moves and shapes from within in the rhythm of the stars and of our lives, is worship.[216]

Precisely for the sake of interreligious dialogue it is of decisive importance, in Ratzinger's view, that other cultures and religions, too, recognize in the glorification of God the reason for creation. Herein one can discern, "often in striking ways", a profound unity between "the great traditions of the peoples"[217] and the biblical belief in creation. Ratzinger sees preserved in these traditions "a primordial human knowledge that is open to Christ", albeit distorted in many ways by the notion "that in worship the human being gives something to the gods that they themselves stand in need of".[218]

If the glorification of God is the goal of creation, then the latter receives its proper structure from the Sabbath.[219] It is, according to Ratzinger, "the summing up of Torah, the law of Israel",[220] since the Sabbath is the day "when the human being, in the freedom of worship, participates in God's freedom, in God's rest, and thus in God's peace".[221] But if the Law and the Sabbath form a unity, then the Decalogue and worship cohere, which is to say that cult and the moral

---

[216] Ibid., 27–28.

[217] Ibid., 28.

[218] Ibid., 28–29.

[219] *Song*, 69–73, citation at 69: "One could actually say that the metaphor of the seven-day week was selected for the creation account because of the Sabbath. By culminating in the sign of the covenant, the Sabbath, the creation account clearly shows that creation and covenant belong together from the start, that the Creator and the Redeemer can only be one and the same God. It shows that the world is not a neutral receptacle where human beings then accidentally become involved, but that right from the start creation came to be so that there would be a place for the covenant. But it also shows that the covenant can exist only if it conforms to the yardstick of creation. From this starting point a merely historical religion or simple salvation history without metaphysics is just as unthinkable as a worldless piety." Karl Barth defines the creation-covenant relationship in a similar way: Creation is the external reason for the covenant; the covenant is the internal reason for creation. Moltmann understands the Sabbath eschatologically as the goal of creation.

[220] *In the Beginning*, 29.

[221] Ibid., 30–31.

order must not be separated from each other but essentially belong together. This is true, however, not only with a view to morality but also in a historical perspective. When Israel speaks about the Torah, it means at the same time its history with God. The Torah itself is, as Ratzinger puts it, "an expression of the covenant, and the covenant is in turn an expression of God's love." [222] Starting from the Torah, Ratzinger builds a bridge directly to Jesus Christ,[223] the incarnate Word of God:

> In Jewish literature it is said of Torah, which embodies the mystery of the covenant and of the history of God's love for humankind, that it was in the beginning, that it was with God, that by it was made all that was made, and that it was the light and the life of humankind. John only needed to take up these formulas and to apply them to him who is the living Word of God, saying that all things were made through him (cf. John 1:3). And even before him Paul had said: "All things were created through him and for him" (Colossians 1:16; cf. Colossians 1:15–23). God created the universe in order to be able to become a human being and pour out his love upon us and to invite us to love him in return.[224]

A response of love in return, however, never occurs in isolation, for man is supposed to recognize that he is "situated in the context of the body of history, which will ultimately become the body of Christ".[225] Ratzinger develops this idea christologically through the image of the relationship of bride and bridegroom, by interpreting history as a love story between man and God:

---

[222] Ibid., 29.

[223] On this subject, see also Christoph Schönborn, *Loving the Church*, trans. John Saward (San Francisco: Ignatius Press, 1998). In his reflections on *LG* 2, which is cited in *CCC* 759, Cardinal Schönborn mentions the following incident: "I can never go past the Great Synagogue without thinking of Israel Zolli, the Chief Rabbi of Rome. On Yom Kippur 1944, as he stood before the shrine of the Torah, Christ the Lord appeared to him and his wife, and at his baptism, out of gratitude to Pope Pacelli [Pius XII], he took the baptismal name Eugenio" (ibid., 89).

[224] *In the Beginning*, 30. If Ratzinger interprets the Torah as existing before time, then logically this is true of the alliance of the twelve tribes of Israel as well, which has its foundations in the Torah. From this is deduced the continuity of the Church's preexistence, starting from the twelve tribes of Israel and leading to the twelve apostles. See Prov 8:22–23.

[225] *In the Beginning*, 34.

God finds and prepares a bride for his Son, the one bride who is the one Church. As a result of the verse from Genesis that says that man and woman will "become one flesh" (cf. Gen 2:24), the image of the bride coalesced with the idea of the Church as the Body of Christ, which in turn has its sacramental basis in eucharistic devotion. The one Body of Christ is prepared; Christ and his Church will "become one flesh", one Body, and thus God will become "everything to everyone" [cf. 1 Cor 15:28; Eph 1:23].[226]

From the image of the union of bride and bridegroom, Church and Christ, Ratzinger immediately concludes that the one universal Church is ontologically prior. For him she is the preexisting Body of Christ, for the purpose of which creation was formed. Against this background it is difficult for Ratzinger to understand the critique of the ontological precedence of the universal Church over the particular Churches.[227]

3. On the ontological precedence of the universal Church over her concrete empirical realizations

The theological debate about the ontological precedence of the universal Church over the local Churches seems—in the opinion of Hermann J. Pottmeyer—to be not very helpful.[228] According to Ladislas Orsy, the question "Which came first, the universal Church or the particular Church?" is even framed incorrectly and proves to be a trap: "Anyone who walks into it must choose either the one or the other. It is like asking: *Which is prior, the body or its members?* A body without members is no body; members that do not form a body are not members."[229]

Despite such objections, which should be taken seriously, ideas such as the unity of creation and redemption, the synthesis of the Old and

---

[226] "Gottesidee", 46.

[227] Cf. ibid. "This ontological precedence of the universal Church, the one Church and the one Body, the one Bride, over the empirical and concrete realizations in the individual particular Churches seems to me so obvious that I find it difficult to understand the objections raised against it."

[228] Cf. Pottmeyer, "Weg", 306f.

[229] L. Orsy, "The Papacy for an Ecumenical Age", *America* 183, no. 12 (2000): 11, quoted in Pottmeyer, "Weg", 306f.

New Testaments,[230] and, last but not least, the finding of comparative religion that worship is the goal of all creation in other religions, too, determine the structure of Ratzinger's argumentation in the discussion about the ontological precedence of the universal Church.

In the next two steps of this presentation I will concentrate, first, on Ratzinger's attempt to find a New Testament basis for the ontological priority of the universal Church. One reason that this is of interest is that Ratzinger himself[231]—perhaps in reaction to Kasper's objection[232]—admits a certain weakness in this approach, given the many-layered complexity of the actual historical data. Second, I will discuss the extent to which Ratzinger sees the ontological priority as having a foundation in the Vatican II Constitution on the Church.

a. The first beginnings in the New Testament

In his search for a New Testament foundation for "God's great idea, the Church",[233] Ratzinger refers not only to the Deutero-Pauline Letters and the Revelation of John, but especially to Galatians 4:26. In that passage of the Letter to the Galatians, "the heart of the great Pauline letters", Paul speaks

> about the heavenly Jerusalem, and not as an eschatological entity, but as something that precedes us: "The Jerusalem above is free, and she is our mother" (Gal 4:26). Heinrich Schlier comments that for Paul, as for the related Jewish tradition, the Jerusalem above is the

---

[230] Cf. *Song*, 69–73, ref. at 72–73: "If one rejects the aspect of creation and the social components along with the Old Testament—that is, in this case along with the Sabbath—then Christianity becomes a clublike pastime."

[231] Cf. "Ecclesiology", 135ff.

[232] Cf. Kasper, "Auseinandersetzung", 797.

[233] "Gottesidee", 46. See also Kasper, "Auseinandersetzung", 797: "In the principal Pauline letters, *ecclesia* means first of all the individual Church or individual congregation; that is why Paul can speak about 'local Churches' in the plural. In his view, the one Church of God is represented in every local congregation. Thus Paul speaks, for instance, about the Church of God that is in Corinth (1 Cor 1:2; 2 Cor 1:1; cf. Rom 16:1). The Church of God is accordingly present at that place in the Church in question. In the imprisonment letters, which are most often described today as Deutero-Pauline, this local Church connotation is almost completely insignificant. The Letters to the Ephesians and the Colossians are in agreement inasmuch as they view the Church as a whole, as the universal Church, and not as a local congregation. For Luke, *ecclesia* can mean both the house assembly and the local congregation; moreover, we find in his writings an early holistic concept of the Church."

new eon. For the Apostle, however, this new eon is already present "in the Christian Church. For him she is the heavenly Jerusalem in her children."[234]

Then, too, "the Lucan depiction of the birth of the Church from the Holy Spirit on Pentecost"[235] in Acts 2 is likewise ontologically significant for him. In this depiction, the Church is "the union of men among themselves through the radical transcendence of self into eternal love",[236] for the dynamic of the Spirit is "a departure into the great unity that envelops mankind of all places and times".[237] The signs of this universal unity are, first, the assembly of the 120 with the "restored fellowship of the Twelve" around Mary, the Mother of Jesus;[238] second, the fact that the Church from the very beginning speaks in *all* languages;[239] and, third, the *Table [List] of Twelve Nations*:

From the first moment on, the Church is *kat'holon*—embracing the whole universe. Accordingly, Luke describes the crowd of listeners as pilgrims from all over the world by means of a table of twelve nations, the purpose of which is to indicate the utterly comprehensive character of the audience; Luke added to this Hellenistic list of nations a thirteenth name: the Romans, whereby he intended, no doubt, to underscore once again the idea of the *orbis*.[240]

In response to the objection of Walter Kasper that the assembly in Jerusalem was "both the universal Church and the local Church in

---

[234] "Gottesidee", 46.

[235] Ibid.

[236] Ratzinger, *Images of Hope: Meditations on Major Feasts*, trans. John Rock and Graham Harrison (San Francisco: Ignatius Press, 2006), 68.

[237] Ibid., 69.

[238] These Twelve are not primarily "members of a local Church" but, rather, apostles and as such signs of the Catholic Church, since they are supposed to bring the gospel to the ends of the earth. A further sign of unity is the number twelve, through which they are, as Ratzinger explains, "simultaneously the old and the new Israel, the one Israel of God, which was contained in principle in the People of God concept from the beginning and hence now spreads to all nations and founds the one People of God among all peoples" ("Gottesidee", 46). On this subject, see pt. 2, sec. 2, chap. 2, § 6.2, in this book, "On the Meaning of the Marian Statements".

[239] Ratzinger, *Images of Hope*, 69: "She speaks on her first day in all languages, in the languages of the planet. She was first universal before she brought forth local churches."

[240] "Gottesidee", 46.

one"[241] and that at the same time "there were several congregations from the very beginning",[242] especially in Galilee, Ratzinger sidesteps the issue, inasmuch as he is not discussing in detail the question of historicity. Ratzinger himself is more concerned with the "inner beginning of the Church in time, which Luke intends to describe and which he traces back beyond all empirical data to the power of the Holy Spirit".[243] Of course Kasper is in no way disputing the ontological priority of the universal Church, since he elaborates:

> The Church is not the result of random intra-historical coincidences, developments, and decisions; she has her foundations in the eternal salvific will and in God's mystery of salvation. This is precisely what the Letters of St. Paul express when they speak about the eternal salvific mystery of God, which was hidden from earlier times but is now revealed in the Church and through the Church (Eph 1:3–14; 3:3–12; Col 1:26f.). A preexistence understood in this way ... is theologically indispensable for an understanding of the Church.[244]

Thus the real point of contention between Ratzinger and Kasper is the fact that Kasper assumes the preexistence of the one Church *"in and formed out of the local Churches"*.[245] From this he derives the thesis of the simultaneity of universal and particular Church.[246]

Arguments quite similar to those of Kasper are advanced also by Hermann Josef Pottmeyer, who, alluding to Yves Congar, states that the one and unique Church preexists in God's plan, "namely, as her defining ideal and absolute essence".[247] This is not meant, however, "as though the universal Church preexisted the particular Churches as one concrete reality precedes other concrete realities".[248] We cannot go any deeper here into this question, which Walter Kasper describes

---

[241] Kasper, "Theologie", 33. See also Kehl, *Wohin geht die Kirche?* 98.

[242] Kasper, "Theologie", 34.

[243] "Gottesidee", 46.

[244] Kasper, "Auseinandersetzung", 801.

[245] Ibid.

[246] See ibid., 802.

[247] Pottmeyer, "Weg", 303. Cf. Y. Congar, *Ministères et communion ecclésiale* (Paris: Éditions du Cerf, 1971), 131.

[248] Pottmeyer, "Weg", 303.

as a controversy about "a Scholastic debate".[249] It is striking, nonetheless, that Ratzinger himself, at the end of the year 2000, assigned a relative value to the question of the "temporal precedence of the universal Church"[250] by saying that he did "not want to exaggerate its importance".[251] Through all the debate, the decisive point for Ratzinger remains the fact that the Church carries universality within herself from the beginning,

> that the Church is born of the one Spirit in the Twelve ... for all peoples and hence even from the first moment is aimed at expressing herself in all cultures and in that way being the one People of God. It is not that one local congregation is slowly expanding; rather, the leaven is always ordered to the whole.[252]

With the reference to that "one local congregation", Ratzinger is taking aim at Walter Kasper's statement that the "original community in Jerusalem was in fact both universal Church and local Church in one".[253]

---

[249] Kasper, "Auseinandersetzung", 800; cf. ibid., 802: "Upon closer inspection, the controversy about the question of the primacy of the universal Church turns out to be a question, not of ecclesial doctrine, but rather of theological opinion and of the various philosophies taken into consideration by those on either side. They proceed either in a more Platonic manner from the primacy of the idea and of the universal, or else, in a more Aristotelian manner, they see the universal realized in the particular. The latter line of thought, of course, has nothing to do with a reduction to the empirical data. The medieval debate between theologians who thought more in Platonic terms and those who were more Aristotelian and Thomistic was a Scholastic debate within the common faith of the Church. Bonaventure and Thomas of Aquinas, who went their different ways in the question of universal papal authority, are both recognized as Doctors of the Church; both are revered as saints. Why should a diversity that was possible in the Middle Ages no longer be possible today?" An early controversy between Ratzinger and Kasper likewise came to a head with Kasper's accusation that Ratzinger in his *Introduction to Christianity* had chosen a "Platonizing point of departure" through which, as Kasper suspects, "the distinctively Christian scandal of the *Logos sarx egeneto* [the Word became flesh] (Jn 1:14), contrary to the author's oft-declared better intentions and despite his constant emphasis on the positive character of Christianity ... , nevertheless comes again and again under the ascendancy and under the laws of the concept of reality found in Greek philosophy." See W. Kasper, "Das Wesen des Christlichen", *ThRv* 65 (1969): 182–88, citation at 185.

[250] "Gottesidee", 46.

[251] Ibid. Cf. Kasper, "Auseinandersetzung", 801. This relativizing could be Ratzinger's reaction to Kasper's critique.

[252] "Gottesidee", 46.

[253] Kasper, "Theologie", 33. See also Kasper, "Auseinandersetzung", 800: Citing M. Theobald, Kasper points out that "on Pentecost the focus is not on the universal Church, but rather on the assembly of the Jewish Diaspora, which ... over the course of time

Ratzinger sees this assumption as the basis for Kasper's "interpretative leap",[254] which supposes that the one universal Church is "covertly identified [by Ratzinger] with the Roman Church, and de facto with the pope and the curia".[255] The suspicion raised by Kasper should arise, in Ratzinger's view, only "if one had already identified the local Church of Jerusalem with the universal Church, that is, if one had already reduced the concept of Church to the empirically evident congregations and had lost sight of its theological depth."[256]

This counterattack by Ratzinger is understandable in view of the above-cited accusation by Kasper.[257] Nevertheless, the exaggerated manner in which both theologians argue contains rhetoric that makes their positions seem more contrary than they are in truth.[258] Therefore, Walter Kasper rejects the charge of a "sociological reduction of the Church to individual congregations" as "a serious misunderstanding and a caricature of my position".[259]

But what is the concern behind Ratzinger's sharp criticism? He laments the widespread inability "to imagine that something concrete is meant by the universal Church, by the one, holy, catholic Church".[260] Not infrequently the only concrete elements associated with the universal Church are "the pope and the Curia, and if they are ranked too high theologically, it is felt to be a threat".[261] In summary, this means that Ratzinger sees the symbolism of the Twelve[262] as the foundation, not primarily for

---

expands through the guidance of the Holy Spirit to become the Church of all nations." Therefore "this whole process, and not just the Lucan account of the beginnings on the first Pentecost, should be considered normative." Cf. M. Theobald, "Der römische Zentralismus und die Jerusalemer Urgemeinde", *ThQ* 180 (2000): 225–28.

[254] "Gottesidee", 46.

[255] Ibid. See also Kasper, "Theologie", 34.

[256] "Gottesidee", 46.

[257] See Pottmeyer, "Weg", 300.

[258] Cf. Kasper, "Auseinandersetzung", 799f.: "Common ecclesiological foundations" shared by Ratzinger and Kasper. Among these Kasper lists: 1. The uniqueness of the Church of Jesus Christ and her subsistence in the Roman Catholic Church. 2. *Ecclesia in et ex Ecclesiae* and *Ecclesiae in et ex Ecclesia* as understood in the eucharistic *communio* ecclesiology. 3. Local Church and universal Church are in perichoresis with one another.

[259] Kasper, "Auseinandersetzung", 797.

[260] "Gottesidee", 46.

[261] Ibid.

[262] Compare pt. 2, sec. 2, chap. 2, § 3.2, of this work, "Jesus Christ as the Patriarch of the New People of God".

an "original congregation in Jerusalem",[263] but rather for the Catholic Church pure and simple, which embraces the old and the new People of God. From this he draws the inference:

> The first thing … is that in the Twelve the old Israel, which is one, becomes the new Israel and that this one Israel of God, through the miracle of tongues, manifests a unity that embraces all times and places, even before the formation of a local Church of Jerusalem occurs. In the pilgrims who are present, who hail from all nations, this new Israel immediately is related to all the peoples of the world.[264]

Because for Ratzinger the unity of the Church is at stake in the question of the ontological precedence of the universal Church, the debate about the treatment of this theme in *Lumen gentium* is not a peripheral matter.[265] This debate, he says, shows concretely what concept of universal Church is found in the Constitution on the Church. For this reason, he asks: "What, concretely, is she—the one universal Church that precedes the local Churches ontologically and temporally? What does she consist of? Where can we see her at work?"[266] Ratzinger sees his questions answered in *Lumen gentium* in the trinitarian constitution of the Church (*Lumen gentium* 2–4), in her inner dynamic leading toward the kingdom of God (*Lumen gentium* 5), and finally in her sacramental structure.

b. Arguments for an ontological priority of the universal Church over the local Churches in *Lumen gentium*

1) *Trinitarian overture as the key to ecclesiology*

The first four articles of *Lumen gentium* are for Ratzinger the key to understanding ecclesiology,[267] which is "talk about God",[268] starting with Christ, the Light of the nations, and leading to the trinitarian mystery:

---

[263] Kasper, "Theologie", 33.
[264] "Gottesidee", 46.
[265] Cf. ibid.
[266] Ibid.
[267] Cf. ibid., 46.
[268] Ibid.

Because ... no one can speak correctly about Christ, the Son, without at the same time speaking about the Father, and because one cannot speak correctly about Father and Son without being attentive to the Holy Spirit, the christological view of the Church necessarily broadens into a trinitarian ecclesiology.[269]

Starting from this trinitarian overture, *Lumen gentium* goes on to explain the inner dynamic of the Church leading to the kingdom of God.[270] But when we inquire with Ratzinger into the concrete and visible features of the ontological precedence of the universal Church over the local Churches, he refers to the sacraments, as does *Lumen gentium*.

2) The ontological priority is visible in the Church's sacramental structure

The ecclesial dimension of the sacraments, which comes from God and leads to him, is for Ratzinger a decisive argument for the ontological priority of the universal Church. In this ecclesial dimension, the deep and irrevocable structure of the People of God is revealed, the fact that it was willed by God from all eternity and hence derives its own legitimacy from him. Because of her sacramental structure, the Church of Jesus Christ is different from a club or a political party. She is distinguished from them in that she has her unity in God. When this is disregarded, ecclesiology becomes flattened into sociology.[271]

This becomes particularly clear in current ways of viewing baptism, the Eucharist, and holy orders. For this reason, Ratzinger emphasizes that baptism is more than incorporation into a given local congregation (in the sense of social initiation into the local Church). Rather, it is "a trinitarian, that is, an utterly theological, event",[272] for in baptism is poured out "the source of pure surrender, the lavish love of God",[273] which proceeds from the Cross of Christ "as a mighty stream through the whole Church and 'makes glad the city of God' (cf. Ps 46:4)".[274] In baptism, accordingly, the one Church of heaven and earth is quite concretely present as a reality that precedes the local Churches

---

[269] Ibid. Cf. Kasper, "Auseinandersetzung", 800.
[270] Cf. "Gottesidee", 46.
[271] See *Report*, 49.
[272] "Gottesidee", 46.
[273] *Dogma*, 341–47, citation at 344f.
[274] Ibid., 345.

and creates them. As a result, the members of this one Church are at home in all local congregations: "Someone who is baptized in Berlin is just as much at home in the Church of Rome or in New York or in Kinshasa or in Bangalore as in his baptismal Church. He does not have to re-register; it is the same Church."[275]

Likewise, the Eucharist is a sacrament that "does not originate from the local Church"[276] and is not limited to it.[277] In the Eucharist, just as in the sacrament of holy orders,[278] which is inseparably bound up with it, the *extra nos* character of the sacrament is made concrete. For the liturgy of the Church, in Ratzinger's view, is always an opening up of the limits of what is our own.

> That is why, however much it lives in the here and now, in a particular place, seeking the consent of the local community, Christian liturgy is essentially Catholic, that is, it proceeds from the whole and leads back to it, it leads to unity with the pope, the bishops and the faithful of all times and places. The Catholic element is not something added on externally ... but something from the Lord himself who seeks everyone and seeks to bring them all together.[279]

Without this openness to the totality, Ratzinger says, the Church would ultimately lose the consciousness that in her sacraments "a supreme authority is operative, an authority which no one can arrogate to

---

[275] "Gottesidee", 46.

[276] Ibid. See also *Song*, 111–27. Ratzinger opposes a concept of the liturgy that is based exclusively on Matthew 18:20 ("For where two or three are gathered in my name, there am I in the midst of them"). "When one isolates this one biblical text and contrasts it with the entire liturgical tradition", Matthew 18:20 is "brought into conflict with an institution having institutional roles and with every 'codified program.' This definition therefore means that the Church does not come before the group, but the group before the Church. It is not the Church as an integral whole that carries the liturgy of the individual group or parish; rather, the group is itself the place of origin for the liturgy. Hence, liturgy does not grow out of a common given either, a 'rite' (which now, as a 'codified program,' has acquired the negative image of lack of freedom); it originates on the spot from the creativity of those gathered" (*Song*, 112).

[277] See pt. 2, sec. 2, chap. 1, §3.2, of this work, "Eucharistic Communities as the Realization of the Church".

[278] Cf. *Song*, 113.

[279] *Feast of Faith*, 148.

himself. In the liturgy the absolutely Other takes place, the absolutely Other comes among us."[280]

§ 5. On the Critique of the Sociological Misunderstanding of the "People of God"

Today the expression "People of God" is not infrequently misunderstood in a purely sociological sense, which prompts statements like: "We are the people" and "We decide."[281] Moreover, the "People of God", as Ratzinger noted as early as 1970, is no longer seen "as the totality of the Church, which exists prior to the division into clergy and laity, but rather exclusively [as] the lay people, who as a group in the Church are now covered by this title".[282] This bifurcation, however, involves at the same time an astonishing overemphasis on the clergy and a fixation on structural issues in the Church:

> Such reform can touch only things of secondary importance in the Church. No wonder, then, that in the end it sees the Church itself as of secondary importance. If we become aware of this, the paradox that has emerged apparently with the present efforts at reform becomes intelligible: the attempt to loosen up rigid structures, to correct forms of Church government and ministry, which derive from the Middle Ages, or, rather, the age of absolutism ... —all these efforts have led to an almost unparalleled over-emphasis on the official elements in the Church.
>
> It is true that today the institutions and ministries in the Church are being criticized more radically than ever before, but in the process they attract more exclusive attention than ever before. For not a few people the Church today seems to consist of nothing but these.[283]

---

[280] Ibid., 150.

[281] Cf. *Salt of the Earth*, 186–90.

[282] "Demokratisierung I", 27. Cf. ibid., 28: According to Ratzinger, the Church exists "in the active voice, as the process of gathering, and therefore she is not called λαός, but εκκλησια, not a people, but an assembly".

[283] Ratzinger, "Why I Am Still in the Church", in *Two Say Why: Why I Am Still a Christian; Why I Am Still in the Church*, by H. U. von Balthasar and J. Ratzinger, trans. John Griffiths, 65–91, citation at 70f. (Chicago: Franciscan Herald Press, 1973).

The fixation on the so-called official Church has led to a fading of ecclesial consciousness, so that in 1971 Ratzinger observed that "the Church is becoming extinguished in men's souls, and Christian communities are crumbling."[284] An investigation of the manifold causes of this "breakdown in communication", which according to Medard Kehl was precipitated by the "still unresolved problem of the relation between the Catholic Church and modern culture",[285] would require a thoroughgoing diagnosis of the present time.[286] Since that is not possible here, I will concentrate on three crucial points that acquired special significance for Ratzinger during the challenges of the postconciliar period, namely: first, the transformation of the People of God concept into something political; second, the question about relativism as a prerequisite for a democratic state; and third, the problem of the majority principle in questions of faith.

1. The transformation of the People of God concept into something political

In order to understand correctly the Council's concept of the People of God, Ratzinger says, this term needs to be applied spiritually[287] to the Church. In his 1986 review of the Council, he cites the Scripture scholar Norbert Lohfink, who has shown that the expression "People of God" does not designate any empirical entity in the Old Testament, either:

Purely empirically no people is the people of God. To set God up as an indicator of descent or as sociological label could only ever be an intolerable presumption and indeed ultimately blasphemy. Israel is described by the term people of God to the extent that it is turned towards the Lord, not just in itself but in the act of relating and transcending itself which alone turns it into what it is not of itself.[288]

In an analogous manner, this means that the Church is the People of God only in communion with Christ. Here, in Ratzinger's view,

---

[284] Ibid., 67.
[285] Cf. Kehl, *Wohin geht die Kirche?* 59–64, ref. at 62.
[286] On this subject, see *Turning Point*, 145–77; Ratzinger, "Gefährliche Spaltung", *Rheinischer Merkur*, no. 6 (February 6, 1998): 25f. See also Kehl, *Wohin geht die Kirche?* 13–58.
[287] Cf. "Demokratisierung 1", 28.
[288] *Church*, 18–19. See also *Salt of the Earth*, 186f.

the *communio sanctorum* plays an important role. By this he understands the communion in the "holy gifts" (*sancta*) that are bestowed on us by the glorified Christ, the crucified and risen Savior, and especially "the holy *thing*, granted to the Church in her eucharistic feast by God as the real bond of unity".[289] This is a real albeit mysterious bond and "the reason why the Church is not *our* Church ... [but] rather, *his* Church".[290]

Against the background that we have just outlined, we are now confronted with the question of whether the concept "People of God" actually can be transformed politically. Ratzinger, at any rate, reflects that in every age certain secular systemic forms were adopted for the Church; from this he concludes: "Hence it would be surprising if the model of the democratic constitutional state were not applied to the Church too and the attempt undertaken to 'democratize' the Church. This is today the actual way in which the conflict over freedom and constraint in the Church takes place."[291]

The realism of Christian freedom recognizes, according to Ratzinger, "that the unrestricted ability to do anything and everything one wants has as its model an idol and not God".[292] For the People of God, therefore, true freedom means being bound to a God who is "bound to himself in threefold love and is thus pure freedom".[293] Many individuals, he says, "have trouble with the Church"[294] because they regard the Church as an institution that restricts their personal freedom.[295] In their view, the Church is supposed to be an "island of

---

[289] *Introduction*, 334. Cf. H. de Lubac, "Credo ... Sanctorum Communionem", in *Credo: Ein theologisches Lesebuch*, ed. J. Ratzinger and P. Henrici, 271–88 (Cologne: Communio, 1992).

[290] *Report*, 48.

[291] *Church*, 193.

[292] Ibid., 255–75, citation at 274.

[293] Ibid.

[294] *Called to Communion*, 134.

[295] On this subject, see *Church*, 194: "When the formal aspect of democratic freedom is elevated into a universal model what is at work is in reality a concept of freedom that presses beyond the constitutional state and its balance of freedoms. This becomes especially clear when the slogan 'more democracy' occurs; here the constitutional form of the constraints and obligations that lead to freedom are seen merely as a stage on the way to man's complete liberation which is meant finally to lead to freedom from all institutions. The concept of grassroots democracy that belongs here seems especially suitable for transfer to the Church because it appears to correspond in its inner nature with the idea of the

the good life, a tiny oasis of freedom"[296] in a society full of anxieties and pressures. Such a demand for freedom is, from their perspective, the way "in which the yearning for redemption and the feeling of unredemption and alienation"[297] are manifested. It is expected of the Church, "in the midst of a world full of harsh discipline and inexorable pressures"—as Ratzinger says—to fulfill the "dream of a better world", so that in the Church they might at least have a "taste of freedom"[298] and a sense of being redeemed.

Because of their longing for the "wholly Other", other people are at the same time unhappy about the fact that "the Church has conformed too much to the standards of the world".[299] According to Ratzinger, this "insistence on what is proper to the Church and different about her",[300] too, has its justification in the Church. When it is a question of societal structures in the Church as the People of God, then we should inquire first into what is characteristic of the Church, as opposed to the understanding of democracy in modern states.

As the first and fundamental difference between the Church and a democratic state, Ratzinger mentions the holder of sovereignty. God himself is to be regarded as the sovereign of the People of God, and not the people.[301] There is a second difference with respect to the purpose of the community: Whereas the state has in view the common good of its own citizens as its highest purpose, the Church is concerned with "the truth of the gospel of Jesus Christ as a reality coming from outside and expropriating mankind for its own sake".[302] Third and finally, official ministry in the Church has a structural place different from the one that it has in the secular state. Anyone who

congregation and thus of the structure of the people of God that is based on the local Church. Satiety with the anonymity of large-scale societies makes its contribution to let the idea of the self-determining small community seem the solution.... The universal Church and its sacramental structure now become the official Church which belongs, along with all other political, social and economic large-scale structures, to the powers that block freedom."

[296] *Called to Communion*, 135.
[297] Ibid., 134.
[298] Ibid., 135.
[299] Ibid., 134.
[300] "Demokratisierung I", 9.
[301] Cf. ibid., 16–18.
[302] Ibid., 18.

ignores this difference is, in Ratzinger's judgment, "from the outset
on the way to misconstruing the matter, because he is starting from a
half-understood analogy and thus from a complete misunderstanding".[303] Specifically, this means:

> Although interest in the state and its well-being is to a great extent
> identical with interest in its institutions, a rightly understood inter-
> est in the Church is primarily directed, not to the Church herself,
> but rather to that from which and for which she exists; in other
> words (to speak in the words of the Augsburg Confession), to ensure
> that the Word of God is proclaimed pure and unadulterated and
> that the liturgy is celebrated correctly. The question of ministries is
> important only insofar as it is a prerequisite for this.... Ministry
> should operate as noiselessly as possible and should not be primarily
> concerned about itself.[304]

The Church bureaucracy's preoccupation with itself has a rather debil-
itating effect on evangelization.[305] For, as Ratzinger noted in 1970,
people are not interested in "how bishops, priests, and full-time Catholics can strike a balance, but rather in what God wants from them in
life and death".[306] In particular he shares the concern of Henri de
Lubac, who toward the end of the Council said, "We could end up
with the positivism of a self-running ecclesial operation, behind which
is hidden a basic loss of the faith."[307] Ratzinger epitomizes this fear
in the formula: "A Church that has people talking much too much
about herself is not talking about what she should be talking about."[308]
Her duty is, rather, to talk about God, that is, "to make room for the
One who is Alive and for his variety".[309]

---

[303] Ibid., 19.

[304] Ibid., 19f., with a reference to the "Confessio Augustana" 7, 1: "Est autem ecclesia congregatio sanctorum, in qua evangelium pure docetur et recte administrantur sacramenta." See also *Die Bekenntnisschriften der evangelisch-lutherischen Kirche* (Göttingen: Vandenhoeck and Ruprecht, 1952), 61.

[305] Cf. Pottmeyer, "Weg", 293–95.

[306] "Demokratisierung 1", 21.

[307] Ibid. See H. de Lubac, "Zur Einführung", in Baraúna, 1:15–22; Ratzinger refers also to the first part of Henri de Lubac, *The Drama of Atheist Humanism*, trans. Edith M. Riley, Anne Englund Nash, and Mark Sebanc from the 7th ed. (San Francisco: Ignatius Press, 1995).

[308] "Demokratisierung 1", 21.

[309] "Demokratisierung 2", 92.

Right before the Council, when the expression "People of God" met with such enthusiasm, it became clear, as Ratzinger recalls, that "the emotion surrounding this discovery far exceeded what the biblical foundations could bear."[310] The consequence was a mutation of "the idea of the Church into a sociological entity",[311] in some cases out of anti-hierarchical and anti-sacramental motives.[312] In this trend a not insignificant role was played by the various intellectual movements of the modern era, such as the Enlightenment, Romanticism, the turn to social and political causes, nationalism, and Communism. For Ratzinger, such historical intellectual movements appear to be "startlingly close . . . to the modern ideas . . . of the grass-roots Church, the 'Church from below', the Church of the people, the congregation as the agent of all campaigns that are religious and political and social at one and the same time".[313] Moreover, he points out interesting connections in intellectual history, for instance, between the spirit of the Enlightenment and the ideas of Latin American traditions,[314] and concludes:

Anyone who tries to grasp the post-conciliar development of the concept of the Church merely on the basis of the classical theological sources will only with difficulty catch sight of the real problems.

---

[310] *Church*, 21.

[311] Ibid. Ratzinger refers here to the remarkable study by the Byzantine scholar Endre von Ivánka, *Rhomäerreich und Gottesvolk*. She finds the earliest roots for the sociological transformation of the People of God concept in the writings of Eusebius of Caesarea, specifically, as Ratzinger summarizes her argument, "in his idea of Christians as the 'third nation' to which the 'two others', the pagans and the Jews, lead up. [Whereas] Clement of Alexandria presented the providential role of the Greeks, what we get with Eusebius is the evaluation of the Roman Empire in terms of salvation history and its classification within God's plan of salvation. On this, Ivánka comments: 'It is an incredible audacity to regard an actual human community, a genuinely existing state, even if it should be the universal Roman *imperium*, simply as the people of God and to clothe it with the aura of the chosen people of the Old Testament.' . . . Ivánka then shows how this conception persisted and was modified in Byzantine theology and its continuation after the fall of Constantinople in the idea of the third Rome" (*Church*, 22; see E. von Ivánka, *Rhomäerreich und Gottesvolk* [Freiburg im Breisgau and Munich: Alber, 1968], 51–57).

[312] See also Ratzinger, "Why I Am Still in the Church", 65–91, ref. at 74.

[313] *Church*, 26.

[314] Cf. ibid., 27: "The Brazilian scholar Ricardo Vélez Rodriguez has shown how in South America it was especially Jean-Jacques Rousseau (1712–1778) and Claude Henri Saint-Simon (1760–1825) who became the 'Fathers of the Church' for a new blend of philosophical and theological, political and religious ideas." See also R. Vélez Rodriguez, "Politischer Messianismus und Theologie der Befreiung", *IKaZ* 13 (1984): 343–54.

The effort to obtain an accurate, biblically based formulation of the concept of the Church must be realized today primarily as an exercise in the self-criticism of the intellectual history of the modern age, with its blendings of what is political and what is religious, of biblical tradition and more recent mythologies. To a greater extent than we had thought both the eastern world on the one hand and the American continent on the other belong to this intellectual history. Such an analysis will not only lead to condemnations: it will be able to discover fruitful new knowledge in what is often a [strange] context. It will not only be condemnation but it must always be purification.[315]

These words written by Ratzinger acquire new meaning and are even more important in light of the changes brought about in the year 1989 with the surprising collapse of the socialist regime in Europe.[316] Hopes that this would produce new opportunities for the Church have not been fulfilled; instead "disillusionment"[317] and "scepticism about great ideals"[318] have increased.

In these few highlights of developments in intellectual history during the second half of the twentieth century, among which the years 1968 and 1989 stand out as "particularly important milestones",[319] it becomes evident that Ratzinger regards the Church in each instance within the context of the societal changes, and it is clear how he does this.[320] The political and philosophical movements of the Enlightenment, as well as Marxism, pragmatism, subjectivism, skepticism, proportionalism, and, last but not least, relativism, were in his judgment influential during the postconciliar period in contributing to the transformation of the concept of the People of God into something political and sociological, especially in Europe and America.[321] Against this background, it becomes clear why "a purification of the concept of the people of God on the basis of the biblical foundations and the

---

[315] *Church*, 27f.
[316] Cf. *Introduction*, 11–29, esp. 11–18.
[317] "New Questions", 117.
[318] *Introduction*, 18.
[319] Ibid., 11.
[320] See also "New Questions", 115–37.
[321] Cf. *Introduction*, 11–26.

[heart] of the [faith] tradition"[322] is one of the chief concerns of Ratzinger's ecclesiology.

In the next few pages of this presentation, I will concentrate first on relativism as an implicit cause for the transformation of the People of God concept into something political, for as the "prevailing philosophy" of the postmodern period it has become "the central problem for faith".[323] In a second step, I will discuss Ratzinger's position on present ecclesial praxis, whereby I will limit myself to his judgment on the transfer of democratic elements to the Church, especially the majority principle.

2. Relativism a prerequisite for democracy?

In an essay looking back on his study entitled "Democratization of the Church?"[324] which caused a sensation when it was published in 1970, Ratzinger writes thirty years later:

> When I . . . took my almost forgotten commentary on the democratization of the Church off the shelf and reread it, I discovered to my surprise that today I stand by everything that I said then, only more so. I myself was astounded at how constant my views have remained during those turbulent thirty years, which after all brought about momentous changes in my own life as well. But it goes without saying that the study could not be rewritten but, rather, would have to be continued, because since then the understanding of democracy in our society has continued to develop and our political system, on account of its progressive involvement in European institutions and the process of globalization, has had to confront new questions about our understanding and practice of democracy.[325]

For Ratzinger, one such open question is whether relativism is a prerequisite for democracy. After the collapse of the twentieth-century totalitarian systems of government in Europe in the years 1945 and 1989, the conviction has spread worldwide that democracy, "while

---

[322] *Church*, 28.
[323] "New Questions", 117.
[324] "Demokratisierung 1", 7–46.
[325] "Demokratisierung 2", 78.

not producing the ideal society, is nevertheless in practice the only suitable system of government",[326] because it protects freedom, "justice, and the good".[327] Admittedly, there are difficulties in implementing it concretely: Many people do not want "the state to impose a particular idea of the good".[328] If "the good" is replaced with the concept of truth, then the same general opinion applies: that it cannot be known but is valid only for the individual or for groups in society in particular situations.

> The attempt to dictate to all what appears to one segment of the citizens as truth is considered the enslavement of conscience: the concept of truth has moved into the zone of anti-democratic intolerance. It is not a public, but only a private good, or perhaps a good belonging to groups but not to the citizenry as a whole. In other words: The modern concept of democracy seems to be inseparably connected with relativism, whereas relativism appears to be the real guarantee of freedom, precisely of the essential core of freedom as well: freedom of religion and freedom of conscience.[329]

In a democratic society, therefore, relativism defines itself "positively on the basis of the concepts of tolerance, dialectic epistemology, and freedom".[330] Ratzinger says that public life in such a society depends on "all the ways acknowledging each other as fragmentary attempts at improvement and trying to agree in common through dialogue".[331] This gives rise to competition between relative positions in a net maximum of societal freedom.[332] Even though Ratzinger largely agrees with this interpretation in the political realm— "what is relative, the construction of a freely ordered common life ... cannot be absolute"[333]—there are nevertheless, as he understands it, rights that have absolute validity. As human rights, they represent the "nonrelativistic core"[334] of democracy.

---

[326] *Prüfsteine*, 65.
[327] Ibid., 67.
[328] Ibid.
[329] Ibid., 67f.
[330] "New Questions", 117.
[331] Ibid.
[332] Cf. ibid.
[333] Ibid.
[334] *Prüfsteine*, 68.

For is it not built around human rights that are inviolable, so that
the granting and safeguarding of these rights is the most profound
reason why democracy is necessary? Human rights, for their part,
are not subject to the commandment of pluralism and tolerance;
they *are* the content of tolerance and freedom. Depriving someone
else of his rights can never become the content of a right and can
never be the object of freedom. That means that a basic store of
truth, namely, of moral truth, seems to be indispensable precisely
for democracy.[335]

But how are these rights to be substantiated? Are they subject to
"the play of majority and minority"?[336] Two radically opposed positions, in several variations, confront each other in the current discussion about political philosophy: the radically relativistic position,[337]
which ultimately recognizes no other principle than majority rule,
and the contrary fundamental position that "truth is not the product
of politics (of the majority) but rather precedes it and illumines it."[338]
Applied to ecclesiology, the following axiom is therefore true, according to Ratzinger: "Praxis does not create truth, but rather truth makes
right praxis possible."[339]
In view of the above-mentioned modern ways of fusing the political with the religious, this political digression proves to be extremely
relevant. According to Ratzinger, at present there are attempts—some
more determined than others—in "the gray pragmatism at work in

---

[335] Ibid. Cf. "Demokratisierung 2", 79: "There are human rights, fundamental human
values, that can never be up for debate; agreement about this common basis is what makes
possible a meaningful debate about whatever has to be regulated."

[336] *Prüfsteine*, 69.

[337] Cf. ibid. This radically relativistic position excludes "the concept of the good (and
thus even more so the concept of the true) from politics", because it is said to "endanger
freedom". " 'Natural law' is rejected as metaphysically dubious, so as to maintain relativism
consistently. According to this way of thinking, there is ultimately no other political principle than the decision of the majority, which replaces the truth in the life of the state."

[338] Ibid., 70.

[339] Ibid. In this context, in my opinion, one should inquire further into the principle of
the normative force of the factual. See also Romano Guardini, *The Spirit of the Liturgy*,
trans. Ada Lane (1930; reprinted, New York: Crossroad, 1998), 85–95, "The Primacy of
the Logos over the Ethos". See also K.-H. Menke, *Die Einzigkeit Jesu Christi im Horizont
der Sinnfrage* (Freiburg: Johannes Verlag, 1995), 95. Similarly, with regard to ecumenical and
interreligious dialogue, Ratzinger is convinced that no progress can be made by starting
with the "primacy of orthopraxis over orthodoxy".

the everyday life of the Church ... to extend the majority principle
to matters of faith and morals".[340] This leads us to the question of to
what extent the rules of democracy are valid for ecclesial praxis and
where its limits are found. Since this topic is very complex, I concentrate, with Ratzinger, on the problem of the majority principle for
reaching decisions in questions of faith.

3. *On the problem of the majority principle*

Whereas, in the wake of the upheaval in the year 1968, democracy
had been trumpeted as a "code word for a doctrine of salvation",[341]
there is now a danger, in Ratzinger's view, of confusing the "many-
layered reality of democracy" with "one of the instruments of its
practical implementation".[342] Specifically this means that nowadays
democracy in practice is equated with the application of the principle of majority rule.[343] In parliamentary democracies, this is foundational for the complex process of arriving at decisions.[344] To rely
on this principle alone, however, would not do justice to political
action in a democracy, either. This is not the place to list all the
components of the democratic structures of a state. With Ratzinger,
we will point out three essential limitations of the majority principle, namely: first, the human rights that were just mentioned;
second, the freedom of the independent courts; and finally, areas
of freedom granted by every state to various societal forces, "the
autonomy of which is in turn a part of the system of mutually
supporting and reciprocally limiting rights to freedom that make
up the democracy".[345] Among these areas is the free space of the
Church, whereby democratic states attribute to the "intrinsic autonomy" of the Church "a special importance, inasmuch as it not only

---

[340] "New Questions", 129.
[341] "Demokratisierung I", 12. On this subject, see K. Rahner, *Freiheit und Manipulation in Gesellschaft und Kirche* (Munich: Kösel, 1970), esp. 9, 16.
[342] "Demokratisierung 2", 79. Cf. *Called to Communion*, 137.
[343] On this subject, see "Demokratisierung 2", 79, where Ratzinger refers in a footnote to the essay by L. Roos, "Demokratie in der Kirche?" in *Christen und Demokratie*, by G. Baadte and A. Rauscher, 125–48, esp. 140 (Graz: Styria, 1991).
[344] Cf. "Demokratisierung 2", 79f.
[345] Ibid., 80.

represents an important force in our educational and social system
but is also the conveyor of value convictions, which in a certain
respect are the inner prerequisite for the fundamental values defined
by the constitution."[346]

Anyone who wants to talk about democratizing the Church, Ratzinger says, should keep in view the contours of democratically ordered
states as just outlined,[347] "so as not to think only about the majority
principle with a one-track mind".[348] Just as in democratic states "the
individual instruments serve the purpose of the whole",[349] namely,
protecting the good of the individual and of the community, so too
analogously the ecclesiastical order enshrined in constitution and law
are subject to the good of the Church and her goal. Hence, as early as
1970, Ratzinger emphatically pointed out the distinctive feature of
ecclesiastical structures, which is evident in the fact that "the truth of
the gospel of Jesus Christ" is a reality that is not immanent, which has
the authority to expropriate mankind for its own sake.[350] Thirty years
later, he expresses the fear "that in the debate about democratization
there is a widespread and growing demand [to formulate] the faith in
terms of the ability to gain assent",[351] with the result that the truth
does not expropriate man, but rather man himself defines what is true
for him. The good and the purpose of the Church, however, are always
a prior given that has been received from God: "This good is, from
God's perspective, the gospel and, from man's perspective, the faith.
The foremost purpose of ecclesiastical order, both constitutional and
legal, must be making it accessible to all, in unadulterated form, as the
light and the strength by which we live."[352]

Allowing for this prior given, in the postconciliar period democratic
elements on a large scale[353] were introduced in the Church (and rightly

[346] Ibid.
[347] Here, in practice, the "systems of economic laws" play in Western democracies a
role that should not be underestimated (cf. ibid., 8of.).
[348] Ibid., 81.
[349] Ibid.
[350] "Demokratisierung 1", 18.
[351] "Demokratisierung 2", 88.
[352] Ibid., 81f. See also "Demokratisierung 1", 18f.
[353] "Demokratisierung 2", 82f. Among the elements of democratization in the Church,
as Ratzinger lists them (ibid., 82), are "the consultative structures, from the parish through
the deanery and the diocese all the way to the umbrella organization, the Central Committee

so, in Ratzinger's view), the purpose of which was to support in various ways "the common good of the Church and the struggle to make the gospel present for the individual and for the entirety".[354] In this way, the Catholic Church is an "extremely many-leveled structure with an amazing wealth of forms and manifold living spaces".[355]

Ratzinger's basically positive outlook on democratic forms of implementation in the Church must not fool us into overlooking his severe criticism of many developments within the Church, which he formulates in expressions such as "pastoral ministry by slogans",[356] "a dangerous mixture of faith and politics",[357] "counter-magisterium",[358] "a dualism" between hierarchy and laity,[359] "political correctness",[360] or a "particular type of idea about unity".[361] In these is manifested the weakness of democratic organizational forms, which try to regulate

---

of German Catholics [*Zentralkomitee der deutschen Katholiken* (ZdK)] ... , the Synods, from the General Synods of the early seventies to the diocesan synods and forums.... Furthermore, we will recall the 'base community movements' such as 'Church from Below' and 'We Are Church'; the latter name is connected with the attempt to mobilize popular petition drives about important, fundamental decisions concerning the faith and life of the Church and thus to set up in the Church the most radical instrument of direct democracy." Ratzinger goes on to mention the new spiritual movements, the synods of bishops, the local Church council, the ecumenical council, and also democratic elements in religious life.

[354] Ibid., 83.

[355] Ibid.

[356] Ibid., 84.

[357] Ibid., 86.

[358] Ibid., 87. Ratzinger refers here to the Central Committee of German Catholics (ZdK) when he remarks, "During the past twenty years there were probably few Roman magisterial decisions that were not promptly followed by a blunt protest from the ZdK.... If one inquires into the theological justification for such magisterial activities of the ZdK, one most often gets two answers. Since Vatican II, the argument usually goes, lay people also have a say in doctrine; the ZdK is the organization suited to this purpose; after all, it is the union of the elected lay representatives of German Catholicism.... It is well known that voter participation in elections for Church governing bodies is minimal, and the atmosphere becomes even more rarefied, the higher one climbs through the various systems of delegates. As for the base constituency, therefore, it is much too narrow to support such grandiose words.... It is even more dubious when the word of the hierarchy is pitted against the word of the laity."

[359] Ibid.

[360] Ibid., 91. Here Ratzinger specifically mentions activities of the BDKJ [the organization that coordinates Catholic conferences in Germany] that are tinged with Church politics.

[361] Ibid.

everything according to the majority principle, without taking into consideration what for Ratzinger is the decisive question of truth, which is ultimately the question of Christ, the way, the truth, and the life. Therefore he argues:

> Not everything has to be regulated, by no means. . . . If everything is subjected to the prevailing patterns of organization, then the fresh spring water of life dries up. Sterility is the necessary result. Democratization in the Church . . . cannot consist of setting up still more voting bodies; it consists, rather, of allowing room for what is alive, in its variety.[362]

This judgment may originate from Ratzinger's experience that hierarchy is often mistaken for a sort of tutelage and therefore has to be replaced by "democratic self-determination".[363] But this results in a "self-made church" that "savors of the 'self', which always has a bitter taste to the other self"[364] and obscures the real thing, which comes from God:

> Everything that men make can also be undone again by others. Everything that has its origin in human likes can be disliked by others. Everything that one majority decides upon can be revoked by another majority. A church based on human resolutions becomes a merely human church. It is reduced to the level of the makeable, of the obvious, of opinion. Opinion replaces faith.[365]

In contrast, Ratzinger senses the freshness of the early Christian Church in an altogether different "democratic" element, which he views as "the real enlivening element in the development of the post-conciliar period":[366] the new ecclesial movements. In them, the power of the Holy Spirit can be discerned, which has restored the dynamic of the People of God at precisely the time when "in fact it had become weary and dispirited after the many debates and the stress of looking for new structures".[367] In his view, this is "a phenomenon that recurs

---

[362] "Demokratisierung 2", 91f.
[363] *Called to Communion*, 139.
[364] Ibid., 140.
[365] Ibid., 139.
[366] Cf. "Demokratisierung 2", 90, and also Ratzinger, "Kirchliche Bewegungen und ihr theologischer Ort", *IKaZ* 27 (1998): 431–48. See also *Principles*, 377f.
[367] Ratzinger, "Kirchliche Bewegungen", 431f.

in various forms periodically in Church history", whereby the Holy Spirit himself desires "again and again to enliven and renew"[368] this system of ecclesial life. The initiative, therefore, lies in the sovereignty of God, who through his Spirit is "quite obviously at work in the Church even today".[369]

When Ratzinger applies the adjective "democratic" to the Church, therefore, it is always presupposed "that we keep in view the special character of this 'people', which does not just act on its own";[370] the distinctive feature is their certainty that God is the real sovereign of his people. As he explains in another passage, the Church always lives "by the call of the Spirit, in the 'crisis' of the transition from the old to the new".[371] The saints give eloquent witness to this. They belong, Ratzinger says, to the Church's "identity that over-arches time" and make up "her real majority".[372] Consequently, the call to holiness is to be lived out only in continuity with the People of God, understood diachronically[373] as he considers it here: a people that defines itself, not politically, but rather in terms of Christ.

§ 6. The Universal Call to Holiness

1. *An increase in faith, hope, and charity as the aim of conciliar ecclesiology*

If we compare Ratzinger's essays from the years 1975, 1985, and 2000, in which he takes stock of the reception of the Second Vatican Council, we cannot help being struck by the fact that they all conclude with the same theme: the universal call of all the members of the People of God to holiness.

---

[368] Ibid., 432.

[369] Ibid., 447.

[370] "Demokratisierung 2", 90.

[371] *Volk Gottes*, 71–90, citation at 85.

[372] *Salt of the Earth*, 189. See also *Called to Communion*, 154: "The fortuitous majorities that may form here or there in the Church do not decide their and our path: they, the saints, are the true, the normative majority by which we orient ourselves." Here Ratzinger refers to J. Meisner, *Wider die Entsinnlichung des Glaubens* (Graz: Styria, 1990), 35.

[373] *Salt of the Earth*, 188f.

In his 1975 retrospect, he recalled a comparison that Karl Rahner had made at the end of the Council:

Huge amounts of pitchblende are needed to produce a small quantity of radium, which is the sole object of the process. In like manner, he said, the tremendous exertion of the Council was, in the last analysis, worthwhile because of the small increase of faith, hope and charity it produced.[374]

Ratzinger concludes from this comparison that whether or not the Council brings about a renewal in the Church "depends only indirectly on texts and organizations".[375] On the one side, throughout Church history the saints have always been the ones "who, by their personal willingness, which cannot be forced, are ready to effect something new and living"[376] by putting the message into practice. For this purpose, the Council "opened ways that lead from all kinds of byways and one-way streets to the real center of Christianity".[377] On the other hand, however, he opposes a naïve postconciliar optimism that, along with the excessive "self-esteem of many", could spoil the anticipated harvest and make the Council a "waste of time"; he refers, moreover, to the history of Church councils, especially to the Fifth Lateran Council, which met from 1512 to 1517 "without doing anything effective to prevent the crisis that was developing".[378] Ten years later, in 1985, Ratzinger warns that it would be nonsensical to base a "theology of the laity" on chapter 2 of the Constitution of the Church, "The People of God", because this section of the document is not discussing a particular state in life; rather, "what is being dealt with here is the Church as a whole and its nature".[379] All the baptized, both lay persons and clerics, belong to this one people, and the call to holiness is addressed to them all. Therefore, at the conclusion he turns his attention especially to Mary, who as an exemplar shows the Church the way.[380] In his report on the Council from the year 2000, which in

---

[374] *Principles*, 367–78, citation at 377.
[375] Ibid.
[376] Ibid.
[377] Ibid., 377–78.
[378] Cf. ibid., 378. The last of the three phrases is quoted from n. 14.
[379] *Church*, 3–20, citation at 20.
[380] Cf. ibid.

particular discusses the ecclesiology of *Lumen gentium*, Ratzinger succinctly declares, along the same lines as the other two retrospective essays:

> No one who wants to understand the characteristics of the Council's ecclesiology can leave out chapters 4 through 7 of the Constitution, which talk about laymen, about the universal call to *holiness*, about religion, and about the eschatological orientation of the Church. In these chapters the inner reason for the Church's existence, what is essential in her life, once more makes its appearance: they are concerned with holiness, that is, with what is fitting for God—in order that space may be made in the world for God, so that he may dwell therein and the world may thus become his "Kingdom".[381]

In these remarks we can discern one of Ratzinger's fundamental intentions, which he puts into words right at the beginning of his essay: What matters to him is the question about God.[382] Hence the vocation to holiness is for him "more than a moral quality"; it is "the dwelling of God with men, of men with God, the setting of God's 'tabernacle' with us and among us (Jn 1:14)".[383] He sees in this the realization of the Church's meaning and of her eschatological dimension, which have their foundations in Scripture: "The Church is there in order that God may come to dwell in the world and in order that 'holiness' may come about: that is what we should be competing for in the Church, not competing for more or less privilege, about sitting in the best places."[384]

Ratzinger is concerned here about the center of Christian vocation, about the question: "What shall I do to inherit eternal life?" (Lk 10:25). In grappling with this crucial question of the Gospel, he deliberately turns his attention first to responsibility in God's sight as a prerequisite for a sincere love of neighbor:

> I must think of the fact that God has a task in mind for me in the world and will ask me afterwards what I have done with my life. Today many people maintain that thinking about eternal life prevents

---

[381] "Ecclesiology", 149.
[382] On this subject, see ibid., 124.
[383] Ibid., 149.
[384] Ibid., 150.

people from doing the right thing in this world. But the opposite is true. If we lose sight of God's standard, the standard of eternity, then all that remains over as a guiding thread is nothing but egotism.[385]

The call to holiness represents for Ratzinger "a kind of Copernican revolution".[386] It means that the individual should not think that he is the real center around which everything has to revolve, but rather he must "leave this error" and act like a brother or a sister, "joining together with all the others in the round dance of love around the one center".[387] Although pathways through life may vary greatly, the Christian must not lose sight of this one goal. The Marian chapter of *Lumen gentium* should also be understood against the background of the vocation of all Christians to holiness. This concluding chapter sees Mary in communion with the whole Church, "not ... as an isolated individual, closed up in herself",[388] but rather as a person who reflects the mystery of the Church.

2. On the meaning of the Marian statements

a. Ratzinger's position during the Council

While the Council was still in session, Ratzinger described the highly controversial vote of the Council Fathers on October 29, 1963, in which a slim majority[389] rejected an independent schema on Mary[390] and incorporated Mariology into the schema on the Church, as "a very positive decision".[391] In his report on the second session, he himself mentions four reasons for including the Marian doctrine in the schema on the Church. The first is that it strengthens the eschatological as well as the spiritual perspective of the Church: "It is now also much clearer that the nature of the Church is not tied up exclusively

---

[385] *To Look on Christ*, 100–105, citation at 100–101.
[386] See ibid., 103.
[387] Ibid., 103–4.
[388] "Ecclesiology", 151.
[389] See Pesch, 192–96, ref. at 193. The majority on October 29, 1963, consisted of 1,114 against 1,074 votes. See also "Marian Doctrine", 22.
[390] The schema on Mary, "De beata virgine matre Dei et matre hominum", can be found in *AS* 1/4: 92–121.
[391] Cf. *Highlights*, 60, 92–95.

with the temporal dimensions nor fully defined in terms of visible institutions, but that it extends into the future, into an area beyond human intervention and disposition."[392]

The second reason, in Ratzinger's opinion, is very closely related to the first. Through the broadened perspective of the connection between the Church's earthly and heavenly life, the "communicantes et memoriam venerantes sanctorum"[393] of the liturgy comes into view. Thus the worshipping community is "encompassed in that cosmic liturgy, where all the world and all the saints adore God".[394]

Third, with the expression "Church of the poor", Ratzinger refers to an essential element that is constitutive of the Church, one that is typologically presented in the lowliness of Mary, the handmaid of the Lord.

> She exemplifies the paradox of grace that touches those who cannot accomplish anything by themselves. She personifies the Church of the poor, the Church that moves through history as a humble servant, and by that very fact is in a position to express the mystery of God's promise and proximity.[395]

Finally, for him the connection between the Old and the New Covenant is evident in Mary. In her person it becomes clear that the Church has "sprung from the root of Israel".[396] On the laborious journey of the People of God, she "carries the hope of the world ... beneath [her] heart", a hope on which mankind "secretly lives".[397]

b. Later complementary statements by Ratzinger

Years later, too, Ratzinger acclaimed the result of the Council Fathers' vote in October 1963, which subsequently "marked an intellectual watershed".[398] In order to make the background to the debate at that time comprehensible, he refers to the historical context of the conciliar decision, specifically to the period between the First World War and the Second Vatican Council, during which "two major spiritual

---

[392] *Highlights*, 60.
[393] Cf. ibid. See the Roman Canon of the *Missale Romanum*.
[394] *Highlights*, 60.
[395] Ibid.
[396] Ibid.
[397] Ibid.
[398] "Marian Doctrine", 22.

movements"[399] within the Church were decisive for the mariological question. The one was influenced by the Marian apparitions in La Salette, Lourdes, and Fatima, and, "by the time it reached its peak under Pius XII, its influence had spread throughout the whole Church."[400] In contrast, the second trend was the liturgical movement, the origins of which are to be found, on the one hand, in the Benedictine reform movement of Solesmes and, on the other hand, in the eucharistic renewal initiated by Pope Pius X. In it, together with the ecumenical movement and the Bible movement, a spiritual force had developed, "the renewal of the Church from the sources of Scripture and the primitive form of the Church's prayer".[401] Both "charismatic"[402] currents (the Marian apparitions and these renewal movements) had to be recognized, Ratzinger says, as "signs of the times" and brought together into a healthy relationship of tension in the conciliar debates:

> Theologically speaking, the majority spearheaded by Cardinal König was right. If the two charismatic movements should not be seen as contrary, but must be regarded as complementary, then an integration was imperative, even though this integration could not mean the absorption of one movement by the other.[403]

As for the reception of *Lumen gentium*, however, Ratzinger recognizes inadequacies with relation to the deeper, Marian understanding

---

[399] Ibid., 19.

[400] Ibid. See also "Einleitung", 18f.: In his commentary, Ratzinger expresses his opinion about "the most controversial statement of them all", the designation of the Mother of God as "Mediatrix of all graces", a title that was not adopted by the Council. The conclusion of his commentary reads: "The outcome of all this is not to chill Catholic Marian devotion in the cold breeze of rationalistic theology or to let it waste away in the iconoclasm of so-called Marian minimalism; this fact is demonstrated clearly enough in the Marian chapter of our Constitution [on the Church], which is richer and more lively than the syllogistic treatises of Scholastic Mariology that are probably on the wrong track when they express their piety by thinking up ever-new privileges for the Mother of God." Cf. *Highlights*, 93f. During the Council, Ratzinger judged rather harshly the Marian devotion of those who invoke Mary as Mediatrix and attributed to them a lack of theological enlightenment.

[401] "Marian Doctrine", 20.

[402] Ratzinger speaks about "charismatic" traits of these very different movements. See ibid., 19, 22.

[403] Ibid., 22. Cardinal Rufino Santos of Manila spoke against this and in favor of an independent schema on Mary.

of ecclesiology, which were largely caused "by a misunderstanding of the conciliar statements on the concept of tradition", which led to talk about the "sufficiency" of Scripture.[404] This notion, he says, was interpreted in the sense of a biblicism that, furthermore, "condemned the whole patristic heritage to irrelevance".[405] Ratzinger characterizes this as an "archaeological mentality",[406] one feature of which is the principle of decline.

> What occurs after a certain point in time appears ipso facto to be of inferior value, as if the Church were not alive and therefore capable of development in every age. As a result of all this, the kind of thinking shaped by the liturgical movement narrowed into a biblicist-positivist mentality, locked itself into a backward-looking attitude, and thus left no more room for the dynamic development of the faith. On the other hand, the distance implied in historicism inevitably paved the way for "modernism"; since what is merely past is no longer living, it leaves the present isolated and so leads to self-made experimentation.[407]

Yet, in Ratzinger's judgment it was not only "biblicistic positivism" that caused a refusal to accept what had been acknowledged in chapter 8 of *Lumen gentium* as a new ecclesiocentric Mariology. This new form of doctrine about Mary in the mystery of Christ and of the Church was still foreign to those Council Fathers, too, who were reckoned as "the principal upholders of Marian piety".[408] The title "Mother of the Church",[409] which was debated among the Council Fathers

---

[404] Ratzinger refers to vol. 17 in the series entitled Quaestiones disputatae, in which he treats this question: Ratzinger, "On the Interpretation of the Tridentine Decree on Tradition", in *Revelation and Tradition*, by K. Rahner and J. Ratzinger [1965], trans. W.J. O'Hara, 26–66 (New York: Herder and Herder, 1966). See also Ratzinger, "Kommentar zu Kapitel 2 der Dogmatischen Konstitution über die göttliche Offenbarung", in *LThK.E*, vol. 2 (Freiburg am Breisgau: Herder, 1967), 515–28.

[405] "Marian Doctrine", 23.

[406] Cf. ibid., 24.

[407] Ibid.

[408] Ibid.

[409] See O. Semmelroth, "Kommentar zu LG Kap. 8", in *LThK.E*, vol. 1 (Freiburg im Breisgau: Herder, 1966), 326–47, ref. at 338–40: "Exkurs". Cf. *Probleme*, 7f. [that is, the foreword to the German ed. of pt. 3 of the *Theological Highlights*]: Ratzinger reckoned Pope Paul's conduct at that time, in proclaiming Mary "Mother of the Church", against the will of the majority of the Council, as one of a series of "unfriendly surprises".

and which Pope Paul VI proclaimed in his concluding address at the
end of the third session of the Council, was equally incapable of pre-
venting the crisis. In summary, Ratzinger concludes that "the victory
of ecclesiocentric Mariology", which he himself welcomed, actually
caused "the collapse of Mariology".[410]

> The decision of 1963 had led de facto to the absorption of Mari-
> ology by ecclesiology. A reconsideration of the text has to begin
> with the recognition that its actual historical effect contradicts its
> own original meaning. For the chapter on Mary (chap. 8) was writ-
> ten so as to correspond intrinsically to chapters 1–4, which describe
> the structure of the Church. The balance of the two was meant to
> secure the correct equilibrium that would fruitfully correlate the
> respective energies of the biblical-ecumenical-liturgical movement
> and the Marian movements.[411]

When the Council is interpreted properly, the inclusion of the Marian chapter in the schema on the Church has a twofold function with
respect to the concept of the Church: First, it recognizes the Church
in her feminine structure as Virgin and Mother, and, second, it acknowledges her as *sponsa Christi*.

Before discussing in more detail these two mariological definitions of
the Church, we should turn our attention to Ratzinger's observation that
the mariological statements of the Church Fathers, which the Council
cites, were originally conceived in ecclesiological terms. They had already
"foreshadowed the whole of Mariology ... , albeit without any mention of the name of the Mother of the Lord: The *virgo ecclesia* [virgin
Church], the *mater ecclesia* [mother Church], the *ecclesia immaculata* [immac-
ulate Church], the *ecclesia assumpta* [assumed Church]".[412] Ever since Bernard of Clairvaux, this "initially anonymous, though personally shaped,
ecclesiology"[413] had been brought into relation with the early statements about Mary in Christology. From this, as Ratzinger remarks, "a

---

[410] "Marian Doctrine", 24. On the problem of integrating Mariology into theology as
a whole during the postconciliar period, see the section entitled "Tendenzen und Probleme der Mariologie nach dem Zweiten Vatikanum", in H. Steinhauer, *Maria als dramatische Person bei Hans Urs von Balthasar: Zum marianischen Prinzip seines Denkens*, STS 17
(Innsbruck: Tyrolia-Verlag, 2001), 56–81, esp. 70.

[411] "Marian Doctrine", 25.

[412] Ibid., 28.

[413] Ibid.

Mariology having an integrity of its own first emerged within theology",[414] and because of its twofold origin, it has both christological and ecclesiological relevance. Indeed, over the course of time the Church recognized that in Mary she had already anticipated what her own destination is. Conversely, it is equally true that "Mary does not stand there as an isolated individual, closed up in herself, but carries within her the whole mystery of the Church."[415] For Ratzinger, the consequences of this, with respect to the ecclesiological relation between person and communion in general, are as follows:

> The person is not being understood as closed and individualistic, nor the community as collective and non-personal; the two merge inseparably together.
> That is true of the apocalyptic woman who appears in the twelfth chapter of the Book of Revelation: it will not do for this woman to be understood exclusively and individualistically as Mary, because in her we are seeing the whole People of God, suffering and yet fruitful through their suffering, the old and the new Israel together; yet equally it will not do to keep Mary, the Mother of the Redeemer, purely separate from this picture.[416]

This "transition and fluidity"[417] between person and community, which is indicated in the Revelation of John and continued by the Church Fathers in their typological interpretation of Scripture, was taken up anew by the Council. Ratzinger locates within this context the revision of a Mariology that concentrated solely on Mary's privileges and thus removed the Mother of God to an unreachable height. Such a divergence of person and community "damaged both Mariology and ecclesiology in equal measure", since the Church, too, was thereby "seen as being nonpersonal and purely institutional".[418] It would be "a thorough misunderstanding", however, of the typological interpretation of the Church Fathers, according to Ratzinger, to "reduce Mary to a mere, hence, interchangeable, exemplification of theological structures",[419] for:

---

[414] Ibid.
[415] "Ecclesiology", 151.
[416] Ibid.
[417] Ibid.
[418] Ibid.
[419] "Marian Doctrine", 27.

In theology, it is not the person that is reducible to the thing, but the thing to the person. A purely structural ecclesiology is bound to degrade Church to the level of a program of action. Only the Marian dimension secures the place of affectivity in faith and thus ensures a fully human correspondence to the reality of the incarnate Logos.[420]

From experience, he knows that it is precisely the personal, heartfelt ties to God that prevent the faith from becoming reified as sociology.[421] Ratzinger is convinced that by looking to the figure of Mary, the Church, of which she is the personal type, is preserved from a "masculinized model that views her as an instrument for a program of social-political action".[422] Thus the Church rediscovers in Mary her own countenance as Mother and Virgin. This will be explained in greater detail in the following sections, in which we look first at the feminine structure of the Church as Virgin and Mother and, second, at the mystery of unity and distinctness in the nuptial act in which Christ and the Church are made one.

1) *The feminine structure of the Church*

Ratzinger interprets the Marian development of ecclesiology as a good arrangement, in which it becomes obvious that the Church cannot be reduced to what is institutional or sociological, since by her very nature she is feminine (*Ecclesia*), namely, Woman and Mother. In contrast, whenever the *Ecclesia* displays only masculine traits, her real mystery,

---

[420] Ibid. Ratzinger continues (ibid.): "Here I see the truth of the saying that Mary is the 'vanquisher of all heresies'. This affective rooting guarantees the bond *ex toto corde*—from the depth of the heart—to the *personal* God and his Christ and rules out any recasting of Christology into a Jesus program, which can be atheistic and purely neutral: the experience of the last few years verifies today in an astonishing way the accuracy of such ancient phrases." See also *Report*, 105–6: "As a young theologian in the time before (and also during) the Council, I had ... some reservations in regard to certain ancient formulas, as, for example, that famous *De Maria nunquam satis*, 'concerning Mary one can never say enough.' It seemed exaggerated to me. So it was difficult for me later to understand the true meaning of another famous expression (current in the Church since the first centuries when—after a memorable dispute—the Council of Ephesus, in 431, had proclaimed Mary *Theotokos*, Mother of God). The declaration, namely, that designated the Virgin as '*the conqueror of all heresies*'. Now—in this confused period ... I understand that it was not a matter of pious exaggerations, but of truths that today are more valid than ever."
[421] Cf. "Marian Doctrine", 34.
[422] *Report*, 108.

which is manifested in virginal love and the wonder of motherhood, is misconstrued.[423]

> The Church is not some piece of machinery, is not just an institution, is not even one of the usual sociological entities. It is a person. It is a woman. It is a mother. It is living. The Marian understanding of the Church is the most decisive contrast to a purely organizational or bureaucratic concept of the Church. We cannot make the Church: we have to be it. And it is only to the extent that faith moulds our being beyond any question of making that we *are* the Church, that the Church is in us. It is only in being Marian that we become the Church.[424]

Mary is the personal realization of the Church, because she was called as a Virgin, in the name of all creation, in "the freedom of the creature, which does not lose its integrity in love",[425] to give her *Fiat,* and because she thus bodily became the Mother of the Lord. Thus Mary "represents saved and liberated man".[426] Yet she does so "precisely as a woman, that is, in the bodily determinateness that is inseparable from man",[427] more

---

[423] Ratzinger refers to the remarks of H. U. von Balthasar, "Who Is the Church?" trans. A. V. Littledale with Alexander Dru, in *Spouse of the Word,* Explorations in Theology 2 (San Francisco: Ignatius Press, 1991), 143–91.

[424] *Church,* 3–20, citation at 20.

[425] "Marian Doctrine", 31.

[426] Ibid.

[427] Ibid. In Ratzinger's view, this difference between the sexes is established irrevocably by the Creator himself. "Male and female he created them" (Gen 1:27). In contrast, liberation movements of the present day would aim at demanding a freedom from human biological determination and thus fall prey to the primordial temptation of man: to be like God (Gen 3:5): "This sexual difference . . . is regarded as a totally irrelevant triviality, as a constraint arising from historically fabricated 'roles', and is therefore consigned to the 'purely biological realm', which has nothing to do with man as such. Accordingly, this 'purely biological' dimension is treated as a thing that man can manipulate at will because it lies beyond the scope of what counts as human and spiritual (so much so that man can freely manipulate the coming into being of life itself). This treatment of 'biology' as a mere thing is accordingly regarded as a liberation, for it enables man to leave *bios* behind, use it freely, and to be completely independent of it in every other respect, that is, to be simply a 'human being' who is neither male nor female" ("Marian Doctrine", 32). But if the biological determination of a human being shrinks to a "despicable trifle" and thus is deducted from what is human, then humanity itself is negated. For this reason, according to Ratzinger, it is really a question "of the legitimacy of maleness as such and of femaleness as such", and "nothing less than the reality of the creature" is at stake (ibid., 32–33). He illustrates this also using the example of motherhood: "Since this biological determinateness of humanity is least possible to hide in motherhood,

particularly in the "intrinsic interwovenness"[428] of the two mysteries of Virgin and Mother that is unique to her. In Mary, along with motherhood, virginity, too, "confirms that the 'biological' is human".[429] In these two gifts, "the mystery of woman receives a very lofty destiny from which she cannot be torn away."[430] The belief in Mary's perpetual virginity,[431] furthermore, according to Ratzinger, protects "the faith—threatened today—in God the Creator", who at any time "can freely intervene also in matter".[432] At the same time, her virginity is a bodily eschatological sign.[433] In Ratzinger's view, therefore, it is no accident that virginity, "although as a form of life it is also possible, and intended for, the man—is first patterned on the woman, the true keeper of the seal of creation, and has its normative, plenary form—which the man can, so to say, only imitate—in her."[434]

Since the Church possesses in Mary her typological form, and everything that is said about Mary is also true analogously of the Church,[435] according to Ratzinger, the Church as Virgin and Mother has a feminine nature.[436] Therefore, from his perspective, three characteristics

---

an emancipation that negates *bios* is a particular aggression against the woman. It is the denial of her right to be a woman. Conversely, the preservation of creation is in this respect bound up in a special way with the question of woman. And the Woman in whom the 'biological' is 'theological'—that is, motherhood of God—is in a special way the point where the paths diverge" (ibid., 33).

[428] Ibid., 29.

[429] Ibid., 33.

[430] *Report*, 108.

[431] Cf. LG 57.

[432] *Report*, 107.

[433] Cf. Ratzinger, "The Sign of the Woman: An Introductory Essay on the Encyclical *Redemptoris Mater*", in *Mary: The Church at the Source*, by Ratzinger and H. U. von Balthasar, trans. Adrian Walker, 37–60, esp. 51 (San Francisco: Ignatius Press, 2005). Ratzinger recognizes at the same time in the eschatological sign of the Woman (according to the principle of "the self-interpretation of Scripture" he advocates) a theological figure of salvation history, which extends from that "mysterious passage that tradition has called the *Protoevangelium*" (Gen 3:15) through the angelic salutation (Lk 1:28) to that apocalyptic Woman (Rev 12).

[434] "Marian Doctrine", 33. In a footnote, Ratzinger refers to a remark by A. Luciani: "The perfecting of the creature as creature occurs in the woman, not in the man." Cf. A. Luciani, *Illustrissimi: Letters from Pope John Paul I* (Boston: Little, Brown, 1978), 121–27, "King Lemuel and the Ideal Woman", esp. 121f.

[435] Cf. "Full of Grace", 66: "Mary is identified with daughter Zion, with the bridal people of God. Everything said about the *ecclesia* in the Bible is true of her, and vice versa."

[436] Of course it should still be noted that the analogy of the correlative terms "Bridegroom" and "Bride" is surpassed in Mary, since Mary's relationship to the incarnate Word

hold true for all basic mariological-ecclesiological figures. First, they are "personalizing"; that is, they view "the Church, not as a structure, but as a person and in person".[437] Second, they are "incarnational", which means "the unity of *bios*, person, and relation to God; the onto-logical freedom of the creature vis-à-vis the Creator and of the 'body' of Christ relative to the head".[438] Finally, these typologies, as the two characteristics just mentioned show, are settled in the realm of the heart. Thus faith is anchored in the emotional sphere, that is, "in the deepest roots of man's being".[439]

In Mary as a person, who is "transparent to God",[440] the nuptial love of the creature for its Creator finds its highest form, insofar as it experiences during Christ's own self-giving the act of being "given away under the Cross"[441] (Jn 19:26). There she is "the living Veronica's veil", an "icon of Christ that brings him into the present of man's heart, translates Christ's image into the heart's vision, and thus makes it intelligible".[442] Thereby Mary lives, as Ratzinger puts it, "into the [true] measure of sacred history, so that what appears in her is, not the narrow and constricted ego of an isolated individ-ual, but the whole, true Israel",[443] "in whom Old and New Cov-enant, Israel and Church, are indivisibly one".[444] Therefore in Mary he discerns a theological figure who, in the Gospel of John, "is addressed simply as *gynē*, 'the woman', if she plays a role beyond that

---

is not in the first place bridal but rather maternal (cf. "Marian Doctrine", 29). Ratzinger situates herein the specific role of the title "Mother of the Church". It "expresses the fact that Mariology goes beyond the framework of ecclesiology and at the same time is cor-relative to it" (ibid.).

[437] Ibid., 34.

[438] Ibid.

[439] Ibid. Cf. ibid., 35f.: "Marian piety will always stand within the tension between theological rationality and believing affectivity. This is part of its essence, and its task is not to allow either to atrophy. Affectivity must not lead it to forget the sober measure of *ratio*, nor must the sobriety of a reasonable faith allow it to suffocate the heart, which often sees more than naked reason. It was not for nothing that the Fathers understood Matthew 5:8 as the center of their theological epistemology: 'Blessed are the pure in heart, for they shall see God.' The organ for seeing God is the purified heart."

[440] "Full of Grace", 66.

[441] "Marian Doctrine", 35.

[442] Ibid.

[443] "Full of Grace", 66, English translation amended.

[444] *Daughter Zion*, 43.

of an individual".⁴⁴⁵ The image of the New Eve shines forth in her:
the "woman clothed with the sun, that is, permeated by the light of
God, dwelling in God—and God in her".⁴⁴⁶ Consequently, she is for
the People of God—as Ratzinger says—a "signpost of hope" ⁴⁴⁷ and of
consolation: "Looking toward the *Mater assumpta*, the Virgin Mother
assumed into heaven, Advent broadens into eschatology. The Incarnation becomes the way, which in the Cross does not revoke the fact that
our Lord took on flesh but, rather, renders this fact definitive." ⁴⁴⁸ In
this definitiveness, the Church, like Mary, appears as a bride adorned,
whom Christ loved and for whom he gave himself up,⁴⁴⁹ whom he sanctified and whom he thus chose to be "Mother of believers".⁴⁵⁰

2) *Sponsa Christi*

It seems to me, at the beginning of my discussion of the nuptial relation between Christ and his Church, that a remark made by Ratzinger clarifies the subject. He notes that Mary was physically the mother
of Jesus but that this is not the only reason why she is the type of the
Church.

> Such an argument would be an unjustifiable simplification of the
> relationship between the orders of being and knowledge. In response,
> one could, in fact, rightly point to passages like Mark 3:33–35 or
> Luke 11:27f. and ask whether, assuming this point of departure, Mary's
> physical maternity still had any theological significance at all.⁴⁵¹

---

⁴⁴⁵ *God and the World*, 297.

⁴⁴⁶ Ratzinger, "Mariä Aufnahme in den Himmel" [Homily on the Solemnity of the
Assumption of the Blessed Virgin Mary, 1993, in Henegauer Park, Regensburg], in *Heiligenpredigten*, ed. Stefan O. Horn (Munich: Wewel, 1997), 70–75, citation at 70. In Mary's
Assumption, "heaven and earth" meet. The sign of mutability ("the moon at her feet") is
"overcome and what is passing is lifted up into everlasting life. And she is part of the
constellation of redemption, for the twelve stars indicate the new family of God, represented by the twelve sons of Jacob, the twelve apostles of Jesus Christ" (ibid.).

⁴⁴⁷ Ibid., 71.

⁴⁴⁸ "Marian Doctrine", 35. The second sentence in the quotation is omitted from the
English edition and has been translated from the original German.

⁴⁴⁹ Cf. Eph 5:25f.

⁴⁵⁰ See J. Ratzinger, " 'Hail, Full of Grace': Elements of Marian Piety according to the
Bible", in Ratzinger and Balthasar, *Mary: The Church at the Source*, 61–79, esp. 64–69.

⁴⁵¹ "Marian Doctrine", 29. "We must avoid relegating Mary's maternity to the sphere
of mere biology. But we can do so only if our reading of Scripture can legitimately presuppose a hermeneutics that rules out just this kind of division and allows us instead to

For Ratzinger, the two approaches, the biological and the theological—as we have already observed with regard to the mystery of the *Assumpta*—are not contradictory but, rather, complementary. Since Christ and the Church "are the hermeneutical center of the scriptural narration of the history of God's saving dealings with man",[452] the Virgin Mary through her *Fiat to the Incarnation* becomes the concrete locus of this salvation history. In other words, Mary, at the moment of her Yes in Nazareth, represents the "personal concretization" of the People of God, namely, "Israel in person ... the Church in person and as person".[453] In her physical motherhood, effected by the Holy Spirit, who comes over her as the power of the Most High that overshadows her (Lk 1:35),[454] is revealed the coming of Jesus as the new creation. "Its novelty" is so radical that, as Ratzinger remarks, "it penetrates to the ground of being",[455] because it is specifically effected by God. For this reason, the physical motherhood of Mary as a biological fact is at the same time, in his view, the expression of a "theological reality", precisely through the fact that in Mary the deepest spiritual content of the covenant[456] has been realized: Through her *Fiat* to the will of God, there is a marvelous agreement between the two ways in which she is called blessed in the Gospel of Luke: "Blessed is she who believed" (Lk 1:45) and "Blessed ... are those who hear the word of God and keep it" (Lk 11:28).[457] With respect to ecclesiology, this means for Ratzinger:

> The affirmation of Mary's motherhood and the affirmation of her representation of the Church are related as *factum* and *mysterium facti*, as the fact and the sense that gives the fact its meaning. The two

recognize the correlation of Christ and his Mother as a theological reality. This hermeneutics was developed in the Fathers' personal, albeit anonymous, ecclesiology that we mentioned just now. Its basis was Scripture itself and the Church's intimate experience of faith" (ibid., 29–30).

[452] Ibid., 30.

[453] Ibid.

[454] Cf. *Daughter Zion*, 44. The image "the power of the Most High will overshadow you" belongs, according to Ratzinger, to the theology of Israel's cult. "It refers to the cloud which overshadows the temple and thereby indicates the presence of God. Mary appears as the sacred tent over whom God's hidden presence becomes effective."

[455] Ibid., 44.

[456] Cf. "Marian Doctrine", 30.

[457] Cf. ibid.

things are inseparable: the fact without its sense would be blind; the sense without the fact would be empty. Mariology cannot be developed from the naked fact, but only from the fact as it is understood in the hermeneutics of faith. In consequence, Mariology can never be purely mariological. Rather, it stands within the totality of the basic Christ-Church structure and is the most concrete expression of its inner coherence.[458]

To summarize, this means: In Ratzinger's argument, from the perspective of salvation history, *Christus* and *Ecclesia*, *sponsus* and *sponsa* form the hermeneutic center of Scripture.[459] He bases this insight on the writings of the Church Fathers. Patristic theology acknowledged this center, which signifies that the salvation established in history by the triune God shines forth in the nuptial relation between Christ and his Church: "Church here meaning the creature's fusion with its Lord in spousal love".[460] In the Bride—Church—Mary, the hope of obtaining divine life is realized by way of faith-filled assent to God's will. The Church, which becomes one Body with Christ and thus, from the perspective of salvation history, consummates "the spousal mystery of Adam and Eve", stands therefore, according to Ratzinger, in the "dynamism of a unity that does not abolish dialogical reciprocity".[461] More particularly, this means:

> Precisely the eucharistic-christological mystery of the Church indicated in the term "Body of Christ" remains within the proper measure only when it includes the mystery of Mary: the mystery of the listening handmaid who—liberated in grace—speaks her *Fiat* and, in so doing, becomes bride and thus body.[462]

In her capacity as Bride, Mary is called to become *one flesh*[463] with him. The latter means, according to Ratzinger, that she is "the body,

---

[458] Ibid.
[459] Cf. ibid., 31.
[460] Ibid., 30.
[461] Ibid., 26.
[462] Ibid., 26–27. On this subject, see also *Church*, 20: "It is only in being Marian that we become the Church. In its origins the Church was not made but was born. It was born when the intention 'Let it be to me according to your word' awoke in the soul of Mary. That the Church should awaken in our souls is the deepest desire of the Council. Mary shows us the way."
[463] Ratzinger refers to Gen 2:24 and 1 Cor 6:17.

the flesh of Christ in the spiritual tension of love, . . . [and] hence in the dynamism of a unity that does not abolish dialogical reciprocity".[464] In her *Fiat*, at the same time, the "relative subsistence" of the Bride is preserved vis-à-vis Christ; "even when she becomes one flesh with Christ in love, [she] nonetheless remains an other before him." [465]

This mutual love is the reason why the personified *Ecclesia* bears her purest name in Mary. She is at the same time, however, according to Ratzinger, that "Daughter Zion" whom Scripture identifies "with the bridal people of God".[466] Already in the Old Testament, Yahweh's covenant with his people is portrayed as marital love, which is irrevocable.[467] This theme running through the Old Testament is fulfilled in the New Testament "in the woman who is herself described as the true holy remnant, as the authentic daughter Zion".[468] In her, the new People of God, too, finds its standard. For this reason Ratzinger says that

> the Church learns concretely what she is and is meant to be by looking at Mary. Mary is her mirror, the pure measure of her being, because Mary is wholly within the measure of Christ and of God, is through and through his habitation. And what other reason could the *ecclesia* have for existing than to become a dwelling for God in

---

[464] "Marian Doctrine", 26.

[465] Ibid., 28.

[466] See "Full of Grace", 66. Ratzinger explains here that "Mary is Zion in person"; that is, "her life wholly embodies what is meant by 'Zion'". In this regard he cites René Laurentin, who has shown that the Evangelist Luke "has used subtle word play to deepen the theme of God's indwelling. Even early traditions portray God as dwelling 'in the womb' of Israel—in the Ark of the Covenant. This dwelling 'in the womb' of Israel now becomes quite literally real in the Virgin of Nazareth. Mary herself thus becomes the true Ark of the Covenant in Israel, so that the symbol of the Ark gathers an incredibly realistic force: God in the flesh of a human being, which flesh now becomes his dwelling place in the midst of creation" (ibid., 65).

[467] On this subject, cf. *Daughter Zion*, 21f.: "Israel herself, the chosen people, is interpreted simultaneously as woman, virgin, beloved, wife and mother. The great women of Israel represent what this people itself is. The history of these women becomes the theology of God's people and, at the same time, the theology of the covenant. . . . The covenant relation of Yahweh to Israel is a covenant of marital love, which—as in Hosea's magnificent vision—moves and stirs Yahweh himself to his heart. He has loved the young maiden Israel with a love that has proved to be indestructible, eternal." See Hos 11:8f.

[468] *Daughter Zion*, 24.

the world? God does not deal with abstractions. He is a person, and the Church is a person. The more that each one of us becomes person, person in the sense of a fit habitation for God, daughter Zion, the more we become one, the more we are the Church, and the more the Church is herself.[469]

Thus, according to Ratzinger, the mariological perspective of the *Ecclesia* and, conversely, the view of Mary in terms of ecclesiology and salvation history lead to Jesus Christ and, in him, to the mystery of the triune God, in which it becomes evident what the vocation to holiness ultimately means: "the dwelling of God in man, and in the world".[470] The Church, which lives in this eschatological tension, is led back again to her "christological and trinitarian starting point"[471] by this Marian view at the conclusion of *Lumen gentium*.

At the end of his 2000 essay on the ecclesiology of *Lumen gentium*, Ratzinger quoted a passage from St. Ambrose. In this dissertation, let it serve as a bridge between the mariological section and the concluding part of this discussion of the Church's holiness.

Stand firm, then, in your inmost heart! ... What it means to stand, the Apostle has taught us, and Moses wrote: "The place on which you are standing is holy ground." No one can stand who is not standing firm in faith. ... And there is another saying written, "But you stand firm with me." You are standing firm with me when you are standing in the Church. The Church is the holy ground upon which we are to stand. ... Stand firm, then, stand in the Church. Stand firm in that place at which I choose to appear to you; there I will stay with you. Where the Church is, there is the firm standing place for your heart. The foundations of your soul are resting in the Church. For in the Church I have appeared to you, as once I did in the thornbush. You are the thornbush, and I am the fire. I am the fire in the burning bush, in your flesh. I am fire to give you light; to burn away the thorny tangles of your sins; to bestow on you the favor of my grace.[472]

---

[469] "Full of Grace", 66. Cf. *Daughter Zion*, 67f.
[470] "Ecclesiology", 152.
[471] Ibid.
[472] Ibid., with a reference to Ambrose, *Ep.* 63, 41.42, in PL 16, 1200 C/D.

3. *"I am black but beautiful"*[473]

In reviewing the Marian dimension of the People of God, we can state that in Mary, the Immaculata, the new Israel appears as a Bride, "holy, immaculate, luminously beautiful".[474] She is an indication of the fidelity of the *Ecclesia* of which Mary is a type. This fidelity of the Bride of Christ, which is preserved for the Church in the power of the Holy Spirit, "is not called in question by the infidelities of her members",[475] as Ratzinger emphasizes. Here we glimpse the mystery that can be labeled with the Scripture verse "I am black *and* beautiful" (Song 1:5, Douay-Rheims version, modified).[476] Within this mystery, the daring image of the *casta meretrix*, the chaste whore, that the Fathers of the Church applied to the Church, symbolizes "the 'nevertheless' of divine grace".[477] Ratzinger characterizes this tension as the genuine hallmark of the New Covenant:

> In Christ, God has bound himself to men, has let himself be bound by them. . . . Because of the Lord's devotion, never more to be

---

[473] See *Volk Gottes*, 71–90, ref. at 82. Cf. H. U. von Balthasar, "Casta meretrix", in *Spouse of the Word*, 193–288. See also Bernard of Clairvaux, Sermon 25 on the Song of Songs, in *On the Song of Songs*, trans. Kilian Walsh, vol. 2 (Spencer, Mass.: Cistercian Publications, 1976), 50–57. Original Latin text in *Sancti Bernardi Opera*, ad fidem codicum recensuerunt J. Leclercq, C. H. Talbot, and H. M. Rochais (Rome: Editiones Cistercienses, 1957–1997), vol. 1. The German translation by H. U. von Balthasar in *Sponsa Verbi*, Skizzen zur Theologie 2 (Einsiedeln: Johannes Verlag, 1961), 257, runs: "Sagte die Braut, dass sie nichts Schwarzes an sich habe, so würde sie sich selber verführen, und die Wahrheit wäre nicht in ihr [Were the bride to say that she had nothing black in her, she would be deceiving herself, and the truth would not be in her (*Spouse of the Word*, 245)]." See also *Theology of History*, 154f. In Bonaventure, the image of the whore represents reason as opposed to wisdom, which is described as the bride.

[474] Cf. *Daughter Zion*, 67, with a reference to Eph 5:27. See also G. L. Müller and K. J. Wallner, *Was bedeutet uns Maria? Die Antwort des Konzils* (Vienna: Rosenkranz-Sühnekreuzzug um den Frieden der Welt, 1994), 68f.

[475] *Report*, 50. This remark by Ratzinger is in keeping with the discussion in GS 43: "Although by the power of the Holy Spirit the Church will remain the faithful spouse of her Lord and will never cease to be the sign of salvation on earth, still she is very well aware that among her members, both clerical and lay, some have been unfaithful to the Spirit of God during the course of many centuries."

[476] On this subject, see *Volk Gottes*, 71–90, ref. at 80.

[477] Ibid., 77. Cf. *Introduction*, 339f.

revoked, the Church is the institution sanctified by him forever, an institution in which the holiness of the *Lord* becomes present among men. But it is really and truly the holiness of the *Lord* that becomes present in her and that chooses again and again as the vessel of its presence—with a paradoxical love—the dirty hands of men. It is holiness that radiates as the holiness of Christ from the midst of the Church's sin.[478]

More particularly this means, as Ratzinger formulates it along with Hans Urs von Balthasar: "Perpetually the Church lives on forgiveness, which recreates her and changes her from a whore into a bride." [479] In and of itself, mankind is in Babylon. By grace it is called forth and reformed into the Bride of Christ.

When we examine Ratzinger's writings on the theme of holiness and sin in the Church, we discover a tension between his statements at the time of the Council and those made after his appointment as prefect of the Congregation for the Doctrine of the Faith; it is possible to tell them apart by the different answers they give to the question of whether or not the name "sinner" can be predicated of the Church herself.[480] I will outline this development by Ratzinger in three steps and, wherever possible, mention the sources on which he relies. My first question concerns the formula: "Ecclesia sancta simul et semper purificanda", used in *Lumen gentium* 8 and, with it, the problem of whether the Church herself can be described as a sinner. In a second step, I will examine the nature of true reform; and in the third and final step, I will demonstrate that morality, forgiveness, and atonement are the personal heart of any Church reform.

---

[478] *Introduction*, 341. See also ibid., where Ratzinger even uses the expression "the Church's sin". "It is holiness that radiates as the holiness of Christ from the midst of the Church's sin. So the paradoxical figure of the Church, in which the divine so often presents itself in such unworthy hands, in which the divine is only ever present in the form of a 'nevertheless', is to the faithful the sign of the 'nevertheless' of the ever greater love shown by God."

[479] *Volk Gottes*, 71–90, citation at 78; cf. Balthasar, "Casta meretrix", *Spouse of the Word*, 204ff., 221–22, 257–58.

[480] Weiler, too (294f.), refers to this tension in the development of Ratzinger's ecclesiology.

a. *Ecclesia peccatrix?*

The idea of an *Ecclesia peccatrix*,[481] a favorite theme in the works of the Church Fathers and in the mysticism of the High Middle Ages,[482] was applied in a restricted sense in post-Reformation Catholic ecclesiology exclusively to the individual sinful member, not to the body of the Church as a whole. Even the conciliar schema *De Ecclesia*,[483] as Günther Wassilowsky shows in his ecclesiological study of Karl Rahner's influence on Vatican II, speaks only about the *peccata membrorum*, but not about the Church as *Ecclesia peccatorum*, much less about the Church as sinner.[484] Therefore Wassilowsky explains that the statement in *Lumen gentium* that the Church is an *Ecclesia* "sancta simul et semper purificanda"[485] probably would have been unthinkable had it not been for the objection of the theologians Karl Rahner and Otto Semmelroth.[486] This should be mentioned beforehand so as to bring to light the circumstances of the theological struggle in which Ratzinger, too, was involved, when in his 1964 retrospect on the second session of the Council he spoke about a sinful Church:

[481] Cf. R. Latourelle, *Le Christ et l'Église: Signes du salut* (Tournai: Desclée; Montreal: Bellarmin, 1971), 206. The reader will find there a survey of studies on this topic by K. Rahner, J. Ratzinger, Y. Congar, and C. Journet.

[482] Cf. Kehl, *Kirche*, 24f. Until the High Middle Ages, the reality of sinfulness in the Church was one of the "most excruciating questions in the theology of the Church", as Karl Rahner calls it. See K. Rahner, *Die Kirche der Sünder* (Vienna: Herder, 1948), 301.

[483] See the *Schema Constitutionis dogmaticae De Ecclesia*, in *AS* 1/4:14f.

[484] See Wassilowsky, 216f.: "The document means to distinguish between *offendere* and *laedere*; the sins of the members, indeed, 'offend' the body of the Church, as though from outside, but cannot really injure it. For the Church, sin—even if it comes from her own members—is an external circumstance, which does affect her, but the guilt would never be capable of harming the holiness of the Church; much less the idea that the Church sins in the sins of her members."

[485] *LG* 8: "... at the same time holy and always in need of being purified".

[486] See Wassilowsky, 217f. Wassilowsky describes the intention of the two Jesuits by saying that they "are seeking an ecclesiology that does not yield normativeness in spite of all facticity. Instead, they are looking for an ecclesiology that systematically weighs the historical experience with the Church and theoretically takes into account the concrete phenomenon of the Church as well" (ibid., 218). On the development of the conciliar statements about the sinfulness of the Church, see M. Becht, "Ecclesia semper purificanda: Die Sündigkeit der Kirche als Thema des II. Vatikanischen Konzils", *Cath(M)* 49 (1995): 218–60. Concerning the influence of the German-speaking theologians on the development of the Constitution on the Church, see Stefan Alberto, "Begriff und Wesen der Kirche in der Entstehung der Kirchenkonstitution *Lumen gentium*", in Naab, *Ex latere*, 153–62.

A Christ-centered Church is thus oriented not merely toward past salvific events; it will always also be a Church moving forward under the sign of hope. Its decisive future and its transformation are still ahead. It must therefore always be open to what comes and always ready to shed fixed formulations with which it was once at home so as to march on toward the Lord who is calling and waiting.

So seen, the Church's image assumes a more human aspect. It is no longer necessary to see it as a sacrosanct entity which must artificially be protected from all criticism and reproach. If the Church means the journey of mankind together with its God, if it is essentially incomplete and always short of its goal, then it is still the sinful Church continually in need of renovation. It must always throw off its earthly bonds and whatever leads to feelings of self-satisfaction.[487]

Already in 1962, on the eve of the Council, Ratzinger took up the theme of the Church's sinfulness in his article "Freimut und Gehorsam: Das Verhältnis des Christen zu seiner Kirche" (Candor and obedience: The relation of the Christian to his Church).[488] In this essay, which he included in almost unaltered form[489] ten years later in his anthology *Das neue Volk Gottes*, he cites in particular Hans Urs von Balthasar[490] and Karl Rahner,[491] who both follow the patristic tradition

---

[487] *Highlights*, 47.

[488] First published in *WuW* 17 (1964): 409–21; later in *Volk Gottes*, 71–90.

[489] See *Volk Gottes*, 71–90, ref. at 89. In the final footnote, Ratzinger tempers his earlier statements about an excess of ecclesiastical standardization.

[490] See Balthasar, "Casta meretrix". See also *Augustinus: Das Antlitz der Kirche*, sel. and trans. Balthasar, 2nd ed. (Einsiedeln: Benziger, 1955).

[491] See K. Rahner, *Kirche der Sünder*; cf. Rahner, "Die Sünde in der Kirche", in Baraúna, 1:346–62. See also Rahner, "Die Gliedschaft der Kirche nach der Lehre der Enzyklika Pius' XII. *Mystici Corporis Christi*", in *Schriften zur Theologie*, vol. 2 (Einsiedeln, Zürich, and Cologne: Benziger, 1964), 7–94; Rahner, "Vergessene Wahrheiten über das Buß-sakrament", in *Schriften zur Theologie* 2:143–83; Rahner, "Die Kirche der Heiligen", in *Schriften zur Theologie* 3:111–26; Rahner, "Kirche und Parusie", *Cath(M)* 17 (1963): 113–28; cf. *Schriften zur Theologie*, vol. 6 (Einsiedeln: Benziger, 1965), 348–67. Rahner, "Gerecht und Sünder zugleich", *GuL* 36 (1963): 434–43; cf. *Schriften zur Theologie* 6:262–76. A detailed study of the theme of "the holy and sinful Church" according to Karl Rahner can be found in M. Kehl, *Kirche als Institution: Zur theologischen Begründung des institutionellen Charakters der Kirche in der neueren deutschsprachigen katholischen Ekklesiologie* (Frankfurt am Main: Knecht, 1978), 216–19, esp. 217: "For Rahner sin is not only a reality 'in' the Church, insofar as the individual believers are sinners, but also a reality of the Church herself: she is a 'sinful Church'." Ibid., 218: "Nevertheless, where she (and really she herself!) appears sinful, she merely makes evident the remaining resistance of

in describing the *Ecclesia* as "the Church of sinners". The Church Fathers testified to the membership of sinners in the Church especially in opposing heresies such as those of Novatian and the Donatists.[492]

Early on, through his scholarly work on Augustine, Ratzinger encountered the question about the "Church of sinners" [*Sünderkirche*],[493] specifically in the dispute between Augustine[494] and the Donatists. For Augustine, "the Church is full of sinners",[495] so that doubts might arise about whether there are any just men left in her at all. In contrast to the Donatist ideal of holiness, he points to the reality of sin even in the lives of the saints.[496] In Ratzinger's dissertation, there is a passage on this subject:

> Naturally, the fact that the Church is a Church of sinners was so obtrusive at that time on both sides of the debate that it was undeniable even for the Donatists. It was just a matter of how one wanted to deal with it. The Donatists rejected Tyconius' attempt to find a Catholic solution, which Augustine had taken up, and wanted to admit that there were only hidden sinners in the Church, whose administration of the sacraments was declared valid through a sort of *supplet Ecclesia*; publicly known sinners, on the other hand, had to be excluded. Later, of course, under the pressure of the facts, it appears that the idea of *tolerare pro pace* prevailed, whereby naturally the Donatist stance was surrendered in practice. For the *tolerare pro pace* was, after all, precisely the argument with which Augustine defended the Catholics' Church of sinners.[497]

---

man within history to the holiness that has been bestowed, even though that resistance has been overcome by Christ."

[492] Cf. Wassilowsky, 214.

[493] *Volk und Haus Gottes*, 127–58, citation at 139.

[494] Augustine defended against the Donatists the Church's teaching that not only saints but also sinners are members of the Church. In doing this, Augustine relied principally on the parables of Jesus. Cf. Augustine, *In Ioan tr.* 6, 12, in CCL 36, 59f.; Augustine, *Enarr. in Ps.* 128, 8, in CSEL 95, 3, 241f.; CCL 40, 1885f.; Augustine, *Ep.* 93, 9, in CSEL 34, 453f.

[495] *Volk und Haus Gottes*, 139.

[496] Ratzinger mentions (ibid., 127–58, esp. 139) the following quotations from Augustine's writings: *C. Ep. Parm.* 2, 7, 14, in CSEL 51, 58f.; ibid., 2, 14, 32: "Quis enim castum se habere glorietur cor? Aut quis glorietur mundum se esse a peccato? ... Sicut autem spe salvi facti sumus, ita spe mundati sumus in perfecta salute et perfecta munditia" (CSEL 51, 85). See also *En. in Ps.* 4, 6, in CSEL 93, 1 A, 98f.; CCL 38, 16; PL 36, 80f. See also the foreword by Ratzinger in *Erneuerung und Mächte der Finsternis*, by L.-J. Suenens, trans. from French into German by P. B. Bayer, 5–7, esp. 5 (Salzburg: Müller, 1983).

[497] *Volk und Haus Gottes*, 127–58, citation at 139f.

This tension between the Church's sinfulness and holiness was formulated most dramatically, in Ratzinger's opinion, by the Donatist Tyconius, who was just mentioned in the quotation. He assumes "that the
Church has a right and a left side, that she is Christ and Antichrist,
Jerusalem and Babylon, all in one".[498] To her is applicable the somewhat modified verse from the Song of Songs: "I am black *and* beautiful", a verse that Ratzinger says had already been used by Origen to
express the "paradoxical and fundamental tension in the life of the
Church".[499] The whole patristic tradition, he says, adopted this idea,
last but not least Augustine, who interpreted the Church's holiness in
increasingly eschatological terms, the more he argued against Pelagius.[500]
For Augustine, driving out sinners is the Lord's business and not the
Church's concern.[501] In this regard, nevertheless, he speaks about the
true Church, the Church of the saints, which, as Ratzinger demonstrates, appears "in the time before the resurrection in a garment of
flesh that at the same time indicates and conceals this truth".[502] Through
the purification of the Church, "in which the Lord will separate the
wheat from the chaff on the last day",[503] the *Ecclesia*, according to
Augustine, arrives at a new unity of love. For this reason, humility is
called for, a willingness to take one's place "in this figure of weakness,
in a Church whose image is darkened by the throngs of sinners who
belong to her".[504]

Entirely along the same lines as the great Church Father, Ratzinger
still argues in 1968 for the concept of the *sinful Church* when in his
Introduction to Christianity he clearly intimates:

> The Second Vatican Council itself ventured to the point of speak-
> ing no longer merely of the holy Church but of the sinful Church,
> and the only reproach it incurred was that of still being far too

---

[498] *Volk Gottes*, 71–90, citation at 82.

[499] See *Volk Gottes*, 71–90, citing Origen, *In Cant. hom.* 2, 4 (*SC*, 2nd ed., 37, 116f.).
Ratzinger cites Origen here in the German version found in Balthasar, "Casta meretrix",
282.

[500] Cf. *Volk Gottes*, 71–90, ref. at 82. Ratzinger again refers to Balthasar, "Casta meretrix", 284.

[501] Cf. *Volk und Haus Gottes*, 127–58, ref. at 146.

[502] Ibid. See also Weiler, 63–65.

[503] *Volk und Haus Gottes*, 151.

[504] Ibid.

timorous; so deeply aware are we all of the sinfulness of the Church. This may well be partly due to the Lutheran theology of sin and also to an assumption arising out of dogmatic prejudgments. But what makes this "dogmatic theology" so reasonable is its harmony with our own experience. The centuries of the Church's history are so filled with all sorts of human failure that we can quite understand Dante's ghastly vision of the Babylonian whore sitting in the Church's chariot; and the dreadful words of William of Auvergne, Bishop of Paris in the thirteenth century, seem perfectly comprehensible. William said that the barbarism of the Church had to make everyone who saw it go rigid with horror: "We are no longer dealing with a bride but with a monster of terrible deformity and ferocity." [505]

In 1971, only three years after this explicit affirmation of the idea of the sinful Church, Ratzinger strikes a different note in his apologia "Why I Am Still in the Church" that suggests instead a certain reserve with regard to the ecclesial self-accusation by the Second Vatican Council, which he had previously characterized as still being insufficiently harsh.

> Today it is clear that ... the Church that has emerged from this process is not a modern but a thoroughly shaky and deeply divided Church. Let us put it very crudely: the first Vatican Council described the Church as a *"signum levatum in nationes"*, as the great eschatological banner that was visible from afar and called and united men. It was (so said the Council of 1870) that for which Isaiah had hoped (Is 11:12): the universally visible sign that every man could recognize and that pointed the way unequivocally to all men. With its astounding expansion, superb holiness, fecundity in all goodness, and invincible stability, it was supposed to be the real miracle of Christianity, its permanent authentication—replacing all other signs and miracles—in the eyes of history.
>
> Today everything seems to have turned to the opposite. There is no marvellous expansion, but only a small-scale, stagnating association ... ; there is no superb holiness, but a collection of all human sicknesses besmirched and humiliated by a history from which no

---

[505] *Introduction*, 339–40. Cf. Balthasar, "Casta meretrix", 189–91, ref. at 191. Furthermore, Balthasar and Ratzinger refer to H. Riedlinger, *Die Makellosigkeit der Kirche in den lateinischen Hoheliedkommentaren des Mittelalters* (Münster: Aschendorff, 1958).

scandal is absent ... , so that anyone who listens to this story can only cover his head in shame; there is no stability, but only involvement in all the streams of history.... These are not signs that evoke faith, but seem to constitute a supreme obstacle to it.[506]

This pessimistic picture of the Church that Ratzinger drew at the beginning of the 1970s, which were marked by the upheavals of the postconciliar period, is brought into proper focus, however, by his call to conversion in Christ. For him, conversion means a spiritual process in which a person not only changes but also assumes responsibility for "the hard work of repentance".[507] In a metaphor that is strongly reminiscent of the beginning of *Lumen gentium*, Ratzinger focuses his attention, not on the Church, but rather on Christ. It is the symbolism of the moon,[508] which he applies to the Church. The former "shines, yet its light is not its own, but the light of another. It is darkness and light both at once."[509] For him, that means that the Church, in and of herself, is dark but receives light through Christ, even though she herself is "only deserts, sand, and rocks".[510]

In retrospect, the call to conversion and repentance was for Ratzinger the essential feature of the reformative intentions of the last Council. Therefore in his 1982 essay "A Review of the Postconciliar Era—Failures, Tasks, Hopes", he explains that the Council understood itself as "a great examination of conscience by the Catholic Church", as an "act of penance, of conversion".[511] This is apparent in "the confessions of guilt, in the intensity of the self-accusations", which Ratzinger describes, however, in negative terms: "this excruciating plumbing of her own depths", combined with an "almost painful willingness to take seriously the whole arsenal of complaints against the Church, to omit none of them".[512] In such rhetoric, his present uneasiness with the predominance of an exclusively "sinful Church" becomes

---

[506] Ratzinger, "Why I Am Still in the Church", 65–90, citation at 74f.

[507] Ibid., 70.

[508] Ratzinger refers to H. Rahner, *Griechische Mythen in christlicher Deutung* (Darmstadt: Wissenschaftl. Buchgesellsch., 1957), 200–224; H. Rahner, *Symbole der Kirche* (Salzburg: Müller, 1964), 89–173; Ambrosius, *Hexaemeron* 4, 8, 32, in CSEL 32, 1, 137f.

[509] Ratzinger, "Why I Am Still in the Church", 77.

[510] Ibid., 78.

[511] *Principles*, 367–77, citation at 371.

[512] Ibid.

apparent. This image heightens the negative view of the Church and fears "as triumphalism whatever might be interpreted as satisfaction with what she had become or what she still was".[513] His criticism goes so far as to level at the sort of ecclesial self-accusation that was prompted by the Council, causing neurotic symptoms,[514] the charge that it lacked an authentic spirit of penance. True repentance always leads to the gospel, "that is, to joy—even to joy in oneself". Ratzinger does recognize that it was necessary "for the Council to put an end to the false forms of the Church's glorification of self on earth and, by suppressing her compulsive tendency to defend her past history, to eliminate her false justification of self". Nonetheless, he misses delight in the Church and would like to see it rekindled by attention to the Church's saints.

We must rediscover that luminous trail that is the history of the saints and of the beautiful—a history in which the joy of the gospel has been irrefutably expressed throughout the centuries.... In a word, it must become clear again that penance requires, not the destruction of one's own identity, but the finding of it.[515]

That requires personal conversion, "which today is very often hidden in the anonymous mass of 'We' ".[516] Symptomatic of this, in Ratzinger's view, is the change in the form of the prayer immediately before the Sign of Peace in the celebration of the Eucharist, from the personal "I" to the impersonal "we". Originally the priest prayed: "Lord, ... look not on *my* sins, but on the faith of *your* Church."[517] This earlier form gives a most poignant expression[518] to the Catholic tradition that speaks about the "fidelity of the Bride of Christ",[519] "which is not called in question by the infidelities of her members".[520] For Ratzinger, the original formulation means:

---

[513] Ibid.
[514] Cf. ibid., 372f. The following citations are found there also.
[515] Ibid., 373.
[516] *Report*, 51.
[517] See "Kirchenverfassung und Umkehr: Fragen an Joseph Kardinal Ratzinger", *IKaZ Communio* 13 (1984): 445.
[518] Cf. ibid.
[519] See *GS* 43.
[520] *Report*, 50.

The one praying is meant personally: "*I* have sinned." He must painfully acknowledge his own guilt precisely in this great moment, in the presence of the Redeemer who has become the Lamb of God. It is important, then, that the Church, in making this a liturgical prayer, presupposes that everyone celebrating the Eucharist has reason to say such a thing. Indeed, until the reform, the prayer was primarily a prayer of the priest: the pope has to say it, just like the bishops, all the priests, and all those who participate in the Eucharist.... To receive Communion means to expose oneself anew to the fire of his nearness and thus to the demand for conversion. From the fact that all the members of the Church have to say the prayer "Forgive us our trespasses", this prayer does not conclude, however, that one can also call the Church *as* Church sinful. Instead, it contrasts "my sins" with the "faith of your Church" as a claim to a favorable hearing.[521]

Now that the prayer has been rewritten in the plural, it can easily be misunderstood. Ratzinger does not see the real problem with this so much in "the change from the *I* to the *We*, from personal to collective responsibility".[522] For him, the decisive thing is the dangerous contrast between an objectively sinful Church and a subjective faith. This fundamentally changed attitude would ultimately lead to the formula: "Look not upon the *sins of the Church* but upon *my faith*."[523]

A review of the argument thus far is appropriate here. In the previous discussion of the Church as *peccatrix*, we were able to point out a clear instance of Ratzinger revising his position, in which he concludes by denying that the Church herself is sinful, since she belongs to the Lord; that is, she is his Church and as such she can be the bearer of the faith.[524] Ratzinger's denial henceforth of an

---

[521] Ratzinger, "Kirchenverfassung und Umkehr", 446.

[522] *Report*, 52.

[523] Ibid.

[524] See Ratzinger, "Kirchenverfassung und Umkehr", 446. Cf. *Report*, 52: "But this in no way means that the Church as such was also a sinner. The Church ... is a reality that surpasses, mysteriously and infinitely, the sum of her members. In fact, in order to obtain Christ's forgiveness, *my sin* was set over against the *faith of his Church*." Ibid.: "We must ... go back to saying to the Lord: 'We sin, but the Church that is yours and the bearer of faith does not sin.' Faith is the answer of the Church to Christ. It is Church in the measure that it is an act of faith. This faith is not an individual, solitary act, a response of the individual. Faith means to believe *together*, with all the Church."

Ecclesia peccatrix, in contrast to his statements before 1970, is according to Medard Kehl ecclesiologically incorrect:

Neither the completely unexpected distinction (almost a division!) between "our Church" and "the Church of Jesus Christ" nor the philosophically and theologically unreflected division between sinful individuals and non-sinful Church can be maintained in light of the patristic tradition and the modern ecclesiological development.[525]

Now, in my opinion, we should nevertheless ask whether these different positions taken by Ratzinger might not in fact be formulations of *one* message that is addressed to *different* listeners. Whereas by his earlier emphasis on the *Ecclesia peccatrix* he intended to express a clear "No to self-glorification"[526] in the Church, without denying her "true holiness",[527] in his later statements, he opposes horizontalizing tendencies, without thereby ignoring the sin in the Church. What remains the same, however, is his profession of the " 'holy Church' that is holy because the Lord bestows holiness on her as a quite unmerited gift".[528] This differing emphasis should be borne in mind in the next two subsections of my dissertation.

In summary, at any rate, we can declare that, according to Ratzinger, the renewal of the Church cannot begin primarily with a change of structures. For "what results from that is something that we ourselves have made: 'our Church'."[529] For him, quite to the contrary, it is a matter of "letting what is ours disappear as much as possible".[530] Briefly, then, I will present the features of true reform, as Ratzinger lists them.

---

[525] M. Kehl, Review of the German edition of *The Ratzinger Report, ThPh* 61 (1986): 609f., citation at 610. Kehl suspects that Ratzinger "is speaking here, for reasons of Church politics, without making too many distinctions, so as to 'dry up' [that is, discredit] theologically the often disloyal and unloving criticism of the Church as such, including her official structures and ministries. For if there is no 'sinful Church', then no criticism of her can be theologically legitimate."

[526] *Volk Gottes*, 71–90, citation at 73.

[527] *Introduction*, 338–47, citation at 342.

[528] Ibid., 344.

[529] Ratzinger, "Kirchenverfassung und Umkehr", 447.

[530] Ibid.

b. The nature of true reform

Even before the end of the Council, Ratzinger spoke with some disillusionment to the Catholic student union in Münster about how the
joy of Pentecost, which was connected with the idea of *aggiornamento*,
had given way to the "difficulties"[531] of ecclesiastical routine. Church
renewal, he said, could not mean supporting the forces of reform, or
conformity to the so-called consciousness of the average man. Together
with Hans Urs von Balthasar, he acknowledged that by *aggiornamento*
alone, "only half the job was done." Equally important is "reflection
on Christianity itself, the clarification, deepening, and focusing of the
idea of it".[532] Only in this way, he said, can we testify to the credibility of Christianity.

Therefore an important criterion for true renewal, in Ratzinger's
opinion, is the discernment of spirits, that is—as he said in 1965—
differentiating between unauthorized "fashionable reforms" and "the
true nature of ecclesial renewal".[533] For him this means

> distinguishing between those who try to deny and do away with
> the Christian scandal as such, under the pretext of removing the
> scandal of Christians, and those who out of the integrity of their
> faith want to uncover the true Christian scandal, which is con-
> cealed by the false scandal of Christendom.[534]

Church reform must not degenerate into "everything is permitted",
the slogan of an arbitrary enthusiasm for change,[535] but rather must
recognize that Christian reform is striving for the renewal of Christianity itself, which "exists essentially in the manner of the Church".[536]

---

[531] *Volk Gottes*, 91–106, citation at 91.
[532] Ibid. See also H. U. von Balthasar, *Rechenschaft* (Einsiedeln: Johannes Verlag, 1965), 7.
Cf. Balthasar, *Cordula oder der Ernstfall*, Kriterien 2 (Einsiedeln: Johannes Verlag, 1966).
[533] *Volk Gottes*, 92.
[534] Ibid.
[535] Cf. ibid. Ratzinger refers to Gnostic tendencies that twisted the Pauline theologoumenon "freedom from the Law" into the idea that "everything is permitted." In this regard,
he cites H. Schlier, *Die Zeit der Kirche* (Freiburg: Herder, 1958), 147–59: "Über das Haupt-
anliegen des Ersten Briefes an die Korinther" (On the chief concerns of the First Letter
to the Corinthians), and ibid., 206–32: "Kerygma und Sophia: Zur neutestamentlichen
Grundlegung des Dogmas" (Kerygma and Sophia: On the New Testament foundation of
dogma).
[536] *Volk Gottes*, 93.

For this reason, Christian renewal is always an ecclesial process, which furthermore "presupposes the faith" and "takes place within the faith".[537] This leads to the question of the inner structure of the Christian faith. In Ratzinger's view, the faith is transtemporal and hence must not be adapted to contemporary tastes but must instead correspond to the truth. This in turn means, for a true renewal: "True reform is one that strives for what is truly Christian but hidden, that lets itself be challenged and formed by it; false reform is one that runs after man instead of leading him and, thus, transforms Christianity into a general store that is not doing well and has to drum up customers." [538]

The standard of true renewal is its origin in Jesus Christ. Therefore, what is great and liberating about the Church cannot be "the product of our own will and invention", but rather it always "precedes us and comes to meet us as the incomprehensible reality".[539] Despite the need for institutional features suited to the current circumstances, this pre-existing reality is the source of the Church's experience of purification, which at the same time signifies real renewal in terms of her origin.

In the next step, Ratzinger relates this knowledge, which is valid for the whole Church, to her individual members by transposing true reform "from the general and objective to the personal".[540] He gives special consideration to forgiveness and penance, grace and personal conversion, for they are indicative of a very real "active-passive event" [541] of change, at the center of which morality, forgiveness, and atonement shine as the personal heart of reform.

c. Morality, forgiveness, and atonement—The personal heart of reform

In 1984 Ratzinger noted an increasingly serious crisis in morality, especially in the so-called Western world, "where money and wealth are the measure of all things".[542] In the early 1990s, along with

---

[537] Ibid., 95.
[538] Ibid., 96.
[539] *Called to Communion*, 140.
[540] Ibid., 148.
[541] Cf. ibid., 149.
[542] *Report*, 83.

Robert Spaemann,[543] he pointed out a dangerous development: since 1989, after the "fall of utopia", a "banal nihilism" was spreading, in which "absolute values and standards no longer exist".[544] Therefore, in this secularized society which is characterized by a permissiveness that corresponds on the moral level to economic liberalism, Catholic ethics is regarded as something that fell to earth from another planet.[545] Moreover, human conscience is reduced to a sort of subjective certainty, without the possibility of any objective reference to the truth.

Those who equate conscience with superficial conviction identify it with a pseudo-rational certainty that is woven out of self-righteousness, the habit of conforming, and laziness. Conscience is demoted to an excusing mechanism, whereas it is in fact the transparency of the personal subject to what is divine and thus represents the genuine worth and greatness of the human being.[546]

Only this transparency to the divine makes it possible for the conscience to make a just admission of guilt. Ratzinger says that not only is guilt manifested by this judgment, along with the resulting inner need, but also "the fact that there is an authority of grace, a power of atonement, that makes guilt vanish and makes truth really redemptive".[547] Therefore, in Ratzinger's view, the chief cause of "the spiritual crisis of our time" lies in "the obscuration of the grace of forgiveness".[548] Morality and forgiveness are genuine only through the atonement of the redemptive work of Jesus Christ.

---

[543] See R. Spaemann, "La Perle précieuse et le nihilisme banal", *Catholica* 33 (1992): 43–50, esp. 45.

[544] *Prüfsteine*, 11–24, citation at 16.

[545] See *Report*, 83.

[546] *Prüfsteine*, 25–62, citation at 39.

[547] Ibid., 61. Ratzinger refers (ibid., 60) to H. U. von Balthasar, *The Glory of the Lord: A Theological Aesthetics*, vol. 4: *The Realm of Metaphysics in Antiquity* (San Francisco: Ignatius Press, 1989), 120f. On this subject, see also *God and the World*, 420–24, esp. 421–22: "The capacity to recognize guilt can be tolerated, and properly developed, whenever there is also healing. And healing, in turn, can only exist when there is absolution.... Only the sacrament, the authority from God, can truly overcome guilt." See also Ratzinger, "Kirchenverfassung und Umkehr", 444–57, ref. at 449ff.

[548] *Called to Communion*, 149. See ibid., 150f., and the reference to A. Görres, "Schuld und Schuldgefühle", *IKaZ* 13 (1984): 430–43, esp. 433f. and 438.

But true forgiveness exists only when the "price", the "equivalent value", is paid, when guilt is atoned by suffering, when there is expiation. The circular link between morality, forgiveness and expiation cannot be forced apart at any point; when one element is missing, everything else is ruined. Whether or not man can find redemption depends on the undivided existence of this circle. In the Torah, the five books of Moses, these three elements are knotted together inseparably, and it is therefore impossible to follow the Enlightenment in excising from this core of the Old Testament an eternally valid moral law, while consigning the rest to past history. This moralistic manner of giving the Old Testament relevance for today is bound to fail. . . .

Jesus, on the other hand, fulfilled the *whole* law, not a portion of it, and thus renewed it from the ground up: he himself, who suffered the whole tale of guilt, is at once expiation and forgiveness and is therefore also the only reliable and perennially valid basis of our morality.[549]

According to Ratzinger, morality, forgiveness, and atonement are the way to renewal for the individual, as well as for the Church and for all mankind. It involves "an event of birth and death"[550] in the Pauline sense: The individual is freed from his isolation and is accepted into "the communion of a new subject",[551] into the Body of Christ. To this communion belong "the men of all places and all times whose hearts stretch out in hope and love to Christ".[552]

Consequently, to Ratzinger's way of thinking, Church reform always starts with Christ and comes to its completion through the Church's sacramental ministry of reconciliation. Finally, another central consideration related to this is the question about God, namely, faith in the one God who really enters into history and who thus remains the real "subject of history".[553] That is why it is for Ratzinger so crucial to hear "that God [himself] addresses us and says: 'Your sins are forgiven' . . . that there really is something that we call grace".[554]

---

[549] *Called to Communion*, 151–52.
[550] Ibid., 153.
[551] Ibid.
[552] Ibid., 154.
[553] Ratzinger and Metz, "God, Sin, and Suffering", 47–53, citation at 50.
[554] Ibid., 51.

Ratzinger mentions three principal reasons for the contemporary crisis of the sacrament of penance—priests and religious are said to be affected by it in a particular way.[555] First, the strangeness of the message, when compared to the "specious watchwords of our age";[556] second, a lack of understanding concerning the form of the Church's ministry; and, finally, the "plight of the ministers, who are morally abandoned".[557] For this reason, it is imperative "to help priests and religious regain an understanding of the reality of the sacrament.... The celebration of the sacrament does not depend on the minister's own achievement but, rather, on the fact that he steps back and makes room for the Greater One, so that it might become 'His Church'".[558]

Based on the discussion thus far, it is clear, according to Ratzinger, that forgiveness and penance, grace and personal conversion are the Church's real answer to the question about renewal. The shepherds are called to go before the People of God on this way of holiness.[559]

---

[555] Cf. Ratzinger, "Kirchenverfassung und Umkehr", 447: "Some years ago Louis Bouyer proposed the thesis that the crisis in the Church today is really a crisis of the priests and religious. That is, of course, a very pointed statement, but it correctly characterizes the focal point of the crisis." Cf. *Report*, 55–58.

[556] Ratzinger, "Kirchenverfassung und Umkehr", 447. Cf. *Report*, 58: According to Ratzinger, today there is pressure on every priest to adapt to the ways of the world. "Such a man, in the end, can grow weary of resisting, with his words and even more with his life-style, the seemingly so reasonable realities that are accepted as a matter of course and that characterize our culture.... Today he could experience the greatness of the Sacred as a burden and long (even unconsciously) to free himself from it, lowering the mystery to his human stature."

[557] Ratzinger, "Kirchenverfassung und Umkehr", 447.

[558] Ibid., 448.

[559] Cf. *LG* 21 and 28.

Chapter 3

The Hierarchical Constitution of the Church,
in Particular with Regard to Episcopal Collegiality

No theme of the Council was so much debated as that of chapter 3 of
Lumen gentium on the hierarchical structure of the Church, in particular the episcopal ministry.[1] Ratzinger, too, underscores this in his
retrospective volume *Ergebnisse und Probleme der dritten Konzilsperiode*
[Results and problems of the third session of the Council]:

> No other issue resulted in so much activity both open and covert;
> nor was any other issue subjected to such a careful and meticulous
> voting. A few figures will verify this: In the entire schema on the
> Church, which comprised eight chapters, ten ballots were taken dur-
> ing the first series of votes on chapters 1–2 and chapters 4–8. In
> contrast, for chapter 3 alone (the chapter containing the teaching
> on collegiality) 41 separate votes were taken. The more important
> sections were voted on sentence by sentence.[2]

The passage of time since the Council makes it possible to discern,
for the following discussion of this problematic subject, four crucial
points that, on the one hand, set forth Ratzinger's view of hierarchy
and collegiality and, on the other hand, demonstrate the development
or even the change of his view on particular questions. As the point

---

[1] On this subject, see B. Kloppenburg, "Abstimmungen und letzte Änderungen der Konstitution", in Baraúna, 1:110–23. See also pt. 1, sec. 1, chap. 2, in this book, "From the
Schema *De Ecclesia* to the Dogmatic Constitution *Lumen gentium*".

[2] *Highlights*, 108f. See also L. Vischer, "Die Rezeption der Debatte über die Kollegialität", in *Die Rezeption des Zweiten Vatikanischen Konzils*, ed. H.J. Pottmeyer, G. Alberigo,
and J.-P. Jossua, 293–312, ref. at 294 (Düsseldorf: Patmos-Verlag, 1986). In this passage,
Vischer mentions the expectation of many bishops and theologians that the "*ecclesia Romana*
... must get rid of a bit of her *romanitas* and make room for the diversity of cultures and
forms of expression".

of departure for his exposition of the hierarchical structure of the Church, Ratzinger chose during Vatican II—and we follow his decision in this—first the fundamental conciliar concern for ecumenism.[3] At that time, he advocated the opinion that through the rediscovery of the idea of collegiality, an ecumenical paradigm could be created that would ultimately serve the cause of Church unity per se. Since this unity is not possible without first confronting obstacles, especially with regard to the sacraments, it would be more realistic to set "intermediate goals".[4] The second central point leads us to the foundation of the Church's hierarchical structure. This, according to Ratzinger, is not a juridical, man-made entity, but rather Jesus Christ as its "sacred origin".[5] He communicates himself and makes himself present through the Church's sacramental structure, supported by the sacrament of orders in apostolic succession. A third leading idea results from the question of the hierarchical constitution of the Church herself, in particular the relation between primacy and collegiality. Here revisions and changes become evident in Ratzinger's development, which then become the subject of the fourth section. On the one hand, Ratzinger remains

---

[3] Cf. J. Ratzinger, *Der gegenwärtige Stand der Arbeiten des Zweiten Vatikanischen Konzils* (Bonn: Katholische Rundfunk- und Fernseharbeit in Deutschland, 1964), 10. In the same passage he summarized in six points the ecumenical possibilities that he hoped would result from the newly formulated teaching on episcopal collegiality: "(a) The ministry of unity, the papal ministry, remains undiminished, even though its function now appears more clearly in its proper context. It should not be a monarchical rule but rather a coordination of the plurality that is an essential part of the Church. (b) The plural of the [local] Churches headed by the bishops is an essential part of the singular of the one Church; it is the inner structure of the latter. (c) Within the unity of the Church, a relative independence is due to the particular Churches, which normally will consist of a sizeable group of local Churches headed by bishops; this independence must be expressed in the liturgical as well as in the administrative sphere. (d) This will be the first step toward making possible, instead of individual conversions, corporate reunions with the Catholic Church, in which the united Churches retain their distinctive character, remain themselves, and can contribute their charism to the universal Church.... Through the restoration of the plurality of local Churches headed by bishops in union with the one Church, a new point of departure for ecumenical work has been gained. (e) At the same time, there is a new possibility of grasping the ecclesial dignity of the Churches that are separated from Rome. (f) There is greater latitude for freedom in the Church."

[4] *Church*, 99–122, citation at 121. In the mid-1980s he spoke more often of a "praxeological model" that guarantees unity in what is already possible and does not ignore the multiplicity in the differences that still exist ("Ecumenical Situation", 266)

[5] *Salt of the Earth*, 190.

true to his ecclesiological approach, which can be called a eucharistic ecclesiology, while, on the other hand, there are aspects of his present teaching that are in tension with statements that he made at the time of the Council, for instance, his assessment of the theological status of episcopal conferences.

§ 1. The Idea of Collegiality as an Ecumenical Paradigm

1. Unity through multiplicity

Even during the Council, given the particular accentuation of the third chapter of the Constitution on the Church, Ratzinger faced the question of whether the principle of the episcopal constitution of the Church set forth therein corresponded to the standard that Pope John XXIII had set for the Council as a whole, namely, the guiding ideas of ecumenism and pastoral renewal.[6] The two were so closely connected with each other at that time that Ratzinger wanted to see the principle of collegiality in particular treated as a "question about the ecumenical value of this teaching".[7] If we bring his statements at the time of the Council concerning the hierarchical structure of the Church to bear on this point, we see what hope Ratzinger associated with the rediscovered principle of episcopal collegiality, since, according to the prototype of the early Church, the ecclesial *communio* was supposed to be characterized by unity in multiplicity.

---

[6] On this subject, see *Highlights*, 109f. Cf. G. Alberigo, "Die Ankündigung des Konzils: Von der Sicherheit des Sich-Verschanzens zur Faszination des Suchens", in Wittstadt, 1:1–60, esp. 1–19. On June 5, 1959, John XXIII expressed the hope that with the Council the "inner structure" of the Catholic Church "might gain new vigor and that all the sheep might hear the voice of the Shepherd and follow him and that that one sheepfold might be built which the Heart of Jesus ardently desires" (Alberigo, "Ankündigung des Konzils", 43f.). See also *AD* 1, 1:16. On the basic pastoral purpose, see "Kommentar", 350. As for the theological competence of a pastoral council, Ratzinger ("Kommentar", 350) presents the opinion of Pope Paul VI and of the majority of the Council Fathers. Even though the Council formulated no new dogma, "that does not mean that the whole thing could be set aside as something nonbinding and merely edifying", as the minority thought. "The documents include ... a serious demand upon the conscience of the Catholic Christian."

[7] *Highlights*, 109.

More important ... is the general principle of collegiality, the meaning of which is not found primarily in the question concerning a governmental authority over the entire Church but is concentrated instead on the need to bring the multiplicity of the particular Churches, in their irreplaceable proper significance, to bear within the unity of the one Church.... With such a view of the Church, it automatically becomes clear that the unity of the Church must include the multiplicity of the Churches (in the early Christian understanding thereof), that there never can and never should be an absolute centralization in the Church, but that the multiplicity must instead retain its proper importance and its proper right within the unity.[8]

This understanding of unity and multiplicity, it was thought, gave new impetus to the ecumenical effort. Unity in multiplicity and multiplicity in unity was for Ratzinger at that time the "genuine focus of the idea of collegiality", which "should bring to bear the proper significance of the 'Churches' in the 'Church', that living variety which is the richness of true unity".[9]

In an interview with the *Internationale Katholische Zeitschrift Communio* in the early 1980s, Ratzinger advocated the view that the ecumenical effort should pursue the goal of striving to make a "plural of local Churches" out of the "plural of confessional Churches [that are] separated from one another".[10] For Ratzinger, though, the assumption of a *sacramental* and thus hierarchical structure is directly connected with the concept of local Church.[11] As early as 1976 he indicated that, therefore, as compared with Orthodoxy, it was much more difficult to build this ecumenical bridge to the Reformation communities. Despite all that, a prior reunion between Catholics and Orthodox would be beneficial for the "Reformation churches"[12] as well, especially since it is impossible, in Ratzinger's view, to look for the

---

[8] "Einleitung", 14.

[9] Ibid.

[10] *Church*, 99–122, citation at 120.

[11] From this fundamental conviction developed the "Ratzinger formula" that was mentioned earlier: "Rome must not demand more from the East by way of doctrine on the primacy than what had been formulated and practiced during the first millennium." See Ratzinger, "Prognosen für die Zukunft des Ökumenismus", in *Mitte*, 181–94, citation at 188.

[12] In 1976, the terminological distinction between "ecclesial communities that resulted from the Reformation" and "Reformation churches" was not yet a compelling one for Ratzinger.

solution "in the renunciation of ancient Church dogma and of the structure of the early Church",[13] as a memorandum of the Study Group of Ecumenical University Institutes suggested in 1973.[14]

Since the sacramentally based, hierarchical structure of the Church is a work of God that belongs to her very nature, ecumenism with the churches of the Reformation will require patience, above all. In contrast to Ratzinger's ecumenical positions during the Council,[15] his later declarations, therefore, became more restrained. In 1982, he recommended setting "realistic intermediate goals, since otherwise ecumenical enthusiasm could suddenly turn into resignation or even into a new embitterment".[16] Accordingly, he speaks in a 1986 letter to Max Seckler about the progress of ecumenism, which, however, cannot be expected to continue at the same pace as during the Council.[17] Indeed, the Council was preceded by "a lengthy process of joint struggle" that at that time suddenly seemed to make possible so much that was "new and hitherto unexpected".[18]

If the sacramental-hierarchical constitution of the Church is essential, then, according to Ratzinger, models such as "grassroots ecumenism" or ecumenism through the action of "the authorities"[19] can

---

[13] *Mitte*, 190.
[14] Cf. H. Fries, H. Küng, P. Lengsfeld, W. Pannenberg, E. Schlink, and H.-H. Wolf, eds., *Reform und Anerkennung kirchlicher Ämter: Ein Memorandum der Arbeitsgemeinschaft ökumenischer Universitätsinstitute* (Munich: Kaiser Verlag; Mainz: Matthias-Grünewald-Verlag, 1973), 11–25, esp. 24, where it says: "Until now, controversies in understanding apostolic succession and ordination were considered decisive obstacles to the mutual recognition of ministries and to communion among churches. Based on the findings of ecumenical theology, a refusal to recognize one another's ministries can therefore no longer be justified, because these conventional differences no longer have to be viewed as dividing churches from one another.... Whether ordination should be designated a sacrament or not is a question of semantics."
[15] On this subject, see *Highlights*, 73–76.
[16] *Church*, 121.
[17] Cf. *Church*, 135–42, ref. at 135.
[18] Ibid.
[19] See ibid., 136. In Ratzinger's view, the model of grassroots ecumenism is correct insofar as "the authorities in the Church cannot create anything that has not already matured in its life in the way of the insight and experience that comes from faith. But when this process of maturation was not meant but instead the dominant idea was the division of the Church into the grassroots Church and the official Church no new unity of any importance could grow." He explains further on (ibid., 137): "This means that neither an isolated grassroots nor an isolated authority comes into consideration as the

ultimately be of no use to the concern for unity, since they are based on a "do-it-yourself" foundation. Instead, it must be recognized that in this ecumenical task we are dealing, not with a *ius humanum* [human law], but rather with a work of God, which is therefore to be understood, in keeping with John 17, as a "theological unity"[20] that cannot be effected merely according to the principles of a diplomatic "ecumenism of negotiation".[21] But how, according to Ratzinger, is the ecumenical task itself to be carried out?

His 1986 answer to the dilemma of unity and multiplicity takes its bearings from Oscar Cullmann,[22] who provided him with a helpful catchword with the expression "unity through multiplicity":

Unity through diversity. True, schism belongs to what is evil, especially when it leads to hostility and to the impoverishment of the Christian witness. But when the poison of hostility is slowly extracted from the schism and when as a result of mutual acceptance what emerges from the difference is no longer just impoverishment but a new wealth of listening and understanding, then it can be in transition towards being seen as a *felix culpa* even before it is completely healed.[23]

In his essay "On the Ecumenical Situation", Ratzinger repeats in 1995 "that division represents not only an evil we have created, and which we ought therefore also to clear away again, but something

---

subject of ecumenical activity; effective ecumenical action presupposes the inner unity of the authorities' action on the one hand and the Church's real life of faith on the other. At this point I see one of the fundamental errors of the Fries-Rahner project: Rahner's view is that Catholics would follow the authorities anyway and that this is provided for by tradition and structure. In practice however things would not be essentially different among the Protestants; if the authorities decreed reunion and campaigned for it sufficiently here too the congregations would not fail to follow." Compare H. Fries and K. Rahner, *Einigung der Kirchen—reale Möglichkeit*, QD 100 (Freiburg im Breisgau: Herder, 1983).

[20] *Church*, 137.

[21] Ibid., 138.

[22] Cf. O. Cullmann, *Einheit und Vielfalt*, 2nd ed. (Tübingen: Mohr, 1990). A Protestant exegete, Cullmann was invited to be an observer at the Council because of his commitment to the reunion of Christians. See H. Raguer, "Das früheste Gepräge der Versammlung", in Wittstadt, 2:201–72, ref. at 214. See also O. Cullmann, "Verwirklichungen des ökumenischen Gedankens auf dem Konzil", in Hampe, *Konzil*, 355–59.

[23] *Church*, 138.

wherein there can be an element of divine 'necessity' ".[24] In this divine demand there is, at the same time, the power to purify, so as to arrive in this way at a God-given unity.

2. Ratzinger's critique of the new paradigm, the priority of praxis

At present, Ratzinger notes a paradigm shift[25] in ecumenism, which he says is the result of the abandonment of the concept of truth.[26] In the previous "so-called consensus ecumenism", it became apparent "how difficult it is to do justice to the demands of truth",[27] since that exceeds our capacities, time and again. Now, however, one remarks in the ecumenical debate the tendency "to invert the relationship between consensus and truth: It is not, they say, truth that creates consensus but consensus that is the only concrete and realistic court of judgment to decide what shall now hold good."[28]

As Ratzinger notes, when this is carried over to the relation between truth and praxis, it leads to the formula: "Action becomes the standard

---

[24] "Ecumenical Situation", 258. With regard to Church history, Ratzinger had likewise spoken in 1986 about a "mysterious and obscure necessity" for divisions ("Einleitung", 14), in the sense intended by the apostle Paul in 1 Corinthians 11:19, "there must be factions". Only "in the many churches outside of the one Church" ("Einleitung", 15) could multiplicity make a place for itself. On this subject, see also Church, 135–42, esp. 138. The passage in question is from an essay that was originally published in ThQ 166 (1986): 243–48 as a letter to Max Seckler. Ratzinger writes: "Towards the end of my years at Tübingen, Professor Seckler, you gave me to read a work prepared under your supervision which presented Augustine's interpretation of that mysterious phrase in Paul, 'there must be factions' (1 Cor 11:19).... It seems to me that the Fathers were not so wrong when they found a statement with more general implications in a remark with an originally very local reference, and even H. Schlier takes the view that as far as Paul was concerned it was a matter of an eschatological and dogmatic proposition [Kittel, ed., Theological Dictionary of the New Testament, 1:182–83]. If one may think in this direction, the exegetical conclusion derives its especial weight from the fact that in the Bible δει always refers in some way to an action of God's or expresses an eschatological necessity [thus, for example, Grundmann, in Kittel, Theological Dictionary 2:21–25]."

[25] Ratzinger refers to K. Raiser, Ökumene im Übergang: Paradigmenwechsel in der ökumenischen Bewegung (Munich: Kaiser, 1989), esp. 51ff.

[26] Ratzinger mentions as an essay of great importance for a new ecumenical consciousness: H. Wagner, "Ekklesiologische Optionen evangelischer Theologie als mögliche Leitbilder der Ökumene", Cath(M) 47 (1993): 124–41.

[27] "Ecumenical Situation", 260.

[28] Ibid.

for truth."[29] The final consequence is that "action is becoming the actual hermeneutic of unity."[30] Thereby, however, an entirely new paradigm of ecumenism is promoted, which understands itself to be not only an interdenominational but also an interreligious effort[31] and which aims, not at substantial convergence, but instead at a worldwide "fellowship of solidarity"[32] for the cause of justice, peace, and the conservation of creation. Ratzinger decisively rejects such a path that prioritizes praxis, for this means the "renunciation of metaphysics"[33] and thus the loss of truth. For this reason orthopraxis either leads eventually to what is nonbinding, thus making itself superfluous, or else it becomes ideology, since it asserts absolute standards and establishes them precisely "where in fact absolutes can have no place",[34] because they lack the requisite metaphysical basis. From this Ratzinger concludes:

It is easy to formulate the great goals—peace, justice, the conservation of creation. Yet if justice falls apart into many justices, and all this occurs only in the plural form, which can never be transcended, then these become empty goals. Almost inevitably they are taken over by the contemporary party attitude, by the dominant ideologies.[35]

---

[29] Ibid.

[30] Ibid.

[31] Cf. "New Questions", 121ff. As an example of this, Ratzinger refers to P. F. Knitter. The latter, he says, tries to simplify interreligious dialogue and make it practically effective by applying to it "the primacy of orthopraxy over orthodoxy" (ibid., 123). Compare on this subject K.-H. Menke, *Die Einzigkeit Jesu Christi im Horizont der Sinnfrage* (Freiburg: Johannes Verlag, 1995), 94–110. In his book, Menke analyzes the ideas of the two chief proponents of the pluralistic theology of religion, J. Hick and P. F. Knitter. See also P. F. Knitter, *Ein Gott—viele Religionen: Gegen den Absolutheitsanspruch des Christentums* (Munich: Kösel, 1988). Knitter argues for a "pluralistic nature of truth" (173). Therefore truth, for him, is not exclusive or all-absorbing: "Rather, what is true will reveal itself by the fact that it can enter into a relation to other statements of the truth and can grow through this relation. Truth is defined, not through exclusion, but rather through relation" (175). See also J. Hick, *Evil and the God of Love*, 4th ed. (Norfolk, 1975), 236–41, esp. 240f.

[32] On this subject, see H. Wagner, "Ekklesiologische Optionen evangelischer Theologie als mögliche Leitbilder der Ökumene", *Cath(M)* 47 (1993): 129f.

[33] "New Questions", 124.

[34] Ibid., 126.

[35] "Ecumenical Situation", 262.

For him, therefore, the principle holds true: "Ethos without logos cannot endure."[36] This is not the least important lesson taught by the collapse of socialism in 1989.

Nevertheless, Ratzinger can also discern something positive for ecumenism in the paradigm shift just outlined. It consists in the readiness "to realize those elements of unity that are now possible and to leave what is not now possible in the sphere of pluralism, which can also have a positive significance".[37] As long as no relativistic ideology is derived from it, an "ecumenism of praxis" has its value in the sense of being the ethical fulfillment of Christ's commandment of love. Thereby faith itself is purified so that it can distinguish better what is essential from what is not.[38]

In summarizing, Ratzinger declares that from the "praxeological model" we should "learn dogmatic patience but without declining into indifference toward the truth and its verbal expression".[39] For the question about truth and faith's claim to truth proves to be for him "the fundamental question for the survival of contemporary Christianity".[40] An ecumenism that renounced truth and, like the Fries-Rahner plan proposed in 1983, contented itself with an "epistemological tolerance"[41] would serve to bring about a formal unity that would lack any actual content. For this reason, Ratzinger pointedly rejected such an undertaking in 1986.

> But as far as things stand with Rahner the possibility of unity rests on nobody knowing any longer exactly whether he ... has correctly understood the Church's teaching (based on the bible), whether he ... has rightly grasped the other's theology. In the present

---

[36] Ibid.

[37] Ibid.

[38] Cf. ibid., 263. A few pages later (ibid., 267) Ratzinger speaks about the positive "crosslinking between groups set up in the individual churches and communities" and mentions in this regard the Focolare Movement as well as the relationship between Catholic religious orders and Protestant brotherhoods. It is a matter of testimonies to the faith in which all are enriched by the gifts of those who join forces.

[39] Ibid., 266.

[40] *Church*, 122–34, citation at 124. Eilert Herms, too, is in agreement with Ratzinger on this point. See E. Herms, "Ökumenische Zeichen der Glaubensfreiheit", *US* 39 (1984): 178–200; Herms, *Einheit der Christen in der Gemeinschaft der Kirchen* (Göttingen: Vandenhoeck and Ruprecht, 1984), esp. 47, 187f.

[41] See Fries and Rahner, *Einigung der Kirchen*, 42.

"intellectual political situation" (what a linguistic monstrosity) all that can be stated is merely that we all have as our point of reference "always still clearly and tangibly ... Jesus as our Christ". Thus there remains the "eschatological hope that the fact that our faith is the same will emerge despite the present (partial) incommensurability of our theologies".[42]

In Ratzinger's judgment, Rahner conceives of unity, not in terms of a common search to know the truth, but rather as something "based on common scepticism".[43] But that is ultimately a "capitulation before the possibility of approaching one another in the truth".[44] At this intersection of truth and the possibility of knowing it, Ratzinger situates the duty of the ecclesial ministry to serve the truth. From this he derives the principle: "An authority that serves the truth, as should be the case with a Church authority based on the sacrament, is an obedient authority. An authority based on scepticism becomes arbitrary and high-handed."[45]

Accordingly, for Ratzinger the sacramental understanding of ministry and the truth of the faith are inseparably connected. The ordained minister must be a witness to the faith of the whole Church, for he represents, not himself, but Christ as the holy origin of the Church.[46] Therefore in the Church "the atmosphere becomes cramped and stifling when her officebearers forget that the sacrament is, not an allocation of power, but dispossession of myself for the sake of the one in whose 'persona' I am to speak and act."[47]

In summary, we can say that Ratzinger derives from the rediscovery of the sacramentally based, collegial constitution of the early Church in *Lumen gentium*—in keeping with the basic ecumenical concern of

---

[42] *Church*, 130f. Ratzinger quotes from Fries and Rahner, *Einigung der Kirchen*, 42. Compare also Fries and Rahner, *Einigung der Kirchen*, 48f. In this passage Rahner finally summarizes as follows: "Given an existential epistemological tolerance—in which radically contradictory things that are taught expressly and explicitly are not forcibly harmonized, but rather leeway is preserved for what has not yet been positively agreed upon but is recognized in hope as being in agreement—a union of Churches from dogmatic points of view is already possible today."

[43] *Church*, 131.

[44] Ibid.

[45] Ibid.

[46] Cf. ibid., 128f.; see also *Called to Communion*, 118f.

[47] *Called to Communion*, 146.

the Council—a new paradigm for ecumenism along the lines of *unity in multiplicity*. He applies this principle especially to the Orthodox Churches, since in them is preserved the sacramental-hierarchical structure that, according to Ratzinger, belongs to the nature of the Church, whereas the Reformation churches display foundational differences in regard to this question. Since unity is a gift of God, it cannot be attained by way of theological compromises but is under an obligation to his truth; therefore, Ratzinger rejects the so-called primacy of orthopraxis over orthodoxy.[48] For then, instead of truth, consensus determines what is valid, and thereby praxis ultimately becomes the standard of what is true. As a positive aspect of this model for the present day, Ratzinger mentions that from it one can learn "praxeological patience", in which the "necessity of divisions" can be endured. This will ultimately be overcome only through the conversion of all to the truth, which is Christ,[49] so that the ecumenical effort is not "a matter of human ingenuity".[50] The unity of the Church, in contrast, can be understood from the outset only as a theological entity[51] and is therefore to be awaited as a gift from God. On account of this self-transcendence toward God, Ratzinger says that even the painful points of a hierarchy understood in sacramental terms and of the papal primacy must not be omitted from ecumenical dialogue.

§ 2. Hierarchy as Holy Origin

1. *The making present of a beginning*

In contrast to a view of hierarchy in purely sociological terms, Ratzinger, along with the Council, emphasizes its sacramental basis. In his view, therefore, the etymological definition of the term "hierarchy" as "sacred origin" corresponds better to the ecclesial use of the

---

[48] Cf. "New Questions", 123.

[49] Cf. Ratzinger, letter to Provincial Bishop Johannes Hanselmann dated March 9, 1993, from "Exchange of Letters between Provincial Bishop Johannes Hanselmann and Joseph Cardinal Ratzinger", in *Pilgrim Fellowship*, 247–52, ref. at 251. Ratzinger emphasizes that there are "wounds" on both sides, and therefore conversion to the truth is necessary for both.

[50] Ibid., 249.

[51] Cf. ibid.

term than the translation "sacred rule".[52] The power implied in this origin is based, not solely on continuity with it, that is to say, through the apostolic succession of the bishops, but also on the presence of this very origin, which communicates itself in the sacrament as a source that is ever present and ever new. Consequently, ministry that has a sacramental basis falls, not primarily under the category of power or authority, but rather under the category of service, in that it must be "a conduit and a making present of a beginning".[53] In this way, the Church is oriented to Jesus Christ, indeed, to the historical Jesus and at the same time to the Christ who is to come. She "is based, on the one hand, utterly and entirely in the fact of the past, in the life, death, and Resurrection of Jesus Christ",[54] while, on the other hand, she is "directed forward to his Second Coming, in which he will fulfill his promise".[55]

This eschatological view of hope, according to Ratzinger, is among "the most important pastoral tasks after the Council".[56] Therefore, he argues against "an idea of ministry as the domination of a ruler on the model of the Enlightenment",[57] which relieves the officeholder of the duty to witness to Christ and makes him answerable only to his own reason:

> Hierarchical service and ministry is thus guarding an origin that is holy, and not making arbitrary dispositions and decisions. The teaching office and indeed ministry in general in the Church is thus not a business of "leading" in the sense of the enlightened ruler who knows that he is in possession of better reason, translates it into regulations and counts on the obedience of his subjects, who have to accept his reason and its articulation as their divinely willed standard. Nor does hierarchical office correspond to a democratic authority in which individuals delegate their will to representatives and thereby declare that they agree that the will of the majority should be law.[58]

---

[52] Cf. *Salt of the Earth*, 190.

[53] Ibid., 191.

[54] *Volk Gottes*, 43–70, citation at 68.

[55] Ibid., 69.

[56] Ibid., 70.

[57] Ratzinger sees such an approach in the Fries-Rahner model of ecumenism; see *Church*, 122–34, esp. 129. On this subject, cf. Fries and Rahner, *Einigung der Kirchen*, 66.

[58] *Church*, 122–34, citation at 128.

Succession in the hierarchical service means for Ratzinger, instead, being enlisted in the service of Christ, the Eternal Word, in order to testify to his presence in word and sacrament and to step back behind the responsibility itself so as to be, as it were, only a voice that makes the eternal Logos "articulate in the world".[59]

2. On the sacramental basis of episcopal collegiality

Since the hierarchical constitution of the Church is structured in an episcopal and collegial manner, the Council first had to clarify to what extent the episcopal ministry in itself should be understood as *sacramental*. Even in the autumn 1962 draft of the schema on the Church, *De Ecclesia*,[60] as Ratzinger explains, "the sacramentality and the collegiality of the episcopal ministry were treated in two separate chapters."[61] The 1962 draft related collegiality *in a purely juridical way* only to those residential bishops who are in communion with the pope.[62] *Lumen gentium*, on the other hand, states that the collegial constitution of the Church has a *sacramental* basis, when it speaks in article 21 about the sacramentality of episcopal consecration, through which "the fullness of the sacrament of Orders is conferred."[63] The following article 22 forms, in Ratzinger's view, "an important passage that combines both ideas and thus invests both with a new significance",[64] for here the sacramentality of episcopal consecration is directly connected to the collegial-juridical constitution of the Church: "One is constituted a member of the episcopal body in

[59] Ratzinger, "Primacy, Episcopate, and Apostolic Succession", in *The Episcopate and the Primacy*, by K. Rahner and J. Ratzinger, 37–63, citation at 47, QD 11 (New York: Herder and Herder, 1962).

[60] On this subject, see Alberigo/Magistretti, 90–111, esp. 90, 103. See also the table contrasting the 1962 draft and the final version of *Lumen gentium* in pt. 1, sec. 1, chap. 2, § 1, of this work, "On the Dynamics at the Council".

[61] "Kollegialität", 47. In an extensive essay in *IKaZ* 10 (1981): 435–45, Ratzinger sets forth "The Church's Doctrine of the *Sacramentum Ordinis*".

[62] Cf. *Highlights*, 126: "Following the initiative of John XXIII, even the draft of the text rejected by the bishops in 1962 attempted to revaluate the office of bishop, and for this purpose submitted two concepts: (1) the sacramentality of the ordination of bishops, and (2) the concept of the college of bishops." See also "Kommentar", 352.

[63] *LG* 21.

[64] *Highlights*, 127.

virtue of sacramental consecration and hierarchical communion with the head and members of the body."[65]

Ratzinger is convinced that this enunciates the "double basis" of episcopal collegiality, that is, juridical and sacramental, "in such a way that these two roots are inseparably connected".[66] This new understanding of episcopal collegiality has consequences also on the exercise thereof through a council. A council cannot be understood juridically as a Church parliament; it is, rather, "a place of witness".[67] Although there is representation in a council, "this representation rests not on the delegation of people's wills but on the sacrament",[68] which obliges the ordained man "to represent the faith of the whole Church, the 'holy origin' ".[69] The sacramental obligation that binds him is an expression of the Church's relation to Christ[70] and, therefore, "involves the elimination of arbitrarily following one's own designs".[71] Therefore, the statements of a council that are passed with moral unanimity are not decisions that invent something new; rather, they bear witness to the Church's faith: "They do not create anything but simply articulate what already exists in the Church of the Lord, and therefore make it publicly binding as a mark by which the *anima ecclesiastica* can be known."[72]

This act of making present what was already received at the beginning of the Church is also the reason why Ratzinger, in keeping with *Lumen gentium*, never reduces the correlation between collegiality and primacy to pragmatic or purely juridical terms; rather, he regards it as having a sacramental basis, thus assigning it to the sphere of what is constitutive of the Church. In doing so, however, he is aware of "how narrow the scope of divine right in the Church really is and how much latitude is given for discretion".[73]

---

[65] *LG* 22.
[66] *Highlights*, 127.
[67] *Church*, 122–34, citation at 129.
[68] Ibid.
[69] Ibid.
[70] On this subject, see J. Meyer zu Schlochtern, *Sakrament Kirche: Wirken Gottes im Handeln der Menschen* (Freiburg im Breisgau: Herder, 1992), 153–90, ref. at 158–60.
[71] *Church*, 129.
[72] Ibid., 130.
[73] "Formen", 155.

§ 3. Collegiality and Primacy

In order to make the tension between the dogmatic foundation and the pastoral implementation of the Church's hierarchical structure a productive one, Ratzinger recommends consulting Scripture and the patristic tradition, because in them shines the truth that must determine the Church's activity.[74] Certainly, over the course of time, and in particular as a result of Ratzinger's transfer from Munich to Rome in the early 1980s, his understanding changed about how the dogmatic statement on the episcopal-collegial structure should be put concretely into pastoral practice. Thomas Weiler elaborates on this subject:

> It is obvious that something has changed in Ratzinger's view. In my opinion two things should be taken into account in attempting to answer this question. First: The situation is different now. In 1963, that is, *before* the approval of the Dogmatic Constitution *Lumen gentium*, it was Ratzinger's task ... to contribute material for the Council Fathers to evaluate. It was a situation of seeking. Meanwhile, however, *Lumen gentium* has been promulgated.... His reflections must now begin with the new reality, the conciliar documents.[75]

Consequently, with regard to the hierarchical constitution of the Church, we should discuss where specifically in Ratzinger's writings changes can in fact be noted and what realities remain for him constitutive and therefore unchangeable. In order to be able to decide these questions fairly, it is crucial to clarify first the dogmatic foundations of collegiality.

1. *Dogmatic foundations of collegiality*

In an article for the first issue of the journal *Concilium* toward the end of the Council, Ratzinger refers in his discussion of "the pastoral implications of the doctrine of the collegiality of bishops"[76] to two historical facts[77] that are fundamental to his argument: namely, the

---

[74] On this topic, see *Volk Gottes*, 43–70, ref. at 56.
[75] Weiler, 333–45, citation at 339.
[76] I quote the essay as reprinted in *Volk Gottes*, 43–70.
[77] See ibid., 43.

collegiality of the apostles and, subsequently, the collegial structure of the episcopal ministry in the early Church.

a. The "collegiality" of the apostles

The collegiality of the apostles, Ratzinger says, is characterized by four essential features. First, it indicates that the officeholders and the People of God belonged together inseparably. Second, it was instituted *sacramentally* by Jesus at the Last Supper. Third, with the sending of the Holy Spirit on Pentecost, it becomes *apostolic* in the strict sense; that is, it has a missionary purpose to proclaim the gospel, and not just a symbolic mission. Linguistically this is expressed by the identification of the Twelve with the names of the apostles, because of which they are later called the "twelve apostles" in the Lucan tradition. Fourth, the three aforementioned characteristics of the *collegium*, or of collegiality, stand on the foundation of the *primatial* structure of the Church's hierarchical constitution.

With respect to the first point: The point of departure for collegiality, according to Ratzinger, is the fact that the apostles are twelve in number, along with the associated eschatological symbolism:[78] "When Jesus called twelve men to be his immediate followers, his gesture was intelligible to everyone. It meant that now the end had arrived; these twelve represented the reestablished, final Israel."[79]

For Ratzinger, it is crucial that the Twelve, according to this view, represent "not only the future bishops and officeholders" but also "and, in fact, primarily the 'new people' that will be called Church".[80] In saying this, he is not advocating a Protestant interpretation, which sees in the Twelve only the universal priesthood of all believers and disregards the fact "that the Twelve were already a select group even during Jesus' lifetime and thus clearly prefigured the special status of the ministry".[81] Instead, Ratzinger sees in this very act of choosing the Twelve a foreshadowing of the fact that the officeholders and the People of God *belong together inseparably*, since as the Twelve they are

---

[78] See *Highlights*, 49ff. Cf. pt. 2, sec. 2, chap. 2, § 3.2.b, of this work.
[79] *Highlights*, 50.
[80] *Volk Gottes*, 45.
[81] Ibid.

appointed to be patriarchs of the new People of God, by analogy with the twelve sons of Jacob, the patriarchs of Israel.

Second, for Ratzinger the *sacramental foundation* of collegiality is decisive. In the Passover of the New Covenant, which in his view should be interpreted, not as an "isolated cultic transaction"[82] of Jesus, but rather as a new covenant act between God and his people, the Twelve receive their ecclesiological-eucharistic appointment:

> The institution of the most holy Eucharist on the evening before the Passion . . . is the making of a covenant and, as such, is the concrete foundation of the new people: the people comes into being through its covenant relation to God. . . . By his eucharistic action, Jesus draws the disciples into his relationship with God and, therefore, into his mission, which aims to reach "the many", the humanity of all places and of all times.[83]

This eucharistic focus is the expression of a development that the schema on the Church underwent with respect to the relation between collegiality and the sacramentality of the episcopal ministry.[84] Whereas in the first draft of *De Ecclesia* in the autumn of 1962, sacramentality and collegiality were still treated in two different sections,[85] the final text of *Lumen gentium* shows the interrelationship between sacramental foundation and the *communio* of Head and members within the *collegium*.[86] Ratzinger says that, with the symbolism of the Twelve, a clearly defined, sacramentally founded and collegially structured community is presented in *Lumen gentium*. In this *communio* unity "the apostles are what they are only by sharing in the community of the twelve."[87]

As a third aspect of collegiality, Ratzinger mentions the fact of being sent in "the ministry of the Twelve", which begins as "*apostolate* in the strict sense"[88] with the Pentecost event. For the word "apostle" is not used until after Pentecost, so that we can conclude that the expression "the Twelve" is the older of the two. The two terms, as Ratzinger

---

[82] *Called to Communion*, 28.
[83] Ibid.
[84] See pt. 1, sec. 1, chap. 2, of this dissertation, "From the Schema *De Ecclesia* to the Dogmatic Constitution *Lumen gentium*".
[85] On this subject, see Alberigo/Magistretti, 90–111, esp. 90, 103.
[86] See "Kollegialität", 47–49.
[87] *Church*, 3–20, citation at 13.
[88] *Volk Gottes*, 43–70, citation at 43.

explains, are first equated "in Lucan theology.... Then, from the two originally separate, albeit overlapping orders"[89] developed the compound title "the twelve apostles", which became common usage in the Church. They, in turn, form the foundation of her collegial-hierarchical structure. From the very beginning, she is structured in terms of Peter's *ministry of primacy*, the special place of which is clearly prominent in the Gospels.[90]

As a result of the foregoing discussion, it is evident that Ratzinger, given his dogmatic approach, considers the concept of *collegium* to be particularly important,[91] much in the same way as *Lumen gentium* 19 does. During the First Vatican Council, this expression still met with resolute objections because of the theological line of demarcation drawn

---

[89] Ibid.

[90] Cf. "Kollegialität", 44f.: "The primordial form of spiritual ministry established by the Lord himself—'the Twelve', as Scripture simply and repeatedly calls it (for example, Mt 11:1; 20:17; 26:14, 20; Mk 3:14, 16; 4:10; 11:11; 14:10, 17, 20, 43; Lk 8:1; 9:1; 18:31; 22:3; Jn 6:67–71; 20:24; Acts 6:2; 1 Cor 15:5)—is collegial; one of the Twelve, Peter, is meanwhile singled out and stands at the head of the others, yet in such a way that he continues to belong to the *collegium*, that is, to the Twelve."

[91] Cf. ibid., 46f., where Ratzinger comments on the adoption of the term *collegium* in the Constitution on the Church. "The Theological Commission thought it right to take into account the misgivings that were voiced again and again about the word *collegium* ... and, following a suggested revision supported in particular by the Italian bishops, added to the description of the company of the Twelve as a *collegium* the words *seu coetus stabilis*: college as a permanent assembly.... For the same reason, it had been decided even in the earlier stages of the drafting to alternate the word *collegium* with the expressions *ordo* and *corpus*, which in the tradition of the early Church are used as synonyms for *collegium*. The alternation of terms can indicate, at any rate, that none of the words that secular legal language places at our disposal is capable of expressing with complete accuracy the state of affairs in the Church, for which there are analogous phenomena in the secular realm, but no exact parallels." In *Highlights*, 123, Ratzinger mentions also the term *fraternitas*. He notes (ibid., 124) a repeated "abridgement and narrowing" of the linguistic usage of the term "fraternity". "The first change involved a gradual developing of various 'layers' within the Christian fraternity. The ordinary Christian could no longer address the cleric, especially the bishop, as 'brother', but instead had to address him as 'papa'." Finally, Ratzinger situates a second narrowing in the suppression of the name "brother" among officeholders in favor of "the formal title of 'colleague' [*collega*], which the bishops now used to address one another. Correspondingly, the concept of brotherhood (fraternity) was replaced by that of collegiality (college). During the fourth and fifth centuries this expression became more and more the customary one for the community of bishops. Other terms coming into use at this time, such as 'order' and 'body', were also borrowed from legal language and indicated the same development" (ibid., 124–25). Cf. "Kommentar", 351. See also *Volk Gottes*, 52f.

in the controversy against the Reformation idea of the complete equality of all members in the Church.[92] Even during Vatican II, therefore, the term "collegiality" was accepted with some skepticism, especially within the Curia.[93] Already during the Council, Ratzinger decisively argued for a rediscovery of the order of the early Church. His concern in doing so was to understand the relation between primacy and episcopacy "against the background of the original spiritual structure of the Church, which is identical to none of the political structures that are familiar to us today".[94] The ancient Church's tradition of episcopal collegiality, which until the Second Vatican Council was neglected in practice,[95] along with its liturgical expression,[96] is of crucial importance in carrying out this task. This is all the more true since this heritage from the early Church was preserved from the fifteenth until the nineteenth century primarily by "Italian-speaking theologians", even though the scholars in question displayed an "emphatically primatial"[97] way of thinking.

---

[92] Besides *Pastor Aeternus*, Vatican I intended to promulgate a second dogmatic constitution on the nature of the Church. The *Schema de Ecclesia Christi* for this second constitution had already been drafted by the Theological Preparatory Commission. The schema comprises fifteen chapters, the tenth of which treats the authority and the hierarchical structure of the Church. In it the schema repudiates the reformers, especially those who advocate a collegial system. On this subject, see F. van der Horst, *Das Schema über die Kirche auf dem I. Vatikanischen Konzil* (Paderborn: Bonifacius-Druckerei, 1963), 296.

[93] Cf. "Kollegialität", 45. On this topic, see G. Ruggieri, "Der schwierige Abschied von der kontroverstheologisch geprägten Ekklesiologie", in Wittstadt, 2:331–419, esp. 355f., 360–63, 368f., 380–82, 391f., 394f.

[94] J. Ratzinger, "Zurück zur Ordnung der Alten Kirche", in Hampe, *Konzil*, 183f., citation at 183.

[95] On this subject, see Ruggieri, "Schwierige Abschied", 2:331–419, esp. 392f. In Ruggieri's opinion, during the controversy over this concept at the beginning of the debate about *De Ecclesia* in December 1962, "the intervention of Cardinal Frings, to which, we may rightly assume, his theologian Ratzinger made his own contribution", was very effective. "It dealt with what was probably the harshest criticism, since here the schema was being torn to shreds precisely with regard to the central claim that it asserted, namely, as to its catholicity. The critique argued that it represented, instead, merely the Latin tradition of the last two centuries, that the Greek and the old Latin traditions, on the contrary, were not represented."

[96] On this subject, see *Church*, 12. The word *ordo* as a formal description for the sacrament of orders means entrance into community service, "into the 'we' of those who serve". Ratzinger indicates here that *ordo* and *collegium* were used synonymously in the early Church.

[97] "Kollegialität", 46.

b. The collegial character of spiritual ministry in the early Church

In the previous section we showed that the collegiality of the apostles and the fact that they are rooted in the Eucharist are for Ratzinger the point of departure for making the *communio* structure of the early Church once again the standard for his ecclesiology. Both for him and for the Council, the ecumenical concern was an important motive for harking back to the heritage of the early Church. In the "still undivided and unseparated Church of the time of the Fathers when the Church was still aware of its direct unity with the apostles", theologians saw the "basis for renewal of the structure of the Church in our time",[98] so as to promote the cause of Church unity. From this order of the early Church, Ratzinger derives the following formula for Church unity:

> The nature of Church unity stands out clearly in the four concepts of *communio—collegium—caput—membra*.... In the juxtaposition of these concepts, it becomes evident which one is the real axis of unity: *communio*, in its full spiritual sense as membership and sharing in the Body of the Lord, which of course must be perfected as *communio hierarchica*, in the binding form of the Church's hierarchically ordered communion. This concept already includes the multiplicity of the local *communiones*, or, to speak the language of the early Church, the multiplicity of *ecclesiae* (*locales, episcopales*), and already excludes the possibility that unity can be determined solely in terms of one's relation to the *caput*. It demands, rather, the ordered structure of the *collegium* as representation of the *ecclesiae* and their intrinsic association.[99]

According to Ratzinger, it is crucial for this ordered structure of the early Church that the particular Church represents a whole in herself yet acquires her completeness only in the openness of *communio* with the other Churches. Applied to episcopal collegiality, this means, first, that the bishop does not lead his local Church as a "fragment" of a larger unit of governance (namely, the universal Church). For in each of the individual local Churches is realized—as has already

---

[98] *Highlights*, 120.
[99] "Kollegialität", 51f.

been noted[100]—"the total reality of the Church".[101] This rediscovery of the local Church is for Ratzinger "one of the most significant and pertinent statements of the doctrine on collegiality".[102] Second, through the collegiality of the bishops is brought about the horizontal connection of the individual local Churches with one another. With relation to the particular Church, this means: "It is complete only when the bishop does not stand alone, but is himself in communion with the other bishops of the other Churches of God."[103]

c. The collegiality of the bishops and the primacy of the pope

When Ratzinger talks about the collegiality of the bishops, at the same time the question arises for him of the Church's principle of unity, the Petrine ministry. Not only in ecumenical dialogue is this "probably the most difficult problem"; within the Catholic Church as well, the Roman primacy has "again and again proved to be a stumbling block, from the medieval struggle between *imperiumi* and *sacerdotium*, through the early modern state Church movements and the nineteenth century's demands for independence from Rome",[104] down to the debate during Vatican II over the nature of the papal primacy and the manner in which it should be exercised.[105] On the one hand, the teaching rediscovered at the Council concerning the collegiality of the bishops brought with it "significant modifications with respect to certain ways of presenting the doctrine on the primacy", while, on the other hand, it was itself instrumental in highlighting the "central theological importance"[106] of the Petrine ministry.

Accordingly, the primacy of the pope cannot be understood in terms of the model of absolute monarchy, as though the Bishop of Rome were the unlimited monarch of a centrally constituted, supernatural state called "Church"; it means, rather, that within the network of the Churches that are in communion with each other, from which

[100] See pt. 2, sec. 2, chap. 1, § 3.2.b, of this dissertation, "The Fulfillment of the Whole Church in Each Celebration of the Eucharist".
[101] *Highlights*, 121.
[102] Ibid.
[103] Ibid., 122. See also "Kollegialität", 55f. Cf. *Volk Gottes*, 43–70, esp. 46–54.
[104] *Called to Communion*, 47.
[105] Cf. *Highlights*, 106–8.
[106] *Volk Gottes*, 54.

the one Church of God is built up, there is an obligatory fixed point, the *sedes Romana*, from which the unity of the faith and of *communio* must take their bearings.[107]

Just as Peter belongs to the company of the apostles and at the same time assumes a special role within it, so too the successor of Peter in the *communio* of the college of bishops. Here, however, Ratzinger says we should keep in mind that the bishops are not apostles, for the "successor is something other than the one from whom the succession proceeds".[108] This principle of irreplaceability, however, is true also for the relation between Peter and the successor of Peter, for the pope is not an apostle, but rather stands, like the bishops, in the order of succession.[109] What distinguishes him from the others pertains to his specific service to the universal Church.[110]

In his definition of the correlation between primacy and episcopate, Ratzinger stresses the twofold duty of the bishops. First, they are ordered to the totality of the one Church and in this way bear a responsibility for the universal Church.[111] Second, in their particular Churches, the totality of the Church is realized "most importantly in the Eucharist and the proclamation of the Gospel".[112] From this twofold efficacy are derived two different structural types of episcopal collegiality, which both made their way into the ecclesiology of the Council and—as Ratzinger explains—ultimately are supposed to serve the same purpose of bringing to bear "the proper significance of the 'Churches'" and thus "that living multiplicity which is the richness of true unity".[113]

---

[107] Ibid., 54f.

[108] "Kollegialität", 55. Ratzinger's dissertation adviser, G. Söhngen, has also made this point forcefully. See G. Söhngen, *Die Einheit in der Theologie* (Munich: Zink, 1952), 305–23.

[109] See Ratzinger's preconciliar discussion of "Primacy, Episcopate, and Apostolic Succession", in Rahner and Ratzinger, *Episcopate and the Primacy*, 37–63, esp. 55ff., "Papal Succession and Episcopal Succession: Their Relation and Differences"; already in the preparatory phase of the Council this monograph in the series Quaestiones disputatae proved to be influential among the Council Fathers. On this subject, see the commentary in *Herderkorrespondenz*, "Das kollegiale Prinzip in der Kirche", *HerKorr* 17 (1962/63): 527–29, ref. at 527. See also the mention of QD 11 by Archbishop Raphael Garcia y Garcia de Castro during the second session of the Council, in *AS* 3/1:578.

[110] Cf. "Kollegialität", 55. See also Söhngen, *Einheit in der Theologie*, 307.

[111] See "Kollegialität", 55.

[112] Ibid., 56.

[113] "Einleitung", 15.

1) *The modern-speculative approach*

The modern-speculative approach starts with the universal Church and the whole episcopal college and is primarily concerned with the *plena et suprema potestas* [full and supreme authority] of the college of bishops and "its equilibrium with the *plena et suprema potestas* of the pope".[114] In contrast to Karl Rahner, with whom Ratzinger collaborated on the question of collegiality during the Council,[115] Ratzinger preferred from the very beginning the approach of the early Church.[116] Karl Rahner,[117] however, defined the episcopal ministry from the modern perspective, Ratzinger says, "as nothing short of the ministry of those who bear such responsibility for the universal Church that they can rightly be counted as members of the *collegium* that governs it".[118] Admittedly, this view causes great difficulties, especially with regard to ecumenism, as is clearly evident in the judgment of the Orthodox theologian N. A. Nissiotis, whom Ratzinger quotes: "For the Orthodox, it is the sign of a dangerous ecclesiological misunderstanding when a council proposes this unbiblical and unhistorical understanding of collegiality for discussion and decides to accept it."[119]

Shortly after the Council, Ratzinger pleaded that such objections should not be ignored. Otherwise, the teaching about episcopal collegiality, which was rediscovered as an *ecumenical* paradigm during the Council, could ultimately, "through a one-sided, systematic treatment, become a new obstacle for the ecumenical effort".[120] In

---

[114] "Kollegialität", 58.

[115] See the notice in Wassilowsky, 390f.

[116] Proof of this is, for example, the article by J. Ratzinger, "Zurück zur Ordnung der Alten Kirche", in Hampe, *Konzil*, 183f.

[117] On this subject, see K. Rahner, *Das Amt der Einheit* (Stuttgart: Schwabenverlag, 1964), 253–57, 272. Rahner correctly notes (255) that the apostles were not bound territorially to one place. From this he concludes "that the college of bishops as such derives its existence and its title from a college" (256). Ratzinger pointed out that Rahner, "contrary to these remarks ... , had set forth in *The Episcopate and the Primacy* 11–36 a foundation for the episcopal ministry based purely on the local Church" ("Kollegialität", 56f.).

[118] "Kollegialität", 56.

[119] N. A. Nissiotis, "Die Ekklesiologie des Zweiten Vatikanischen Konzils in orthodoxer Sicht und ihre ökumenische Bedeutung", *KuD* 10 (1964): 153–68, citation at 157. See "Kollegialität", 58.

[120] Ibid.

contrast to Rahner, he refers to the theology of the Church Fathers. There the idea of the universal college is secondary.

2) The early Church's approach to episcopal collegiality

In contrast to the modern approach just described, the approach taken by the early Church, according to Ratzinger, proceeds in the opposite direction:

> Every "particular Church" is not just a part, but is truly Church; no political system has anything comparable to this special peculiarity of the Church of Jesus Christ, which is defined in terms of the Word and the Eucharist and which is opposed to speculative constitutional structures. Consequently, the man who stands at the head of one Church necessarily has a significance also for the Church as a whole, which lives in the particular Churches.[121]

Since both structural types of collegiality are found in *Lumen gentium*,[122] in his view determining the theological emphases is a matter of interpretation and reception, so that the "serious responsibility of the commentators"[123] is unmistakable. As he sees it, two basic rules for the practical implementation of episcopal collegiality result from the foundation of the *communio* structure in the early Church—rules that are still valid today:

> The necessity of the particular Churches as vital fundamental expressions of ecclesiastical life must be seen as a fundamental precondition and as a goal of the Church's constitution.

---

[121] Ibid., 57.

[122] Two representative texts from *Lumen gentium* may illustrate this: For the modern type of collegiality, see *LG* 22: "The order of bishops, which succeeds to the college of apostles and gives this apostolic body continued existence, is also the subject of supreme and full power over the universal Church, provided we understand this body together with its head the Roman Pontiff and never without this head." The Council refers to the *relatio* of Zinelli at the First Vatican Council in Mansi 52, 1109 C. For the early-Church type, see *LG* 23: "The individual bishops, however, are the visible principle and foundation of unity in their particular churches, fashioned after the model of the universal Church, in and from which churches comes into being the one and only Catholic Church." *Lumen gentium* [supplementary n. 31] argues with Cyprian (*Ep.* 66, 8, in CSEL [Hartel] 3, 2, 733): "The bishop in the Church and the Church in the bishop".

[123] "Kollegialität", 57.

This individual life of the particular Churches must of course be of such a nature that they do not live shut in on themselves but are in themselves "Catholic" and so are open to the whole in the living out of their life.[124]

With that, we arrive with Ratzinger at the question of how this dogmatic teaching about collegiality can be implemented concretely in pastoral practice.

2. Pastoral implications of the episcopal-collegial structure

During the Council, Ratzinger already noted an "amalgamation of pragmatic concerns and theologically framed questions".[125] He describes as follows the ambivalence of this entanglement:

> There was something positive to this process, insofar as it clearly brought to light the hidden sociological presuppositions that no doubt had operated, along with others, in preparing the groundwork for the theoretical debate.... It also contained a risk, however, because one was tempted to define the desired praxis under consideration at the moment in the loftiest possible theological terms and to make it unassailable by relegating it to the sphere of divine right [ius divinum]. As a matter of fact, there is no doubt a temptation here for both sides, and it could lead to questionable conclusions if one were to allow oneself to be swept away by it.[126]

For this reason, Ratzinger advocated distinguishing clearly what is purely pragmatic from what is dogmatic, so as to avoid "turning the pragmatic into an ideology".[127]

Before I explain the concrete practice of episcopal collegiality and its relation to the primacy and point out, where necessary, different positions taken by Ratzinger, I will first discuss briefly those three aspects in which, according to his view, the correlation of dogmatic and pastoral application stands out with particular clarity. These aspects

---

[124] *Church*, 46–62, citation at 56.
[125] "Formen", 155.
[126] Ibid.
[127] Ibid., 156.

make it clear that for Ratzinger the principle of "unity in multiplicity", which is derived from the relation between collegiality and primacy, is, not something arbitrary, but rather an essential structural element of the whole Church as well as of the particular Church. Since the task of representation, that is, of embodying this unity in multiplicity, belongs to the bishops together with the successor of Peter, the first aspect highlights collegiality as a sign of the "we" structure of the faith, which is founded upon the Church's *communio*. The second aspect of the correlation of collegial teaching and practice consists of the fact that the ecclesial "we" cannot be separated from personal witness.[128] In particular, it is a question of the witness structure of the episcopal ministry, which finds its expression in the responsibility of the individual member of the college of bishops as well as in the totality of the college. The third aspect concerns episcopal collegiality from an ecumenical perspective. Although we cannot go into detail here, this approach of Ratzinger should be considered, insofar as he sees in the structural principle "unity in multiplicity" the indication of a path to unity for the Orthodox Churches.

a. Collegiality as the expression of the "we" structure of the faith

The collegial structure of the Church becomes visible for Ratzinger in the "three colleges", "congregation—presbyterate—episcopate", which are "nested one within the other and in each case specifically connected with the other two".[129] They give expression to the fact that the "I" in the Church "always exists in the plural, in a 'we' that actually gives meaning to the individual 'I'".[130] Ratzinger says that this is true both for the spiritual ministry in the Church, which is always a ministry of *communio* with others, and also for every baptized person; this is why he declares:

It is not that a particular bishop succeeds a particular apostle, but rather that the college of bishops is the continuation of the college of apostles. Thus one is not alone as bishop but essentially with

---

[128] This second aspect is of decisive importance for Ratzinger's different opinions on the theological status of episcopal conferences. On this subject, see pt. 2, sec. 2, chap. 3, § 4.2, of this dissertation, "Concrete Forms of Episcopal Collegiality, as Variously Interpreted".
[129] "Demokratisierung 1", 43.
[130] *Volk Gottes*, 43–70, citation at 57.

others. That is true also of the priest. One is not alone as a priest; to become a priest means to enter into the priestly community that is united to the bishop. Ultimately, a basic principle of Christianity itself is evident here: it is only in the community of all the brothers and sisters of Jesus Christ that one is a Christian, not otherwise.[131]

The real reason for this "we" character of the Church and of Christianity in general, Ratzinger says, is the triune God himself, who in the Church's profession of faith is understood, not as "an absolute and indivisible ego shut in on itself", but as "unity in the trinitarian relationship of I-you-we".[132] For this reason "being we as the fundamental form of God precedes all earthly forms of this relationship and being made in the image of God is from the start referred to this kind of being we."[133] Because the law of mutual relationship rules, no officeholder in the Church is an autocrat. Ratzinger supports his view with Cyprian's remark "nihil sine episcopo", which prompts Cyprian to act as a bishop toward his presbyterium according to the axiom "nihil sine consilio vestro" or, with regard to the congregation, "nihil sine consensu plebis".[134]

This principle of ecclesial *communio*, which Ratzinger takes up here, corresponds to the central statement in *Lumen gentium* 4, which likewise professes with Cyprian: "Thus, the Church has been seen as 'a people made one with the unity of the Father, the Son and the Holy

---

[131] *Principles*, 367–77, citation at 375.

[132] *Church*, 29–45, citation at 31.

[133] Ibid. In this context, Ratzinger refers to Henri de Lubac, *Catholicism: Christ and the Common Destiny of Man*, trans. Lancelot C. Sheppard and Sister Elizabeth Englund, O.C.D. (San Francisco: Ignatius Press, 1988); H. Mühlen, *Una mystica persona: Die Kirche als Mysterium der Identität des Heiligen Geistes in Christus und der Kirche; Eine Person in vielen Personen* (Paderborn: Schöningh, 1964; 3rd ed., 1968); see also *Introduction*, 162–90.

[134] Cyprian, *Ep.* 14, 4, in CSEL 3, 2, 512; CCL 3, B 83: "Ad id vero quod scripserunt mihi conpresbyteri nostri Donatus et Fortunatus et Novatus et Gordius, solus rescribere nihil potui, quando a primordio episcopatus mei statuerim nihil sine consilio vestro et sine consensu plebis mea privatim sententia gerere." (But I could not reply alone to what our fellow priests Donatus, Fortunatus, Novatus, and Gordius wrote to me, since from the beginning of my episcopate I resolved to do nothing according to my own private opinion without your advice and without the consent of the people.) Cf. Cyprian, *Ep.* 66, 8 in CSEL 3, 2, 733; CCL 3, C 443: "Unde scire debes episcopum in ecclesia esse et ecclesiam in episcopo et si qui(s) cum episcopo non sit in ecclesia non esse." (Hence you should know that the bishop is in the Church and the Church in the bishop, and that if anyone is not with the bishop then he is not in the Church.) ("Demokratisierung 1", 44.)

Spirit'."[135] In keeping with patristic theology, Ratzinger in 1965 used the concept of perichoresis to express the "we" of ecclesial *communio*, "whereby this unity represents a perpetual, dynamic overflowing into one another, the mutual penetration from mind to mind, from love to love".[136] Consequently, episcopal collegiality fulfills its purpose only when the *communio* is put into living practice by the individual bishop, and thus "a bit of the ecclesial fullness is truly contributed by him to ecclesial unity as a whole."[137] In this way, the bishop becomes a witness to unity and "fraternal solidarity"[138] in the Church.

b. The witness structure of ministry

Out of the "we" structure of the faith grows, in Ratzinger's view, the need "to link the theology of community which has developed out of the idea of collegiality more clearly once again with a theology of personality",[139] which already has its foundations in the Old Testament and in the New Testament is related in a new way to the individual person, since the People of God now no longer functions as a "kind of large-scale individual" but rather is "marked by a new structure of personal responsibility which is seen in the personalization of worship".[140]

> From now on everyone is called by his ... name in the sacrament of penance, and on the basis of the personal baptism which he ... received as being a particular person is called to personal repentance by name, and for this the general statement "We have sinned" can no longer suffice. Also corresponding to this structure, for example, is the fact that the liturgy does not just talk of the Church in general but presents it by name in the eucharistic prayer, with the names of the saints and of those who bear the responsibility of unity.[141]

---

[135] *LG* 4 cites Cyprian, *De Orat. Dom.* 23 in CSEL 3, 1, 285; CCL 3, A, 105; PL 4, 553. See also Augustine, *Serm.* 71, 20, 33 in PL 38, 463f.; John Damascene, *Adv. Iconocl.* 12, in PG 96, 1358 D.

[136] *Volk Gottes*, 43–70, citation at 58. If, on the other hand, one reads the opinion on this subject that Ratzinger formulated thirty-five years later ("Absurd", 51), one is struck by the fact that he distances himself from direct application of trinitarian formulas to the Church.

[137] *Volk Gottes*, 59.

[138] Ibid.

[139] *Church*, 29–45, citation at 32.

[140] Ibid., 33.

[141] Ibid.

This line of argument is supported also by the fact that, already at the beginning of the second century, lists of bishops were compiled, so as to prove to the judgment of history "the personal responsibility of the witnesses of Jesus Christ".[142] In this, Ratzinger recognizes a characteristic feature of the Christian faith.

> Corresponding to *the* witness Jesus Christ are *the* witnesses who, because they are witnesses, vouch for him by name. Martyrdom as response to the cross of Christ is nothing other than the final confirmation of this principle of named personal responsibility that cannot be transferred. Being a witness implies this personal particularity, but as response to the cross and resurrection being a witness is anyway the original basic form of Christian discipleship. With this, however, this principle is now anchored fast in the trinitarian belief in God itself, since the trinity becomes meaningful and in fact recognizable for us through the fact that in his Son as man God himself has become witness to himself.[143]

In this context, Ratzinger refers to the theology of Peter in the New Testament.[144] Peter is considered to be the first witness, who "in his own name and as a person" made his profession of faith in Christ, the Son of the living God (Mt 16:16).[145] He declares this profession "in the name of the Twelve"[146] and afterward is charged with the special task of serving as the Rock. Thus, according to Ratzinger, to the ministry of the Twelve, which is considered to be an eschatological sign, is added a second sign, namely, that of the Rock, which was likewise recognizable as an eschatological symbol of Israel.[147] For in the rabbinical writings, the image of the rock, as a symbol of the end times, was applied to Abraham,[148] the father of

---

[142] Ibid., 34.

[143] Ibid. Ratzinger cites Philippians 2:7 as a typical New Testament declaration of this.

[144] On this subject, see also the chapter "The Primacy of Peter and the Unity of the Church", in *Called to Communion*, 47–74, esp. 48–65.

[145] See *Church*, 35.

[146] *Called to Communion*, 61. Cf. *Church*, 35.

[147] See *Church*, 3–20, ref. at 13.

[148] Cf. Is 51:1–2: "Listen to me, you who pursue deliverance, you who seek the LORD; look to the rock from which you were hewn, and to the quarry from which you were dug. Look to Abraham your father and to Sarah who bore you; for when he was but one I called him, and I blessed him and made him many." Ratzinger cites J. Jeremias, *Golgotha und der heilige Fels* (Leipzig: Pfeiffer, 1926), 74.

faith, who "holds back chaos, the onrushing primordial flood of destruction, and thus sustains creation".[149] For this reason, the conferral of the title "Cephas" upon Simon should be understood, not pedagogically or psychologically, but rather "in terms of mystery, that is to say, christologically and ecclesiologically".[150]

To summarize what has been said thus far: Simon, as the first witness, personally professes his faith in Christ and receives from Jesus the title "Cephas", Rock. Based on the parallel to Isaiah 51:1, where Abraham is described as "Rock", Ratzinger concludes from the New Testament application of the same image in Matthew 16:18 that Peter has an "Abrahamic faith, which is renewed in Christ".[151] The two forms of witness, the Petrine ministry and the ministry of the Twelve, together guarantee the credibility of the Church's Creed. This duality of the ministry of the first witness and the collegial ministry of witness, which through the writings of Irenaeus[152] became part of the early Church's self-understanding, resulted logically, according to Ratzinger, in the fact "that the primacy of the Bishop of Rome, according to its original meaning, is not opposed to the collegial constitution of the Church but rather is a *communio* primacy".[153] Moreover, collegiality and primacy

---

[149] *Called to Communion*, 56.

[150] Ibid., 55.

[151] Ibid., 56. This means, according to Ratzinger, that both Simon and Abraham are called to stand as a rock of faith "against the impure tide of unbelief and its destruction of man" (ibid.). See also ibid., 60, where Ratzinger proceeds on the assumption that linguistically Matthew 16:16–18 contains a play on the word *kepha* in the original Aramaic, which is not completely successful in the Greek translation because of the change in gender between *Petros* and *petra*. According to Ratzinger, this detail allows us to conclude that in this passage we can "perceive the voice of Jesus himself" (ibid.).

[152] Ratzinger, "Primacy, Episcopate, and Apostolic Succession", 37–63, esp. 55f. Ratzinger refers to Irenaeus, *Adversus haereses*, 3, 3, 1f., in PG 7, 844ff., esp. 848.

[153] *Volk Gottes*, 43–70, citation at 55. See also Ratzinger, "Das geistliche Amt und die Einheit der Kirche", in *Die Autorität der Freiheit: Gegenwart des Konzils und Zukunft der Kirche im ökumenischen Disput*, ed. J. C. Hampe, 2:417–33, esp. 430 (Munich: Kösel-Verlag, 1967). As Ratzinger explained in 1967, the primacy of the pope means, "as the case may be, the ability and the right to decide in a binding way within the 'communio network' where witness is being borne correctly to the Word of the Lord and consequently where there is true *communio*. According to the Catholic understanding of the Church, such a ministry not only is rendered legitimate but is demanded by the fact that the Lord himself, by means of the twofold structure of Peter's apostolic commission and special commission, instituted the twofold office of witness and first witness, which continues in the twofold structure of episcopate and primacy."

are always connected with persons, or, as Ratzinger puts it, they are constituted martyrologically.[154]

This is clearly brought into focus by the commemoration of the diocesan bishop and of the pope by name in the Eucharistic Prayers of the Church, a practice that is far more than a "mere ornament"; it is, rather, "the intrinsically necessary expression of the κοινωνια of what takes place in the Eucharist".[155] As a result of this eucharistic ecclesiology, the collegial form is not only decisive for the hierarchical structure of the Church, but it even becomes, so to speak, the essential feature of ecclesial unity and multiplicity in the Church in general.

c. Unity in multiplicity as a structural question for the Church

The theme "unity in multiplicity" has already been discussed several times in this study.[156] In the following paragraphs, this criterion, which according to Ratzinger represents a structural element of the Church, will be highlighted as an aspect of collegiality, since this is of decisive importance especially with regard to ecumenism. In 1965, Ratzinger still formulated pointedly the idea that "the Church of unity" must not impede the unity of the Church.

> This is a statement that has a very broad scope that extends from the constitution of the universal Church down to the daily life of the individual parishes. With respect to the constitution of the universal Church, it becomes evident here that it is not a matter of deducing it from some political model or other and that the all-too-popular attempts to justify the primacy by means of a political philosophy based on Aristotle and Plato (according to which the monarchy is the best form of rule) are just as mistaken as the attempt to describe the Church in terms of the category of monarchy, which is inappropriate to her. The relations between sacrament and order, Petrine ministry and episcopal ministry, episcopal collegiality and Christian fraternity, the multiplicity of Churches and the unity of

---

[154] For this reason, Ratzinger says that the personal responsibility in [these ecclesial features] must not be masked by anonymous bureaucratic structures. On this subject, see *Church*, 29–45, ref. at 37–40.

[155] *Volk Gottes*, 64.

[156] See pt. 2, sec. 2, chap. 1, § 2, of this dissertation, " 'Body of Christ' as the Key to the Ecclesiology of *Lumen gentium*" and § 4, "The Church as a *Communio* Unity".

the Church ... transcend too much all the categories of political philosophy.[157]

For this reason, Ratzinger demanded then an "ordered multiplicity"[158] in unity. He said that episcopal collegiality had the task of making visible the reciprocal ordering, that is, the *communio* unity of all the particular Churches in the one Church. From this notion, it becomes clear that Ratzinger had in mind a harking back to the *communio* structure of the early Church in her sacramental constitution. How is this *communio* structure to be realized within the Catholic Church herself? When the collegial element in the Church is realized concretely, what form should it assume? There are various answers to these questions in Ratzinger's writings, depending on differences in time, place, degree of ecclesial responsibility, and theological development. In the next subsection, therefore, we will examine several of Ratzinger's opinions, taking care to distinguish clearly the statements of the young theologian at the Council from those made by the "later" Ratzinger,[159] since there is tension between the former and the latter.

§ 4. Aspects during the Council in Tension with the Later Perspective

1. The "shadow" of the "Preliminary Note of Explanation"

As in liturgical questions[160] or ecumenical issues,[161] so too in ecclesiology we can discern a clear progression in Ratzinger's thought from

---

[157] Cf. *Volk Gottes*, 43–70, ref. at 65f.

[158] Ibid., 67.

[159] Here the focus is not on statements that Ratzinger published as prefect of the Congregation for the Doctrine of the Faith, but rather on his own theological publications.

[160] On this subject, see Ratzinger's critical remarks concerning the inaugural liturgy of the Second Vatican Council. "The observer could not help thinking that a barometer of the success of the Council would be the extent to which the concluding liturgy differs from the one on the day when the Council opened." See Ratzinger, *Gegenwärtige Stand*, 5–8; cf. *Highlights*, 6f. For a contrasting view, see *Feast of Faith*, 79–95, esp. 87f., on the concept of *participatio actuosa*. Cf. *Song*, 111–27, esp. 115: "The belief that the spirit of the Council points in this direction has been able to gain acceptance in many a liturgical office and its agencies, although it is indisputable that these ideas cannot be supported by the text of the Second Vatican Council. In the sense just described, the opinion is all too widely

462 II/2. Recurring Themes in Ratzinger's Ecclesiology

the reform-happy conciliar theologian to the shepherd responsible for preserving the faith. This is particularly evident in his judgment on the relation between primatial and collegial structures in the Church.[162] In the judgment of Hermann J. Pottmeyer, Ratzinger is one of the conciliar theologians who during and immediately after the Council "represented most effectively a *communio* ecclesiology and the idea of episcopal collegiality".[163] At that time, Ratzinger considered it the Council's most important task "to bring clearly to light again the *communio* structure of the Church and, with it, the collegial structure of the episcopal ministry",[164] the primacy of the pope being assumed. Therefore he was all the more miffed at the "Preliminary Note of Explanation" to *Lumen gentium* that the General Secretary, Archbishop Pericles Felici, communicated to the General Assembly on November 16, 1964, and which represents the core of the Council's proclamations on this subject. Ratzinger's critique was aimed, on the one hand, at the manner of proceeding and, on the other hand, with the contents of the announcement, which principally regulated the relation between primacy and episcopal collegiality. The following quotation illustrates his stress and disappointment at that time.

But didn't the Council lose face with the pope's interventions during the final weeks of the session? Didn't even the best texts have a bitter aftertaste due to the impression that in the final analysis the

held today that so-called creativity, the active participation of all present, and the relationship to a group in which everyone is acquainted with and speaks to everyone else are the real categories of the conciliar understanding of the liturgy. Not only assistant pastors but even some bishops think they are not being faithful to the Council if they pray everything just the way it is found in the Roman Missal; at least *one* 'creative' formulation must be inserted, regardless of how trite it may be." See also *Spirit of the Liturgy*, 74–84, 166–70.

[161] On this subject, see *Highlights*, 61–76, esp. 73: "A basic unity—of Churches that remain Churches, yet become *one* Church—must replace the idea of conversion, even though conversion retains its meaningfulness for those in conscience motivated to seek it."

[162] See the dissertation by K.-J. E. Jeon, *Die Kirche bei Joseph Ratzinger: Untersuchungen zum strukturierten Volk Gottes nach der Kirchenlehre Joseph Ratzingers* (unpublished dissertation, Innsbruck, 1995), 195f. In this study, there is no reference to an actual change in Ratzinger's perspective. O. H. Pesch, in contrast, points out course corrections made by Ratzinger (Pesch, 262).

[163] H. J. Pottmeyer, "Der theologische Status der Bischofskonferenz—Positionen, Klärungen und Prinzipien", in Müller/Pottmeyer, 44–87, citation at 54.

[164] J. Ratzinger, "Zurück zur Ordnung der Alten Kirche", in Hampe, *Konzil*, 183f., citation at 184.

pope could and would do whatever suited him? These were the half-gloating, half-anxious questions heard again and again. To answer them in a way neither cheaply edifying nor grossly oversimplified was certainly no easy thing.[165]

With regard to the manner of proceeding, Ratzinger noted back then with astonishment that in the *regolamento*, that is, in the conciliar rules of procedure, one could find "no legal guidelines for ways the pope might bring his opinion into play", and he saw therein a "statutory omission" that manifested its "dangerous disadvantages".[166] Even though the Preliminary Note of Explanation did not fundamentally change the text of the Constitution on the Church[167] but rather served to achieve the largest possible consensus among the Council Fathers,[168] whereby the concerns of the minority in particular were brought to bear in the preliminary remarks, Ratzinger was skeptical about such an undertaking, last but not least for ecumenical reasons.

It is certain, however, that no one would want what happened during that week in November, 1964, to ever happen again. For those interventions showed without doubt that [the Church had not yet found a way of putting the primacy into action (and of formulating the doctrine of primacy) that would be] capable, for example, of

---

[165] *Highlights*, 106. The first sentence of paragraph 4 of the Preliminary Note of Explanation reads: "As Supreme Pastor of the Church, the Supreme Pontiff can always exercise his power at will [*ad placidum*], as his very office demands." Ratzinger criticizes this expression, *ad placidum*, as "an unfortunate formulation; it will surely be regretted that the Theological Commission did not stand by the position that it formulated during the summer" ("Kommentar", 357).

[166] *Highlights*, 106.

[167] On this subject, see "Kollegialität", 62. Ratzinger suggests that the Note is "a document of the Commission, not a document of the Council". "The [Preliminary] Note [of Explanation] does not speak a conciliar language, but rather the language of textbooks, of scientific distinction and clarification, not of the authoritative development of a teaching" (ibid.).

[168] On this subject, see "Kommentar", 349: "In retrospect it will be evident that this was not only supposed to curb the more far-flung interpretations of the idea of collegiality but that the gesture was likewise addressed to the minority that was opposed to collegiality and that in light of the Note was supposed to recognize that their opposition was groundless and to be encouraged to agree to the document, which in fact happened.... Only the future elaboration and development of what is set forth in the Constitution will be able to show whether this success was purchased at too high a price through an excessive weakening of the doctrine."

convincing the Eastern Churches that a union with Rome would not mean subjection to a papal monarchy but rather the restoration of mutual communion with the See of Peter as a See presiding in brotherhood over the many-faceted unity of the Churches of God, knowing no worldly kind of dominion but rather—to use the words of the *Constitution on the Church*—acting as a community in the bond of unity, love and peace.[169]

At the end of the Council, Ratzinger speaks of a dialectic in *Lumen gentium*, which has bearing particularly in the Preliminary Note of Explanation, resulting in a dual aspect of episcopal collegiality. This ambivalence reflects the unsuccessful attempt "to reconcile the conflicting tendencies",[170] namely, on the one hand, a way of thinking "that looks at the whole spectrum of Christian tradition", and, on the other hand, a purely systematic, legal way of thinking that "takes the current legal status of the Church as the only standard for its considerations . . . [and] regards any change beyond these limits as an extremely dangerous step".[171]

It is striking that Ratzinger as an archbishop and cardinal no longer articulates these obvious ambiguities in the conciliar documents but, rather, calls for a "return to the authentic texts of the original Vatican II".[172] Ten years later, after "the cultural revolutions and the social convulsions that the Fathers in no way could have foreseen",[173] there is no more mention in his writings of the opposition between the traditional outlook and the systematic-juridical view dating back to the end of the Council. In 1975, another antithesis affected the postconciliar situation: As opposed to an "anti-historical, utopian interpretation of the Council", Ratzinger called for "a creative, spiritual understanding" of the conciliar documents "in living unity with authentic tradition".[174]

If we compare Ratzinger's challenge here with his efforts during the Council to give voice to the entire tradition of the Church, we

---

[169] *Highlights*, 107. [The words in brackets spell out a distinction missing from the summary English translation.—TRANS.]

[170] Ibid., 115.

[171] Ibid.

[172] *Report*, 31.

[173] Ibid., 34.

[174] *Dogma*, 439–47, citation at 443.

can observe at this point in his thinking a continuity in the essentials. As opposed to the postconciliar forms of progressivism and traditionalism, the forces that made the Council possible, in his view, were the ones whose theology and piety "were based essentially on Sacred Scripture, on the Church Fathers, and on the great liturgical heritage of the universal Church".[175] Enlivening this "great stream of tradition in its totality"[176] was his endeavor, which he formulated in 1972, ten years after the beginning of the Council, and to which he devoted all of his theological efforts. Nevertheless, there are also important particular questions in ecclesiology on which Ratzinger has taken varying positions. They do not ultimately depend on the different possibilities for interpretation inherent in the documents of Vatican II. One example of this sort of question is the issue of determining episcopal authority. In the text of the Preliminary Note of Explanation, it says in paragraph 2 (emphasis added):

> In his *consecration* a person is given an ontological participation in the *sacred functions* [*munera*]. . . . The word "functions [*munera*]" is used deliberately instead of the word "powers [*potestates*]," because the latter word could be understood as a *power fully ready to act*. But for this power to be fully ready to act, there must be a further *canonical* or *juridicial determination* through the hierarchical authority. This determination of power can consist in the granting of a particular office or in the allotment of subjects, and it is done according to the *norms* approved by the supreme authority.

In 1965, Ratzinger interpreted this wording of the Note so as to leave room "for the various ways in which the ordering of the individual bishop to the entirety of the episcopal ministry was secured in practice in Church history".[177] Therefore, he comes to the conclusion "that the form that has been customary in the Latin Church for a long time, that is, appointment exclusively by the pope, is not the sole possible method of juridically determining the competency of a bishop".[178] Since the appointment of bishops is a fundamental task of the ecclesial *communio*—so goes the interpretation of Medard Kehl—the

---

[175] Ibid., 445.
[176] Ibid.
[177] "Kollegialität", 64.
[178] Ibid.

young conciliar theologian Ratzinger thought that all who held responsibility for the *communio* had to be involved in this process, according to the model of the election of bishops in the early Church.[179] Thirty years after the Council, however, in his response to the so-called Petition of the People of the Church, Ratzinger conspicuously avoids addressing the focal point of the campaign, namely, "the appointment of bishops".[180] In an earlier discussion with Cardinal König, which Hans-Jakob Stehle moderated in 1991, he nevertheless admitted:

> While it is true that a bishop, who indeed has to represent the Church and the faith of all ages, is not elected democratically, still his appointment should grow out of the knowledge and hearing of the people— that is the meaning of the consultation process. Yet every system does have its weaknesses.[181]

A second example involves the concrete form of the *communio hierarchica*. Although in the following pages we will discuss chronologically and theologically disparate commentaries by Ratzinger on questions concerning the *realization* of the *communio hierarchica*,[182] we of course should not overlook the constant basic line of argument, which regards the *mysterium* of *communio* as the sacramentally based juridical and ontological form of the Church, as Ratzinger has always maintained, in agreement with *Lumen gentium*.[183] In his commentary on number 2 of the Preliminary Note of Explanation of the Constitution on the Church, he characterizes the sacramental foundation of episcopal collegiality as one of the "most difficult problems in the canonical and constitutional history of the Church, which is at the same time of crucial

---

[179] M. Kehl formulates Ratzinger's concerns along these lines in Kehl, *Wohin geht die Kirche? Eine Zeitdiagnose* (Freiburg im Breisgau: Herder, 1996), 88. On the question of appointing bishops, see also Quinn, *Reform*, 117–39.

[180] Cf. *Salt of the Earth*, 181–213.

[181] H. Stehle, F. König, and J. Ratzinger, "Die Botschaft Jesu für alle Zeiten", in *Zivilcourage in der Kirche*, by W. Bühlmann, 166–72, citation at 171 (document no. 10) (Graz: Styria, 1992). The original essay appeared in the German weekly newspaper *Die Zeit*, no. 49 (November 29, 1991).

[182] "Kommentar", 353. The addition of the adjective *hierarchica* to *communio*, although unknown in "the linguistic usage of tradition" (ibid.), does serve the purpose, according to Ratzinger, of clarifying the argument along traditional lines. See Pottmeyer, *Rolle*, 98.

[183] See *LG* 22: "One is constituted a member of the episcopal body in virtue of sacramental consecration and hierarchical communion with the head and members of the body." Cf. also the Preliminary Note of Explanation, par. 2.

theological importance".[184] For Ratzinger, the formula of the *communio hierarchica* that was discovered by *Lumen gentium* is constitutive for episcopal collegiality:

> Thereby collegiality is anchored in the sacramental principle *also*, the idea of *iurisdictio* is connected with that of *communio*, and inasmuch as the law enters again into a direct relation with the sacramental principle, it also ceases, for its part, to appear as an entity subject to manipulation by centralizing tendencies, in that it shares in the necessary plurality of the sacramental sphere and thus bears within itself the "collegial" aspect from the very beginning. The measure in which the legal idea is bound or loosed vis-à-vis the sacramental idea determines at the same time whether there is an exclusively centralistic or an intrinsically collegial structure of law in the Church.[185]

In this way, Ratzinger says in this commentary on the Note, people's consciousness will be raised concerning "the importance of what takes place in the particular Church".[186]

Whereas during the time of the Council Ratzinger emphasized, for the sake of the Church's sacramental structure, the plural of the local Churches in which the Church is realized on any given occasion, nowadays he calls attention to the *communio* unity of the universal Church, likewise based on his sacramental understanding. In the following subsection, therefore, we will articulate his different hermeneutic approaches with regard to the concrete forms of the Church's episcopal-collegial *communio* structure.

2. *Concrete forms of episcopal collegiality, as variously interpreted*

a. Unbraiding the three papal offices—The totality of the Church in her universal dimension

Of the positions taken by Ratzinger during the Council, one is struck especially by his endeavor to propose the standard of the early Church as a means of identifying ways to reform the relation between the pope and the college of bishops. One approach along these lines that

---

[184] "Kommentar", 352.
[185] Ibid.
[186] Ibid., 357.

was important to him in November 1963 was the plan to "unbraid" the interwoven strands of the originally threefold fundamental form of the papal ministry. According to this concept, the pope is:

1. Bishop of Rome, the bishop of a local Church "that is in communion with the various other local Churches and together with them builds up the one Church of God".[187]

2. His second office is that of patriarch of the West, that is, of the Latin Church, whereby it was thought, according to Ratzinger, that "at this level ... Rome had in principle the same rank as the other ancient patriarchs." It is especially important to keep in mind "that a series of functions we usually view today as emanations of the primacy were originally understood as the consequence of the patriarchal dignity". Among these Ratzinger lists "the right of liturgical legislation, participation in the appointment and deposal of bishops, and similar powers at the level of discipline".

3. The third office of the pope is to be "the successor of Peter" and along with this to exercise "a primatial ministry, instituted by the Lord himself, over the entire Church ... , the concrete duties of which, admittedly, occupy per se a much smaller compass than they do in practice today as a result of a complicated historical development".[188]

At the time of the Council, Ratzinger considered it an important goal to differentiate again among these three spheres in a way that viewed the local Church and the patriarchate in a subsidiary relationship to the primacy, without detriment to the Petrine ministry established by Christ. That is why he made at that time a suggestion that, in light of his stance today, strikes us as revolutionary: "to abolish the Latin patriarchate in its present scope and to replace it with several patriarchal districts".[189] This idea of Ratzinger's was even echoed[190]

---

[187] This and the following quotations are found in "Formen", 156.

[188] Ibid., 158. For the historical development, see ibid., 157.

[189] Ibid., 158f.

[190] During the second session of the Council, Ratzinger suggested the formation of regions ("patriarchal districts") "whose autonomy would correspond approximately to that of the earlier patriarchates, the governance of which, however, could lie with the appropriate conference of bishops, which in turn would naturally have to answer to the universal college of bishops and the pope" (ibid., 159). Only in the final version of the Constitution on the Church is this idea taken up. On this subject, see Alberigo/ Magistretti, 116. See also Weiler, 238–42.

in the Constitution on the Church *Lumen gentium*, which reads at the end of article 23:

By divine Providence it has come about that various churches, established in various places by the apostles and their successors, have in the course of time coalesced into several groups, organically united, which, preserving the unity of faith and the unique divine constitution of the universal Church, enjoy their own discipline, their own liturgical usage, and their own theological and spiritual heritage. Some of these churches, notably the ancient patriarchal churches, as parent-stocks of the Faith, so to speak, have begotten others as daughter churches, with which they are connected down to our own time by a close bond of charity in their sacramental life and in their mutual respect for their rights and duties. This variety of local churches with one common aspiration is splendid evidence of the catholicity of the undivided Church. In like manner the episcopal bodies of today are in a position to render a manifold and fruitful assistance, so that this collegiate feeling may be put into practical application.[191]

Even though in this passage the Council addresses the patriarchates in the Eastern Churches first, one should not overlook the fact that this teaching was referred analogously by Ratzinger to the episcopal conferences of the Latin Church as well. Gisbert Greshake, along with Klaus Mörsdorf, even portrays the conciliar teaching about the patriarchal Churches as a "norm on the order of constitutional law for the Church in every age".[192] To what extent did Ratzinger later, as prefect of the Congregation for the Doctrine of the Faith, distance himself not only from his own point of view but also from the intended meaning of the Constitution on the Church? That will be the topic of discussion in the next subsection about the so-called patriarchal districts and the theological status of the episcopal conferences.

[191] *LG* 23.
[192] G. Greshake, "Weltkirche und Ortskirche: Bemerkungen zu einem problematischen Verhältnis", *ThGl* 91 (2001): 528–42, citation at 542. See also K. Mörsdorf, "Die Autonomie der Ortskirche", *AKathKR* 138 (1969): 388–405, esp. 393. On this question, see also F. R. Gahbauer, "Die Patriarchalstruktur auf dem Zweiten Vatikanischen Konzil", in *Das Dienstamt der Einheit in der Kirche*, ed. A. Rauch and P. Imhof, 377–415 (St. Ottilien: EOS-Verlag, 1991).

First, though, I would like to refer to the lecture that he gave in Graz, Austria, in 1976, "Prognoses for the Future of Ecumenism".[193] At that time, Ratzinger was making similar proposals about rethinking the relationship between primacy and collegiality as these were understood during the first Christian millennium. As Stephan Otto Horn explains, his approach was based on the conviction "that already in the first millennium in the West and in the East, indeed, very early on, a common ground for Church unity and also for the acknowledgment of the Petrine status of the Church of Rome"[194] had been manifest. Against the background of this ecumenical paradigm, which has even been described as the "Ratzinger formula",[195] Ratzinger's present demand for a preeminence of the universal Church over the local Churches stands out conspicuously.[196]

Along with this concern and the resulting emphasis on the papal primacy, the problem of "Roman centralism" is simultaneously at the center of the current debate. Ratzinger does not deny that this danger exists, but he clarifies the reason for posing the question at present as follows: Today the relation between the universal Church and the local Churches is not infrequently reduced in a purely sociological way to the question of assigning competencies. Through a superficial perspective of this sort, one loses sight of *"the whole in its depth dimension"*.[197] Based on this experience, Ratzinger argues theologically. Starting with the Last Supper of Jesus, in which the eucharistic structure of the *whole* Church was founded, he emphasizes the

---

[193] J. Ratzinger, "Prognosen für die Zukunft des Ökumenismus", in *Mitte*, 181–94, ref. at 188. First published in *Ökumenisches Forum: Grazer Hefte für konkrete Ökumene* 1 (1977): 31–41.

[194] Stephan O. Horn, "II. Ökumenische Dimensionen—Einführung", in *Mitte*, 175–80, citation at 175. Horn goes on to say that Ratzinger is later obliged "to oppose an interpretation of his thesis that makes out of it something that is essentially different from what he intended: a perspective in which the First Vatican Council appears to be the result of a particular development of the Latin Church and no longer the expression of the faith of the universal Church. Such a perspective would necessarily mean, however, that the Church of the second millennium had lost the ability to articulate the faith in a new way in the face of new challenges."

[195] See Kasper, "Auseinandersetzung", 798.

[196] See pt. 2, sec. 2, chap. 3, § 4.2, in this book, "Concrete Forms of Episcopal Collegiality, as Variously Interpreted".

[197] Stephan O. Horn and V. Pfnür, "Introduction", in *Pilgrim Fellowship*, 9–16, citation at 12.

ontological priority of the universal Church over the local Churches.[198] This, however, is "not a declaration in favor of any particular form of distribution of responsibility within the Church, not a declaration that the local Church of Rome should seek to acquire as many privileges as possible".[199] After all, the local Church of Rome "is not herself the universal Church" but only has been entrusted with "a special responsibility for the whole Church".[200] In contrast, someone who makes only a sociological inquiry into the allocation of competencies overlooks the real question about God and ends up discussing "our favorite topic", namely, "the question of our privileges".[201] With regard to the Church, this means:

> Anyone who always just turns straight to the question of the distribution of power has utterly missed the mystery of the Church. No, this is strictly a matter of theology, not of juridical questions or of Church politics: the fact that God's idea of the Son's one bride, eschatologically oriented toward the eternal wedding feast, is the first and the one essential idea of God that is at stake in matters to do with the Church, while the concrete realization of the Church in local Churches constitutes a second plane that is subsequent to the first and always remains subordinated to it.[202]

The sacramental structure means that "the Church ... lives as 'a vessel of the Holy Spirit', founded on the Lord, and is constantly being re-created."[203] The bishop is the witness to this *extra nos* character of the sacrament,[204] since his own ministry, as a result of his sacramental association with the Lord, not only is related to the local Church but represents, precisely in its *universal communio*, the connection to the universal Church.

---

[198] This eucharistic approach served Ratzinger during the Council as an argument in favor of emphasizing the autonomy of the local Churches. See pt. 2, sec. 2, chap. 1, § 3.2, below, "Eucharistic Communities as the Realization of the Church".

[199] Damaskinos and Ratzinger, "Exchange of Letters", 239.

[200] Ibid.

[201] "Ecclesiology", 133.

[202] Damaskinos and Ratzinger, "Exchange of Letters", 239.

[203] J. Ratzinger, "Church Movements and Their Place in Theology", reprinted in *Pilgrim Fellowship*, 176–208, citation at 201.

[204] See pt. 2, sec. 2, chap. 1, § 3.2, of this work, "Eucharistic Communities as the Realization of the Church".

Does this ecclesiological approach taken by Ratzinger in the year 2000 contradict his remarks at the time of the Council? A pointed answer would be: The eucharistic approach is the same, then as now. Granted, his understanding of the concrete form of collegiality during the Council was influenced by the ideal of *communio* in the early Church, whereas Ratzinger today is primarily concerned that the Church could lose her distinctive feature, namely, her sacramental *extra nos*, and at the same time exchange her universal dimension for one that is too particularistic,[205] which is also why Ratzinger's understanding with regard to the function of the episcopal conferences is different today from the one that he had advocated while still a theologian at the Council.

b. "Patriarchal districts"—On the theological status of the episcopal conferences

In his slim retrospective volume from the year 1965, Ratzinger considered that one of the principal goals of Vatican II was to make the structure of the Church in the patristic era productive again for the present day. From the two ecclesiological criteria mentioned above, namely, the principle of the local Church and the principle of the mutual association of the bishops, he derived the following conclusion during the time of the Council:

> The collegiality of the bishops, as a medium for achieving unity and plurality and as an expression for the upbuilding of the one Church of God from the many local Churches, supplies the normal pattern of orderly life in the Church. This collegiality can take many forms. The early Church established the various synods and instituted the patriarchate; today the same reality takes a new form in bishops' conferences.[206]

Ratzinger admitted in 1964, however, that the bishops themselves "in many instances have resisted the establishment of an effective episcopal conference"[207] because they feared the restriction of their own rights. At that time he himself did not yet share this misgiving but, rather, viewed the episcopal conference, inasmuch as it "harks back to

---

[205] On this subject, see Horn and Pfnür, "Introduction", 12.
[206] *Highlights*, 129–30.
[207] "Formen", 161.

the model of the synodal structure in the early Church ..., as the expression of the collegial structural element"[208] for our time. The same outlook was still on display in 1965, one year later, when he asked: "Why should it not be possible for bishops' conferences to have something to say to each other as well, by way of thanks, mutual encouragement, perhaps also in the form of correction, when the wrong paths are being followed?"[209]

At that time, Ratzinger optimistically described the episcopal conferences as the "optimal means"[210] of realizing multiplicity in unity concretely. At the same time, he rejected the opinion that the bishops' conferences have no theological foundation whatsoever and therefore cannot oblige the individual bishop, since the term "college" can be "applied only to the entire episcopate when it acts in unison".[211] Although Ratzinger himself adopted this argument in 1984,[212] he responded to it in 1965 as follows:

Of course the "suprema potestas in universam Ecclesiam" [supreme authority over the universal Church] that is attributed to the ecumenical council in canon 228 §1 of the [1917] Code of Canon Law can pertain only to the college of bishops as a whole together with its head, the bishop of Rome. But is it only a question of "suprema potestas" in the Church? That would be fatally reminiscent of the quarrel among the disciples about who was the first. We shall have to say, rather, that the concept of collegiality ... suggests a manifold and adaptable element that belongs as a matter of principle to the constitution of the Church.[213]

At that time, therefore, Ratzinger attributed to the bishops' conferences a theological significance also as partial realizations of collegiality, and he described this with the dogmatic term "perichoresis".[214]

---

[208] Ibid., 162.

[209] *Volk Gottes*, 43–70, citation at 66.

[210] Ibid., 67.

[211] Ibid.

[212] See *Report*, 59: "We must not forget that the episcopal conferences have no theological basis, they do not belong to the structure of the Church, as willed by Christ, that cannot be eliminated; they have only a practical, concrete function."

[213] *Volk Gottes*, 67.

[214] Gisbert Greshake takes a similar approach in "Weltkirche und Ortskirche: Bemerkungen zu einem problematischen Verhältnis", *ThGl* 91 (2001): 528–42, esp. 533. Hence Greshake

The bishops' conferences, he said, are supposed to exist, not side by side, but rather in perichoresis, that is, in a mutual exchange, which "becomes all the more important, the more the each ecclesial district develops its individual character".[215] Moreover, the primacy also acquires the new task of supporting or bringing about such an exchange.

Hermann J. Pottmeyer and Walter Kasper[216] are correct in assuming that Henri de Lubac, who like Ratzinger regarded the inter-ecclesial activity of the bishops as an important realization of the collegial element, influenced Ratzinger to revise his own view of collegiality.[217] The basis for this is the thesis proposed by de Lubac as early as 1971 that "in recent years the idea of episcopal collegiality has been too closely tied, if not altogether assimilated in public opinion, to that of episcopal conferences, just as to that of all supra-diocesan organizations",[218] since collegiality had been confused with collective forms of governance.

---

criticizes Ratzinger's explanation in "Absurd", 51, when the latter says, "Above all, though, I am decidedly against the increasingly fashionable trend of applying the trinitarian mystery directly to the Church. It does not work. We would end up believing in three Gods." Greshake objects to this view in *ThGl* 91 (2001): 533. "For fear that the universal Church could be understood as 'the result of the mutual recognition of the particular Churches', the 1992 *Letter to the Bishops of the Catholic Church on Some Aspects of the Church Understood as Communion* issued by the Congregation for the Doctrine of the Faith turns literally on their heads the crystal-clear conciliar statements [*LG* 23] about the Church as a perichoretic unity 'in these [particular Churches] and formed out of them', by maintaining that the universal Church is 'a reality preexisting every particular Church ontologically and chronologically'. Accordingly, Cardinal Ratzinger denies—decidedly, as he puts it—that the Church is structured perichoretically, in the image of the Trinity, at all. For even theologians who are critical of the Church, for example, Herbert Vorgrimler, vehemently reject this structural reflection of the Trinity. This is not surprising for critics of the Church, but it certainly is in Cardinal Ratzinger's case. For in spite of everything, he agreed to the dialogue statement, 'The Mystery of the Church and of the Eucharist in Light of the Mystery of the Trinity', issued jointly by the Roman Curia and the Orthodox Churches in 1982."

[215] *Volk Gottes*, 68.

[216] Cf. W. Kasper, "Nochmals: Der theologische Status der Bischofskonferenzen", *ThQ* 168 (1988): 237–40, ref. at 237.

[217] Cf. H. J. Pottmeyer, "Der theologische Status der Bischofskonferenzen—Positionen, Klärungen und Prinzipien", in Müller/Pottmeyer, 44–87, esp. 47–54.

[218] H. de Lubac, *The Motherhood of the Church, Followed by Particular Churches in the Universal Church and an Interview Conducted by Gwendoline Jarczyk*, trans. Sr. Sergia Englund, O.C.D. (San Francisco: Ignatius Press, 1982), 233–55, citation at 260. See also M. Figura, "Die Beziehung zwischen Universalkirche und Teilkirchen nach Henri de Lubac", *IKaZ* 30 (2001): 468–83, esp. 475.

Against the background of such an understanding, we can trace the reasons for Ratzinger's change of perspective twenty years after the opening of the Council. In his essay "Review of the Postconciliar Era—Failures, Tasks, Hopes", written in 1982, he paints a skeptical, negative picture with regard to the collegial structures that have developed since the Council and were suggested by the Council itself.

In place of the informal meetings of bishops that had taken place up to that time, for instance, a strictly juridical and carefully organized bureaucracy, the episcopal conference, was created. The synod of bishops, a kind of council with regular meetings, was created to express the solidarity of all episcopal conferences. The national synods met and declared their intention of developing into permanent organizations of the Church in their respective countries. Councils of priests and pastoral counselors were formed in the dioceses and community councils in the parishes. No one will deny that the basic concept was a good one and that community realization of the Church's mission is necessary.... But neither will anyone doubt that their uncoordinated multiplication led to an excess of duplication, to a senseless mountain of paper work and to much wasted time during which the best efforts were consumed in endless discussions.... The limitations of this paper-dominated Christianity and of the reform of the church by paper have meanwhile become clear.[219]

Ratzinger's main argument for his negative attitude toward bureaucratic arrangements is the restriction of the personal responsibility and the personal intuition[220] of the individual. Hans Urs von Balthasar, too, argues along very similar lines in 1986, acknowledging that "more than ever before" the freedom of the individual bishop "to make decisions has been curtailed from below as well as from above."[221] On the one hand, Balthasar laments the bureaucratization or "curialization" of the bishops' chanceries, whereby the diocesan bishop is "severely hampered", since he must "avail himself of expert advice from all the proper organizations" for every one of his movements and each of his

[219] *Principles*, 367–378, citation at 375.
[220] See ibid. Compare *Called to Communion*, 98.
[221] Hans Urs von Balthasar, *Test Everything: Hold Fast to What Is Good*, trans. Maria Shrady (San Francisco: Ignatius Press, 1989), 60.

decisions.[222] On the other hand, he views with skepticism the work of the permanent administrative offices of the bishops' conferences, "which are supposed to free the individual bishop of much work. Alas, it is work proper to the individual bishop, responsibilities which have been withdrawn from him, a regrettable fact as far as the good of the Church is concerned."[223] These arguments are identical with those of Ratzinger in the early 1980s. It is difficult to determine who influenced whom; the congruence of their opinions, nevertheless, is evident.

It would be shortsighted, though, to portray Ratzinger as an opponent of the collegial principle. In 1990, he emphasized that he was not criticizing collegiality per se, which is an essential part of the episcopal ministry on account of its catholic and apostolic roots,[224] but rather the manner in which collegiality is being realized at present.[225] As with the positions that he took during the Council, he supports his view again by harking back to the early Church. The emphases are different, however, from those in his earlier arguments: First, he now calls attention especially to the event-character of the assemblies of bishops in the early Church, and, second, he stresses Rome's primatial status.[226] With respect to these two "fundamental forms"[227] of implementing collegiality, he now writes:

---

[222] See ibid., 61.

[223] Ibid.

[224] Ratzinger speaks here about the "togetherness" of the bishops in the " 'we' formed by all the successors", whereby he clearly differentiates between the successors of Peter and the successors of the other apostles: "Only the bishop of Rome is the successor of a particular apostle—of Saint Peter—and is thus given responsibility for the whole Church. All the remaining bishops are successors of the *apostles* in general; they do not succeed a certain apostle but are members of the college that takes the place of the apostolic college, and this fact makes each single one of them a successor of the apostles" (*Called to Communion*, 97).

[225] Cf. ibid., 98.

[226] Cf. ibid., 98f. In his n. 21 (p. 98), Ratzinger notes, "The 'primacies' having a Petrine foundation spring from ancient theological tradition and include the special primacy of Rome. They are to be distinguished from the idea of the patriarchate developed in Byzantium; this notion was at first categorically refused by Rome and was adopted for that city only with hesitation". Ratzinger cites J. Richards, *Consul of God: The Life and Times of Gregory the Great* (London, Boston: Routledge and Kegan Paul, 1980), pp. 217–227, esp. 221. He refers also to A. Garuti, *Il Papa Patriarca d'occidente? Studio storico dottrinale* (Bologna, 1990).

[227] *Called to Communion*, 97.

First of all there is the special bond uniting the neighboring bishops of a region, who in a shared political and cultural context seek to plot a common course for their episcopal ministry. This was the origin of the synods (assemblies of bishops), which in the North Africa of Saint Augustine's time, for example, met together twice a year. In a certain sense, it is quite legitimate to compare them with today's bishops' conferences. There is, however, a hardly minor difference: these synods had no permanent institutional infrastructure. There were no bureaus or permanent administrative bodies, only the assembly taking place at the moment, in which the bishops alone ... attempted themselves to find answers to urgent questions....

The second figure in which the "we" of the bishops took form in the sphere of action consisted in their relationship to the "primacies", to the normative episcopal sees and their occupants. In particular, this relationship included measurement by the standard of Rome and harmony with the testimony of faith of the successor of Peter.[228]

Ratzinger presents an idealized picture of the relation between Rome and the other ecclesial provinces headed by bishops; this is demonstrated by a historical review of the poor reception met with by the pertinent canons of the Council of Serdica[229] (around 343), which expressly declared the preeminence of the Bishop of Rome in the collegial order of bishops both in the East and in the West. Of course, this is not the place to discuss the historical development of the relation between primacy and collegiality. Instead, the question arises of why Ratzinger, in his assessment of the Church's collegial structure, backed away from his perichoretic model of ecclesial provinces in communion with one another, in favor of the primatial status of Rome and also of the individual bishop. He clearly articulates this change in his view during an interview in the year 2000, when he answers the question, "Are there going to be patriarchates in the Catholic Church as well?" as follows:

---

[228] Ibid., 97f. The Council of Nicaea had already designated for the whole Church that two provencial synods a year should be held, one before Easter and the other in the fall. On this, see H.J. Sieben, "Selbstverständnis und römische Sicht der Partikularsynode: Einige Streiflichter auf das erste Jahrtausend", in Müller/Pottmeyer, 10–35, ref. at 15.

[229] See DH 133–36. On the relation between Rome and a particular synod, see Sieben, "Selbstverständnis und römische Sicht", 21. See also W. Brandmüller, "Petrus und seine Nachfolger", in Mysterium Kirche: Sozialkonzern oder Stiftung Christi? ed. Brandmüller, 135–62, esp. 156f. (Aachen: MM Verlag, 1996).

Whether this is the form by which great continental units will have
to be organized—as I used to think—does in fact seem more and
more questionable to me. The roots of these patriarchates lay, after
all, in their connection with their respective place of apostolic origin. The Second Vatican Council, on the contrary, has already defined
the *bishops' conferences* as the form giving concrete shape to such
supraregional units. Continental units have come in, in addition to
them. Not only Latin America but also Africa and Asia have in the
meantime developed various structures of episcopal association at
the continental level. Perhaps these offer possibilities better adapted
to the current situation. There have to be supraregional structures
of cooperation, in any case, that remain more of a loose association
and do not degenerate into great bureaucracies or lead to domination by officials. But there is no doubt that we need such supraregional associations, which can then take over some of the work
from Rome.[230]

Besides the influence of Henri de Lubac mentioned earlier in this
subsection, Ratzinger himself gives three reasons that led him to this
modified assessment of the bishops' conferences: first, the recognition
that episcopal conferences have no teaching authority in matters of
faith and morals, so that, second, their majority decisions are not binding for the individual bishops, since (third and finally) the "conscience
of faith"[231] obliges a person only to the truth. It is worth examining
these three arguments in more detail.

1) *No magisterial competence in questions of faith and morals*

During the Council, Ratzinger situated the bishops' conference, as an
instrument of collegiality, in the sphere of a modified "arrangement
of church law",[232] but he attributed to it the competence to create
distinctive "pastoral sectors" within the one Church and at the same
time to "integrate the power of the individual bishop into the framework of the collegial structure of his office".[233] Twenty years later, in
contrast, he cites the 1983 Code of Canon Law, stressing the purely
practical function of the episcopal conference:

---

[230] *God and the World*, 384.
[231] *Church*, 46–62, citation at 59.
[232] "Formen", 162.
[233] *Highlights*, 57.

[This] is ... confirmed in the new Code of Canon Law, which prescribes the extent of the authority of the conferences, which cannot validly act "in the name of all the bishops unless each and every bishop has given his consent." ... The collective, therefore, does not substitute for the persons of the bishops. ... "No episcopal conference, as such, has a teaching mission; its documents have no weight of their own save that of the consent given to them by the individual bishops."[234]

Why does Ratzinger in 1984 insist so much on this magisterial competence of the individual bishop? He himself refers to "the very nature of the Catholic Church, which is based on an episcopal structure and not on a kind of federation of national churches",[235] for in the Catholic Church there is a "balance between the *community* and the *person*, in this case between the community of individual particular churches united in the universal Church and the *person* of the responsible head of the diocese".[236] Almost contemporaneously, Hans Urs von Balthasar argued in very similar terms:

Were we not told that the true *Communio* within a country or continent was embodied by the bishops' conference, of which each bishop is a "member"? Viewed from such a perspective, one cannot help but conclude that the Universal Church consists of the sum total of national churches, and hence is not supranational but international.[237]

---

[234] *Report*, 60. Ratzinger refers to *CIC*, cann. 455 and 753. This argument is contested by Heribert Schmitz: "It is a mistake to conclude from the language '*Episcopi* ... *congregati*', without taking into account the complicated syntactical structure of canon 753 *CIC*, that bishops, while gathered in one place at particular councils or bishops' conferences, act only as individuals." See Schmitz, "Die Lehrautorität der Bischofskonferenz gemäß c. 753 CIC", in Müller/Pottmeyer, 196–235, citation at 211.

[235] *Report*, 60. See also A. Nichols, *The Theology of Joseph Ratzinger: An Introductory Study* (Edinburgh: T. and T. Clark, 1988), 141: "Ratzinger was, then, deeply exercised by the theme of the Church's unity, an international unity with a salvific significance in its very transcending of the merely national. He looked back to the world of Christian antiquity to find his bearings on this topic, with its obvious contemporary relevance in the temptation of post-conciliar Catholicism to see itself as a vine carrying discreet clusters of dioceses, bunched together on a broadly national basis." As early as 1971, Ratzinger pointed out this problem in Ratzinger, *Die Einheit der Nationen: Eine Vision der Kirchenväter* (Munich: Pustet, 1971).

[236] *Report*, 60.

[237] Balthasar, *Test Everything*, 20.

In contrast, Gisbert Greshake, following Karl Rahner, sees the episcopal conferences as "intermediate authorities",[238] that is to say, "not
simply and solely *juris humani* [of human right]", but *"divina providen-
tia"*[239] according to *Lumen gentium* 23.

2) *No binding majority decisions*

Ratzinger presupposes that episcopal conferences lack magisterial competence; the logical consequence of this is that their majority decisions cannot bind the individual bishop, because in questions of faith
and morals no one, as a matter of principle, can be bound by majority
decisions. For him, this is the real reason "why bishops' conferences
do not have any teaching authority and cannot as conferences make
teaching binding".[240] Furthermore, Ratzinger clarifies the case of ecumenical councils, which

> can only decide on matters of faith and morals in moral unanimity,
> since one cannot establish the truth by resolution but can only rec-
> ognize and accept it. The pattern whereby truths are defined as
> such is not the majority decision but the recognition becoming gen-
> erally clear that the guardians of the faith united in sacramental com-
> munion jointly recognize a statement as the consequence of this
> faith they hold. Where this kind of unity arises it should be judged
> as a sign that this reality is an expression of the faith of the Church
> which as the Church and as a whole cannot err in matters of faith.
> This is the inner foundation of theological definitions. The idea of
> consciences being bound by a teaching through a majority decision
> is an impossibility in human as well as theological terms.[241]

---

[238] On this subject, see Karl-Rahner Stiftung, ed., *Karl Rahner: Sämtliche Werke*, vol. 19,
Selbstvollzug der Kirche: Ekklesiologische Grundlegung praktischer Theologie, ed. K.-H. Neufeld
(Solothurn, Düsseldorf, and Freiburg im Breisgau: Herder, 1995), 144–46. Karl Rahner
considers it conceivable that Rome itself might habitually delegate to the bishops' conferences "certain competencies that according to the law currently in force are reserved to
the pope" (ibid., 145).
[239] G. Greshake, "Weltkirche und Ortskirche: Bemerkungen zu einem problematischen
Verhältnis", *ThGl* 91 (2001): 528–42, citation at 541.
[240] *Church*, 46–62, citation at 58.
[241] Ibid., 58f. See also *Prüfsteine*, 25–62, citation at 55f.: "The true meaning of the pope's
teaching authority consists in the fact that he is the advocate or attorney of the Christian
memory. The pope does not interpret from outside but, rather, unfolds the Christian memory and defends it. Therefore one really ought to propose a toast to conscience before

Therefore, as Ratzinger sees it, the moral unanimity with which conciliar decisions are reached, "according to the classic concept of the council, does not possess the character of a vote but that of a testimony"[242] to the truth of the faith. Hermann Joseph Pottmeyer objects that one cannot deny the witness-character of a vote on a doctrinal question in a bishops' conference that results in moral unanimity. The difference between a council and a bishops' conference lies instead, he says, in the restricted "representation" afforded by the latter. Pottmeyer supports this argument as follows:

> The council has the authority to speak for the whole Church; its definitive doctrinal declaration is therefore infallible. The episcopal conference does not have this authority, and therefore its doctrinal statement does not possess the same binding character, either. Yet its moral unanimity does constitute a witness when these bishops abide and act in communion with the college of bishops; hence a voting procedure, understood in this way, cannot be forbidden, just as a particular council is not forbidden, even though it likewise represents only a restricted area.[243]

If we read Ratzinger's explanation of his negative assessment from the year 1984, we find that he refers to the psychological pressure exerted by the "group spirit" and occasionally by a desire to conform or to be irenic, which cause bishops to allow themselves to be manipulated, as it were.[244] This misgiving, however, as Pottmeyer retorts, would also tell "against particular councils and especially against ecumenical councils."[245] What is the meaning of Ratzinger's remark that

---

drinking one to the pope, because without conscience there would be no papacy at all. All the authority that he has is the authority of conscience—a service to the twofold recollection on which faith rests and which must again and again be unified, extended, and defended against the destruction of memory, which is threatened both by a subjectivity that forgets its own foundation and also by the pressure of social and cultural conformity."

[242] *Report*, 62.

[243] H. J. Pottmeyer, "Das Lehramt der Bischofskonferenz", in Müller/Pottmeyer, 116–33, citation at 117.

[244] Cf. *Report*, 62. In his concern about this, Ratzinger cites his personal experience: "I know bishops who privately confess that they would have decided differently than they did at a conference if they had had to decide by themselves. [Going along with the group dynamics,] they shied away from the odium of being viewed as a 'spoilsport', as 'backward', as 'not open'. It seems very nice always to decide *together*" (ibid.).

[245] Pottmeyer, "Lehramt der Bischofskonferenz", 117.

during the Council only about "10 percent intervened actively by taking the floor in the debate",[246] while the other 90 percent formed the silent, voting majority? Pottmeyer asks, can this be interpreted as "social-psychological group dynamics",[247] applied by Ratzinger to the Council as well? We cannot answer this question here, but we merely recall the principle, which is for Ratzinger ineluctable, "that truth cannot be created through ballots. A statement is either true or false. Truth can only be found, not created."[248] This brings us to the third point: The conscience of faith can be obliged only to the truth.

3) The conscience of faith, obliged only to the truth

For Ratzinger, conscience is the place "where faith dwells".[249] Applied to the collegial constitution of the Church, this means, in his view, that the individual diocesan bishop most fully represents both the local and the universal Church when he follows his conscience. That does not mean, however, that he is following "an ego raised to an absolute but an open, alert and listening conscience of faith".[250] On account of this personal responsibility to the truth of the faith, the individual bishop cannot delegate his doctrinal responsibility.[251] During the Council, on the other hand, Ratzinger (presupposing obedience to the conscience of the faith) did not yet have any objections of this sort against the possibility of delegating episcopal responsibility; in 1964 he demanded with regard to the structure of an "episcopal synod" that one "should not insist all too much on the doctrinaire question of to what extent this synod of bishops can represent in the strict sense the college of bishops".[252]

c. The "episcopal synod" (synod of bishops) as congubernium—The commission on behalf of the universal Church cannot be delegated

The "episcopal council", which was described by the Council itself as the "synod of bishops", corresponded to Pope Paul VI's objective of bringing episcopal collegiality to bear beyond the parameters of the

---

[246] *Report*, 61.
[247] Pottmeyer, "Lehramt der Bischofskonferenz", 118.
[248] *Report*, 61.
[249] *Church*, 46–62, citation at 59.
[250] Ibid., 59.
[251] *Report*, 63. Ratzinger refers to *CIC*, can. 756 § 2.
[252] "Formen", 159.

Council assembly. As early as September 21, 1963, the Pope announced to the Curia a reform, whereby diocesan bishops especially were to become involved in the work and responsibility of leading the Church.[253] Surprisingly, by means of the motu proprio *Apostolica Sollicitudo*,[254] Paul VI instituted this synod of bishops as a purely consultative body— six weeks before the Decree on the Pastoral Office of Bishops, *Christus Dominus*, was promulgated on October 28, 1965. Even though the synod of bishops in its operations is associated with the primacy, being dependent on the pope, because in every instance he has to determine the time, place, and agenda of the synod, it was for Ratzinger at the conclusion of the Council "a positive development"[255] with relation to episcopal collegiality as well, although it fell far short of his earlier ideas of a collegial organization for governing the universal Church. He deemed it especially fortunate in a lecture he gave in Rome on the day when *Christus Dominus* was promulgated (October 28, 1965) that the members of the synod of bishops "will be designated only in a few cases by papal appointment and for the large part will be delegated by the episcopal conferences".[256] At that time Ratzinger personally hoped that the synod of bishops would be a permanent *concilium*[257] modeled on the institution

---

[253] See M. von Galli and B. Moosbrugger, *Das Konzil: Von Johannes XXIII zu Paul VI: Chronik der zweiten Sessio; Die Pilgerfahrt ins Heilige Land* (Olten: Walter, 1964), 87–93: "Papst Paul VI über die Reform der Römischen Kurie (21. September 1963)" (Pope Paul VI on the reform of the Roman Curia).

[254] Pope Paul VI, motu proprio *Apostolica Sollicitudo*, dated September 15, 1965, in *AAS* 57 (1965): 775–80.

[255] J. Ratzinger, *Probleme der vierten Konzilsperiode* (Bonn: Katholische Rundfunk- und Fernseharbeit in Deutschland, 1965), 15.

[256] Ibid. On this subject, see also the insightful contemporary journalistic view of H. Linnerz, *Das Konzil hat gesprochen: Themen—Texte—Tendenzen* (Kevelaer: Butzon, 1966), 234–36.

[257] In Ratzinger's view, the synod of bishops "is not supposed to be a subdivision or super-committee [supervisory panel] within the curia, but rather be a counterpart to it. It was not supposed to be part of the papal bureaucracy.... It would be something like a Council extended into the Church's everyday life" (*Highlights*, 58). As prefect of the Congregation for the Doctrine of the Faith, Ratzinger recognizes instead that it runs the risk of becoming a second Curia, which would also stand in the way of the residence requirement of diocesan bishops. On this subject, see Nichols, *Theology of Joseph Ratzinger*, 252: "One idea is that the Pope should delegate decision-making power to the Synod on a regular and systematic basis. But this would be a second, reduplicated Curia. It would also deprive local churches of their residential bishops for considerable periods, thus resurrecting that figure buried by the Council of Trent, the late mediaeval absentee bishop."

of the synod in Christian antiquity, which over the course of history had assumed "its most impressive form in the permanent synod of Constantinople".[258] In the name *synodus episcoporum*, therefore, Ratzinger recognized at the same time an ecumenical sign to the Orthodox Churches:

> Through this nomenclature the episcopal synod is detached from political models and connected with the tradition of the early Church and of the Eastern Churches. It has thereby acquired an ecumenical profile, in that it now represents a renewal of structures from the early Church and thus employs again to greater effect the common basis of divided Christianity.[259]

On the other hand, Ratzinger then viewed it as problematical "that the pope is solely responsible for convoking the synod and thus there is no canonically determined guarantee that it would operate regularly".[260] One year earlier, in 1964, he was even advocating a sort of collegial co-governance of the bishops in leading the universal Church. He cited historical precedents as well, which justified from the papal perspective the establishment of such a panel of bishops that would be distinct from the Curia. Among them he listed the synods of bishops in Christian antiquity, the consistory of cardinals as the real senate of the pope in the Middle Ages, and in the modern era "the *congubernium* of the bureaucracy and the Curial offices".[261] He expressed an opinion on the fundamental problem concerning the delegation of episcopal-collegial competence in the same article, which we quote verbatim:

> Often the objection is raised that the synod of bishops cannot be the representative of the college of bishops at all, since it is impossible for the latter to delegate its authority. Consequently, such a panel could derive its authority in the first place only from a delegation of papal authority. But here the formalism of our usual canonical thinking fails. . . . If we take the historical facts seriously, we can determine that the absolute division into papal authority and

---

[258] Ratzinger, *Probleme der vierten Konzilsperiode*, 15.
[259] Ibid.
[260] Ibid.
[261] "Formen", 160.

episcopal authority, according to which everything that surpasses the competence of the individual bishop must be of papal right, is by no means capable of grasping the matter properly. Instead of that, we find in history manifold models of a collegial authority, which cannot simply be derived from the pope alone or from the individual bishop but are the expression of the collegial element in the Church as an effective and canonically significant factor, which created for itself concrete manifestations especially in two formations: the patriarchate and the synod.[262]

Ratzinger's remarks twenty years later sounded quite different, when he read a paper,[263] originally in Latin, on the "Purposes and Structure of the Synod of Bishops"[264] to the Standing Committee of the Synod of Bishops. The point of departure for his exposition is the canonical form of the synod of bishops laid down by the 1983 Code of Canon Law.[265] At the very start, Ratzinger himself points out a modification of the theological and/or canonical competence of the synod of bishops. The currently valid form of the synod of bishops "does indeed take up the idea of regularly involving the bishops of the universal Church collectively in the formation of policy on major questions affecting the Church as a whole", but in doing so, it "canonically and theologically ... follows a different model. It advises the pope; it is not a small-scale Council, and it is not a collegial organ of leadership for the universal Church."[266] Basing his argument on the systematic presentation in the Code of Canon Law, Ratzinger emphasizes that the synod of bishops is treated, not among the canons concerning the particular Churches, but rather in the section dealing with the "supreme authority of the Church",[267] the agents of which are the pope and the college of bishops. According to canon 342, as he explains it, there are three fundamental aspects or relations involved in the synod of

---

[262] Ibid., 160f. See also Weiler, 240f.

[263] The report was published in Italian under the title "Scopi e metodi del Sinodo dei Vescovi", in *Sinodo dei Vescovi: Natura, metodo, prospettive*, ed. J. Tomko, 45–58 (Vatican City: Libreria Editrice Vaticana, 1985).

[264] A revised German version appeared in *Kirche, Ökumene und Politik*; English trans. in *Church*, 46–62.

[265] *CIC*, cann. 342–348.

[266] *Church*, 46–62, citations at 46.

[267] Ibid., 47. See also W. Aymans, "Bischofssynode", in *LThK*, 3rd ed., 2:502–4.

bishops, which, he says, at the same time correspond to the Second Vatican Council's concept of the Church:

> The first [aspect] is the internal relationship of the pope and the college of bishops. To put it another way, the synod serves the right relationship of the Church's unity and catholicity and therefore of that living unity which corresponds to the vitality of the living organism that is living and growing in the many cells of the local Church. The second consists of assisting and co-operating in the task of the pope; the third in the Church's activity with regard to the world. One could talk of the Church's collegial, primatial and external aspects: the relationship of the college of bishops to the pope, of the pope to the universal Church, and of the Church to the world. According to the canon this triple framework of relationships forms the one object that bears the name "synod of bishops".[268]

Like the Code of Canon Law, Ratzinger subsumes this threefold statement of the purpose of the synod under "the one juridical category of the assistance"[269] with which the bishops throughout the world provide the pope in his universal ministry. This makes for closer ties between the pope and the bishops, as well as among the bishops themselves, whereby their witness in the world becomes more effective. He explicitly refers to the supplementary provisions of the Code of Canon Law in canon 344 and canon 345. There the advisory function of the synod of bishops is spelled out, and thus its canonical status is defined. Even though "in certain cases the pope can confer on the synod a power of decision", this power to decide remains a papal prerogative and, as Ratzinger emphasizes, "is not the expression of powers inherent in the college of bishops".[270] With reference to the general secretariat of the synod of bishops described in canon 348 and the council that assists it, the change in Ratzinger's point of view becomes especially clear in comparison to his statements during the Council. At that time he still spoke literally of the synod of bishops as "an organ of the world episcopate",[271] whereas twenty years later this is precisely the interpretation he cannot accept.

---

[268] *Church*, 48–49. On this subject, see also the discussion in Weiler, 336–40.
[269] *Church*, 49.
[270] Ibid.
[271] *Highlights*, 58.

The secretariat's job is to prepare meetings of the synod and to implement things undertaken by it and connected with it. The co-operation in this of the bishops ... guarantees coherence with the needs and desires of the local Churches. But it is obvious that this "council" does not offer any kind of pre-figurement of a "permanent synod" in the way that many would like to understand it; it serves the secretariat and is in no way an organ for sharing with the pope in governing the Church, however important it may be for him to meet these representatives of the universal Church regularly.[272]

In 1985, while presenting the regulations of canon law, Ratzinger nevertheless concedes that "the theological and the legal patterns do not overlap completely and that often the theological framework is drawn more broadly than the legal".[273] Ratzinger asks, furthermore, whether this must be so: "Or should not the legal pattern have the same breadth as the theological aims? Is there not here perhaps a starting-point for extending and reforming the synod?"[274]

This question of Ratzinger's could encourage a revision of the canonical framework of the synod of bishops along the lines proposed by Medard Kehl, who in 1992 suggested that the canonical structure of the synod of bishops should be classified as being simultaneously collegial and primatial, since "the current status ... basically only reinforces the unbalanced structure of the Church's governing and teaching office, so that the initiatives of the Second Vatican Council toward establishing an equilibrium can hardly be made productive."[275] For Ratzinger, however, there is no reason to revise the 1983 Code of Canon Law on this question. He asks instead about the reason "why the legal framework is drawn more tightly than the theological and pastoral one and in what form the college of bishops

---

[272] *Church*, 50.
[273] Ibid.
[274] Ibid., 50–51.
[275] Kehl, *Kirche*, 378f. Kehl repeats the same arguments in Kehl, *Wohin geht die Kirche?* 84f. See also R. Puza, "Kanonistisches zur Streitkultur in der kirchlichen Communio", in *Was ist heute noch katholisch? Zum Streit um die innere Einheit und Vielfalt der Kirche*, ed. A. Franz, 135–59, ref. at 146f., QD 192 (Freiburg im Breisgau: Herder, 2001). Richard Puza suggests investigating the extent to which decision-making competence could be within the province of the synod of bishops.

can become effective as a legal source".[276] He supports his answer
with a reference to the definitions of the Second Vatican Council in
Lumen gentium 22:

> According to the Council there are only two ways in which the
> college of bishops can act with legal force, that is, as plenipotentiary
> for the universal Church: an ecumenical council, and by all the bish-
> ops dispersed around the world acting together....
>   If things are so, then the college of bishops cannot delegate its
> powers; it can only exercise them itself, as a whole, either in a
> council or in practice. Included in this once again is the corollary
> that the college may be able to be involved generally in some
> process as a spiritual reality but that it cannot ever be a legal source
> for any kind of representation of itself. This however means that
> in actual fact it is only the pope who can be the legal source for
> the synod.[277]

The inevitable logical consequence of this, for Ratzinger, is a "dichotomy between the theological and pastoral framework"[278] of the synod
of bishops.

In assessing the extent to which Ratzinger abandoned his earlier
position, we must take into account this distinction between theological doctrine and canonical framework and, furthermore, the fact that
the situation before the promulgation of *Lumen gentium* and *Christus
Dominus* was different from the one after the magisterial publication
of these conciliar documents. Therefore, one must also always take
into account Ratzinger's intention in arguing on any particular occasion. As Thomas Weiler explains, in 1963 the Council was concerned,
"not primarily with the *canonical* definition of episcopal collegiality,
but above all with the (*theological*) doctrine about the collegiality of
bishops"[279] with moral unanimity, despite the opposition of a minority. On the other hand, in 1985, after the promulgation of the new
Code of Canon Law, Ratzinger's intention was aimed at clarifying
theological problems that resulted from the canonical definition of the
synod of bishops.

---

[276] *Church*, 51.
[277] Ibid.
[278] Ibid.
[279] Weiler, 339.

Is Ratzinger now in fact, with his modified argument, calling into question the fundamental conciliar concern about collegiality? Before an answer to this question can be given, we must present his line of argument from the year 1985, a time when the new Code of Canon Law had already regulated the nature and purposes of the synod and the 1985 Extraordinary Synod of Bishops[280] was taking place in Rome, standing right in the spotlight of Vatican II. Twenty years after the end of the Council, that extraordinary synod focused its review of the conciliar heritage on the central concept of the Church's *communio* structure.

In his 1985 exposition of the task of the synod of bishops,[281] Ratzinger starts with the unsatisfactory approaches, then explains the collegial structure as a *communio* union of local Churches, and finally discusses the problem of why the synod of bishops is canonically ordered to the primacy, even though theologically it belongs to the sphere of collegiality.

1) *Inadequate models for the synod*

On the initial question of the suitability or unsuitability of alternative models for the synod, Ratzinger argues first against the demand that the synod should be vested with general decision-making authority. He rejects this demand for two reasons. First, from a theological perspective, it is true that such decision-making authority "would—unavoidably, as has been shown—be by delegation from the pope and not the right of the synod itself", and hence such a synod of bishops would be, as Ratzinger understands it, "simply a second Roman curia".[282] The second reason is a practical one: In Ratzinger's opinion, within the four weeks when the synod would be in session,[283] "the thorough preparation of

---

[280] On the synod, see *Zukunft der Kirche aus der Kraft des Konzils: Die außerordentliche Bischofssynode '85*, the documents with a commentary by Walter Kasper (Freiburg im Breisgau: Herder, 1986).

[281] *Church*, 46–62.

[282] Ibid., 53.

[283] On this subject, see also the description of the proceedings and structure of a synod of bishops in Quinn, *Reform*, 110–16. Quinn is suspicious of the Curia's intention of restricting the competence of the synod as much as possible. Instead, he calls for a "genuine evangelical prudence and authentic discernment" (ibid., 114).

documents or decrees is not possible".[284] Furthermore, an extension of
the synod would be opposed to the canonically established residency
requirement for bishops. In Ratzinger's view, though, this obligation is
not just a juridical specification but rather "at its core a requirement of
divine law",[285] since it has a sacramental basis. From these two premises, therefore, he draws the conclusion:

> Bishops remain bishops, responsible to their particular Churches.
> The variable elements of the Church's constitution do not include
> the possibility of building up a second central power within it that
> would do far less damage to the importance of the papal ministry
> than to that of the episcopal ministry and would in fact eliminate
> the latter.[286]

For the reasons stated, giving general decision-making authority to
the synod of bishops would *not* be an appropriate *modus operandi* in
Ratzinger's opinion, nor would the suggestion of establishing as a "permanent synod" the council made up of bishops that assists the synod
secretariat. Here again the problem arises of the bishops' residency
requirement and/or the development in practice of a second curia of
international composition. For the aforementioned reasons, Ratzinger
considers this suggestion unrealistic. Nevertheless, he is able to find
one positive feature in it, namely, that it is "desirable ... for the existing curia to have as international a membership as possible, with the
opportunity for its members to change places. This would in fact bring
about what is called for under the wrong label of a permanent synod." [287]

2) *The collegial structure as a* communio *union of local Churches*

Ratzinger's second main argument against an enhancement of the synodal principle in the Church, in the direction of a decision-making
panel that would represent the universal Church, is the theological
connection between the collegiality of the bishops and the *communio*
of the Churches, for "the concept of the college of bishops, which
describes the hierarchical aspect of the Church, presupposes the

---

[284] *Church*, 53.
[285] Ibid., 54.
[286] Ibid.
[287] Ibid., 55.

reality of communion as the Church's vital and constitutional fundamental form."[288] That means: "A collegial structure exists in the Church
because the Church lives in the communion of Churches and because
this structure of communion implies bishops belonging to one another
and thus forming a college."[289]

From this, Ratzinger derives two fundamental rules: It must be the
goal of the Church's constitution to strengthen the vitality of the individual local Church. The latter, however, must not remain self-
enclosed but must be open to the totality of the Church. The axiom
that Ratzinger championed in 1965—that the Church is a network of
"Churches in communion with each other",[290] which, on the one
hand, stand in direct relation to one another and, on the other hand,
are held together by the *communio* primacy of the bishop of Rome—
accordingly gives expression to the fact that in the Church the law of
the totality and of the personal holds true. In his essay on Ratzinger,
"Die Communio und das Ganze" [The *communio* and the totality],
Miroslav Volf formulated this as follows:

> As opposed to any individual or communal particularism, Rat-
> zinger underscores the totality: A Christian, a local Church, and
> also a bishop are always constituted in terms of the whole and are
> directed toward the whole. It cannot be otherwise, since the pri-
> mary category of his ecclesiology is *Christus totus*. It follows from
> this that the totality is to be understood in terms of the principle
> "individual". This principle has a soteriological and a christological
> basis. . . . An ecclesiology of universal communion therefore calls for
> an ecclesiology of the responsible personality—not least of all on
> the level of the individual who answers for the totality.[291]

Ratzinger's line of argument here follows that of *Lumen gentium* 23,
where the twofold principle of the whole and of personal responsibility mentioned in the passage quoted above is stated with reference
to the bishops, who contribute most efficaciously "to the welfare of
the whole Mystical Body" by "governing well their own church as a

---

[288] Ibid., 56.
[289] Ibid.
[290] *Volk Gottes*, 43–70, citation at 55.
[291] M. Volf, *Trinität und Gemeinschaft: Eine ökumenische Ekklesiologie* (Mainz: Matthias-
Grünewald-Verlag, 1996), 26–69, citation at 55.

portion of the universal Church".[292] For Ratzinger, "the first and fundamental collegial action consists of a bishop governing his Church well according to the responsibility assigned to him in the sacrament and as a good shepherd maintaining the vitality of his portion of the universal Church by leading it towards the Lord and thus into the co-operative community of the whole."[293] From this Ratzinger insight derives the formula: "Governing the local Churches is to share in governing the Church as a whole."[294]

3) The twofold ordering of the synod of bishops: Canonically to the primacy— Theologically to collegiality

This assertion—that diocesan bishops by being personally responsible for the governance of their local Churches simultaneously realize their collegial responsibility for the universal Church—makes it possible to understand, finally, Ratzinger's thesis in 1985 that the association of the bishops in the synod of bishops, on the one hand, serves the "relationship of the Churches among themselves" and thus "belongs theologically to the sphere of collegiality", while on the other hand the synod "derives its legal basis from the primacy".[295] This two-track structure prompts Ratzinger to ask whether it would not be possible to turn the synod itself "into a genuine organ of the college of bishops".[296] He no longer speaks, as he did in 1964, about a formalism of canonical thinking but, rather, strictly adheres to the legal principle that "the college's right of governing cannot be delegated because by its nature it cannot be centralized."[297] The reason for this, again, is the principle of personal responsibility, which is left solely to the individual conscience.[298]

Therefore, in contrast to his views during the Council, Ratzinger sees the goal of the synod of bishops, no longer to be a form of *congubernium* [collaborative government], but rather to be a collegial witness to faith, hope, and charity, so as to ensure "an increase in the

---

[292] LG 23.

[293] *Church*, 46–62, citation at 57.

[294] Ibid.

[295] Ibid., 57. See also the conclusion of the second paragraph of LG 22. See also "Kommentar", 355.

[296] *Church*, 46–62, citation at 57.

[297] Ibid.

[298] On this subject, see ibid., 58–62.

real presence of the gospel in the Church and in the world".²⁹⁹ This, of course, is the main goal of Christian life; he places it in the context of three concrete short-term goals for the synod of bishops: It facilitates the exchange of information, mutual correction, and finally "encouragement"³⁰⁰ in truth and love. With that he leads the discussion back from the juridical to the theological level. At the same time, he also indicates that the problem of "a Roman centre that appears all too strong"³⁰¹ cannot be solved by a central synodal government, but only through the assumption of personal responsibility by the individual bishop in his particular Church in a manner that is open to the *Ecclesia Catholica*.³⁰²

3. *Critical review*

In looking back over the subsection entitled "Aspects during the Council in Tension with the Later Perspective", we recognize that Ratzinger's description of the Church's hierarchical structure has not changed *essentially* in the decades of his theological career—nor has it changed in his own judgment. Taking as its basis the *communio* approach to ecclesiology in the early Church,³⁰³ his view continues to be grounded

---

²⁹⁹ Ibid., 46–62, citation at 61. See also Ratzinger, "Demokratisierung 2", 83, where Ratzinger lists a series of organizations that are constitutive of the universal Church and the particular Churches, for example, "the synod of bishops as the concrete form of the meeting of the world's bishops with one another and with the pope and his organs of governance", and he arrives at the conclusion: "All these are ways of contributing to the common good of the Church, to the struggle to make the gospel present for the individual and for the totality."

³⁰⁰ *Church*, 46–62, citation at 62.

³⁰¹ Ibid.

³⁰² With unvarnished candor, Pottmeyer addresses (*Weg*, 297) "the well-known and the misunderstood causes of centralism". He says, among other things, that a majority of the bishops simply drift into playing "the role of a letter-carrier to the Curia.... If they do not consider these concerns and suggestions to be right, they should confront their diocesan priests and not hide behind Rome's authority. But if they consider the recommendations justified and helpful, they should advocate them vigorously and persistently, together with other bishops, in Rome.... Anyone who speaks to members of the Curia hears the complaint about the all-too-frequent inquiries made by the bishops to Rome, specifically in matters that very likely fall within the competence of the local Church."

³⁰³ See "Kommentar", 353: "*Communio* is the expression of the canonical structure of the early Church, defined in terms of the sacraments.... The canonical building up of the Church is accomplished in the communion with one another of the *Ecclesiae* headed by bishop, thus in a hierarchical association that has a sacramental content—this is precisely

at the same coordinates of sacramental *communio* and the resulting relation between primacy and collegiality. Nevertheless, in his theological characterization of the status of bishops' conferences, Ratzinger departs from his original standpoint.[304] On this point, he even distances himself from *Lumen gentium*, even though at the time of the Council he was one of those influential in formulating the conciliar statement that bishops' conferences could, much like the old patriarchal Churches, lead to "this collegiate feeling [being] put into practical application."[305]

These revisions in his assessment of the *practical implementation* of the *communio* structure are obvious, so that it is possible to speak of an "earlier" and a "later"[306] Ratzinger. The quondam Council theologian emphasized the "plural *communio* structure of the Church"[307] and gave expression at that time to his regret that the primatial status of the pope was being accentuated, especially by the Preliminary Note of Explanation to *Lumen gentium*. Nevertheless, shortly after the Council, he saw the danger of centralism as being limited both by the *communio* primacy,[308] which is characterized by a separation of the three offices of the pope, and also by the "importance of what happens in the particular Church".[309] By the latter, Ratzinger meant, not primarily collegial acts in the strict sense (for example, at an ecumenical council), but rather a gradated collegial activity that was not subject to "the conditions of the *actus stricte collegialis*".[310] The Constitution on the Church speaks in

---

the meaning of the expression *hierarchica communio*, which should make relevant for all times and so also for today with the utmost clarity the early Church's concept of *communio* as the fundamental juridical and ontological form of the Church."

[304] On this subject, see Quinn, *Reform*, 106f.

[305] *LG* 23.

[306] See Quinn, *Reform*, 107f. "In any case, it is interesting that both the later Ratzinger and the later Hamer appear to base their changed and negative views on the works of two other authors: Henri de Lubac and Willy Onclin, a professor of canon law at Louvain." Quinn notes here that de Lubac did not take into consideration the following summary of Onclin's thought: "Local councils and episcopal conferences may therefore be considered the juridical expression of the bishops' responsibilities as members of the college of bishops and of their concern for all the Churches. As such they are a manifestation of episcopal collegiality." See W. H. J. Onclin, "Die Kollegialität der Bischöfe und ihre Struktur", *Conc(D)* I (1965): 664–69.

[307] Cf. "Kommentar", 357.

[308] *Volk Gottes*, 43–70, ref. at 55. See "Kommentar", 357. Cf. Pottmeyer, *Rolle*, 103.

[309] "Kommentar", 357.

[310] Ibid.

similar terms about these "mutual relations of the individual bishops with particular churches and with the universal Church", in which "collegiate union"[311] is demonstrated, inasmuch as it refers in the same article to bishops' conferences in particular. Furthermore, the conciliar Decree on the Pastoral Office of Bishops in the Church, *Christus Dominus*, mentions the so-called council or synod of bishops,[312] an institution that—like the bishops' conferences—demonstrates the collegial *communio* structure of the Church. In October 1965, Ratzinger's joy over this *synodus episcoporum* was unmistakable.[313]

The "later" Ratzinger, in contrast, no longer attributed the same importance to those two institutions. Influenced by de Lubac, he continued as archbishop and cardinal to speak out for the collegial *communio* structure of the Church, but in doing so he emphasized the personal responsibility of the individual bishop, which must not disappear in "anonymous governing boards".[314] For this reason, collegiality and primacy are interdependent, according to Ratzinger, and must not dissolve "into each other".[315] The pope and the bishops, he says, being witnesses to the gospel, are not subject to majority decisions in matters of faith and morals but, rather, are obliged to follow their conscience, as informed by faith. In 1984, when Ratzinger even denied that bishops' conferences have any magisterial function,[316] his statement evoked protest.[317]

The fundamental rules of personal responsibility in the Church and of the residential requirement for bishops caused Ratzinger to agree

---

[311] *LG* 23.

[312] *CD* 5.

[313] See Ratzinger, *Probleme der vierten Konzilsperiode*, 15.

[314] J. Ratzinger, "Der Primat des Papstes und die Einheit des Gottesvolkes", in *Dienst an der Einheit: Zum Wesen des Petrusamtes*, ed. Ratzinger, 165–79, citation at 178, Schriften der katholischen Akademie in Bayern 85 (Düsseldorf, 1978).

[315] Ibid. Cf. Nachtwei, 187–93, citation at 189: "Ratzinger clearly emphasizes that because of this *communio* experience that is based on God's trinitarian being, the 'I' is not absorbed in an anonymous 'we'. Precisely in this dialogical relationship, the individual experiences himself irreplaceably and uniquely as someone called by God personally, as a martyr, as a witness. Personal responsibility and intuition can be neither replaced nor suppressed by collegiality."

[316] Cf. *Report*, 60.

[317] See, for example, Quinn, *Reform*, 110: "Reading the aggregate of the council teaching and the Code of Canon Law, it is difficult to see how one could reach the conclusion that episcopal conferences are not a true realization of episcopal collegiality and that they do not have a true teaching role. The apostolic letter on episcopal conferences affirms this teaching role but sets severe limits on its exercise."

II/2. Recurring Themes in Ratzinger's Ecclesiology

to the canonical classification of the synod of bishops in the section on papal primacy according to the 1983 Code of Canon Law. Thus the later Ratzinger denied what the earlier Council theologian had regarded as a possibility for *congubernium*; in his opinion now, episcopal collegiality is intended, not to create an organ of centralized government for the Church, but rather to build sacramental solidarity in the one *communio* of the Church. In saying this, however, he is not denying collegiality per se. According to Pottmeyer, the later Ratzinger is concerned about putting collegiality into action as the expression of a "living organism [made up] of a multiplicity of local Churches".[318] Here, though, Ratzinger sees the relation of bishop to bishop or to the successor of Peter as playing the crucial role. Furthermore, even greater centralization could result if an additional central organ—a second curia, so to speak—were created.[319]

With regard to the question of collegiality, therefore, Ratzinger is concerned, not with allocating competencies,[320] but rather with the mystery of the Church's sacramental *communio*. This is experienced in the local Churches, which are truly Church because they are associated with one another in the one *communio* of the one Church. This essential form runs through all of his ecclesiological writings, based on the ecclesiology of the early Church.

Obviously the modern problems involved in legislating for and administering the universal Church are different today from those of the early Church. The earlier Ratzinger saw the separation of the primatial and patriarchal competencies of the pope as an important step toward a solution.[321] Even more decisive though, it seems to me, is the later Ratzinger's call for safeguarding episcopal responsibility as personal responsibility so as to serve genuine *communio*.[322]

---

[318] Pottmeyer, *Rolle*, 106.

[319] Cf. ibid. "Anyone who tried to overcome papal centralism by setting up a collegial central organization alongside the pope would only introduce a new and cruder centralism and subject the Church to the logic of modern governmental theories."

[320] "Gottesidee", 46.

[321] Cf. Pottmeyer, *Rolle*, 107: "It is not a question of replacing papal centralism with a collegial centralism, but rather ... of shaping the central legislation and administration in a collegial way and, as far as possible, of minimizing them in favor of regional authorities."

[322] Cf. Pottmeyer, "Weg", 298.

PART THREE

SYNOPSIS AND SUMMARY

Having arrived at the end of my dissertation, I will summarize my findings under three headings, in keeping with the preceding discussion. First I will compare *Lumen gentium* with Ratzinger's main ecclesiological themes, focusing on the overall train of thought in both. Therefore, it is not possible to analyze the individual points again here; instead I will sketch the fundamental agreements and differences between Ratzinger and *Lumen gentium* and give a nuanced answer to the question of continuity or discontinuity in Ratzinger's thinking. This first finding leads to the second point of my summary, in which I will try to show what issues in the intellectual history of the modern era provide the background for Ratzinger's ecclesiological thought. The contours of the subject matter should become clearer against a more comprehensive backdrop. At the same time, mentioning these issues is the prerequisite for a comparison of Ratzinger's ecclesiology with other contemporary outlines—a comparison going beyond the parameters of this summary. The third point, finally, will single out the liturgy as the *locus* and concrete realization of his eucharistic *communio* ecclesiology and thus show the definiteness and the purpose [*Bestimmtheit und Bestimmung*] that belong specifically to Ratzinger's ecclesiology.

1. *Comparison between the main lines of* Lumen gentium *and of Ratzinger's ecclesiology*

a. Preliminary remark: On the compromises in the conciliar documents

Before I compare the main lines of *Lumen gentium* with Ratzinger's ecclesiology, it is crucial to examine the following statement by Ratzinger from the year 1964 concerning the Second Vatican Council's schema on the Church, which at that time had still not been completed:

> To understand the text ... , it may be useful to realize that it was mainly the work of Belgian theologians who belonged to Cardinal Suenens' circle. It reflected their position, midway between Roman and Spanish scholasticism, and the boldly modern writings of

German and French theologians. Like any man-made text, it was
not free of weaknesses and it left room for criticism, particularly in
view of the fact that a Council document is supposed to be for all
future time part of the essential record of the Church.[1]

In this comment, Ratzinger points out the problem—and this is an
initial finding of my investigation—that in reading the conciliar documents, we are constantly dealing with texts that represent compromises.[2] Consequently, and quite logically, in 1964 he says that it would
be unrealistic for "a perfectionist"[3] to expect from these documents
the same uniformity and systematic order as could be found, for example, in the drafts by individual Council theologians or by the groups
associated with them.[4] It seems to him all the more important, then,
for later interpreters "to recognize ... the stated direction that the
Council had in mind as it worked."[5]

The protracted debate about the authentic explanation of the Council sometimes gives the impression, admittedly, that the later Ratzinger identified his own interpretation with the Council's ecclesiology.
Even though a great similarity between the two approaches can be
observed over long stretches, it should not be overlooked[6] that the
text of *Lumen gentium* must be understood as the unification of different ecclesiological approaches that are in tension with each other
and that this fact makes it possible to accentuate different elements in
interpreting the document.

In order to comply in my summary as closely as possible with this
careful attention to the "intended meaning" that Ratzinger called for
during the Council, I will concentrate in the following comparison of
Lumen gentium and Ratzinger's ecclesiology on the statements that he

---

[1] *Highlights*, 44.
[2] On this subject, see also W. Beinert, "Kirchenbilder in der Kirchengeschichte", in *Kirchenbilder, Kirchenvisionen: Variationen über eine Wirklichkeit*, ed. Beinert, 112 (Regens-burg: Pustet, 1995).
[3] *Highlights*, 44.
[4] See the informative chart showing the development of the second schema of *De Eccle-sia* (1963), in Wassilowsky, 369. See also ibid., 401.
[5] *Rückblick*, 25. [Translated directly from the German, since the English translation at *Highlights*, 44, is itself a tendentious reinterpretation of Ratzinger's remark—TRANS.] Cf. *Highlights*, 131.
[6] See Weiler, 344f.

made at the time of the Council on the themes of mystery, the People of God, and collegiality, so as to contrast these, where necessary, with his later deviations.

b. Comparison with regard to "mystery"

In contrast to the first draft of *De Ecclesia* (1962), which in its basic train of thought still bears all the hallmarks of a Neoscholastic ecclesiology of an apologetic cast, *Lumen gentium* gains a brand new *leitmotiv* with its first chapter on the *mysterium* of the Church. Anyone who wants to understand the Constitution on the Church correctly must—as Ratzinger always stresses—begin with its first sentence. He sees the "one-sided"[7] view of the Church's nature up to that time, in its conventional hierarchical-juridical, Counter-Reformation form, being broken open by this christological prelude in favor of a *sacramental* understanding of the Church. For him it is indicative of the Council's program that "the conciliar Constitution [highlights] again the distinctive feature of the 'communion of saints' ",[8] which he understands in the original sense of "the holy gifts, the holy *thing*, granted to the Church in her eucharistic feast by God as the real bond of unity".[9] This centering on the Eucharist—which should be noted carefully as our first point—is a constant characteristic feature in Ratzinger's explanations of the mystery character of the Church, and it is more explicit in his writings than in *Lumen gentium* itself. From his perspective, he interprets the Church's sacramentality in the Augustinian sense, as a sign of God that points beyond itself.[10]

Relying on Augustine's theology, Ratzinger therefore interprets the Church as a sacramental Body of Christ communion. As understood by the Church Fathers, this perspective is for him—in agreement here with *Lumen gentium* 7—a hermeneutic key to understanding *Lumen gentium* in its entirety.[11] The sacramental explanation of the Church as

---

[7] *Highlights*, 45.

[8] "Einleitung", 9.

[9] *Introduction*, 334.

[10] On this subject, see *Highlights*, 48.

[11] Stefano Alberto also comes to this conclusion in his dissertation: *"Corpus Suum mystice constituit" (LG 7): La Chiesa Corpo Mistico di Cristo nel primo capitolo della "Lumen gentium"; Storia del Testo dalla "Mystici corporis" al Vaticano II con riferimenti alla attività del P. Sebastian Tromp S.J.* (Regensburg: Pustet, 1996), esp. 540–44. Alberto underscores the

Corpus Christi overcomes the fixation on an institutional view understood in purely juridical terms, in that it simultaneously testifies to the presence of the Holy Spirit, who does not allow the Church to be utterly absorbed in organizational matters but, rather, causes her to become his organism. In keeping with his Augustinian cast of mind, Ratzinger emphasizes that only the person who abides in the Body of Christ can receive the Spirit of Christ. In this construction of a bridge from the christological to the "pneumatological understanding of the Church", the "earlier Ratzinger" shortly after the Council sees the possibility—second point—of overcoming the corporate rigidity by means of multiple transitions. In the biblical understanding of πνευμα-σωμα [that is, the soul-body unity], he is able to discern "precisely the opposite of corporeality within history":[12] "That could facilitate an initial opening-up of ecclesiology, which, although it quite often starts with questions about the thought of the Eastern Churches, also allows us to take in hand in a new way the problems that arise in the dialogue with the Reformation Christians."[13]

The spirit and body of Christ open up for Ratzinger the trinitarian mystery of the Church's unity, which should be understood universally, in accordance with the conciliar Constitution (*LG* 1–4). Therefore, the universality that makes its appearance in *Lumen gentium* 13–16 from the perspective of creation theology, ecumenism, and interreligious dialogue is supported, in his reading, by the aspect of the totality—the third point of our summary—that runs through all his theological writings. Since the totality of the Church is realized, according to Ratzinger, in every celebration of the Eucharist, he reasons that universality itself has a eucharistic basis also. Ratzinger recognizes in the eucharistic *communio* ecclesiology that was influenced by the Church Fathers the heart of *Lumen gentium* and of his own teaching about the Church as well.

Ratzinger's *communio* ecclesiology, fourth, is in opposition to a functional model of the Church, which endangers the Church's essence as

---

central theological dimension that the image of the Body of Christ has in the ecclesiology of *Lumen gentium*.

[12] J. Ratzinger, "Kirche als Tempel des Heiligen Geistes", in *Mitte*, 152. The citation is from a lecture that Ratzinger had presented in Salzburg in 1967, which was published in 1997 in abridged and slightly revised form (ibid., 148–59).

[13] Ibid., 153.

mysterium in that it brings about a "departure from the metaphysics" of history through the so-called primacy of praxis.[14] That is the real reason why he interpreted the *subsistit* formula (which was not inserted into *Lumen gentium* 8 until 1964) ontologically, especially in the debate with ecclesiological relativism[15] and other sociological models of the Church, without ignoring, however, the Church's relation to history.

This ontological orientation meant for him at the same time— fifth—emphasizing the priority of the universal Church over the local Churches. The accusation of centralism that was leveled against him on that account came to a head in his debate with Walter Kasper and at the same time was clarified somewhat by it, inasmuch as both theologians acknowledged that there was no insurmountable difference in their views. As a matter of principle, they both proceed on the assumption that the Church is not the result of accidental historical developments but, rather, was based from all eternity on the salvific will and soteriological mystery of God. There is evidence for the thesis—as I have explained in this dissertation[16]—that Ratzinger's philosophically reasoned understanding agrees with the intended meaning of the Council Fathers, who testified by means of the *subsistit* formula to the visibility of the one Church in the Catholic Church and interpreted this visibility metaphysically in terms of that concept. Hence the only explanation for Hermann Häring's retort that Ratzinger was contradicting the spirit of the Council and advocating an ideology of uniqueness and universality is the fact that Häring presupposes a different form of the visibility of the one Church from that of the Council Fathers (and of Ratzinger in agreement with them).

Nevertheless, in the writings of the "later Ratzinger"—sixth—we can note a certain contrast with *Lumen gentium* 8; whereas the conciliar document says that even outside the visible confines of the Catholic Church there are "many elements of sanctification and of

---

[14] On this subject, see *Dogma*, 441.

[15] Leonardo Boff should be mentioned as one proponent of such relativism. On this subject, see pt. 2, sec. 2, chap. 1, § 4.4.a, in this dissertation, "The Difference between *Subsistit* and *Est*".

[16] Ibid.

truth" which, as "gifts belonging to the Church of Christ ... are forces impelling toward catholic unity", Ratzinger diminishes the originally positive import of this ecumenical statement by immediately mentioning misgivings.[17] The reason behind the change in his attitude since the time of the Council was his experience that—contrary to the intended meaning of *Lumen gentium*—the concept of subsistence was used as a pretext for that ecclesiological relativism which, in Ratzinger's view, causes its proponents to lose sight of the question of truth.

c. Comparison with regard to the "People of God"

In contrast to the term "mystery", the concept of the "People of God" received the most attention in the postconciliar period. In effect, it replaced the image of the Body of Christ, which had been heavily emphasized during the reign of Pope Pius XII, and it simultaneously became an ecumenical bridge. In using this expression, *Lumen gentium* meant to make clear the intrinsic continuity in salvation history between the first Chosen People, Israel, and the Church. Moreover, it was possible to understand the Church as the pilgrim People of God, whose eschatological perfection is yet to come. What was new about this concept was the fact that it formed a model of the Church that initially declares the true equality of all members of this people, before making any differentiation among them (*LG* 32).

Even though Ratzinger agrees with these connotations of the People of God concept in *Lumen gentium*, it is striking—and this is the first point to note in this subsection—that he rather infrequently[18] or only indirectly articulates another important aspect, namely, the participation of all the baptized in the priestly, prophetic, and kingly mission of Jesus (*LG* 10–13). To the extent that he addresses this issue, his focus is mainly on *participatio actuosa*,[19] which "again brings to light

---

[17] See Ratzinger, "Presentation of the Declaration *Dominus Iesus* in the Press Conference Room of the Holy See, on September 5, 2000", in *Pilgrim Fellowship*, 209–16, esp. 213f. Even though Ratzinger speaks here about seeds of truth, he refers in the same breath to the "errors and illusions" in other religions.

[18] Ratzinger outlines this universal vocation in only three sentences in "Einleitung", 12. He describes the "universal priesthood" in terms of the "particular priesthood" in *Called to Communion*, 125–28.

[19] Cf. *SC* 14, 30, 48, 50, 114; *GE* 4.

the universal call and empowerment to the service of worship, as opposed to false clericalization".[20]

Secondly, the dignity of the laity (LG 30–38), which was formulated for the first time by Vatican II,[21] is emphasized by Ratzinger especially in terms of their missionary responsibility for the world,[22] and, in accordance with chapter 5 of *Lumen gentium* (LG 39–42), he connects this with the aspect of striving for holiness.

Thus for him, thirdly, it is decisive—in keeping with chapter 7 of the Constitution on the Church (LG 48–51)—that the eschatological hope of the People of God represents, not a this-worldly utopia, but rather a God-given goal that must be preceded by the gathering and purification of the people, since it is the Church's lot on her pilgrimage always to experience "weakness and sin", and she therefore needs "God's forgiving kindness".[23] Her destination is Jesus Christ, who is at the same time the origin of this people. This emphasis of Ratzinger's is aimed—usually in generalized terms— against political theologies, especially against the tenets of liberation theology.

Ratzinger's salvation-history approach—a *leitmotiv* that runs through all of his theology—expresses, fourth, the unity of the two Testaments. For this reason, the biblical understanding of the People of God concept is crucial for him, as it is in *Lumen gentium*, and he contrasts it with political reinterpretations that flatten the notion. The later Ratzinger mentions relativism as the implicit reason for

---

[20] *Volk Gottes*, 118. Compare *Spirit of the Liturgy*, 171–77, esp. 175: "If the various external actions (as a matter of fact, there are not very many of them, though they are being artificially multiplied) become the essential in the liturgy, if the liturgy degenerates into general activity, then we have radically misunderstood the 'theo-drama' of the liturgy and lapsed almost into parody.... True liturgical education cannot consist in learning and experimenting with external activities. Instead one must be led toward the essential *actio* that makes the liturgy what it is, toward the transforming power of God, who wants, through what happens in the liturgy, to transform us and the world. In this respect, liturgical education today, of both priests and laity, is deficient to a deplorable extent."

[21] Cf. also the Decree on the Lay Apostolate (*AA*).

[22] On this subject, see J. Ratzinger, "Konzilsaussagen über die Mission außerhalb des Missionsdekretes", in *Das neue Volk Gottes: Entwürfe zur Ekklesiologie* (Düsseldorf: Patmos-Verlag, 1969), 376–403, esp. 388. This essay was not incorporated in the later paperback edition (*Volk Gottes*).

[23] *Highlights*, 47.

this distortion and notes that, as the prevailing philosophy of the postmodern era, it has become "the central problem for faith".[24] He describes a relativistic dialectic that assumes that Jesus himself did not intend to found a new People of God and that therefore the plurality of Churches is historically justifiable; in Ratzinger's judgment, such a dialectic treats the divisions among the Churches as harmless and reduces to nonsense the necessary search for the unity demanded by the gospel.

In connection with the political transformation of the "People of God" concept, we note as the fifth point of this summary that Ratzinger considers the principle of majority rule in secular democracies to be a valuable instrument, which can be applied only conditionally, however, to ecclesial praxis, because the faith is always a prior given, the truth of which is independent of majority decisions. One very important reason for this is that political systems can be particularly susceptible to developing "sick majorities".[25] Therefore, according to Ratzinger, the primacy of orthodoxy over orthopraxis always holds true for the People of God.

In much the same way as with the *mysterium* of the Church, the original "salvation history" accentuation of the People of God concept is, sixth, turned into a metaphysical orientation of ecclesiology, in contrast with the perspective of *Lumen gentium*. Ratzinger himself called attention to this change in 1982, when he said in reference to one of his essays[26] from the early postconciliar period:

> In view of the fundamental meaning of this "is", I would stress more strongly today than I have in these pages the irreplaceability and preeminence of the ontological aspect and, therefore, of metaphysics as the basis of any history.... The fact that the first article of faith forms the basis of all Christian belief includes, theologically, the basic character of the ontological statements and the

---

[24] "New Questions", 117.

[25] Ratzinger, "Glauben im Kontext heutiger Philosophie: Ein Gespräch mit dem Philosophen Vittorio Possenti", *IKaZ* 31 (2002): 266–73, citation at 270.

[26] Ratzinger, "Heilsgeschichte und Eschatologie: Zur Frage nach dem Ansatz des theologischen Denkens", in *Theologie im Wandel: Festschrift zum 150-jährigen Bestehen der Katholisch-Theologischen Fakultät an der Universität Tübingen, 1817–1967*, ed. J. Neumann and J. Ratzinger, 68–89 (Munich and Freiburg im Breisgau: Wewel, 1967).

indispensability of the metaphysical, that is, of the Creator God who
is before all becoming.[27]

Ratzinger derives this priority of the ontological, first, from patristic
theology, which saw creation as having an inner teleology leading to the
Church, since God has only one will and one salvific plan, and, second,
from the rabbinical teaching about the preexistence of the Torah and of
Israel, which the Fathers applied to the Church, and finally—connected
with this—with respect to creation theology from the rabbinical conviction that creation is for the sake of divine worship, in that it tends
toward the Sabbath. Ratzinger sees the last-mentioned argument for his
ontological preference confirmed also by comparisons with other religions, because it becomes evident in them as a unifying element that not
only Christianity and Judaism but also other religions acknowledge that
the reason and purpose for creation is the glorification of God.

d. Comparison with regard to "collegiality"

As in the two preceding points of comparison, Ratzinger's ontological
preference—this should be noted as an important finding—also plays
an important role in his characterization of the Church's collegial structure. This is evident in his emphasis on the universal Church over the
local or particular Churches. His reasoning for this priority is trinitarian (he cites *LG* 1–3) and also biblical, based on the concept of the
kingdom of God (*LG* 5), and finally sacramental as well. When we
contrast the later Ratzinger with the stated direction of the earlier
Council theologian, it is easy to distinguish his comments then about
the relation between primacy and collegiality from those in his recent
writings, for instance, concerning the separation of the three offices of
the pope as successor of Peter, patriarch of the West, and finally as
bishop of Rome, or concerning the theological status of the synod of
bishops or of bishops' conferences. With regard to the latter, he even
departs from *Lumen gentium*. For that document, reflecting his influence back then,[28] used language to the effect that "the episcopal bodies of today" (*LG* 23), much like the ancient patriarchal Churches,

---

[27] *Principles*, 171–190, citation at 190, n. 172. On this subject, compare Ratzinger, *The God of Jesus Christ: Meditations on God in the Trinity*, trans. Robert J. Cunningham (Chi-cago: Franciscan Herald Press, 1978), 20–21 and 30–41.
[28] "Formen", 155–59, esp. 159.

could be a concrete way of witnessing today to the collegial structure of the Church.

Article 23 of *Lumen gentium* is of decisive importance for episcopal collegiality in order to express the multiplicity and universality of the Church. In this article, textbook examples of Ratzinger's two ecclesiological approaches are found side by side, which once again makes it clear that various ecclesiologies are interwoven in the Constitution on the Church yet remain in tension with one another. Besides the enhanced status of the bishops' conferences just mentioned, one finds also in *Lumen gentium* 23 the core statement in support of the collegial approach, to wit, that the one and unique Catholic Church exists and is formed out of the particular Churches. Two other sentences from *Lumen gentium* 23 seem to me, however, to support the later Ratzinger's view that focuses on the universal Church and the individual bishop, namely:

> The individual bishops ... are the visible principle and foundation of unity in their particular churches, fashioned after the model of the universal Church....
>
> By governing well their own church as a portion of the universal Church, they themselves are effectively contributing to the welfare of the whole Mystical Body, which is also the body of the churches.

These two quotations articulate Ratzinger's present concerns, first, that episcopal responsibility cannot be delegated but must be exercised personally and, second, that the office of bishop, like that of the apostle, has a universal structure.

Does the later Ratzinger contradict the earlier theologian by such a shift of emphases? The answer that my dissertation gives to this question is nuanced. On the one hand, as a result of his eucharistic ecclesiology in an Augustinian mold, Ratzinger consistently adheres to the early Christian *communio* structure of the Church and furthermore recognizes in it an ecumenical opportunity for dialogue with the Orthodox Churches. On the other hand, he derives from this eucharistic approach the universal structure of the Church as a whole[29] and thus

---

[29] On this subject, see *Called to Communion*, 83–94, where Ratzinger focuses especially on the individual apostle's responsibility for the universal Church, a responsibility that is carried over to the individual bishop, who is himself "the ligature of catholicity" (ibid., 88).

at the same time her ontological priority. He is constant in maintaining that the "Totally Other" appears among us in the Church's intimate sacramental relation with her Founder—as the last point of my dissertation will demonstrate.

Summarizing what has been said thus far, we can say that Ratzinger's tendency today has changed and gives preference in the aforementioned points to the primatial approach in *Lumen gentium* over the collegial approach. The following subsection on the historical and theological context of Ratzinger's work will clarify why this preference developed.

2. Ratzinger's ecclesiology against the background of issues in intellectual history

No serious survey of Ratzinger's ecclesiology can ignore the historical theological background in response to which his theology takes on its own contours. In his life in the Church, Ratzinger directly confronted the tensions of the controversies that broke out in the wake of Vatican II and made it clear that the Church herself is going through a time of transition. Concretely this means that we must inquire into the central issues of intellectual history that, on the one hand, informed this ecclesial assembly and, on the other hand, had an important influence on Ratzinger's reception of the Council. This topic would provide ample material for further monographs on what can be indicated only in outline form in my summary.

At the outset of this discussion, I want to mention, first, as a premise, one of the results of my dissertation thus far: The Second Vatican Council is—as Wolfgang Beinert says—"neither the beginning nor the end; it is, rather, a milestone that concludes one stretch of the Church's journey through time and at the same moment opens up a new one." [30] That also means, however, that the Council itself is not a completely new beginning; rather, in it and through it several basic philosophical and theological trends are manifested that form the background for my remarks about Ratzinger's ecclesiology.

---

[30] W. Beinert, "Grundströmungen heutiger Theologie", in *Tendenzen der katholischen Theologie nach dem Zweiten Vatikanischen Konzil*, ed. G. Kaufmann, 9–23, citation at 9 (Munich: Kösel, 1979).

This theological-historical outline, secondly, cannot comment on the entire spectrum of the postconciliar intellectual debates and is restricted geographically to Europe first and foremost.[31] This is not to subscribe to a Eurocentrism that at the time of the Council was still deeply rooted in the Church and in society. My purpose, rather, is to examine more closely the interwoven strands of the discussion in which Ratzinger himself has taken part.

a. The paradigm of historical thinking

The most telling feature in the intellectual-historical context of Ratzinger's theology is the challenge of a changed historical consciousness; it is impossible to imagine scholarly debates since the nineteenth century without historical criticism. Instead of "the Scholastic equation *verum est ens* (being is truth)", a new formula was advanced: "*verum quia factum*. That is to say, all that we can truly know is what we have made ourselves."[32] This change in attitude toward the truth, according to Ratzinger, is symptomatic of the modern mind, which thereby rejects the metaphysical approach.

This thesis of Ratzinger from the year 1968, which shapes his entire theology, especially his ecclesiology, brings us face to face with the question (left unanswered by the Council) of the relation between "historical research and dogmatic tradition".[33] In 1976, Ratzinger declared this to be the real problem of contemporary theology, exemplified by the writings of Hans Küng.[34] In entering this controversy,

---

[31] Cf. ibid., 10. An analysis of the postconciliar development that likewise concentrates on the European scene is provided by G. Alberigo, "Das II. Vatikanum und der kulturelle Wandel in Europa", German trans. by Sigrid Müller, in *Das II. Vatikanum—christlicher Glaube im Horizont globaler Modernisierung: Einleitungsfragen*, ed. P. Hünermann, 139–57 (Paderborn: Schöningh, 1998). An approach in terms of the history of theology can be found in G. Ruggieri, "Zu einer Hermeneutik des Zweiten Vatikanischen Konzils", *Conc(D)* 35 (1999): 4–17. See also K. Rahner, "Theologische Grundinterpretationen des II. Vatikanischen Konzils", in *Schriften zur Theologie*, vol. 14 (Einsiedeln, Zürich, and Cologne: Benziger, 1980), 287–302.

[32] *Introduction*, 59. Ratzinger quotes here the Italian philosopher Giambattista Vico (1688–1744), "who was almost certainly the first to formulate a completely new idea of truth and knowledge" (ibid.).

[33] Ratzinger, "Einleitung zur Dogmatischen Konstitution über die göttliche Offenbarung", in *LThK.E*, vol. 2 (Freiburg am Breisgau: Herder, 1967), 498–503, citation at 499.

[34] On this subject, see his controversy with Hans Küng in J. Ratzinger, "Wer verantwortet die Aussagen der Theologie? Zur Methodenfrage", in *Diskussion über Hans Küngs*

his goal is, not the wholesale rejection of the historical-critical method[35] in theology, but rather the drawing of boundaries between what it can and cannot accomplish. Therefore, this kind of research is determined "in a theologically legitimate way by the Christian concept of God, which is shaped by the idea of the Incarnation".[36] On the other hand, though, theology cannot be reduced to "the 'historical' in the strict sense of the word", since this, according Ratzinger, represents a restriction of the investigation "to the phenomenon (the demonstrable)".[37] He regards such a positivistic reduction as one consequence of Kantian philosophy and also of the Enlightenment, both of which arrive at their judgments according to the maxim: "Reason cannot answer the question 'What is it?' but only the question 'How does it function?'"[38]

Such an axiom implies a profound breach with the ontological approach of metaphysics, which defined philosophy from antiquity until the beginning of the modern period. After this rupture, the question about being is replaced, in keeping with the rules of the natural sciences, by the question of becoming, of how a thing came to be that way.[39] This departure from metaphysics is evident especially in the philosophy of Hegel (1770–1831), since in his intellectual approach being and time are interwoven: "Being itself now is regarded as time; the logos becomes itself in history. It cannot be assigned, therefore, to

---

"Christ sein", by H. U. von Balthasar et al., 7–18, esp. 16 (Mainz: Matthias-Grünewald-Verlag, 1976), where Ratzinger writes: "The specific note of Küng's thought is that, with his book on infallibility, he has decided as a matter of principle that that dogma is not a permanently binding statement, and hence theological studies cannot be pursued at all in terms of that dogma or of the Church's community of believers. But what has become a matter of principle in Küng's writings is, practically speaking, widely prevalent in other theological circles as well—not due to ill will on the part of its proponents, but rather because the methodological problem has not been clarified."

[35] Cf. Ratzinger, "Schriftauslegung im Widerstreit: Zur Frage nach Grundlagen und Weg der Exegese heute", in Schriftauslegung im Widerstreit, ed. Ratzinger, 15–44, esp. 21–24, QD 117 (Freiburg im Breisgau: Herder, 1989).

[36] "Einleitung zur Dogmatischen Konstitution über die göttliche Offenbarung", in LThK.E 2:499.

[37] Introduction, 197.

[38] Kaes, 115. See also Church, 152–64, esp. 154f.

[39] Cf. Ratzinger, "Zur Frage nach der Geschichtlichkeit der Dogmen", in Martyria, Leiturgia, Diakonia: Festschrift für Hermann Volk zum 65. Geburtstag, ed. O. Semmelroth, 59–70, esp. 62 (Mainz: Matthias-Grünwald-Verlag, 1968).

any particular point in history or be viewed as something existing in itself outside of history." [40]

This means, according to Ratzinger, that the truth becomes "a function of time"; that is, "the true is not that which simply is true, for truth is not simply that which is; it is true for a time because it is part of the becoming of truth, which *is* by becoming." [41] For Ratzinger, however, truth is always something that outlasts the ages, independently of our limited capacity to know. [42]

If truth is only a truth adapted to the given historical moment, then there is no room in this deistic mind-set for the intervention of the Totally Other into history. [43] In contrast, this inquiry about the personal God, who even became flesh in order to be close to mankind, is the constant and abiding theme in Ratzinger's approach. Starting from that, the Christ-event is established within the coordinates of history through revelation and, finally, through the tradition of the truth that is Christ. Nevertheless, the truth remains at the same time above us

[40] *Principles*, 15–27, citation at 16. Cf. P. Hünermann, "Zu den Kategorien 'Konzil' und 'Konzilsentscheidung'", in Hünermann, *II. Vatikanum*, 67–81, esp. 75. According to Hünermann, Hegel's solution of mediating between being and time "by a dialectic totality" does not bear closer inspection, because reality proves to be "more multifarious and complex, indeed, more mysterious" than that. Hünermann cites Hans-Georg Gadamer, who, "for all his emphasis on tradition, points out how the history of [the] influence [of an idea or a philosophy] occurs through a continual series of new intellectual productions and not simply through transmission. Finally, Richard Schaeffler has demonstrated in a transcendental reflection on how experience in every case is mediated through and in the midst of what is unexplained and incomprehensible.... In reference to theology's understanding of tradition, this means that the sameness of the faith is mediated precisely by ever-new explanations of the faith, in such a way that the innovations that follow from the potential of tradition are in turn establishing continuity. The testing [*Bewährung*, as opposed to the preservation, *Bewahrung*] of the faith tradition in the explanation thus has the character of a validation [*Wahr-Machens*], of a making-permanent [*Be-währens*]" (ibid.). For Hünermann, the reception [of the contents of tradition] has such great importance that the validity of the Council's instruction is dependent on its probation [and acceptance]. But should there not also be a truth that is independent of the reception of the moment? And which *sensus fidelium* decides a question? The sense of the faith of the Christian faithful, understood synchronically, or diachronically in view of the saints of all times? For Ratzinger, as a matter of principle, universality is both "synchronic and diachronic: it unites men and cultures of all places and of all times. It is a force for unity in a world threatened by particular ideologies and allegiances." See Ratzinger, "Glauben im Kontext", 269.
[41] Ibid.
[42] Cf. Kaes, 65–67.
[43] On this subject, see Ratzinger, "Schriftauslegung", 16.

by dint of the *extra nos* of what is sacramental, which we ourselves have not made. Therefore, it can never be exhaustively defined within time.

From this we can conclude that historical thinking in Ratzinger's work does not contradict ontological thinking. Having recognized this, we can conclude with Dorothee Kaes:

> If in all the diversity there were no unity, one could not honestly speak about history at all. The only thing left would be chronology— the past event reduced to a fact that can be verified and documented yet eludes the question about the meaning that lies in the event but simultaneously transcends it. Against this background, an understanding of history of the sort found in the writings of R. Bultmann (1884–1976) or of proponents of political theology is rejected. For they understand history as an ever newly occurring Logos event or else exclusively as the future, whereby the past is devalued and is turned into a theological neutral entity.[44]

In keeping with the tradition of the Tübingen school,[45] Ratzinger tries to respond to the challenge of this historical paradigm bearing the stamp of German Idealism by means of "a new approach to history as the locus of God's self-revelation";[46] he understands history itself as an organic whole, as salvation history, which is intrinsically characterized by the ontological priority of the universal as the expression of the True. This means that theology has to take as its hermeneutic point of departure "the question about the unity of truth in the variety of its historical transmissions".[47] From this develops, in Ratzinger's writings, a synthesis of reflection on salvation history and speculative thinking—a characteristic of the Tübingen school—which, as a result of its confrontation with the primacy of

---

[44] Kaes, 85.

[45] In the present context, we should mention in particular F. A. Staudenmaier (1800–1856) and H. Schnell (1850–1906) as representatives of this school.

[46] Kaes, 222.

[47] Ibid., 72. For Ratzinger, what is at stake here is ultimately a christological problem, which is why he understands Christ as "the true center and the turning-point of history" (*Theology of History*, 118), as Bonaventure does. Bonaventure regards time as the time of salvation with "two corresponding movements ... *egressus* and *regressus*. Christ stands at the turning point of these movements and as the center who both divides and unites" (ibid., 142–43).

orthopraxis[48] advocated by political theologies and with theological and ecclesiological relativism (for example, in his debate with Leonardo Boff), led to a preference for the metaphysical approach.

In these controversies, Ratzinger is concerned above all with the intrinsic reasonableness of Christianity, which abolishes the division between *ratio* and *religio*, not by postulating "the ideal of 'religion within the limits of mere reason'",[49] in the spirit of the Enlightenment, but rather by the fact that Christianity itself, through the Divine Logos, further extends the radius of human reason.[50] Through Logos-oriented faith, *ratio* itself can be restored to health, since one important function of faith, according to Ratzinger, is that it offers "healing for the reason as reason, not to overpower it or to remain outside it, but in fact to bring it to itself again".[51]

b. Harking back to patristic theology

Ratzinger's shift of emphasis toward the metaphysical approach of Scholasticism should be understood along the lines of two theologians from Tübingen, Johann Adam Möhler (1796–1838) and Matthias Joseph

---

[48] Cf. Beinert, "Grundströmungen heutiger Theologie", 9–23, esp. 14, where Beinert sees a root cause of the primacy of orthopraxis in the fact that the experience of World War II had given "priority to ethical-practical problems over systematic-theoretical considerations".

[49] J. Ratzinger, "Gefährliche Spaltung", *Rheinischer Merkur*, no. 6 (February 6, 1998): 25.

[50] Ratzinger is of the opinion ("New Questions", 136) that "the neoscholastic rationalism that was trying to reconstruct the *praeambula fidei*, the approach to faith, with pure rational certainty, by means of rational argument that was strictly independent of any faith, has failed.... In that sense, Karl Barth was right when he rejected philosophy as a basis for faith that is independent of faith itself: for in that case, our faith would in the end be based on changing philosophical theories. Yet Barth was mistaken in declaring faith on that account to be a sheer paradox, which can only ever exist contrary to reason and quite independent of it." Cf. Ratzinger, "Gefährliche Spaltung", 26, where Ratzinger alludes to Schleiermacher's view that religion is a matter of feelings: "When man ... can no longer inquire rationally about where he came from and where he is going, about what he should and may do, about life and death, but rather must leave these crucial problems to a feeling that is detached from reason, then he does not exalt reason but dishonors it. The disintegration that is thereby set in motion gives rise to the pathology of religion and to the pathology of science as well. It is obvious today that the separation of religion from responsibility to reason is resulting increasingly in pathological forms of religion." See also Ratzinger, "Das Christentum wollte immer mehr sein als nur Tradition: Die Kirche muss den Glauben vernünftig machen, damit er an den Enden der Erde verstanden werden kann: Ein Gespräch mit Joseph Kardinal Ratzinger", *FAZ*, no. 57 (March 8, 2000): 52.

[51] "New Questions", 136.

Scheeben (1835–1888); both of them restated in a new way the sacramental view of the Church in the writings of the Latin and Greek
Fathers of the Church. Möhler sees the Church as an *incarnatio continua*, by way of analogy with the Incarnation of the Divine Logos.[52]
Scheeben, too, adopted this incarnational idea and, despite his more
pronounced speculative tendency, maintains the reference to history,
inasmuch as he "adopts the Augustinian and Alexandrinian heritage
and places at the center of his reflections the notion of man restored
to grace as the image of the intratrinitarian life".[53] The works of
E. Mersch[54] and S. Tromp,[55] who upon the patristic foundation developed the ecclesiological image of the Body of Christ, also had a lasting impression on Ratzinger.

This line of thought from patristic theology is also continued by
Yves Congar, Henri de Lubac, and his "pupil" Hans Urs von Balthasar. In it the reductively historical understanding of the nineteenth
century is opened out, in that history is once again understood as
salvation history, at the center of which stands the Cross.[56] Among
Lutherans, Oscar Cullmann represents a similar salvation-history
approach, in that he depicts the eschatological tension between the
"already" and the "not yet".[57] Ratzinger was impressed by these
theologians, also and above all by his teacher Gottlieb Söhngen. The

---

[52] Cf. R. G. Geiselmann, ed., *J. A. Möhler: Symbolik* (Cologne: Hegner, 1960), 632f.

[53] Kaes, 222.

[54] Cf. E. Mersch, *Le Corps mystique du Christ: Études de théologie historique*, 2 vols. (Louvain: Museum Lessianum, 1933).

[55] Cf. S. Tromp, *Corpus Christi, quod est Ecclesia*, 3 vols. (Rome, 1937–1960). The Jesuit
Sebastian Tromp was the principal author of the encyclical *Mystici Corporis* of Pope Pius
XII and of the first draft of *De Ecclesia* (1962).

[56] On this subject, see H. U. von Balthasar, *Das Ganze im Fragment: Aspekte der Geschichtstheologie* (Einsiedeln: Johannes Verlag, 1963), 352. See also K. J. Wallner, *Gott als Eschaton:
Trinitarische Dramatik als Voraussetzung göttlicher Universalität bei Hans Urs von Balthasar* (Heiligenkreuz: Verein der Heiligenkreuzer Hochschulfreunde, 1992), 348f. and 366–73.

[57] On this subject, see Kaes, 223. Concerning Cullmann, see also Avery Dulles, S.J.,
Revelation Theology: A History (New York: Herder and Herder, 1969), 123–125, esp. 124,
where Dulles writes: "Cullmann ... holds that the Biblical revelation has as its primary
theme God's redemptive action in history.... In focussing on redemptive history as the
chief content of revelation, Cullmann opposes the Rationalists, who conceive of revelation
as timeless truth; the Barthians, who take refuge in primal history or meta-history (*Urge-
schichte* and *Übergeschichte*); and the Bultmannians, who tend to separate faith from belief in
past historical occurrences."

last-mentioned theologian—by way of controversy with M. D. Koster[58] over the term "People of God"—led his student to Augustine and eventually inspired him with enthusiasm for Bonaventure's theology of history. This approach had a decisive influence both on Ratzinger's eschatology and on his understanding of revelation, which includes ecclesial reception as an essential feature.[59]

c. Ecumenical perspective

Patristic theology was an important formative influence on Ratzinger's ecumenical consciousness as well. His thesis, that unity between the Roman Catholic Church and the Orthodox Churches could be restored through reflection on the heritage of the first Christian millennium, became the paradigm especially for *rapprochement* with Eastern Christianity. Ratzinger is intent on countering a "denominationalism of division" with a "hermeneutic of unification".[60]

However, once an incorrectly understood "ecumenism of consensus" had led to the alternative of a praxeological priority, the standard of truth was no longer considered relevant and praxis itself became the hermeneutic of unity. Thereby—in Ratzinger's judgment—all ecumenism is dissolved along with ecclesiology itself, whereas he abides by the axiom that the truth of the faith is not something that can be made relative.

> The belief that there is indeed truth, valid and binding truth, within history itself, in the figure of Jesus Christ and in the faith of the Church, is referred to as fundamentalism, which appears as the real assault upon the spirit of the modern age and, manifested in many forms, as the fundamental threat to the highest good of that age, freedom and tolerance.[61]

Unlike the proponents of "consensus ecumenism", Ratzinger is concerned about finding the common center and what unites the various

---

[58] M. D. Koster, *Ekklesiologie im Werden* (Paderborn: Bonifacius-Druckerei, 1940). This work was reprinted in the anthology of Koster's essays compiled by H.-D. Langer and O. H. Pesch and published under the title *Volk Gottes im Werden* (Mainz: Matthias-Grünewald-Verlag, 1971).

[59] Cf. *Milestones*, 127.

[60] Stephan O. Horn, "II. Ökumenische Dimensionen—Einführung", in *Mitte*, 175–80, citation at 178.

[61] "New Questions", 120.

Christian denominations by means of purification and renewal. In the hermeneutic of unity that he calls for, there is an increased effort to read "the statements of both parties in the context of the whole tradition and with a deeper understanding of scripture".[62] In this search for unity among the Churches, the question should be asked to what extent "decisions [made] since the separation have been stamped with a certain particularisation both as to language and thought—something that might well be transcended without doing violence to the content of the statements."[63] According to Ratzinger, the splendor that is proper to truth must be allowed to shine, so that truth is not confused with useful customs; Tertullian warned about this when he said, "Christ did not call himself the Custom, but rather the truth (*Virg.* 1, 1)."[64] God himself—and this is Ratzinger's hope—can awaken faith "in such a way that it overflows from one to the other, and the one Church is there."[65] Ratzinger is persuaded that "the basic shape of this one Church is given us in the Catholic Church." She, too, is called to turn to the Lord. For this reason, Ratzinger advocates, not an ecumenism of annexation, but rather an onward "march . . . in faith under the leadership of the Lord".

3. Liturgy as a topic for theological ecclesiology

The Church as a divine institution with human features is not primarily subject to the law of human feasibility; rather, first and foremost she is defined sacramentally; that is, she grows by means of the Word of God that has been spoken into history as well as through the efficacy of the liturgy, which together "afford a transparent view of the salvific work of Jesus Christ and thus allow the eternal to shine through into the temporal; indeed, they allow it to become present as

---

[62] *Church*, 65–88, citation at 82.

[63] Ibid.

[64] Ratzinger, "Glauben im Kontext", 272. See Tertullian, *Virg.* 1, 1, in CSEL 76, 79; CCL 2, 1209. On this subject, see also J. Ratzinger, "Christentum wollte", 52. Here Ratzinger broadens the ecumenical aspect to include all mankind by pointing out that the Christian faith has an inner dynamic that not only hands down culture and traditions but also "can address a universal human expectation, a common capacity for perception that then feels that it has really been understood and thereby bursts into bloom, so to speak, and opens up into Christ and thus helps mankind arrive at an interior unity."

[65] *God and the World*, 452. The following two quotations are found in the same paragraph, 452–53.

III Synopsis and Summary

the genuinely productive reality."[66] This statement by Ratzinger—made in 1966, immediately after the Council—can be understood at the same time as a synthesis of his ecclesiology, corresponding to the theological axiom *lex orandi—lex credendi*. It is true, according to this rule, that the Church, which by her very nature is constituted by the Eucharist, must recognize God's primacy as her *extra nos*, on which she lives. For Ratzinger, the liturgy is "the worship of an open heaven".[67] The universality of the liturgy is based on its openness toward God and is concentrated in the self-giving love of the crucified and risen Christ. He is the new and universal temple, "whose outstretched arms on the Cross span the world, in order to draw all men into the embrace of eternal love".[68] In the years following the Council, Ratzinger says, these biblically founded and sacramentally based ecclesiological formulas for identifying the Church were trivialized and to some extent replaced with meaningless interpretations of the concept Church.[69]

a. The demand that liturgy be "consistent with being"[70]

One of Ratzinger's fundamental concerns is that the liturgy become "more substantial" [*wesentlicher*], in the sense in which Romano Guardini used the expression, which is to say that it should be understood in terms of "its inner demands and form—as the prayer of the Church, a prayer moved and guided by the Holy Spirit himself, a prayer in which Christ unceasingly becomes contemporary with us, enters into our lives".[71] Thereby, in Ratzinger's view, the liturgy becomes the existential expression of the Church, to which the personal, what is one's own, has to surrender. Along this same line of thought, he quotes a passage from Guardini that brings into sharp focus and expresses his own understanding of Church and of the experience of being struck by the truth she conveys:

---

[66] Ratzinger, *Der sakramentale Begründung christlicher Existenz*, 2nd ed. (Meitingen and Freising: Kyrios-Verlag, 1967), 16.

[67] *Spirit of the Liturgy*, 49.

[68] Ibid., 48.

[69] On this subject, see J. Ratzinger and K. Lehmann, *Living with the Church*, trans. Zachary Hayes, O.F.M. (Chicago: Francisco Herald Press, 1978), 16–20.

[70] "Liturgie", 135.

[71] *Spirit of the Liturgy*, 7.

Therefore there must be an objective tribunal that can retrieve my answer from every nook where self-assertion might hide. But there is only one such tribunal: the Catholic Church in her authority and precision. The question of keeping or surrendering the soul is decided ultimately, not in the presence of God, but in the presence of the Church.[72]

Following Guardini, Ratzinger is concerned about turning to the truth itself, that is, about a metaphysical approach to thinking, in which the liturgy is "the call of the substance, the path to the truth, because it corresponds to being" and not merely "aesthetic game-playing or a sort of communal self-affirmation or pragmatic indoctrination".[73] Therefore he speaks, together with Romans 12:1, about a "worship characterized by logos",[74] a λογικη λατρεια. He interprets this expression in terms of the theology of the cross and at the same time eucharistically:

The Logos, who is the Son, makes us sons in the sacramental fellowship in which we are living. And if we become sacrifices, if we ourselves become conformed to the Logos, then this is not a process confined to the spirit, which leaves the body behind it as something distanced from God. The Logos himself has become a body and gives himself to us in his Body. That is why we are being urged to present our bodies as a form of worship consistent with the Logos, that is to say, to be drawn into the fellowship of love with God in our entire bodily existence, in bodily fellowship with Christ.[75]

---

[72] R. Guardini, *Berichte über mein Leben* (Düsseldorf: Patmos, 1984), 72. Cf. ibid.: "Then it seemed to me as if I were carrying everything in my hands—really 'everything', my whole life—as though in a balanced scale: 'I can let it tilt to the right or to the left. I can surrender my soul or keep it. . . .' And then I let the scale tilt toward the right." Cf. "Liturgie", 123.

[73] "Liturgie", 135. Ratzinger sees this intellectual approach as the "breakthrough out of the Kantian perspective" (ibid., 134) that had first been accomplished by Edmund Husserl and his circle of phenomenologists. On Kant, see Dulles, *Revelation Theology*, 58. Kant presupposes that pure reason cannot prove "the existence of transcendent realities". The "ideas of pure speculative reason, such as soul, freedom, and God" are "unverifiable", and yet as such they form "the indispensable basis of morality and religion" (ibid.). The true Church, for Kant, is "not the external one but the internal one—and it is confined to the rational union of morally upright wills" (ibid.).

[74] J. Ratzinger, "Eucharist and Mission", in *Pilgrim Fellowship*, 90–122, ref. at 114–18; citation at 115.

[75] Ibid., 117. On this subject, see also *Spirit of the Liturgy*, 45–48, esp. 46f., where Ratzinger, refuting Gnostic interpretations that leave the body behind as though it were something insubstantial, points out that the Christian idea of the Logos sacrifice "becomes a full

Thereby—as Ratzinger puts it, echoing Augustine—a "metamorphosis" is accomplished through which we are taken "beyond this world's scheme of things, beyond sharing in what 'people' think and say and do", and are reshaped "into union with the will of God".[76] This "will of God is truth, and entering into it is thus breaking out into freedom."[77] Hence Ratzinger interprets unity in the Church as unity in the Body of the one living Christ.

As a necessary consequence of this openness to Logos-Being, Ratzinger acknowledges revealed truth, "God's *prius*" [that is, the fact that God is prior to everything], as a fundamental category of his own thinking, as opposed to praxeological approaches. For him worship is derived from the objective claim of the truth that is to be perceived.[78] Thus the very worship of God becomes the "heart of our perception and acceptance of the truth", and that in turn means, according to Ratzinger, "the precedence of Logos before ethos, of being before doing".[79]

b. Liturgy as an expression of the "universal"

In Ratzinger's view, there is nothing theoretical about the truth that takes place in the liturgy; rather, it is revealed—to borrow a phrase from Guardini—in "what is living and concrete",[80] namely, in the Person of Jesus Christ, in his death and Resurrection, which are present

---

reality only in the *Logos incarnatus*, the Word who is made flesh and draws 'all flesh' into the glorification of God" (ibid., 47). Ratzinger recognizes that Logos here does not mean simply "the 'Meaning' behind and above things" in the Hellenistic sense. Furthermore, the Logos is not merely "the representation of something else, of what is bodily"; rather, "in Jesus' self-surrender on the Cross, the Word is united with the entire reality of human life and suffering." Then, too, the worship of God is no longer exclusively spiritual, as it was during Israel's time of exile (Ps 51[50]); rather, "the vicarious sacrifice of Jesus takes us up and leads us into that likeness with God, that transformation into love, which is the only true adoration." From these remarks Ratzinger concludes that "the Eucharist is the meeting point of all the lines that lead from the Old Covenant, indeed from the whole of man's religious history."

[76] *Pilgrim Fellowship*, 117f.

[77] Ibid., 118.

[78] On this topic, see "Liturgie", 137. Cf. also *Spirit of the Liturgy*, 16, where Ratzinger argues in terms of salvation history that the real goal of Israel's Exodus out of the Egypt was not the possession of the promised land, but rather "worship, which can only take place according to God's measure and therefore eludes the rules of the game of political compromise".

[79] "Liturgie", 137. See also *Spirit of the Liturgy*, 18f.

[80] "Liturgie", 141.

in every celebration of the Eucharist. For Ratzinger the "entire liturgy is ... nothing other than beholding the Pierced One".[81] The risen and glorified Lord "does not assemble the parish community in order to enclose it"[82] but, rather, to open it up for all. Thus for Ratzinger, liturgy is the place in which the Church is realized, and at the same time it is the expression of her universality and catholicity, which should not be understood externally (that is, in the juridical sense); rather, it is one of her essential features:

> The man who allows himself to be "assembled" by the Lord has plunged into a river which will always be taking him beyond the limits of his self at any one time. ... It is a favorite theme of our time that the Church is "wherever two or three are gathered in my name", but the reverse is also true: the community is only "with the Lord" and "gathered in his name" provided it is entirely at one with the Church, wholly part of the whole. That is why, however much it lives in the here and now, in a particular place, seeking the consent of the local community, Christian liturgy is essentially Catholic, that is, it proceeds from the whole and leads back to it, it leads to unity with the pope, the bishops and the faithful of all times and places.[83]

Therefore, liturgy in its ecclesial dimension is never a private worship-gathering—which, as Ratzinger remarks, "would have spared the Christians a lot of trouble" during the persecution by the Roman Empire, since private cultic practices "were permitted by Roman law".[84] Instead, the Church has understood from the very beginning that she is by nature universal.

c. Liturgy as *actio* of the Completely Other

Ratzinger understands the *participatio actuosa*[85] called for by the Council in such a way that the faithful do not necessarily participate in the

---

[81] Ratzinger, *Meditationen zur Karwoche* (Meitingen and Freising: Meitinger Kleinschriften, 1969), 5.
[82] *Feast of Faith*, 148.
[83] Ibid.
[84] *Dogma*, 275–79, citation at 277. "Christians are convinced that in the Eucharist it is not a group or circle of friends that meets, but rather the public dimension of the People of God" (ibid.).
[85] Cf. *SC* 14, 30, 48, 50, 114; *GE* 4.

liturgy through external activity but, rather, share in the principal activity, namely, in the great prayer that the Church Fathers called *oratio*, which constitutes the "center and fundamental form"[86] of the eucharistic celebration.

> This *oratio*—the Eucharistic Prayer, the "Canon"—is ... *actio* in the highest sense of the word. For what happens in it is that the human *actio* (as performed hitherto by the priests in the various religions of the world) steps back and makes way for the *actio divina*, the action of God. In this *oratio* the priest speaks with the I of the Lord— "This is my Body", "This is my Blood." He knows that he is not now speaking from his own resources but in virtue of the Sacrament that he has received, he has become the voice of Someone Else, who is now speaking and acting. This action of God, which takes place through human speech, is the real "action" for which all of creation is in expectation. The elements of the earth are transubstantiated, pulled, so to speak, from their creaturely anchorage, grasped at the deepest ground of their being, and changed into the Body and Blood of the Lord. The New Heaven and the New Earth are anticipated.[87]

The active participation of all the faithful does not mean, therefore, according to Ratzinger, that the liturgy has to be " 'made' by the community ... if the liturgy is to be the work of the community".[88] Since no one can carry out Christ's *actio* on his own, instead, "these words can be pronounced only in the sacrament of the Church as a whole, with the authority that she alone, in her unity and her fullness, possesses."[89] This liturgy in keeping with the Logos is the accomplishment of Christ's salvific work in the *communio* of the Father in the Holy Spirit. In this way, Christ in the Eucharist "builds up the Church as his body, and through his body that rises again he unites us with God the Trinity and with each other."[90]

Without any fault line, this eucharistic approach of Ratzinger's ecclesiology can be documented both in his early and in his later statements.

---

[86] *Spirit of the Liturgy*, 172.
[87] Ibid., 172–73.
[88] *Feast of Faith*, 149.
[89] *Eucharist*, 54.
[90] "Ecclesiology", 131.

For him, as for Augustine,[91] the formula that he coined during the Council holds true: "The Church is the People of God which lives on the Body of Christ and which itself becomes the Body of Christ in the celebration of the Eucharist."[92]

To summarize, we can say that the essence of Ratzinger's eucharistic *communio* ecclesiology is to be found in the fact that the Church does not derive her status as an acting subject from herself; rather—as *Lumen gentium*[93] also emphasizes—she receives it from her "union with Christ".[94] Hence Ratzinger's ecclesiological approach provides an answer to the question of the existence of a faith that emerges from the "autonomy of arbitrary thinking"[95] and acting into the truth[96] that we receive from God alone. In every celebration of the Eucharist, the Church is taken into this *extra nos* of the sacrament, into the Totally Other, that is, into Christ's *oratio*, and thus abides with Christ and, through him, shares in the dialogue between the Father and the Son in the Holy Spirit. She becomes "Church through worship, and worship, although it must be thought of in terms of Christ, is always trinitarian."[97]

[91] Cf. *Volk und Haus Gottes*, 211–15.

[92] Ratzinger, "Zeichen unter den Völkern", in *Wahrheit und Zeugnis: Aktuelle Themen der Gegenwart in theologischer Sicht*, ed. M. Schmaus and A. Läpple, 456–66, citation at 459 (Düsseldorf: Patmos-Verlag, 1964).

[93] On this subject, see esp. *LG* 1.

[94] *Principles*, 132.

[95] "Liturgie", 142.

[96] On this subject, see *Turning Point*, 174, where Ratzinger points out that M. Horkheimer and T. W. Adorno, "with the clear sight of the outsider, have denounced the attempt by theologians to sneak past the core of the faith, removing the provocatory character of the Trinity and life beyond death ... by reducing these to the level of symbols. They tell us that when theologians bracket off dogma, what they say has no validity; they bow to that 'fear of the truth' in which the spiritual and intellectual decline of the present day has its roots."

[97] "Liturgie", 138. On this subject, see also Ratzinger's eschatological perspective on the liturgy in *Song*, 128–146, esp. 129: "Liturgy is anticipated Parousia, the 'already' entering our 'not yet', as John described it in the account of the wedding at Cana. The hour of the Lord has not yet come; all that must happen is not yet fulfilled; but at Mary's—the Church's—request Jesus does give the new wine now and already bestows in advance the gift of his hour."

ABBREVIATIONS

Abbreviations [for example, for German scholarly journals] not specifically listed here, including the acronyms for the documents of
the Second Vatican Council, are taken from the "Abkürzungsver-
zeichnis" in the third edition of the *Lexikon für Theologie und Kirche*
(Freiburg am Breisgau: Herder, 1993).

1. Abbreviations for the Working Documents of the Second Vatican Council

AD 1   *Acta et documenta Concilio Oecumenico Vaticano II apparando*, series
1: *Antepraeparatoria, cura et studio Secretariae Pontificale Commissionis centralis praeparatoriae Concilii Vaticani II*, vol. 1: *Acta Summi
Pontificis Ioannis XXIII* [printed as 2 vols.]; vol. 2: *Consilia et
vota Episcoporum ac Praelatorum* [printed as 8 vols.] with an
appendix to vol. 2: *Analyticus conspectus consiliorum et votorum
quae ab Episcopis et Praelatis data sunt* [printed as 2 vols.]; vol. 3:
Proposita et monita: Sacrarum Congregationum Curiae Romanae;
vol. 4: *Studia et vota: Universitatum et Facultatum Ecclesiasticarum
et Catholicarum* [printed as 3 vols.]; *Indices* (Typis polyglottis
Vaticanis, 1960–1961).

AD 2   *Acta et documenta Concilio Oecumenico Vaticano II apparando*, series
2: *Praeparatoria, cura et studio Secretariae Generalis Concilii Oecumenici Vaticani II*, vol. 1: *Acta Summi Pontificis Ioannis XXIII*;
vol. 2: *Acta Commissionis Centralis Praeparatoriae Concilii Oecumenici Vaticani II* [printed as 4 vols.]; vol. 3: *Acta Commis-
sionum et Secretariatuum Praeparatoriorum Concilii Oecumenici
Vaticani II* [printed as 2 vols.] (Typis polyglottis Vaticanis,
1964–1995).

AS   *Acta synodalia sacrosancti Concilii Oecumenici Vaticani II, cura et
studio Archivi Concilii Oecumenici Vaticani II*, vol. 1: *Periodus*

prima [printed as 4 vols.]; vol. 2: *Periodus secunda* [printed as
6 vols.]; vol. 3: *Periodus tertia* [printed as 8 vols.]; vol. 4: *Periodus quarta* [printed as 6 vols.]; *Indices, Appendix, Appendix
altera* (Typis polyglottis Vaticanis, 1970–1998).

KlKK   *Kleines Konzilskompendium*, ed. K. Rahner and H. Vorgrimler, 29th ed. (Freiburg in Breisgau: Herder, 2002).

2. Abbreviations of Other Magisterial Documents

CCC   *Catechism of the Catholic Church*, English trans. for the United
States, 2nd ed. (Vatican City: Libreria Editrice Vaticana; Washington, D.C.: United States Catholic Conference, 2000).

DI   Congregation for the Doctrine of the Faith, declaration *Dominus Iesus: On the Unicity and Salvific Universality of Jesus Christ
and the Church*, *L'Osservatore Romano*, weekly ed. in English,
no. 36 (September 6, 2000), special insert.

3. Abbreviated Titles of Frequently Cited Works
by Ratzinger in Alphabetical Order
[English translations are cited whenever possible; see the
bibliography for original German titles.]

"Absurd"   "'Es scheint mir absurd, was unsere lutherischen Freunde jetzt wollen.' Die Pluralität relativiert nicht den Anspruch des Wahren: Joseph
Kardinal Ratzinger antwortet seinen Kritikern", *FAZ* 221 (September 22, 2000): 51f.

Behold   *Behold the Pierced One: An Approach to a Spiritual Christology*, trans. Graham Harrison (San
Francisco: Ignatius Press, 1986).

Called to Communion   *Called to Communion: Understanding the Church
Today*, trans. Adrian Walker, 2nd ed. (San Fran-
cisco: Ignatius Press, 1996).

Church   *Church, Ecumenism and Politics: New Essays in
Ecclesiology*, trans. Robert Lowell and Dame

Frideswide Sandemann, O.S.B. (New York: Crossroad, 1988).

Daughter Zion *Daughter Zion: Meditations on the Church's Marian Belief*, trans. John M. McDermott, S.J. (San Francisco: Ignatius Press, 1983).

"Demokratisierung 1" "Demokratisierung der Kirche?", in *Demokratie in der Kirche: Möglichkeiten und Grenzen*, by Ratzinger and H. Maier, 7–46 (Limburg and Kevelaer: Lahn-Verlag, 2000).

"Demokratisierung 2" "Demokratisierung der Kirche—Dreißig Jahre danach", in *Demokratie in der Kirche: Möglichkeiten und Grenzen*, by Ratzinger and H. Maier, 78–92 (Limburg and Kevelaer: Lahn-Verlag, 2000).

Dogma *Dogma und Verkündigung* (Munich and Freiburg: Wewel, 1973).

Dogma and Preaching *Dogma and Preaching*, sel. ed., trans. Matthew J. O'Connell (Chicago: Franciscan Herald Press, 1985).

"Ecclesiology" "The Ecclesiology of the Constitution *Lumen gentium*", in *Pilgrim Fellowship*, 123–52.

"Ecumenical Situation" "On the Ecumenical Situation", in *Pilgrim Fellowship*, 253–69.

Einheit "Kommentar zur These I–VIII", in *Die Einheit des Glaubens und der theologische Pluralismus*, ed. Internationale Theologenkommission, 17–51 (Einsiedeln: Johannes Verlag, 1973).

"Einleitung" "Einleitung", in *Zweites Vatikanisches Konzil, Dogmatische Konstitution über die Kirche: Authentischer lateinischer Text: Deutsche Übersetzung im Auftrag der deutschen Bischöfe*, 7–19 (Münster: Aschendorff, 1965).

Eucharist	*God Is Near Us: The Eucharist, The Heart of Life*, ed. Stephan Otto Horn and Vinzenz Pfnür, trans. Henry Taylor (San Francisco: Ignatius Press, 2003).
Feast of Faith	*The Feast of Faith: Approaches to a Theology of the Liturgy*, trans. Graham Harrison (San Francisco: Ignatius Press, 1986).
"Formen"	"Konkrete Formen bischöflicher Kollegialität", in Hampe, *Konzil*, 155–63.
"Full of Grace"	" 'Hail, Full of Grace': Elements of Marian Piety according to the Bible", in *Mary: The Church at the Source*, by Ratzinger and H. U. von Balthasar, trans. Adrian Walker, 61–80 (San Francisco: Ignatius Press, 2005).
"Geist und Kirche"	"Der Heilige Geist und die Kirche", in *Servitium pietatis: Festschrift für Hans Hermann Kardinal Groer zum 70. Geburtstag*, ed. A. Coreth and I. Fux, 91–97 (Maria Roggendorf: Sal Terrae, 1989).
God and the World	*God and the World: Believing and Living in Our Time; A Conversation with Peter Seewald*, trans. Henry Taylor (San Francisco: Ignatius Press, 2002).
"Gottesidee"	"Die große Gottesidee 'Kirche' ist keine Schwärmerei: Nicht nur eine Frage der Kompetenzverteilung; Das Verhältnis von Universalkirche und Ortskirche aus der Sicht des Zweiten Vatikanischen Konzils", *FAZ* 298 (December 22, 2000): 46.
Highlights	*Theological Highlights of Vatican II*, trans. Henry Traub, S.J., et al. (New York: Paulist Press, 1966).
"Holy Spirit"	"The Holy Spirit as Communion: On the Relationship between Pneumatology and Spirituality in the Writings of Augustine", in *Pilgrim Fellowship*, 38–59.

"Identification"	"Identification with the Church", in *Living with the Church*, by Ratzinger and Karl Lehmann, trans. Zachary Hayes, O.F.M., 9–28 (Chicago: Franciscan Herald Press, 1978).
In the Beginning	*In the Beginning: A Catholic Understanding of the Story of Creation and the Fall*, trans. Boniface Ramsey, O.P., new expanded ed. (Grand Rapids, Mich.: Eerdmans, 1995).
Introduction	*Introduction to Christianity*, trans. J. R. Foster (San Francisco: Ignatius Press, 2004).
"Kollegialität"	"Die bischöfliche Kollegialität: Theologische Entfaltung", in Baraúna 2:44–70.
"Kommentar"	"Kommentar zu den 'Bekanntmachungen, die der Generalsekretär des Konzils in der 123. Generalkongregation am 16. November 1964 mitgeteilt hat' ", in *LThK.E*, vol. 1 (Freiburg im Breisgau: Herder, 1966), 348–59.
"Liturgie"	"Von der Liturgie zur Christologie: Romano Guardinis theologischer Grundansatz und seine Aussagekraft", in *Wege zur Wahrheit: Die bleibende Bedeutung von Romano Guardini*, ed. Ratzinger, 121–44 (Düsseldorf: Patmos-Verlag, 1985).
Many Religions	*Many Religions—One Covenant: Israel, the Church, and the World*, trans. Graham Harrison (San Francisco: Ignatius Press, 1999).
"Marian Doctrine"	"Thoughts on the Place of Marian Doctrine and Piety in Faith and Theology as a Whole", in *Mary: The Church at the Source*, by Ratzinger and H. U. von Balthasar, trans. Adrian Walker, 19–36 (San Francisco: Ignatius Press, 2005).
Milestones	*Milestones: Memoirs (1927–1977)*, trans. Erasmo Leiva-Merikakis (San Francisco: Ignatius Press, 1998).

Mitte	*Vom Wiederauffinden der Mitte: Grundorientierungen: Texte aus vier Jahrzehnten*, published by the association of former students, ed. S. O. Horn, V. Pfnür, et al. (Freiburg im Breisgau: Herder, 1997).
Nature	*The Nature and Mission of Theology: Essays to Orient Theology in Today's Debates*, trans. Adrian Walker (San Francisco: Ignatius Press, 1995).
"New Questions"	"The New Questions That Arose in the Nineties: The Position of Faith and Theology Today", in *Truth and Tolerance: Christian Belief and World Religions*, trans. Henry Taylor (San Francisco: Ignatius Press, 2004), 115–37.
Pilgrim Fellowship	*Pilgrim Fellowship of Faith: The Church as Communion*, ed. Stephan Otto Horn and Vinzenz Pfnür, trans. Henry Taylor (San Francisco: Ignatius Press, 2005).
Principles	*Principles of Catholic Theology: Building Stones for a Fundamental Theology*, trans. Sister Mary Frances McCarthy, S.N.D. (San Francisco: Ignatius Press, 1987).
Probleme	*Ergebnisse und Probleme der dritten Konzilsperiode* (Cologne: Bachem, 1965).
Prüfsteine	*Wahrheit, Werte, Macht: Prüfsteine der pluralistischen Gesellschaft* (Freiburg im Breisgau: Herder, 1993).
Report	*The Ratzinger Report: An Exclusive Interview on the State of the Church*, by Ratzinger and Vittorio Messori, trans. Salvator Attanasio and Graham Harrison (San Francisco: Ignatius Press, 1985).
Rückblick	*Das Konzil auf dem Weg: Rückblick auf die zweite Sitzungsperiode des Zweiten Vatikanischen Konzils* (Cologne: Bachem, 1964).
Salt of the Earth	*Salt of the Earth: Christianity and the Catholic Church at the End of the Millennium; An Interview with Peter*

Seewald, trans. Adrian Walker (San Francisco: Ignatius Press, 1997).

Song   *A New Song for the Lord: Faith in Christ and Liturgy Today*, trans. Martha M. Matesich (New York: Crossroad, 1997).

Spirit of the Liturgy   *The Spirit of the Liturgy*, trans. John Saward (San Francisco: Ignatius Press, 2000).

Theology of History   *The Theology of History in St. Bonaventure*, trans. Zachary Hayes, O.F.M., 2nd ed. (Chicago: Franciscan Herald Press, 1989).

Turning Point   *A Turning Point for Europe? The Church in the Modern World—Assessment and Forecast*, trans. Brian McNeil, C.R.V. (San Francisco: Ignatius Press, 1994).

Volk Gottes   *Das neue Volk Gottes: Entwürfe zur Ekklesiologie*, 2nd ed. (Düsseldorf: Patmos-Verlag, 1977).

Volk und Haus Gottes   *Volk und Haus Gottes in Augustins Lehre von der Kirche* (St. Ottilien: EOS-Verlag, 1992).

"Wesen"   "Wesen und Grenzen der Kirche", in *Das Zweite Vatikanische Konzil*, essays by Walther Kampe, Johannes Hirschmann, Joseph Ratzinger, Joseph Pascher, and Karl Rahner, ed. K. Forster, 47–68, Studien und Berichte der Katholischen Akademie in Bayern, vol. 24 (Würzburg: Echter-Verlag, 1963).

4. Other Abbreviated Titles

Alberigo/Magistretti   G. Alberigo and F. Magistretti, eds., *Constitutionis dogmaticae Lumen gentium Synopsis historica* (Bologna: Istituto per le scienze religiose, 1975).

Baraúna 1   G. Baraúna, ed., *De Ecclesia*, vol. 1 (Freiburg im Breisgau: Herder, 1966).

Baraúna 2	G. Baraúna, ed., *De Ecclesia*, vol. 2 (Freiburg im Breisgau: Herder, 1966).
Fahey	M. Fahey, "Joseph Ratzinger als Ekklesiologe und Seelsorger", *Conc(D)* 17 (1981): 79–85.
Grillmeier 1	A. Grillmeier, "Kommentar zu LG Kap. 1", in *LThK.E*, vol. 1 (Freiburg im Breisgau: Herder, 1966), 156–76.
Grillmeier 2	A. Grillmeier, "Kommentar zu LG Kap. 2", in *LThK.E*, vol. 1 (Freiburg im Breisgau: Herder, 1966), 176–209.
Hampe, *Konzil*	J. C. Hampe, *Ende der Gegenreformation? Das Konzil: Dokumente und Deutung* (Mainz: Matthis-Grünewald-Verlag, 1964).
Häring, *Ideologie*	H. Häring, *Theologie und Ideologie bei Joseph Ratzinger* (Düsseldorf: Patmos, 2001).
Kaes	D. Kaes, *Theologie im Anspruch von Geschichte und Wahrheit: Zur Hermeneutik Joseph Ratzingers*, dissertation, Theologische Reihe, vol. 75 (St. Ottilien: EOS-Verlag, 1997).
Kasper, "Auseinandersetzung"	W. Kasper, "Das Verhältnis von Universal- und Ortskirche: Freundschaftliche Auseinandersetzung mit der Kritik von Joseph Kardinal Ratzinger", *StZ* 125 (2000): 795–804.
Kasper, "Theologie"	W. Kasper, "Zur Theologie und Praxis des bischöflichen Amtes", in *Bischofsbestellung: Mitwirkung der Ortskirche?* ed. B. Körner, 18–39 (Graz: Styria, 2000).

Kehl, *Kirche*

M. Kehl, *Die Kirche: Eine katholische Ekklesiologie*, 3rd ed. (Würzburg: Echter-Verlag, 1994).

Klausnitzer

W. Klausnitzer, *Das Papstamt im Disput zwischen Lutheranern und Katholiken: Schwerpunkte von der Reformation bis zur Gegenwart*, ITS 20 (Innsbruck: Tyrolia-Verlag, 1987).

Lohaus

G. Lohaus, "Das Verhältnis von Ortskirche und Universalkirche bei Joseph Ratzinger: Ein Beitrag zum nachkonziliaren Streit um die universale und partikulare Kirche", *Pastoralblatt für die Diözesen Aachen, Berlin, Essen, Hamburg, Hildesheim, Köln, Osnabrück* 45, no. 8 (1993): 234–45.

Müller/Pottmeyer

H. Müller and H.J. Pottmeyer, eds., *Die Bischofskonferenz, theologischer und juridischer Status* (Düsseldorf: Patmos, 1989).

Nachtwei

G. Nachtwei, *Dialogische Unsterblichkeit: Eine Untersuchung zu Joseph Ratzingers Eschatologie und Theologie*, EThSt 54 (Leipzig: St. Benno Verlag, 1986).

Pesch

O.H. Pesch, *Das Zweite Vatikanische Konzil: Vorgeschichte, Verlauf, Ergebnisse, Nachgeschichte* (Würzburg: Echter, 1994).

Peters/Urban

T.R. Peters and C. Urban, eds., *The End of Time? The Provocation of Talking about God: Proceedings of a Meeting of Joseph Cardinal Ratzinger, Johann Baptist Metz, Jürgen Moltmann, and Eveline Goodman-Thau in Ahaus*, trans. and ed. J. Matthew Ashley (New York: Paulist Press, 2004).

Pottmeyer, *Rolle*

H.J. Pottmeyer, *Die Rolle des Papsttums im Dritten Jahrtausend*, QD 179 (Freiburg im Breisgau: Herder, 1999).

Pottmeyer, "Weg"

"Der mühsame Weg zum Miteinander von Einheit und Vielfalt im Verhältnis von Gesamtkirche und Ortskirchen", in *Was ist heute noch katholisch? Zum Streit um die innere Einheit und Vielfalt der Kirche,* ed. A. Franz, 291–310, QD 192 (Freiburg im Breisgau: Herder, 2001).

Quinn, *Reform*   J. R. Quinn, *The Reform of the Papacy: The Costly Call to Christian Unity* (New York: Crossroad, 1999).

Richter, *Konzil*   K. Richter, ed., *Das Konzil war erst der Anfang: Die Bedeutung des II. Vatikanums für Theologie und Kirche* (Mainz: Matthias-Grünewald-Verlag, 1991).

Sandfuchs   W. Sandfuchs, ed., *Das neue Volk Gottes: Eine Einführung in die Dogmatische Konstitution "Über die Kirche",* with contributions by Heinrich Fries et al. (Würzburg: Arena-Verlag, 1966).

Teuffenbach   A. von Teuffenbach, *Die Bedeutung des* subsistit in *(LG 8): Zum Selbstverständnis der katholischen Kirche* (Munich: Wissenschaft, 2002).

tztD5/II   P. Neuner, ed., *Ekklesiologie II: Von der Reformation bis zur Gegenwart,* Texte zur Theologie: Dogmatik, ed. W. Beinert (Graz: Styria, 1995).

Wagner/Ruf   K. Wagner and A. H. Ruf, *Kardinal Ratzinger: Der Erzbischof von München und Freising in Wort und Bild: Mit dem Beitrag "Aus meinem Leben"* (Munich: Pfeiffer, 1977).

Wassilowsky   G. Wassilowsky, *Universales Heilssakrament Kirche: Karl Rahners Beitrag zur Ekklesiologie des II. Vatikanums* (Innsbruck: Tyrolia-Verlag, 2001).

Weiler   T. Weiler, *Volk Gottes—Leib Christi: Die Ekklesiologie Joseph Ratzingers und ihr Einfluss auf das Zweite Vatikanische Konzil* (Mainz: Matthias-Grünewald-Verlag, 1997).

Wittstadt 1   K. Wittstadt, ed. of German ed., *Die Geschichte des Zweiten Vatikanischen Konzils (1959–1965),* vol. 1: *Die katholische Kirche auf dem Weg in ein neues Zeitalter: Die Ankündigung und Vorbereitung des Zweiten*

Vatikanischen Konzils (Mainz: Matthias-Grünewald-Verlag, 1997).

Wittstadt 2   K. Wittstadt, ed. of German ed., *Die Geschichte des Zweiten Vatikanischen Konzils (1959–1965)*, vol. 2: *Das Konzil auf dem Weg zu sich selbst: Erste Sitzungsperiode und Intersessio: Oktober 1962–September 1963* (Mainz: Matthias-Grünewald-Verlag, 2000).

BIBLIOGRAPHY

I. CHURCH DOCUMENTS AND SOURCES

1. Councils

Decrees of the Ecumenical Councils. Original texts and English translations. Edited by Norman P. Tanner. Vol. 2, *Trent to Vatican II.* London: Sheed and Ward; Washington, D.C.: Georgetown University Press, 1990.

Das Zweite Vatikanische Konzil: Dokumente und Kommentare. In *LThK.E.* 3 vols. Freiburg im Breisgau: Herder, 1966–1968.

2. Papal Pronouncements in Chronological Order

Pius XI. Encyclical *Quadragesimo anno.* In *AAS* 23 (1931): 177–228.
Pius XII. Encyclical *Mystici Corporis.* In *AAS* 35 (1943): 193–248.
———. *Litterae encyclicae no. 2: De mystico Iesu Christi corpore deque nostra in eo cum Christo coniunctione "Mystici Corporis Christi".* June 29, 1943. 4th ed. Uberrimisque documentis illustravit Sebastianus Tromp S.I. Rome: Pont. Universitatis Gregorianae, 1963.
———. *Encyclical Letter of His Holiness Pius XII on the Mystical Body of Christ and Our Union in It with Christ, Mystici Corporis.* June 29, 1943. Boston: St. Paul Editions, 1943.
———. Encyclical *Humani generis.* In *AAS* 42 (1950): 561–78.
John XXIII. Encyclical *Ad Petri cathedram.* In *AAS* 51 (1959): 497–531. English translation in *The Encyclicals and Other Messages of John XXIII*, arranged and edited by the staff of *The Pope Speaks* magazine (Washington, D.C.: TPS Press, 1964), 24–56, and also at the Vatican website, ⟨http://www.vatican.va/holy_father/ john_xxiii/encyclicals/documents/hf_j-xxiii_enc_29061959_ad-petri_en.html⟩.

———. Apostolic constitution *Humanae salutis*. In *AAS* 54 (1962): 7–10. English translation in *The Encyclicals and Other Messages of John XXIII*, arranged and edited by the staff of *The Pope Speaks* magazine (Washington, D.C.: TPS Press, 1964), 386–97.

———. Motu proprio *Concilium*. In *AAS* 54 (1962): 65f.

———. Opening address of John XXIII on October 11, 1962. In *AAS* 54 (1962): 786–96. English translation in *Council Daybook: Vatican II, Sessions 1 and 2*, ed. Floyd Anderson (Washington, D.C.: National Catholic Welfare Conference, 1965), 25ff.

———. "Radio Message to the Catholics of the World". September 11, 1962. In *AAS* 11 (1962): 678–85. English translation of excerpts in *The Pope Speaks* 8, no. 3 (1963): 233–34.

Paul VI. "Address at Opening of the Second Session of the Second Vatican Council on September 29, 1963". In *AAS* 55 (1963): 841–59. English translation in *Council Daybook: Vatican II*, edited by Floyd Anderson, vol. 1 (Washington, D.C.: National Catholic Welfare Conference, 1965), pp. 143–50.

———. Encyclical *Ecclesiam suam*. In *AAS* 56 (1964): 626–36. English translation in *The Papal Encyclicals: 1958–1981*, edited by Claudia Carlen, I.H.M. (Ann Arbor, Mich.: Pierian Press, 1990), 135–60.

———. Motu proprio *Apostolica sollicitudo*. In *AAS* 57 (1965): 775–80.

John Paul II. Encyclical *Sollicitudo rei socialis*. Boston: Pauline Books and Media, 1987.

———. "Address to the Roman Curia, December 20, 1990". In *AAS* 83 (1991): 745–47.

———. Encyclical *Ut unum sint*. Vatican translation. Boston: Pauline Books and Media, 1995.

3. Magisterial Documents in Chronological Order

[1973] Congregation for the Doctrine of the Faith. Declaration *Mysterium Ecclesiae*. In *AAS* 65 (1973): 396–408.

[1984] ———. *Instruction concerning Certain Aspects of Liberation Theology*. August 6, 1984. Vatican and EWTN websites.

[1985] ———. "Notification on the Book *Church: Charism and Power* by Father Leonardo Boff, O.F.M.: Essay on Militant Ecclesiology". March 11, 1985. Vatican and EWTN websites.

[1986] *Zukunft der Kirche aus der Kraft des Konzils: Die außerordentliche Bischofssynode '85.* The documents of the 1985 Extraordinary Synod of Bishops with a commentary by W. Kasper. Freiburg im Breisgau: Herder, 1986.

[1992] Congregation for the Doctrine of the Faith. *Letter to the Bishops of the Catholic Church on Some Aspects of the Church Understood as Communion.* May 28, 1992. Vatican and EWTN websites.

[1997] Congregation for the Clergy and seven other dicasteries. *Instruction on Certain Questions regarding the Collaboration of the Nonordained Faithful in the Sacred Ministry of the Priests.* August 15, 1997. Vatican and EWTN websites.

[2000] *Catechism of the Catholic Church.* 2nd ed. English translation for the United States. Vatican City: Libreria Editrice Vaticana; Washington, D.C.: United States Catholic Conference, 2000.

Congregation for the Doctrine of the Faith. Declaration *Dominus Iesus: On the Unicity and Salvific Universality of Jesus Christ and the Church. L'Osservatore Romano,* weekly ed. in English, no. 36 (September 6, 2000), special insert.

II. THE WORKS OF JOSEPH RATZINGER

1. Separate Publications in Chronological Order

These works are arranged by the date when they were first published. This section is based on the recent (2002) Ratzinger bibliography in *Pilgrim Fellowship of Faith,* 299–379. [When available, an English translation is listed after the original German title.]

[1954] *Volk und Haus Gottes in Augustins Lehre von der Kirche.* Munich: Zink, 1954. Unamended reprint, with a new preface, St. Ottilien: EOS-Verlag, 1992.

[1959] *Die Geschichtstheologie des heiligen Bonaventura.* Munich: Schnell and Steiner, 1959. Unamended reprint, with a new preface, St. Ottilien: EOS-Verlag, 1992. Translated by Zachary Hayes,

O.F.M., as *The Theology of History in St. Bonaventure*, 2nd ed. (Chicago: Franciscan Herald Press, 1989).

[1963] *Die erste Sitzungsperiode des Zweiten Vatikanischen Konzils: Ein Rückblick*. Cologne: Bachem, 1963. This volume and the next three marked with an asterisk were translated into English without their respective forewords and published in one volume as *Theological Highlights of Vatican II*, translated by Henry Traub, S.J., et al. (New York: Paulist Press, 1966).

[1964] *Der gegenwärtige Stand der Arbeiten des Zweiten Vatikanischen Konzils*. Lecture given on October 1, 1964. Bonn: Katholische Rundfunk- und Fernseharbeit in Deutschland, 1964.

Das Konzil auf dem Weg: Rückblick auf die zweite Sitzungsperiode des Zweiten Vatikanischen Konzils. Cologne: Bachem, 1964.

[1965] *Ergebnisse und Probleme der dritten Konzilsperiode*. Cologne: Bachem, 1965.

Probleme der vierten Konzilsperiode. Lecture given on October 28, 1965, in Rome. Bonn: Katholische Rundfunk- und Fernseharbeit in Deutschland, 1965.

[1966] *Die letzte Sitzungsperiode des Konzils*. Cologne: Bachem, 1966.

[1967] *Die sakramentale Begründung christlicher Existenz*. 2nd ed. Meitingen and Freising: Kyrios-Verlag, 1967.

[1968] *Einführung in das Christentum: Vorlesungen über das Apostolische Glaubensbekenntnis*. Munich: Kösel Verlag, 1968; new edition with a new preface, 2000. Translated by J. R. Foster as *Introduction to Christianity*, new ed. with new preface (San Francisco: Ignatius Press, 2004).

[1969] *Meditationen zur Karwoche*. Meitingen and Freising: Meitinger Kleinschriften, 1969.

Das neue Volk Gottes: Entwürfe zur Ekklesiologie. Düsseldorf: Patmos-Verlag, 1969; 2nd abridged pocket ed., 1977.

[1970] *Glaube und Zukunft*. Munich: Kösel, 1970. Translated into English as *Faith and Future* (Chicago: Franciscan Herald Press, 1971).

[1971] *Die Einheit der Nationen: Eine Vision der Kirchenväter*. Salzburg and Munich: Pustet, 1971.

[1973] *Dogma und Verkündigung*. Munich and Freiburg: Erich Wewel Verlag, 1973. Translated by Matthew J. O'Connell as *Dogma and Preaching*, selective edition (Chicago: Franciscan Herald Press, 1985).

[1975] *Prinzipien christlicher Moral*. With Heinz Schürmann and Hans Urs von Balthasar. Einsiedeln: Johannes Verlag, 1975. Translated by Graham Harrison as *Principles of Christian Morality* (San Francisco: Ignatius Press, 1986).

[1977] Eschatologie—Tod und ewiges Leben. KKD, vol. 9. Regensburg: Friedrich Pustet Verlag, 1977; 6th enlarged ed., Regensburg: Pustet, 1990. Translated by Michael Waldstein as *Eschatology: Death and Eternal Life* (Washington, D.C.: Catholic University of America Press, 1988).

Der Gott Jesu Christi: Betrachtungen über den Dreieinigen Gott. 2nd ed. Munich: Kösel-Verlag, 1977. Translated by Robert J. Cunningham as *The God of Jesus Christ: Meditations on God in the Trinity* (Chicago: Franciscan Herald Press, 1978).

Die Tochter Zion: Betrachtungen über den Marienglauben der Kirche. Einsiedeln: Johannes Verlag, 1977. Translated by John M. McDermott, S.J., as *Daughter Zion: Meditations on the Church's Marian Belief* (San Francisco: Ignatius Press, 1983).

[1978] *Eucharistie—Mitte der Kirche*. Munich: Wewel, 1978.

[1979] "Was ihr von Anfang an gehört habt, soll in euch bleiben". Homily, December 31, 1979. Munich: Pressereferat der Erzdiözese München-Freising [Press Office of the Archdiocese of Munich and Freising], 1980.

[1980] "Lasst das Netz nicht zerreißen". Homily, December 31, 1980. Munich: Pressereferat der Erzdiözese München-Freising, 1981.

[1981] *Christlicher Glaube und Europa*. Twelve homilies. Munich: Pressereferat der Erzdiözese München-Freising, 1981.

Das Fest des Glaubens: Versuche zur Theologie des Gottesdienstes. Einsiedeln: Johannes Verlag, 1981. Translated by Graham Harrison as *The Feast of Faith: Approaches to a Theology of the Liturgy* (San Francisco: Ignatius Press, 1986).

[1982] *Theologische Prinzipienlehre: Bausteine zur Fundamentaltheologie*. Munich: Erich Wewel Verlag, 1982. Translated by Sister Mary Frances McCarthy, S.N.D., as *Principles of Catholic Theology: Building Stones for a Fundamental Theology* (San Francisco: Ignatius Press, 1987).

[1983] *Die Krise der Katechese und ihre Überwindung: Rede in Frankreich*. Lectures by Joseph Cardinal Ratzinger, Archbishop Dermot J. Ryan (Dublin), Godfried Cardinal Danneels (Malines/

Brussels), and Franciszek Cardinal Macharski (Krakow). Einsiedeln: Johannes Verlag, 1983. Translated by Michael J. Miller as *Handing on the Faith in an Age of Disbelief* (San Francisco: Ignatius Press, 2006).

Zeitfragen und christlicher Glaube. Eight homilies given in Munich. 2nd ed. Würzburg: Naumann, 1983.

[1984] *Schauen auf den Durchbohrten.* Einsiedeln: Johannes Verlag, 1984. Translated by Graham Harrison as *Behold the Pierced One: An Approach to a Spiritual Christology* (San Francisco: Ignatius Press, 1986).

[1985] *Rapporto Sulla Fede.* Milan: Edizioni Paoline, 1985. Translated by Salvator Attanasio and Graham Harrison from the original German manuscript as *The Ratzinger Report: An Exclusive Interview on the State of the Church*, 2nd ed. (San Francisco: Ignatius Press, 1986).

Suchen, was droben ist: Meditationen das Jahr hindurch. Freiburg im Breisgau: Herder, 1985. Translated by Graham Harrison as *Seek That Which Is Above: Meditations through the Year* (San Francisco: Ignatius Press, 1986).

[1986] *Im Anfang schuf Gott: Vier Predigten über Schöpfung und Fall; Konsequenzen des Schöpfungsglaubens.* Munich: Erich Wewel Verlag, 1986. 2nd, enlarged ed., Freiburg: Herder; Einsiedeln: Johannes Verlag, 1996. Translated by Boniface Ramsey, O.P., as *In the Beginning . . . : A Catholic Understanding of the Story of Creation and the Fall* (Huntington, Ind.: Our Sunday Visitor, 1990; 2nd, enlarged ed., Grand Rapids, Mich.: Eerdmans, 1995).

[1987] *Kirche, Ökumene und Politik: Neue Versuche zur Ekklesiologie.* Einsiedeln: Johannes Verlag, 1987. Translated by Robert Lowell and Dame Frideswide Sandemann, O.S.B., as *Church, Ecumenism and Politics: New Essays in Ecclesiology* (New York: Crossroad, 1988).

[1988] *Diener eurer Freude: Meditationen zur priesterlichen Spiritualität.* Freiburg im Breisgau: Herder, 1988. Translated into English as *Ministers of Your Joy: Scriptural Meditations on Priestly Spirituality* (Ann Arbor, Mich.: Redeemer Books, 1989).

[1989] *Auf Christus schauen: Einübung in Glaube, Hoffnung, Liebe.* Freiburg im Breisgau: Herder, 1989. Translated by Robert Nowell as

To Look on Christ: Exercises in Faith, Hope, and Love (New York: Crossroad, 1991).

[1991] *Wendezeit für Europa? Diagnosen und Prognosen zur Lage von Kirche und Welt.* Einsiedeln: Johannes Verlag, 1991. Translated by Brian McNeil, C.R.V., as *A Turning Point for Europe? The Church in the Modern World—Assessment and Forecast* (San Francisco: Ignatius Press, 1994).

Zur Gemeinschaft gerufen: Kirche heute verstehen. Freiburg im Breisgau: Herder, 1991. Translated by Adrian Walker as *Called to Communion*, 2nd ed. (San Francisco: Ignatius Press, 1996).

[1993] *Wahrheit, Werte, Macht: Prüfsteine der pluralistischen Gesellschaft.* Freiburg im Breisgau: Herder, 1993.

Wesen und Auftrag der Theologie: Versuche zu ihrer Ortsbestimmung im Disput der Gegenwart. Einsiedeln: Johannes Verlag, 1993. Translated by Adrian Walker as *The Nature and Mission of Theology: Essays to Orient Theology in Today's Debates* (San Francisco: Ignatius Press, 1995).

[1995] *Evangelium—Katechese—Katechismus: Streiflichter auf den Katechismus der katholischen Kirche.* Munich: Verlag Neue Stadt, 1995. Translated into English as *Gospel, Catechesis, Catechism: Sidelights on the* Catechism of the Catholic Church (San Francisco: Ignatius Press, 1997).

Ein neues Lied für den Herrn: Christusglaube und Liturgie in der Gegenwart. Freiburg im Breisgau: Herder, 1995. Translated by Martha M. Matesich as *A New Song for the Lord: Faith in Christ and Liturgy Today* (New York: Crossroad, 1997).

[1996] *Salz der Erde: Christentum und katholische Kirche an der Jahrtausendwende: Ein Gespräch mit Peter Seewald.* Stuttgart: Deutsche Verlags-Anstalt, 1996. Translated by Adrian Walker as *Salt of the Earth: Christianity and the Catholic Church at the End of the Millennium; An Interview with Peter Seewald* (San Francisco: Ignatius Press, 1997).

[1997] *Bilder der Hoffnung: Wanderungen im Kirchenjahr.* Freiburg im Breisgau: Herder, 1997. Translated by John Rock and Graham Harrison as *Images of Hope: Meditations on Major Feasts* (San Francisco: Ignatius Press, 2006).

La mia vita: Ricordi (1927–1977). Milan: Edizioni San Paolo, 1997. Translated from the German by Erasmo Leiva-Merikakis as *Milestones: Memoirs (1927–1977)* (San Francisco: Ignatius Press, 1998).

Vom Wiederauffinden der Mitte: Grundorientierungen; Texte aus vier Jahrzehnten. Published by the association of former students. Edited by S. O. Horn, V. Pfnür, et al. Freiburg im Breisgau: Herder, 1997.

[1998] *Die Vielfalt der Religionen und der Eine Bund.* Hagen: Verlag Urfeld, 1998. Translated by Graham Harrison as *Many Religions— One Covenant: Israel, the Church, and the World* (San Francisco: Ignatius Press, 1999).

[2000] *Einführung in den Geist der Liturgie.* Freiburg im Breisgau: Herder, 2000. Translated by John Saward as *The Spirit of the Liturgy* (San Francisco: Ignatius Press, 2000).

Gott und die Welt: Glauben und Leben in unserer Zeit; Ein Gespräch mit Peter Seewald. Stuttgart: Deutsche Verlags-Anstalt, 2000. Translated by Henry Taylor as *God and the World: Believing and Living in Our Time; Conversations with Peter Seewald* (San Francisco: Ignatius Press, 2002).

[2001] *Gott ist uns nah. Eucharistie, Mitte des Lebens.* Edited by S. O. Horn and V. Pfnür. Augsburg: Sankt Ulrich Verlag, 2001. Translated by Henry Taylor as *God Is Near Us: The Eucharist, The Heart of Life* (San Francisco: Ignatius Press, 2003).

[2002] *Weggemeinschaft des Glaubens: Kirche als Communio.* Edited by S. O. Horn and V. Pfnür. Augsburg: Sankt Ulrich Verlag, 2002. Translated by Henry Taylor as *Pilgrim Fellowship of Faith: The Church as Communion* (San Francisco: Ignatius Press, 2005).

2. Pieces in Collective Works and Periodicals in Chronological Order

A. Essays, Interviews, and Letters

[1961] "Kirche". In *LThK*, 2nd ed., 6:172–83. Freiburg im Breisgau: Herder, 1961.

"Primat, Episkopat und Successio Apostolica". In *Episkopat und Primat*, by K. Rahner and J. Ratzinger, 37–59. QD 11. Freiburg im Breisgau: Herder, 1961. Translated by Kenneth Barker et al. as "Primacy, Episcopate, and Apostolic Succession", in

The Episcopate and the Primacy, 37–63, QD 4 (New York: Herder and Herder, 1962).

[1963] "Wesen und Grenzen der Kirche". In *Das Zweite Vatikanische Konzil*, essays by Walther Kampe, Johannes Hirschmann, Joseph Ratzinger, Joseph Pascher, and Karl Rahner, edited by K. Forster, 47–68. Studien und Berichte der Katholischen Akademie in Bayern, vol. 24. Würzburg: Echter-Verlag, 1963.

[1964] "Konkrete Formen bischöflicher Kollegialität". In Hampe, *Konzil*, 155–63.

"Zeichen unter den Völkern". In *Wahrheit und Zeugnis: Aktuelle Themen der Gegenwart in theologischer Sicht*, edited by M. Schmaus and A. Läpple, 456–66. Düsseldorf: Patmos-Verlag, 1964.

"Zurück zur Ordnung der Alten Kirche". In Hampe, *Konzil*, 183f.

[1965] "Ein Versuch zur Frage des Traditionsbegriffs". In *Offenbarung und Überlieferung*, by K. Rahner and J. Ratzinger, 25–69. QD 25. Freiburg im Breisgau: Herder, 1965. Translated by W. J. O'Hara as *Revelation and Tradition*, QD 17 (New York: Herder and Herder, 1966).

[1966] "Die bischöfliche Kollegialität: Theologische Entfaltung". In Baraúna 2:44–70.

"Kommentar zu den 'Bekanntmachungen, die der Generalsekretär des Konzils in der 123. Generalkongregation am 16. November 1964 mitgeteilt hat'". In *LThK.E* 1:348–59. Freiburg im Breisgau: Herder, 1966.

[1967] "Einleitung zur Dogmatischen Konstitution über die göttliche Offenbarung". In *LThK.E* 2:498–503. Freiburg im Breisgau: Herder, 1967.

"Das geistliche Amt und die Einheit der Kirche". In *Die Autorität der Freiheit: Gegenwart des Konzils und Zukunft der Kirche im ökumenischen Disput*, edited by J. C. Hampe, 2:417–33. Munich: Kösel-Verlag, 1967.

"Heilsgeschichte und Eschatologie: Zur Frage nach dem Ansatz des theologischen Denkens". In *Theologie im Wandel: Festschrift zum 150jährigen Bestehen der Katholisch-Theologischen Fakultät an der Universität Tübingen: 1817–1967*, edited by J. Neumann and J. Ratzinger, 68–89. Munich and Freiburg im Breisgau: Wewel, 1967. Expanded version in *Theologische Prinzipienlehre*, 180–99. Translated into English in *Principles*, 171–90.

"Kirche als Tempel des Heiligen Geistes". In *Mitte*, 148–57. Abridged and slightly revised version of the lecture "Aspekte der Kirche" given on September 29, 1967, in Salzburg.

"Kommentar zu Kapitel 2 der Dogmatischen Konstitution über die göttliche Offenbarung". In *LThK.E* 2:515–28. Freiburg im Breisgau: Herder, 1967.

[1968] "Kommentar zu Artikel 11–22 der Pastoralkonstitution Gaudium et spes". In *LThK.E* 3:313–54. Freiburg im Breisgau: Herder, 1968.

"Zur Frage nach der Geschichtlichkeit der Dogmen". In *Martyria, Leiturgia, Diakonia: Festschrift für Hermann Volk zum 65. Geburtstag*, edited by O. Semmelroth, 59–70. Mainz: Matthias-Grünwald-Verlag, 1968.

[1969] "Begegnung lutherischer und katholischer Theologie nach dem Konzil". *Oecumenica* 4 (1969): 251–70.

[1970] (Joseph Ratzinger and Hans Maier.) *Demokratie in der Kirche: Möglichkeiten und Grenzen.* 1970; new expanded edition, Limburg and Kevelaer: Lahn-Verlag, 2000.

"Demokratisierung der Kirche?" In *Demokratie in der Kirche: Möglichkeiten und Grenzen*, by J. Ratzinger and H. Maier, 7–46. Limburg and Kevelaer: Lahn-Verlag, 2000.

[1971] "Das Ganze im Fragment: Gottfried Söhngen zum Gedächtnis". *Christ in der Gegenwart* 23 (1971): 398f. Reprinted under the title "Von der Wissenschaft zur Weisheit", in *Cath(M)* 26 (1972): 2–6.

"Die Situation der Kirche heute—Hoffnungen und Gefahren". In *Festvortrag beim Priestertreffen (J. Ratzinger) und Ansprache beim Pontifikalamt (Kardinal J. Höffner) anlässlich des 60jährigen Priesterjubiläums von Kardinal Josef Frings*, edited by the Presseamt des Erzbistums Köln, 7–22. Cologne, 1971.

"Warum ich noch in der Kirche bin". In *Zwei Plädoyers: Warum ich noch ein Christ bin: Warum ich noch in der Kirche bin*, by H. U. von Balthasar and J. Ratzinger, 55–75. Munich: Kösel, 1971. Translated by John Griffiths as *Two Say Why: Why I Am Still a Christian; Why I Am Still in the Church* (Chicago: Franciscan Herald Press, 1973).

[1972] "Einheit der Kirche—Einheit der Menschheit: Ein Tagungsbericht". *IKaZ* 1 (1972): 78–83.

"Das Gewissen in der Zeit". *IKaZ* 1 (1972): 432–42.

"Was eint und was trennt die Konfessionen?" *IKaZ* 1 (1972): 171–77.

[1973] "Kommentar zur These I–VIII". In *Die Einheit des Glaubens und der theologische Pluralismus*, edited by the Internationale Theologenkommission, 17–51. Einsiedeln: Johannes Verlag, 1973.

[1974] "Der Heilige Geist als communio: Zum Verhältnis von Pneumatologie und Spiritualität bei Augustinus". In *Erfahrung und Theologie des Heiligen Geistes*, edited by C. Heitmann and H. Mühlen, 223–38. Hamburg: Agentur des Rauhen Hauses; Munich: Kösel, 1974. Translated by Henry Taylor as "The Holy Spirit as Communion: On the Relationship between Pneumatology and Spirituality in the Writings of Augustine", in *Pilgrim Fellowship of Faith*, 38–59.

"Ökumenisches Dilemma? Zur Diskussion um die Erklärung 'Mysterium Ecclesiae' ". *IKaZ* 3 (1974): 56–63.

[1975] "Der Weltdienst der Kirche: Auswirkungen von 'Gaudium et spes' im letzten Jahrzehnt". *IKaZ* 4 (1975): 439–54. Reprinted in *Zehn Jahre Vaticanum II*, edited by A. Bauch et al. (Regensburg: Pustet, 1976), 36–53.

[1976] "Die kirchliche Lehre vom sacramentum ordinis". *IKaZ* 10 (1981): 435–45. First published in *Pluralisme et oecuménisme en recherches théologiques: Mélanges offerts au R. P. Dockx, O.P.* (Gembloux: Duculot, 1976).

[1977] "Der Bischof ist ein Christus-Träger: Predigt bei der Bischofsweihe im Münchener Liebfrauendom am 23. Juli 1977". In Wagner/Ruf, 36–40.

"Identifikation mit der Kirche". In *Mit der Kirche leben*, by J. Ratzinger and K. Lehmann, 9–40. Freiburg im Breisgau: Herder, 1977. Translated by Zachary Hayes, O.F.M., as "Identification with the Church", in *Living with the Church* (Chicago: Franciscan Herald Press, 1978), 9–28.

"Kirche als Heilssakrament". In *Zeit des Geistes*, edited by J. Reikerstorfer, 59–70. Vienna: Dom-Verlag, 1977.

"Prognosen für die Zukunft des Ökumenismus". In *Mitte*, 181–94. First published in *Ökumenisches Forum: Grazer Hefte für konkrete Ökumene* 1 (1977): 31–41.

[1978] "Der Primat des Papstes und die Einheit des Gottesvolkes". In *Dienst an der Einheit: Zum Wesen des Petrusamtes*, edited by J. Ratzinger. Schriften der katholischen Akademie in Bayern, vol. 85, 165–79. Düsseldorf: Patmos-Verlag, 1978.

"Theologie und Kirchenpolitik". *IKaZ* 9 (1980): 425–34.

[1982] "Wagt den Lebensstil, der Zukunft hat: Abschieds-Hirtenbrief des Erzbischofs von München und Freising, Joseph Cardinal Ratinger, an die Gemeinden". In *Wir leben vom Ja: Dokumentation der Verabschiedung von Joseph Kardinal Ratzinger*, edited by Pressereferat der Erzdiözese München-Freising, 117–19. Munich: Pfeiffer, 1982.

[1983] "Schwierigkeiten mit der Glaubensunterweisung heute: Interview mit J. Ratzinger". In *Krise der Katechese und ihre Uberwindung*, by Ratzinger et al., 63–79. Einsiedeln: Johannes Verlag, 1983. Translated by Michael J. Miller as "Difficulties in Teaching the Faith Today: Interview with Joseph Cardinal Ratzinger", in *Handing on the Faith in an Age of Disbelief* (San Francisco: Ignatius Press, 2006), 65–82.

[1984] "Kirchenverfassung und Umkehr: Fragen an Joseph Kardinal Ratzinger". *IKaZ* 13 (1984): 444–57.

[1985] "Scopi e metodi del Sinodo dei Vescovi". In *Sinodo dei Vescovi: Natura, metodo, prospettive*, edited by J. Tomko, 45–58. Vatican City: Libreria Editrice Vaticana, 1985.

"Von der Liturgie zur Christologie: Romano Guardinis theologischer Grundansatz und seine Aussagekraft". In *Wege zur Wahrheit: Die bleibende Bedeutung von Romano Guardini*, edited by J. Ratzinger, 121–44. Düsseldorf: Patmos-Verlag, 1985.

[1987] "Buchstabe und Geist des Zweiten Vatikanums in den Konzilsreden von Kardinal Frings". *IKaZ* 16 (1987): 251–65.

[1989] "Der Heilige Geist und die Kirche". In *Servitium pietatis: Festschrift für Hans Hermann Kardinal Groër zum 70. Geburtstag*, edited by A. Coreth and I. Fux, 91–97. Maria Roggendorf: Sal Terrae, 1989.

"Schriftauslegung im Widerstreit: Zur Frage nach Grundlagen und Weg der Exegese heute". In *Schriftauslegung im Widerstreit*, edited by J. Ratzinger, 15–44. QD 117. Freiburg im Breisgau: Herder, 1989.

[1990] "Glaube—eine Antwort auf die Urfrage des Menschen: Die Instruktion über die kirchliche Berufung des Theologen". *OR (D)* 20 (1990): 6–7.

[1991] (H. Stehle, F. König, and J. Ratzinger.) "Die Botschaft Jesu für alle Zeiten". In *Zivilcourage in der Kirche*, by W. Bühlmann, 166–72 (document no. 10). Graz: Styria, 1992. The essay first appeared in the German weekly newspaper *Die Zeit* 49 (November 29, 1991).

[1992] "Communio—ein Programm". *IKaZ* 21 (1992): 454–63.

"Probleme von Glaubens- und Sittenlehre im europäischen Kontext". In *Zu Grundfragen der Theologie heute*, edited by the Erzbischöfliches Generalvikariat Paderborn, Presse- und Informationsstelle, 7–17. Paderborn, 1992.

[1993] "Brief an Landesbischof J. Hanselmann vom 9. März 1993". In *Weggemeinschaft des Glaubens: Kirche als Communio*, by Ratzinger, edited by S. O. Horn and V. Pfnür, 215–19. Augsburg: Sankt Ulrich Verlag, 2002. Translated by Henry Taylor as "Letter to Provincial Bishop Johannes Hanselmann dated March 9, 1993", in *Pilgrim Fellowship of Faith*, 247–52.

"Damit Gott alles in allem sei und alles Leid ein Ende habe". In *Kleines Credo für Verunsicherte*, edited by J. Hoeren and N. Kutschki, 121–40. Freiburg im Breisgau: Herder, 1993.

"Hinführung zum Katechismus der Katholischen Kirche". In *Kleine Hinführung zum Katechismus der Katholischen Kirch*, by J. Ratzinger and C. Schönborn, 7–34. Munich: Verlag Neue Stadt, 1993. Translated by Adrian Walker as "Introduction to the Catechism of the Catholic Church", in *Introduction to the Catechism of the Catholic Church* (San Francisco: Ignatius Press, 1994), 9–36.

"Mariä Aufnahme in den Himmel: Predigt am Fest Mariä Himmelfahrt 1993 im Hegenauerpark in Regensburg". In *Heiligenpredigten*, by J. Ratzinger, ed. Stefan O. Horn, 70–75. Munich: Wewel, 1997.

[1994] "Grenzen kirchlicher Vollmacht: Das neue Dokument von Papst Johannes Paul II. zur Frage der Frauenordination". *IKaZ* 23 (1994): 337–45.

[1995] "Zur Lage der Ökumene". In *Perspectives actuelles sur l'oecuménisme*, edited by J.-L. Leuba, 231–44. Louvain-la-Neuve: Artel, 1995.

Translated by Henry Taylor as "On the Ecumenical Situation", in *Pilgrim Fellowship of Faith*, 253–69.

[1997] "'Du bist voll der Gnade': Elemente biblischer Marienfröm-
migkeit". In *Maria—Kirche im Ursprung*, by J. Ratzinger and
H. U. von Balthasar, 53–70. Einsiedeln: Johannes Verlag, 1997.
Translated by Adrian Walker as "'Hail, Full of Grace': Ele-
ments of Marian Piety according to the Bible", in *Mary: The
Church at the Source* (San Francisco: Ignatius Press, 2005), 61–80.

"Erwägungen zur Stellung von Mariologie und Marienfröm-
migkeit im Ganzen von Glaube und Theologie". In *Maria—
Kirche im Ursprung*, by J. Ratzinger and H. U. von Balthasar,
14–30. Einsiedeln: Johannes Verlag, 1997. Translated by Adrian
Walker as "Thoughts on the Place of Marian Doctrine and
Piety in Faith and Theology as a Whole", in *Mary: The Church
at the Source* (San Francisco: Ignatius Press, 2005), 19–36.

"Das Zeichen der Frau: Versuch einer Einführung zur Enzyklika 'Redemptoris Mater'". In *Maria—Kirche im Ursprung*,
by J. Ratzinger and H. U. von Balthasar, 31–52. Einsiedeln:
Johannes Verlag, 1997. Translated by Adrian Walker as "The
Sign of the Woman: An Introductory Essay on the Encyclical *Redemptoris Mater*", in *Mary: The Church at the Source*
(San Francisco: Ignatius Press, 2005), 37–60.

[1998] "Eucharistie und Mission". *FoKTh* 14 (1998): 81–98; subsequently reprinted in *Weggemeinschaft des Glaubens: Kirche
als Communio*, by Ratzinger, edited by S. O. Horn and V.
Pfnür, 79–106. Augsburg: Sankt Ulrich Verlag, 2002. Translated by Henry Taylor as "Eucharist and Mission", in *Pilgrim Fellowship of Faith*, 90–122.

"Gefährliche Spaltung". *Rheinischer Merkur* 6 (February 6, 1998):
25f.

"Kirchliche Bewegungen und ihr theologischer Ort". *IKaZ* 27
(1998): 431–48. Translated by Henry Taylor as "Church Movements and Their Place in Theology", in *Pilgrim Fellowship of
Faith*, 176–208.

[1999] "Der Glaube ist kein Parteiprogramm: Zur Lage von Glaube
und Theologie heute". In *Stets war es der Hund, der starb. . . .
Die Kirche zur Jahrtausendwende: Gefahren, Irrwege und Perspektiven*, edited by M. Müller, 33–53. Aachen: MM-Verlag, 1999.

Translated by Henry Taylor as "The New Questions That Arose in the Nineties: The Position of Faith and Theology Today", in J. Ratzinger, *Truth and Tolerance: Christian Belief and World Religions* (San Francisco: Ignatius Press, 2004), 115–37.

(J. Ratzinger and J. B. Metz.) "Gott, die Schuld und das Leiden: Gespräch". In *Ende der Zeit? Die Provokation der Rede von Gott: Dokumentation einer Tagung mit Joseph Kardinal Ratzinger, Johann Baptist Metz, Jürgen Moltmann und Eveline Goodman-Thau in Ahaus*, edited by T. R. Peters and C. Urban, 50–55. Mainz: Matthias-Grünewald-Verlag, 1999. Translated by J. Matthew Ashley as "God, Sin, and Suffering: A Conversation", in Peters/Urban, 47–53.

"Ohne Glaube an Christus zerfällt alles in reine Tradition: Die anderen Religionen, die Ökumene, der Dialog mit den Juden: Ein Gespräch mit Kardinal Joseph Ratzinger über den Wahrheitsanspruch des Christentums". *Die Tagespost* 52 (October 23, 1999): 5.

(J. Ratzinger, J. B. Metz, J. Moltmann, and E. Goodman-Thau.) "Die Provokation der Rede von Gott: Diskussion–Moderation: R. Leicht". In *Ende der Zeit? Die Provokation der Rede von Gott: Dokumentation einer Tagung mit Joseph Kardinal Ratzinger, Johann Baptist Metz, Jürgen Moltmann und Eveline Goodman-Thau in Ahaus*, edited by T. R. Peters and C. Urban, 77–93. Translated by J. Matthew Ashley as "The Provocation of Talking about God: A Discussion, Moderated by Robert Leicht", in Peters/Urban, 78–99.

[2000] "Christentum: Der Sieg der Einsicht über die Welt der Religionen". *30 Tage* 18, no. 1 (2000): 33–44.

"Das Christentum wollte immer mehr sein als nur Tradition: Die Kirche muss den Glauben vernünftig auslegen, damit er an den Enden der Erde verstanden werden kann; Ein Gespräch mit Joseph Kardinal Ratzinger". *FAZ* 57 (March 8, 2000): 51f.

"Demokratisierung der Kirche—Dreißig Jahre danach". In *Demokratie in der Kirche: Möglichkeiten und Grenzen*, by J. Ratzinger and H. Maier, 78–92. Limburg and Kevelaer: Lahn-Verlag, 2000.

" 'Es scheint mir absurd, was unsere lutherischen Freunde jetzt wollen.' Die Pluralität relativiert nicht den Anspruch des Wahren: Joseph Kardinal Ratzinger antwortet seinen Kritikern". *FAZ* 221 (September 22, 2000): 51f.

"Die große Gottesidee 'Kirche' ist keine Schwärmerei: Nicht nur eine Frage der Kompetenzverteilung; Das Verhältnis von Universalkirche und Ortskirche aus der Sicht des Zweiten Vatikanischen Konzils". *FAZ* 298 (December 22, 2000): 46.

"Kommentar zur Erklärung 'Dominus Iesus' im Pressesaal des Vatikans". In *Erklärung Dominus Iesus: Über die Einzigkeit und Heilsuniversalität Jesu Christi und der Kirche*, by the Kongregation für die Glaubenslehre, 38–44. Stein am Rhein: Christiana-Verlag, 2000. Translated by Henry Taylor as "Presentation of the Declaration *Dominus Iesus* in the Press Conference Room of the Holy See, on September 5, 2000", in *Pilgrim Fellowship of Faith*, 209–16.

"Nur die Wirklichkeit der Vergebung macht das Bekenntnis der Sünden möglich". *30 Tage* 18, no. 3 (2000): 24–27.

"Über die Ekklesiologie der Konstitution 'Lumen gentium': Welchen Begriff das Konzil von der Gesamtkirche hatte". *Die Tagespost* 53 (March 11, 2000): 1–8. Reprinted with supplementary notes in *Weggemeinschaft des Glaubens: Kirche als Communio*, by Ratzinger, edited by S. O. Horn and V. Pfnür, 107–31. Augsburg: Sankt Ulrich Verlag, 2002. Translated by Henry Taylor as "The Ecclesiology of the Constitution *Lumen gentium*", in *Pilgrim Fellowship of Faith*, 123–52.

"Wie weit trägt der Konsens über die Rechtfertigungslehre?" *IKaZ* 29 (2000): 424–37.

[2001] (Metropolit Damaskinos and J. Kard. Ratzinger.) "Ein Briefwechsel zwischen Metropolit Damaskinos und Kardinal Ratzinger". *IKaZ* 30 (2001): 282–96. Translated by Henry Taylor as "Exchange of Letters between Metropolitan Damaskinos and Cardinal Joseph Ratzinger", in *Pilgrim Fellowship of Faith*, 217–41.

"The Local Church and the Universal Church: A Response to Walter Kasper". *America: A Jesuit Magazine* 185, no. 16 (2001): 7–11.

[2002] "Glauben im Kontext heutiger Philosophie: Ein Gespräch mit dem Philosophen Vittorio Possenti". *IKaZ* 31 (2002): 266–73.

B. Introductions, Forewords, and Epilogues

[1965] "Einleitung". In *Zweites Vatikanisches Konzil, Dogmatische Konstitution über die Kirche: Authentischer lateinischer Text: Deutsche Übersetzung im Auftrag der deutschen Bischöfe*, 7–19. Münster: Aschendorff, 1965.
[1972] "Einleitung". In *Die Frage nach Gott*, edited by J. Ratzinger, 5–8. QD 56. Freiburg im Breisgau: Herder, 1972.
[1983] "Vorwort". In *Erneuerung und Mächte der Finsternis*, by L.-J. Suenens, translated from French into German by P. B. Bayer, 5–7. Salzburg: Müller, 1983.
[1993] "Vorwort" (co-authored with Christoph Schönborn). In *Kleine Hinführung zum Katechismus der katholischen Kirche*, by J. Ratzinger and C. Schönborn, 5–6. Munich: Neue Stadt, 1993. Translated by Adrian Walker as "Foreword", in *Introduction to the Catechism of the Catholic Church* (San Francisco: Ignatius Press, 1994), 7–8.
[1997] "Geleitwort". In Weiler, xiii–xvi.
[1998] "Geleitwort". In *Leben für die Kirche*, by C. Schönborn, 9f. Freiburg in Breisgau: Herder, 1997. [Translated from the original Italian edition, without Ratzinger's foreword, by John Saward as *Loving the Church* (San Francisco: Ignatius Press, 1998).
[1999] "Geleitwort". In *Komm, Schöpfer Geist: Betrachtungen zum Hymnus Veni Creator Spiritus*, by R. Cantalamessa, 11–14. Freiburg im Breisgau: Herder, 1999.

III. SECONDARY LITERATURE ON VATICAN II

Alberigo, G. "Die Ankündigung des Konzils: Von der Sicherheit des Sich-Verschanzens zur Faszination des Suchens". In Wittstadt 1:1–60.
———. "Die Konstitution in Beziehung zur gesamten Lehre des Konzils". In *Die Kirche in der Welt von heute: Untersuchungen und Kommentare zur Pastoralkonstitution "Gaudium et spes" des*

II. Vatikanischen Konzils, edited by G. Baraúna. Salzburg: Müller, 1967.

———. "Die konziliare Erfahrung: Selbständig lernen". In Wittstadt 2:679–98.

———. "Das Zweite Vatikanische Konzil (1962–1965)". In *Geschichte der Konzilien: Vom Nicaenum bis zum Vaticanum II*, edited by Alberigo, 413–69. Düsseldorf: Patmos, 1993.

———. "Das II. Vatikanum und der kulturelle Wandel in Europa". Translated by Sigrid Müller. In *Das II. Vatikanum—christlicher Glaube im Horizont globaler Modernisierung: Einleitungsfragen*, edited by P. Hünermann, 139–57. Paderborn: Schöningh, 1998.

——— and F. Magistretti, eds. *Constitutionis dogmaticae Lumen gentium Synopsis historica*. Bologna: Istituto per le scienze religiose, 1975.

Alberto, S. "Begriff und Wesen der Kirche in der Entstehung der Kirchenkonstitution 'Lumen gentium': Einige Anmerkungen zu drei Voten der Fuldaer Bischofskonferenz (1960–1963)". In *Ex latere: Ausfaltungen communialer Theologie*, edited by E. Naab, 149–75. Eichstätt: Franz-Sales-Verlag, 1993.

———. *"Corpus Suum mystice constituit" (LG 7): La Chiesa Corpo Mistico di Cristo nel prima capitolo della "Lumen gentium": Storia del Testo dalla "Mystici Corporis" al Vaticano II con riferimenti alla attività conciliare del P. Sebastian Tromp S.J.* Regensburg: Pustet, 1996.

Auer, A. "Die Laien". In Sandfuchs, 55–71.

Aymans, W. "Bischofssynode". In *LThK*, 3rd ed., 2:502–4. Freiburg im Breisgau: Herder, 1994.

Balthasar, H. U. von. *Cordula oder der Ernstfall*. Kriterien 2. Einsiedeln: Johannes Verlag, 1966. English: *The Moment of Christian Witness*. San Francisco: Ignatius Press, 1994.

———. *Rechenschaft*. Einsiedeln: Johannes Verlag, 1965.

———. *Test Everything: Hold Fast to What Is Good*. An interview with Angelo Scola. Translated by Maria Shrady. San Francisco: Ignatius Press, 1989.

———. "Who Is the Church?" In *Spouse of the Word*, translated by A. V. Littledale with Alexander Dru, 148–202. Explorations in Theology, vol. 2. San Francisco: Ignatius Press, 1991.

Baraúna, G., ed. *De Ecclesia*. 2 vols. Freiburg im Breisgau: Herder, 1966.

———. "Die heiligste Jungfrau im Dienste des Heilsplanes". In Baraúna 2:459–76.

———. "Vorwort". In Baraúna 1:7–11.

Becht, M. "Ecclesia semper purificanda: Die Sündigkeit der Kirche als Thema des II. Vatikanischen Konzils". *Cath(M)* 49 (1995): 218–60.

Beinert, W. "Grundströmungen heutiger Theologie". In *Tendenzen der katholischen Theologie nach dem Zweiten Vatikanischen Konzil*, edited by G. Kaufmann, 9–23. Munich: Kösel, 1979.

Berg, W. " 'Volk Gottes'—ein biblischer Begriff?" In *Kirche sein: Nachkonziliare Theologie im Dienst der Kirchenreform: Für Hermann Josef Pottmeyer*, edited by W. Geerlings and M. Seckler, 13–20. Freiburg im Breisgau: Herder, 1994.

Betti, U. "Die Entstehungsgeschichte der Konstitution". In Baraúna 1:45–70.

Congar, Y. "Die Kirche als Volk Gottes". *Conc(D)* 1 (1965): 5–16.

———. *Ministères et communion ecclésiale*. Paris: Éditions du Cerf, 1971.

———. "Schlusswort". In Baraúna 2:589–97.

Cullmann, O. "Verwirklichungen des ökumenischen Gedankens auf dem Konzil". In Hampe, *Konzil*, 355–59.

De Smedt, E. J. "Das Priestertum der Gläubigen". In Baraúna 1:380–92.

Döring, H. "Der ökumenische Aufbruch". In *Erinnerung an einen Aufbruch: Das II. Vatikanische Konzil*, edited by N. Kutschki, 66–79. Würzburg: Echter, 1995.

Fries, H. "Das Konzil: Grund ökumenischer Hoffnung". In *Die bleibende Bedeutung des Zweiten Vatikanischen Konzils*, edited by F. König, 107–21. Düsseldorf: Patmos, 1986.

J. Frings. *Für die Menschen bestellt: Erinnerungen des Alterzbischofs von Köln*. Cologne: Bachem, 1973.

———. *Das Konzil und die moderne Gedankenwelt*. Cologne: Bachem, 1962.

Froitzheim, D., ed. *Kardinal Frings, Leben und Werk*. 2nd ed. Cologne: Wienand, 1980.

Gahbauer, F. R. "Die Patriarchalstruktur auf dem Zweiten Vatikanischen Konzil". In *Das Dienstamt der Einheit in der Kirche: Primat, Patriarchat, Papsttum*, edited by A. Rauch and P. Imhof, 377–415. St. Ottilien: EOS-Verlag, 1991.

Galli, M. von, and B. Moosbrugger. *Das Konzil: Von Johannes XXIII. zu Paul VI.—Chronik der zweiten Sessio: Die Pilgerfahrt ins Heilige Land*. Olten: Walter, 1964.

Garijo-Guembe, M. M. "Konsequenzen des Dialogs mit der Orthodoxie für die römische Ekklesiologie". In Richter, Konzil, 140–58.

Giblet, J. "Die Priester 'zweiten Grades' ". In Baraúna 2:189–213.

Girault, R. "Die Rezeption des Ökumenismus". In Die Rezeption des
Zweiten Vatikanischen Konzils, edited by H.J. Pottmeyer, G.
Alberigo, and J.-P. Jossua, 180–217. Düsseldorf: Patmos-
Verlag, 1986.

Grillmeier, A. "Geist, Grundeinstellung und Eigenart der Konstitution 'Licht der Völker' ". In Baraúna 1:140–54.

———. "Kommentar zu LG Artikel 28". In LThK.E 1:247–55. Freiburg
im Breisgau: Herder, 1966.

———. "Kommentar zu LG Kap. 1". In LThK.E 1:156–76. Freiburg
im Breisgau: Herder, 1966.

———. "Kommentar zu LG Kap. 2". In LThK.E 1:176–209. Freiburg
im Breisgau: Herder, 1966.

Grootaers, J. "Zwischen den Sitzungsperioden: Die 'zweite Vorbereitung' des Konzils und ihre Gegner". In Wittstadt 2:421–617.

Hampe, J. C. Ende der Gegenreformation? Das Konzil: Dokumente und
Deutung. Mainz: Matthias-Grünewald, 1964.

Hebblethwaite, P. Paul VI: The First Modern Pope. New York: Paulist
Press, 1993.

Heim, M. "Nur Tinte oder substantielle Erkenntnis? Zur ekklesiologischen Diskussion um den Begriff der Subsistenz". In Auditorium Spiritus Sancti: Festschrift zum 200-Jahr-Jubiläum der
Philosophisch-Theologischen Hochschule Heiligenkreuz, edited by
K.J. Wallner, 241–78. Grevenbroich: Bernardus-Verlag Langwaden, 2004.

Heinz, H. "Wer steht der Ökumene im Wege? Einsprüche gegen einen
ökumenischen Stillstand". In Zweites Vatikanisches Konzil: Das
bleibende Anliegen, edited by J. Piegsa, 77–115. St. Ottilien: EOS
Verlag, 1991.

Hemmerle, K. "Einheit als Leitmotiv in 'Lumen gentium' und im
Gesamt des II. Vatikanums". In Glaube im Prozess: Christsein
nach dem II. Vatikanum; Festschrift für Karl Rahner, edited by E.
Klinger and K. Wittstadt, 207–20. Freiburg im Breisgau: Herder,
1984.

———. "Erste Überlegungen zu möglichen Themen für den Dresdener Katholikentag". In Klaus Hemmerle—Weggeschichte mit dem

Zentralkomitee der deutschen Katholiken, edited by the General-sekretariat des Zentralkomitees der deutschen Katholiken, 39–52. Bonn: Generalsekretariat des Zentralkomitees der deutschen Katholiken, 1994.

———. "Ist das Konzil schon angekommen? Zum Schlussdokument der Außerordentlichen Bischofssynode 1985". In *Gemeinschaft als Bild Gottes: Beiträge zur Ekklesiologie*, edited by R. Feiter, 60–84. Ausgewählte Schriften, vol. 5. Freiburg im Breisgau: Herder, 1996.

———. "Pilgerndes Gottesvolk—Geeintes Gottesvolk: Eine Weg-Skizze". In *Gemeinschaft als Bild Gottes: Beiträge zur Ekklesiologie*, edited by R. Feiter, 85–103. Ausgewählte Schriften, vol. 5. Freiburg im Breisgau: Herder, 1996.

Hernández, O. G. "Das neue Selbstverständnis der Kirche und seine geschichtlichen und theologischen Voraussetzungen". In Baraúna 1:155–85.

Hödl, L. " 'Die Kirche ist nämlich in Christus gleichsam das Sakrament …': Eine Konzilsaussage und ihre nachkonziliare Auslegung". In *Kirche sein: Nachkonziliare Theologie im Dienst der Kirchenreform: Für Hermann Josef Pottmeyer*, edited by W. Geerlings and M. Seckler, 163–79. Freiburg im Breisgau: Herder, 1994.

Hünermann, P. "Zu den Kategorien 'Konzil' und 'Konzilsentscheidung': Vorüberlegungen zur Interpretation des II. Vatikanums". In *Das II. Vatikanum—christlicher Glaube im Horizont globaler Modernisierung: Einleitungsfragen*, edited by Hünermann, 67–82. Paderborn: Schöningh, 1998.

Huyghe, G. "Autorität der Kirche durch Dienst an den Mitmenschen". In *Die Autorität der Freiheit: Gegenwart des Konzils und Zukunft der Kirche im ökumenischen Disput*, edited by J. C. Hampe, vol. 1. Munich: Kösel-Verlag, 1967.

Jedin, H. "Die Geschäftsordnung des Konzils". In *LThK.E* 3:610–23. Freiburg im Breisgau: Herder, 1968.

Kasper, W. "Kirche als communio: Überlegungen zur ekklesiologischen Leitidee des Zweiten Vatikanischen Konzils". In *Die bleibende Bedeutung des Zweiten Vatikanischen Konzils*, edited by F. König, 62–84. Düsseldorf: Patmos-Verlag, 1986.

———. "Nochmals: Der theologische Status der Bischofskonferenzen". *ThQ* 168 (1988): 237–40.

———. *Theologie und Kirche.* Mainz: Matthias-Grünewald-Verlag, 1987.

———. "Zur Theologie und Praxis des bischöflichen Amtes". In *Bischofsbestellung: Mitwirkung der Ortskirche?* edited by B. Körner, 18–39. Graz: Styria, 2000. Previously published in *Auf neue Art Kirche sein: Festschrift für Bischof Homeyer,* edited by W. Schreer and G. Steins, 32–48. Munich: Bernward bei Don Bosco, 1999.

——— and J. Drumm. "Kirche, II. Theologie- u. dogmengeschichtlich". In *LThK*, 3rd ed., 5:1458–65. Freiburg im Breisgau: Herder, 1996.

Kaufmann, G., ed. *Tendenzen der katholischen Theologie nach dem Zweiten Vatikanischen Konzil.* Munich: Kösel, 1979.

Kehl, M. *Die Kirche: Eine katholische Ekklesiologie.* 3rd ed. Würzburg: Echter-Verlag, 1994.

Kienzler, K. " 'Communio' zwischen Gott und den Menschen—zum Kirchenbild des 2. Vatikanischen Konzils". In *Zweites Vatikanisches Konzil: Das bleibende Anliegen,* by J. Piegsa, 117–40. St. Ottilien: EOS-Verlag, 1991.

Kirchner, H. *Die römisch-katholische Kirche vom II. Vatikanischen Konzil bis zur Gegenwart.* Leipzig: Evangelische Verlagsanstalt, 1996.

Klausnitzer, W. *Das Papstamt im Disput zwischen Lutheranern und Katholiken: Schwerpunkte von der Reformation bis zur Gegenwart.* ITS 20. Innsbruck: Tyrolia-Verlag, 1987.

Klinger, E., and R. Zerfaß, eds. *Die Kirche der Laien: Eine Weichenstellung des Konzils.* Würzburg: Echter, 1987.

Kloppenburg, B. "Abstimmungen und letzte Änderungen der Konstitution". In Baraúna 1:106–39.

Klostermann, F. "Kommentar zu LG Kap. 4". In *LThK.E* 1:260–83. Freiburg im Breisgau: Herder, 1966.

"Das kollegiale Prinzip in der Kirche". *HerKorr* 17 (1962/1963):527–29.

Komonchak, J. A. "Der Kampf für das Konzil während der Vorbereitung (1960–1962)". In Wittstadt 1:189–401.

König, F. "Das Vatikanum II—wegweisend für die Zukunft der Kirche". In *Die bleibende Bedeutung des Zweiten Vatikanischen Konzils,* ed. König, 131–42. Düsseldorf: Patmos-Verlag, 1986.

———. *Der Weg der Kirche.* Düsseldorf: Patmos-Verlag, 1986.

Küng, H. "Die charismatische Struktur der Kirche". *Conc(D)* 1 (1965): 282–90.

Latourelle, R. *Le Christ et l'Église: Signes du salut*. Tournai: Desclée; Montreal: Bellarmin, 1971.

Lercaro, G. "La Signification du Décret 'De Œcumenismo'". *Irén* (1964): 467–86.

Linnerz, H. *Das Konzil hat gesprochen: Themen—Texte—Tendenzen*. Kevelaer: Butzon, 1966.

Lobkowicz, N. *Was brachte uns das Konzil?* Würzburg: Naumann, 1986.

Lubac, H. de. *De Lubac: A Theologian Speaks*. Interview conducted by Angelo Scola. Los Angeles, Calif.: Twin Circle Publishing Company, 1985.

———. "Zur Einführung". In Baraúna 1:15–22.

Metz, J. B. "Das Konzil—'der Anfang eines Anfangs'?" In Richter, *Konzil*, 11–24.

Mieth, D., and C. Theobald. "Unbeantwortete Fragen". *Conc(D)* 35 (1999): 1–3.

Moeller, C. "Die Entstehung der Konstitution, ideengeschichtlich betrachtet". In Baraúna 1:71–105.

Molinari, P. "Der endzeitliche Charakter der pilgernden Kirche und ihre Einheit mit der himmlischen Kirche". In Baraúna 2:435–56.

Mörsdorf, K. "Der hierarchische Aufbau der Kirche". In Sandfuchs, 38–54.

Mühlen, H. "Der Kirchenbegriff des Konzils". In *Die Autorität der Freiheit: Gegenwart des Konzils und Zukunft der Kirche im ökumenischen Disput*, edited by J. C. Hampe, 1:291–313. Munich: Kösel-Verlag, 1967.

———. *Una mystica Persona: Die Kirche als das Mysterium der Identität des Hl. Geistes in Christus und den Christen; Eine Person in vielen Personen*. Munich: Schöningh, 1964.

———. "Das Verhältnis zwischen Inkarnation und Kirche in den Aussagen des Vaticanum II". *ThGl* 55 (1965): 171–90.

Müller, G. L., and K. J. Wallner. *Was bedeutet uns Maria? Die Antwort des Konzils*. Vienna: Rosenkranz-Sühnekreuzzug um den Frieden der Welt, 1994.

Neuner, P. "Die Kirche: Mysterium und Volk Gottes". In *Erinnerungen an einen Aufbruch: Das II. Vatikanische Konzil*, edited by N. Kutschki, 37–50. Würzburg: Echter, 1995.

Nissiotis, N. A. "Die Ekklesiologie des Zweiten Vatikanischen Konzils in orthodoxer Sicht und ihre ökumenische Bedeutung". *KuD* 10 (1964): 153–68.

Onclin, W. H. J. "Die Kollegialität der Bischöfe und ihre Struktur". *Conc(D)* 1 (1965): 664–69.

Ott, H. "Das Mysterium der Kirche". In Hampe, *Konzil*, 164–70.

Persson, Per Erik. "Der endzeitliche Charakter der pilgernden Kirche und ihre Einheit mit der himmlischen Kirche". In *Die Autorität der Freiheit: Gegenwart des Konzils und Zukunft der Kirche im ökumenischen Disput*, edited by J. C. Hampe, 1:338–43. Munich: Kösel-Verlag, 1967.

Pesch, O. H. *Das Zweite Vatikanische Konzil: Vorgeschichte, Verlauf, Ergebnisse, Nachgeschichte*. Würzburg: Echter, 1994.

Philips, G. *L'Église et son mystère au II Concile du Vatican*. Vol. 1. Paris: Desclée, 1967.

———. "Die Geschichte der Dogmatischen Konstitution über die Kirche 'Lumen gentium'". In *LThK.E* 1:139–55. Freiburg im Breisgau: Herder, 1966.

Plate, M. *Weltereignis Konzil: Darstellung-Sinn-Ereignis*. Freiburg im Breisgau: Herder, 1966.

Pottmeyer, H. J. "Die Frage nach der wahren Kirche". In *HFTh*, 2nd ed., 3:159–84. Tübingen: Francke, 2000.

———. "Der Heilige Geist und die Kirche: Von einer christomonistischen zu einer trinitarischen Ekklesiologie". *Tutzinger-Studien* 2 (1981): 44–55.

———. "Kirche als Communio: Eine Reformidee aus unterschiedlichen Perspektiven". *StZ* 117 (1992): 579–89.

———. "Das Lehramt der Bischofskonferenz". In Müller/Pottmeyer, 116–33.

———. "Die Mitsprache der Gläubigen in Glaubenssachen: Eine alte Praxis und ihre Wiederentdeckung". *IKaZ* 25 (1996): 134–47.

———. "Modernisierung in der katholischen Kirche am Beispiel der Kirchenkonzeption des I. und II. Vatikanischen Konzils". In *Vatikanum II und Modernisierung: Historische, theologische und soziologische Perspektiven*, edited by F.-X. Kaufmann and A. Zingerle, 131–46. Paderborn: Schöningh, 1996.

———. *Die Rolle des Papsttums im Dritten Jahrtausend*. QD 179. Freiburg im Breisgau: Herder, 1999.

———. "Der theologische Status der Bischofskonferenz—Positionen, Klärungen und Prinzipien". In Müller/Pottmeyer, 44–87.

———. "Die Voten und ersten Beiträge der deutschen Bischöfe zur Ekklesiologie des II. Vatikanischen Konzils". In *Der Beitrag der deutschsprachigen und osteuropäischen Länder zum Zweiten Vatikanischen Konzil*, edited by K. Wittstadt and W. Verschooten, 143–55. Louvain: Bibliotheek van de Faculteit der Godgeleerdheid, 1996.

———. "Die zwiespältige Ekklesiologie des Zweiten Vatikanums—Ursache nachkonziliarer Konflikte". *TThZ* 92 (1993): 272–83.

———, G. Alberigo, and J.-P. Jossua, eds. *Die Rezeption des Zweiten Vatikanischen Konzils*. Düsseldorf: Patmos-Verlag, 1986.

Raguer, H. "Das früheste Gepräge der Versammlung". In Wittstadt 2:201–72.

Rahner, H. *Symbole der Kirche: Die Ekklesiologie der Väter*. Salzburg: Müller, 1964.

Rahner, K. *Das Amt der Einheit*. Stuttgart: Schwabenverlag, 1964.

———. "Kommentar zu LG Artikel 18 bis 27". In *LThK.E* 1:210–46. Freiburg: Herder, 1966.

———. "Die Sünde in der Kirche". In Baraúna 1:346–62.

———. "Theologische Grundinterpretationen des II. Vatikanischen Konzils". In *Schriften zur Theologie* 14:287–302. Einsiedeln, Zürich, and Cologne: Benziger, 1980.

———. "Volk Gottes". In *Herders Theologisches Taschenlexikon*, edited by Rahner, 8:65–68. Freiburg im Breisgau: Herder, 1973.

———. "Das Volk Gottes". In Sandfuchs, 27–37.

——— and E. Schillebeeckx. "Wozu und für wen eine neue internationale theologische Zeitschrift?" *Conc(D)* 1 (1965): 1–3.

——— and H. Vorgrimler. "Allgemeine Einleitung". In *KlKK*, edited by Rahner and Vorgrimler, 13–33.

Reuter, H. *Das II. Vatikanische Konzil: Vorgeschichte—Verlauf—Ergebnisse, dargestellt nach Dokumenten und Berichten*. Cologne: Wort und Werk, 1966.

Richter, K. "Liturgiereform als Mitte einer Erneuerung der Kirche". In Richter, *Konzil*, 53–74.

———, ed. *Das Konzil war erst der Anfang: Die Bedeutung des II. Vatikanums für Theologie und Kirche*. Mainz: Matthias-Grünewald-Verlag, 1991.

Rigaux, B. "Das Mysterium der Kirche im Lichte der Schrift". In Baraúna 1:199–219.

Rousseau, O. "Die Konstitution im Rahmen der Erneuerungsbewegungen in Theologie und Seelsorge während der letzten Jahrzehnte". In Baraúna 1:25–44.

Ruggieri, G. "Der schwierige Abschied von der kontroverstheologisch geprägten Ekklesiologie". In Wittstadt 2:331–419.

———. "Zu einer Hermeneutik des Zweiten Vatikanischen Konzils". *Conc(D)* 35 (1999): 4–17.

Sandfuchs, W., ed. *Das neue Volk Gottes: Eine Einführung in die Dogmatische Konstitution "Über die Kirche"*. With contributions by Heinrich Fries et al. Würzburg: Arena-Verlag, 1966.

Scheffczyk, L. *Aspekte der Kirche in der Krise: Um die Entscheidung für das authentische Konzil*. Quaestiones non disputatae 1. Siegburg: F. Schmitt, 1993.

———. "Die Kollegialität der Bischöfe unter theologischem und pastoralpraktischem Aspekt". In *Episcopale Munus: Recueil d'études sur le ministère épiscopal offertes en hommage à Son Excellence Mgr J. Gijsen*, edited by P. Delhaye and L. Elders, 83–99. Assen: Van Gorcum, 1982.

Schillebeeckx, E. *Besinnung auf das Zweite Vatikanum: Vierte Session: Bilanz und Übersicht*. Vienna: Herder, 1966.

Schmiedl, J. *Das Konzil und die Orden: Krise und Erneuerung des gottgeweihten Lebens*. Vallendar-Schönstatt: Patris-Verlag, 1999.

Schmitz, H. "Die Lehrautorität der Bischofskonferenz gemäß c. 753 CIC". In *Die Bischofskonferenz, theologischer und juridischer Status*, with contributions by I. Führer et al. Edited by H. Müller and H.J. Pottmeyer, 196–235. Düsseldorf: Patmos, 1989.

Schulte, R. "Erneuertes Kirchen- und Priesterverständnis als aktueller Auftrag: Zur Wegweisung der Dogmatischen Konstitution 'Lumen gentium'—Über die Kirche". In *Aufbruch des Zweiten Vatikanischen Konzils heute*, edited by J. Kremer, 73–102. Innsbruck, Vienna: Tyrolia-Verlag, 1993.

———. "Das Ordensleben als Zeichen". In Baraúna 2:383–414.

Seeber, D. A. *Das Zweite Vaticanum: Konzil des Übergangs*. Freiburg im Breisgau: Herder, 1966.

Semmelroth, O. "Die Kirche, das neue Gottesvolk". In Baraúna 1:365–79.

———. "Kommentar zu LG Kap. 7". In *LThK.E* 1:314–25. Freiburg: Herder, 1966.

———. "Kommentar zu LG Kap. 8". In *LThK.E* 1:326–47. Freiburg: Herder, 1966.

———. "Maria im Geheimnis Christi und der Kirche". In Sandfuchs, 102–14.

Seybold, M. Foreword to *"Corpus Suum mystice constituit" (LG 7): La Chiesa Corpo Mistico di Cristo nel primo capitolo della "Lumen gentium"; Storia del Testo dalla "Mystici Corporis" al Vaticano II con riferimenti alla attività conciliare del P. Sebastian Tromp S.J.*, by S. Alberto, 13–18. Regensburg: Pustet, 1996.

Sieben, H. J. "Selbstverständnis und römische Sicht der Partikularsynode: Einige Streiflichter auf das erste Jahrtausend". In *Die Bischofskonferenz, theologischer und juridischer Status*, with contributions by I. Führer et al., edited by H. Müller and H. J. Pottmeyer, 10–35. Düsseldorf: Patmos, 1989.

Smulders, P. "Die Kirche als Sakrament des Heils". In Baraúna 1:289–312.

Teuffenbach, A. von. *Die Bedeutung des* subsistit in *(LG 8): Zum Selbstverständnis der katholischen Kirche.* Munich: Wissenschaft, 2002.

Tromp, S. *Corpus Christi, quod est Ecclesia.* 4 vols. Rome: Universitas Gregoriana, 1937–1972.

Vaucelles, L. de. "Der Katholizismus in der Zeit nach dem Konzil: Veränderungen des gesellschaftlichen Umfelds". In *Die Rezeption des Zweiten Vatikanischen Konzils*, edited by H. J. Pottmeyer, G. Alberigo, and J.-P. Jossua, 66–84. Düsseldorf: Patmos-Verlag, 1986.

Vischer, L. "Die Rezeption der Debatte über die Kollegialität". In *Die Rezeption des Zweiten Vatikanischen Konzils*, edited by H. J. Pottmeyer, G. Alberigo, and J.-P. Jossua, 293–312. Düsseldorf: Patmos-Verlag, 1986.

Vorgrimler, H. "Kommentar zu LG Artikel 29", in *LThK.E* 1:256–59. Freiburg: Herder, 1966.

———. "Theologische Positionen Karl Rahners im Blick auf Hans Urs von Balthasar". Lecture given on January 12, 2000, at the Karl Rahner Akademie in Cologne.

———. "Vom 'Geist des Konzils'". In Richter, *Konzil*, 25–52.

———. "Zur Einführung". in *LThK.E* 1:7f. Freiburg: Herder, 1966.

Wassilowsky, G. "Die 'Textwerkstatt' einer Gruppe deutscher Theologen auf dem II. Vatikanum". In *Die deutschsprachigen Länder und das II. Vatikanum*, edited by H. Wolf and C. Arnold, 61–87. ITS 59. Paderborn: Schöningh, 2000.

———. *Universales Heilssakrament Kirche: Karl Rahners Beitrag zur Ekklesiologie des II. Vatikanums*. Innsbruck: Tyrolia-Verlag, 2001.

Witte, J. L. "Die Kirche 'Sacramentum unitatis' für die ganze Welt". In Baraúna 1:420–52.

Wittstadt, K. "Am Vorabend des II. Vatikanischen Konzils (1. Juli–10. Oktober 1962)". In Wittstadt 1:457–560.

———, ed. of the German edition. *Geschichte des Zweiten Vatikanischen Konzils (1959–1965)*. Vol. 1: *Die katholische Kirche auf dem Weg in ein neues Zeitalter: Die Ankündigung und Vorbereitung des Zweiten Vatikanischen Konzils* (Mainz: Grünewald, 1997); vol. 2: *Das Konzil auf dem Weg zu sich selbst: Erste Sitzungsperiode und Intersessio: Oktober 1962–September 1963* (Mainz: Grünewald, 2000).

———. "Perspektiven einer kirchlichen Erneuerung—Der deutsche Episkopat und die Vorbereitungsphase des II. Vatikanums". In *Vatikanum II und Modernisierung—Historische, theologische und soziologische Perspektiven*, edited by F.-X. Kaufmann and A. Zingerle, 85–106. Paderborn: Schöningh, 1996.

Wulf, F. "Die allgemeine Berufung zur Heiligkeit in der Kirche: Die Ordensleute". In Sandfuchs, 72–85.

———. "Kommentar zu LG Kap. 5 u. 6". In *LThK.E* 1:284–313. Freiburg: Herder, 1966.

———. "Theologische Phänomenologie des Ordenslebens". *MySal* 4/2 (1973): 450–87.

IV. SECONDARY LITERATURE ON JOSEPH RATZINGER

Allen, J. L. *Cardinal Ratzinger: The Vatican's Enforcer of the Faith*. New York and London: Continuum, 2000.

Baier, W., et al., eds. *Weisheit Gottes—Weisheit der Welt: Festschrift für Joseph Kardinal Ratzinger zum 60. Geburtstag*. 2 vols. St. Ottilien: EOS Verlag, 1987.

Batlogg, A. "Christentum als Neuheitserlebnis: Zur jüngsten Veröffentlichung von Joseph Ratzinger". *ZKTh* 119 (1997): 323–32.

Beinert, W. "Eine Kirche, die so bleibt, bleibt nicht: Tradition und Wandel in der Glaubensgemeinschaft". In *Im Spannungsfeld von*

Tradition und Innovation: Festschrift für Joseph Kardinal Ratzinger, edited by G. Schmuttermayr et al., 219–48. Regensburg: Pustet, 1997.

Boff, L. *Manifest für die Ökumene: Ein Streit mit Kardinal Ratzinger*. Düsseldorf: Patmos-Verlag, 2001.

Fahey, M. "Joseph Ratzinger als Ekklesiologe und Seelsorger". *Conc(D)* 17 (1981): 79–85.

Frieling, R. "Der Ökumenismus Ratzingers". *MdKI* 33 (1982): 64–70.

Greiner, F. "Vorwort". *IKaZ* 1 (1972): 1–3.

Greshake, G. "Weltkirche und Ortskirche: Bemerkungen zu einem problematischen Verhältnis". *ThGl* 91 (2001): 528–42.

Hahn, V. "Strukturen der Kirche—Zur Identitätsproblematik der Kirche". In *Weisheit Gottes—Weisheit der Welt: Festschrift für Joseph Ratzinger zum 60. Geburtstag*, edited by W. Baier et al., 2:979–97. St. Ottilien: EOS Verlag, 1987.

Häring, H. "Eine katholische Theologie? J. Ratzinger, das Trauma von Hans im Glück". In *Katholische Kirche—wohin? Wider den Verrat am Konzil*, edited by N. Greinacher and H. Küng, 241–58. Munich: Piper, 1986.

———. *Theologie und Ideologie bei Joseph Ratzinger*. Düsseldorf: Patmos, 2001.

Horn, S. O. "II. Ökumenische Dimensionen—Einführung". In *Mitte*, 175–80.

———. and V. Pfnür. "Introduction". In *Pilgrim Fellowship of Faith*, translated by Henry Taylor, 9–16. San Francisco: Ignatius Press, 2005.

Jeon, K.-J. E. *Die Kirche bei Joseph Ratzinger: Untersuchungen zum strukturierten Volk Gottes nach der Kirchenlehre Joseph Ratzingers*. Unpublished dissertation. Innsbruck, 1995.

Jüngel, E. "Nur Wahrheit befreit". *Deutsches Allgemeines Sonntagsblatt* 37 (October 15, 2000): 20–22.

Kaes, D. *Theologie im Anspruch von Geschichte und Wahrheit: Zur Hermeneutik Joseph Ratzingers*. Dissertation. Theologische Reihe, vol. 75. St. Ottilien: EOS Verlag, 1997.

Karger, M. "Kirche als Leib Christi und als Volk Gottes verbunden: Zum siebzigsten Geburtstag von Kardinal Joseph Ratzinger, dem Präfekten der römischen Kongregation für die Glaubenslehre". *Deutsche Tagespost* 50 (April 15, 1997): 5.

Kasper, W. "Das Verhältnis von Universal- und Ortskirche: Freund-
   schaftliche Auseinandersetzung mit der Kritik von Joseph Kar-
   dinal Ratzinger". *StZ* 125 (2000): 795–804.
———. "Das Wesen des Christlichen". *ThRv* 65 (1969): 182–88.
Kehl, M. "Review of J. Ratzinger, *Zur Lage des Glaubens*". *ThPh* 61
   (1986): 609f.
Küng, H. "Kardinal Ratzinger, Papst Wojtyla und die Angst vor der
   Freiheit (1985): Nach langem Schweigen ein offenes Wort".
   In *Katholische Kirche—wohin? Wider den Verrat am Konzil*, edited
   by N. Greinacher and H. Küng, 389–407. Munich: Piper,
   1986.
———. "Theologe und Vatikankritiker: 'Dieser Papst redet mit Haider,
   nicht mit Küng', Gespräch von D. Hemberger mit H. Küng".
   Die Furche 57, no. 1 (2001): 11.
Lohaus, G. "Kirche und Pastoral bei Joseph Ratzinger: Die pastoral-
   theologische Relevanz seines konziliaren Kirchenbegriffs (Teil
   1)". *Pastoralblatt für die Diözesen Aachen, Berlin, Essen, Ham-
   burg, Hildesheim, Köln, Osnabrück* 53, no. 5 (2001): 131–41.
———. "Das Verhältnis von Ortskirche und Universalkirche bei Joseph
   Ratzinger: Ein Beitrag zum nachkonziliaren Streit um die uni-
   versale und partikulare Kirche". *Pastoralblatt für die Diözesen
   Aachen, Berlin, Essen, Hamburg, Hildesheim, Köln, Osnabrück* 45,
   no. 8 (1993): 234–45.
Marnach, G. "Wächter des Glaubens: Joseph Kardinal Ratzinger". In
   *Wie sie wurden, was sie sind: Zeitgenössische Theologinnen und
   Theologen im Portrait*, edited by L. Baucherochse and K. Hofmeis-
   ter, 210–29. Gütersloh: Gütersloher Verlag-Haus, 2001.
Meyer zu Schlochtern, J. *Sakrament Kirche: Wirken Gottes im Handeln
   der Menschen*. Freiburg im Breisgau: Herder, 1992.
Moll, H. "Sekundärliteratur: Rezeption und Auseinandersetzung mit dem
   theologischen Werk von Joseph Cardinal Ratzinger". In *Mitte*,
   309–15.
Nachtwei, G. *Dialogische Unsterblichkeit: Eine Untersuchung zu Joseph Rat-
   zingers Eschatologie und Theologie*. EThSt 54. Leipzig: St. Benno
   Verlag, 1986.
Nichols, A. *The Theology of Joseph Ratzinger: An Introductory Study*.
   Edinburgh: T. and T. Clark, 1988.
Pfnür, V. "Einführung". In *Mitte*, 17–24.

Schmuttermayr, G., et al., eds. *Im Spannungsfeld von Tradition und Innovation: Festschrift für Joseph Kardinal Ratzinger*. Regensburg: Pustet, 1997.

Seeber, D. "Kardinal Ratzinger: Wechsel nach Rom". *HerKorr* 36 (1982): 4–7.

Seigfried, A. "Volk Gottes als ekklesiale Gestalt der Gnade". In *Im Spannungsfeld von Tradition und Innovation: Festschrift für Joseph Kardinal Ratzinger*, edited by G. Schmuttermayr et al., 249–68. Regensburg: Pustet, 1997.

Söhngen, G. *Die Einheit in der Theologie*. Munich: Zink, 1952.

Toiviainen, S. *Subjektista objektiin: Painopisteen muutos Joseph Ratzingerin transsendentaalisessa ajattelumuodossa 1954–1981*. Helsinki: Helsinki Suomalainen teologinen kirjallisuusseura, 1993.

Utz, A. F. "Der christliche Glaube als Voraussetzung des demokratischen Pluralismus: Eine sozialethische Würdigung der wissenschaftlichen Arbeiten von Joseph Kardinal Ratzinger". In *Glaube und demokratischer Pluralismus im wissenschaftlichen Werk von Joseph Kardinal Ratzinger: Zur Verleihung des Augustin-Bea-Preises 1989*, im Auftrag der Internationalen Stiftung *Humanum*, edited by Utz, 11–44. Bonn: WBV, 1991.

Volf, M. *Trinität und Gemeinschaft: Eine ökumenische Ekklesiologie* (Mainz: Matthias-Grünewald-Verlag, 1996).

Wagner, K., and A. H. Ruf. *Kardinal Ratzinger: Der Erzbischof von München und Freising im Wort und Bild: Mit dem Beitrag "Aus meinem Leben"*. Munich: Pfeiffer, 1977.

Weiler, T. *Volk Gottes—Leib Christi: Die Ekklesiologie Joseph Ratzingers und ihr Einfluss auf das Zweite Vatikanische Konzil*. Mainz: Matthias-Grünewald-Verlag, 1997.

Wiedenhofer, S. "I. Theologische Grundlegung—Einführung". In *Mitte*, 123–26.

V. ADDITIONAL LITERATURE

Adam, K. *Das Wesen des Katholizismus*. 13th ed. Düsseldorf: Patmos-Verlag, 1957.

Aubert, R. *Vaticanum I*. Translated into German by K. Bergner. Mainz: Matthias-Grünewald-Verlag, 1965.

Balthasar, H. U. von. "Casta meretrix". Translated by John Saward. In *Spouse of the Word*, 193–288. Explorations in Theology 2. San Francisco: Ignatius Press, 1991.

———. *Elucidations*. Translated by John Riches. San Francisco: Ignatius Press, 1998.

———. *The Glory of the Lord: A Theological Aesthetics*. Vol. 4, *The Realm of Metaphysics in Antiquity*. Translated by Brian McNeil, C.R.V., et al. San Francisco: Ignatius Press, 1989.

———. *The Office of Peter and the Structure of the Church*. Translated by Andrée Emery. San Francisco: Ignatius Press, 1986.

———. *A Theological Anthropology*. New York: Sheed and Ward, 1967.

Basil the Great. *On the Holy Spirit*. Crestwood, N.Y.: St. Vladimir's Seminary Press, 1980.

Beinert, W. "Autorität um der Liebe willen". In *Priester heute*, edited by K. Hillenbrand, 32–66. Würzburg: Echter, 1990.

———, ed. *Kirchenbilder, Kirchenvisionen: Variationen über eine Wirklichkeit*. Regensburg: Pustet, 1995.

Bellarmine, R. *Controrsarium de conciliis IV/2*. In *Opera*, edited by J. Fèvre. Paris, 1870; photostatic reprint (Frankfurt, 1965).

Berger, K. "Keine Ohrfeige für Protestanten: Warum *Dominus Iesus* auch für protestantische Christen nützlich sein kann". *Die Tagespost* 53 (November 25, 2000): 6.

Bernard of Clairvaux. *On the Song of Songs*. Translated by Kilian Walsh. 4 vols. Spencer, Mass.: Cistercian Publications, 1976; Latin text in *Sancti Bernardi Opera*, ad fidem codicum recensuerunt J. Leclercq, C. H. Talbot, H. M. Rochais, vol. 1 (Rome: Editiones Cistercienses, 1957).

Berz, A., trans. "Das neue Gesicht des 'Concilium' ". *Conc(D)* 8 (1972): 705–7.

Betti, U. *La costituzione dommatica "Pastor aeternus" del Concilio vaticano I*. Rome: Pontificio Ateneo "Antonianum", 1961.

Beyerhaus, P. "Der kirchlich-theologische Dienst des Albrecht-Bengel-Hauses". *Diakrisis* 17 (1969): 9f.

Blank, J., P. Hünermann, and P. M. Zulehner. *Das Recht der Gemeinde auf Eucharistie*. Trier: Paulinus-Verlag, 1978.

Boff, L. *Church: Charism and Power; Liberation Theology and the Institutional Church*. Translated by John W. Diercksmeier. New York: Crossroad, 1985.

Böttigheimer, C. "Mysterium Christi und sakramentales Amt: Zur Problematik von Gemeinden ohne sonntägliche Eucharistiefeier". *StZ* 122 (1997): 117–28.

Bouyer, L. "Die Einheit des Glaubens und die Vielheit der Theologien: Eine historische Hinführung". In *Die Einheit des Glaubens und der theologische Pluralismus*, edited by the Internationale Theologenkommission, 166–79. Einsiedeln: Johannes Verlag, 1973.

Brandmüller, W. "Petrus und seine Nachfolger". In *Mysterium Kirche: Sozialkonzern oder Stiftung Christi?* Edited by Brandmüller, 135–62. Aachen: MM Verlag, 1996.

Bulgakov, S. "Le Ciel sur la terre". *US* 3 (1927): 43.

Casel, O. *Das christliche Kultmysterium.* 4th ed. Regensburg: Pustet, 1960.

Collet, G. "Befreiungstheologie I: Historische, geographische und politische Wurzeln". In *LThK*, 3rd ed., 2:130–32. Freiburg im Breisgau: Herder, 1994.

Congar, Y. "Ecclesia ab Abel". In *Abhandlungen über Theologie und Kirche: Festschrift für Karl Adam*, edited by M. Reding, 79–108. Düsseldorf: Patmos-Verlag, 1952.

———. *Die Lehre von der Kirche: Vom Abendländischen Schisma bis zur Gegenwart.* HDG 3/3d. Freiburg: Herder, 1971.

Courth, F. *Die Sakramente: Ein Lehrbuch für Studium und Praxis der Theologie.* Freiburg im Breisgau: Herder, 1995.

Cullmann, O. *Einheit und Vielfalt.* 2nd ed. Tübingen: Mohr, 1990.

Degenhardt, J.J., H. Tenhumberg, and H. Thimme, eds. *Kirchen auf gemeinsamem Wege.* Bielefeld and Kevelaer: Luther-Verlag, 1977.

Dibelius, O. *Das Jahrhundert der Kirche.* 6th ed. Berlin: Furche-Verlag, 1928.

Dulles, A., S.J. *Revelation Theology: A History.* New York: Herder and Herder, 1969.

Eckert, M. "Bloch, Ernst". In *LThK*, 3rd ed., 2:527. Freiburg im Breisgau: Herder, 1994.

Elsässer, M., trans. and ed. *A. M. S. Boethius: Die theologischen Traktate.* Hamburg: Meiner, 1988.

Faber, E.-M. "Mysterium. III. Systematisch-theologisch". In *LThK*, 3rd ed., 7:579–81. Freiburg im Breisgau: Herder, 1998.

Fernandez, C. "Metaphysica Generalis". In *Philosophiae Scholasticae Summa*, edited by L. Salcedo and C. Fernandez, 3rd ed., vol. 1. Madrid: Ed. Católica, 1964.

Figura, M. "Die Beziehung zwischen Universalkirche und Teilkirche nach Henri de Lubac". *IKaZ* 30 (2001): 468–83.

———. "Kirche und Eucharistie im Licht des Geheimnisses des dreifaltigen Gottes". *IKaZ* 29 (2000): 100–119.

Forte, B. *La Chiesa—icona della Trinità: Breve ecclesiologia.* Brescia: Queriniana, 1984.

Fries, H., H. Küng, P. Lengsfeld, W. Pannenberg, E. Schlink, and H.-H. Wolf, eds. *Reform und Anerkennung kirchlicher Ämter: Ein Memorandum der Arbeitsgemeinschaft ökumenischer Universitätsinstitute.* Munich: Kaiser Verlag; Mainz: Matthias-Grünewald-Verlag, 1973.

Fries, H., and K. Rahner. *Einigung der Kirchen—reale Möglichkeit.* QD 100. Freiburg im Breisgau: Herder, 1983.

García, A. "Die lateinamerikanische Theologie der Befreiung". *IKaZ* 2 (73): 400–423.

Geiselmann, R. G., ed. *Symbolik,* by J. A. Möhler. Cologne: Hegner, 1960.

Görres, A. "Schuld und Schuldgefühle". *IKaZ* 13 (1984): 430–43.

Gredt, J. *Elementa Philosophiae Aristotelico-Thomisticae.* Vol. 2. Barcelona, Freiburg, and Rome: Herder, 1961.

Greiner, F. "Internationale katholische Zeitschrift 'Communio'". *IKaZ* 1 (1972): 1–3.

Greshake, G. *An den drei-einen Gott glauben.* Freiburg im Breisgau: Herder, 1998.

———. *Der dreieine Gott: Eine trinitarische Theologie.* Freiburg im Breisgau: Herder, 1997.

———. *Priestersein.* Freiburg im Breisgau: Herder, 1982.

———. *Priester sein in dieser Zeit: Theologie—Pastorale Praxis—Spiritualität.* 2nd ed. Freiburg im Breisgau: Herder, 2000.

———. "Weltkirche und Ortskirche: Bemerkungen zu einem problematischen Verhältnis". *ThGl* 91 (2001): 528–42.

Guardini, R. *Berichte über mein Leben.* Düsseldorf: Patmos, 1984.

———. *The Spirit of the Liturgy.* Translated by Ada Lane. London: Sheed and Ward, 1930; reprinted, New York: Crossroad, 1998.

———. *Vom Sinn der Kirche.* Mainz, 1922; new ed., Mainz: Grünewald; Paderborn: Schöningh, 1990.

Gutiérrez, G. *A Theology of Liberation: History, Politics, and Salvation.* Translated and edited by Sr. Caridad Inda and John Eagleson. Maryknoll, N.Y.: Orbis Books, 1973.

Hallermann, H. "Priesterliche Identität gewinnen in Abgrenzung oder in Kooperation?" *Diak* 29 (1998): 200.

Herder Verlag, ed. *"Wir sind Kirche": Das Kirchenvolks-Begehren in der Diskussion.* Freiburg im Breisgau: Herder, 1995.

Herms, E. *Einheit der Christen in der Gemeinschaft der Kirchen.* Göttingen: Vandenhoeck and Ruprecht, 1984.

———. "Ökumenische Zeichen der Glaubensfreiheit". *US* 39 (1984): 178–200.

Herwegen, I. *Lumen Christi.* Munich: Theatiner-Verlag, 1924.

Hick, J. *Evil and the God of Love.* 4th ed. Norfolk, 1975.

Hoppe, R. "Das Mysterium und die Ekklesia: Aspekte zum Mysterium-Verständnis im Kolosser- und Epheserbrief". In *Gottes Weisheit im Mysterium: Vergessene Wege christlicher Spiritualität,* edited by A. Schilson, 81–101. Mainz: Matthias-Grünewald-Verlag, 1989.

Horn, C. "Subsistenz". In *HWPh,* vol. 10, cols. 486–93.

Horst, F. van der. *Das Schema über die Kirche auf dem I. Vatikanischen Konzil.* Paderborn: Bonifacius-Druckerei, 1963.

Hünermann, P. "Hinweise zum theologischen Gebrauch des 'Denzinger'". In *DH* 9–13.

———. "Rationale Begründungsverfahren in der Dogmatik und kirchliches Lehramt". In *Glaubenswissenschaft? Theologie im Spannungsfeld von Glaube, Rationalität und Öffentlichkeit,* edited by P. Neuner, 77–98. QD 195. Freiburg im Breisgau: Herder, 2002.

———. "Theologische Reflexionen zu einem umstrittenen römischen Lehrdokument". In *Was ist heute noch katholisch? Zum Streit um die innere Einheit und Vielfalt der Kirche,* edited by A. Franz, 65–86. QD 192. Freiburg im Breisgau: Herder, 2001.

Imhof, P., and H. Biallowons, eds. *Glaube in winterlicher Zeit: Gespräche mit Karl Rahner aus den letzten Lebensjahren.* Düsseldorf: Patmos, 1986.

Internationale Theologenkommission, ed. *Mysterium des Gottesvolkes.* Einsiedeln: Johannes Verlag, 1987.

Ivánka, E. von. *Rhomäerreich und Gottesvolk.* Freiburg im Breisgau and Munich: Alber, 1968.

Jeremias, J. *Die Abendmahlsworte Jesu.* Göttingen: Vandenhoeck and Ruprecht, 1960.

———. *Golgotha und der heilige Fels.* Leipzig: Pfeiffer, 1926.

————. *Neutestamentliche Theologie*. Vol. 1. Gütersloh: Gütersloher Verlagshaus G. Mohn, 1971.

John Paul II. *Crossing the Threshold of Hope*. Edited by Vittorio Messori. Translated by Jenny McPhee and Martha McPhee. New York: Alfred A. Knopf, 1994.

Kasper, W. "Die Kirche als universales Sakrament des Heils". In *Glaube im Prozess: Christsein nach dem II. Vatikanum: Festschrift für Karl Rahner*, edited by E. Klinger and K. Wittstadt, 221–39. Freiburg im Breisgau: Herder, 1984.

Kehl, M. *Kirche als Institution: Zur theologischen Begründung des institutionellen Charakters der Kirche in der neueren deutschsprachigen katholischen Ekklesiologie*. Frankfurt am Main: Knecht, 1978.

————. *Die Kirche: Eine katholische Ekklesiologie*. 3rd ed. Würzburg: Echter-Verlag, 1994.

————. *Wohin geht die Kirche? Eine Zeitdiagnose*. Freiburg im Breisgau: Herder, 1996.

Kertelge, K. "Kirche: I. Neues Testament". In *LThK*, 3rd ed., 5:1453–58. Freiburg im Breisgau: Herder, 1996.

Knitter, P. F. *Ein Gott—viele Religionen: Gegen den Absolutheitsanspruch des Christentums*. Munich: Kösel, 1988.

Körner, B. "Extra ecclesiam nulla salus: Sinn und Pröblematik dieses Satzes in einer sich wandelnden fundamentaltheologischen Ekklesiologie". *ZKTh* 114 (1992): 274–92.

————. "Mitgestaltung, nicht Demokratisierung? Eine erste Auswertung des Forschungsschwerpunktes 'Demokratische und synodale Strukturen in der Kirche'". In *Bischofsbestellung: Mitwirkung der Ortskirche?* edited by Körner, 124–60. Graz: Styria, 2000.

Koster, M. D. *Ekklesiologie im Werden*. Paderborn: Bonifacius-Druckerei, 1940. Reprinted in the anthology of Koster's essays edited and published under the title *Volk Gottes im Werden*, by H.-D. Langer and O. H. Pesch, 195–272 (Mainz: Matthias-Grünewald-Verlag, 1971).

Küng, H. *Christ sein*. Munich: Piper, 1974.

————. "Ein Welt-Katechismus?" *Conc(D)* 29 (1993): 273f.

Lehmann, K. *Neuer Mut zum Kirchesein*. Freiburg im Breisgau: Herder, 1982.

Lohfink, N. "Beobachtungen zur Geschichte des Ausdrucks 'Am Jahwe'".
In *Probleme biblischer Theologie: Gerhard von Rad zum 70. Geburtstag*, edited by H. W. Wolff, 275–305. Munich: Kaiser, 1970.

Loisy, A. *L'Évangile et l'Église*. Paris: Fishbacher, 1902.

Löser, W. "'Jetzt aber seid ihr Gottes Volk' (1 Petr 2,10): Rechtfertigung und sakramentale Kirche". *ThPh* 73 (1998): 321–33.

Lubac, H. de. *Catholicism: Christ and the Common Destiny of Man*. Translated by Lancelot C. Sheppard and Elizabeth Englund. San
Francisco: Ignatius Press, 1988.

————. *The Christian Faith: An Essay on the Structure of the Apostles' Creed*.
Translated by Richard Arnandez. San Francisco: Ignatius Press,
1986.

————. *Corpus mysticum: L'Eucharistie et l'Église au moyen âge; Étude
historique*. Paris: Aubier, 1944.

————. "Credo ... Sanctorum Communionem". In *Credo: Ein theologisches Lesebuch*, edited by J. Ratzinger and P. Henrici, 271–88.
Cologne: Communio, 1992.

————. *The Drama of Atheist Humanism*. Translated by Edith M. Riley.
New York: Sheed and Ward, 1950.

————. "Der Glaube der Kirche". In *Geheimnis aus dem wir leben* [an
anthology of de Lubac's essays on the Church selected and
translated into German by Hans Urs von Balthasar], 49–82.
Einsiedeln: Johannes Verlag, 1967.

————. *The Motherhood of the Church, Followed by Particular Churches in
the Universal Church and an Interview Conducted by Gwendoline
Jarczyk*. Translated by Sr. Sergia Englund, O.C.D. San Francisco: Ignatius Press, 1982.

————. *The Splendor of the Church*. Translated by Michael Mason. San
Francisco: Ignatius Press, 1999.

Menke, K.-H. *Die Einzigkeit Jesu Christi im Horizont der Sinnfrage*.
Freiburg: Johannes Verlag, 1995.

Mersch, E. *Le Corps mystique du Christ: Études de théologie historique*.
2 vols. Louvain: Museum Lessianum, 1933.

Metz, J. B. *Zur Theologie der Welt*. Mainz: Matthias-Grünewald-Verlag,
1968.

Möhler, J. A. *Symbolik oder Darstellung der dogmatischen Gegensätze der
Katholiken und Protestanten nach ihren öffentlichen Bekenntnißschriften*. Regensburg: Manz, 1882.

Moll, H. "Die Internationale Theologische Kommission im Spiegel ihrer Publikationen". *ThG* 33 (1990): 284–90.

Moltmann, J. *Der gekreuzigte Gott*. Munich: Kaiser, 1972.

———. *Theologie der Hoffnung*. Munich: Kaiser, 1964.

Morawa, J. *Die Communio-Kirche als Sakrament des Heils in und für die Welt: Zum erneuerten Verständnis der Sendung der Kirche in der Gegenwart im Werk Walter Kaspers*. Frankfurt am Main: Lang, 1996.

Mörsdorf, K. "Die Autonomie der Ortskirche". *AKathKR* 138 (1969): 388–405.

Mühl, M., and J.-H. Tück. "Stellungnahmen zu 'Dominus Iesus': Ein erster bibliographischer Überblick". In *"Dominus Iesus": Anstößige Wahrheit oder anstößige Kirche? Dokumente, Hintergründe, Standpunkte und Folgerungen*, edited by M. J. Rainer, 336–45. 2nd ed. Münster: Lit, 2001.

Müller, G. L. *Katholische Dogmatik für Studium und Praxis der Theologie*. Freiburg im Breisgau: Herder, 1996.

———. *Mit der Kirche denken: Bausteine und Skizzen zu einer Ekklesiologie der Gegenwart*. Würzburg: Naumann, 2001.

———. *Priesthood and Diaconate: The Recipient of the Sacrament of Holy Orders from the Perspective of Creation Theology and Christology*. Translated by Michael J. Miller. San Francisco: Ignatius Press, 2002.

——— and H. J. Pottmeyer, eds. *Die Bischofskonferenz: Theologischer und juridischer Status*. Dusseldorf: Patmos, 1989.

Neuner, P., ed. *Ekklesiologie*. Vol. 2, *Von der Reformation bis zur Gegenwart*, edited by W. Beinert. Texte zur Theologie: Dogmatik. Graz: Styria, 1995.

———. "Ekklesiologie—Die Lehre von der Kirche". In *Glaubenszugänge: Lehrbuch der katholischen Dogmatik*, edited by W. Beinert, 2:399–578. Paderborn: Schöningh, 1995.

———. *Der Laie und das Gottesvolk*. Frankfurt: Knecht, 1988.

Nocke, F.-J. "I. Allgemeine Sakramentenlehre". In *Handbuch der Dogmatik*, edited by T. Schneider, 2:188–225. Düsseldorf: Patmos-Verlag, 1992.

Orlandis Rovira, J. *Stürmische Zeiten: Die katholische Kirche in der zweiten Hälfte des 20. Jahrhunderts*. Translated from Spanish by G. Stein. Aachen: MM-Verlag, 1999.

Pottmeyer, H. J. "Der eine Geist als Prinzip der Einheit der Kirche in Vielfalt: Auswege aus einer christomonistischen Ekklesiologie". *PthI* 5 (1985): 253–84.

———. "Kirche—Selbstverständnis und Strukturen: Theologische und gesellschaftliche Herausforderung zur Glaubwürdigkeit". In *Kirche im Kontext der modernen Gesellschaft*, edited by Pottmeyer, 99–123. Munich and Zürich: Schnell und Steiner, 1989.

———. "Der mühsame Weg zum Miteinander von Einheit und Vielfalt im Verhältnis von Gesamtkirche und Ortskirchen". In *Was ist heute noch katholisch? Zum Streit um die innere Einheit und Vielfalt der Kirche*, edited by A. Franz, 291–310. QD 192. Freiburg im Breisgau: Herder, 2001.

Puza, R. "Kanonistisches zur Streitkultur in der kirchlichen Communio". In *Was ist heute noch katholisch? Zum Streit um die innere Einheit und Vielfalt der Kirche*, edited by A. Franz, 135–59. QD 192. Freiburg im Breisgau: Herder, 2001.

Quinn, J. R. *The Reform of the Papacy: The Costly Call to Christian Unity*. New York: Crossroad, 1999.

Rahner, H. *Griechische Mythen in christlicher Deutung*. Darmstadt: Wissenschaftl. Buchgesellsch., 1957.

———. *Maria und die Kirche*. Innsbruck: Tyrolia-Verlag, 1962.

———. *Symbole der Kirche: Die Ekklesiologie der Väter*. Salzburg: Müller, 1964.

Rahner, K. *Freiheit und Manipulation in Gesellschaft und Kirche*. Munich: Kösel, 1970.

———. "Gerecht und Sünder zugleich". *GuL* 36 (1963): 434–43.

———. "Die Gliedschaft der Kirche nach der Lehre der Enzyklika Pius' XII. 'Mystici Corporis Christi'". In *Schriften zur Theologie* 2:7–94. Einsiedeln, Zürich, and Cologne: Benziger, 1964.

———. "Die Kirche der Heiligen". In *Schriften zur Theologie* 3:111–26. Einsiedeln, Zürich, and Cologne: Benziger, 1964.

———. *Die Kirche der Sünder*. Vienna: Herder, 1948; first published in *StZ* 140 (1947): 163–77.

———. "Kirche und Parusie". *Cath(M)* 17 (1963): 113–28.

———. *Kirche und Sakramente*. QD 10. Freiburg im Breisgau: Herder, 1960.

———. "Vergessene Wahrheiten über das Bußsakrament". In *Schriften zur Theologie* 2:143–83. Einsiedeln, Zürich, and Cologne: Benziger, 1964.

Rahner (Karl)-Stiftung, ed. *Karl Rahner: Sämtliche Werke.* Vol. 19, *Selbst-vollzug der Kirche: Ekklesiologische Grundlegung praktischer The-ologie,* edited by K.-H. Neufeld. Solothurn, Düsseldorf, and Freiburg im Breisgau: Herder, 1995.

Rainer, M.J., ed. *"Dominus Iesus": Anstößige Wahrheit oder anstößige Kirche? Dokumente, Hintergründe, Standpunkte und Folgerungen.* 2nd ed. Münster: Lit, 2001.

Raiser, K. *Ökumene im Übergang: Paradigmenwechsel in der ökumenischen Bewegung.* Munich: Kaiser, 1989.

Richards, J. *Consul of God: The Life and Times of Gregory the Great.* London and Boston: Routledge and Kegan Paul, 1980.

Riedlinger, H. *Die Makellosigkeit der Kirche in den lateinischen Hoheliedkommentaren des Mittelalters.* Münster: Aschendorff, 1958.

Roos, L. "Demokratie in der Kirche?" In *Christen und Demokratie,* by G. Baadte and A. Rauscher, 125–48. Graz: Styria, 1991.

Sattler, D. "Ökumenische Annäherungen an die Ecclesia ab Abel vor dem Hintergrund *Dominus Iesus*". In *Was ist heute noch katholisch? Zum Streit um die innere Einheit und Vielfalt der Kirche,* edited by A. Franz, 87–113. QD 192. Freiburg im Briesgau: Herder, 2001.

Scheeben, M.J. *Die Mysterien des Christentums.* Freiburg: Herder, 1941.

Scheffczyk, L. "Kirche als Weinstock und Leib Christi: Die Wurzel des Mysteriums". In *Mysterium Kirche: Sozialkonzern oder Stiftung Christi?* edited by W. Brandmüller, 85–106. Aachen: MM-Verlag, 1996.

———. "Die Kirche—das Ganzsakrament Jesu Christi". In *Christus-begegnung in den Sakramenten,* edited by H. Luthe. Kevelaer: Butzon und Bercker, 1981.

———. "Zur Einführung". In *Dominus Iesus: Über die Einzigkeit und Heilsuniversalität Jesu Christi und der Kirche,* by the Kongrega-tion für die Glaubenslehre, 6–10. Stein am Rhein: Christiana-Verlag, 2000.

Schlier, H. *Der Brief an die Galater.* Göttingen: Vandenhoeck and Ruprecht, 1962.

———. *Die Zeit der Kirche.* Freiburg: Herder, 1958.

Schnackenburg, R. "Kirche: I. Die K. im NT". In *LThK,* 2nd ed., 6:169f. Freiburg im Breisgau: Herder, 1961.

Schönborn, C. *Loving the Church.* Translated by John Saward. San Francisco: Ignatius Press, 1998.

———. "Major Themes and Underlying Principles of the Catechism of the Catholic Church". In *Introduction to the Catechism of the Catholic Church*, by J. Ratzinger and C. Schönborn, 37–57. San Francisco: Ignatius Press, 1994.

Schulz, H.-J. "Überlieferung—Wesensvollzug der Kirche". In *Mysterium Kirche: Sozialkonzern oder Stiftung Christi?* edited by W. Brandmüller, 63–83. Aachen: MM-Verlag, 1996.

Schüssler Fiorenza, E. *Bread, Not Stones: The Challenge of Feminist Biblical Interpretation*. Boston: Beacon Press, 1984.

———. "Ecclesia semper reformanda: Theologie als Ideologiekritik". *Conc(D)* 35 (1999): 70–77.

Seckler, M. "Außerhalb der Kirche kein Heil?" In *Hoffnungsversuche*, edited by Seckler, 105–15. Freiburg im Breisgau: Herder, 1974.

———. "Glaubenssinn". In *LThK*, 2nd ed., 4:945–48. Freiburg im Breisgau: Herder, 1960.

———. *Im Spannungsfeld von Wissenschaft und Kirche: Theologie als schöpferische Auslegung der Wirklichkeit*. Freiburg im Breisgau: Herder, 1980.

Söll, G. *Mariologie*. HDG 3/4. Freiburg im Breisgau: Herder, 1978.

Spaemann, R. "La Perle précieuse et le nihilisme banal". *Catholica* 33 (1992): 43–50.

Steinhauer, H. *Maria als dramatische Person bei Hans Urs von Balthasar: Zum marianischen Prinzip seines Denkens*. STS 17. Innsbruck: Tyrolia-Verlag, 2001.

Stockmeier, P. "Kirche unter den Herausforderungen der Geschichte". In *HFTh*, 2nd ed., 3:85–108. Tübingen: Francke, 2000.

Tewes, E., ed. *Kardinal Julius Döpfner: Weggefährte in bedrängter Zeit; Briefe an Priester*. Munich: St.-Michaels-Bund, 1986.

Vagaggini, C. *Theologie der Liturgie*. Einsiedeln: Benziger, 1959.

Vélez Rodriguez, R. "Politischer Messianismus und Theologie der Befreiung". *IKaZ* 13 (1984): 343–54.

Verweyen, H. *Gottes letztes Wort: Grundriss der Fundamentaltheologie*. Düsseldorf: Patmos-Verlag, 1991.

———. *Der Weltkatechismus: Therapie oder Symptom einer kranken Kirche?* Düsseldorf: Patmos-Verlag, 1993.

Vliet, C. T. M. *Communio sacramentalis: Das Kirchenverständnis von Yves Congar*. Mainz: Matthias-Grünewald-Verlag, 1995.

Wagner, H. "Ekklesiologische Optionen evangelischer Theologie als
    mögliche Leitbilder der Ökumene". *Cath(M)* 47 (1993): 124–41.

Waldenfels, H. "Autorität und Erkenntnis". *Conc(D)* 21 (1985): 255–61.

Wallner, K. J. *Gott als Eschaton: Trinitarische Dramatik als Voraussetzung
    göttlicher Universalität bei Hans Urs von Balthasar.* HKSR 7. Heil-
    igenkreuz: Verein der Heiligenkreuzer Hochschulfreunde, 1992.

Warnach, W. "Mysterientheologie". in *LThK*, 2nd ed., 7:729–31.
    Freiburg im Breisgau: Herder, 1962.

Werbick, J. *Kirche: Ein ekklesiologischer Entwurf für Studium und Praxis.*
    Freiburg im Breisgau: Herder, 1994.

Weß, P. *Ihr alle seid Geschwister: Priester und Kirche.* Mainz: Matthias-
    Grünewald-Verlag, 1983.

Wiedenhofer, S. *Politische Theologie.* Stuttgart: Kohlhammer, 1976.

Ziegenaus, A. "Kirche—Stiftung Jesu Christi". In *Mysterium Kirche:
    Sozialkonzem oder Stiftung Christi?* edited by W. Brandmüller,
    41–61. Aachen: MM-Verlag, 1996.

Zulehner, P. M. "Das geistliche Amt des Volkes Gottes". In *Priesterkirche*,
    edited by P. Hoffmann. Düsseldorf: Patmos-Verlag, 1987.

———, ed. *Kirchenvolks-Begehren (und Weizer Pfingstvision): Kirche auf
    Reformkurs.* Düsseldorf, Innsbruck, and Vienna: Tyrolia, 1995.

———. *Pastoraltheologie.* Vol. 2, *Gemeindepastoral: Orte christlicher Praxis.*
    Düsseldorf: Patmos-Verlag, 1989.

———. *Sie werden mein Volk sein: Grundkurs gemeindlichen Glaubens.* Düs-
    seldorf: Patmos-Verlag, 1986.

INDEX

Abraham, 327n512, 336–38, 351, 458–59
Absolutism, 170n58, 382
Adam, 251n21, 327n513, 344n73, 356n143
  Christ as second, 251n120, 254n139, 369n210, 370
  and unity, 250–52, 254n139, 258–59, 411
Adam, Karl, 22
Adoration, 108, 264, 268, 273n243, 280, 337–38, 520n75
  See also Love; Worship
Adorno, Theodor, 182n109, 523n96
Advent, 409
Africa, 165n37, 208n11, 477–78
Aggiornamento, 23–28, 168, 183n114, 191, 425
Agnosticism, 198
Alberigo, Guiseppe, 24–25, 33, 39n1, 133n107, 165n17, 316, 432n6, 510n31
Alberto, Stefano, 50–51n58, 51n61, 78n1, 501–2n11
Alienation, 341n48, 369n210, 385
Allen, John L., 154–55n2
Ambrose of Milan, St., 233n15, 413
America, 388
  See also Latin America; North America
Anamnesis, 274
Anglican Church, 201n92, 281n284
"Anonymous" Christianity, 178n91, 223
Anselm of Canterbury, 158
Anthropology, 220, 261
Apostles, 277–78, 290, 294, 355, 469
  bishops and, 451, 452n117, 453n122, 455–56, 476n224
  collegiality of, 445–49
  communio and teaching of the apostles, 294–96
  grace of, 279n222
  lot of the apostle, 209
  Peter's role, 451

and Scripture, 335n16
teaching of, 290, 294–96
the Twelve, 353–54, 373n224, 375n238, 409n446
the word "apostle", 446
  See also Apostolic succession; Disciples; individual names
Apostolic succession, 276–78, 294, 308n430, 309n431, 312, 431, 441
  and ecumenism, 434n14
  and the Eucharist, 282–83
Apostolic tradition, 324
Aristotle, 158, 315, 377n249, 460
Asia, 478
Atheism, 198, 267, 291, 405n420
Atonement, 415, 426–29
Auer, Alfons, 97
Augustine, St., 40, 46n35, 54, 93, 107n150, 270, 335, 344n74
  beast of burden metaphor, 227
  and the Body of Christ, 244–46, 270, 285–86, 305
  on the Church, 261
  and the Donatists, 238, 247n94, 305, 418–19
  on God's faithfulness, 337
  and the Holy Spirit, 257
  on love and faith, 246
  on love for the Church, 251
  on Old and New Testaments, 368
  and People of God concept, 331–32, 334n74
  Ratzinger's dissertation on, 158–59, 244, 286, 331–32, 344n74, 418
  and Ratzinger's ecclesiology, 238, 244–47, 331–32, 501–2, 508, 515–16, 520, 523
  and sin in the Church, 418–19
  synods in time of, 477
  and unity, 238, 247, 286, 305, 419, 436n24
Austria, 179n58, 201, 281, 479

Authority, 139–40
  "authority of life", 96
  Church, 45, 94–95, 109, 263–64, 282,
      290, 350–51, 359, 439, 519, 522
      (see also Bishops; Hierarchy;
      Magisterium; Papacy)
    councils and, 139, 481
    episcopal, 70, 119–39 passim, 452,
        465, 473–90 passim, 493n302
    episcopal office of governing,
        130–31
    freedom and, 169
    papal, 120–21, 129, 133n107,
        377n249, 480–81n241, 484–85,
        489
    Ratzinger on, 437
    supreme, 32, 118–21, 130, 134,
        381–82, 452–53, 465, 473, 485
    teaching, 32, 94, 129, 480–81n241
        (see also Magisterium)
    Vatican II and, 118–20
  and "college", the term, 133
  of grace, 69, 427
  "of representation", 281
  and service, 441
  See also Government; Law; Politics;
      State
Autobiography of Joseph Ratzinger. See
    Milestones: Memoirs 1927–1977

Balthasar, Hans Urs von, 174, 177–78,
    214, 233, 406n423, 427n547
  on bishops, 475, 479
  on the Church's sinfulness, 415, 417–18
  on communio (concept), 141
  and Communio (journal), 177–78
  on the last two ecumenical councils,
      141
  on liberation through integration, 141
  and the patristic tradition, 417–18, 515
  and Karl Rahner, 178n91
  and Ratzinger's ecclesiology, 156–57
  and renewal, 425
Baptism, 36, 40n4, 66, 71, 237, 246,
    372, 380–81
  baptismal grace, 89n53, 103
  common priesthood of all the
      baptized, 85–86

formation into likeness of Christ
    through, 52
  as fundamental sacrament, 53, 241,
      251, 256, 347, 380
  "indelible character" of, 90–91
  the laity and, 85–86, 90–91, 98
  and membership in the Church,
      47n75, 71, 86, 109, 112, 303–4, 334
  necessity of, 110
  and non-Catholics, 112, 303
  and personal responsibility, 457
  See also Sacrament
Baraúna, Guilherme, 32, 37n34, 105n40
Barth, Karl, 48, 83n24, 371n219,
    514n50, 515n57
Barthians, 515n57
Basil of Caesarea, 45n32, 267n208
Batlogg, A., 15n2
Bavaria, 154, 174–75, 177n88, 207n7, 209
Bea, Augustine Cardinal, 165n37, 303
Beast of burden metaphor, 227
Beauty, 422
  "black but beautiful", 414–29
Beinert, Wolfgant, 13, 173n75, 509,
    514n48
Benedict, St. (XLIII), 268, 371
Benedictines, 401
Benedict XVI, Pope. See Ratzinger,
    Joseph
Benelli, Giovanni, 208n11
Berg, Werner, 79
Bernard of Clairvaux, St., 51n60, 403,
    414n471
Bertrams, W., 132
Betti, U., 132n100, 311n447
Beyerhaus, Peter, 171n61
Bible. See Scripture
Bishop of Rome, 468
  See also Papacy
Bishops,
  apostles and (see under Apostles:
      bishops and)
  apostolic succession (see Apostolic
      succession)
  college of, 117–25 (see also
      Collegiality)
    and apostolic college, 117–18
    mutual relations among bishops in,
        120–25

and Petrine office, 118–20
and primacy, 444–61, 450–54
conferences, episcopal, 472–82
  and majority decisions, 480–82
  no magisterial competence re. faith
    and morals, 478–80
  theological status of, 472–82
and conscience of faith, 482
consecration of, 119, 125–27, 133, 207
  as sacrament, 115, 117, 125–28,
    133n108, 442–43, 466n183
episcopal-collegial structure, pastoral
  implications of, 454–61, 478, 483,
  487–88, 495
episcopal office, 129–31
  of governing, 130–31
  of preaching, 129–30
  of sancitfying, 130
function vs. power, 126–27
one priesthood, union with, 138–39
pastoral implications of episcopal-
  collegial structure, 454–61
and personal responsibility (see under
  Personal responsibility: bishops and)
Ratzinger on, 491–92, 508
synod of, 124, 483–93
  collegial structure as communio
    union of local Churches, 490–92
  as congubernium, 482–89
  inadequate models for, 489–90
  twofold ordering of, 492–93
three interwoven munera of as rooted
  in sacramental ordination, 127–31
See also Collegiality; Hierarchy;
  specific topics, e.g., Grace
"Black but beautiful," 414–29
Bloch, Ernst, 171–72, 184
Blood and water, 47, 66, 241, 256, 273
Body of Christ (Church as), 237–71
  Church constituted as Body of Christ
    through Eucharist, 284–86
  Corpus Christi, patristic interpretation
    as point of departure, 244–47
  caritas as consequence of unity,
    246–47
  Church as true Body of Christ,
    244–46
  doctrine of, consequences for
    ecclesiology, 260–70

Christ's Church, not men's, 268–70
  Church's identity crisis as God
    crisis, 265–67
  and identification with the
    Church, 260–61
  roots of current crisis in the
    Church, 262–65
  and the eucharistic Body of Christ,
    245n84, 284–86
  and Lumen gentium ecclesiology,
    243–70
Pauline teaching about, 248–60
  Holy Spirit, Church as organism
    of, 250–54
  nuptiality, theme of, 254–56
  unity in the Spirit as goal of all
    gifts, 256–60
"People of God" image and, 333–44
Ratzinger's ecclesiology, summary of,
  523 (see also Ecclesiology,
  Ratzinger's; specific topics)
the term, 237
three "historical rings" of Body of
  Christ concept in relation to
  Church membership, 300–303
  institutional-hierarchical
    perspective, 301
  mystical perspective, 301–3
  sacramental perspective, 300–301
See also Church; People of God
Body of Christ (Eucharist). See
  Eucharist
Boethius, 313n451
Boff, Leonardo, 200–201, 217n49,
  311nn445–47, 313, 321–23, 326n506,
  503n15, 513–14
Bonaventure, St., 158, 377n249,
  414n473, 513n47, 516
  Ratzinger's thesis, 160–63
Bonn, 163
Bouyer, Louis, 175, 177n87, 429n555
Brecht, Bertolt, 341n48
Bride,
  Church as bride of Christ in the
    Holy Spirit, 48–50, 67, 101,
    253–56, 357, 372–73, 420, 471
  fidelity to, 422
  Mary and, 407n436, 409, 411, 414,
    415

Bride (continued)
    spousal love between Christ and
        Church, 249, 254–56, 411,
        414n474
    Israel as, 254n137, 412n467, 414 (see
        under Israel: as bride)
    wisdom as, 414n473
Buchberger, M., 267n210
Bulgakov, S., 41n13
Bultmann, R., 10n8, 170, 273n243,
    513, 515n57
Bultmannians, 515n57

Called to Communion (Ratzinger),
    250n120, 476n224
    See also specific topics
Call to Holiness. See Holiness,
    Universal Call to
Canon, Roman, 274–75, 522
Canon law, 222, 334, 473, 478–79
Capitalism, 23n13, 180, 485–89,
    495n317, 496
Cardinals, 484
    See also individual names
Caritas, 246–47
Casel, Odo, 41
Cassiodorus, 313n451
Catechesis, 214–16
Catechism of the Catholic Church, 214–17
Catholic Church, 212, 227
    Catholic theology, duty of, 319n473
    as communion, 149, 157
    crisis in, 169–70, 192
    and ecumenical activity, 176n85, 222
    freedom and, 154–55n2
    in Germany, 157, 216
    Ratzinger on being Catholic, 149
    regarding Church unity, 227
    subsistit formula and, 226 (see also
        Subsistence)
    as "the Church", 309
    truth outside, 34, 51n61, 75, 504
    understanding of herself, 333–34
    See also Church; specific topics, e.g.,
        Papacy
Catholicity, 78n2, 177n86, 304n406,
    448n95, 486, 508n29, 521
    and ecumenism, 108–13, 123, 469,
    486

Celibacy, 216
    the diaconate and, 34, 139n137, 281
    evangelical counsel of, 102
    See also Virginity
Centralism. See Roman centralism
Chalcedon, Council of, 150–51, 151
Charismatic movements, 401
Charisms,
    as basic ecclesiological theme, 237n46
    of choosing and practicing evangelical
        counsels, 103
    Church, charismatic structure of, 94
    diaconal orientation of, 94–95
    Holy Spirit and, 68–69, 92, 94–95,
        270n222
    and unity, 62, 68–69, 79, 92, 94–95,
        270n222, 431n3
    vocation and, 97
    See also Gifts
Charity, 246, 248n106, 286n312, 469,
    492
    Vatican II and, 396–99
    See also Love
Chaste whore, symbol of, 414–15
Chastity. See Celibacy; Virginity
Children, 92
    See also Family; Youth
Christ. See Jesus Christ
Christian formation, 90
Christianity, 161n23, 167, 186, 191,
    212, 216n46
    "anonymous", 178n91, 223
    appeal of, 213
    becoming a Christian, 175
    characteristics of, 458
    being a Christian, 216n46, 259, 284
    Christian life
        foundation for, 214, 251
        main goal of, 492–93
    core of, 176, 182n109
    and the Cross, 191
    and culture, 196, 517n64
    discipleship, 458
    God, Christian concept of, 511
    inherent reasonableness of, 514 (see
        also under Reason: faith and)
    politics and (see under Politics: faith
        and)
    and social responsibility, 218–19

as "soul of the world", 100
and tradition (see Tradition)
and truth, 176, 185, 204, 207–8n9,
    213
See also Church; Faith; People of
    God; Theology; specific topics, e.g.,
    Ecumenism; Ethics
Christian memory, 480–81n241
Christian unity. See Ecumenism; Unity
Christian vocation. See under Vocation,
    Christian
Christian witness. See Witness
Christology, 238–49, 267, 349, 362n168,
    405n420
    biblical metaphors for Church with
        christological reference, 49–52
    as center of ecclesiology, 237, 347
    christological development of image
        of preexistent People of God,
        370–73
    and Church, understanding of,
        248–60
    and communio ecclesiology, 285
    direction for, 239
    hypostasis, 313
    and liberation theology, 218
    Mary in, 403
    and pneumatology, 159, 163, 238–43,
        248–60, 502
    Ratzinger's goal and foundation, 205
    trinitarian approach of, 237, 238
Church, 209, 214–15, 230–330,
    296–300
    biblical metaphors for, 49–52
    birth of, 375, 377–79
    "black but beautiful", 414–29
    as Body of Christ, 238–71 (see also
        Body of Christ)
    as Bride of Christ in the Holy Spirit
        (see under Bride: Church as)
    Catholic Church as, 309
    and Christ, distinguishing from,
        44–45 (see also under Jesus Christ:
        and the Church)
    christological and pneumatological
        understanding of, 248–60, 502
    as Christ's, not men's, 268–70
    and Christ's kingdom, 46–49
    classical marks of, 305n406

as communio (see Communio)
as communion, 149, 157, 193n47,
    256, 289
as "complex reality", 140–41
crisis in, roots of, 265–67
desecularized, 195–96
duty of, 286
early (see Early Church)
economy of salvation, 45–46
eschatological character of, 58,
    339–44
and the Eucharist (see under
    Eucharist)
as Eucharist, 271n228
feminine structure of, 254n137, 405–9
founding of, 43, 340
goal and origin of, 348–57
growth process of, 252–53
hierarchical constitution of (see
    Hierarchy)
Holy Spirit and (see under Holy
    Spirit: and the Church)
identity crisis of, 265–67
inner predestination of creation for,
    368–73
juridical view of (see Juridical view of
    the Church)
Last Supper as origin of, 272–75
as living memory, 148
as locus of faith, 147–50
Lumen gentium on, 60, 70, 237
Mary and (see Mary)
membership (see Church membership,
    below)
ministry of (see Ministry)
mission of (see Mission of the
    Church)
as mystery (see under Mystery: Church
    as)
non-Catholic Christians and (see
    Non-Catholic Christians)
origin and goal of, 348–57
particular Churches and universal
    Church, 121–22
as People of God (see People of God)
plural Churches and the one Church
    of Jesus Christ, 306–10
pneumatological and christological
    understanding of, 248–60, 502

Church (*continued*)
   Ratzinger's ecclesiology (*see*
      Ecclesiology, Ratzinger's; *specific
      topics*)
   renewal (*see* Renewal)
   as sacrament, 54 (*see also under*
      Sacrament: Church, sacramental
      understanding of)
   and salvation, 57, 236, 292
   as sign of faith and mystery of faith
      (Ratzinger's ecclesiology),
      230–330 (*see also* Body of Christ;
      Communio; Eucharist; Subsistence)
   "sinful Church" concept, 414–29
   sociological view of, 267
   subsistit formula and (*see* Subsistence)
   as temple of the Holy Spirit (*see
      under* Holy Spirit: temple of)
   and theology, 205 (*see also* Theology)
   universal (*see* Universal Church)
   Vatican II view of, 110
   See also Body of Christ; Catholic
      Church; *Communio;* People of
      God; Universal Church; *specific
      topics*, e.g., Unity; Renewal;
      Subsistence
Church membership, 303–6, 334
   communio and, 300–310
   and non-Catholic Christians, 112, 303
   and the sacraments, 47n75, 71, 86,
      109, 112, 303–4, 334
   three "historical rings" of Body of
      Christ concept in relation to,
      300–303
   various degrees of, 109–11
Ciappi, Luigi, 208n11
Cicognani, Amleto Giovanni Cardinal,
   132, 208n11
Clement of Alexandria, 158, 387n311,
   515
Clement of Rome, Pope St., 369n207
College,
   the term, 133
   See also under Bishops: college of;
      Collegiality
Collegiality, 119–20, 200, 433
   of the apostles, 445–48
   collegial structure as *communio* union
      of local Churches, 490–92

concrete forms of, 467–92
   patriarchal districts; theological
      status of episcopal conferences,
      472–82
   the three papal offices; totality of
      Church in her universal
      dimension, 467–72
dogmatic foundations of, 444–54
   the early Church's approach to,
      453–54
   as ecumenical paradigm, 431–40, 450
   episcopal, sacramental basis of, 442–43
   Lumen gentium compared with
      Ratzinger's ecclesiology, 507–9
   the modern-speculative approach,
      452–53
pastoral implications of
   episcopal-collegial structure,
   454–61
and primacy, 444–61
Ratzinger and, 474, 496
of spiritual ministry in the early
   Church, 449–50
and synod of bishops, twofold
   ordering of, 492–93
Vatican II and, 448
and "we" structure of the faith,
   455–57
See also under Bishops: college of
Commandments, Ten. *See* Ten
   Commandments
Communio (ecclesiology), 288–90, 290
   accomplishment of Christ's salvific
      work in *communio* of the Father in
      the Holy Spirit, 522
   and apostles, teaching of, 294–96
   Christology and, 285
   the Church as, 296–300
      Church as *communio* unity, 286–88
      Church as mystery of trinitarian
         communio, 69–73
   collegial structure as *communio* union
      of local Churches, 490–92
   divine-human *communio* as realized in
      Christ, 66–67
   early Church acceptance of concept,
      70–71
   ecclesiology of *communio*,
      consequences of, 291–300

eucharistic ecclesiology as *communio*
  ecclesiology, 286
the Father as calling men to share in
  trinitarian *communio*, 65–66
the Holy Spirit as effecting, 68–69,
  522
joy of, 289, 291–92
as liturgical community, 292–94
as *Lumen gentium* theme, 62
meaning of, 288–90
and membership in the Church,
  300–310
Ratzinger's ecclesiology and, 522–23
sacramental structure as sign and
  instrument of, 63–65
and suffering, 76–77
and the Trinity
  accomplishment of Christ's salvific
    work in *communio* of the Father
    in the Holy Spirit, 522
  Church as mystery of trinitarian
    communio, 69–73
  communio as belief in the Trinity,
    147–48
  communio as image of Trinity,
    71–73
  the Father as calling men to share
    in trinitarian *communio*, 65–66
  trinitarian *communio* as source and
    goal of ecclesial *communio*,
    65–69
as Vatican II central idea, 60–61, 269,
  271, 287n316, 300
See also Unity
Communio (periodical),
  founding of, 176–78
Communion,
  Church as, 149, 157, 193n47, 256, 289
  ecclesial, 177, 213
  the Incarnation and, 285, 289
  truth and, 152
  See also Unity
Communion, Holy. See Eucharist
Communism, 387
  See also Marx, Karl
Community,
  Catholic, 212
  global, 212n22
  international, 25n18

of mankind, 25n18
parish, 359
See also Ecclesia
Concilium, 146, 174–80, 183, 186
  Ratzinger's break with, 146, 174,
    178–83, 186–87
Conferences, episcopal. See under
  Bishops: conferences, episcopal
Confession of faith, 90, 324
Confession of guilt, 421
Confirmation, 53n68
Congar, Yves Cardinal, O.P., 41n13,
  45n32, 111–12, 130n89, 165n37,
  271n231, 376, 515
Congregation for the Doctrine of the
  Faith (CDF), 89n53, 145n2, 191–92,
  357, 358nn149–50, 364–65, 474n215
  documents of, 204
  office of prefect, 193n47, 202, 214–27
  Ratzinger as Cardinal Prefect, 204–6,
    211–27, 361, 415, 461n159, 469,
    483n257
    catechesis and catechism, 214–16
    and ecumenism, 222–27
    and liberation theology, 217–21
    and traditionalism, 222
  See also Dominus Iesus
Congregations, 122, 138, 145n2, 360,
  376, 378, 381, 435n19
Conscience, 96, 427, 462n161
  bishops and, 482, 492, 495
  ecumenical councils and, 480
  of faith, 478, 482
  freedom and, 155n2, 390
  Hitler and, 155n2
  individual, 96, 492
  the papacy and, 480–81n241, 495
  of pastors and teachers, 204n111
  Ratzinger and, 482
  subjectivity and, 427
  truth and, 390, 478, 482
  Vatican II and, 32, 421, 432n7
Consecrated religious, 36, 97, 99, 102
  sixth chapter of *Lumen gentium*, 30,
    36, 103–5
Consecration, 90, 103, 128n79, 465
  laity and, 99
  participation in consecration and
    mission of Christ, 136–37

Consecration (*continued*)
  priests and, 136–38
  See also under Bishops: consecration of
"Consensus ecumenism", 436, 516–17
Conservatism, 181–82, 196, 298
  Ratzinger and, 168n49, 186, 200,
    205, 209
  Vatican II and, 196
Conversion, 44, 213, 295, 298, 426,
  431n3, 440
  intellectual insight and, 236n34
  personal, 422, 426, 429
  Ratzinger and, 421
  and receiving Communion, 423
  and repentance, 421
  and unity, 259, 462n161
Copernicus, 399
"Corporate personality", 250–52
Corpus Christi, 244–47
  See also Body of Christ
the Council. *See* Vatican II
Councils, ecumenical. *See* Ecumenical
  councils
Counter-Reformation, 31n8, 41, 304,
  501
Courage,
  of conversion, 259
  of faith, 177
  and faith's hope, 219
  and reality, 219n58
  and truth, 208n9, 209
Courth, F., 40n4
Covenants, Old and New. *See* New
  Testament; Old Testament; *specific
  topics*
Creation, 147, 258, 371n219, 502
  the Church and, 356–57, 368–74, 507
  communion with, 275
  conservation of, 437
  goal of, 371
  inner predestination of creation for
    the Church, 368–73
  Mary and, 406–7, 410, 412
  reason and purpose for, 370, 507
  and redemption, 373
  responsibility of People of God for,
    96–97
  theology of, 502, 507
  worship and, 507

the Creed, 150–53, 214, 304
the Cross, 63n111, 82, 171n61, 256,
  298–99, 337–38, 380, 518–20
  and the Eucharist, 137, 249, 272n237,
    273–74, 280, 290
  martyrdom, 458
  Mary and, 106, 408–9
  mystery of, 191
  and salvation, 45–47, 50
  and salvation history, 515
  scandal of, 168, 191
  theology of, 519–20
  See also Death and Resurrection of
    Christ
Cullmann, Oscar, 435, 515
Culture, 25n18
  Christian faith and, 196, 517n64
  civic, 36
  diversity, 133, 327, 371, 430n2
  modern, 282, 383
  multiculturalism, 216
  priests and, 556
  and universality, 377, 510n40 (*see also*
    Universality)
  world, 221n66
Curia, Roman, 116, 169, 201, 211, 263,
  448, 474n214
  bishops and, 475, 483–84, 489–90,
    493n302, 496
  Ratzinger as curial theologian,
    170n58
  universal Church and, 364–66, 378
  Vatican II and, 30, 116
Cyprian of Carthage, St., 69–71,
  453n122, 456–56
Cyril of Alexandria, St., 246n89

Damaskinos, Metropolitan, 204
Daniel, 355n134
Daniélou, J., 165n37, 271n231
Das neue Volk Gottes (Ratzinger), 174,
  231, 283n295, 417
Daughter Zion, 407–8n435, 412–13
Daughter Zion (Ratzinger), 408n444,
  410n454, 412n467–68
Deacons; the diaconate, 86n38, 135–37,
  139–40
  the celibacy obligation, 34, 139n137,
    281

charisms, diaconal orientation of,
94–95
See also Orders, Holy
Death, 76, 295, 299, 386, 428
and eternal life, 182n109
and freedom to choose, 211
love and, 299
symbol of, 421
Death and Resurrection of Christ, 141,
149–50, 273n243, 274, 514n50, 520
baptism and, 95
and the Church, 66, 289, 340, 441
and Church as communion, 289
and covenant with Abraham, 337
as Easter mystery, 292
and the Eucharist, 137, 273n243, 274
Johannine theology, 241
Mary and, 106
See also Cross; Paschal Mystery
Debate. *See* Dialogue; *specific topics*, e.g.,
Liberation theology; Orthodoxy
Decalogue. *See* Ten Commandments
Decourtray, Albert, 214
De Ecclesia, 29–35, 39, 55n75, 78, 135,
164n34, 304n407
contrasted to *Lumen gentium*, 30, 501
debate about, 448n95
deliberations of Council concerning,
302
1962 draft of, 442, 446
and *Ecclesia peccatrix* concept, 416
Deism, 264–65, 265, 363, 512
See also Enlightenment, the
Delhaye, Philippe, 175
de Lubac, Henri, S.J. *See* Lubac, Henri
de, S.J.
Democracy, 81, 281, 384–85, 389, 441,
506
the majority principle (*see* Majority
principle)
relativism and, 38, 383, 389–92
Denominations, 22, 83n24, 177n86,
202–3, 303, 306–8, 324, 437
denominationalism, 203, 516
Ratzinger and, 516–17
See also Dialogue; Ecumenism;
Non-Catholic Christians;
Protestantism
Descartes, R., 250n120

De Smedt, E.J., 90n60
Diaconate. *See* Deacons
Dialogue, 187–88
the Catholic Church and, 176n85
the concept, 187–88
Concilium and, 179
goal of, 188
interreligious, 113, 152n35, 212n22,
221
of love, 210
the Magisterium and, 225
with Protestant Churches, 112n173,
333
Ratzinger and, 201, 209–11, 224–25
the "Ratzinger formula", 201
subsistence formula and, 310–30
truth and, 227
Vatican II documents and, 113
with world religions, 212n22
See also Ecumenism
Dibelius, Otto, 22–23
Dietzfelbinger, W., 311n447
Dignity, 189n26, 209
of Christ, 107
Gaudium et spes and, 25n18
of the human person, 25n18
of the laity, 505
of marriage and family, 25n18
of non-Catholic Churches, 309
patriarchal, 468
of People of God, 62, 66, 72, 83–84,
86, 95, 97, 287n313
Diocese, 121–22, 130, 138, 210,
393n353, 475, 479
Diplomacy,
Vatican II and, 168
See also Politics
Disciples, 240n57, 324, 353, 446, 473
discipleship, 336n21, 458
Ratzinger and, 353
seventy, 355n136
See also Apostles
Dissertations, Ratzinger's, 158–61, 244,
286, 331–32, 344n74, 418
Diversity, 50n56, 89n53, 377n249,
430n2, 435
reconciled, 63, 226, 324
unity through, 57, 62, 86, 99, 109,
223, 513

Divorce, 216
Doctors of the Church, 377n249
Doctrine,
    Vatican II and, 27
    See also specific topics, e.g.,
        Collegiality; Trinity
Documents of Vatican II. See Vatican II
    documents
Dogma and Preaching (Ratzinger),
    151n24, 174
Dogmatic Constitution on the Church.
    See Lumen gentium
Dogmatic theology, 158, 160, 163, 170,
    174, 179–80, 420
    historical research in relation to
        dogmatic tradition, 510–11
    See also under Ratzinger, Joseph: as
        professor
"Domestic church", 92
Dominicans (order), 271n231
Dominus Iesus, 200, 309, 320–21,
    326–27, 504n17
    controversy of, 225–26, 309, 326–28
    structure of, 326n508
Donatist schism, 238, 247n94, 305,
    418–19
Döpfner, Julius Cardinal, 33, 168n49, 207
Döring, H., 111n170
Drumm, J., 31n8
Dulles, Avery, 515n57

Early Church, 70–71, 449–50
    See also specific topics, e.g., Renewal
Earth,
    and heaven (see under Heaven: and
        earth)
    new, 522
    See also Creation; World
Easter, 154, 238, 243, 292, 477n228
Eastern bloc countries, 102n22, 214n35
Eastern Churches, 41, 43, 85n34, 116,
    134, 214n35, 309, 388, 502
    and common priesthood, 85n34
    and communio, 61, 112n174
    ecumenism and, 112n174, 230, 309,
        463–64, 469, 484, 502, 516
    eucharistic ecclesiology of, 283
    pneumatology of, 237–38
    the "Ratzinger formula", 14n29, 470

and Ratzinger's ecclesiology, 200–203
    passim, 329
    trinitarian understanding of the
        Church, 230, 238, 393n492
    and Western ecclesiology, 112n174,
        230, 237–38, 283, 323n492
    See also Orthodox Churches
Ecclesia, 344–46
    as community, 159n16
    Ecclesia peccatrix, 416–24
    and Israel's preexistence, 368–70
    and the Torah, 368–70
    understanding of, 368–70
Ecclesia, De (schema). See De Ecclesia
Ecclesiology, 379
    Christology as center of, 237, 347
    core of, 269
    Eastern and Western, 112n174, 230
    eucharistic ecclesiology as communio
        ecclesiology, 286
    trinitarian theology and, 251
    of Vatican II, 267, 286, 396–99 (see
        also Vatican II; specific topics)
    See also Theology; specific topics and
        doctrines, e.g., Body of Christ;
        Eucharist
Ecclesiology, Ratzinger's, 146, 159, 183,
    186n12, 230–330, 523
    as Augustinian (see under Augustine,
        St: and Ratzinger's ecclesiology)
    against background of issues in
        intellectual history, 509–17
    ecumenical perspective, 516–17
    paradigm of historical thinking,
        510–14
    and patristic theology, 514–16
    character of, 203
    essence and summary of, 271, 522–23
    eucharistic approach of, 271, 502,
        522–23
    as lifelong occupation, 159
    themes in, recurring (see under
        Theology, Ratzinger's: themes in,
        recurring)
    thesis from 1968 as shaping, 510
    See also Theology, Ratzinger's; specific
        topics, e.g., People of God
        concept: Ratzinger's ecclesiology
        and

Economics, 25n18
Economy of salvation, 45–46
 Mary's role in, 105–7
Ecumenical councils, 121, 201n92, 480
 the last two, 141
 See also Vatican II; *specific council names*, e.g., Chalcedon
Ecumenism, 108–13, 199
 collegiality as ecumenical paradigm, 432–40
 "consensus", 436, 516–17
 Decree on, 34n18, 71, 111
 ecumenical dialogue (*see* Dialogue)
 the ecumenical movement, 22
 and eschatological character of the Church, 111
 the Fries-Rahner plan, 202
 Gaudium et spes and, 25n18
 kingdom of God and, 48–49
 Lumen gentium and, 35, 74–75, 108–13
 and Marian devotion, 108
 and morality, 177n86, 202–3
 and non-Catholic Christians, 37, 51n61, 111n170, 112, 303, 322n489, 323n494
 "of return", 112n176
 paradigm shift in, 222n85, 436–40
 particular Churches and, 121
 and People of God concept, 112n173
 Ratzinger and, 201–3, 214, 222–27, 516–17
 schema *De Ecclesia* and, 30
 solidarity, fellowship of, 437
 task of, 225
 truth outside the Catholic Church, 51n61
 Vatican II and, 112
 and world religions, 187, 221n66
 See also Dialogue; Unity; *specific topics*, e.g., Eastern Churches; Protestants
Education, 392–93
 liturgical, 505n20
Egotism, 259
 See also Individualism
Encyclicals,
 of John Paul II, 125, 217n51
 of John XXIII, 23–24nn13–14, 27n27, 27n29

 of Paul VI, 23–24n13, 73n163, 174n75
 of Pius XII, 50, 78, 234n19, 515n55
the Enlightenment, 180n103, 262, 264, 387–88, 428, 441, 511, 514
 See also Deism; Reason
Environment, 221n66
Ephesus, Council of, 405n420
Epiphany, 335n19
Episcopate. *See* Bishops
Error, 253, 260, 327n512, 399, 504n17
 See also Heresy; Schism; Sin
Eschatology,
 eschatological fulfillment, 162
 Eschatological Nature of the Pilgrim Church and its Union with the Church in Heaven (seventh chapter of *Lumen gentium*), 36–37, 111
 factions, 223
 kingdom of God as eschatological gathering and cleansing, 348–51
 liberation theology and, 218
 Ratzinger's writing and, 174
 the term "eschatological", 36n28, 339, 343
 and utopia, 160, 162–63, 172
Eschatology: Death and Eternal Life (Ratzinger), 172n66, 174
Eternal life, 85, 182n109, 398–99
 See also Heaven
Ethics, 175–76, 427, 438, 514n48
 deism and, 265
 and the Eucharist, 246n89
 See also Morality; *specific topics*
Eucharist, 148, 226, 246, 256n156, 271–86, 381, 522–23
 as Body of Christ, 245n84
 Christ in, 522
 Church as, 271n228
 Church as eucharistic communion, 193
 Church constituted as Body of Christ through, 284–86
 conversion and receiving Communion, 423
 the Cross and (*see under* Cross: and the Eucharist)
 ethics and, 246n89

Eucharist (*continued*)
  eucharistic communities as realization
      of the Church, 276–84
    fulfillment of whole Church in
      each celebration of Eucharist,
      283–84
    legitimacy as union with the
      pastors, 276–78
  eucharistic ecclesiology as *communio*
      ecclesiology, 286
  as fundamental sacrament, 53, 241,
      251, 256, 347, 380
  institution (beginning) of, 273n243
  the Last Supper as founding the
      Church, 272–75
  mystery of, 226
  Paul and, 248n106
  prayer, Roman Canon, 274–75, 522
  Ratzinger's ecclesiology, eucharistic
      approach of, 271, 502, 522–23
  totality of Church as realized in every
      celebration of, 502
  Vatican II and, 286
  worship and, 520
  See also Sacrament
Europe, 33n13, 103n124, 180, 220, 265,
    388–89, 510
  See also Western world.
Eusebius of Caesarea, 387n311
Evangelical counsels, 102–5, 105
Evangelization, 386
  See also Witness
Evil, 181n108, 199, 327n512, 435
Excommunication, 222
Existentialism, 170–71
the Exodus, 218, 520n78
Expiation, 428
Extreme unction, 53n68

Factions, 223
Fahey Michael, 174, 180–81, 193,
    200
Faith, 212–14
  aim of, 218
  behaviors contrary to, 210–11
  Church as locus of, 147–50
  and courage, 177, 219
  crisis of, 177n86, 216
  existentialism and, 170n56

hope of, 219
  and love, 246
  and magisterial competence, 478–80
  path of, 203
  and philosophy, 514n50
  politics and (*See under* Politics: and
      faith)
  purification of, 438
  Ratzinger's, 150–52, 204n11
  Ratzinger's ecclesiology and, 522–23
  and reason, 212n22, 219, 221n70,
      408n439, 511, 514, 519n73
  of "simple folk", 150
  as social, 157
  supernatural sense of faith belonging
      to whole People of God, 92–94
  truth and, 176, 209, 213
  Vatican II and, 396–99
  as virtue, 161n25
  and the world, 210–11
  See also Christianity
Family, 92
  dignity of, 25n18
  "domestic church", 92
  of God, 352–53
Fascism, 154n2
the Father, God as,
  accomplishment of Christ's salvific
      work in *communio* of in the Holy
      Spirit, 522
  See also Trinity
Fathers of the Church, 66, 145, 156–60
    passim, 175, 210n5, 501–3 passim,
    507, 522
  writings of, 515
  See also individual names; specific topics,
      e.g., Heresy
Faulhaber, Michael Cardinal, 159
*Feast of Faith: Approaches to a Theology of
    the Liturgy* (Ratzinger), 208–9
Felici, Pericles, 132n102, 462
Fellermeier, Jakob, 157n10
Fellowship (*Communio*). See *Communio*
Feminism, 220
Fernandez, Clemente, 314
Figura, Michael, 94
Fiorenza, Elizabeth Schüssler, 281n284
Fire, 259, 413, 423
First Vatican Council. *See* Vatican I

First World War. *See under* World Wars:
  World War I
Focolare movement, 350n106, 438n38
Forcellini, A., 313
Forgiveness, 350–51, 426–29
  and expiation, 428
  grace and, 350, 427–28
  penance and, 203
  and reform, 415, 426–29
Formation, Christian, 90
Forte, B., 71n156
France; French theologians, 29n4,
  214n35, 271n231, 499–500
Franciscan tradition, 145, 161n25
Francis of Assisi, St., 145, 161n25,
  162n27
Frankfurter Allgemeine Zeitung, 226,
  367
Freedom,
  academic, 212
  the Catholic Church and, 169
  of the children of God, 95–96
  and conscience, 155n2, 390
  empty, 211
  liberation theology and, 221n66
  and truth, 211
Freising, 156–63 passim, 205–11
Frieling, R., 193
Fries, Heinrich, 202, 434n14, 435n19,
  438, 439n42, 441n57
  the Fries-Rahner plan, 202,
  434–35n19, 438–39, 441n57
Frings, Josef Cardinal, 29n3, 33, 37n35,
  163–66, 169n53, 191, 448n95
  Ratzinger as theological advisor to,
  163–66
Fundamentalism, 181–82, 263, 326,
  516

Gabhauer, G. R., 469n192
Gadamer, Hans-Georg, 512n40
Gantin, Archbishop Bernardin, 208n11
Garijo-Guembe, M. M., 283n295,
  311n447
Gaudium et spes, 13–14, 24–25, 57, 171,
  187–88, 194, 223–24n83
  and People of God concept, 79n7
  themes and central ideas of, 25n18
  See also Vatican II documents

Germany, 53n66, 281
  Catholics in, 61n102, 157, 216,
    393–94n353, 394n358, 394n360
  German theologians, 29n4, 33, 234,
    416n486, 499–500 (*see also individ-
    ual names*, e.g., Rahner, Karl)
  Idealism, German, 513
  Lumen gentium, German translation,
    88
  Ratzinger's background in, 154–59
  See also specific topics and locations, e.g.,
    Munich
Giblet, J., 136n119
Gifts,
  belonging to the Church, 34, 67–69,
    75, 305, 330, 504
  eucharistic, 285, 384, 501
  gift as name for Holy Spirit, 257
  holiness as, 102
  individual, 94–95, 150, 239, 248n107,
    270n22
  Mary and, 407
  and mutual enrichment, 438n38
  unity in Spirit as goal of, 256–60
  See also Charisms
Giono, Jean, 291
Girault, R., 176n85
Globalization, 212n22, 325, 366, 389
Glorification of God, 371, 507, 520n75
Gnosticism, 216, 250–51n120, 425n535,
  519–20n75
God,
  action in history, 159
  Christian concept of, 511
  faithfulness of, 337
  glorification of, 371, 507, 520n75
  Kingdom of (*see* Kingdom of God)
  mystery of, 215n41
  Word of (*see* Word of God)
  See also Trinity; *specific topics*, e.g.,
    Creation; Love; Worship
God and the World (Seewald), 154–55n2,
  207–8n9, 225n89, 227n1
"God is dead" mentality, 181n108
Gogarten, Friedrich, 184
Gonzáles Hernandez, Olegario, 21n2,
  31, 48
Goodness, 104, 106, 181n108, 327, 393,
  420

Görres, A., 177n88
Gospel, 147, 168, 179, 188, 200, 216,
    335n16
  the Church and, 21n2, 260, 385
  De Ecclesia and, 30
  inculturation of, 113, 221
  "Jesus of the Gospels", 262
  joy, 422
  mission of proclaiming, 32, 44, 113,
    122, 356, 445
  real presence of, 492–93
  rejuvenating power of, 67
  repentance and, 422
  truth of, 385, 393
  Vatican II and, 26, 32, 34
  as "Word of life", 263n189
  See also New Testament; specific topics
Government, 389–94
  episcopal office of governing,
    130–31
  See also Authority; Bishops;
    Collegiality; Democracy;
    Magisterium; Papacy; Politics;
    State
Graber, Rudolf, 207
Grace, 28, 36, 51, 69, 96, 108, 176,
    196n64
  baptismal, 89n53, 103
  bishops and, 109, 130
  and change/renewal, 426, 429
  Christ and, 196n64, 263, 269n219,
    336n21, 342
  Church as sign and instrument of,
    52, 90, 106
  Church as visible form of, 54
  doctrine on, 269n219
  forgiveness and, 350, 427–28
  fruits of, 102
  and guilt, 269n219, 427
  Mary and, 106, 108, 400, 411
  Old and New Covenant, 82
  restoration to, 515
  sacramental, 90–91, 139, 287
  theology of, 304–5
  and unity, 71, 86, 284, 287, 291–92
  and works, 102
Graz, Austria, 201
Greco, J., 165n37
Gredt, Joseph, 314–15

Greek Fathers of the Church, 45n32,
    515. See also Fathers of the Church;
    individual names; specific topics
Greek tradition and culture, 345–46,
    369n210, 377n249
  the Greek philosophers, 377n249
  See also specific topics and concepts
Gregory the Great, 46n35
Greiner, Franz, 177–78
Greshake, Gilbert, 62, 71–73, 76,
    88–89, 469, 473–74n214, 480
Grillmeier, Alois Cardinal, 317–18n467
  on Body of Christ, erroneous
    interpretations, 67
  on the Church, 110n168, 317–18n467
  on Lumen gentium, 25, 34, 38, 42,
    44–46, 70, 73, 86
  charisms, 88, 92n67
  common priesthood, 88
  communio, 62, 66, 112n174, 135–36
  Ecclesia Christi, 81n18
  People of God, 82n21, 86, 109
  relation of particular Churches to
    one Church, 109
  patristic theology, 40n8
  on Vatican II view of the Church,
    110n168
Growth of the Church, 252–53
Guardini, Romano, 22, 150n20, 182,
    269, 518–20
Guilt, 102, 196n64, 416n484, 421, 423,
    427–28
  and grace, 427
Gutiérrez, Gustavo, 217n49

Habilitation thesis, 160–63
Haider, 170n58
Hanselmann, Johannes, 440n49
Häring, Hermann, 186n10, 186n12,
    190n33, 193–94, 201, 326–28 passim,
    503
  analysis of Dominus Iesus, 320–21
Heaven, 36n28, 341n48, 343
  Church in, 338–39
  and communion of saints, 344
  Daniel's vision, 355n134
  and earth, 256n156, 259, 380, 400,
    409n446
  kingdom of (see Kingdom of God)

liturgy as worship of open heaven, 518
new, 340, 522
See also Eschatological Nature of the Pilgrim Church and its Union with the Church in Heaven; Eternal life
Heavenly Jerusalem, 113, 256n155, 273n45, 338, 353n125, 374–75
Hegel, Georg Wilhelm Friedrich, 162, 328n520, 511–12
Heidegger, M., 170–71
Heinz, Hanspeter, 112n176, 113
Hell, 36n28, 343
Hemberger, D., 170n58
Hemmerle, Klaus, 60n99, 61n102, 63n116
Heresy, 70n152, 71n154, 134, 247, 335n16, 418
See also Error; Schism
Herms, Eilert, 438n40
Hernandez, Olegario Gonzáles, 21n2, 31, 48
Hick, J., 437n31
Hierarchy, Church, 229, 304
Ratzinger's ecclesiology, 183, 430–96
collegiality and primacy, 444–61
collegiality as ecumenical paradigm, 432–40
Council and later perspective on, 461–96
hierarchy as holy origin, 440–43
liberation theology and, 217n50
third chapter of Lumen gentium, 35, 114–41
Church as "complex reality", 140–41
main themes of, 117–31
college of bishops, 117–25
sacramentality of episcopal consecration, 125–27
three munera of the bishop as rooted in sacramental ordination, 127–31
premises for, 114–17
priests and deacons, 135–40
See also specific topics for more detailed information, e.g., Bishops; Collegiality

Hilary of Poitiers, 246n89
"Historical" Jesus, 262, 264
History,
Bonaventure's theology of, 160–63
dogmatic tradition, historical research in relation to, 510–11
God's action in, 159
historical thinking, paradigm of, 510–14
intellectual, and Ratzinger's ecclesiology, 509–17
paradigm of historical thinking, 510–14
salvation (See Salvation history)
See also Tradition; specific topics, e.g., Reformation
Hitler, Adolf, 154–55n2
See also Third Reich
Hödl, L., 79n3, 81n17
Höfl, Helmut, 167n45
Holiness, vocation to, 83, 86, 396–399, 413
Holiness, universal call to, 396–429
fifth chapter of Lumen gentium, 36, 101–2
Holy Communion. See Eucharist
Holy Mass. See Mass, Holy
Holy Orders. See Orders, Holy
Holy Spirit, 162
accomplishment of Christ's salvific work in communio of the Father in, 522
and the Church, 21n2
Church as Bride of Christ in, 67
Church as organism of, 250–54
Church as organization vs. organism of Holy Spirit, 250–54
Church as temple of, 47, 68, 72, 95, 237–38
and growth of the Church, 252–53
communio, as effecting, 68–69
as fire, 259
and the liturgy, 150n20
as love, 246, 251, 270n22
"Spirit", the term, 254
temple of, 47, 68, 72, 95, 237–38
union in, 203n105
as goal of all gifts, 256–60

Holy Spirit (*continued*)
  Vatican II and, 168, 194
  Word of God and, 208
  See also Pneumatology; Trinity; *specific topics*, e.g,, Gifts
Hope, 161n25, 341
  Church as sign of, 58
  eschatological view of, 341, 441
  of faith, 219
  faith as, 157, 219
  liberation theology and, 211n66
  the Our Father and, 214
  reform and, 200
  renewal and, 205
  "theology of", 184
  Vatican II and, 396–99
Horkheimer, M., 182n109, 523n96
Horn, C., 313n451
Horn, Stephan Otto, S.D.S., 9nn3–4, 10n7, 201, 203, 409n446, 470, 472n205, 516n60
Human rights, 390–92
Humility, Christian, 96, 182, 208n9, 419
Hünermann, P., 171n63, 262–63, 512n40
Husserl, Edmund, 519n73
Huyghe, G., 22n2

Idealism, German, 513
Imhof, P., 199nn76–77
Imperfection, 219, 342
the Incarnation, 55, 66n129, 197, 238, 289, 328n520, 519
  and Body of Christ concept, 50, 237, 284
  and the Catholic Church's understanding of herself, 333–34
  and being a Christian, 284
  and Christian concept of God, 511
  the Church and, 56n77, 66, 83n24, 324, 329, 333–34, 409
  communion and, 285, 289
  "incarnational", the term, 408
  Mary and, 106, 409–10
  mystery of, 284–86, 311, 329
  ongoing, 56
  scandal of, 261
  See also Jesus Christ; Logos

Inculturation, 113, 221
Individualism, 291–92
  egotism, 259
Individual responsibility. *See* Personal responsibility
Infallibility, 92–94, 115–16, 129–30, 481
Injustice, 219
  See also Justice
International Catholic Journal Communio. See *Communio*
International community, 25n18, 479
International relations. *See* Politics
International Theological Commission, 151, 175–78
Interreligious dialogue. *See* Dialogue
"In the Beginning. . .": A Catholic Understanding of the Story of Creation and the Fall (Ratzinger), 251n122, 351n114, 368n204, 369n209, 370n215, 371n220, 372nn224–25
Introduction to Christianity (Ratzinger), 173, 194, 377n249, 419–20
Irenaeus of Lyons, St., 67, 459
Islam, 113, 280, 327
Israel, 159n16, 298, 335n19, 412n66, 504, 507, 520n75, 520n78
  birth of, 272
  as bride, 254n137, 412n467, 414
  Christ and, 340n41, 354–57
  and the Church, 65, 340, 344–46, 351, 400
  cult, theology of, 410n454
  and the *Ecclesia*, understanding of, 368–70
  faith of, 340
  Mary and, 400, 404, 408, 410
  new, 354–57, 375n238, 379, 404, 408
  New Testament and, 351
  as People of God, 80–82, 332, 344–46, 383
  preexistence of, 368–72
  Rock as symbol of, 458
  and salvation history, 340
  and temple worship, 353
  women and, 412n467
  See also Exodus; Jerusalem; Judaism
Italy, 163, 177, 230
Ivánka, Endre von, 387n311

Jedin, H., 166n41
Jeon, Kwan-Jin Elamus, 12n20,
   306n417, 310n437, 462n162
Jeremias, J., 272n238, 349, 458n148
Jerome, St., 126
Jerusalem, 335n19, 419
   beginning of Church in, 375, 377–79
   destruction of Temple in, 289
Jerusalem, new. See Heavenly Jerusalem
Jesuits, 33, 165n37, 271n231, 416n486,
   515n55
Jesus Christ,
   and the Church (see also Body of
      Christ)
      Church, distinguishing from, 44–45
      Church as Bride of Christ in the
         Holy Spirit, 67
      Church as sacramental
         re-presentation of, 59–60
      Church as seed and beginning of
         Christ's kingdom, 46–49
      as origin and goal of the Church,
         348–57
      as patriarch of new People of God,
         351–57
      as sacramental center of People of
         God, 346–48
      death and Resurrection of (see Death
         and Resurrection of Christ)
      divine-human communio as realized in,
         66–67
      in the Eucharist, 522 (see also Eucharist)
      "family of God" as a favorite image
         of, 352–53
      "historical", 262
      mission of (see Mission of Christ)
      mystery of, 22, 195–97, 269
      new Israel, as patriarch of, 354–57
      salvific work, accomplishment of, 522
      Second Coming of (see Second
         Coming)
      the twelve appointed by, 353–54
      See also Incarnation; Logos; Trinity;
         specific topics, e.g., Salvation
Jews. See Judaism
Joachim of Fiore, 161n25, 162
Johannine theology, 241
John Chrysostom, St., 100n109,
   245n84, 246n89

John Damascene, St., 46n35
John of Parma, Bl., 161n25
John Paul II, Pope, 34n19, 125, 211,
   215, 223, 357–58, 365
John the Baptist, St., 349
John XXIII, Pope Bl., 164, 179, 190,
   194, 303n402, 442
   aggiornamento, 23–24n13
   and Church unity, 26n26
   and dialogue, 34n19, 38n39
   encyclicals, 23–24n13–14, 27n27,
      27n29
   and Lumen gentium, 36–37
   on Lumen gentium, 34n19
   optimism of, 167
   and renewal, 28
   and Vatican II, 23–28, 44, 188, 432
Joy, 27
   communio and, 289, 291–92
   of Pentecost, 425
   repentance and, 422
Judaism, 100, 113, 254n137, 327,
   335–37, 355, 377–78n253, 387n311
   early Christians and, 346
   and heavenly Jerusalem concept,
      374–75
   salvation as from, 335
   See also Israel; Torah; specific topics,
      e.g., Passover
Judgment, 218
   the Last Judgment, 343
Jüngel, Eberhard, 323n492
Juridical view of the Church, 21, 31,
   33n13, 41–42, 71n154, 101, 116–18,
   130
   bishops and, 293, 442–43, 465, 475,
      486, 490, 493, 494n306
   and Church as corporate body, 245n87
   and Church membership, 304, 334
   and "Church", the title, 316n463
   and "college", the term, 133–34
   collegiality and, 442–43
   communio and, 494n303
   and "gathering of the people", 345
   and the hierarchical communio of the
      Church, 135
   the papacy and, 234–35, 293
   Ratzinger and, 231–32, 431, 466,
      471, 501–2, 521

Juridical view of the Church (*continued*)
  and unity, 74
  Vatican II and, 464
  as Western view, 283
Justice, 181n108, 219, 437
  of God, 254n137
  liberation theology and, 221n66 (*see
    also* Liberation theology)
  social, 390, 437
  See also Social responsibility
Justification by faith doctrine, 224

Kaes, Dorothee, 10–11, 194, 326n505,
  369n210, 370, 515n53, 515n57
Kant, Immanuel, 511, 519n73
Karger, Michael, 222
Käsemann, Ernst, 333
Kasper, Walter,
  on bishops, 27, 125, 126n67, 130–31
  on Church as sacrament, 54
  on *communio*, 62–63
  on *Dominus Iesus*, 326n507
  on *Lumen gentium*, 116
  on particular Churches and universal
    Church, 122, 293n353, 364–68,
    374
  on the Petrine office, 125
  on Ratzinger, 293n353, 474
  on the "Ratzinger formula", 201
  Ratzinger's debate with, 364–68,
    374–79, 503
  on Vatican II, 118–19
Kehl, Medard,
  on bishops, 465–66, 487–88
  on blood and water, 66
  on charisms, 69
  on the Church, 59–60, 64
  on Church and modern culture, 383
  on the laity, 97–99 passim
  on priesthood, common and
    ministerial, 88–89
  on Ratzinger's ecclesiology, 424
  "trinitarian signature", 43n19
Kertelge, Karl, 81
Kingdom of God,
  ecumenical importance of idea, 48–49
  as eschatological gathering and
    cleansing, 348–51
  kingdom, the word, 218

Kirchner, Hubert, 217nn50–51, 222
Klausnitzer, W., 6, 33n13, 112–21
  passim, 126–28, 134, 139n134
Klinger, E., 54n73, 98n93
Kloppenburg, B., 2n2, 117n20, 135n113
Klostermann, Ferdinand, 89, 99,
  100n109
Knitter, P. F., 437n31
Koinonia. See *Communio*
Komonchak, Joseph A., 28n30, 29n2,
  303n402
König, Franz, 62n107, 75n175,
  105n140, 199, 308, 401, 466
Körner, Bernhard, 5–6, 8, 75n176,
  110–11
Koster, M. D., 516
Küng, Hans, 95n81, 170, 180n105,
  193n51, 261n184, 434n14, 510–11

Laity, 78, 96–100
  calling of, 99
  and common priesthood, 90
  and consecration, 99
  dignity of, 505
  fourth chapter of *Lumen gentium*, 30,
    36, 92–93, 96–100
  mission of, 83, 87n42, 96, 98–99
  responsibility of, 84, 96–97
  Vatican II and, 84, 86, 87n42
  See also specific topics, e.g., Witness
Langer, H. D., 269n219, 516n58
Language, 23, 224n86, 375, 517
  and handing on faith, 263n189
  magisterial, 326n501
Läpple, Alfred, 156–57, 523n92
Last Judgment, 343
the Last Supper, 239–40, 270, 299, 351,
  356, 445, 470
  as origin of the Church, 272–75
the Last Things, 36n28, 343
Latin America, 387, 478
  liberation theology (*see* Liberation
    theology)
Latin Church, 201n92, 468–70 passim
Latin Fathers of the Church, 515
  See also Fathers of the Church;
    individual names; specific topics
Latourelle, R., 416n481
Laurentin, René, 412n466

Law, 218
    love and, 219, 232
    See also Authority; Canon law; Old
        Testament; Ten Commandments
Law, Bernard Cardinal, 215n41
Lectures, 204n111
Lécuyer, J., 303n402
Lefèbvre, M., 200, 222
Léger, Paul-Emil, 165n37
Le Guillou, M., 175, 177n87
Lehmann, Karl Cardinal, 177nn87–88,
    178n91, 518n69
Leicht, Robert, 147n8, 172n67
Lengsfeld, P., 434n14
Leo XIII, Pope, 42
Lercaro, Giacomo Cardinal, 45n32,
    165n37
Liberalism, 427
Liberation theology, 160–63 passim,
    180–81, 214, 217–21
    basic themes of, 221n66
    concept of, 217n49
    and hierarchical model, 217n50
Licheri, Gianni, 199
Liénart, Achille, 33, 74
Linnerz, H., 483n256
Listening, importance of, 223, 435
    See also Dialogue
Liturgy, 84, 139, 150n20, 181, 200, 246,
    273
    as accomplishment of Christ's salvific
        work in the communio of the
        Father in the Holy Spirit, 522
    and "Body of Christ", 51
    as celebration of the mystery, 41
    Christian liturgy as essentially
        Catholic, 521
    Church ministry and, 386
    and deist perspective, 264
    education, liturgical, 505n20
    in Holy Mass, 280
    Holy Spirit and, 150n20
    and Old Testament theology of
        sacrifice, 280, 339–39
    in patristic theology, 40
    as prayer of the Church, 150n20,
        518
    Ratzinger on, 150n20, 269, 339,
        381–82, 400, 457, 505n20

Ratzinger's ecclesiology and, 200,
    499, 517–23
    as actio of the Completely Other,
        521–23
    "consistent with being", 518–20
    as expression of the universal,
        520–21
    Sacrosanctum Concilium, 23, 27, 90–91
    The Spirit of the Liturgy (Guardini),
        150n20
    task of, 181
    and unification of People of God,
        343–44
    at Vatican II, 461–62n160
    Vatican II and, 268
    as worship, 518
Lobkowicz, N., 172n66
Logos, 50, 149, 251n120, 442, 511, 515,
    519–20
    complete union with, 251n120
    Dominus Iesus, 326n508
    "ethos without logos", 438
    faith, logos-oriented, 514
    faith in, 328n520
    in history, 328n520, 513
    liturgy and, 522
    Marian dimension and, 405
    seeds of, 327n512
    theology of, 274–75n247
    worship and, 519
    See also Jesus Christ; Word of God
Lohaus, Gerd, 193, 213, 270–71,
    284–87, 290
Lohfink, Norbert, 336n25, 383
Loisy, Alfred, 348–49
Lord's Supper. See Eucharist
Love, 27n27, 55n75, 89, 100, 102, 104,
    254–56, 256, 519–20
    caritas, 246–47
    of Christ for Church, 67, 91, 101,
        249, 254–56
    Christ's self-giving, 66, 273n243, 292,
        299, 337, 338, 412, 518
    for the Church, 251
    the Church and, 63, 232, 249,
        255–56, 360, 375, 411, 415
    Church as sign of God's, 83
    commandments to, 83, 104, 336n21,
        438

Love (continued)
conversion of heart and, 295n362
and death, 299
dialogue of, 210
eternal, 280, 289, 337–38, 375, 518
faith and, 246
freedom and, 384
of God, 66, 83, 251, 289, 297–99,
336–37, 372, 380
Holy Spirit as, 246, 251, 270n222
for human family, 188n21
law and, 219, 232
loss of transcendence and, 181n108
Mary and, 106, 399, 406, 408–9,
411–12
missionary life of, 298
of neighbor, 104, 398–99
nuptiality, Pauline theme of, 249,
254–56
and renewal, 27n27
spousal love between Christ and
Church, 249, 254–56, 411,
414n474 (see also under Bride:
Church as)
and study of the Church, 33
and three fundamental themes of
truth, unity, and peace, 27n28
trinitarian, 149
truth and, 251
and unity, 69, 245–57 passim,
270n22, 286–95 passim, 319, 325,
360, 399, 419, 428, 457
virtue of, 161n25, 256
See also Adoration; Charity
Lubac, Henri de, S.J., 162n29, 271, 515
and Body of Christ concept, 243n76,
271, 276–77
and Church as sacrament, 234n91
and collegiality, 474
as conciliar theologian, 271n231, 386
and individual faith, 148n10
the International Theological
Commission, 175
the journal Communio, 177n87
patristic theology, 515
on pilgrim People of God concept
and Vatican II, 79
and Ratzinger's ecclesiology, 148n10,
156–57, 474, 478, 495, 515

and restoration, 197n68, 199
on salvation, 291
Lubich, Chiara, 350n106, 438n38
Lüdemann, Gerd, 225n88
Luke, St.; Lucan theology, 375, 377n253
Lumen gentium, 19–141
"Body of Christ" as key to
ecclesiology of, 243–70
chapter topics (principal themes),
39–141, 229
list and summary of, 30, 33–38
(See under these specific
themes/chapter topics for more
detailed information)
Church, as shedding light on, 331
communio, theme of, 62
De Ecclesia, contrast with, 30, 501
ecclesiology of, 243–70
and the liturgy (see Liturgy;
Sacrosanctum Concilium)
"new" aspects of, 31–32
and People of God concept, 112
purpose of, 42
Ratzinger's theology and (see under
Theology, Ratzinger's: Lumen
gentium compared with)
as "the work of the Council", 32–38
universalism of, 35
See also Vatican II; specific topics, e.g.,
Universal Church
Lustiger, Jean-Marie, 214
Luthe, Herbert, 53n69, 166
Luther, Martin, 184, 224, 308n430,
369n210
Lutheranism, 171, 216n46, 225n88, 307,
308n430, 311n444, 420, 515
Joint Declaration with Catholic
Church on the Doctrine of
Justification, 224

Maccarone, M., 166n42
Magisterium, 93–94, 176n83, 186, 191,
212n22, 221n68, 225
and interdenominational dialogue,
225
limited authority of, 221n68
Ratzinger and, 192, 201
theology and, 205, 211
the truth and, 221n68

Vatican II and, 196
See also Apostolic succession; Bishops:
    college of; *specific topics*
Magistretti, F., 28n32, 39n1, 306n415,
    316, 442n60, 446n85, 468n190
Maier, Friedrich Wilhelm, 158
Maier, Hans, 174, 177n88, 178n91
the Majority principle, 392–96, 506
    episcopal conferences and, 480–82
    See also Democracy
Malula, G., 165n37
Marcuse, H., 181
Mariology, 37, 399–414
    Daughter Zion, 407–38n408, 412–13
    Marian devotion and ecumenism, 108
    Marian statements, meaning of, 399–414
        Ratzinger's position during the
            Council, 399–400
        statements by Ratzinger, later,
            400–413
        feminine structure of the Church,
            405–9
        Sponsa Christi, 409–13
    Mary in the Mystery of Christ and
        the Church (eighth chapter of
        Lumen gentium), 105–8
    cult of the Blessed Virgin, 107–8
    economy of salvation, role in,
        106–7
    model for the Church, 107
    redemption, role in, 37n34
    Theotokos, 37, 405n420
    See also under specific topics, e.g.,
        Grace; Love
Marnach, Gitta, 205n114
Marriage, 91–92, 216
    Adam and Eve, spousal mystery of,
        411
    dignity of, 25n18
    matrimony, sacrament of, 53n68, 91
    nuptiality, Pauline theme of, 249,
        254–56
    spousal love between Christ and
        Church, 249, 254–56, 411,
        414n474
Martyrdom, 102, 458, 460, 495n315
Marx, Karl; Marxism, 156, 162, 170–72,
    181, 217–18, 220, 341n48, 388
Mary. *See* Mariology

Mass, Holy, 137, 282
    and Liturgy of the Word, 280
    prayer and, 137, 274–75
    See also Eucharist
Matrimony, sacrament of, 53n68, 91
    See also Marriage
Media, 326n507
Medina, Jorge, 175, 177n87
Meditation, 203, 347
Meisner, J., 396n372
Membership, Church. *See* Church
    membership
Memoirs. *See* *Milestones: Memoirs
    1927–1977*
Memory,
    Christian, 480–81n241
    Church as living, 148
    purification of, 223
Menke, K.-H., 437n31
Mercy, 83, 254n137, 342
Merit (works), 102
Mersch, E., 515
Messori, Vittorio, 34n19, 186, 198,
    217
Metaphysics, 189, 194, 369n210,
    371n219, 391n337, 437, 511
    and truth, 437
    See also specific topics, e.g., Subsistence
Metz, Johann Baptist, 148n12, 172n66,
    178n91, 187n15, 189n26, 216n46,
    266
    "theology of the world", 184
Meyer zu Schlochtern, Josef, 433n70
Middle Ages, 82, 160, 245n87, 301,
    377n249, 382, 416, 484
Mieth, D., 182n114
Milestones: Memoirs 1927–1977, 206n1
    See also specific topics
Ministry,
    early Church, spiritual ministry of,
        449–50
    witness structure of, 457–60
Mission, individual, 141
Mission of Christ, 45–46
    priestly, prophetic, and kingly, 84–97
    priests' participation in, 136–38
Mission of the Church, 195
    missionary attitude, Vatican II
        transition to, 196

Mission of the Church (*continued*)
  missionary spirit of the Church, 205
  unification and, 205
  See also under Gospel: mission of
    proclaiming; Pastoral mission of
    the Church
Modernism, 31n8, 271n231, 402
Modernity, 151, 169n53, 178, 181
  and liberation theology, 180
  and pluralism, 210
  the post-modern era, 506
  reconciliation and, 180
  role of Church in modern world,
    25n18
  theology and, 173, 212
Moeller, Charles, 33, 132–33nn102–103
Möhler, Johann Adam, 45n32, 47n43,
  56, 231n10, 514–15
Moll, Helmut, 7, 12–13n20
Moltmann, Jürgen, 147n8, 171–72,
  371n219
Moon, symbolism of, 409n446, 421
Moosbrugger, B., 483n253
Moralism, 156–57, 220
Morality, 90, 372, 415, 426–28
  deism and, 265
  ecumenism and, 177n86, 202–3
  Jesus and, 354
  Kant and, 519n73
  and magisterial competence, 478–80
  and reform, 415, 426–29
Morawa, J., 40n4
Mörsdorf, Klaus, 158, 469
Mucci, G., 311n447
Mühl, M., 200n86, 226n93, 309n434
Mühlen, Heribert, 34, 68n142, 74,
  311n447, 456n133
Müller, Gerhard Ludwig, 69n147,
  105n139, 140n138, 325n503
Multiculturalism, 216
Multiplicity. *See under* Unity: in
  multiplicity
Munich, 156–58, 163, 206–11
  Ratzinger as Archbishop, 205–11
Münster, 168–70, 194
Mystery, 147, 152n35, 229
  central, of salvation, 149
  of Christ, 22, 195–97, 269
  of the Church, 82

Church as sign of faith and mystery
  of faith, Ratzinger's ecclesiology
  of, 230–330 (*see also under* Body
  of Christ; *Communio;* Eucharist;
  Subsistence)
of the Church (first chapter of *Lumen
  gentium*), 33–34, 39–77
  three perspectives of, 44–77
    Christ and the Church, 44–52
    the Church as sacrament, 52–60
    the Church's unity, 60–73
of the Cross, 191
of death and Resurrection of Jesus,
  150
Easter, 292
Eucharistic, 226
fundamental concepts of, 82
of God, 215n41
of the Incarnation, 284–86, 311, 329
liturgy as celebration of, 41
in *Lumen gentium*, 39–40
Lumen gentium compared with
  Ratzinger's ecclesiology, 501–4
the Paschal Mystery, 256–57, 289
saving, of Christ, 22
the term, 39–42
theology of, 41
trinitarian, 149, 237
Mystical Body of Christ. *See* Body of
  Christ (Church as).
Mystici Corporis (Pius XII, encyclical),
  50–51, 78, 234n19, 515n55
Mysticism, 245n87, 270, 301, 303, 416
  and Church membership, 301–3
Myth, 341, 388

Nachtwei, Gerhard, 174n77, 193,
  246n91, 329, 339n40, 340, 495n315
Nationalism, 366, 387
Nazis. *See* Hitler; Third Reich
Neighbor, love of, 104, 398–99
Neo-conservatism. *See* Conservatism
Neoscholasticism, 41, 158, 169n53, 175,
  314, 501, 514n50
Neuner, P., 22n2, 72n159, 98n93
New Age Movement, 221
New Jerusalem. *See* Heavenly Jerusalem
Newman, John Henry Cardinal, 158,
  252

New Testament, 162, 171n61
  beginnings of Church in, 374–79
  and liberation theology, 218
  Old Testament, unity with, 280, 368
  See also Gospel; specific topics, e.g.,
    People of God
"New Theology", 271n231
Nicaea, Council of, 477n228
Nichols, A., 479n235, 483n257
Nietzsche, 181n108, 341n48
Nihilism, 487
1968, student revolt of, 145, 170–72,
  174
  See also Paradigm shift, late sixties
Nirvana, 259
Nissiotis, N. A., 452
Nocke, F.-J., 40n7
Non-Catholic Christians, 37, 111n170,
  112, 303, 322n489, 323n494, 330
  Vatican II and, 112
  See also Protestants; Truth: outside
    the Catholic Church
Non-Christians; non-Christian
  religions, 113, 199, 305n414,
  327n512, 504n17
  See also specific religions
Nonconformism, 196
North America, 180, 265–66, 388
  See also Western world
Nuptiality, Pauline theme of, 249,
  254–56

Obedience of faith, 27, 93–94, 102–6,
  129, 141
Old Testament, 162, 218
  and liberation theology, 218
  New Testament, unity with, 280,
  368
  See also specific topics, e.g., People of
    God
Onclin, W. H. J., 494n306
Ontological priority of the Universal
  Church. See Universal Church
Ontology, 369n210
Optimism, 167, 187–88, 397
Orders, Holy, sacrament of, 69, 347,
  360, 380, 431
  and the episcopal office, 30, 125–236,
  133n108

priests and, 137
  See also Bishops; Deacons; Priests;
    Sacrament
Origen, 236, 259, 294, 419
Original sin, 251n21, 291
Orlandis Rovira, J., 124n58, 222n74
Örsy, Ladislas, 373
Orthodox Churches, 108, 200, 329,
  452, 474n214
  ecumenism and, 41, 48, 433–34, 455,
  484, 508, 516
  Ratzinger's theology and, 200, 329
  structure of, 440
  See also Eastern Churches
Orthodoxy, 163n339, 175–76, 185, 217,
  433, 437n31, 440, 506
Orthopraxis, primacy of orthodoxy
  over. See Orthodoxy.
Ott, H., 311n444
Ottaviani, Alfred Cardinal, 28n32,
  29nn3–4, 75, 132, 165, 165n37, 303
the Our Father, 214, 353

Pacelli, Eugenio Cardinal. See Pius XII,
  Pope
Pannenberg, Wolfhart, 434n14
Papacy, 234–35
  authority of, 120–21, 129, 133n107,
  377n249, 480–81n241, 484–85,
  489
  papal primacy, 125
    and collegiality of bishops, 118–20,
    450–54
    the "Ratzinger formula", 14n29,
    470
    and synod of bishops, twofold
    ordering of, 492–93
  the three papal offices, 467–72
    Bishop of Rome, 468
    patriarch of the West (the Latin
    Church), 468
    the successor of Peter, 468
  See also Catholic Church; individual
    pope.
Parables, 349
Paradigm shift, late sixties, 170–71,
  182–83, 192, 224n85, 235
Paris, 214
Parish community, 359

Parousia. *See* Second Coming
Pascal, B., 158
Paschal Mystery, 256–57, 289
Pascher, Josef, 158
Passover, 272–74, 288, 353, 356, 446
Pastoral Constitution on the Church.
  See *Gaudium et spes*
Pastoral mission of the Church,
  after the Council, 441
  and Church's teaching office, 27
  episcopal-collegial structure, pastoral
    implications of, 454–61, 478, 483,
    487–88, 495
  and hierarchical structure, 97, 444
  "pastoral approach by slogans",
    189n28, 216, 394
  pastoral schism between hierarchy
    and simple faithful, 97
  priests and, 136, 138
  Ratzinger and, 200
  and renewal, 432
  the term "pastoral", 25
  Vatican II and, 23–28, 135, 183n114,
    436n6
Patriarchal districts, 472–82
Patriarch of the West, 468
  See also Papacy
the Patriarchs, 335n19, 336, 446, 468
  See also individual names, e.g.,
    Abraham
Patristic theology, 40, 368, 514–16, 515
Paul, St.,
  Church as Body of Christ, 248–60
  and the Eucharist, 248n106
  factions, 223
  the lot of the apostle, 209
  Mary, 106
  nuptiality, theme of, 249, 254–56
Paul VI, Pope, 50–51n58, 179, 207–8
  encyclicals, 23–24n13, 23n13, 73n163,
    174n74
  and *Lumen gentium*, 28n32, 34n19,
    50n58, 331n1
  Roman Curia under, 262–63
  and synod of bishops, 124, 482–83
  and Vatican II, 119, 132, 402–3,
    432n6
  and World Council of Churches,
    176n85

Peace, 27, 333
  the Church and, 63, 70n150, 72, 96,
    124, 360, 464
  ecumenism and, 437
  Jesus as source of, 64, 83, 226,
    236n38, 291, 325, 351
  laity and, 36, 100
  Mary and, 108
  Sign of, 422
Penance, 203, 223, 426, 429
  the sacrament, 53n68
Pentecost, 43, 45, 48, 68, 125, 445–46
  and the Jewish Diaspora, 377n253
  joy of, 425
  Lucan depiction of, 375, 377n253
  a new, 194n58
People of God concept, 229
  Israel and, 80–82, 332, 344–46, 383
  Lumen gentium as rediscovering, 112
  New Testament and, 159n16
  political transformation of, 506
  purification of, 388
  Ratzinger's ecclesiology and,
    331–429, 523
    Augustine and, 331–32
    christological development of
      image of preexistent People of
      God, 370–73
    Church as "pilgrim people of
      God", 333–34
    conciliar ecclesiology, aim of,
      396–99
    creation, inner predestination of
      for the Church, 368–73
    ecclesia, 344–46, 368–270
    Ecclesia peccatrix, 416–24
    eschatological character of pilgrim
      Church, 339–44
    holiness, universal call to, 396–429
    "I am black but beautiful",
      414–29
    image as revision of
      Body-of-Christ idea, 333–44
    inner continuity of salvation
      history through, 335–39
    inner predestination of creation for
      the Church, 368–73
    Jesus as origin and goal of the
      Church, 348–57

People of God concept (*continued*)
  Jesus as patriarch of new People of
    God, 351–57
  Jesus as sacramental center of,
    346–48
  kingdom of God as eschatological
    gathering and cleansing, 348–51
  Lumen gentium compared with,
    504–7
  Marian statements, meaning of,
    339–414
  Ratzinger as accused of Roman
    centralism, 364–68
  reform, nature and heart of,
    425–29
  sociological misunderstanding of,
    382–96
  summary of, 523
  universal call to holiness, 396–429
  universal Church, ontological
    priority of, 357–82
  second chapter of *Lumen gentium*, 35,
    78–113 (*see also* Consecrated
    religious; Holiness, call to; Laity;
    Mariology)
  Catholicity of, 108–13
  charisms of, 94–95
  and ecumenism, 108–13
  freedom of, 95–96
  kingly service in, 95–97
  participation in Christ's priestly,
    prophetic, and kingly mission,
    84–97
  prophetic ministry of, 92–95
  Ratzinger's ecclesiology compared
    with, 504–7
  responsibility of for creation and
    the world, 96–97
  in salvation history, 80–84
  supernatural sense of faith
    belonging to, 92–94
  See also Church; *specific topics for more
    detailed information*, e.g., Laity
Perfection,
  the Church and, 46–47, 59, 81, 83,
    101, 147, 197, 342
  Church as signifying, 111
  De Ecclesia and, 30
  love and, 102

  vocation to, shared, 86
  worldly, 160n20
Perfect society. *See* Utopianism
Perichoresis, 72, 122, 378n258, 457,
    473–74
Peritus, 166, 306n415
Persecution, 76
Personal responsibility,
  baptism and, 457
  bishops and, 457–58, 460n154, 475,
    482, 491–93, 495–96
Persson, Per E., 48–49n50
Pesch, Otto Hermann,
  on Church as sacrament, 54
  on *communio*, 85
  on *Lumen gentium*, 34n18, 37n30, 85,
    118n117
  on Mariology, 37–38n18
  on mystery, 39
  on *sensus fidei*, 94n76
  on subsistence, 34n18
  on Vatican II, 135n115, 179, 189n29,
    190
Peter, St., 350, 356
  ministry of primacy, 447
  pope as successor to, 468
  role among apostles, 451
  theology of, 458–59
  See also Papacy
Peter Lombard, 125–26
Peterson, E., 348n99
Petrine office. *See* Papacy
Pfau, Hubert, 155n2
Pfnür, Vinzenz, 9nn3–4, 10n7, 256n153,
    470n197, 472n205
Philips, Msgr. Gérard, 29n4, 32–38
  passim, 75, 78n2, 295, 311n444,
    324
Philosophy, 150, 157, 181, 315, 370,
    388–89, 503, 509
  faith and (Barth), 514n50
  the Greek philosophers, 377n249
  ontological approach of metaphysics
    and, 511–12
  political (*see under* Politics: political
    philosophy)
  *See also individual philosophers,
    philosophies, and topics*, e.g.,
    Relativism

Pilgrim Fellowship of Faith: The Church as Communion (Ratzinger), 326n505, 440n49, 504n17
Pius IX, Pope Bl., 188
Pius X, Pope St., 401
Pius XI, Pope, 25
Pius XII, Pope, 263, 317, 372n223, 504
 and the Church, 42, 55
 encyclical *Mystici Corporis*, 50–51, 78, 109, 234n19, 334, 515n55
 Marian spiritual movement during papacy of, 401
 Roman Curia under, 262–63
 and Vatican I, resumption of, 25
Plato, 158, 288, 377n249, 460
Pluralism, 152, 210, 325–29 passim, 363, 366, 391, 437–38
Pneumatology, 242–43
 and christology, 159, 163, 238–43, 248–60
 and Church, understanding of, 248–60
 See also Holy Spirit
Politics,
 faith and, 172, 175, 218, 221
 People of God concept and, 383–89
 political philosophy, 391, 460–61
 and theology, 171–72
 See also specific topics, e.g., Democracy
the Poor. *See* Poverty
Popes. *See* Papacy; *individual names*
Positivism, 181, 386, 402, 511
Post-modern era, 506
Pottmeyer, Hermann Josef, 5
 on bishops, 124n60, 366n193, 481–82
 on centralism, 193–94, 366–67, 493n302, 496n319
 on Church as mystery, 82
 on *communio*, 72n158, 124n62, 286n313, 358, 462
 on holiness, 102
 on individual vocation and mission, 141
 on *Lumen gentium*, 116
 on the Magisterium, 93
 on office *vs.* function, 133n108
 on the primacy, 125
 on Ratzinger's theology, 366, 368, 462, 474, 496

 on traditionalist opposition to renewal, 57n80
 on unity, 56–57
 on universal Church and local Churches, 361, 373, 376
 on Vatican I, 115–16
 on Vatican II, 56–57, 73n164, 115–18 passim, 120n39, 124n60, 358, 462
Poverty, 100
 Christ's passion and, 298
 "Church of the poor", 76, 400
 the Church sharing, 76
 of desecularized Church, 195
 evangelical counsel of, 102–3, 105
 in Latin America, 180n103
 liberation theology and (*see* Liberation theology)
 orthodoxy and, 217
 Ratzinger and, 219
Power,
 the Church and, 195, 208
 democracy and (*see* Democracy)
 See also Authority; State
Pragmatism, 181n108, 184–85, 213, 388, 391, 443, 454, 519
 and truth, 189, 329n521
Prayer, 84–85, 91, 99, 104, 200, 223, 353
 Church as communion united through, 353
 Eucharist and, 337–38, 422–23, 457, 460
  the Roman Canon, 274–75, 522
 and founding of the Church, 258
 Israel's, 346
 liturgy as, 150n20, 518
 and Mass, celebration of, 137
 New Testament liturgy of, 338
 the Our Father, 353
 prayer groups, 282
 primitive form of, 401
 Psalm 22, 298
 Ratzinger's ecclesiology and, 200
 temple worship and, 353
 and unity, 249, 256
Preaching, office of, 129–30
Predestination, 42
Prefect, Ratzinger as. *See under* Congregation for the Doctrine of the Faith: Ratzinger as Cardinal Prefect

Priesthood,
  common priesthood, actuation in
    sacraments and in life of virtue,
    90–92
  common priesthood of all the
    baptized, 85–86
  common priesthood *vs.* ministerial
    priesthood, 87–90
  one priesthood in union with bishop,
    138–39
  ordained, 178n91
  women and, 221n68
  See also Priests, below.
Priestly, prophetic, and kingly mission
    of Christ. See Mission of Christ
Priests, 135–39
  consecration of, 136–38
  "Co-workers of the Truth", 207–8
  future, formation of, 210
  participation in the consecration and
    in the threefold mission of Christ,
    136–38
  Ratzinger and, 207–8, 210
  See also Priesthood, above
Prignon, A., 165n37
Primacy, papal. See under Papacy: papal
    primacy
Principles of Catholic Theology
    (Ratzinger), 211–12
Professor, Ratzinger as. See under
    Ratzinger, Joseph: as professor
Proportionalism, 388
Protestants; Protestantism, 48, 216n46,
    327n517
  brotherhoods, relationship with
    Catholic religious orders, 438n38
  Church, view of, 41–42, 304n406,
    309–9, 334
  dialogue with, 112n173, 333
  Holy Spirit and, 51n6, 203n105
  and Mariology, 37
  and the Twelve, 445
  at Vatican II, 435n22
  See also Dialogue; Ecumenism;
    Non-Catholic Christians; *specific
    denominations specific topics,* e.g.,
    Sola scriptura
Przywara, E., 269n219
Psalm 22, 298

Purgatory, 36n28, 343
Purification, 203, 223, 351, 505
  of the Church, 334n10, 388, 419,
    426
  and Church as sinner concept,
    415–16
  of faith, 438
  of the heart, 408n439
  of memory, 223
  of People of God concept, 388
  as reform, 350
  and unification, 349–50, 516–17
Puza, Richard, 487n275

Quinn, J.R., 132n102, 201n92,
    489n283, 494n306, 495n317
Qumran, 349

Rad, G. von, 272n235
Rahner, Hugo, 257, 421n508
Rahner, Karl, 33, 165n37, 178n91, 184,
    231, 416–18
  being an "anonymous Christian",
    178n91
  and authority in the Church, 120–21
  and von Balthasar, 178n91
  on the Church as not sum of
    members, 102
  and Church as sacrament, 54, 60–61
  and the Church of sinners, 417–18
  on collegial unity of particular
    Churches and universal Church,
    122n48
  and concilar texts, 23n12, 30
  as conciliar theologian, 165–66,
    187n15, 190, 231n5, 397, 416, 452
  and *Ecclesia peccatrix* concept, 416
  and ecumenism, 360n157 (*see also
    under* the subentry Fries-Rahner
    plan, below)
  on the episcopate, 126–27, 452–53,
    480
  the Fries-Rahner plan, 202,
    434–35n19, 438–39, 441n57
  on individuals, 165n39, 231n5
  on Israel as People of God, 80n12
  on *Lumen gentium*, 30, 114–15, 117,
    123–24
  on purification and renewal, 76–77

Rahner, Karl (*continued*)
  and "restoration", the term, 198–99
  on the sacraments, 91
  on salvation, 83n27
  on sinfulness of the Church, 416–18
  on truth outside the Catholic
    Church, 75n177
  and unity, 438–39
  on Vatican II, 139n134, 397
  See also *Concilium*.
Rainer, M. J., 200n86
Rationalism, 215n41, 401n400, 514n50,
    515n57
  See also Reason
Ratzinger, Georg (brother), 159
Ratzinger, Joseph Aloysius Cardinal
    (Pope Benedict XVI)
  archbishop of Munich and Freising,
    206–11
  Communio, founding of, 176–78
  as conciliar theologian, 164–68, 462
  Concilium, break with, 178–83
  dissertations (*see* Dissertations,
    Ratzinger's)
  ecclesiological plan, 145–227
  faith of, 150–52, 204n11
  German background of
    childhood and youth, 154–57
    education, 156–59
  goal and foundation of, 205
  International Theological
    Commission, appointment to,
    175–76
  as *peritus*, 166, 306n415
  as Prefect of the Congregation for
    the Doctrine of the Faith (CDF),
    204–6, 211–27, 361, 415, 461n159,
    469, 483n257
  as professor, 158–63, 169–83
    in Münster, 169–70
    in Regensburg, 174–83
    in Tübingen, 170–74
  reputation of, 168n49, 186, 200, 205,
    209
  Vatican II, reason for change in
    attitude after, 504
  as writer, 174, 204n111, 211, 263
  See also Theology, Ratzinger's; *specific
    topics*

the "Ratzinger formula", 14n29, 470
The Ratzinger Report (Messori), 186,
    424n525
Real presence,
  of Christ, 264, 283
  of God in the world, 147
  of the Gospel, 492–93
Reason, 511, 514, 519n73
  Christianity, inherent reasonableness
    of, 514
  faith and, 212n22, 219, 221n70,
    408n439, 514, 519n73
  See also Enlightenment; Rationalism
"Reconciled diversity". See under
    Diversity: "reconciled"
Reconciliation, 180, 223, 268, 282–83,
    428
Redemption, 147, 197, 218, 221n66
  creation and, 373
  liberation theology and, 221n66
  Mary's role in, 37n34
Reform, 231n10, 350, 382, 415, 475
  personal heart of, 415, 426–29
  Ratzinger on, 175, 194–95, 200, 205,
    424–28
  renewal and, 205, 428
  repentance and, 175
  true, nature of, 425–26
  unification and, 205
  See also Renewal
the Reformation, 21n2, 201–3, 266,
    305n413, 308, 321, 448, 502
  anti-Reformation view of the
    Church, 116
  post-Reformation ecclesiology, 42,
    109n164, 416
  Reformation Churches, 433–34, 440
Regensburg, 174–83, 267n210
Relativism, 227, 312, 327, 330, 503–6,
    506, 514, 516
  and democracy, 383, 388–92
  subsistit formula as alternative to, 167,
    220n64, 320–25
  truth and, 181–82
Religion, 327
  comparison of religions, 507
  need for, 212n22
  non-Christian religions, 327n512,
    504n17

world religions, 187, 221n66
See also Dialogue; Ecumenism;
Non-Christians; specific religions
Religious, consecrated. See Consecrated
religious
Rénard, A., 135–36
Renewal, 24n13, 28, 145, 164, 168n49,
198n72, 203n105, 516–17
the early Church and, 449, 484
grace and, 429
growth of Church as tension between
continuity and, 253
love and, 27n27
Lumen gentium and, 34, 36n28, 77
personal, 194–95
Pius X and, 401
Ratzinger's view of, 174–75, 194–200
passim, 205, 253, 332–34 passim,
342, 424–29 passim, 516
reform and, 205
renewal movements, reception of
new, 230–43, 401
traditionalist opposition to, 57n80
Vatican II and, 32, 164, 397, 432
the way to, 428
World War I and, 22
Repentance, 175
conversion and, 421–22
Reputation, Ratzinger's. See under
Ratzinger, Joseph: reputation of
Responsibility. See Personal
responsibility; Social responsibility
Restoration, 183, 197–205
Resurrection of Jesus Christ. See Death
and Resurrection of Jesus Christ
Reuter, H., 29n3
Revelation, 58, 73n162, 80, 92, 160–62,
262–63, 294, 327
believing in, 152, 335
Church worship and, 341
"college" and, 133
Dei Verbum, 23
Dominus Jesus, 326n508
Lumen gentium and, 43
primary theme of, 515n57
and Scripture, 161
Revelation and Tradition (Ratzinger),
161n23, 402n404
Richards, J., 476n226

Richter, Klemens, 178n91, 187n15,
193n51, 275n251
Ricken, F., 311n447
Righteousness, 218
Robert Bellarmine, St., 109n164, 304,
317n465
Rock, image of, 458–59
Roegele, O. B., 177n88
Roman Canon, 274–75, 522
Roman Catholic Church. See Catholic
Church; Church
Roman centralism, 193–94, 364–68,
471, 493n302, 496n319
Roman Congregation for the Doctrine
of the Faith. See Congregation for
the Doctrine of the Faith
Roman Curia. See Curia, Roman
Romanticism, 301, 387
Rousseau, Jean-Jacques, 387n314
Rousseau, O., 41n13, 45n32
Ruf, A. H., 155n4, 158n14, 164n33,
165n36, 173n71, 178n90,
207–8nn8–11, 207n6
Ruffini, E., 165n37
Ruggieri, G., 448n95, 510n31
Russia, 41

Sabbath, 370–71, 374n230, 507
creation and, 370–71
Sunday worship, 282
Sacrament, 54, 152, 214–15, 271n228,
304
Church, sacramental understanding
of, 52–60, 234–38, 248, 291–92,
300, 380–82
meaning of "Church as
sacrament", 54, 271n228
sacramental re-presentation of
Jesus, 59–60
sacrament of salvation, 57
sacrament of unity, 291
common priesthood, actuation of in,
90–92
episcopal collegiality, sacramental
basis of, 442–43
grace, sacramental, 90–91, 139, 287
Jesus as sacramental center of People
of God, 346–48
mysticism and, 270

Sacrament (*continued*)
  sacramental structure as sign and
    instrument of *communio*,
    63–65
  "sacramental", the term, 234
  sacramental *vs.* functional perspective,
    234–38
  the seven sacraments, 53n68
  the fundamental sacraments, 53,
    241, 251, 256, 347, 380
  See also specific sacraments, e.g.,
    Baptism; Eucharist
Sacrosanctum Concilium, 23, 27, 90–91
Saints, 94, 343–44, 396–97, 400,
    418–19, 422, 457, 512n40
  communion of, 235, 246, 261, 274,
    344, 501
  veneration of, 36–37
  See also individual saints
Saint-Simon, Claude Henri, 387n314
Salaverri, G., 166n42
Salcedo, Leovigildo, 314
Salt of the Earth (interview), 151n26,
    281nn282–84, 351n113,
    396nn372–73, 431n5
  See also specific topics
Salvation, 83, 175, 224
  Catholic and Protestant concepts,
    227, 291
  central mystery of, 149
  Christ's salvific work,
    accomplishment of, 522
  the Church and, 21n2, 45–46, 110
  Church as instrument of, 83
  Church as sign of, 236
  Church as universal sacrament of,
    57–58, 82
  "helmet of", 208
  individualistic notion of, 227, 291
  Jesus as author of, 236n38
  Mary's role in, 106–7
  mystery of, 149
  being "saved", 227
  the Word and, 208
  See also Economy of salvation;
    Salvation history; *specific topics*,
    e.g., Reform
Salvation history, 179, 194, 515
  the Cross and, 515

inner continuity through one People
    of God, 335–39
  Lumen gentium and, 504
  the People of God in, 80–84,
    335–40, 506
  Ratzinger's ecclesiology and, 505, 513
  See also specific topics, e.g., Exodus
Sanctification, 26, 102
  as Christian vocation, 36
  episcopal office of sanctifying, 130
Santos, Rufino, 105n140, 401n403
Scandal of the cross. *See under* Cross:
    scandal of
Schaeffler, Richard, 512n40
Scheeben, Matthias Joseph, 56, 514–15
Scheffczyk, Leo, 52–53, 56, 71
  the Schema *De Ecclesia*. See *De Ecclesia*
Schillebeeckx, Edward, 68n38, 165n37,
    178–80
Schism, 71, 90n58, 97, 134, 222, 247,
    318, 435
  the Donatists, 238, 247n94, 305,
    418–19
  See also Error
Schleiermacher, Friedrich Daniel Ernst,
    514n50
Schlier, Heinrich, 223, 346n84, 348n99,
    374, 425n535, 434n14, 436n24
Schlink, E., 434n14
Schmälzle, U. F., 193n51
Schmaus, Michael, 158, 160n21,
    303n402
Schmitz, Heribert, 479n234
Schnell, H., 513n45
Scholasticism, 29n4, 164, 315, 499, 510,
    514
  Neoscholasticism, 41, 158, 169n53,
    175, 314, 501, 514n50
  truth and, 210
Schönborn, Christoph Cardinal, 8, 194,
    215n41, 372n223
Schulte, Raphael, 43, 87–88
Schultz, H.-J., 39n1
Schüssler Fiorenza, Elizabeth, 281n284
Science, 208n9
Scola, Angelo, 79n10, 199
Scripture, 335n16
  catechesis and, 215
  literalness of, 215n88

Old and New Testaments,
  interrelationship and continuity
  between, 368
  as polyphony, 335n16
  Ratzinger's faith and, 151
  and revelation, 161
  totality of, 335n16
  and tradition (*See under* Tradition:
    Scripture and)
  and unity, 203
  See also New Testament; Old
    Testament; Word of God; *specific
    topics*
Seckler, Max, 222, 434, 436n24
the Second Coming, 36n38, 46,
  340–41, 343, 352, 441
Secular authority. *See* Politics; State
Secularism, 180n105, 181
  liberation theology and, 162, 218,
    219n58
  truth and, 181
Seeber, David Andreas, 131–32, 193
Seewald, Peter, 151, 227
Seigfried, Adam, 82, 87n43
Self-denial, 91, 200
Seminaries, 210
Semmelroth, Otto, 33
  and Church as sacrament, 54, 58n89,
    59, 112n175
  and *De Ecclesia*, 33
  and *Ecclesia peccatrix* concept, 416
  on Marian devotion, 106, 108,
    402n409
Serdica, Council of, 477
Seybold, M., 50n58
Shepherds, 164, 210n15, 429
Sin, 102, 264, 416n484
  in the Church, 418–19
  concept of Church as sinner, 414–29
  original sin, 251n21, 291
  personal renewal and, 194–95
  See also Forgiveness; Guilt; Penance;
    Repentance
Skepticism, 151, 153, 388
Smulders, P., 56n77
Social doctrine, 219
Socialism, 388, 438
Social justice, 390, 427
Social responsibility, 218–19, 219

Sociology, 267
  and Church, view of, 267
  and People of God, misunderstanding
    of, 382–96
  truth and, 178–83
Sohm, Rudolf, 232
Söhnen, Gottlieb, 11n13, 158, 160,
  331n2, 451n108, 515
Sola scriptura, 161n25, 225
Solidarity, fellowship of, 437
Son of God; sonship, 251
  See also Jesus Christ; Trinity
Spaemann, Robert, 426–27
Spirit,
  the term, 254
  See also Holy Spirit
The Spirit of the Liturgy (Guardini),
  150n20
The Spirit of the Liturgy (Ratzinger),
  280n278, 337n33, 339n37, 505n20,
  518–22 passim
Stangl, Josef, 207
State, 257n161, 268, 385–87, 389–93, 390
  See also Authority; Democracy;
    Politics
"State Church", 266, 450–51
Staudenmaier, Franz Anton, 513n45
Stehle, Hans-Jakob, 466
Steinhauer, Hilda, 6, 403n410
Stoicism, 257
Subjectivism; subjectivity, 181, 208n9,
  227, 388, 427
Subsistence, 34, 74–76, 306, 310–30,
  378n258
  and Ratzinger's change in attitude
    since Vatican II, 504
  "relative subsistence", 412
  relativism, as alternative to, 320–25
  subsistit, meaning of, 312–20
  and truth, 326–30
Successio apostolica. See Apostolic
  succession
Suddeutsche Zeitung, 151n25, 209
Suenens, L.-J., 165n37, 499
Suffering, 298, 404, 428
  of Christ, 148–49, 298, 520n75
  communio and, 76–77
  idea of world without suffering, 181
Sullivan, F., 311n447

Sunday worship, 282
  See also Sabbath
Supernatural sense of faith, 92–94, 93
Superstition, 328
Symbol, 49, 182n109, 273, 312, 356,
    455, 523n96
  blood and water, 47, 66
  the number twelve, 352, 354–56, 378,
    446
  religious orders and, 100
  and Vatican II ecclesiology, 22, 49
  See also specific topics and descriptions,
    e.g., Rock
Synod, episcopal. See under Bishops:
  synod of

Teaching authority of the Church, 32,
    94, 129, 480–81n241
  See also Magisterium
the Temple, 272–73, 280, 289, 337–39,
    353, 410n454
  new, 272–73, 280, 337–39, 518
Temple of the Holy Spirit. See under
  Holy Spirit: temple of
Ten Commandments, 214, 265n198
  love, commandments to, 83, 104,
    336n21, 438
  See also Law
Tertullian, 40n4, 517
Teuffenbach, Alexandra von, 29n4,
    74–75, 306n419, 311n447, 312n449,
    313n453, 315n458
Tewes, Ernst, 207
Theobald, C., 182–83n114
Theobald, M., 377n253
Theology, 182n109, 205, 212
  Catholic, 319n473
  the Church and, 205 (see also
    Ecclesiology)
  contemporary, problem with, 510
  dogmatic (see Dogmatic theology)
  historical identity of, 263
  "of hope", 184
  liberation (see Liberation theology)
  the Magisterium and, 205, 211
  and the modern world, 173, 212
  of mystery, 41
  "New Theology", 271n231
  patristic (see Patristic theology)

political, 171–72
postwar, 170n56
pragmatic approach to (see
    Pragmatism)
Ratzinger on, 263
task of, 218
and tradition, 212n22
Western, 237
"of the world", 184
See also specific topics
Theology, Ratzinger's, 145–205
  characteristics of, 190, 200, 205, 510,
    522–23
  Church as locus of the faith, 147–50
  as conciliar theologian, 166–68
  consistency of, 184–205, 508–9
    accusations of betrayal of former
        positions, 190–92
    corrections through change of
        perspective, 192–94
    renewal, view of, 194–97
    and "restoration", the term,
        197–205
  Creed as form and content of the
    existential plan, 150–53
  development of, 194
  ecclesial dimension of, 190 (see also
    Ecclesiology, Ratzinger's)
  key to understanding, 379–80
  Lumen gentium compared with,
    379–80, 499–509
    collegiality, 504–9
    mystery, 501–4
    People of God, 504–7
  path of, 154–83
  themes in, recurring, 229–496,
    499–509
    Church as People of God,
        331–429, 504–7 (see also People
        of God)
    the Church—sign of faith and mys-
        tery of faith, 230–330 (see also
        under Body of Christ; Com-
        munio; Eucharist; Subsistence)
    the hierarchical constitution of the
        Church, 430–96 (see also
        Hierarchy)
  thesis from 1968 as shaping, 510
  and Vatican II, 186–90

See also more detailed information under specific themes and topics, e.g., Collegiality

Theology of Liberation (Guttieriez), 162n9, 217n49

Theotokos, 37

Third World. *See* Latin America; Liberation theology

Thomas Aquinas, St., 158, 246, 313n453, 335n19, 377n249

Thomism, 184

Tittmoning, 154

Toiviainen, S., 193n51

To Look on Christ (Ratzinger), 162n29, 212–13, 399n385

Tomašek, František, 208n11

Torah, 335n19, 336n21, 351, 357, 368–72, 428, 507

Totalitarianism, 154–55n2, 389

Tradition, 159–61, 222
  Chalcedon and, 151
  Christianity and, 161n23
  dogmatic tradition, historical research in relation to, 510–11
  meaning of, 21, 184
  and progress, 184
  Ratzinger's theology and, 185, 205, 222
  Scripture and, 161–62n25, 225
  theology and, 212n22
  Vatican II and, 184–85, 187
  See also specific topics

Traditionalism, 214, 222

Transcendence, 181n108, 184–85, 212n22, 219n58

Traunstein, 154–56

Trent, Council of, 21n2, 27, 183n114

Trinity, 182n109, 240n57, 259n171
  accomplishment of Christ's salvific work in *communio* of the Father in the Holy Spirit, 522
  belief in, 147
  Christ in the Eucharist uniting us with, 522
  Christology and, 238
  Church as work of trinitarian economy of salvation, 45–46
  communio as belief in, 147–48

Church as mystery of trinitarian *communio*, 69–73
  communio unity of Church as image of, 71–73
  the Father as calling men to share in trinitarian *communio*, 65–66
  trinitarian *communio* as source and goal of ecclesial *communio*, 65–69

ecclesiology, as direct standard for, 251
and God's action in history, 159
interrelationship of, 240n57
love, trinitarian, 149
Lumen gentium on, 379–80
mystery of, 149, 237
and Ratzinger's ecclesiology, 522–23, 523
theology of, 251
worship as trinitarian, 523
See also God; Holy Spirit; Jesus Christ

Tromp, Sebastian, 28n32, 29, 74–75, 165n37, 234n19, 315n458, 515

Truth, 27n27, 152
  bearing witness to, 188
  Christianity and, 176, 185, 207–8n9, 213
  communion and, 152
  and conscience, 390, 478, 482
  conversion to, 440
  courage and, 208n9, 209
  and dialogue, 227
  and ecumenical dialogue, 227
  and faith, 176, 204, 213
  fear of, in theology, 182n109
  freedom and, 211
  of the Gospel, 385, 393
  and heresy, 335n16
  Holy Spirit and, 240n57
  and love, 251
  metaphysics and, 437
  outside the Catholic Church, 34, 51n61, 75, 327, 504
  pragmatism and, 189, 329n521 (*see also* Pragmatism)
  question of, 326–30
  Ratzinger's ecclesiology and, 211, 522–23
  Ratzinger's motto, *Co-workers of the Truth*, 211

Truth (*continued*)
    and relativism (*see* Relativism)
    revealed, propagation of, 26
    and sociology, 178–83
    subsistence and, 326–30
    and worship, 520
    See also specific theologies and philosophies
Tübingen, 22, 159, 169–74, 436n24,
    513–15
Tück, J.-H., 200n86, 226n93
A Turning Point for Europe (Ratzinger),
    182n109, 218nn54–55, 219n60,
    220n63
Twelve, the number, 351–56, 372n224,
    375, 377–79, 445–47, 458–59,
    499n446
    the twelve apostles, 353–54, 372n224,
        375n238, 409n446 (*See also*
        Apostles)
Tyconius, 418–19

Unbelievers. *See* Non-Christians
United States. *See* North America;
    Western world
Unity, 26, 27n27, 60–73
    Adam and, 250–52, 254n139, 258–59,
        411
    caritas as consequence of, 246–47
    Catholic Church and, 227
    Christ in the Eucharist uniting us
        with God the Trinity and with
        each other, 522
    Church as *communio* unity, 286–88
    Church as sacrament of, 291
    conversion and, 259, 462n161
    as goal of all gifts, 256–60
    in multiplicity, 109, 223, 432–36,
        460–61, 513 (*see also* Diversity)
    purification and, 349–50, 516–17
    Ratzinger's ecclesiology and, 520, 521
    See also Communio; Ecumenism;
        specific topics, e.g., Grace: and unity
Universal Call to Holiness. *See*
    Holiness, Universal Call to
Universal Church,
    Lumen gentium and, 379–82
    as not sum of Churches, 359–68
    ontological precedence of over con-
        crete empirical realizations, 373–82

ontological priority of, 357–82
    particular Churches and, 121–22
    See also Church
Universality, 57, 277, 377, 502–3, 508,
    512n40, 520–21
    and Christian worship, 338–39
    Dominus Iesus, 326–27
    of the liturgy, 518, 520–21
    salvation and, 57, 80
Uppsala, 176
Utopianism, 160–63 passim, 172, 184,
    189, 221n70, 320, 325, 505
    and Council, interpretation of, 464
    eschatological hope *vs.*, 341
    "fall of", 427

Vatican I, 25, 27, 55n75, 132n100, 135,
    141, 448n92
    and Vatican II themes, 115–17,
        120n39, 182–83n174
Vatican II, 21–23, 141, 182–83n174,
    268, 416
    aim and goals of, 396–99
        doctrinal purpose of, 24–28
        main goal of, 24
        pastoral goal of, 24–28
        primary concern of, 267
    "beginning of the beginning", 186–90
    and *communio* concept, 60–61, 269,
        271, 287n316, 300
    core of, 286
    documents of (*see* Vatican II
        documents, below)
    as ecclesiological turning point, 76
    ecclesiology of, 267, 396–99
    and ecumenism, 112
    leitmotiv of, 60–61
    and Marian devotion, 108
    Marian statements, meaning of,
        399–400
    and minority opinions, 132
    missionary attitude, transition to, 196,
        298
    pastoral approach of, 23–28, 135,
        183n114, 432n6
    Ratzinger as conciliar theologian,
        164–68, 462
    reason for Ratzinger's change in
        attitude after, 504

and tradition, 184–85
as transitional council, 182–83n174
and Vatican I themes, 94n36, 115–17,
    120n39, 182–83n174
view of the Church, 110n168
See also under specific topics, e.g.,
    Ecumenism; Liturgy
Vatican II documents, 21–25, 38, 61,
    79, 184, 189
and Catholic conscience, 432n6
central idea of, 269
and *communio* ecclesiology, 269,
    287n316, 300
compromises in, 499–501
dialogue, references to, 113
and *Dominus Iesus*, 367n507
postconciliar treatment of, 187, 189
principal document on the Church
    (see *Lumen gentium*)
Ratzinger and, 14, 444, 464–65, 488
Ratzinger's participation in, 164–65
See also *Gaudium et spes; Lumen
    gentium; specific topic.*
Vaucelles, L. de, 171n62
Vélez Rodriguez, Ricardo, 387n314
Veluti sacramentum, 52–55
Vico, Giambattista, 510n32
Virgin, Blessed, 107–8
See also Mariology
Virginity,
    evangelical counsel of, 102–3, 105
    of Mary, 105, 107
    See also Celibacy
Virtue,
    common priesthood, actuation of in
        life of virtue, 90–92
    divine virtues, 161n25
Vischer, L., 430n2
Vocation,
    of all mankind, 57
    Christian, 36, 398–99
    of the Church, 255
    common, 95–97 passim
    to holiness, 83, 86, 90, 100, 398–99,
        413
    individual, 79, 84, 91–92, 140–41
    to perfection, 86
    religious life and, 103–4
Volf, Miroslav, 491

Volk, Hermann, 168
*Volk and Haus Gottes in Augustins Lehre
    von der Kirche*, 158–59, 504n20
von Balthasar, Hans Urs. *See* Balthasar,
    Hans Urs von
Vorgrimler, Herbert
    on *Communio* and *Concilium*, 178n91
    on Ratzinger as conservative, 186
    on the *Ratzinger Report*, 186n11
    on the Trinity, 474n215
    on Vatican II, 23n121, 60–61,
        139n134, 199

Wagner, H., 436n26
Wagner, K., 155n4, 158n14, 164n33,
    165n36, 173n71, 178n90,
    207–8nn8–11, 207n6
Waldenfels, Hans, 96
Wallner, Karl, 6
War, 25n18
    See also Peace; World Wars
Wassilowsky, Günther, 53n66, 165n38,
    166n42, 233n18, 416, 500n4
Weiler, Thomas, 11–12
    on Body of Christ, 244
    on *De Ecclesia*, 29n4
    on episcopal collegiality, 444, 488
    on Ratzinger as conciliar theologian,
        11–12, 164n34, 188
    on Ratzinger's theology, 11–12,
        238n50, 244, 317n464, 319n473,
        444
    on Vatican II, 166n42, 188, 444, 488
Western ecclesiology. *See under*
    Ecclesiology: Eastern and Western
Western world,
    crisis of, 169–70
    theologians from, 180
    See also Europe; North America
Whore, 414–15, 420
Wickert, Ulrich, 171n61
Wiedenhofer, S., 173n66, 203
William of Auvergne, 420
Wilmsen, Arnold, 157n10
Wisdom, 414n473
Witness, 147, 182, 188, 209, 435
    evangelization, 386
    the laity and, 93, 98
    and ministry, 457–60

Witness (*continued*)
  See also under Gospel: mission of
    proclaiming
Witte, J. L., 23n9, 64n119
Wittstadt, K., 23n9, 165n37, 271n231,
  432n6
Wolf, H.-H., 434n14
Women,
  feminine structure of the Church,
    254n137, 405–9
  feminism, 220
  Israel and, 412n467
  and ordination, 68, 216, 281
Word of God,
  consolidation through, 207–9
  as helmet of salvation, 208
  living, 197
  Logos (*see* Logos)
  See also Jesus Christ; Scripture
Works (merit), 102
World, 98
  laity and, 98
  responsibility of People of God for,
    96–97
  situation of man in, 25n18
  the term, 187, 210–11
  "theology of", 184
  See also Creation; *specific topics*, e.g.,
    Religion: world religions
World Council of Churches, 176,
  176n85, 225
World Wars,
  time between, 158–59, 269–70

World War I, 22, 333
  and renewal, 22
World War II, 154n2, 156, 514n48
  the postwar generations, 169–70
  Ratzinger during, 156
Worship,
  creation and, 507
  the Eucharist and, 520
  as goal of Israel's Exodus, 520n78
  liturgy as, 518
  logos and, 519
  primacy of, 268
  Ratzinger's ecclesiology and, 520,
    522–23
  as trinitarian, 523
  truth and, 520
  as universal, not private, 521
  Vatican II and, 268
  See also Adoration; Eucharist; Liturgy
Wrath of God, 224
Writing, Ratzinger's, 174, 204n111, 211,
  263
  See also specific titles and topics
Wulf, Friedrich, 101–3 passim

Youth, 24n13, 67n133, 104
  1968 student revolt, 170, 172, 174
  youth movement, 22

Zerfass, R., 98n93
Ziade, Archbishop Ignatius, 112n174
Ziegenaus, Anton, 44
Zulehner, P. M., 98n93